STUDIES IN THE BIBLE
AND JEWISH THOUGHT

Photograph by Ilya Dolgopolsky; Moscow, October 1991.

JPS דור דור
SCHOLAR ודורשיו
OF DISTINCTION
SERIES

MOSHE GREENBERG

STUDIES IN THE BIBLE
AND JEWISH THOUGHT

 The Jewish Publication Society
Philadelphia • Jerusalem 5755/1995

Library of Congress Cataloging-in-Publication Data

Greenberg, Moshe.
    Studies in the Bible and Jewish thought / Moshe Greenberg.—1st ed.
        p.   cm. — (JPS scholar of distinction series)
    Includes bibliographical references and index.
    ISBN 0-8276-0504-8
    1. Bible. O.T.—Criticism, interpretation, etc. 2. Bible. O.T.—Criticism, interpretation, etc., Jewish. I. Title. II. Series.
BS1171.2.G73   1995
221.6—dc20   93-47361
                                                              CIP

Designed by Adrianne Onderdonk Dudden

הַבִּיטוּ אֶל־צוּר חֻצַּבְתֶּם
וְאֶל־מַקֶּבֶת בּוֹר נֻקַּרְתֶּם

Look to the rock you were hewn from,
To the quarry you were dug from.

Isaiah 51:1

Publication of this volume was made possible through gifts from Robert S. Rifkind and Jerome J. Shestack in memory of Dr. Simon Greenberg, *z"l.*

Contents

THE BIBLE IN JEWISH THOUGHT

Acknowledgments

The author expresses thanks to the following organizations that kindly permitted the republication of these papers that first appeared under their auspices:

World Union of Jewish Studies, The Hebrew University, for "Can Modern Critical Bible Scholarship Have a Jewish Character?" (in Hebrew), from *Proceedings, Eighth World Congress of Jewish Studies*, 1983; the Ecumenical Theological Research Fraternity in Israel, for the English version, from *Immanuel*, Winter 1982/3.

Neukirchener Verlag des Erziehungsvereins GmbH, for "Three Conceptions of the Torah in Hebrew Scriptures," from *Festschrift für Rolf Rendtorff, zum 65, Geburtstag*, 1990.

The Magnes Press, The Hebrew University, for "Some Postulates of Biblical Criminal Law," from *Yehezkel Kaufmann Jubilee Volume*, 1960, and *The Jewish Expression*, Judah Goldin, ed., Bantam Books, 1970.

Scholars Press, for "The Biblical Conception of Asylum," from *Journal of Biblical Literature*, Vol. LXXVIII, Part II, 1959.

Eisenbrauns, Inc., for "Biblical Attitudes Toward Power: Ideal and Reality in Law and Prophets," from *Religion and Law: Biblical-Judaic and Islamic Perspectives*, Edwin B. Firmage, et al., eds., 1990.

Association for Jewish Studies, Harvard University, for "On the Refinement of the Conception of Prayer in Hebrew Scriptures," from *AJS Review*, Vol. 1, 1976.

Jewish History Publications, Ltd., (receivers), for "Religion: Stability and Ferment," from *The World History of the Jewish People: The Age of the Monarchies: Culture and Society*, ed., A. Malamat, ed., 1979.

JUDAISM: A Quarterly Journal of Jewish Life and Thought, Vol. 13, No. 1, Winter Issue, 1964, for "Kaufmann on the Bible: An Appreciation."

American Oriental Society, for "The Stabilization of the Text of the Hebrew Bible," *JAOS* 76:157–167, 1956.

E. J. Brill, for "The Use of the Ancient Versions for Interpreting the Hebrew Text," from *Congress Volume, Goettingen, 1977*, Supplements to Vetus Testamentum XXIX, 1978, pp.131–148.

KTAV, for "Reflections on Interpretation: The Vision of Jerusalem in Ezekiel 8–11," from *The Divine Helmsman*, J. L. Crenshaw and S. Sandmel, eds., 1980.

World Union of Jewish Studies, The Hebrew University, for "To Whom and For What Should a Bible Commentator Be Responsible?" from *Proceedings of the Tenth World Congress of Jewish Studies, Div. A, The Bible and Its World*, 1990.

JUDAISM: A Quarterly Journal of Jewish Life and Thought, Vol. 12, No. 2, Spring Issue, 1963, for "The New Torah Translation."

Scholars Press, for "Another Look at Rachel's Theft of the Teraphim," from *Journal of Biblical Literature*, Vol. LXXXI, Part III, 1962.

American Oriental Society, for "Hebrew s^{e}gullā: Akkadian *sikiltu*," from "Brief Communications," *JAOS* 71:172-174, 1951.

The Magnes Press, The Hebrew University, for "The Decalogue Tradition Critically Examined," from *The Ten Commandments in History and Tradition*, Ben-Zion Segal, ed.; English version, Gershon Levi, ed., 1985.

American Oriental Society, for "Idealism and Practicality in Numbers 35:4–5 and Ezekiel 48," from *Essays in Memory of E. A. Speiser*, William W. Hallo, ed. Published simultaneously as *JAOS* 88:59-65, 1968, and as *American Oriental Series*, Vol. 53, 1968.

The Jewish Publication Society, for "Reflections on Job's Theology," from *The Book of Job*, 1980.

Harvard University Press, for "Job," from *The Literary Guide to the Bible*, Robert Alter and Frank Kermode, eds., 1987.

Charles Scribner's Sons, an imprint of Macmillan Publishing Company (U.S. rights), and Balkin Agency, Inc. (world rights), for "Exegesis," from *Contemporary Jewish Religious Thought*, Arthur A. Cohen and Paul Mendes-Flohr, eds., 1987.

E. J. Brill, for "Mankind, Israel and the Nations in the Hebraic Heritage," from *No Man Is Alien: Essays on the Unity of Mankind*, J. Robert Nelson, ed., 1970, pp. 15–40.

JUDAISM: A Quarterly Journal of Jewish Life and Thought, Vol. 19, No. 1, Winter 1970, for "Rabbinic Reflections on Defying Illegal Orders: Amasa, Abner and Joab."

Scholars Press, for "Jewish Conceptions of the Human Factor in Biblical Prophecy," from *Justice and the Holy: Essays in Honor of Walter Harrelson*, D. A. Knight and P. J. Paris, eds., 1989.

Annenberg Research Institute, for "Bible Interpretation as Exhibited in the First Book of Maimonides' *Code*," from *The Judeo-Christian Tradition and the U.S. Constitution:* Proceedings of a Conference at Annenberg Research Institute, November 16–17, 1987.

Introduction

Jewish Bible (TANAKH) scholarship has long been a stepchild in the academies of Jewish learning. The talmudic sages held that Bible study was for beginners, while the 19th-century proponents of the modern study of Judaism (*Wissenschaft des Judentums*) regarded the critical study of the Bible—largely a Protestant achievement—as tainted with animosity toward Judaism (which it was and sometimes still is). Jews who entered the field were either joining the enemy or pursuing apologetics. As a result the modern study of the Bible had, until the mid-20th century, only a minor input from Jewish scholars. The Jewish student of the 1940s and 1950s who aspired to be a biblical scholar had to overcome internal and external prejudices that appeared as challenges worthy to be met.

Representative of the traditional Jewish attitude is this ranking of the stages of learning attributed to Rabbi Shim'on bar Yohai, one of the great sages of the Mishnah (2nd c. C.E.): "Study of the Bible—hardly a virtue; of the Mishnah—for that one is rewarded; of the Talmud—there is no greater virtue than that" (Pal. Talmud, Shabbat 15c). The Bible is ranked low, explained Rabbi Judah the Pious (12th-c. Germany), "because one pays exclusive attention to the plain sense [of the biblical text, which, unlike the Mishnah and Talmud, is not normative]" (*Sefer Ḥasidim*, ed. Wistinetzki, # 748). Yet a bit further on he qualifies this: "At times, study of the Bible is worthier than that of the Talmud—as when one is among the unlearned or others who do not study Talmud, and if one would not teach them Bible they would learn nothing at all" (ibid., #765). More generous is the hierarchy that compares the Scriptures to water, the Mishnah to wine, and the Talmud to spiced wine—"all three are necessary and the rich partake of all three" (*Soferim* 15.6; 8th-c.).

In spite of this traditional view, medieval Jewish scholars were increasingly attracted to the intellectual challenge of making out the plain sense of Scripture—whether as an exercise of the new Hebrew linguistics or esthetics (developed through emulation of Arabic scholarship), or by way of response to the Karaites who claimed to understand the Scriptures better than the mainstream Jewish scholars (the Rabbinites), or in order to counter the allegorical, christocentric reading of the Christians. Or they were attracted to Scripture simply out of conviction that the primary sense of the text, unelaborated by talmudic-midrashic interpretation, was worthy of study as the prophetic word of God:

> Know that when the prophecies (= the holy Scriptures) were committed to writing everything necessary for understanding them was included, so that future generations should not be perplexed.... We have no need of external aid or midrash.... Whoever cannot make out the plain sense of Scripture but resorts to some midrashic explanation is like someone caught in a powerful river current... who grasps at anything to be saved. If he really set his heart on God's word he would have searched after the plain sense and found it (Joseph Kara, 11th-c. France; comment to 1 Sam. 1:17).

Notwithstanding such bold assertions of independence from tradition, study of the Bible alone was rarely a Jewish mode of scholarship. All the major plain-sense (*peshat*) exegetes of Scripture were familiar with other branches of Jewish learning—be it Talmud and Midrash, theology-philosophy, linguistics, or mysticism. Those branches, repositories of centuries of reflection and maturation of biblical faith and text study, bridged the gap between the Scriptures and contemporary significance. The assumption, held by all exegetes, that the Scriptures were prophetic—that is, divinely inspired—implied (to them) that they equaled the best in contemporary thought; hence, some elements of those branches of learning were reflected in their commentary. The premodern exegete worked within a tradition and for a faith community constituted by that tradition. His reading of Scripture, the fountainhead of the tradition, aimed at enhancing its worth in the eyes of the community; hence he read it in the light of the best and worthiest in contemporary thought.

Modern critical Bible scholarship differs in its all-pervasive historical consciousness and in its address predominantly to a peer group of scholars. Its agenda is autonomous: not so much answering questions (difficulties linguistic and ideational) pertaining to the surface meaning of the text, as asking questions aimed at disclosing what lies behind or beneath the text. For example: To what genre does it belong? Is it a unity or a compilation? In what circumstances did its components originate, and by what process did they come together? Whose views and interests does it represent? Historical perspective and plurality of voices are gained as the previously assumed unity and univocality of the Bible are lost. Of late a reaction to the fragmentation resulting from such critical operations has set in, in the shape of (a) attention to the art and design exhibited by the final form of the literature, and (b) doubts about the soundness of the assumptions underlying these operations.

Critical biblical scholarship is chary about examining the truth and value claims of the Bible. It is especially wary of claims of uniqueness—which have too often proven groundless in the light of the progressive discovery of the high cultures surrounding ancient Israel. The problem of distinguishing what was common to Near Eastern cultures from what was peculiar to ancient Israel becomes increasingly complex as new extrabiblical material comes to light.

The essays collected here present my endeavor to be true to the task of the classical Jewish Bible scholar: to enhance the Bible in the eyes of the faith/cultural community by (a) seeking to set forth existential values embodied in biblical narratives, laws and rituals; (b) pointing to the continuities and transformations of the biblical materials in later Jewish creativity. At the same time I have tried to be true to the task of the critical scholar in (a) using historical, linguistic, and comparative methods that seek to understand the Bible in its ancient context; (b) presenting and dealing with material uncongenial to my predilections; (c) reviewing the goals and reflecting on the assumptions underlying the procedures of criticism. Through loyalty to both tasks I hope to have said some things of interest to all who regard the Bible as a supreme spiritual-cultural treasure.

In accord with the title of the series in which this volume appears, the essays in it were chosen to exemplify the range and nature of the author's scholarly work: the phenomenology of biblical religion and law; the biblical text and the theory and practice of its interpretation; the Bible in Jewish thought (including the history of exegesis). Consideration was shown to essays not readily available—such as those appearing in jubilee volumes, collective works, or learned periodicals. From the above-mentioned criteria the policy on exclusion derived; not included here are (1) educational and topical articles and book reviews; (2) essays that go over ground covered in books of mine; (3) articles appearing in encyclopaedias. Only essays available in English have been included.

Previously published essays have been edited for correction of errors, gender neutrality and stylistic uniformity (e.g., in citation and transliteration), but I am aware that at least the latter two have not been consistently achieved. Dedications to honorees of jubilee volumes have been retained as memorials of my relations with and sentiments toward them. At the end of most articles I have added a note referring to subsequent studies that bear on my treatment of (some aspect of) the subject.

Translations of biblical passages are my own. I have generally followed the New JPS *Tanakh*, but, as a member of one of the translation committees of that version, I have reserved the right to differ at times from my colleagues and teachers.

I am grateful to The Jewish Publication Society for having included this collection in its Scholar of Distinction series and to its editorial staff for their help along the way.

I dedicate this book to the memory of my parents, Rabbi Simon and Betty Greenberg, who died while it was aborning.

Moshe Greenberg
Jerusalem

Abbreviations

AASOR	*Annual of the American Schools of Oriental Research*
ANEP	J. B. Pritchard, ed., *The Ancient Near East in Pictures*
ANET	J. B. Pritchard, ed., *Ancient Near Eastern Texts Relating to the Old Testament*[3] (1969)
AO	*Archiv Orientální*
ASTI	*Annual of the Swedish Theological Institute*, Jerusalem
ATD	Das Alte Testament Deutsch
BASOR	*Bulletin of the American Schools of Oriental Research*
BK	Biblischer Kommentar Altes Testament
BZAW	Beihefte zur Zeitschrift für die Alttestamentliche Wissenschaft
CAH	Cambridge Ancient History
CB	Cambridge Bible for Schools and Colleges
CBQ	*Catholic Biblical Quarterly*
CJ	*Conservative Judaism*
EB	*Encyclopaedia Biblica* (Hebrew)
EncBrit	*Encyclopaedia Britannica*
EncJud	*Encyclopaedia Judaica* (1971)
HAR	*Hebrew Annual Review*
HAT	Handbuch zum Alten Testament
HSS	Harvard Semitic Studies
HTR	*Harvard Theological Review*
HUCA	*Hebrew Union College Annual*
IB	Interpreter's Bible
ICC	International Critical Commentary

IDB	Interpreter's Dictionary of the Bible
IEJ	*Israel Exploration Journal*
Int	*Interpetation*
JANES	*Journal of the Ancient Near Eastern Society of Columbia University*
JAOS	*Journal of the American Oriental Society*
JBL	*Journal of Biblical Literature*
JBR	*Journal of Bible and Religion*
JCS	*Journal of Cuneiform Studies*
JJS	*Journal of Jewish Studies*
JQR	*Jewish Quarterly Review*
JT(h)S	*Journal of Theological Studies*
KAT	Kommentar zum Alten Testament
KHAT	Kurzgefasstes exegetisches Handbuch zum Alten Testament
OBO	Orbis Biblicus et Orientalis
OTL	Old Testament Library
OTS	*Oudtestamentische Studiën*
PAAJR	Proceedings, American Academy for Jewish Research
RA	*Revue d'assyriologie et d'archéologie orientale*
RB	*Revue biblique*
SBT	*Studies in Biblical Theology*
TDNT	G. Kittel and G. Friedrich (eds.), *Theological Dictionary of the New Testament*
UF	*Ugarit-Forschungen*
VTSup	*Vetus Testamentum: Supplements*
ZAW	*Zeitschrift für die alttestamentliche Wissenschaft*

STUDIES IN THE BIBLE
AND JEWISH THOUGHT

Prologue: Can Modern Critical Bible Scholarship Have a Jewish Character?

1983

Modern critical Bible scholarship is a creation of Christian Europe; its Jewish embodiment is derivative. However, it appears that Jews who wished to be regarded as critical scholars did not take over all the elements of this scholarship as it developed in Europe, but singled out one for emulation, as essential. Consideration of this transmutation will help us clarify for ourselves the course we have taken till now.

There are two approaches to biblical research in Europe and America, both equally scholarly and respected in the academic community; neither negates nor excludes the other. A given scholar may by temperament be more inclined toward one of the two, but he or she is not barred from adopting the other on occasion. There seems to be a consensus that both are needed, and it is due to their concomitance that Bible scholarship has played a role in shaping European culture.

These two approaches coexist in the joint Bible project of the British churches known as *The New English Bible*, whose publication was completed in 1970. One is reflected in the translation of the "Old Testament" (i.e., our Hebrew Bible or *Tanakh*) and in its introduction, the other in the translation of the New Testament and its introduction.[1] We shall examine each introduction—its main topics and the spirit that animates it—then compare each with a sample of actual translation.

This paper was originally one of several delivered at the Opening Session of the Eighth World Congress of Jewish Studies in Jerusalem, August 1981. The Hebrew text of the lecture appeared in the *Proceedings* of the Congress. The author has made slight changes in the English version.

3

The introduction to the Old Testament opens with an exposition of the factors that put a distance between us and Scripture: the original text has been lost; the language is full of obscurities; the subject matter is alien to us. Since "it is certain that [the present text] does not always represent what was originally written," the translator "must often go behind the traditional text to discover the writer's meaning."[2] The resources available to the scholar are described: He is portrayed as an expert in ancient languages and literature while the Bible itself is the arena in which he exercises his expertise. He begins with the establishment of correct readings either from the testimony of ancient translations or by speculative emendation of the text on the basis of its context and with the help of other Semitic languages and archeology. Emphasis is placed on the authority of the scholar to add, delete, and change in order to obtain a professional goal—the maximum possible approximation to the lost original, that is, a philological-historical goal. In this endeavor to close the gap between ourselves and the lost original, the connecting links—the traditional understanding of the Bible, and even the received text itself—serve only as points of departure toward the ideal, and so have in themselves only derivative value. With its focus on the current state of the art, it is not surprising that the introduction ignores the work of predecessors. We are given to feel that this project is a triumph of philological talent, a landmark in the history of a science that, like archeology, strives to restore ruins and recover the pristine shape of antiquity.

To sample the result of this approach, we examined the footnotes to the translation of the Book of Deuteronomy, and compared them with a list of "readings which served as a basis for the translation," published separately in a quasi-internal publication.[3] In Deuteronomy, there are a total of thirty notes with the rubric "or," giving alternative translations. By contrast, there are eighty-one text emendations. (Here we must observe that the introduction states that every correction of the text more substantial than a change in vocalization will be recorded in the notes,[4] yet fifty-nine emendations involve changes of letters or words, additions, or deletions, and of these only ten are mentioned in the notes. There are eighteen changes of vowel, and four of these are also recorded.)

By taking account of the notes, and referring as well to the "internal" list of readings, one will thus receive the impression that the Hebrew text of Deuteronomy contains a good number of ambiguities, but more than twice as many corrupt passages whose texts may be corrected to a "probable reading" on the basis of the Samaritan Pentateuch, the Septuagint, the Peshitta, etc. Moreover, despite the statement in the introduction that every correction involving letters or words will be recorded in a note, only ten out of fifty-nine are in fact so noted. The lay reader is "exempted" by the scholar from under-standing precisely what is being dished up. To paraphrase Proverbs 25:2, "It is the glory of scholars to conceal things." Thus, the scholarly expert exercises his prerogative to speak *ex cathedra*.

Let us turn to the New Testament introduction. Its main concerns are to depict the difficulty of the translators' task and the methods they used for deciding among possibilities. With regard to the text, it con-cludes: "The problem of restoring a form of text as near as possible to the vanished autographs now appears less simple than it did to our predecessors. There is not at the present time any [consensual] critical text . . . nor has the time come . . . to construct such a text, since new material constantly comes to light, and the debate continues."[5] How, then, did the translators operate? They chose among the existing testi-monies, noting in the margins alternative readings worthy of consider-ation. Knowledge of New Testament Greek has greatly improved since the time of the translations currently in use so that, while the general message of the Scripture has not changed, both greater flexibility and greater exactness than our predecessors imagined has become possi-ble. The problem is to avoid slavish literalness on the one hand and paraphrase on the other: The happy inconsistency of the Authorized (King James) Version is worthy of emulation. The conclusion of the in-troduction deserves quotation in full:

> The translators are as conscious as anyone can be of the limitations and imperfections of their work. No one who has not tried it can know how impossible an art translation is. Only those who have meditated long upon the Greek original are aware of the richness and subtlety of meaning that may lie even within the most apparently simple sen-tence . . . Yet we may hope that we have been able to convey to our readers something at least of what the New Testament has said to us during these years of work, and trust that under the providence of Almighty God this translation may open the truth of Scriptures to many who have been hindered in their approach to it by barriers of language.[6]

We examined the translation of the Gospel According to Luke, whose length is comparable to that of the Book of Deuteronomy. The total number of notes in Luke is eighty, of which twenty-eight bear the rubric "or," that is, alternative possibilities of translation, while two are "literally." The remaining fifty notes all have the rubric "some witnesses read" or the like[7]—that is, alternative readings "worthy of consideration." There is not a single conjectural emendation of the text. The impression received by the reader is of the multiplicity of meanings of the text and, even more, of uncertainty with regard to the reading, coupled with unwillingness on the part of the scholars to discredit alternative testimonies.

Let us compare these two approaches to the study and translation of the Bible with one another. The former sees Scripture as a field on which to parade expert knowledge. Scripture is damaged wares requiring the treatment of experts to restore it to its pristine wholeness; stress is put on the remove of the present text from its "sources." As is the wont of experts, doubts and the tentative character of the product are concealed from the lay reader. Scholars project an image of sovereignty; they decide with authority. Their work is characterized by disinterested objectivity—the hallmark of academic professionalism. There is not a single expression of positive evaluation of Scripture, since critical scholars are distinguished by their challenging and rejecting of accepted positions. Finally, one is struck by the indifference toward the motivations and apprehensions of those whom the translation is supposed to serve. There is no sign of a sense of responsibility to any community, nor to any tradition other than that of academic scholarship.

The second approach may be described as a mission—to uncover the wealth of meaning in Scripture, Scripture itself being perceived as a trove of secrets whose treasures can be ferreted out only by patient searching. To accomplish this, scholars have been trained up under public auspices, and are supported by them. The lay reader is the scholar's brother. The scholar labors in order to provide him with information, divulging doubts and the tentative nature of the conclusions. As an expert, the scholar must make decisions, but he also sets out alternatives to the reader, thus making sure he is aware of the uncertainty surrounding the decisions.

Such scholars feel responsible toward the community of their brethren, who are unable to handle the original—which in their eyes enshrines the "truth." They are sensitive to the sacred status of Scripture in the eyes of the public, and they seek to uncover the grounds of that esteem in the text. They regard themselves as a link in a continuing chain of interpreters of the message of the Bible to their brothers.

Their sense of mission and of responsibility to the public imposes upon them modesty; dogmatism and authoritarianism are foreign to them. They recognize that new data constantly change the contours of their field, and that disagreement about their interpretation continues. This awareness dictates humility.

In *The New English Bible* these two approaches dwell side by side:

the former approach is taken to the Hebrew Bible, the latter to the New Testament. We would not at this time speculate upon the reason for this remarkable difference, when by nature these approaches are not determined by subject. The relevant fact is that European Bible scholarship has historically run on two tracks: the academic-professional, centered upon the scholar and his or her discipline and motivated by pursuit of renown for the profession and its practitioners; and the Christian track, centered upon the community that reveres the Book, and motivated by a sense of mission to create a bridge of understanding between the venerated text and the community eager for its message—a bridge of insight into the reason why this book has been and remains a source of inspiration, challenge, and hope to those who hold fast to it.

In Europe, professional-academic Bible scholarship has been applied to both Testaments, and its results hold an honored place in the halls of learning in the Western world. Christian Bible scholarship has also been applied to the two Testaments, but its results—a source of spiritual sustenance to the Christian religious community—are difficult for us Jews to accommodate.

We have adopted academic scholarship, established chairs and trained up students in it. But where is the seat of Jewish scholarship that is characterized by the qualities (shown below) that we have found in Christian scholarship?

Humility—that is, an openness to the new and the innovative, and to continuing debate that entails modesty and lack of dogmatism.

Respect for the text, expressed in a systematic search for its "truth", in the universal-human sense as well as the particularistically Jewish; for the wealth of meanings, past and present, contained in it; and for its art of expression.

Finally, and most important, a sense of responsibility toward a community whose members, the scholars' brethren, await their disclosure to them of the Scriptural message.

The voice of such a Jewish Bible scholarship is beginning to be heard in the land. It is incumbent upon us, as members of the profession, first to recognize the right of this voice to be heard, then to encourage its development, and finally to prepare ourselves for the fruitful confrontation between the two approaches to the study of the Bible. Only when Jewish Bible scholarship (possessing the qualities we have listed above) will flourish alongside the professional-academic sort practiced by Jews, only then will Bible scholarship become a factor shaping our culture as it has been in its birthplace abroad.

NOTES

1. The *New English Bible*, Oxford and Cambridge, 1970. "Introduction to the Old Testament," pp. xv–xviii, by G. R. D[river]: "Introduction to the New Testament," pp. v–viii, by C. H. D[odd].

2. Ibid., p. xvi.

3. L. H. Brockington, *The Hebrew Text of the Old Testament:* the readings adopted by the translators of the New English Bible, Oxford and Cambridge, 1973.

4. Op. cit., p. xvii.

5. Ibid., NT, p. v.

6. Ibid., NT, p. viii.

7. "Some witnesses read/add/insert/omit" etc.

PHENOMENOLOGY OF BIBLICAL RELIGION AND LAW

Three Conceptions of the Torah in Hebrew Scriptures

1990

Rolf Rendtorff's character is defined for me by his study of modern Hebrew and his utilization of classical Jewish texts in his Bible commentary. Few Christian Bible scholars of my generation have regarded these as requisite for their work. That he has, testifies to his deep respect for Jewish religiosity and understanding of our common Scriptures. Out of affection for him and appreciation of his interconfessional outlook I dedicate this essay to him, delineating, from a Jewish perspective, a central biblical concept.

When the psalmist declared: "Your decrees I possess as a heritage (נחלתי) forever" (Ps. 119:111), he was seconding (perhaps unwittingly) the bold figure of Deuteronomy 33:4–a verse that stands out of its context for its clarity:

Moses charged us with the Torah,
A heritage [for us], the congregation of Jacob.[1]

The spiritualization of מורשה "heritage" in the second verset, elsewhere used of territorial possession (e.g., Exod. 6:8; Ezek. 11:15; 25:4), is less notable than the concept of God's Torah as the patrimony of the entire Israelite community. In early rabbinic Judaism the idea was taken to its ultimate conclusion:

Rabbi Judah said in the name of Rab [mid 3rd c., Babylonia]:
Whoever withholds a legal rule from a student is as if he robbed him of his heritage נחלה, as it is said [Deut. 33:4 is cited, then glossed]: a heritage for all Israel from the time of creation.

In the following anecdote our verse serves as the basis of a trenchant (self-) critique of scholarly arrogance:

> On a journey, Rabbi Yannai [3rd c. Palestine] met up with a very wealthy man, and invited him to his home. "As you please," he replied; so he brought him into his house. He questioned him about the Bible and found him ignorant; about mishnah, and found him ignorant; about talmud, and found him ignorant; about haggada, and found him ignorant. When he invited him to say grace, the man replied, "Let Yannai say grace in his own house." Said Yannai, "Can you repeat after me?" "Yes". "Then say, 'A dog has eaten of Yannai's bread.'" Thereupon the man seized Yannai, saying "What! My heritage (ירושה) is with you and you insult me!" He retorted, "What heritage of yours is with me?" He answered, "Schoolchildren say, 'Moses charged us with the Torah, a heritage [for us]'–the congregation of Yannai is not what is written there, but 'the congregation of Jacob' [= every Jew]." (Leviticus Rabba 9.3)

That the Torah as a body of covenant-laws belongs to every member of the community is a concept rooted in the Bible, although modern biblical scholarship's focus on the history of the text rather than on its present sense has shifted attention away from the fact. This essay describes three conceptions of the Torah as a public property embodied in the Hebrew Bible as presently shaped.

Torah in its collective sense–a body of divine instructions for the people at large (e.g., Exod. 24:12)–serves as the rule or discipline of Israel as a priestly order. That is how the covenant stipulations are conceived of in Exodus 21–23, in the book of Deuteronomy, and in the priestly corpus. They are intended to convert the entire people into an order of priesthood, "a kingdom of priests, a holy nation" (Exod. 19:6). This concept will be enlarged upon below.

The classical prophets suppose that this conception of the Torah as directed to the education of the whole people was known to their audiences. Such evidence is seldom found in the narratives of the book of Kings. For while the classical prophets address the people at large, including, at times, the king and his court, the prophets in the book of Kings speak almost exclusively to or about kings. The rationale of the prophetic rebuke in the book of Kings is the royal obligation to uphold the laws and the commandments of God. That obligation is stated in David's charge to Solomon ("to obey his statutes, his commandments and his rules and his decrees as written in Moses' Torah," 1 Kings 2:3. In verse 4 this is paraphrased, "to go before me sincerely with all their hearts and with all their souls". It is repeated in God's responses to Solomon's prayers (3:14; 9:4ff.), and in Ahia's prophecies to Jeroboam (11:38; 14:8). It underlies most of the doom prophecies (cf. 2 Kings

10:31, where the narrative accuses Jehu of not following "the Torah of YHWH, God of Israel"). It is the king's duty to see that the covenant between God and Israel is maintained. Failure on the king's part will result in calamity to himself and to the people. When the king performs his duty, he brings blessing on himself and his people. Accordingly, the rebuke and the threats in the prophecies of the book of Kings are focused on the figure of the monarch; the people at large, when they are mentioned, are adjuncts of the sinful king (e.g., 1 Kings 14:16; 2 Kings 21:11, 16; and elsewhere).

A few passages in which the people's wrongdoing is not expressly ascribed to the king–such as 1 Kings 14:22–24; 2 Kings 17:7–20—appear to be afterthoughts, adjusted to a more discriminating theodicy. In the latter passage prophetic missions to the people are mentioned: "YHWH warned Israel and Judah by every prophet . . . 'Obey my commandments, my laws, all in accord with the Torah with which I charged your fathers'" (2 Kings 17:13–15). This agrees more closely with the role of the classical prophets than with that of the prophets in the book of Kings. Justification of the fall of Israel by imputing sin to the people at large and their defiance of prophetic admonition through the ages is characteristic of the Chronicler's historiography.[2]

Throughout the book of Kings what is fateful for Israel and Judah is the behavior of their kings. They are responsible to God for the people, and hence the relationship between heaven and earth is narrowed simply to that between God and the kings.

A notable exception is the depiction of Elijah's vindication of God on Mount Carmel (1 Kings 18). Elijah demands that Ahab convene "all Israel" to Mount Carmel together with the prophets of Baal and Asherah (18:19). It seems that Elijah intends to go over the head of the king to the people, who have fallen away from God. This agrees with the rest of the story, which represents the people of Israel at large as having broken the covenant with God (19:10, 14). And that accords with Elijah's desire to reestablish the covenant between God and the people (18:37). This story has no parallel in the rest of the Book of Kings. The prophets after Elijah, both in the North and in the South, are depicted in the book of Kings as "king-centered". It may be a historical fact, that with Elijah a turning point occurred, because the subsequent classical prophets of the North (Amos, Hosea) continued to address the people and not primarily the king. That southern classical prophecy followed this pattern (e.g., Isaiah and Micah), may reflect the influence of the North upon the South, particularly after the fall of the northern kingdom.

The assumption of the classical prophets is that the covenant obligation of loyalty to God was known to all the people. Hence they arraign the people for having rejected or rebelled against God's Torah and commandments. Some relevant passages from the eighth century prophets are the following:

> Amos 2:4: "For their rejecting YHWH's Torah, and their not obeying his laws" (including the social laws, whose violation is mentioned in 2:6–8);

> Hosea 8:1: "Because they transgressed my covenant and rebelled against my Torah";

> Hosea 8:12: "The many [injunctions] of my Torah that I wrote for him [Ephraim] have been treated as something alien" (note the indication of a written Torah collection);

> Isaiah 5:24: "Because they rejected the Torah of YHWH [of] hosts, spurned the word of the holy one of Israel";

> Isaiah 24:5: "They transgressed *Torot*, violated laws, broke the ancient covenant" (the parallelism suggests that *Torot* = Torah in its collective sense);

> Isaiah 30:9: "For it is a rebellious people, faithless sons who would not obey YHWH's Torah".

Jeremiah and Ezekiel take it to be common knowledge that from its beginning the Israelite people received divine injunctions that it spurned, e.g.,

> Jeremiah 7:22–23: "[At the Exodus God enjoined the people] 'Go only in the way that I command you'";

> Ezekiel 20:11: "[In the wilderness] I gave them my laws and informed them of my rules".[3]

One of the unanswered questions of biblical antiquity is, How did the people at large get to know "Torah and commandments, laws and rules," which the prophets rebuke them for not having obeyed? Jewish tradition assumes that the later practice of public instruction on Sabbaths and holidays already existed in biblical times. Modern scholars–without knowing it–have postulated something similar in their reconstructions of festivals and ceremonies, as occasions for teaching and preaching the covenant-laws.[4]

Our interest lies in the support that this prophetic assumption gives to what the Pentateuch traditions say about the publication of the laws. According to those traditions, from the outset the stipulations of the covenant were public property. Whereas the law collections of other ancient Near Eastern peoples are formulated impersonally, in the Bible the law is an address by the legislator to the audience for whom he is legislating. More important, the law is embedded in a narrative framework, which tells of God's command that every law be proclaimed to the Israelites. That is, every law must be published immediately, and the primary form of ancient publication—as we know from the ancient Greeks as well—was oral.[5] Every issuance of the law in the Pentateuch must be communicated orally to the people: "The Lord spoke to Moses: Speak to the Israelites and say to them (such and such a law)." This sentence or its equivalent is repeated throughout the Pentateuch. Publication is manifestly of the essence of lawgiving.[6]

The vast majority of laws are addressed to the Israelites as a whole or to their representative elders. A few laws are addressed to the priests, to Aaron and his sons.[7] Now, it has been observed, that the closest analogies to the address form of lawgiving are the vassal treaties of antiquity, and instructions to officeholders found among the Hittite documents. Both are, of course, simply variations on a common form: the commandments of a sovereign to his subject. What is particularly interesting to us, however, is the double metaphor suggested by these forms. On the one hand, the people of Israel are treated as a vassal of God, and the stipulations of the covenant therefore establish "international relations" between the "foreign" sovereign and his subject people. But that form pervades the social laws as well, those laws regulating the internal relations of Israelite society. Such legislation is the domain of royal authority within a given nation (like the Hittite instructions to officials), and metaphorizes God as king of the Israelite nation. In Mesopotamia, the literary form such intranational legislating takes is the law collection (such as that issued by the Babylonian King Hammurabi). And indeed, as has been observed, the biblical law collections bear resemblances to the treaty and instruction form on the one hand and to the law collection on the other. God is at once a treaty partner and the proper King of Israel.[8]

Why is it that God not only regulates Israel's relation to him (his worship and its institutions), but also the relations of Israelites to each other—the social laws—and in both cases addresses the Israelites directly and insists that all hear his commandments? The answer would seem to lie in the equivalent status of Israel at large to that of a priesthood, which is already suggested by the parallel in the address-formulas: "Speak to the Israelites" and "Speak to Aaron and his sons."

The lawgiving to the people serves the same purpose for the laity as it does for the priests. Just as with the priests it is a regimen that must be learned in preparation for taking office, so in the case of Israel the law is a regimen, a discipline that must be learned and followed in order to enable Israel to fulfill its office as God's people.

In the various collections of law in the Torah, this office is called an office of holiness (e.g., in Exod. 22:30 "holy men," in Lev. 20:26 "holy," in Deut. 14:2 "a holy people"). The chief statement occurs in Exodus 19:3–6, the passage in which God proposes his covenant to Israel. His purpose in so doing is to turn Israel into a "kingdom of priests and a holy nation" (verse 6). The phrase is parallelistic: it doesn't mean two things, but one and the same thing, namely that all Israel is to become the kingdom of God and its people are to be in the status of priests.

This phrase has been obfuscated by much discussion, but it seems quite plain: Israel as a whole is to live in dedication to God after the manner of priests.[9] Here and there in the laws this is spelled out. Just as priests are to avoid pollutions by unclean food (Lev. 22:8), so are the Israelites at large (Exod. 22:30). Just as the priests must avoid profanation through certain mourning customs (Lev. 21:5), so must the Israelites at large (Lev. 19:27–28; Deut. 14:1). And the law in each case is grounded in Israel's holiness: You must be holy in accord with God's having elected you (Deut. 14:2); or not make yourselves unclean with unclean food (Exod. 22:30). The reason given is identical with the reason for the parallel priestly prescriptions: the obligation to be holy (Lev. 21:6). But these are merely explicit expressions of an idea that appears throughout the priestly legislation, with its detailed prescriptions of purity for every lay Israelite. The idea that every Israelite has to maintain a level of priestly purity is analogous to Moses' exclamation "Would that all of YHWH's people were prophets!" (Num. 11:29). Both regard the entire people as ideally to be brought close to God and his service.

How do priests qualify for service? By learning and obeying the rules of their order. The same holds true for the folk-priesthood of Israel. The folk must learn regulations, hence they must all hear them and understand them. That is the reason for the publication of the law: It is to function as a pedagogue, a trainer in a course of life.

The publication of biblical law sets it apart from all other ancient legislation. Elsewhere, in the ancient Near East the collections of laws were designed to ensure justice, and to demonstrate that the king had performed his duty to uphold justice. In the epilogue of Hammurabi's code, the king invites any person who believes that he has been wronged to come to the monument on which the laws are written and read his rights as the king stated them there. That is something similar to the publication of Israelite laws. But the similarity is remote, and the invitation fictitious. How many people could read cuneiform? How many people could enter into the temple where the monument stood and understand what was written on it? This is in reality rather part of the king's apology for himself, an affirmation before his god that he had given his people just laws.[10]

Hammurabi's law is expressly retrospective: after some wrong has been committed the monument is available for people to come and find what the law is in their cases. Biblical law is prospective. It aims at teaching duties in advance, not at restoring rights after they have been violated. Therefore, the law of the Torah cannot be left to lawyers, a class of experts in litigation. It must be published to the people at large so as to train them, to qualify them for the righteous and holy life that they must lead.

This published character of the Torah in its narrative setting must reflect in some way its place in life. From the very first, the covenant stipulations must have been proclaimed publicly by the lawgiver. And those first laws must have included the idea of calling the people to live the type of consecrated life that demanded instructions in a rule of behavior. Only such an assumption can, in my judgment, explain the fact that the entire body of developed law in the Torah has this character.

So much for the ideal portrait of the ancient covenant. Now this ideal created a problem: How do you in fact make the law public property? How do you in fact inculcate this ideal of holiness into the people? The Book of Deuteronomy goes farthest in attempting to realize the ideal. In Deuteronomy the idea of a holy people gave rise to educational institutions. The primary natural educational institution is the family. Deuteronomy, Chapter 6, makes the family an institution for teaching the Torah. The *Shema Yisrael* passage continues: "Take to heart these instructions with which I charge you this day, impress them on your children, recite them when you stay at home and when you are away, when you lie down and when you get up. Bind them as a sign on your hand; let them serve as a symbol on your forehead; inscribe them on the doorposts of your house and on your gates" (v.6ff.).

At the end of Chapter 6 parents are instructed in how to answer a child who asks, "What is the meaning of the customs and the laws that we practice?" The passage, starting at verse 20, runs: "When in time to come your children ask you, 'What mean these decrees, laws and rules, that the Lord, our God, has enjoined upon you,' you shall say to your children: We were slaves to Pharaoh in Egypt and the Lord freed us from Egypt with a mighty hand . . . "; then follows the whole history of salvation, from the Exodus, through the wandering in the wilderness, the lawgiving, the gift of the land and the promise of reward for the observance of the law. Thus the natural educational institution of the family was enlisted by the framers of the Israelite idea of the covenant in the service of communicating to generations the content of the Torah.

Completely innovative is the institution of the king's education. All over the ancient Near East, royal princes were given an education. Some Mesopotamian kings boast of their literacy.[11] And indeed, how was a prince prepared for his future tasks? Since he didn't have to work for a living, before he became king he had leisure to learn. Without doubt the Israelite kings were also trained, both in the practical laws of administration and in the traditional lore of their people.[12] The education of the king is conceived in Deuteronomy to be a life-long task, and is enlisted in the service of the Torah. We read in Chapter 17: "When the king is seated on his royal throne, he shall have a copy of this Teaching (Torah) written for him on a scroll by Levitical priests. Let it remain with him, and let him read it all his life, so that he may learn to revere the Lord his God, to observe faithfully every word of this Teaching as well as these laws. Thus he will not act haughtily toward his fellows or deviate from the Teaching to the right or to the left, to the end, that he and his descendants may reign long in the midst of Israel (Duet. 17:18–20)."

Finally, adult education "retreats," to use a modern term, were ordained by the law of Deuteronomy. Once every seven years there was to be a gathering of all the people for a public reenactment of the covenant-ceremony of Sinai. In the light of modern discussion of the place of women in religion, and in ancient Israel in particular, the conception of Deuteronomy 31 as to who should participate in the ceremony is noteworthy: "Every seventh year, the year set for remission of debts, you shall read this Teaching (Torah) aloud in the presence of all Israel. Gather the people, men, women, children and the strangers in your communities, that they may hear and so learn to revere the Lord, your God, and observe faithfully every word of this Teaching. Their children, too, who have not had the experience, shall hear and learn to revere the Lord, your God, as long as they live in the land that you are about to cross the Jordan to possess" (Deut. 31:10–13).

A post-exilic account of a royal campaign of public education in connection with a judicial reform appears in 2 Chronicles 17:7ff. King Jehoshaphat of Judah sent emissaries throughout his kingdom to instruct the people in the Torah.[13]

So much for the early ideal of the covenant and some indications about how this ideal was supposed to be carried out. The information is unfortunately too sparse to speak with confidence, but the tendency of the literature is clear. The purpose of the covenant is to make Israel over into a kingdom of priests, a holy nation, and that was to be achieved by institutional innovations. In contrast, the "real" history of Israel, as it is set out in the books of Samuel and Kings and the pre-exilic prophets, is the story of the failure of the people to realize this ideal. We turn now to Jeremiah and Ezekiel who give us extreme reactions to the failure.

Jeremiah and Ezekiel diagnose the failure as ultimately due to human nature: human nature is too weak to fulfill God's purpose. The only way therefore that his purpose can be fulfilled is to change human nature. As Jeremiah puts it in 31:30–33—the Torah will in time to come no longer be external, that is, written on scrolls and books and impressed (in-pressed) on the minds of resisting students, but God will imprint it on people's minds: "See a time is coming, declares the Lord, when I will make a new covenant with the house of Israel and the house of Judah. It will not be like the covenant I made with their fathers, when I took them by hand to lead them out of the land of Egypt, a covenant which they broke, so that I rejected them—declares the Lord. But such is the covenant I will make with the House of Israel after these days–declares the Lord. I will put My Teaching (Torah) into their inmost being and inscribe it upon their hearts, then I will be their God, and they shall be My people. No longer will they need to teach one another and say to one another, 'Heed the Lord', for all of them from the least of them to the greatest, shall heed Me–declares the Lord. For I will forgive their iniquities, and remember their sins no more."

This is meant quite literally. The old Torah was written on papyrus with ink, on parchment and on stone. It was read off these and had to be taught and learned. The new covenant will not be different in content,[14] but it will be inscribed on the hearts and on the minds of the future Israel. This is a counsel of despair. There is no hope that humans in their present nature can observe the Torah. Salvation will come only when God intervenes and makes observing the Torah natural, so that it will no longer be necessary to learn it. There will be no Talmud Torah in the time to come in the way that we know it: a teacher and a student, a parent and a child.

Ezekiel has a similar idea. Describing the return of Israel to its homeland in the future salvation, he says (36:24–26): "I will take you from among the nations and gather you from all the countries, and I will bring you back to your own land. I will sprinkle clean water upon you and you shall be clean . . . And I will give you a new heart and put a new spirit into you. I will remove the heart of stone from your body and give you a heart of flesh." A heart of flesh, unlike of stone, can receive impressions; stone is obdurate. Verse 27 continues: "and I will put my spirit into you. Thus I will cause you to follow my laws and faithfully to observe my rules." There is a unique construction here, emphasizing the divine coercion: literally, "I will make it that you follow my laws"; that is, You will have no alternative but to obey my laws.

God will no longer gamble with Israel as he did in old times, and Israel rebelled against him; in the future–no more experiments! God will put his spirit into them, he will alter their hearts (their minds) and make it impossible for them to be anything but obedient to his rules and his commandments. This again is a counsel of despair, befitting the years in which ancient Israel's kingdom was extinguished. All hope in the capability of Israel in its present state to live up to its ideal purpose has been lost.

Alongside the conception of the Torah as a God-given regimen, a discipline Israel is charged to obey, ran, in late monarchic times, a completely different conception that identified the Torah with divine wisdom. In Deuteronomy 4:6 we have the first indication that the Torah might be conceived of not only as divine rules, but as an embodiment of wisdom, which one did not have to be an Israelite to appreciate. Moses urges the Israelites to observe the ordinances of the Torah faithfully, "for that will be the proof of your wisdom and your discernment to other peoples, who when they hear of all these laws will say: 'Surely that great nation is a wise and a discerning people.'"

The Israelites know that these are God's laws, but the gentiles, when they hear of them, not knowing who really established them, will praise Israel on their account for being a wise and a discerning people. The rationality of the Torah, the light that radiates from it–the light of justice, kindness, and social solidarity–will be evident to all the nations of the world. And when they see the Israelites fostering the Torah and enjoying well-being they will declare the Israelites a wise and discerning people.[15]

This is the earliest identification of the divine law with general wisdom, which can be appreciated even by non-Israelites. As such the Torah is at a first remove from national particularity; the next step to its abstraction is to regard it as an end in itself, not merely a means to mold behavior. Psalm 19 appreciates the Torah of God not only because it leads to right conduct, but also because it is intrinsically good: "The teaching of the Lord is perfect, renewing life. The decrees of the Lord are enduring, making the simple wise. The precepts of the Lord are just, rejoicing the heart. The instruction of the Lord is lucid, making the eyes light up. The fear of the Lord is pure, abiding forever. The judgments of the Lord are true, righteous altogether. More desirable than gold, than much fine gold, sweeter than honey, than drippings of the comb."

Here is a view of the Torah not merely as an instrument leading to righteousness and holiness. It is rapturously affirmed that being a student of the Torah, reciting it, meditating on it, is a delight to the soul. It rejoices the heart; it is sweeter than honey; it is more desirable than gold. This is the view of the Torah set forth in Psalm 1 as well. But it is Psalm 119 that enlarges on the theme, as it expands these few verses of Psalm 19.

Psalm 119 is unique in form: it is an alphabetic acrostic with eight verses for each letter of the alphabet, in all 176 verses celebrating the happiness of those who follow the teaching of the Lord. This happiness includes a new Torah-centered religiosity that I shall illustrate in a few scattered citations.[16]

Verse 19: "I am only a sojourner in the land. Do not hide your commandments from me." Alienation from God is expressed commonly in Scripture as God's hiding his face.[17] The face of God is replaced here by his commandments.

Verse 24: "Your decrees are my delight, my intimate companions." There are very few other occurrences of the word translated "delight." Most of them are in this psalm and they denote the law or the decrees of God. The word is found elsewhere in Proverbs 8:30–31 in which Wisdom is described as the delight of God and the delight of human beings. But here the Torah is the psalmist's delight, the decrees of God.

Verse 30: "I have chosen the way of faithfulness. I have set your rules before me." Elsewhere the psalmist says, "I have set God before me" (16:8); here it is God's rules.

Verse 31: "I cling to your decrees, O Lord, let me not be put to shame." Nowhere else is the phrase "cling to God's decrees" found. One clings to God (Ps. 63:9); to do so is the commandment of Deuteronomy 10:20 and elsewhere.

Verse 42: "I shall have an answer for those who taunt me, for I have put my trust in your word." Elsewhere it is God in whom one trusts (e.g., Ps. 31:15); here it is in the word of God.

Verse 45: "I will walk about at ease, for I have turned to your precepts." Elsewhere (e.g., Ps. 9:11) one turns or has recourse to God, not to his precepts.

Perhaps the most astonishing expression occurs in verse 48: "I reach out for your commandments, which I love; I study your laws." "I reach out" is literally, in Hebrew, "I stretch out my hands toward," an act of prayer! Here the address of prayer is "your commandments, which I love"; everywhere else, one "stretches out hands" to God.

There is a new religiosity in this psalm. Religious sentiment, religious emotion–love, delight, clinging to–are now focused on the Torah, the Teaching, but God is not therewith displaced; on the contrary, the entire psalm is addressed to God. "You" in the psalm is God, and "your Torah," "your precepts," "your commandments," are praised. The Torah does not come between the psalmist and God; it serves to link them. God's Torah, his commandments, rules, precepts, testimonies, words–all these are available on earth to the religious Is-raelites, enabling them at all times to feel contact with God. God's presence is assured within the human community through his Torah that he has bestowed on Israel. The closeness to God through preoccu-pation with Torah is regarded by the psalmist as the most precious ex-perience he can have: through meditation on the Torah, through the love of, and the clinging to it, to feel the presence of God.

From this it is but a step to the talmudic conception of God and his court studying Torah in the heavenly yeshivah (e.g., Baba Meṣiʿa 86a).[18] Here the Torah is an absolute value as an embodiment of di-vine wisdom, in which all the celestials can delight. No greater dis-tance can be imagined from the instrumental conception–the Torah as a means for sanctification for human behavior–than the notion that God and heavenly court study it. The divine beings are already perfect in holiness. If nonetheless they study the Torah, it is because Torah is as intrinsically delightful to them as it is to human beings. "Imitation of God" in this context means two things: The Israelite in the academy below imitates God's behavior, and God in the academy on high imi-tates human behavior in studying the Torah, a spiritual exercise of eternal value.

NOTES

1. My rendering follows S. D. Luzzatto's *Commentary to the Pentateuch* (in He-brew), newly edited by P. Schlesinger (1965), 565, who, following Mendelsohn, takes לנו "(for) us" of the first verset as serving the second verset as well. The versions, fol-lowed by many moderns, extend the dative expressed by לנו to the second verset: "a heritage *for* the congregation," etc. This is slightly less elegant in that it entails a change from second to third person. How the line is to be integrated into its context remains a puzzle. *Tanakh: A New Translation of the Holy Scriptures according to the Traditional He-brew Text* (The Jewish Publication Society, 1985) translates our verse: "When Moses charged us with the Teaching/As the heritage of the congregation of Jacob." This En-glish version of Hebrew Scriptures is for the most part followed in the rest of my article.
2. See E. Bickermann, in: L. Finkelstein (ed.), *The Jews: Their History, Culture and Religion*, vol. 1 (1949):79–80; S. Japhet, *The Ideology of the Book of Chronicles* (in He-brew) (1977), 145–66.
3. Michael Fishbane judiciously surveys the use of the term *torah* in the prophets in the article *torah* in: EB, vol. 8:472–75. The modern critical tendency to credit the early existence of a concept of divine norms obligating Israel is exemplified in R. E. Clements, *Prophecy and Covenant*, SBT 43 (1965), especially chapter iv, "The Law in the Pre-exilic Prophets," 69–85. Note too W. Rudolph's defense of the authenticity of the above cited Amos 2:4 in his commentary in: KAT XIII/2 (1971):121. Bible critics and theologians have been hampered in their evaluation of the biblical law collections by too narrow a view of their possible status (based on western conceptions of legisla-tion); a corrective is Bernard S. Jackson's comparative survey, "From *Dharma* to Law," *American Journal of Comparative Law* 23 (1975):490–512.
4. For the Jewish tradition, see Josephus, *Against Apion* II:17 (§175); Acts 15:21; Pal. Talmud Megillah iv:1 (75a). The putative ancient Israelite covenant festival is con-veniently described in K. Koch, *The Growth of Biblical Tradition*, translated by S. M. Cupitt (1969), 29–33.

5. M. Hadas, *Ancilla to Classical Reading* (1954), 50–60.

6. The national address of the covenant law is stressed by Y. Kaufmann, *The Religion of Israel* (1960), 234. Influenced by Justice M. Silberg's exposition of the "prospective" educative nature of Jewish law (*Principia Talmudica* [Hebrew: כך דרכו של תלמוד] (1961), 52, 55f., 88–94), I connected the two features of biblical law in an article on "The Impact of the New Translation" in the *Jewish Publication Society Bookmark* 11/4 (December 1964):4f. and again in EncJud, vol. 9:1066. See further, S. Paul, *Studies in the Book of the Covenant*, VT Sup 18 (1970):38–39.

7. E.g., Leviticus 6:2, 18; 21:1; 22:2, 18; Numbers 6:23; 8:2. But that the community may have an interest even in such specifically priestly laws is suggested by the third-person formulation of many of these laws (e.g., in Lev. 21–2), the shift to a nonpriestly addressee in 21:8, and the express inclusion of "the Israelites" in the closing formula of Leviticus 21:24 ("Moses spoke to Aaron and to his sons and to all the Israelites"). The implication is that the community is to supervise the priests and to see to their observance of their particular rules (so Rashi, at 21:24, after Sifra, ad loc.).

H. L. Ginsberg infers from the secrecy of Babylonian priestly literature (he cites the colophon of the New Year's rite in ANET 331a) that the Israelite priestly Torah was secret (*New Trends in the Study of the Bible*, Essays in Judaism Series 4 (n.d.): 23; see also C. Cohen, "Was the P Document Secret?" JANES 1 [1969]: 39–44). Whether or not this may at some time have been the case, the present P document is for the most part addressed not only formally, but in substance to the community at large (e.g., the sacrifice list of Leviticus 1–5; the holy day sacrifice list of Numbers 28–29).

8. M. Weinfeld, *Deuteronomy and the Deuteronomic School* (1972), 146–57.

9. For a survey of renderings of the phrase, see W. L. Moran, "A Kingdom of Priests," in: J. L. McKenzie (ed.), *The Bible in Current Catholic Thought* (1962), 7–20 (Moran opts for the strange concept of "a royalty of priests"); D. Muñoz León, "Un reino de Sacerdotes y una nación santa (Exod. 19, 6)," EstB 37 (1978):149–212 (obligation to holiness of all members of God's people).

10. See Paul (note 6), 21–6.

11. E. G. Shulgi (Ur III dynasty, end of third millennium B.C.E.)—see S. N. Kramer, *The Sumerians* (1963), 69; Assurbanipal (Assyria, seventh century B.C.E.)–D. D. Luckenbill, *Ancient Records of Assyria and Babylonia* II (1927; reprint 1968):378–79.

12. See the engaging reconstruction of the Israelite "royal school": in A. Lemaire, *Les écoles et la formation de la Bible dans l'ancien Israël*, OBO 39 (1981):78–9.

13. Lemaire (note 12), 40–41, concurs with the critical doubts concerning the historicity of this account.

14. This is justly emphasized in G. von Rad, *Old Testament Theology*, translated by D. M. G. Stalker, vol. 2 (1965):212–15; see now Y. Amir, "Jeremias Wort vom Neuen Bund: Eine jüdische Auslegung," in: E. Brocke/H.-J. Barkenings (eds.), *Wer Tora vermehrt, mehrt Leben*. Festschrift, H. Kremers (1986), 159–71.

15. Thus is resolved what Weinfeld (note 8), 256, regards as "paradoxical," namely that, "laws . . . given by God are here regarded as . . . the wisdom and understanding of Israel."

16. The following draws upon the insightful essay of Y. Amir, "Psalm 119 als Zeugnis eines protorabbinischen Judentums," in: idem, *Studien zum Antiken Judentum, Beiträge zur Erforschung des AT und des Antiken Judentums* 2 (1985):1–34 (Hebrew version in: B. Uffenheimer [ed.], Te'uda II: *Bible Studies, Y. M. Grintz in Memoriam* [1982], 57–82).

Jon Levenson ("The Sources of Torah: Psalm 119 and the Modes of Revelation in Second Temple Judaism," in: *Ancient Israelite Religion*. Festschrift, F. M. Cross [1987], 559–574) argues that in Psalm 119 "the likelihood is that the Psalmist's Torah lacks a constant identity" (565); "[the commandments] are most likely the general maxims [like תורה and מצוה in Proverbs] . . . rather than the covenant stipulations of the Pentateuchal codes" (567). He remarks the absence of allusions to a book or to the covenant. But it is far from clear how one can compare the psalm terminology that always binds Torah and its synonyms to God (God's Torah, etc.) with Proverbs' terms, that are either unbound or bound to parents or the sage ("The sage's Torah is a fountain of life," Prov. 13:14). Moreover, what the devotee of Psalm 119 receives "from unmediated spiritual experience" (566) is not the laws but the understanding of God's laws already in hand (Levenson seems to confuse the two). It is these given laws of God that he constantly rehearses, and that he asks to be taught and to understand. In verses 99–100 he says, not that "he receives the laws from his teachers and elders" rather than from the Moses book (566), but that the study of God's Torah makes him wiser than his teachers and his elders, just as in verse 98 he says that it made him wiser than his enemies (מן of comparison, not of source). The absence of reference to a book agrees quite well with the speeches of Moses in the first part of Deuteronomy, where the very specific commandments of God are to be taught not from a book but by hearing them (4:9; 6:7; 11:19) and (exactly as in Psalm 119) by repeating them again and again. The absence of allusion to the covenant anticipates the situation in talmudic Judaism where the terminology of laws and commandments virtually excludes the term ברית; where it does not refer to a biblical passage, the term normally signifies circumcision ("the covenant of father Abraham").

17. Discussed by R. E. Friedman, "The Biblical Expression *mastir panim*," *HAR* 1 (1977):139–47.

18. See entry "Academy on High" in EncJud, vol. 1:208.

Additional note:

V.A. Hurowitz argues in his forthcoming monograph, "*Inu Anum sirum*: Literary Structures in the Non-Juridical Sections of Codex Hammurabi," that the unclear expression in Code V 20–21 means "Truth and justice (= my laws) I taught the people of the land" (note 39). This in turn he takes to mean oral alongside written publication. If he is right, the idea of the law as a means of public education has its first appearance here. How, when, and where such publication took place is not said, and there is no evidence outside the Code to support such a singular claim. In note 52 Hurowitz quotes G. Bottero with respect to an educative intent of the Code, but Bottero does not say that the Code was aimed at the public at large. He says, rather, that it was meant to have "the value of a model—instructive, educative, in the judicial order . . . a treatise on the exercise of judicial power by example." The passage from the Epilogue, to which I refer, in which a wronged citizen is invited to find the just verdict in this case on the stele is not consonant with the claim that the public had been taught the laws orally. I thank Dr. Hurowitz for putting his work at my disposal.

Shalom Paul noted (JBL 88 [1969] 73f.) that an inscription of Sargon (Luckenbill, *Ancient Records of Assyria and Babylonia*, II, 122) tells of his "teaching" the foreign settlers in his newly founded capital "correct instruction in serving god and king." He correctly sees in this a measure of forced Assyrianization and religious homogenization. Comparison of this policy with the publication of the laws of the Pentateuch seems remote—whether with respect to content, intent, or mode of effectuation (yet such a comparison has been made by John Welch in E.B. Firmage, et al., *Religion and Law*, Winona Lake: Eisenbrauns, 1990, 118).

Some Postulates of Biblical Criminal Law*
1960

Among the chief merits of Professor Kaufmann's work is the tremendous impetus it has given to the study of the postulates of biblical thought. The debt that the present paper owes to this stimulus and to the lines of investigation laid down by Professor Kaufmann is patent. It is a privilege to have the occasion to offer it to him in grateful tribute.

The study of biblical law has been a stepchild of the historical-critical approach to the Bible. While the law had been a major preoccupation of ancient and medieval scholars, in modern times it has largely been replaced by, or made to serve, other interests. No longer studied for itself, it is now investigated for the reflexes it harbors of stages in Israel's social development, or it is analyzed by literary-historical criticism into strata, each synchronized with a given stage in the evolution of Hebrew religion and culture. The main interest is no longer in the law as an autonomous discipline, but in what the laws can yield to the social or religious historian. It is a remarkable fact that the last comprehensive juristic treatment of biblical law was made over a century ago.[1]

The sociological and literary-historical approaches have, of course, yielded permanent insights, yet it cannot be said that they have exhausted all the laws have to tell about the life and thought of Israel. Too often they have been characterized by theorizing that ignores the

°From M. Haran, ed., *Yehezkel Kaufmann Jubilee Volume*, Jerusalem, Magnes Press, The Hebrew University, 1960, 5–28.

realities of early law and society as we know them at first hand from the written records of the ancient Near East. Severities in biblical law are alleged to reflect archaic notions that in fact have no echo in either ancient civilized, or modern Bedouin law. Humane features are declared the product of urbanization, though they have no parallels in the urban codes of Mesopotamia. Inconsistencies have been discovered and arranged in patterns of historic evolution where a proper discrimination would have revealed that the laws in question dealt with altogether separate realms.

The corrective to these errors is readily available. It is that considerable body of cuneiform law—especially the law collections[2]—which lends itself admirably to elucidate the meaning and background of the biblical law corpora. The detailed studies of these cuneiform collections, made chiefly by European scholars, furnish the student of the Bible with models of legal analysis, conducted without the prejudgments that frequently mar discussions of biblical law.

No clearer demonstration of the limits of literary-historical criticism can be found, for example, than that afforded by the studies made upon the laws of Hammurabi. Inconsistencies no less glaring than those that serve as the basis of analyzing strata in the Bible are found in this greatest corpus of Mesopotamian law. In this case, however, we know when, where, and by whom the laws were promulgated. We know, as we do not in the case of the Bible, that the code as we now have it was published as a whole, and intended—at the very least—as a statement of guiding legal principles for the realm of the king. When like discrepancies were pointed out in biblical laws it had been possible to defend stopping short with a literary-historical analysis by arguing that the discrepancies and inconsistencies of the present text were not found in the original documents that went into it. Attempts to interpret the biblical laws as a coherent whole were regarded as naive and unscholarly. It was not possible to argue this way in the case of Hammurabi's laws. The discrepancies were there from the beginning, and though, to be sure, they may well have originated in earlier collections, the fact remained that there they were, incorporated side by side in one law. Two attitudes have been taken toward this problem in the Code of Hammurabi. One, represented best by Paul Koschaker, is historical-critical. It aims at reconstructing the original laws that have gone into the present text and have caused the discrepancy. Having attained this aim, its work is done. The other, represented by Sir John Miles, is that of the commentator, whose purpose is to attempt "to imagine how this section as it stands can have been interpreted by a Babylonian court."[3] The commentator is compelled in the interest of coherence to look for distinctions of a finer degree than those made by the literary historian. Such distinctions are

not merely the recourse of a modern harmonist to escape the contradictions of the text; they are, it would seem, necessary for understanding how an ancient jurist, how the draftsman himself, understood the
law.[4] It must be assumed that the laws of Hammurabi were intended as
a consistent guide to judges, and had to be interpreted as they stand
in as consistent a manner as possible.

The realization that careful discrimination between apparently
contradictory laws is needed for this most carefully drafted ancient
law corpus is highly pertinent for an understanding of biblical law. The
literary-historical aim leads all too readily to a disregard of distinctions
in favor of establishing a pattern of development. Only by endeavoring
to interpret the laws as they now stand does one guard oneself against
excessive zeal in finding discrepancies that involve totally different
subjects rather than a historical development. Adopting the method of
the commentator, then, we are thrown back much more directly upon
the laws themselves. Recourse to literary-critical surgery is resisted
until all efforts at making distinctions have failed.

Another virtue of the commentator is the insistence on understanding a given body of law in its own terms before leaping into comparisons with other law systems. To do so, however, means to go beyond
the individual rules; for it is not possible to comprehend the law of
any culture without an awareness of its key concepts, its value judgments.[5] Yet much of the comparative work done in Israelite-Near Eastern law has been content with comparing individual laws rather than
law systems or law ideologies. But until the values that the law embodies are understood, it is a question whether any individual law can be
properly appreciated, let alone profitably compared with another in a
foreign system.

In the sequel I shall attempt to indicate some instances of the gain
accruing to the study of biblical law from the application of these two
considerations: the insistence, first, upon proper discriminations, and
second, upon viewing the law as an expression of underlying postulates or values of culture. The limitations of the sociological and literary-historical approaches will emerge from the discussion. My remarks
are confined to the criminal law, an area that lends itself well to comparative treatment, and in which the values of a civilization come into
expression with unmatched clarity.

Underlying the differing conceptions of certain crimes in biblical and
cuneiform law is a divergence, subtle though crucial, in the ideas concerning the origin and sanction of the law.

In Mesopotamia the law was conceived of as the embodiment of
cosmic truths (*kīnātum*, singular *kittum*). Not the originator, but the

divine custodian of justice was Shamash, "the magistrate of gods and men, whose lot is justice and to whom truths have been granted for dispensation."[6] The Mesopotamian king was called by the gods to establish justice in his realm, and to enable him to do so, Shamash inspired him with "truths."[7] In theory, then, the final source of the law, the ideal with which the law had to conform was above the gods as well as humans; in this sense "the Mesopotamian king . . . was not the source of the law but only its agent."[8]

However, the actual authorship of the laws, the embodying of the cosmic ideal in statutes of the realm, is claimed by the king. Hammurabi repeatedly refers to his laws as "my words which I have inscribed on my monument"; they are his "precious" or "choice" words, "the judgment . . . that I have judged (and) the decisions . . . which I have decided."[9] This claim is established by the name inscribed on the stele, and Hammurabi invokes curses upon the man who should presume to erase his name.[10] Similarly, in the case of the laws of Lipit-Ishtar: Lipit-Ishtar has been called by the gods to establish justice in the land. The laws are his, the stele on which they are inscribed is called by his name. The epilogue curses him "who will damage my handiwork . . . who will erase its inscription, who will write his own name upon it."[11] While the ideal is cosmic and impersonal, and the gods manifest great concern for the establishment and enforcement of justice, the immediate sanction of the laws is by the authority of the king. Their formulation is his, and his too, as we shall presently see, is the final decision as to their applicability.

In accord with the royal origin of these laws is their purpose: "to establish justice," "that the strong might not oppress the weak," "to give good government," "stable government," "to prosper the people," "abolish enmity and rebellion"[12]—in sum, those political benefits that the constitution of the United States epitomizes in the phrases, "to establish justice, ensure domestic tranquillity, promote the general welfare."

In the biblical theory the idea of the transcendence of the law receives a more thoroughgoing expression. Here God is not merely the custodian of justice or the dispenser of "truth" to man, he is the fountainhead of the law, and the law is a statement of his will. The very formulation is God's; frequently laws are couched in the first person, and they are always referred to as "words of God," never of humankind. Not only is Moses denied any part in the formulation of the Pentateuchal laws; no Israelite king is said to have authored a law code, nor is any king censured for so doing.[13] The only legislator the Bible knows of is God; the only legislation is that mediated by prophets (Moses and Ezekiel). This conception accounts for the commingling in the law corpora of religious and civil law, and—even more distinctively biblical—of legal enactments and moral exhortations. The entire normative realm, whether in law or morality, pertains to God alone. So far as the law corpora are concerned there is no source of norm-fixing outside of him. Conformably, the purpose of the laws is stated in somewhat different terms in the Bible than in Babylonia. To be sure, observance is a guarantee of well-being and prosperity (Exod. 23:20ff.; Lev. 26; Deut. 11:13ff., etc.), but it is more: it sanctifies (Exod. 19:5f.; Lev. 19) and is accounted as righteousness (Deut. 6:25). There is a distinctively religious tone here, fundamentally different in quality from the political benefits guaranteed in the cuneiform law collections.

In the sphere of the criminal law, the effect of this divine authorship of all law is to make crimes sins, a violation of the will of God. "He who acts willfully (against the law) whether he belongs to the native-born or the aliens, is reviling the Lord" (Num. 15:30). God is directly involved as legislator and sovereign; the offense does not flout a humanly authored safeguard of cosmic truth but an explicit utterance of the divine will. The way is thus prepared to regard offenses as absolute wrongs, transcending the power of men to pardon or expunge. This would seem to underlie the refusal of biblical law to admit of pardon or mitigation of punishment in certain cases where cuneiform law allows it. The laws of adultery and murder are cases in point. Among the Babylonians, Assyrians, and Hittites the procedure in the case of adultery is basically the same. It is left to the discretion of the husband to punish his wife or pardon her. If he punishes his wife, her paramour also is punished; if he pardons her, the paramour goes free too. The purpose of the law is to defend the right of the husband and provide him with redress for the wrong done to him. If the husband, however, is willing to forgo his right, and chooses to overlook the wrong done to him, there is no need for redress. The pardon of the husband wipes out the crime.[14]

In biblical law it is otherwise: "If a man commits adultery with the wife of another man, both the adulterer and the adulteress must be put to death" (Lev. 20:10; cf. Deut. 22:22, 23–24)—in all events. There is no question of permitting the husband to mitigate or cancel the punishment. For adultery is not merely a wrong against the husband, it is a sin against God, an absolute wrong. To what extent this view prevailed may be seen in a few extra-legal passages: Abimelech is providentially kept from violating Abraham's wife, Sarah, and thereby "sinning against God"—not a word is said about wronging Abraham (Gen. 20:6). Joseph repels the advances of Potiphar's wife with the argument that such a breach of faith with his master would be a "sin against God" (39:8f.). The author of the ascription of Psalm 51—"A psalm of David, when Nathan the prophet came to him after he had gone in to Bath-sheba"—finds it no difficulty that verse 6 says,

"Against thee only have I sinned." To be sure the law also recognizes that adultery is a breach of faith with the husband (Num. 5:12), yet the offense as such is absolute, against God. Punishment is not designed to redress an injured husband for violation of his rights; the offended party is God, whose injury no human can pardon or mitigate.

The right of pardon in capital cases that Near Eastern law gives to the king[15] is unknown to biblical law (the right of the king to grant asylum to homicides in extraordinary cases [cf. 2 Sam. 14] is not the same). This would seem to be another indication of the literalness with which the doctrine of the divine authorship of the law was held in Israel. Only the author of the law has the power to waive it: in Mesopotamia he is the king; in Israel, no man.

Divergent underlying principles alone can account for the differences between Israelite and Near Eastern laws of homicide. The unexampled severity of biblical law on the subject has been considered primitive, archaic, or a reflex of Bedouin vendetta customs. But precisely the law of homicide cannot be accounted for on any such grounds.

In the earliest law collection, the Covenant Code of Exodus, it is laid down that murder is punishable by death (Exod. 21:12ff.). If homicide is committed by a beast—a goring ox is spoken of—the beast must be stoned, and its flesh may not be eaten. If it was known to be vicious and its owner was criminally negligent in failing to keep it in, the owner is subject to death as well as the ox, though here the law allows the owner to ransom himself with a sum fixed by the slain person's family (vv. 28ff.). This is the sole degree of culpability in which the early law allows a ransom. It is thus fully in accord with a later law of Numbers (35:31) which states, "You shall not take a ransom for the life of a murderer who is guilty of death, but he shall be surely put to death." A ransom may be accepted only for a homicide not committed personally and with intent to harm. For murder, however, there is only the death penalty.

These provisions contrast sharply with the other Near Eastern laws on homicide. Outside of the Bible, there is no parallel to the absolute ban on composition between the murderer and the next of kin. All Near Eastern law recognizes the right of the slain person's family to agree to accept a settlement in lieu of the death of the slayer, Hittite law going so far as to regulate this settlement minutely in terms of the number of souls that must be surrendered as compensation.[16] Bedouin law is no different: among the Bedouin of Sinai, murder is compensated for by a tariff reckoned in camels for any life destroyed.[17] The Qur'an is equally tolerant of composition: "Believers," it reads (2:178), "retaliation is decreed for you in bloodshed: a free man for a free man, a slave for a slave, and a female for a female. He who is pardoned by his aggrieved brother shall be prosecuted according to usage and shall pay him a liberal fine." In the Babylonian law of the goring ox, otherwise closely paralleling that of the Bible, no punishment is prescribed for the ox.[18]

On both of these counts biblical law has been regarded as exhibiting archaic features.[19] To speak in terms of legal lag and progress, however, is to assume that the biblical and nonbiblical laws are stages in a single line of historical development, a line in which acceptance of composition is the stage after strict talion. This is not only incapable of being demonstrated; the actual history of the biblical law of homicide shows that it followed an altogether different principle of development from that governing Near Eastern law.

A precise and adequate formulation of the jural postulate underlying the biblical law of homicide is found in Genesis 9:5f.: "For your lifeblood I shall require a reckoning; of every beast shall I require it. . . . Whoever sheds the blood of a man, by man shall his blood be shed; for in the image of God was man made." To be sure, this passage belongs to a stratum assigned to late times by current critical opinion; however that may be, the operation of the postulate is visible in the very earliest laws, as will be seen immediately. The meaning of the passage is clear enough: that humans were made in the image of God—the exact significance of the words is not necessary to decide here—is expressive of the peculiar and supreme worth of humankind. Of all creatures, Genesis 1 relates, humans alone possess this attribute, bringing them into closer relation to God than all the rest and conferring upon them the highest value. The first practical consequence of this supremacy is set forth in Genesis 9:3f.: Man may eat beasts. The establishment of a value hierarchy of human beings over beasts means that humans may kill them—for food and sacrifice only (cf. Lev. 17:4)—but the beasts may not kill humans. A beast that kills a human destroys the image of God and must give a reckoning for it. Now this is the law of the goring ox in Exodus: It must be stoned to death. The religious evaluation inherent in this law is further evidenced by the prohibition of eating the flesh of the stoned ox. The beast is laden with guilt and is therefore an object of horror.[20]

Babylonian law on the subject reflects no such theory as to the guilt the peculiar value of human life imposes on all who take it. Babylonian law is concerned with safeguarding rights in property and making losses good. It therefore deals only with the liability of the owner of the ox to pay for damages caused by the ox. The ox is of no concern to the law since no liabilities attach to it. Indeed, one could reasonably argue that from the viewpoint of property rights the biblical law is unjust: Is it not unduly hard on the ox owner to destroy his ox for its first offense? Ought one to suffer for an accident he could in no way have foreseen and for which one therefore cannot be held responsible?

This view of the uniqueness and supremacy of human life has yet another consequence. It places life beyond the reach of other values. The idea that life may be measured in terms of money or other property, and *a fortiori* the idea that persons may be evaluated as equivalences of other persons, is excluded. Compensation of any kind is ruled out. The guilt of the murderer is infinite because the murdered life is invaluable; the kin of the slain person are not competent to say when that person has been paid for. An absolute wrong has been committed, a sin against God that is not subject to human discussion. The effect of this view is, to be sure, paradoxical: because human life is invaluable, to take it entails the death penalty.[21] Yet the paradox must not blind us to the judgment of value that the law sought to embody.

The sense of the invaluableness of human life underlies the divergence of the biblical treatment of the homicide from that of the other law systems of the Near East. There the law allows and at times fixes a value on lives, and leaves it to the kin of the slain to decide whether they will have revenge or receive compensation for their loss in money or property. Perhaps the baldest expression of the economic valuation of life occurs in those cases where punishment of a murderer takes the form of the surrender of other persons—a slave, a son, a wife, a brother—"instead of blood," or "to wash out the blood," or to "make good" the dead person, as the Assyrian phrases put it.[22] Equally expressive are the Hittite laws that prescribe that the killer has to "make amends" for the dead persons by "giving" persons in accord with the status of the slain and the degree of the homicide. The underlying motive in such forms of composition is the desire to make good the deficiency in the fighting or working strength of the community that has lost one of its members.[23] This seems to be the meaning of Hittite law 43: "If a man customarily fords a river with his ox, another man pushes him aside, seizes the tail of the ox and crosses the river, but the river carries the owner of the ox away, they (i.e., the authorities of the respective village or town) shall receive that very man." The view of life as a replaceable economic value here reaches its ultimate expression. The moral guilt of the homicide is so far subordinated to the need of restoring the strength of the community that the culprit is not punished but incorporated;[24] this is the polar opposite of the biblical law that requires that not even the flesh of the stoned homicidal ox may be eaten.

That the divergence in law reflects a basic difference in judgments of value, rather than stages in a single line of evolution, would seem to be borne out by examining the reverse of the coin: the treatment of offenses against property. Both Assyrian and Babylonian law know of offenses against property that entail the death penalty. In Babylonia, breaking and entering, looting at a fire, night trespass—presumably for theft—and theft from another's possessions are punished by death; Assyrian law punishes theft committed by a wife against her husband with death.[25] In view of this, the leniency of biblical law in dealing with all types of property offenses is astonishing. No property offense is punishable with death. Breaking and entering, for which Babylonian law prescribes summary execution and hanging of the culprit at the breach, is punished in biblical law with double damages. If the housebreaking occurred at night, the householder is privileged to slay the culprit caught in the act, though this is not prescribed as a punishment (Exod. 22:1f.).[26]

This unparalleled leniency of biblical law in dealing with property offenses must be combined with its severity in the case of homicide, just as the leniency of nonbiblical law in dealing with homicide must be taken in conjunction with its severity in dealing with property offenses. The significance of the laws then emerges with full clarity: in biblical law life and property are incommensurable; taking of life cannot be made up for by any amount of property, nor can any property offense be considered as amounting to the value of a life. Elsewhere the two are commensurable: a given amount of property can make up for life, and a grave enough offense against property can necessitate forfeiting life. Not the archaicness of the biblical law of homicide relative to that of the cuneiform codes, nor the progressiveness of the biblical law of theft relative to that of Assyria and Babylonia, but a basic difference in the evaluation of life and property separates the one from the others. In the biblical law there is a religious evaluation; in nonbiblical law, an economic and political evaluation predominates.

Now it is true that in terms of each viewpoint one can speak of a more or a less thoroughgoing application of principle, and, in that sense, of advanced or archaic conceptions. Thus the Hittite laws would appear to represent a more consistent adherence to the economic-political yardstick than the law of Babylonia and Assyria. Here the principle of maintaining the political-economic equilibrium is applied in such a way that even homicides (not to speak of property offenses) are punished exclusively in terms of replacement. It is of interest, therefore, to note that within the Hittite system there are traces of an evolution from earlier to later conceptions. The Old Kingdom edict of Telepinus still permits the kin of a slain person to choose between retaliation or composition, while the later law of the code seems to recognize only replacement or composition.[27] And a law of theft in the code (par. 23) records that an earlier capital punishment has been replaced by a pecuniary one.

In the same way it is legitimate to speak of the law of the Bible as archaic in comparison with postbiblical Jewish law. Here again the jural postulate of the biblical law of homicide reached its fullest expression only later: The invaluableness of life led to the virtual abolition of the death penalty. But what distinguishes this abolition from that just described in the Hittite laws, what shows it to be truly in accord with the peculiar inner reason of biblical law, is the fact that it was not accompanied by the institution of any sort of pecuniary compensation. The conditions that had to be met before the death penalty could be inflicted were made so numerous, that is to say, the concern for the life of the accused became so exaggerated, that in effect it was impossible to inflict capital punishment.[28] Nowhere in the account of this process, however, is there a hint that it was ever contemplated to substitute a pecuniary for capital punishment. The same reverence for human life that led to the virtual abolition of the death penalty also forbade setting a value on the life of the slain person. (This reluctance either to execute the culprit or to commute his or her penalty created a dilemma that Jewish law cannot be said to have coped with successfully.)[29]

Thus the divergences between the biblical and Near Eastern laws of homicide appear not as varying stages of progress or lag along a single line of evolution, but as reflections of differing underlying principles. Nor does the social-political explanation of the divergence seem to be adequate in view of the persistence of the peculiarities of biblical law throughout the monarchial, urbanized age of Israel on the one hand, and the survival of the ancient nonbiblical viewpoint in later Bedouin and Arab law on the other.

Another divergence in principle between biblical law and the nonbiblical law of the ancient Near East is in the matter of vicarious punishment—the infliction of a penalty on the person of one other than the actual culprit. The principle of talion is carried out in cuneiform law to a degree that at times involves vicarious punishment. A creditor who has so maltreated the distrained son of his debtor that he dies, must lose his own son.[30] If a man struck the pregnant daughter of another so that she miscarried and died, his own daughter must be put to death.[31] If through faulty construction a house collapses, killing the householder's son, the son of the builder who built the house must be put to death.[32] A seducer must deliver his wife to the seduced girl's father for prostitution.[33] In another class are penalties that involve the substitution of a dependent for the offender—the Hittite laws compelling a slayer to deliver so many persons to the kin of the slain, or prescribing that a man who has pushed another into a fire must give over his son; the Assyrian penalties substituting a son, brother, wife, or slave of the murderer "instead of blood."[34] Crime and punishment are here defined from the standpoint of the *pater-familias:* Causing the death of a child is punished by the death of a child. At the same time the members of the family have no separate individuality vis-à-vis the head of the family. They are extensions of him and may be disposed of at his discretion. The person of the dependent has no independent footing.

As is well known, the biblical law of Deuteronomy 24:16 explicitly excludes this sort of vicarious punishment: "Parents shall not be put to death for children, nor children for parents; each shall be put to death for his own crime." The proper understanding of this requires, first, that it be recognized as a judicial provision, not a theological dictum. It deals with an entirely different realm than Deuteronomy 5:9 and Exodus 20:5, which depict God as "holding children to account to the third and fourth generations for the sins of their parents."[35] This is clear from the verb יומת, "shall be put to death," referring always to judicial execution and not to death at the hand of God.[36] To be sure, Jeremiah and Ezekiel transfer this judicial provision to the theological realm, the first promising that in the future, the second insisting that in the present, each person die for his or her own sin—but both change יומת to ימות (Jer. 31:29; Ezek. 18:4; and passim).

This law is almost universally considered late. On the one hand, it is supposed to reflect in law the theological dictum of Ezekiel; on the other, the dissolution of the family and the "weakening of the old patriarchal position of the house father" that attended the urbanization of Israel during the monarchy.[37] This latter reasoning, at any rate, receives no support from the law of the other highly urbanized cultures of the ancient Near East. Babylonian, Assyrian, and Hittite civilization was surely no less urbanized than that of monarchial Israel, yet the notion of family cohesiveness and the subjection of dependents to the family head was not abated by this fact.

A late dating of the Deuteronomic provision is shown to be altogether unnecessary from the simple fact that the principle of individual culpability in precisely the form taken in Deuteronomy 24:16 is operative in the earliest law collection of the Bible. What appears as a general principle in Deuteronomy is applied to a case in the Covenant Code law of the goring ox: After detailing the law of an ox who has slain a man or a woman, the last clause of the law goes on to say that if the victims are a son or a daughter the same law applies (Exod. 21:31). This clause is a specific repudiation of vicarious punishment in the manner familiar from cuneiform law. There a builder who, through negligence, caused the death of a householder's son must deliver up his own son; here the negligent owner of a vicious ox who has caused the death of another's son or daughter must be dealt with in the same way as when he caused the death of a man or woman, to wit: the owner is to be punished, not his son or daughter.[38] This principle of individual culpability in fact governs all of biblical law. Nowhere does the criminal law of the Bible, in contrast to that of the rest of the Near East, punish secular offenses collectively or vicariously. Murder, negligent homicide, seduction, and so forth, are punishable solely on the person of the actual culprit.

What heightens the significance of this departure is the fact that the Bible is not at all ignorant of collective or vicarious punishment. The narratives tell of the case of Achan who appropriated objects devoted to God from the booty of Jericho and buried them under his tent. The anger of God manifested itself in a defeat of Israel's army before Ai. When Achan was discovered, he and his entire household were put to death (Josh. 7). Saul's sons were put to death for their father's massacre of the Gibeonites in violation of an oath by YHWH (2 Sam. 21). Now these instances are not a matter of ordinary criminal law but touch the realm of the deity directly.[38a] The misappropriation of a devoted object—חרם—infects the culprit and all who come into contact with him with the taboo status of the חרם (Deut. 7:26; 13:16; cf. Josh. 6:18). This is wholly analogous to the contagiousness of the state of impurity, and a provision of the law of the impurity of a corpse is really the best commentary on the story of Achan's crime: "This is the law: when a man dies in a tent every one that comes into that tent, and every thing that is in the tent, shall be unclean" (Num. 19:14). Achan's misappropriated objects—the story tells us four times in three verses (Josh. 7:21, 22, 23)—were hidden in the ground under his tent. Therefore he, his family, his domestic animals, and his tent had to be destroyed, since all incurred the חרם status. This is not a case, then, of vicarious or collective punishment pure and simple, but a case of collective contagion of a taboo status. Each of the inhabitants of Achan's tent incurred the חרם status for which he was put to death, though, to be sure, the actual guilt of the misappropriation was Achan's alone.

The execution of Saul's sons is a genuine case of vicarious punishment, though it too is altogether extraordinary. A national oath made in the name of God has been violated by a king. A drought interpreted as the wrath of God has struck at the whole nation. The injured party, the Gibeonites, demand life for life and expressly refuse to hear of composition. Since the offending king is dead, his children are delivered up.

These two cases—with Judges 21:10f. the only ones in which legitimate collective and vicarious punishments are recorded in the Bible[39]—show clearly in what area notions of family solidarity and collective guilt are still operative: the area of direct affronts to the majesty of God. Crimes committed against the property, the exclusive rights, or the name of God may be held against the whole family, indeed the whole community of the offender. A principle that is rejected in the case of judicial punishment is yet recognized as operative in the divine realm. The same book of Deuteronomy that clears parents and children of each other's guilt still incorporates the dictum that God holds children to account for their parents' apostasy to the third and fourth generation (5:9). Moreover, it is Deuteronomy 13:16 that relates the law of the חרם of the apostate city, ordaining that every inhabitant be destroyed, including the cattle. For the final evidence of the concurrent validity of these divergent standards of judgment, the law of the Molech worshiper may be adduced (Lev. 20:1–5): a man who worships Molech is to be stoned by the people—he alone; but if the people overlook his sin, "Then I," says God, "will set my face against that man, and against his family. . . ." (This interpretation of Leviticus 20:5, understanding the guilt of the family before God as due merely to their association with the Molech-worshiper, is open to question. The intent of the text may rather be to ascribe the people's failure to prosecute the culprit to his family's covering up for him; see Rashi and Ibn Ezra. In that case "his family" of 5a is taken up again in "all who go astray after him" of 5b, and the family is guilty on its own.)

The belief in a dual standard of judgment persisted into late times. Not only Deuteronomy itself, but the literature composed after it continues to exhibit belief in God's dooming children and children's children for the sins of the parents. The prophetess Huldah, who confirms the warnings of Deuteronomy, promises that punishment for the sins of Judah will be deferred until after the time of the righteous king Josiah (2 Kings 22:19f.). Jeremiah, who is imbued with the ideology of Deuteronomy, and who is himself acutely aware of the imperfection of the standard of divine justice (Jer. 31:28f.), yet announces to his personal enemies a doom that involves them and their children (Jer. 11:22; 29:32). And both Jeremiah and the Deuteronomistic compiler of the Book of Kings ascribe the fall of Judah to the sin of Manasseh's age (Jer. 15:4; 2 Kings 23:26f.; 24:3f.). Even Job complains that God lets the children of the wicked live happily (21:7ff.). Thus there can be no question of an evolution during the biblical age from early to late concepts, from "holding children to account for the sins of parents" to "parents shall not be put to death for children," etc. There is rather a remarkable divergence between the way God may judge humans and the way humans must judge each other. The divergence goes back to the earliest legal and narrative texts and persists through the latest.

How anomalous the biblical position is can be appreciated when set against its Near Eastern background. A telling expression of the parallel between human and divine conduct toward wrongdoing is the following Hittite soliloquy:

> Is the disposition of men and of the gods at all different? No! Even in this matter somewhat different? No! But their disposition is quite the same. When a servant stands before his master . . . [and serves him] . . . his master . . . is relaxed in spirit and is favorably inclined (?) to him. If, however, he (the servant) is ever dilatory (?) or is not observant (?), there is a different disposition towards him. And if ever a servant vexes his master, either they kill him, or [mutilate him]; or he (the master) calls him to account (and also) his wife, his sons, his brothers, his sisters, his relatives by marriage, and his family . . . And if ever he dies, he does not die alone, but his family is included with him. If then anyone vexes the feeling of a god, does the god punish him alone for it? Does he not punish his wife, his children, his descendants, his family, his slaves male and female, his cattle, his sheep, and his harvest for it, and remove him utterly?[40]

To this striking statement it need only be added that not alone between master and servant was the principle of vicarious punishment applied in Hittite and Near Eastern law, but, as we have seen, between parents and children and husbands and wives as well.

In contrast, the biblical view asserts a difference between the power of God, and that of human, over human. Biblical criminal law foregoes entirely the right to punish any but the actual culprit in all civil cases; so far as humans are concerned all persons are individual, morally autonomous entities. In this too there is doubtless to be seen the effect of the heightened stress on the unique worth of each life brought about by the religious-legal postulate that human beings are made in the image of God. "All persons are mine, says the Lord, the person of the father as well as that of the son; the person that sins, he shall die" (Ezek. 18:4). By this assertion Ezekiel wished to make valid in the theological realm the individual autonomy that the law had acknowledged in the criminal realm centuries before. That God may impute responsibility and guilt to the whole circle of a person's family and descendants was a notion that biblical Israel shared with its neighbors. What was unique to Israel was its belief that this was exclusively the way of God; it was unlawful arrogation for humans to exercise this divine prerogative.

The study of biblical law, then, with careful attention to its own inner postulates, has as much to reveal about the values of Israelite culture as the study of Psalms and Prophets. For the appreciation of this vital aspect of the biblical world, the riches of cuneiform law offer a key that was unavailable to the two millennia of exegesis that preceded our time. The key is now available and the treasury yields a bountiful reward to those who use it.

NOTES

1. J. L. Saalschütz, *Das Mosaiche Recht, mit Berücksichtigung des spätern Jüdischen*, 2 vols. (Berlin, 1848).

2. The following law collections are pertinent to the discussion of the criminal law of the Bible: the laws of Eshnunna (LE), from the first half of the nineteenth century B.C.E.; the code of Hammurabi (CH), from the beginning of the eighteenth century; the Middle Assyrian laws (MAL), 14th–11th centuries; and the Hittite laws (HL), latter half of the second millennium. All are translated in J. B. Pritchard, ed., *Ancient Near Eastern Texts Relating to the Old Testament* (Princeton, 1955), 159ff. Henceforth this work will be referred to as ANET.

3. G. R. Driver and J. C. Miles, *The Babylonian Laws*, 2 vols. (Oxford, 1952, 1955), henceforth cited as BL. The citation is from I:99; cf. also p. 275, where Koschaker's approach is characterized and Miles' approach contrasted.

4. Contrast, the historical explanation of the discrepancies in the laws of theft given by Meek in ANET, 166, note 45, with Miles's suggestions in BL I:80ff. The historical explanation does not help us understand how the draftsman of the law of Hammurabi conceived of the law of theft.

5. The point is made and expertly illustrated in E. A. Hoebel, *The Law of Primitive Man* (Harvard, 1954); cf. especially chapter 1.

6. Inscription of Yaḥdun-lim of Mari, *Syria* 32 (1955):4, lines 1ff. I owe this reference and its interpretation to Professor E. A. Speiser, whose critique of this part of my discussion has done much to clarify the matter in my mind; cf. his contribution to *Authority and Law in the Ancient Orient* (Supplement to JAOS, No. 17 [1954]), especially 11ff.

7. Cf. CH xxvb:95ff.: "I am Hammurabi, the just king, to whom Shamash has granted truths." We are to understand the laws of Hammurabi as an attempt to embody this cosmic ideal in laws and statutes. (After writing the above I received a communication from Professor J. J. Finkelstein interpreting this passage as follows: "What the god 'gives' the king is not 'laws' but the gift of the perception of kittum, by virtue of which the king, in distinction from any other individual, becomes capable of promulgating laws that are in accord or harmony with the cosmic principle of *kittum*.")

8. Speiser, op.cit., 12; this Mesopotamian conception of cosmic truth is a noteworthy illustration of Professor Kaufmann's thesis that "Paganism conceives of morality not as an expression of the supreme, free will of the deity, but as one of the forces of the transcendent, primordial realm which governs the deity as well" (תולדות האמונה הישראלית, I/2:345).

9. CH xxivb:76f., 81; xxvb:12f., 64ff., 78ff., 99; xxvib:3f., 19ff.

10. Ibid., xxvib:33f. It is not clear, in the face of this plain evidence, how it can still be maintained that the relief at the top of the law stele depicts Shamash dictating or giving the code to Hammurabi (E. Dhorme, *Les religions de Babylon et d'Assyrie* [Paris, 1949], 62; S. H. Hooke, *Babylonian and Assyrian Religion* [London, 1953], 29). The picture is nothing more than a traditional presentation scene in which a worshiper in an attitude of adoration stands before, or is led by another deity into, the presence of a god; it may be inferred from the context (i.e., the position of the picture above the code) that the figures of this highly conventionalized scene represent Hammurabi and Shamash. See the discussion in H. Frankfort, *The Art and Architecture of the Ancient Orient* (1954), 59 (note that Frankfort does not even go so far as Meek who sees in the scene "Hammurabi in the act of receiving the commission to write the law-book from . . . Shamash" [ANET, 163]). For this and similar representations see J. B. Pritchard, ANEP (Princeton, 1954), numbers 514, 515, 529, 533, 535, 707. Miles aptly sums up the matter of the authorship of the laws thus (BL, 39): "Although [Shamash and Marduk] . . . are mentioned a number of times, they are not said to be the authors of the Laws;

Hammurabi himself claims to have written them. Their general character, too, is completely secular, and in this respect they are strongly to be contrasted with the Hebrew laws; they are not a divine pronouncement nor in any sense a religious document."

11. Epilogue to the laws of Lipit-Ishtar, ANET, 161.

12. See the prologue and epilogue of the laws of Lipit-Ishtar and Hammurabi.

13. The point is made in Kaufmann, op. cit., I/1:67.

14. CH 129; MAL 14–16; HL 198; cf. W. Kornfield, "L'adultère dans l'orient antique," RB 57 (1950):92ff.; E. Neufeld, *Ancient Hebrew Marriage Laws* (London, 1944), 172ff.

15. HL 187, 188, 198, 199; cf. LE 48.

16. HL 1–4.

17. A. Kennett, *Bedouin Justice* (Cambridge, 1925), 49ff.

18. LE 54; CH 250, 251.

19. Strict retaliation of life for life is "primitive," a "desert principle"; cf. Th. J. Meek, *Hebrew Origins* (New York, 1936), 66–8; A. Alt, *Die Ursprünge des israelitischen Rechts*, in *Kleine Schriften zur Geschichte des Volkes Israel* (München, 1953), 305ff.; A. Kennett, op. cit., 49; on the goring ox, cf. BL I, 444; M. Weber, *Ancient Judaism* (Glencoe, 1952), 62. For the widely held theory of the development of punishment that underlies this view see BL I, 500.

20. The peculiarities that distinguish this biblical law from the Babylonian are set forth fully by A. van Selms, "The Goring Ox in Babylonian and Biblical Law," AO 18 (1950):321ff., though he has strangely missed the true motive for stoning the ox and tabooing its flesh.

21. From the comment of Sifre to Deuteronomy 19:13a, it is clear that this paradox was already felt in antiquity.

22. Driver-Miles, *The Assyrian Laws* (Oxford, 1935), 35.

23. Ibid., 36; Kennett, op. cit., 26f., 54f.

24. This interpretation follows Goetze's translation (ANET, 191, cf. especially note 9). Since no specific punishment is mentioned, and in view of the recognition by Hittite law of the principle of replacing life by life (cf. HL 44) there does not seem to be any ground for assuming that any further punishment beyond forced incorporation into the injured community was contemplated (E. Neufeld, *The Hittite Laws* [London, 1951], 158).

25. CH 21, 25; LE 13 (cf. A. Goetze, *The Laws of Eshnunna*, Annual of the American Schools of Oriental Research 31 [New Haven, 1956]:53); CH 6–10; MAL 3. Inasmuch as our present interest is in the theoretical postulates of the law systems under consideration, the widely held opinion that these penalties were not enforced in practice, while interesting in itself, is not relevant to our discussion.

26. The action of verse 1 occurs at night; cf. verse 2 and Job 24:16. Verse 2 is to be rendered: "If it occurred after dawn, there is bloodguilt for (killing) him; he must make payment only (and is not subject to death); if he can not, then he is to be sold for his theft" (but he is still not subject to death–contrast CH 8). For the correct interpretation see Ibn Ezra and U. Cassuto, *Commentary on Exodus* (Jerusalem, 1951), ad loc. (Hebrew); Cassuto points out (ibid., 196) that this law is an amendment to the custom reflected in CH's laws of theft–a fact that is entirely obscured by the transposition of verses in the Chicago Bible and the Revised Standard Version. Later jurists doubtless correctly interpreted the householder's privilege as the result of presumption against the burglar that he would not shrink from murder; the privilege, then, is subsumed under the right of self-defense (Mechilta, ad loc.).

27. O. Gurney, *The Hittites* (London, 1952), 98.

28. Mishnah Sanhedrin 5.1ff., Gemara, ibid., 40b bottom; cf. Mishnah Makkoth 1.10.

29. To deal with practical exigencies it became necessary to invest the court with extraordinary powers that permitted suspension of all the elaborate safeguards that the law provided the accused; cf. J. Ginzberg, *Mishpatim Le-israel, A Study in Jewish Criminal Law* (Jerusalem, 1956), part I, chap. 2; part II, chap 4 (Hebrew).

30. CH 116.

31. CH 209–210; cf. MAL 50.

32. CH 230.
33. MAL 55.
34. HL 1–4, 44; see also note 22 above.
35. Ibn Ezra in his commentary to Deuteronomy 24:16 already inveighs against the erroneous combination of the two dicta; the error has persisted through the centuries (cf. B. D. Eerdmans, *The Religion of Israel* [Leiden, 1947], 94).
36. Later jurists differed with regard to but one case חרם (Num. 1:51; 3:10; 18:7) according to Gemara Sanhedrin 84a (cf. Mishnah Sanhedrin 9.6); but the scholar to whom the Gemara ascribes the opinion that והזר הקרב יומת here means by an act of God (R. Ishmael) is quoted in the Sifre to Numbers 18:7 as of the opinion that a judicial execution is intended (so Ibn Ezra at Num. 1:51). The unanimous opinion of the rabbis that Exodus 21:29 refers to death by an act of God (Mechilta) is a liberalizing exegesis; see the ground given in Gemara Sanhedrin, 15b.
37. J. M. Powis Smith, *The Origin and History of Hebrew Law* (Chicago, 1931), 66; Weber, op.cit., 66.
38. Cassuto, commentary ad loc.; P. J. Verdam, "On ne fera point mourir les enfants pour les pères en droit biblique," *Revue internationale des droits de l'antiquité* 2/3 (1949):393ff. Professor I. L. Seeligmann calls my attention to the fact that this interpretation was earlier advanced by D. H. Müller, *Die Gesetze Hammurabis* (Wien, 1903), 166ff. A. B. Ehrlich's interpretation (in his *Randglossen*, ad loc.) taking בן and בת to mean "free man" and "free woman" in contrast with עבד, אמה of verse 32 may now be set aside, ingenious as it is (though forced as well: the suggested parallels John 8:35 and Proverbs 17:2 [Seeligmann] deal with matters of inheritance and ownership where son [not "free man"!] and slave are apt contrasts; not so here. Note also the particle או in Exodus 21:31, indicating the verse to be an appendix to the foregoing, rather than connecting it with the new clause, verse 32, beginning with אם).
38a. Recognized by Verdam, op. cit., 408, and already by S. R. Driver in his commentary to Deuteronomy (ICC, 1909), 277.
39. The massacre of the priestly clan at Nob (1 Sam. 22:19) and the execution of Naboth's sons (2 Kings 9:26) are not represented as lawful. Both cases involve treason, for which it appears to have been customary to execute the whole family of the offender. This custom, by no means confined to ancient Israel (cf. Jos. Antiq. 13.14.2), is not to be assumed to have had legal sanction, though it was so common that Amaziah's departure from it deserved to be singled out for praise (2 Kings 14:6).
40. Gurney, op. cit., 70f.

Additional note:

This essay was subjected to extensive criticism by B.S. Jackson, "Reflections on Biblical Criminal Law," *JJS* 24 (1973) 8–38; revised in his *Essays in Jewish and Comparative Legal History* Leiden: Brill, (1975), 25–63. I replied to his and others' criticism in "More Reflections on Biblical Criminal Law," in S. Japhet, ed., *Studies in Bible: 1986*, Scripta Hierosolymitana 31 (Jerusalem: Magnes Press, 1986), 1–17. Some lines were mistakenly omitted from the text of my reply:
Page 5, line 2, after "can," read: make up for loss of life, and a grave enough offense against property can.
Page 11, before line 1 insert: committed by his ox"; and for one liable only to Heaven the alternative of.
Recently Dale Patrick has called attention to the unfinished business of biblical scholarship respecting the conceptual coherence of biblical law in "Studying Biblical Law as a Humanities," in *Thinking Biblical Law*, Semeia 45 (1989), 27–47. After noting that my essay set an agenda, he singles out David Daube, J.J. Finkelstein, Shalom Paul, Y. Muffs and Jacob Milgrom as "exemplary practitioners of conceptual interpretation" (29f.) It is not accidental that Jewish scholars should have taken the lead in seeking out the ideas and values embodied in biblical law.

The Biblical Conception of Asylum

1959

The laws of the Bible treat of the right of asylum in three passages.[1] In Exodus 21:12–14, it is promised that the accidental homicide will have a place appointed for him for flight. The nature of this place is not further defined, it being clear only that it is other than the altar of YHWH which is referred to in verse 14. For that verse says that the murderer is to be taken away for execution even from the altar; evidently, then, the aforementioned place is not that altar.

Numbers 35:9–34 says nothing of the altar, but prescribes that six Levitical cities, three on each side of the Jordan, are to be appointed as asylums—the term employed is ערי מקלט "cities of intaking"—for the accidental homicide. The "assembly"—a tribunal outside of the asylum—tries the fugitive slayer, and if it finds him innocent of murder, it rescues him from the avenger and returns him to the city of refuge. There the slayer must remain until the death of the high priest. If he leaves the city before, he may be slain with impunity by the avenger. No ransom may be accepted from the slayer in lieu of his stay in the asylum.

The law of Deuteronomy 19:1–13 stresses the responsibility of the community to establish easily accessible asylums for the slayer, and keep murderers from enjoying immunity in them. Nothing is said of the Levitical character of the cities of refuge, or of the requirement that the slayer be detained in them until the death of the high priest.

The humanitarian purpose of these laws is obvious, and their aspiration to control vengeance by making it possible for public justice to intervene between the slayer and the avenger has long been recognized as an advance over the prior custom of regarding homicide as a

43

purely private matter to be settled between the families of the two parties.[2]

On the basis of this humanitarian and political understanding it has generally been assumed that the laws bear the following relation to each other: The law of Exodus, speaking of an altar, is compared with the flight of Adonijah and Joab to the tent sanctuary of Jerusalem, there to lay hold of the corners of the altar for protection from Solomon (1 Kings 1:50, 2:28). With good reason it is supposed that the law of Exodus reflects the earliest custom of seeking asylum at the local sanctuaries that filled ancient Palestine before the Josianic reform. The vague "place" of the Exodus law is accordingly interpreted to mean sanctuary site.

When the Deuteronomist proposed to abolish the local sanctuaries, "in order not to abolish the right of asylum along with the altars, he appoints special cities of refuge for the innocent who are pursued by the avenger of blood."[3] The six cities of refuge are the Deuteronomist's means of replacing the local sanctuaries as asylums, for—it is argued—while the local altars and sanctuaries were in existence, what need was there of six special cities of refuge?

Inasmuch as Numbers also speaks of cities, it is to be inferred that it followed Deuteronomy. The priestly interest reflected in the law of Numbers likewise is taken as a reflex of a later age. That the death of the high priest is the signal for the release of the slayer signifies that "his death marks an epoch; it is when the high priest—not the king—dies that the fugitive slayer obtains his amnesty. . . . What now can be the meaning of this fact . . . but that the civil power has been withdrawn from the nation and is in the hands of foreigners . . . ?"[4] In other words, the law reflects the theocratic organization of the Persian province of Judah. Again, the evidently punitive character of the slayer's stay in the city of refuge, so foreign to the humanitarian interest of the early laws, bespeaks a later transformation of the entire concept of asylum.[5]

Various details of this theory have been criticized. The altar, it has been pointed out, cannot have provided a permanent refuge for the slayer, so that for the Deuteronomic provision of cities there was good practical ground even when many altars were available.[6] The priestly law that the slayer not be released until the death of the high priest has been interpreted alternatively—following ancient exegesis (see below)—as an expiation, which has nothing to do with the political importance of the high priest in post-Exilic times.[7] But the inability of scholars to define convincingly either the nature of this expiation or its necessity has led to the general retention of the original Wellhausenian position.[8]

Now that position is open to question on several grounds. That a high priest's *death* should be the occasion of an amnesty is an odd idea. Amnesties, it has been observed,[9] occur at the accession of new rulers, being a politic device for ingratiating themselves with the populace. Moreover, Wellhausen's interpretation disregards the whole tenor of the law: if there is anything characteristic of the priestly law of Numbers it is the insistence upon the absolute nature of the crime of homicide, and the impermissibility of mitigating its penalties by any human agency.

> You shall not take a ransom for the life of a murderer who is liable to death, but he shall be put to death. And you shall accept no ransom for him who has fled to his city of refuge, that he may return to dwell in the land before the death of the high priest. You shall not thus pollute the land in which you live; for blood pollutes the land, and no expiation can be made for the land for the blood that is shed in it, except by the blood of him who shed it. (Num. 35:31–33)

This would seem definitely to exclude the idea that any human authority was empowered to expunge the guilt of the homicide in a manner so savoring of political expediency as is implied by the notion of amnesty.

Indeed the Achilles' heel of the critical position is its failure to take into account adequately the religious presuppositions of the asylum law. The provisions of that law are not wholly accounted for on humanitarian or political grounds.

It must first be recognized that whenever an innocent person is slain, the law considers the slayer guilty in a measure. Shedding an innocent person's blood, even unintentionally, involved bloodguilt, and no slayer was considered clear of this guilt. This appears, first, in the Deuteronomic law that does not regard as actionable the avenger's killing the slayer on the way to the city of refuge. To be sure, the community is held responsible if the slayer, who did not deserve to die, was caught owing to the failure of the people to make the city of refuge accessible (Deut. 19:10). Yet the avenger is not regarded as a murderer. Why? Because the slayer was not guiltless. The law of Numbers makes this point explicit: if the avenger finds the slayer outside the city of refuge and slays him, he shall not be guilty of bloodshed (35:27). The most striking legal expression of the objectivity of bloodguilt—i.e., its incurrence even without criminal intent—is the law of Exodus 21:28ff. concerning the homicidal ox. Here, where there can be no intent since the killer is a brute, the law nonetheless regards the animal as bloodguilty and requires that it be stoned. Now this law is but the application of the principle of Genesis 9:5: "For your lifeblood

I will surely require a reckoning; of every beast will I require it." And since that principle, laid down in a priestly passage, is incorporated in the Covenant Code—by universal agreement the earliest law collection—we are advised to pause before mechanically assigning ideas that occur in P to late times.

The accidental homicide is, then, guilty, though not guilty of death. How is this guilt to be expiated? Illumination is thrown upon our subject from another quarter. In ancient Greece a strikingly parallel notion of the objectivity of bloodguilt was held. Every bloodshed was polluting; a miasma lay on the slayer, as well as on the family and even the city of the slain, that had somehow to be purged away. The law of involuntary homicide of ancient Greece is set forth as follows by Demosthenes:

> The man who is convicted of involuntary homicide shall, on certain appointed days, leave the country by a prescribed route, and remain in exile until he is reconciled to one of the relatives of the deceased. Then the law permits him to return . . . it instructs him to make sacrifice and to purify himself, and gives other directions for his conduct. (*Against Aristocrates* [XXIII]:72; trans. J. H. Vince, Loeb Classical Library)

Let us apply these concepts to ancient Israel. Condemnation to exile outside the country is not a penalty found in biblical law, for the reason that exile meant being cut off from YHWH, and, in the worst case, being forced to worship other gods (1 Sam. 26:19; Deut. 4:27f.). The Israelite analogue to banishment could only have been the enforced exile of the slayer from his hometown. On the other hand, the punishment of homicide, as has been said, was not subject to human decision. The kin of the slain are not allowed to come to terms with the slayer, either in a monetary or any other fashion. They cannot pardon his act and expunge his sin. This is the explicit law of Numbers 35, but it is not a late idea of the priestly writer; it is a principle informing all of biblical law. Exodus 21:30 must specifically sanction the acceptance of ransom from the negligent owner of a homicidal ox because the rule is that homicides generally cannot be ransomed; an exception is here made only because the owner of the ox did not personally and with malice commit the slaying. Deuteronomy 19:12f. has entirely replaced the right of the kin to dispose as they wish of the murderer with the unconditional death penalty. True, the avenger is the executioner, but he has no say in the sentence; once the man has been convicted of murder the matter is out of the avenger's hands. It is the same in the case of the accidental homicide: the kin are not to say when his guilt is expunged.

Now the city of refuge, as conceived in Numbers, at once takes account of the whole situation in which the accidental homicide finds himself. In contrast with the temporary asylum provided by the altar, the city secures the life of the slayer for an indefinite period. At the same time it provides for the expiation of guilt: first, by an enforced detention—the slayer may not buy his way out of the city of refuge. The punitive character of this detention was fully recognized by later writers. Both Philo (*De spec. leg.* III:123) and Josephus (*Antiq.* 4.7.4.) use the term φυγή "banishment" to describe the stay of the slayer in the city of refuge; tannaitic law uses the equally expressive גלות "exile."

What is the meaning of the peculiar limit set to the term of banishment—the death of the high priest? Later Jewish jurists discussed the question in the following illuminating passage:

> MISHNAH: If after [the slayer] has been sentenced as an accidental homicide and the high priest dies, he need not go into exile.

> GEMARA: . . . But is it not exile that expiates?—It is not exile that expiates, but the death of the high priest. (Bab. Talmud, Makkoth, 11b)

This interpretation accords fully with the biblical view of the incommutability of the penalties of homicide. "He who sheds the blood of man, by man shall his blood be shed, for in the image of God made He man" (Gen. 9:6). This statement, the ideological basis of the law's refusal to recognize the translatability of life into any other terms, occurs in the priestly writings. Again, however, it is no late conceit, but a principle that animated the earliest lawmakers of Israel as well. The clearest expression of this is the remarkable leniency with which property offenses are dealt with in biblical law. No crime against property is punished with death. The insistence of life for life, to the exclusion of monetary compensation—a severity unparalleled in ancient Near Eastern law—has its counterpart in the refusal to consider any offense against property worthy of the death penalty— equally unheard of in all Near Eastern systems but the Hittite. In biblical law, life and property are incommensurable.[10]

Taking life, then, imposes a guilt that cannot be expiated by any means short of death. But whose death can expiate the bloodguilt of the slayer who is not liable to capital punishment? A religious guilt such as bloodguilt can be expiated only in religious terms. Can the Israelite slayer offer—like his Greek counterpart—a purificatory sacrifice? The incommensurability of human with animal life forbids it. It is a remarkable fact that, while biblical, like Greek, law regards bloodshed as polluting, it does not prescribe a purificatory sacrifice to purge any slayer of guilt. And, although it is precisely for unintentional and unwitting sins that the sin and guilt offerings of Leviticus 4–5 and Numbers 15:22–29 are designed, the unintentional homicide is not required to make such a purgatorial offering. Only another human life can expiate the guilt of accidental slaying.

The sole personage whose religious-cultic importance might endow his death with expiatory value for the people at large is the high priest. During his life the priest expiates one type of religious guilt incurred by the people at large through the gold plate that he wears on his forehead: "It shall be on Aaron's forehead, and Aaron shall bear the iniquity committed in the holy things, which the children of Israel shall hallow . . . and it shall always be upon his forehead, that they may be accepted before YHWH" (Exod. 28:36ff.).[11] By his death he expiates the guilt that can be expiated only through death, but that could not be so expiated before. A later jurist expresses the underlying conception thus: "Just as the clothing of the high priest expiates, so the death of the righteous expiates."[12]

It appears, then, that the city of refuge as conceived in Numbers is the necessary adjunct to, rather than a replacement of, the local altars. The altar gives temporary asylum from the immediate danger of pursuit by the avenger; the city alone provides for the expiation of bloodguilt, which every stratum of biblical law associates with homicide.

What finally, is the relation of the law of Numbers to that of Deuteronomy? It has already been suggested that the six cities named in Joshua 20:7f. as Levitical cities of refuge were the sites of important sanctuaries (this is certain for Hebron and Shechem) that had become popular refuges.[13] The six were all part of Israelite territory only during the heyday of the united monarchy, shortly before and after the death of David. The united monarchy may also be considered a likely time for such a national program for regulating blood revenge to have been conceived, though the conception of asylum that it incorporates, apart from the specification of the six cities, is doubtless older. It is interesting, in passing, to note that the idea of punitive confinement to a city area, coupled with a notion of special grace, is also attested to at this time: Solomon's confinement of Shimei to Jerusalem on pain of death if he leaves is a sort of grim variation on the theme of the asylum (1 Kings 2:36f.). In both cases persons are involved who, though they have committed a guilty act, are saved from the death penalty, the one by royal, the other by divine grace. The city of their confinement has at once the attributes of a prison and an asylum.[14]

In perfect accord with pre-Josianic conditions, Numbers represents the cities of refuge as Levitical cities (35:6), a reflex of the fact that all were the sites of important priestly families who were the hereditary priesthoods of the local sanctuaries. The expiatory death of the high priest—it is left unclear whether of the city of refuge or of the slayer's hometown[15]—also accords best with a multiplicity of local priesthoods. Deuteronomy, on the other hand, has wholly transformed the ancient conception by effacing its sacerdotal side. The Levitical character of the cities of refuge (i.e., their being sanctuary sites) as well as the role of the high priest's death are ignored by Deuteronomy, whose doctrine of centralized worship entailed the virtual secularization of the concept of asylum. In Deuteronomy it does indeed become a purely humanitarian institution. But the law of Numbers, whatever be the date of its present formulation,[16] preserves intact the cultic and expiatory features that are the earmarks of antiquity and that, indeed, are made necessary by the idea of the bloodguilt of homicide that prevails in the earliest laws of Israel.

Thus, although there is no mention of cities of refuge outside of the laws, nothing stands in the way of assuming that the laws concerning them reflect the conceptions, perhaps even the custom, of the earliest age of Israel. The law of Numbers is to be understood as amplifying the vague "place" to which Exodus promises that the slayer will be able to flee, and is designed as a final disposition of the fugitive who has fled for temporary protection to a local altar. Deuteronomy takes its departure from the law of Numbers, but by stripping the cities of their sacred status as sanctuary sites, and by its disregard of the religious-cultic provisions of Numbers, it is seen to be later revision.

NOTES

1. Outside the legal corpora the subject is referred to again in Joshua 20. Since that passage is evidently dependent upon the formulations of Numbers 35 and Deuteronomy 19 ("probably a secondary compilation out of both these sources" [Noth, *Das Buch Josua*, HAT (1938), 97; cf. M. David, "Die Bestimmungen über die Asylstädte in Josua XX," OTS, IX (1951):48]; the dating of this passage will depend, of course, on that of its constituents; that nothing in the Numbers [or Deuteronomy] passage necessitates a post-exilic dating is argued below), and since it sheds no new light on the concept of asylum it will not be discussed here.

2. Cf. E. Merz, *Die Blutrache bei den Israeliten* (Leipzig, 1916):88ff., 103ff.

3. J. Wellhausen, *Prolegomena* (English trans.; Edinburgh, 1885), 33.

4. Ibid., 150.

5. Merz, op. cit., 132; David, op. cit., 45.

6. David, op. cit., 38; G. B. Gray, *Numbers*, ICC (1903), 474. Merz (op. cit., 91) seeks to meet this difficulty by adducing evidence from Arabia and Greece for the inclusion of much more than merely the sanctuary building within the sacred precinct that gave asylum. It must be admitted, however, that there is no biblical evidence for such a widening of the sacred area, nor are the cities of refuge ever denoted sacred, sanctified territory.

7. Merz, op. cit., 132; N. M. Nicolsky, "Das Asylrecht in Israel," ZAW, XLVIII (1930):168ff.; Y. Kaufmann, תולדות האמונה הישראלית (Tel Aviv, 1937–[1956]), I:140.

8. Cf. David, op. cit., 40ff.; R. De Vaux, *Les Institutions de l'Ancien Testament* (Paris, 1958), I: 248ff.

9. Kaufmann, loc. cit.

10. That this is a distinctive feature of biblical law will be shown in a forthcoming article ["Some Postulates of Biblical Criminal Law"].

11. The significance of this passage was noted by Nicolsky (op. cit., 169).

12. Dictum of R. Elazar b. Pedath (Palestine, 3rd century), Bab. Talmud, Moed Katan, 28a (cf. Zebahim, 88b). The expiatory death of the righteous is again referred to in Bereshith Rabba 44.5 end; Samuel Jaffe's commentary (*Yefe To'ar*), ad loc., adduces other rabbinic and biblical illustrations, among which latter are Isaiah 53 and Ezekiel 4:4ff. It is interesting to note that in prophetic and rabbinic literature the worth of the expiatory victim is moral, not, as in the ancient law, intrinsic-cultic.

13. Noth, op. cit., 96; W. F. Albright, "The List of Levitic Cities," *Louis Ginzberg Jubilee Volume*, English Section (1945), 49ff.

14. Both M. Löhr, *Das Asylwesen im Alten Testament*, Schriften der Königsberger Gelehrten Gesellschaft, VII/3 (1930):34, and S. Klein, ערי הכהנים והלויים וערי מקלט, קובץ החברה העברית לחקירת ארץ-ישראל ועתיקותיה, לזכר א. מ. מזיא, ירושלים, תרצ"ה, 81–94. date the list of Levitical cities to the early monarchy. To this Kaufmann (op cit., IV:383) has objected that the absence of Jerusalem is inexplicable on the basis of this dating. But it may be that Jerusalem and its royal chapel had not yet attained the popular status that the older sanctuaries had by the early monarchy.

15. The obscurity arises from P's insistence on speaking in terms of the desert age (in spite of its occasional recognition of post-settlement conditions, e.g., in its notion of Levitical cities). At that time there was but one עדה and one high priest. What was to be done when, after the settlement, there would be many עדות, each having its own sanctuary and high priest, is not made explicit.

That P speaks in terms that are archetypical for local communities and sanctuaries has been persuasively argued by Kaufmann (op. cit., I:114ff.; this is, e.g., the only plausible context for the law of the slaughtering in Leviticus 17), who is of the opinion that the high priest belongs to the slayer's town (ibid., 140).

16. The possibility that it is later than Deuteronomy's formulation is suggested by the presence in it of the technical term that is not yet found in Deuteronomy. This would not seem to be sufficient ground for dating the law to post-exilic times.

Biblical Attitudes Toward Power: Ideal and Reality in Law and Prophets

1990

Throughout the Torah ("the Law") and the Prophets, the relation between God and humanity is bedeviled by the issue of power.[1] Tension inheres in the conception that while God has dominion in heaven and earth he has made man in his image and given him dominion over the earth and its resources.

> YHWH our Lord,
> How majestic is your name throughout the earth,
> You who have covered the heavens with your splendor! . . .
> When I behold your heavens, the work of your fingers,
> the moon and stars that you set in place,
> what is man that you have been mindful of him,
> mortal man that you have taken note of him,
> that you have made little less than divine,
> and adorned him with glory and majesty;
> You have made him master over your handiwork,
> laying the world at his feet. (Ps. 8:2, 4–7)

Competition between the two dominions pervades the opening stories of the book of Genesis. Adam and Eve transgressed God's ban in the hope that they would become "like divine beings." A later generation planned to build a tower whose top would reach heaven. The Pharaoh of the Exodus, when commanded by God to let the Israelites worship, retorts insolently, "Who is YHWH that I should obey him? I do not recognize YHWH nor shall I let Israel go!" (Exod. 5:2). The stories show a keen awareness of the pitfalls along the way of a human-

51

ity ambitious for power. So humans are in a quandary: they must dispose of power in order to fulfill their commission of dominating the earth, yet the exercise of power induces delusions of grandeur that lead to destruction.

THE IDEAL OF POWER IN THE LAW

In the biblical view, power belongs properly to God, and he puts it to two purposes: (1) the creation and sustenance of the world, and (2) the maintenance of the moral order. To promote the second purpose, God advises people–first Adam and Eve, then Noah and his family–of the conditions of their happiness in the form of a few prohibitions: in exchange for accepting limitations on the exercise of their power (thus acknowledging God's sovereignty), they will attain happiness. God demands, and has trouble in obtaining, human acquiescence in his supremacy and human acceptance of the order he would impose, for human nature inclines to assert autonomy and thwarts God by refusing to recognize limits to the exercise of human power. But as the generation of the Flood proved, rebellion against God's order inflicts harm only on them: "The earth was filled with violence" (Gen. 6:11). Human aggression had expanded beyond the domain of its proper object–the earth–to impinge upon fellow humans. The race thus became monstrous and was wiped out in the Flood.

God then sought an alternative means to establish his order on earth; out of all the families of the earth he chose that of Abraham, Isaac, and Jacob as the human arena of his self-revelation. Among them he would reign; their descendants he would draw near to him, consecrating them as his kingdom of priests, his holy nation. By his deeds in this modest arena his Godhood would be manifest, and all people would come to see the blessing he conferred on those who acknowledge him.

In Israel, God embodied his order in a legal and moral program–the collections of law comprising the bulk of the Torah. It is formulated in a variety of styles: rulings for hypothetical cases, positive and negative commandments, and rhetorical elements designed to move the recipients to obedience. What distinguishes the style of the Torah from that of all the other treaties and law collections of the ancient East with which it has been compared is the profusion of motive clauses in all its law corpora. Here are some examples from the "Covenant Code" of Exodus:

> You must not wrong the alien or oppress him, for you were aliens in the land of Egypt. (Exod. 22:20)

If you take the garment of your fellow as a pledge, by sunset you must return it to him; for it is his only clothing, the sole cover of his skin; wherein shall he lie down? (Exod. 22:25–26)

Six days you shall do your work but on the seventh you must cease, so that your ox and your ass may rest, and the son of your maidservant and the alien may be refreshed. (Exod. 23:12)

Here is an example from the priestly laws:

Do not make yourselves detestable by eating any swarming creature. Do not defile yourselves with them so as to become unclean, for I am YHWH your God; so sanctify yourselves and be holy, for I am holy. (Lev. 11:43–44)

The rhetorical element in the book of Deuteronomy is so prominent that one scholar has said of its legal corpus, "It is law preached."[2] Two examples will suffice to convey an impression:

[Three cities of refuge must be appointed for the accidental slayer] lest the redeemer of blood pursue the slayer, for his mind will be inflamed, and, catching up with him . . . he will kill him though he is not liable to the death penalty for he was not his [victim's] enemy previously. (Deut. 19:6)

But if the man came upon the betrothed girl in open country and took her by force and lay with her, only the man must die, you must not do anything to the girl; she has not committed any mortal offence. Her case is like that of one attacked by another with intent to murder: he came upon her in open country; the girl [is presumed to have] cried out but there was no one to save her. (Deut. 22:25–27)

The endeavor to persuade goes with the published character of the legislation. According to the narrative framework, the bodies of law were from the first promulgated and done so in a manner accessible to all—by proclamation. To be sure, the laws were written down as a testimony for later times, but first Moses proclaimed them in the hearing of all Israel. God introduces the "Covenant Code" with this charge to Moses: "These are the rulings you must set out before them" (Exod. 21:1). Individual laws are regularly preceded by the formula: "YHWH spoke to Moses saying, 'Speak to the Israelites and say to them'" such and such a law. The dissemination of the laws is of their essence: unlike other ancient systems of law (or modern ones for that matter), the biblical one is designed to educate the public, to mold the national character. Having undertaken to become a holy nation, Israel must be trained to a holy life. The laws of the Torah constitute the regimen and rule of the people conceived as a priestly order. Since the success of God's venture depends on each individual Israelite both knowing the rule and willingly obeying it, it is not only published but suffused with rhetoric calculated to move the individual to assent to its exacting demands.[3]

In the divinely ordained polity provided for Israel, power is dispersed among the members of society and many devices prevent its accumulation and concentration.[4] The society envisaged in the Torah lacks a strong, prestigious focus of power; on the contrary, dignity and authority are distributed. The prestige of parents is guaranteed in the Decalogue; a child who injures them or rebels against them is liable to the death penalty (Exod. 20:12, 21:15, 17; Deut. 21:18–21). Every town ("gate") in Israel has its tribunal of elders, authorized to judge and punish and even to inflict the death penalty (Deut. 16:18, 22:15ff.). Insult to tribal chiefs is paired with insult to God: "You must not revile God or lay a curse upon a chief among your people" (Exod. 22:27). No central government is recognized in the laws, except for an isolated paragraph in Deuteronomy that treats the monarchy; the purpose of that paragraph is to curb the king's appetite for power and prestige.

> He must not have many horses, so as not to return the people to Egypt in order to add to his horses; he must not have many wives so that his mind not be diverted; nor may he have much silver and gold. When he ascends his royal throne he must have a copy of this teaching written for him under the aegis of the Levite priests; it shall be with him and he must read it all his life in order that he may learn to fear YHWH his God . . . that his heart not grow haughty toward his brothers and that he not deviate from the commandments to the right or to the left. (Deut. 17:16–20).

Such a conception of a humble king seems paradoxical, if not quixotic. It is unparalleled in antiquity and remained in Israel also an unrealizable attempt to break human pride for the good of society and the greater glory of God.

Accumulation of economic power is also severely impeded by the laws of the Torah. The foundation of ancient economy being ownership of land, God grants the Israelites a land for their possession, but he conditions their continued tenancy on obedience to his laws. If in the future the people boastfully take the credit for their prosperity, saying, "My power and the might of my hand got me this wealth"; if, forgetting that "It is YHWH your God who has given you the power to get wealth," they are disloyal to him, then they are told "you shall perish as did those nations that YHWH caused to perish before you" (Deut. 8:17–20).

The correlate of God's ownership of the land is the duty of the Israelites to reflect his benevolence in their tenancy of it. The weekly Sabbath rest, for instance, instituted "so that your ox and your ass may rest and the son of your maidservant and the alien may be refreshed," is in force even during the critical, busy seasons of plowing and harvest (Exod. 23:12). Material considerations, which presumably are foremost in the mind of an enterprising farmer, may not prevail against God's benign provision for the needy.[5]

Furthermore, the Israelite must share the wealth gained from the land with unfortunate fellow citizens. The farmer is obliged to let the land lie fallow once in seven years, "so that the needy of your people may eat [its crop];" thus "the Sabbath [-yield] of the land shall serve to feed you and your manservant and your maidservant, your hireling, and the alien resident among you" (Exod. 23:11; Lev. 25:6). The fullest realization of the idea that God owns the land–and a serious curb on economic initiative–is the jubilee, every fiftieth year, in which all sales of land (occasioned in ancient Israel by bankruptcy) are annulled and all real estate reverts to its original owner (who received it in accord with the divine allocation of the land of Canaan among the tribes of Israel at the time of the conquest): "The land shall not be sold permanently, for the land is mine and you are aliens resident with me" (Lev. 25:23). Who will want to buy land when all one actually gets from the purchase is crop years to the next jubilee? Who will invest in a plot of purchased ground when any improvement will in the end redound to its original owner? Such a constraint prevents the accumulation of real property (the basis of economic power); its effect is to keep the economic strength of all families roughly equal (or at least static).

Similar dampening of economic enterprise and growth must result from the ban on interest, by which all loans are converted into charity; that is, money cannot be used to make money (Exod. 22:24; Lev. 25:35ff.). The rule that slaves must be emancipated after seven years or at the jubilee (Exod. 21:2–6; Lev. 25:25–28; Deut. 15:12–18) prevents the accumulation of human capital, "for the Israelites are my slaves," says God, "mine, whom I liberated from the land of Egypt" (Lev. 25:55).

Add to these such provisions as the poor tithe (Deut. 14:28–29), the septennial cancellation of debts (Deut. 15:1–6), the injunction to lend money generously to the needy at no interest (Deut. 15:7–11), and it emerges that the sometimes explicit purpose of the laws to assert God's sovereignty and their implicit reflection of his attributes eventuate in measures that distribute material resources among the people with a clear tendency toward equalization. A focus of human power to rival that of God is precluded.[6]

Finally, such accumulation of power as flows from control of information is counteracted by the regime of the Torah. I have already documented the concern of the legislator to disseminate knowledge of the laws among all the people. The fruit of this concern is Deuteronomy's imposition on parents of a duty to teach the divine commandments to their children (Deut. 6:7, 11:19) and its institution of a septennial public recitation of the Torah ("assemble the people, men, women and children and the alien resident in your towns")–a reenactment of the lawgiving at Mount Horeb (Deut. 31:10–13). That this institution is entrusted to the Levite priests together with the care of the written Torah strikingly contravenes their partisan interest to monopolize sacred lore.

The published laws include the regulation of human authorities and their subjection to divine authority. All Israel knows of God's admonition to judges not to take bribes or pervert justice or ignore the claim of the helpless (Exod. 23:6–8); the ground is thus laid for public supervision and criticism of the judiciary. King Hammurabi of Babylon invited

> any oppressed man who has a cause [to] come into the presence of the statue of me, king of justice, and then read carefully my inscribed stela [of laws], and give heed to my precious words, and may my stela make the case clear to him; may he understand his cause: may he set his mind at ease.[7]

But since the stela stood inside a temple, well out of public view, and was written in the esoteric cuneiform script that necessitated long schooling to read, this invitation amounts to little more than a (boastful) rhetorical gesture. The Torah's regulations concerning the judiciary (to take one example) are calculated to work an entirely different effect. Their oral publication reaches everyone, and empowers whoever feels himself or herself a victim of judicial malfeasance to claim redress, armed with a publicly known divine sanction.

In like manner, broadcasting the king's subjection to God's Torah and the opprobrium attached to his accumulating symbols of prestige and power cannot but undercut his absolute sway over the people. And the publication of the priestly perquisites (e.g., Deut. 18:1–5) and the cause of disqualification from divine service (Lev. 21:13–23) must set limits to priestly authority and prestige in the eyes of the populace.

The promulgation of the Torah serves, in the first instance, the ideal of making Israel a kingdom of priests; it is also the basis of the common responsibility of each for all (e.g., the collective penalty imposed on the community that failed to prosecute a notorious idolater, Leviticus 20:4–5). But at the same time it implicitly heightens the worth and weight of the individual: by imparting information to her or him, both individual accountability and individual power are increased. Duties toward others are matched by the rights one may claim from others. Knowing the boundaries set by God to human authorities makes it impossible for the ruler to assert an absolute sway over the individual. Both are ultimately subject to the same divine sovereign whose laws are designed to keep all humans conscious of their creaturehood.

In its aversion to the concentration of power and its tendency to equalize resources among the citizenry, the system of biblical law resembles democracy. It resembles it, too, in the aspiration to create a society united voluntarily around shared values, in whose achievement all are called on to participate and share responsibility. It resembles it, finally, in its regard for the individual, whose freedom, person, and property it protects with a solicitude unparalleled in ancient societies. On the other hand, since sovereignty and the authority to legislate belong only to God, the biblical person is ideally heteronomous, not autonomous. Moreover, the collective responsibility of members of the covenant community invites mutual surveillance and pressure to conform to divine norms, as oppressive to the individual as any tyranny.

Material benefits, including victory in war, are held out in the Torah not as the purpose for which society is organized and regulated, but as the divine reward for Israel's attaining its spiritual goal of becoming a holy nation (Exod. 23:27–33; Lev. 26:3–13; Deut. 28:1–14). God granted the land of Canaan to the patriarchs and their descendants as a gift; under Joshua, the people, loyal to God, succeeded in conquering most of the land aided by constant miracles. Completion of the conquest was contingent on the continued devotion of Israel to its holy calling, as Joshua expresses it in his farewell speech:

> Now you have seen all that YHWH your God did to all these nations on your behalf—for it is YHWH your God who has fought for you. See I have allotted these nations to you as possessions of your tribes ... YHWH your God will drive them away and dispossess them on your behalf, and you will take possession of your land as YHWH your God promised you. Now be strong and carefully observe all that is written in the Torah of Moses, without deviating to the right or left. Do not mingle with these nations that remain with you; do not invoke the names of their gods ... and do not serve or worship them; but cleave to YHWH your God as you have done to this day—and God has dispossessed great and numerous nations on your behalf. ... A single man of

you put a thousand of them to flight, for it is YHWH your God who has fought for you. . . . So take good care to love YHWH your God, for if you turn away and cleave to these remaining nations . . . know well that YHWH your God will not continue to dispossess these nations on your behalf. (Joshua 23:3–13)

This doctrine applies the lesson learned under Moses to the future: victory is not achieved through clever strategy or effective organization (witness Pharaoh's defeat at the Sea of Reeds, or the rout of Amalek, which had more to do with the rise and fall of Moses' arms than with Joshua's generalship). And similarly the sustenance of Israel in the wilderness owed nothing to social organization, but was the direct provision of God, "in order to make you know that it is not on bread alone that mankind may live, but on whatever God may wish to decree" (Deut. 8:3).[8] The goal of Israel's existence is spiritual; polity and institutions are to be dedicated to attaining it; material blessings are God's reward for its attainment.

THE REALITY OF POWER IN THE PROPHETS

Thus far I have described the program of the Torah and the story of its realization in the Torah and the book of Joshua—both program and story being idealized constructions. What was the reality as described in the Prophets?

Israel's polity during the period to which most of the books of the prophets belong was a monarchy, which arose in the tenth century B.C.E. to free Israel from the control of the well-organized league of Philistine towns. Its goals were to save Israel from its enemies and to preserve a just social order: "Give us a king," the people demand of the prophet Samuel, "who will judge us and lead us forth and fight our battles" (1 Sam. 8:6, 20). The attempt to reconcile the kingship of God, of whom the prophet was the spokesman, with the kingship of a human, by subjecting the latter to the dictate of the former, produced intolerable tension. Where did royal freedom to initiate and decide end, and where did royal obligation to obey God's word conveyed through the prophet begin? Saul's kingship foundered on rigorous tests set by Samuel: would the king obey God's orders when the king judged them to be in conflict with the interests of the state? There was no personal clash between the two men, only a quarrel over ill-defined functions: Samuel is depicted as fond of Saul until the day he died; even afterward it was to Samuel's ghost that Saul applied in his last crisis.

The monarchy could attain its goals only by becoming a national focus of power. That entailed mobilization of public resources, including confiscation of private property and levies on workers for the army and public works. A class of royal officials developed, entitled to make exactions from the people and use them as they saw fit. Some confused the public good with their personal gain. The concentration of resources led to social inequality, and as the prestige of the court and of the officialdom grew, so did their insolence and insouciance toward the mass of the people. The people became estranged from their leaders, who in the northern kingdom eventually degenerated into soldiers of fortune. All the impositions that Samuel said would be necessitated by "the rule of the king" came to pass:

> He will seize your sons and appoint them over his chariots and horses, and they will run before his chariot. He will make them his captains of thousands and fifties, to do his plowing and harvesting, and to make his weapons and chariots. He will take your daughters for perfumers, cooks and bakers. He will take your best fields and give them to his courtiers. Your male and female servants, your best youths, and your asses he will take and use for his works. He will tithe your flocks; and you will be his slaves. (1 Sam. 8:11–17)

The policy of the monarchy subordinated the ideal of becoming a holy nation to the achievement of national prestige and security. It was concerned with building up the military and establishing alliances with powerful neighbors. In the end it subverted the institutions of religion into instruments of royal policy. The story of the nonconforming prophet Micaiah ben Imlah (1 Kings 22) shows how northern kings coopted prophecy for state purposes–in that instance to support a military campaign into territory disputed between Aram and Israel. "Don't you know," says the Israelite king to his staff, "that Ramot Gilead belongs to us?" (1 Kings 22:3). Four hundred prophets–evidently his pensioners–cry their approval and thus conscript God into the army of Israel.[9]

Against these social, political, and spiritual abuses, classical prophecy, beginning with Amos (mid-eighth century), directed its critique. The prophets saw themselves as the spokesmen of Israel's ancient values; since they were not interested in adjusting those values to changed circumstances, they may be called regressive rather than progressive. They denounced the insolent, exploitative, tyrannical use of royal power and prerogative. They denounced the enlisting of God and religion to serve state ends. Hosea was "the first man in history to condemn militarism as a religious-moral sin" (Hos. 8:14, 10:13–14, 14:4).[10] Isaiah put power politics on the same footing as idolatry; he denounced reliance on arms, fortresses, and alliances with great powers. He urged trust in God and quietism that waits on God's salvation.

He foresaw universal peace as the goal toward which history moves—an age in which nations would give up their trust in power and idols, and seek the instruction of God at Zion, the mountain of his holy temple (Isa. 2). Jeremiah and Ezekiel gave voice to God's terrible decision that the present Israel was so degenerate that he could realize his original purpose for the people only by wiping the slate clean and starting over again with renovated survivors.[11]

In the Torah and Prophets, I see an attitude toward power torn between ideal and reality. The conflict could be reconciled only by a creative interpretation of the legislation, applying the old ideal to changed circumstances. Israel's prophets mercilessly exposed the gap between ideal and reality, but did not offer a reconciliation.

The unresolved conflict, along with other issues left open in the canon of Hebrew Scripture, was bequeathed to the Jews of the Second Temple period. The various parties of early Judaism, from the Hasmonean dynasts through the Pharisaic quietists, to the Messianic-apocalypticists, all took distinct positions on the pursuit of power and held consequent attitudes toward the Torah that sought to tame it.

NOTES

1. In this essay the terms Torah and Prophets are literary concepts that define biblical writings by their function. Torah is mainly legislating, constitutional literature, laying down in God's name rules and standards of individual and corporate behavior, aimed at fashioning Israel into a holy people. Although this literature came into being— according to the judgment of modern critics—over generations, it is a unity as regards its estimate of political power, as will emerge in the sequel.

Prophets comprises "Former Prophets" (the books of Joshua, Judges, Samuel, and Kings), which narrate the history of Israel from its settlement of the land of Canaan until the destruction of the First Temple. Composed of heterogeneous elements, this corpus views some six centuries of Israelite history as a disastrous failure: Israel failed to fulfill the conditions of its covenant with God, on which its well-being depended. The corpus of "Latter Prophets" comprises the oracles of named prophets proclaimed from the middle of the monarchic period (mid-eighth century B.C.E.) to the Restoration after the Babylonian Exile (end of the sixth century B.C.E.). These oracles expound a consistent interpretation of the events that befell Israel from the viewpoint of God, with warnings and consolations related to this interpretation. From the Prophets the conflict between the religious ideal and the political reality can be observed. The evidence gathered from these various sources is consistent with respect to the theme of this essay.

For a survey of the nature and composition of this literature, see M. Weinfeld, "Literary Creativity," *The Age of the Monarchies: Culture and Society* (ed. A. Malamat; World History of the Jewish People 4b; Jerusalem: Massada, 1979), 27–58.

2. G. von Rad, *Studies in Deuteronomy* (SBT 9, Chicago: H. Regnery, 1953), 16.

3. On motive clauses, see the pioneering study of B. Gemser, "The Importance of the Motive Clause in Old Testament Law," *Congress Volume: Copenhagen 1953* (VTSup 1; Leiden: Brill, 1953), 50–66; R. Sonsino, *Motive Clauses in Hebrew Law: Biblical Forms and Near Eastern Parallels* (Society of Biblical Literature Dissertation Series 45; Chico, CA: Scholars Press, 1980).

4. In the following paragraphs my observations on power have been shaped by these analyses: H. Heller, "Power, Political," *Encyclopedia of the Social Sciences* 13 (New York: Macmillan, 1934), 300–05; B. Russell, *Power; A New Social Analysis* (London: George Allen and Unwin, 1938); F. W. Frey, "Political Power," EncBrit 14 (15th ed., 1974): 697–702; and G. Tinder, *Political Thinking* (Boston: Little, Brown, 1979).

5. Cf. the humanitarian motive of the Sabbath commandment in the Decalogue of Deuteronomy 5:14, "so that your manservant and maidservant may rest as you do."

6. See the illuminating study of N. W. Soss, "Old Testament Law and Economic Society," *Journal of the History of Ideas* 34 (1973):323–44.

7. Epilogue to the Laws of Hammurabi (trans. T. J. Meek, ANET, 178). G. R. Driver (in G. R. Driver and J. C. Miles, *The Babylonian Laws*, Oxford: Clarendon Press, 1955, vol. II) translates, "and then have the inscription on my monument read out" (97). After defending the reading grammatically he observes: ". . . the meaning must be that the man shall have the text read to him by someone else . . . ; this agrees with the fact that few litigants are likely to have been able to read it for themselves" (286).

8. "In order to make you know the power and greatness of God, who can sustain his creatures by all sorts of things apart from bread" (Commentary to Deuteronomy of Meyuhas bar Elijah, Greece, twelfth century CE. [ed. J. M. Katz; Jerusalem: Kook, 1968], 32). This correct sense of the verse in its original context has been overshadowed by its application in the New Testament, e.g., Matthew 4:4, where Jesus responds to Satan's challenge to turn stones into bread by citing this verse. Jesus' meaning is given thus by J. L. McKenzie: "The answer of Jesus (Deut. 8:3) does not deny that ordinary needs should be met by ordinary means, but subordinates even basic physical necessities to the revealed word of God. Jesus does not fulfill his mission by providing for basic physical necessities, but by proclaiming the word that is life" ("The Gospel according to Matthew," *The Jerome Biblical Commentary*, 2 [ed. R. E. Brown, J. A. Fitzmyer, and R. E. Murphy; Englewood Cliffs, NJ: Prentice-Hall, 1968]:69). From this comes the common use of the expression in the sense of: "Supplying man's physical needs does not answer all of an individual's needs; there is also a spiritual side that needs spiritual sustenance."

9. The degeneration of institutionalized prophecy is described by W. Eichrodt, *Theology of the Old Testament* 1(2 vols.; Philadelphia: Westminster, 1961): 332–37.

10. Y. Kaufmann, *The Religion of Israel* (trans. M. Greenberg; Chicago: University of Chicago Press, 1960), 375.

11. Morris Silver, *Prophets and Markets: The Political Economy of Ancient Israel* (Boston: Kluwer-Nijhoff, 1983), vigorously indicts Israel's prophets for having demoralized the people, thereby contributing substantially to their collapse. The weak link in this intriguing argument is his assumption that the prophets' messages were effective.

Additional note:

On the uniqueness of the biblical idea that the law was published to the entire people, see additional note to "Three conceptions of the Torah."

Aspects of *Biṭṭaḥon* in Hebrew Thought

1976 (unpublished)

Especially for Judy Blanc,
who liked it

Haim Blanc was an unsentimental man, yet he could appreciate senti-ment. Expressions of idealism or "high" thought did not flow naturally off his tongue, but when uttered genuinely by others he did not scoff. Occasionally I read to him studies of mine on religious themes. He would listen attentively and comment briefly, usually on matters of language, aphorisms, or folklore.

The following essay is on confidence, a quality of the ideal believer that Haim, an "unbeliever," appeared to possess abundantly (presum-ably on other grounds). In its original form, the essay was a lecture de-livered in Jerusalem in February 1976, to the Ecumenical Theological Research Fraternity in Israel.

Invitations to speak to this group have often stimulated me to artic-ulate thoughts that had long been rattling about shapelessly in my mind. The present subject has been with me for as many years as I have been living here–about six now–since the conceptions of security and insecurity that an outlander from the United States brings to this country give him small help in dealing with the local reality. I have had to adjust to a state of insecurity for which nothing in my past pre-pared me. Therefore, I thought it beneficial to consider some biblical and Jewish aspects of this universal, yet very particular, problem. I propose to study with you the verbal and nominal derivates of the He-brew root *b-ṭ-ḥ*.[1]

The Hebrew notion of security and safety is inseparable from the subjective notion of assurance and confidence. Both inhere in *b-t-h* whose noun derivates are *betah, bitha, bittahon,* conventionally rendered "security" and "confidence"; and *mibtah,* "source of security/confidence." The verb *batah* is rendered "be secure, without fear" on the one hand, and "trust, rely on" on the other. The primary meaning of *b t h,* surmised from biblical and comparative evidence, would appear to be "fall," and from that "throw oneself on" leading to "rely on." This is supported by an interlinguistic parallel: in Hebrew, a synonym for *batah* is *šaqet* "be tranquil" (Judg. 18:7; Isa. 30:15; Ezek. 38:11)–of which Arabic *saqata* "fall" is a cognate.[2] When *batah* is used in the sense of "trust, rely on" the implication of assured help is present. Security/safety, an objective situation, and the subjective notions of assurance and confidence are bound up together in the term.

Security in the Bible in an equivocal notion, easily shifting from reality to illusion. People may be described as living, or situated (*la)betah,* when they are in fact on the verge of disaster. Of the city of Shechem, about to be attacked by Jacob's sons, it is said, "They came upon the city when it was secure"(*betah;* Gen. 34:25)–meaning, of course, in the minds of its citizens. On the eve of Gideon's assault on the Midianites "the [Midianite] encampment was secure" (*betah;* Judg. 8:11). The Danite scouts, in search of a new area for their hard-pressed tribe to settle, arrive at Laish where "they see the towns-people in its midst living secure" (*labetah;* Judg. 18:7), when in reality their fall was close at hand. The prophet (Isa. 47:8) derides Babylon, which faces imminent disaster, as "the [delicate] one who lives *labetah.*" In all these cases the assurance and fearlessness of the people in question are an illusion.

Labetah describes Israel enjoying God's blessing and protection in the past. Psalm 78:53 says that "He led them in security (*labetah*), so that they were unafraid." Under Solomon the Israelites "lived *labetah*" (1 Kings 5:5). One may find it strange, but in 1 Sam. 12:11 the prophet Samuel looks back on the period of the judges as a time when God "rescued you from the power of your enemies on all sides so that you lived *betah.*" If that period of intermittent peace can be spoken of so, it may be doubted whether the sense of *betah* is adequately conveyed by "security/safety."

The above-cited passages are almost all in which the term is used of the past; with the more common future reference, *betah* is a state contingent on obedience to God. One of the promises conditional on the observance of the covenant with God reads, "You shall dwell on your land *labetah*" (Lev. 25:18). The majority of passages in which such terms are used are prophetic descriptions of the end-time; for example:

For the work of righteousness shall be peace,
And the effect of righteousness, calm and confidence (*beṭaḥ*) forever.
Then my people shall dwell in peaceful homes,
In secure (*mibṭaḥim*) dwellings
In untroubled places of rest (Isa. 32:17–18)[3]

And so it is in over a dozen oracles: once in Isaiah, several times in Jeremiah, frequently in Ezekiel, and once again in Zechariah. What had been promised conditionally in the covenant documents—"you shall dwell in your land in security"—became in prophecy the sure predictions of the future. The most frequent occurrences of (*la*)*beṭaḥ* are thus in contexts describing a state that is to come.

The term appears three times in the Book of Proverbs, as wisdom's promise:

But he who listens to me will dwell *beṭaḥ*,
Untroubled by the terror of misfortune (1:33; of 3:23)

and as the effect of integrity:

He who lives blamelessly lives *beṭaḥ*,
But he who walks a crooked path will be found out (10:9)

and as a potentially illusory state:

Do not devise harm against your fellow
Who lives trustfully (*labeṭaḥ*) with you (3:29)

The noun *mibṭaḥ*, "source of security/confidence" is also equivocal, denoting both a true and an illusory source. Because *mibṭaḥ* is something in which people put their trust rightly or wrongly, and it covers both senses impartially, it is not translatable by any English word. Here is a homely parable, Proverbs 25:19: "Like a loose tooth and an unsteady leg/Is a treacherous *mibṭaḥ* in time of trouble." Job, affirming his blamelessness, declares: "Did I put my reliance on gold,/Or regard fine gold as my *mibṭaḥ*?" (31:24) Time and again it is asserted that God is the only trustworthy *mibṭaḥ*. The classic passage is Jeremiah 17:5–8, as follows:

Thus said the LORD:
Cursed is he who trusts (*yibṭaḥ*) in man,
Who makes mere flesh his strength,
And turns his thoughts from the LORD.
He shall be like a bush in the desert,
Which does not sense the coming of good:

It is set in the scorched places of the wilderness,
In a barren land without inhabitant.
Blessed is he who trusts in the LORD,
Whose trust (*mibṭaḥo*) is the LORD alone.
He shall be like a tree planted by waters,
Sending forth its roots by a stream:
It does not sense the coming of heat,
Its leaves are ever fresh;
It has no care in a year of drought,
It does not cease to yield fruit.

Here we interject a comment of the medieval commentator David Kimḥi (Provence, ca. 1160–1235) which, while explaining Jeremiah's simile, reveals some later refinements of the notion under discussion. Kimḥi asks why it was necessary, in the first sentence, to add the clause "and turns his thoughts from the LORD"? Kimḥi replies:

> For if he does not *turn his thoughts from the LORD* he is not wrong in putting his trust in man to help him, so long as his intention is that with the help of God humans will be enabled to help him, and no other way.

Medieval Jewish reflection on the duty of trust in God sought to harmonize it with regard for human work, which is equally grounded in the Bible (for example, Ps. 128:2: "You shall enjoy the fruit of your labors; you shall be happy and you shall prosper"). Kimḥi finds that the apparently superfluous final clause of the first sentence is there to indicate that trust in man is not unconditionally wicked; it is only *exclusive* trust in man with one's thought "turned from the LORD" that is so. Trust in man with the understanding that human help, to the extent that it is effective, is an agency of God is legitimate and allowed. (Compare the admonition of Deuteronomy 8:14–18: ". . . [beware] lest your heart grow haughty and you forget the LORD your God . . . and you say to yourselves, 'My own power and the might of my own hand have won this wealth for me.' Remember that it is the LORD your God who gives you the power to get wealth. . . .") Kimḥi's comment epitomizes the resolution of the conflict of apparent incompatibles—reliance upon God and the use of God-given faculties to help ourselves and one another.

Following the nominal forms of *b-ṭ-ḥ* we are led to the narrative of 2 Kings 18–19 with its unparalleled concentration of derivatives of that root. This is the exemplary tale of *biṭṭaḥon*, "confidence" (18:19). The hero is King Hezekiah of Judah, who is introduced thusly: "He trusted (*baṭaḥ*) only in the LORD God of Israel; there was none like him among all the kings of Judah after him, nor among those before him"

(18:5). This introduction indicates that trust in God will be the theme of the story. We read of Hezekiah's rebellion against Assyria, its failure, and of the Assyrian attempt to take Jerusalem after subjugating all of Judah. Much attention is given to the psychological warfare of the Assyrians and how it was countered by the faith of the prophet Isaiah and the king. The Assyrian Rabshakeh opened the war of nerves against Jerusalem with a speech containing the following lines:

> You tell Hezekiah: Thus said the Great King, the King of Assyria: What makes you so confident (*ma habbiṭṭaḥon hazze 'ᵃšer baṭaḥta*). . . . on whom are you relying (*baṭaḥta*). . . . You rely (*baṭaḥta*), of all things, on Egypt, that splintered reed of a staff. . . . And if you tell me: "We are relying (*baṭaḥnu*) on the Lᴏʀᴅ our God," he is the very one whose shrines and altars Hezekiah did away with. . . . Don't let Hezekiah make you rely (*yabṭaḥ*) on the Lᴏʀᴅ, saying: the Lᴏʀᴅ will surely save us; this city will not fall into the hands of the king of Assyria. (2 Kings 18:19–30).

The entire speech revolves around derivatives of *b-ṭ-ḥ*. On what does the *assurance* that inspired this rebellion rest? On whom does Hezekiah rely? Chapter 19 of 2 Kings tells of a second Assyrian embassy and a second campaign of psychological warfare waged by means of a letter to this effect:

> Tell this to King Hezekiah of Judah: Do not let your God, on whom you are relying (*boṭeᵃḥ*) mislead you into thinking that Jerusalem will not be delivered into the hands of the king of Assyria. . . . Were the nations that my predecessors destroyed . . . saved by their gods? (19:10–12)

Assyrian dismissal of all the sources of Judah's assurance is met by the unshakable faith of Isaiah that infects and inspires King Hezekiah. We should notice how the Rabshakeh (Assyrian: chief "cupbearer") has constructed his argument. He begins with Egypt, which he dismisses with the observation that it has always proven itself a disappointment. Next he shows why Israel's God cannot be counted on: he has been alienated by Hezekiah's reform of the institutions of worship. In the second round, the Assyrian argument escalates to blasphemy: it seeks to nullify Isaiah's encouraging oracle by belittling the power of its author, the God of Israel. He will prove to be as impotent as all the other gods whose nations were destroyed by previous kings of Assyria.

The cumulative force of this climactic, empirically grounded argument subjects Hezekiah's faith to its supreme test: Fortified by another heartening oracle, Hezekiah throws himself on God, and is delivered. That is why the historiographer singles him out of all the kings for "trusting only in the LORD the God of Israel; there was none like him among all the kings of Judah after him, nor among those before him."

To sum up what has been said so far: Safety and security, in Hebrew thought, are aspects of confidence and fearlessness; that is, they are basically psychic concepts. *Beṭaḥ, biṭṭaḥon* are internal, subjective states that have an external basis to be sure, but whose chief referent is a state of mind, a state of soul. When this state of mind is founded on trust in God, it is anchored in reality; if on trust in humans, power, gold, or other substitutes for God, it is an illusion.

The Psalms are the main repository of expressions of the root *b-ṭ-ḥ*, its derivatives occurring there some forty times. Twice as many refer to the individual as to the collective. In other words, the concept belongs primarily to lyrical prayer and its chief sphere is private, personal religion. We turn then to the Psalms for direct expressions of *biṭṭaḥon.*

What is *biṭṭaḥon* based on? Most frequently, on God's *ḥesed*—another charged term, formerly translated "loving-kindness" but now "steadfast love," "(covenant) loyalty," "faithfulness"—and other terms deemed more suitable to the context.[4] Before considering *biṭṭaḥon*-psalms, then, we do well to attend to the celebration of God's *ḥesed* in Psalm 103:

> Bless the LORD, O my soul,
>> all my being, his holy name.
> Bless the LORD, O my soul
>> and do not forget all his bounties.
> He forgives all your sins,
>> heals all your diseases.
> He redeems your life from the Pit,
>> surrounds you with *ḥesed* and mercy . . .
>
> The LORD executes righteous acts
>> and judgments for all who are wronged.
> He made known his ways to Moses,
>> his deeds to the children of Israel.
> The LORD is compassionate and gracious,
>> slow to anger, abounding in *ḥesed*.
> He will not contend forever
>> or nurse his anger for all time.
> He has not dealt with us according to our sins,
>> nor has he requited us according to our iniquities.
> For as the heavens are high above the earth,
>> so great is his *ḥesed* toward those who fear him.

As east is far from west,
    so far has he removed our sins from us.
As a father has compassion for his children,
    so the LORD has compassion for those who fear Him.
For he knows how we are formed;
    he is mindful that we are dust.

Man, his days are like those of grass;
    he blooms like a flower of the field;
    a wind passes by and it is no more,
    its own place no longer knows it.
But the LORD's *ḥesed* is for all eternity
    toward those who fear him,
    and his beneficence is for the children's children
    of those who keep his covenant
    and remember to observe his precepts . . .

God's *ḥesed* was experienced, then, as care, compassion, and forgiveness both in the history of Israel as well as in the lives of individuals. From this sprang the conviction that the relation between God and the pious pray-er (or the community) was unconditional—as a father's is to his children. This emboldened the psalmists to throw themselves on him in adversity and have confidence of safety in his help.

For the effect of *biṭṭaḥon* on one who had it we turn to Psalm 62:

Truly my soul waits quietly for God;
    my deliverance comes from him.
Truly he is my rock and deliverance,
    my haven; I shall never be shaken.
How long will all of you attack a man,
    to crush him, as though he were
    a leaning wall, a tottering fence?
They lay plans to topple him from his rank;
    they delight in falsehood;
    they bless with their mouths,
    while inwardly they curse.
Truly, wait quietly for God, O my soul,
    for my hope comes from him.
He is my rock and deliverance,
    my haven; I shall not be shaken.
I rely on God, my deliverance and glory
    my rock of strength;
    in God is my refuge.
Trust (*biṭḥu*) in him at all times, O people;
    pour out your heart before him;
    God is our refuge.

Men are mere breath;
    mortals, illusion;
    placed on a scale all together
    they weigh even less than a breath.
Do not trust (*tibṭᵉḥu*) in violence
    or put false hopes in robbery;
    if force bears fruit pay it no mind.
One thing God has spoken;
    two things have I heard:
    that might belongs to God
    and faithfulness (*ḥesed*) is yours, O Lord,
    to reward each man according to his deeds.

The effect of *biṭṭaḥon* is unshakable strength in time of trouble. At the end of the psalm a further effect is mentioned, which will be spelled out in the next (and last) psalm to be presented; namely, eschewal of a quick but crooked means of helping oneself. Though ungodly recourses are ready to hand, these are recognized as illusory.

How *biṭṭaḥon* shapes one's view of God's governance of the world is set forth in the contemplative Psalm 37. Its first sentence states its theme:

Do not be vexed by evil men;
    do not be incensed by wrongdoers;
    for they soon wither like grass
    like verdure fade away.
Trust (*bᵉṭaḥ*) in the LORD and do good,
    abide in the land and remain loyal.
Seek the favor of the LORD,
    and he will grant you the desires of your heart.
Leave all to the LORD;
    trust (*bᵉṭaḥ*) in him; he will do it.
He will cause your vindication to shine forth like the light,
    the justice of your case like the noonday sun.
Be patient and wait for the LORD,
    do not be vexed by the prospering man
    who carries out his schemes.
Give up anger, abandon fury;
    do not be vexed,
    it can only do harm.
For evil men will be cut off,
    but those who look to the LORD—
    they shall inherit the land.
A little longer and there will be no wicked man;
    you will look at where he was—
    he will be gone.

But the lowly shall inherit the land,
    and delight in abundant well-being.
The wicked man schemes against the righteous,
    and gnashes his teeth at him.
The LORD laughs at him,
    for he knows that his day will come.

The steps of a man are made firm by the LORD,
    when he delights in his way.
Though he stumbles, he does not fall down,
    for the LORD gives him support.
I have been young and am now old,
    but I have never seen a righteous man abandoned,
    or his children seeking bread.
He is always generous and lends,
    and his children are held blessed.
Shun evil and do good,
    and you shall abide forever.
For the LORD loves what is right,
    he does not abandon his faithful ones.
They are preserved forever,
    while the children of the wicked will be cut off.

I saw a wicked man, powerful,
    well-rooted like a robust native tree.
Suddenly he vanished and was gone;
    I sought him, but he was not to be found.
Mark the blameless, note the upright,
    for there is a future for the man of integrity.
But transgressors shall be utterly destroyed,
    the future of the wicked shall be cut off . . .

I conclude with some remarks on the divergence between the providential order on which *biṭṭaḥon* is based and the real world as it is perceived by the unprepossessed observer.

The Jewish grace after meals ends with a series of assertions of God's providence, capped by Psalm 37:25: "I have been young and am now old,/but I have never seen a righteous man abandoned,/or his children seeking bread." While the rest of the grace may be said aloud these verses may not, because there may be a needy person at the table who would be embarrassed by the implication that he was not righteous. I used to resent this compromise: if the verses could not be said aloud, why say them at all? Worse, they offered a Pollyannish view of the world in which good is rewarded and evil punished, at odds with all experience. Indeed, not only verse 25 of Psalm 37 but the whole psalm, which is of a piece with it, could not be taken seriously, since the doctrine propounded there was the very one found wanting when advocated by the friends of Job. Then, in the course of preparing myself for writing this essay, I came across the following passage in the *Republic* of Plato:

> This, then, must be our conviction about the just man, that whether he fall into poverty or disease or any other supposed evil, for him all these things will finally prove good, both in life and in death, for by the gods assuredly that man will never be neglected who is willing and eager to be righteous, and by the practice of virtue to be likened unto God so far as that is possible for man. (X, 613 a–b)

The concurrence of Plato with the "simpleminded" psalmist ought to give us pause; is he as naive as he seems?

To begin with, we note that the psalmist does not ignore reality altogether; he exhorts to "Be patient and wait for the Lord,/do not be vexed by the prospering man/who carries out his schemes." He thus acknowledges that the present reality is not the ideal and calls on his hearers to trust that God "will do it"–in the future. He also recognizes that the righteous may "stumble"–though "he does not fall down," much as the author of Proverbs recognizes that "Seven times the righteous man falls–and gets up/while the wicked are tripped by one misfortune" (24:16). Righteousness is thus no shield against troubles, but trouble is not the final card dealt to the righteous.

The issue here is how to sustain belief amidst adversity. The author of Psalm 73 describes how he achieved it: at first he felt that he had wasted his life by following a godly course, for while the wicked prospered he did not. Then one day he visited the Temple, and there he was granted an insight into the truth–that the wicked and their gains are transient; they cannot maintain themselves. Plato, in the sequel to the above-cited passage, says the same: he likens the wicked to short-winded runners; they start with great sprints but soon break down "and in the end are laughed to scorn." This view combines idealism and realism: it is realistic—that is, empirical—that evil eventually consumes itself, contains the seeds of its own destruction; to that extent there is an observable moral order. The idealism is manifested in the assertion that this process occurs within the life span of the righteous, so that they will live to see their vindication. This combination of realism and idealism makes up the myth of the believer; it is the core of his worldview and the standard by which he judges reality. Whenever he sees the downfall of the wicked, he feels that his myth is confirmed; when the wicked prosper, he makes the necessary adjustments.

Theology has devised various explanations for the long-term survival of the wicked. The postbiblical doctrine of a judgment in the after-life opened new possibilities. Typical of them is a talmudic explanation that the prosperity of the wicked in this life is their full reward for whatever good they have done, so that in the afterlife they will get nothing but punishment. As a corollary, the suffering of the righteous in this world is their requital for whatever sins they have committed, so that in the hereafter they will enjoy unending bliss.[5] This is a piquant example of the devices by which the believing mind makes existence in this vale of tears bearable. Through them, *biṭṭaḥon* is sustained and behavior in accord with what is right and just is rationalized, even if it is not rewarded in the here and now.

NOTES

1. Adequate lexical treatment will be found in F. Brown, S. R. Driver, C. A. Briggs, *A Hebrew and English Lexicon of the Old Testament* (Oxford: Clarendon Press, 1952, 2nd ed.), 105. A standard conceptual discussion is E. Gerstenberger's, in E. Jenni, C. Westermann, *Theologisches Handwörterbuch zum Alten Testament* I (München: Chr. Kaiser, 1971):300–05. A. Jepsen's competent survey, in G. J. Botterweck, H. Ringgren, *Theological Dictionary of the Old Testament* II, translated by J. T. Willis (Grand Rapids: W. B. Eerdmans, 1975):88–94, notes in conclusion: "Above all it is not clear how this root can have such a varied connotation that almost always it can have a negative meaning when applied to man [as the object of trust] and a positive meaning when applied to God." A comprehensive discussion, embracing later Jewish and Islamic thought, can be found in R. J. Zvi Werblowski, "Faith, Hope and Trust: A Study in the Concept of Bittahon," J. G. Weiss, editor, *Papers of the Institute of Jewish Studies, London* (Jerusalem: Magnes, 1964), 95–139).
2. L. Kopf, "Arabische Etymologien und Parallelen zum Bibelwörterbuch," VT 8 (1958), 165–68.
3. Here and in the sequel, translation follows *The Prophets . . . A New Translation of the Holy Scriptures According to the Masoretic Text* (Philadelphia: The Jewish Publication Society of America, 1978), and *The Writings* (Philadelphia: The Jewish Publication Society of America, 1982). Lᴏʀᴅ represents the quadriconsonantal name of God (YHWH). I have not capitalized pronouns referring to God and at times have transliterated key terms instead of translating them.
4. For a survey of scholarly grappling with this perhaps overstudied term, see G. A. Larue's introduction, "Recent Studies in *Hesed*," to N. Glueck, *Ḥesed in the Bible*, trans. by A. Gottschalk (Cincinnati: Hebrew Union College, 1967), 1–34. For the connection of *biṭṭaḥon* and *ḥesed* see Psalms 21:8; 13:6; 52:10.
5. The Talmudic rationalization occurs in Leviticus Rabba, section 27.1 (to Leviticus 22:27; Margulies edition, 614, where parallels are noted). The *biṭṭaḥon* underlying it is equivalent to "faith" as described in Hebrews 11:1: "faith gives substance (or: assurance) to our hopes, and makes us certain of realities we do not see" (New English Bible). The contents of *biṭṭaḥon*/faith answer not to observed realities but to intuited ideals that are experienced as truths more real than the imperfect empirical reality. See W. Cantwell Smith, "Religion as Symbolism," EncBrit: "Propaedia" (Chicago, 1974), 498–500. Pertinent to our theme is E. Voegelin, "Immortality: Experience and Symbol," HTR 60 (1967), 235–79. Though often obscure, it is redeemed by flashes of insightful, suggestive formulations. Voegelin's thesis is that religious language symbols do not refer to objects existing in time and space but to a "truth about a nonexisting reality" that the coiner and pristine user of the symbol are (were) conscious of having experienced. "The symbols convey no other truth but that of the engendering consciousness"; their mean-

ing can be understood only if they evoke the engendering reality; their truth belongs to the nonexistent experience that articulates itself.

If we consider that the author of Psalm 37, like all humans, did not go about conscious of the finitude of his life, his faith in the vindication of God's *hesed* "in his lifetime" becomes more understandable. Such a normal "intimation of immortality" approaches the formally articulated postbiblical belief in a hereafter with a divine judgment. Insofar as it provides a "long run" for God's providence to be realized, it functions as an equivalent to immortality.

On the Refinement of the Conception of Prayer in Hebrew Scriptures

1976

Prophetic intercessory prayer was vividly described some years ago by Yochanan Muffs in an essay that collected and interrelated the wrestlings with God that characterize prophetic prayer from Moses through Samuel to Jeremiah. Earlier, Sheldon Blank studied "the Promethean element in biblical prayer," an allusion to the independent, even defiant stance taken by certain biblical pray-ers.[1] To modern Western man, this sort of prayer best corresponds to his ideal image of himself: autonomous, self-assertive, courageous, ready to stand on a principle even against God. However, it would be a mistake to forget the special status of such intercessors within their faith-communities and infer from their conduct a model for the common man. They are "men of God," persons standing in a particularly intimate relation to God as a result of election or prolonged devotion to him. Of Honi the circle-maker—a later representative of this class—it was censoriously said that he was like a child who cajoles his father. Any other man presuming to act that way, the same censor concluded, would deserve excommunication.[2]

We have only to recall Moses' exploitation of his special status with God in his great intercession after the episode of the golden calf: "You have said, 'I have singled you out by name, and you have, indeed, gained my favor.' Now, if I have truly gained your favor, pray let me know your ways . . ." (Exod. 33:12f.); and again, "If I have gained your favor, O LORD, pray let the LORD go in our midst . . ." (34:9). These heroes of faith have achieved a standing with God that ordinary mortals do not enjoy. They bank on their closeness to God and their consciousness of being in his good graces—and upon their utter selfless-ness, their readiness to sacrifice all, themselves included, upon the altar of faith. Having nothing they are not prepared to lose, they can be reckless.

The situation of the ordinary mortal is quite different. With nei-ther a vocation to God's service nor the heroism of these figures of legend, self-assertiveness and autonomy in relation to God would be considered presumptuous. In fact, the attitude of the common wor-shiper was far removed from the Promethean; the storming of heaven by prophets hardly served as a model for the ordinary (or even the ex-traordinary) pious Israelite.

There are several avenues to understanding the meaning of worship to the people of biblical times. The terms denoting acts of worship may be studied, noting whether they are exclusively used with respect to God-human relations, or whether they denote social relations too. Whether, again, they have levels of refinement, e.g., from plain to metaphoric use. In the case of prayer, the literary records of prayer are sources of the first importance for revealing the mind and the mo-tives of pray-ers. Polemics against the people's worship are another in-dication of meaning, with the advantage of disclosing nonstandard, vulgar conceptions otherwise missing from the canonical material. It must be borne in mind, however, that polemicists tend to exaggerate or distort the object of their fulminations.

In the following inquiry, something of all these avenues will be taken. First we shall examine the term *'abad 'et YHWH*, "to serve the Lord." Then we shall study some biblical critiques of modes of wor-ship, following them to their conclusions. As we seek to ascertain the attitude of mind of certain biblical pray-ers, we shall be interested to see wherein they differ from childish, unreflecting conceptions. Ulti-mately, our inquiry will bear on the question: How much of biblical prayer reflects ideas and experiences that can be shared by present-day seekers after God?

Prayer is a form of service of God.[3] This is indicated by the parallelism in such passages as Job 21:15:

> What is the Almighty, that we should serve him?
> And what does it profit us that we pray to him?

or Isaiah 44:17:

> . . . he bows to [his idol] and prostrates himself before it; he prays
> to it, saying, "Save me for you are my God!"

In the future, God will give the nations a "purified speech,"

> So that all of them may call upon the name of the Lord,[1]
> And serve him unanimously. (Zeph. 3:9)

The chief form of divine service in Scripture is the sacrificial cult, but prayer of petition and praise is frequently associated with it. Samuel's cry to God for help from the Philistines follows a sacrifice (1 Sam. 7:9); Solomon's praises and petition at the inauguration of the temple precede a sacrifice (1 Kings 8:62). Sacrifice and prayer are linked closely in the private worship of Hannah at Shiloh (1 Sam. 1). So closely were the two interrelated that the late prophet whose message is contained in the latter part of the book of Isaiah could exchange them:

> I will bring them to my holy mountain,
> And will make them joyful in my house of prayer;
> Their burnt-offerings and their sacrifices shall be welcome upon my
> altar,
> For my house shall be called a house of prayer for all the peoples.
> (Isa. 56:7)

Moreover, the psalmist could expressly equate the two:

> Take my prayer as an offering of incense,
> My upraised hands as an evening sacrifice. (Ps. 141:2)

No less than the sacrificial cult might prayer too be regarded as a divine commandment, a duty ordained by God. This is the case not only with the exiles, addressed by God in Jeremiah 29:12 thus:

> You shall call me, and go and pray to me, and I will listen to you . . .

It is also the demand of God in Psalm 50:15: "Call upon me in time of trouble."

In ancient Mesopotamia, too, prayer was considered on the same footing as the sacrificial cult. The sufferer in the composition "I Will Praise the Lord of Wisdom" described his piety in these terms:

> For myself, I gave attention to supplication and prayer;
> To me prayer was discretion, sacrifice my rule. (II 23f.; ANET 597)

We are entitled, therefore, to start our inquiry into the character of prayer by examining the character of divine service in general in Hebrew Scripture. The attitude of one praying to God and that of one sacrificing to him were as closely linked as the phenomena themselves.

A remark on the method to be pursued in this inquiry is here in order. Our aim is to discover the highest expressions of the scriptural understanding of prayer, those peaks arrived at through insight and reflection, which stand out as the spiritual achievements of the biblical age in ancient Israel. The criterion is the degree of removal from simple anthropopathism—naïve, unreflecting ascription to God of human sentiments and the consequent conception of his service in terms of that done for a human being. That ancient Israel harbored such conceptions is a certainty, on the basis both of polemic against them and their appearance even in the canonical literature. Thus, for example, the *do ut des* ("I give so that You give") of Malachi 3:10:

> Bring the whole tithe into the treasury
> That there may be food in my house,
> And test me now therein, says the LORD of hosts,
> Whether I do not then open the windows of heaven
> And pour out for you blessing without limit.

That level of religion is here taken for granted, and will not be considered save as a background for inquiry into the higher levels. The focus on the peaks carries further the method of G. F. Moore in his classic *History of Religions*, as set forth in the preface to the second volume:

> In this . . . volume it is primarily the religion of intelligent and religious men that is described. . . . Such men are always the minority, but they are the true representatives of their religion in any age, teachers and examples to their fellows. No religion has ever succeeded in bringing all of its adherents to its standards of right living, or within sight of its intellectual and spiritual ideals; and in the highest religions the gulf between the intellectual and moral leaders and the superstitious and depraved sediment of society is widest. But it is not from ignorance and superstition that anything can be learned about a religion; at that end they are all alike. (xi)

Our standard is even more selective; it is the farthest limit to which spiritual refinement developed the germinal conceptions whose gross concretizations are common to all religion.

The sources for such peaks are, generally speaking, in the later literature, from the late monarchy onward and in the Psalms. But it is not to be expected that an evolution can always be traced within these sources, from earlier crude concepts to later refined ones. Both kinds may appear in the same source; our task will be to set forth the ideational relation of the less to the more refined concept, rather than their historical interrelation. We cannot arrange the material in a historical sequence; we can arrange it in an ideational climax.

The Sumero-Babylonian conception of service of the gods, well defined and well attested as it is, can serve as a foil to set off its scriptural counterpart. "[The Sumerian thinkers]," writes S. N. Kramer, "were firmly convinced that man was fashioned of clay and created for one purpose only: to serve the gods by supplying them with food, drink, and shelter so that they might have full leisure for their divine activities."[5] In the various Mesopotamian cosmogonies, this thought is clearly expressed. In *Enuma Elish*, the cosmogonic paean to Marduk, the hero declares his purpose to create man.

> Upon him shall the service of the gods be imposed
> That they may be at rest. (vi 8)

A later bilingual cosmogony goes into greater detail. After the creation of heaven and earth, the gods contemplate the creation of man:

> In Uzumua, the bond of heaven and earth,
> Let us slay (two) Lamga gods.
> With their blood let us create mankind.
> The service of the gods be their portion,
> For all times—
> To maintain the boundary ditch,
> To place the hoe and the basket
> Into their hands
> For the dwelling of the great gods . . .
> To mark off field from field . . .
> To raise plants in abundance . . .
> To increase the abundance in the land,
> To celebrate the festivals of the gods,
> To pour out cold water
> In the great house of the gods, which is fit to be an exalted
>   sanctuary . . .[6]

It is a question whether this idea was always accepted with complacency. Kramer believes it was: "Convinced beyond all need of argument that man was created by the gods solely for their benefit and leisure, the Sumerians accepted their dependent status just as they accepted the divine decision that death was man's lot and that only the gods were immortal."[7] However, Mesopotamian myths telling of the loss of immortality (or eternal youth) suggest that the latter decision was not accepted without protest.[8] Be that as it may, this conception of the purpose of man's creation placed the relation of gods and humans on a thoroughly instrumental footing; humans were the explicit means of giving rest and leisure to the gods. Benefit accrued to the gods from humans—a circumstance that suggested a motive for the gods to be of benefit to them as well. A letter of a man to his personal god puts the matter bluntly:

> To the god, my father, say:
> So says Apiladad, your servant:
> Why have you neglected me?
> Who will give you another
> Who is toward you like me?[9]

The ultimate conclusion of this conception is drawn in the eighth stanza of the "Dialogue of Master and Servant," in which the pros and cons of service to the gods are argued. The piece represents the dissolution of the Babylonian world of values.

> "Slave, oblige me!" "Yes, yes, my lord!"
> "Forthwith fetch and hand me water for my hands! I will offer a
>   sacrifice to my god!"
> "Offer, my lord, offer! The man who offers a sacrifice to his god,
>   his heart is glad;
> He makes investment upon investment."
> "No, slave, I will not, in truth, offer a sacrifice to my god!"
> "Do not, my lord, do not!
> Thou mightest accustom the god to follow thee like a dog,
> Asking of thee either 'my due!' or 'Didst thou not ask?' or anything
>   else."[10]

The mutual alienation that results from instrumental relationships between persons here attains its perfect expression; both the sacrificer and the gods are means for each other's ends. Each party utilizes the other, wields control over and needs the other at the same time. Reverence, awe, even affection can and did arise from such a relationship; it is less easy, however, to conceive of selfless devotion, of longing for everlasting communion with the god as its fruit.

The initial impression of a survey of the term *'abad 'et* YHWH, "to serve the LORD," is of parallelism to the concept of serving human rulers.

> Because you would not serve the LORD your God joyously and willingly in the abundance of everything, you shall serve your enemies . . . in hunger, thirst, nakedness and want of everything; and he shall put an iron yoke on your neck. (Deut. 28:47f.)

> I will break the yoke off their neck . . . and they shall serve aliens no more, but shall serve the LORD their god, and David, their King, whom I will raise up for them. (Jer. 30:8f.)

Nevertheless, they shall be [Shishak's] servants that they may know the difference between my service and the service of the kingdoms of the earth. (2 Chron. 12:8)

The concepts being parallel, examination of the ideational content of the service of human rulers can help us to understand that of the service of God. An expression such as "The nation that will bring its neck under the yoke of the king of Babylon and will serve him" (Jer. 27:11) shows that basically it is compliant acceptance of rule and lordship, analogous to the subjugation of an ox to its master. The contrary is expressed by "He rebelled against the king of Assyria and would not serve him" (2 Kings 18:7). Service to a human ruler is a political concept—subjection expressed by recognition of authority and loyal obedience. This is by no means a negative concept; there is a form of subjection affirmed by the Bible: subjection to a legitimate king.

The king's right to authority and obedience is grounded, in the Bible, on a signal benefaction, particularly rescue from oppression, that he performed for his fellows. Jotham condemned the Shechemites' complicity in the overthrow of Gideon's family, "seeing that my father fought for you . . . and rescued you from the hands of Midian" (Judg. 9:17f.). God raised Saul to kingship to "deliver my people from the hand of the Philistines" (1 Sam. 9:16). The people anointed him after he saved Jabesh Gilead from shameful subjection to the Ammonite king (11:14f.). David's legitimacy was acknowledged by the people after Absalom's death, when they recalled that "The king delivered us from the hand of our enemies, and he freed us from the power of the Philistines" (2 Sam. 19:10). A king's demand of loyal obedience is justified by his benefactions to his subjects and his preserving justice among them. These may properly be demanded of him, as in Jeremiah's admonition:

Hear the word of the LORD O house of David! . . .
Morning by morning give righteous judgment,
And deliver the spoiled from the hand of the oppressor. (21:11f.)

The righteous attributes of the king are the basis of his rule:

Your royal scepter is a scepter of equity.
You love righteousness and hate wickedness;
Rightly has God, your God, chosen to anoint you
With oil of gladness over all your peers. (Ps. 45:7f.)

O God, endow the king with your judgments,
The king's son with your righteousness;

That he judge your people rightly,
Your lowly ones, justly...
Let him champion the lowly among the people,
Deliver the needy folk, and crush those who wrong them...
Let all kings bow to him,
And all nations serve him.
For he saves the needy who cry out,
The lowly who have no helper.
He cares about the wretched needy,
He brings the needy deliverance.
He redeems them from fraud and lawlessness;
The shedding of their blood weighs heavily upon him.
(Ps. 72:1f., 4, 11ff.)

The king's right to the loyalty of his subjects and their obligation to render it are thus based on his positive attributes: he is a good shepherd, a righteous judge, a provider and protector. Therefore, submission to his rule is but the due of gratitude he deserves. The effectiveness of this conception is manifest in the condition the northern tribes made for accepting Rehoboam as their king: "Now lighten the galling service of your father and the burdensome yoke he laid upon us and we will serve you" (1 Kings 12:4). Complete the thought: and if you do not show fairness and fail to consider our welfare, we will not serve you!

The very same conceptions belong to the service of God. Consider, first, the Deuteronomic verb chains:

To stand in awe of the LORD your God, to walk in his ways, love him, serve [him] with all your heart and soul, and keep the commands of the LORD. (Deut. 10:12)

It is the LORD your God whom you must follow; of him you must stand in awe; his commands you must keep; his injunctions you must heed; him you must serve; and to him you must hold fast. (13:5)

Service of God is thus devotion to him in loyal obedience. The national sin is defined as exchanging one sovereign for another; e.g., "They served the Baals . . . abandoning the LORD and not serving him" (Judg. 10:6). The basis of the requirement to serve God is the deliverance and benefactions Israel experienced from him. The people artlessly cry to him, "Save us from the hand of our enemy and we will serve you" (1 Sam. 12:10). God's privilege of demanding Israel's service flows from his freeing them from Egypt and his providence for and protection of them since then: "I am the LORD your God from the land of Egypt; you have experienced no God but me, and have had no deliverer except me" (Hos. 13:4).[11] All the beneficent attributes of the king are found in him:

> The LORD executes righteous acts
> And judgments for all who are wronged. (Ps. 103:6)

> The LORD watches over the stranger;
> He gives courage to the orphan and widow. (146:9)

> He saves the poor from one stronger than he;
> The poor and the needy from his despoiler. (35:10)

Therefore serving him is but recognition of a debt of gratitude, and forsaking him is at once faithlessness and foolishness.

> Be aghast, O heavens, at this . . .
> For my people have committed two wrongs:
> They have forsaken me, the fountain of living water,
> To hew for themselves cisterns, broken cisterns, that can hold no
>   water. (Jer. 2:12f.)

Yet Israel's experience of God contained another element that lent the relation between them a more sublime character. Some passages in the Pentateuch ascribe the deliverance from Egypt to God's compassion and his mindfulness of his covenant with the fathers (Exod. 2:24; 3:7ff.). But Deuteronomy and related passages in Hosea ascribe it to God's love of Israel. "When Israel was a youth," says Hosea, "I loved him . . . I drew him with ropes of love" (11:1, 4); in the future, "I will love them as a freewill offering" (14:5), but at present "I will not continue to love them" (9:15). Deuteronomy speaks in a similar vein:

> The LORD set his heart on your fathers to love your fathers and
>   choose their descendants, even you . . . (10:15)

> Not because you were greater than any other people did the LORD set
> his heart on you and choose you . . . but because the LORD loved you,
> and would keep the oath he swore to your fathers. (7:7f.)

> The LORD your God turned [Balaam's] curse into a blessing for you, be-
> cause the LORD your God loved you. (23:6)

From there, the conception passed to Jeremiah ("I have loved you everlastingly, therefore I tendered you loving kindness" [31:2]), to the (post) exilic Isaiah ("By his love and his pity he redeemed them" [63:9]), and to Malachi ("I love you, says the LORD" [1:2]). The perception of God's acts in Israel as the fruits of love opened the way to lending the service of God the quality of returned love. It has been pointed out by W. Moran[12] that the commandment of loving God in Deuteronomy is analogous to the demand of loyalty made in similar language in ancient Near Eastern vassal treaties. But M. Weinfeld has rightly observed[13] that the context of Deuteronomy indicates a sentiment more refined than political loyalty. God's demand "to stand in awe of the LORD your God, to walk in his ways, love him, serve him with all your heart and soul, and keep his commands" stands in the context of the statement that "the LORD set his heart on your fathers to love them" (Deut. 10:12, 15). Surely there is a connection between these two loves.

At its peak, the concept of serving God includes a constant mental attitude, a permanent awareness of God that is embodied, among other ways, in one's moral character:

> You shall again distinguish between the righteous and the wicked,
> Between him who serves God and him who does not. (Mal. 3:18)

The parallelism indicates that to serve God is not merely to perform at given times certain rites honoring God, but to exhibit service and submission by one's moral character. Equally interesting is a passage showing that awe of God is a state of mind desired by God's servants; Nehemiah 1:11 speaks of "your servants who desire to stand in awe of your name." The servant of God wants the steady consciousness of God's presence; he longs to feel the awe of God.

A delicate statement of the meaning of serving God is found in Psalm 123:

> As the eyes of slaves follow their master's hand,
> As the eyes of a slave-girl follow the hand of her mistress,
> So our eyes are toward the LORD our God,
> Waiting for his favor...

By concentrating upon the eyes, the poet focuses the figure of master-slave upon its, to him, essential aspect: the utter dependence that the slave feels toward his master. Nothing is left of the usefulness of the slave to the master that belongs to the figure in its fullness (its pagan fullness). All is now the servant's dependence and waiting upon the master. That is the purified figure of the human servant of God: not one who ministers to him, but the dependent one, waiting for his favor.

What are the practical expressions of service?

Bowing prostrate ("outstretching of hands and feet"),[14] the plainest self-diminution and degradation, is the typical bodily attitude of service, whether to humans or God. Isaac foretells for Jacob that "Peoples shall serve you, nations bow prostrate before you" (Gen. 27:29). Similar in import is the downcast head (as its opposite, the upraised head, symbolizes self-assertion and defiance [e.g., Ps. 83:3]); the pious complain:

> It is vain to serve God, and what have we gained from keeping his charge,/And from going about with bowed head before the Lord of hosts? (Mal. 3:14)

The posture bespeaks an attitude of humble subjection and self-depreciation.

Offering tribute is another characteristic act of service to a ruler. In the case of human rulers, tribute regularly served to maintain the ruler's household and his administrative establishment. Israel's service of Eglon, king of Moab, entailed a tribute so large it required a troop of carriers (Judg. 3:14–18). The tribute that came in annually to Solomon went to support an extensive court and royal officialdom (1 Kings 5:1ff.; 10:24f.). The heavy imposts paid by the Judeans to the king of Persia are called his "service" in Nehemiah 5:18. But not every tribute to a ruler was a contribution to upkeep. There was also the tribute that expressed submission only, characterized by dispensability. Joseph's brothers are instructed by Jacob to bring a tribute to the Egyptian viceroy—choice confections of the land of Canaan (Gen. 43:11f.). Clearly, the viceroy did not need these gifts to maintain himself; they were but tokens of acknowledgment of his power over the brothers.

Service of God too included offerings made to him, as we learn from such passages as "to perform the service of the Lord before him by our burnt offerings, sacrifices and peace-offerings" (Josh. 22:27), or by Absalom's vow "to serve the Lord" in Hebron (2 Sam. 15:8), by which a sacrifice is intended. That such offerings were not God's upkeep must have been clear to the Israelite from both narrative tradition and law. The well-known Exodus story stated expressly that God was not worshiped in sacrifice during the Egyptian sojourn (Exod. 8:21ff.); Amos assumes it to be common knowledge that there was no regular sacrificial worship during the desert wandering (Amos 5:25). Hosea's threat of exile explicitly enumerates the various items comprising the entire temple worship that will cease—clearly implying its dispensability to God (Hos. 9:3ff.). The regular daily offering prescribed in the priestly law is much too small to have suggested to anyone that it was God's daily maintenance (a yearling lamb in the morning and one other at evening [Num. 28:3ff.]). Later midrash legitimately combined this datum with the rhetorical questions of Psalm 50:13 ("Do I eat the flesh of bulls? . . .") in this extrapolation: "Does he experience hunger? (cf. Ps. 50:12). And he goes on to say, 'If I should experience hunger, is the lamb that you offer at morning and the lamb at evening enough for me?'" (Tosefta Menaḥot 7:6). More will be said concerning Psalm 50 below, but enough has been said here to warrant the conclusion that in the matter of tribute offerings, only a partial symmetry exists between the conception relative to human rulers and the conception relative to God. Offerings to human rulers may be for maintenance or for expressing submission; offerings to God are never more than tokens of submission.

There is, finally, the service of God in his sanctuary performed by the temple personnel. J. Milgrom has traced the distribution of the several meanings of *ᵃboda* in cultic contexts, from its basic sense of labor to that of cult-service.[15] This sort of service lies outside our field of inquiry, since it belongs entirely to the realm of the temple rites performed by priests, Levites, and other temple servants. In passing, however, we note that the daily praise of God in song is included in the levitical service of the temple (e.g., 1 Chron. 23:30; cf. v. 28).

Thus far, practical expressions of service common to God and humans have been surveyed. There are forms of service peculiar to God alone, and these are characterized by the absence of any idea of benefit to the recipient, God; on the contrary, they all answer needs of the server.

The annual commemoration of God's liberation of Israel from Egypt is called a service:

> . . . You must observe this service. When your children say to you, "What do you mean by this service?" you shall say, "It is the passover-sacrifice to the LORD" . . . (Exod. 12:25ff.)

> When the LORD brings you into the land . . . you must hold this service in this month . . . (13:5)

Whatever the primary significance of the passover sacrifice (evidently apotropaic), the text makes it clear that its annual repetition has a purely commemorative function, recalling to later generations the wondrous benefactions of God to Israel. Its aim was to arouse in later times the sentiments of gratitude and devoted loyalty to God.

Another form of service peculiarly offered to God is the joyous singing of his praises.[16] It was noted above that the levitical daily praise-singing is called a service; similarly in Psalm 100:

> Serve the LORD in gladness;
> Come into his presence with shouts of joy . . .
> Enter his gates with praise;
> Praise him; bless his name!

Evaluation of the purpose of praise of God in the psalms must take account of C. Westermann's observation[17] that, in contrast to the practice of extra-biblical ancient Near Eastern hymnody, biblical praise does not precede petition; that is, it is not a means of conciliating and appeasing the deity prior to laying a request before him. In Hebrew Scripture, the praise of God forms a class of hymns unto itself, with no petitional element. When it enters into petitions it is as a foretaste of the acknowledgment of God's help to be made after the petition is granted, or (as will be enlarged upon later) as a ground of hope amidst distress.

In this respect, the psalms differ notably from prayers embedded in the narratives. The latter often preface petition by a laudatory epithet or a more or less extensive statement of praise (e.g., 2 Sam. 7:22ff.; 1 Kings 8:23f.; 2 Kings 19:15). The later Jewish rule concerning petitions—"one should always set forth the praise of God first, then pray (i.e., make petition)" [Berakot 32a]—is modeled explicitly upon Moses' entreaty in Deuteronomy 3:24: "O LORD, GOD. You let your servant see the first works of your greatness and your mighty hand—you whose powerful deeds no god in heaven or on earth can equal! Let me, I pray, cross over and see the good land on the other side of the Jordan. . . ." The motive of such praise (before it became mere convention) is transparent and identical with its pagan hymnal correspondents. But since this collocation of praise-petition does not appear in the psalms, there is room to inquire whether the motive of psalmic praise may not (at least at times) be different. It would indeed appear to be so.

A prime motive of praise, given repeatedly in the psalms, is the sheer joy experienced in God's benefactions. For the psalmist, the song of praise is the necessary expression of his overflowing feeling:

> It is good to praise the LORD,
> To sing hymns to your name, O Most High . . .
> For you have gladdened me by your deeds. . . .
> I shout for joy at your handiwork.
> How great are your works, O LORD,
> How very subtle your designs! (92:2f., 5f.).

> Bless the LORD, O my soul.
> And do not forget all his bounties. (103:2)

So conjoined are the experience of God's goodness and the outburst of acknowledging praise that even inanimate creation is imagined as responding to God's blessing in this way:

> You crown the year with your bounty;
> Fatness is distilled in your paths;
> The pasture lands distill it;
> The hills are girded with joy.
> The meadows are clothed with flocks,
> The valleys mantled with grain;
> They raise a shout, they break into song . . . (65:12ff.)

Since heightened consciousness of God's presence and work in the world characterizes spiritual men, not a few of the psalmists assert a resolve constantly to praise God; for them, to live is to acknowledge God's benefactions:

> I bless the LORD at all times;
> Praise of him is ever in my mouth. (34:2)

> I will sing to the LORD as long as I live;
> All my life I will chant hymns to my God. (104:33)

Psalm 71 is singularly filled with such expressions:

> I sing your praises always,
> My mouth is full of praise to you,
> Glorifying you all day long . . .
> My mouth tells of your beneficence,
> Of your deliverance all day long . . .
> I come with praise of your mighty acts . . .
> I celebrate your beneficence, yours alone.
> You have taught me, God, from my youth,
> Until now I have proclaimed your wondrous deeds;
> And even in hoary old age do not forsake me, God,
> Until I proclaim your strength to the next generation,
> Your mighty acts to all who are to come. . . .
> All day long my tongue shall recite your beneficent acts . . .

These sentiments are of a piece with assertions made elsewhere of a desire to dwell forever in the house of God (Pss. 23:6; 27:4; 61:8)— i.e., to be a permanent temple-servant. They bespeak a soul so filled with an awareness of God as to be unwilling to sever communion with him for even a moment. We are reminded of the postbiblical image of the heavenly beings whose eternal occupation is to sing hymns to God:

> And in that place my eyes saw the Elect one ...
> And all the righteous and elect before him shall be strong as fiery
> lights, and their mouths shall be full of blessing, and their lips
> extol the name of the Lord of Spirits ...
> And here my eyes saw all those who sleep not: they stand before
> him and say, Blessed be thou and blessed be the name of the
> Lord forever and ever ... (1 Enoch 39:6, 7, 13f.)

Praise of God has here reached the farthest remove from flattery and appeasement. As in the psalms cited above (and others not cited), it is the blissful experience of God that motivates praise, not the anxiety of need. In the case of postbiblical imagery, the angelic status of the praises makes it plain that they stand in no need, that their praise is therefore without ulterior motive. The basis of that imagery, however, must be some human experience; the disinterested praise of the psalmists, the outpouring of their joy and wonder at God's deeds, supplies the antecedent human model of the later imagery.

Another feature that distinguished biblical songs of praise from their Babylonian and Egyptian counterparts (in other respects strikingly similar) is the large number of summonses to praise that occur in them. Doubtless this is connected with the fact that Israel's praises were congregational, sung by lay celebrants, not only by professional temple singers (cf. Ps. 42:5, ". . . how I walked with the crowd, moved with them, the festive throng, to the house of God with joyous shouts of praise"). But that cannot by itself explain why out of fifty-three hymns and praise-songs of the community, twenty-eight contain a summons, addressed to the hearers, to praise, sing, shout for joy, chant hymns, raise a shout, clap hands, or bless. Even four of the fifteen praises of the individual contain such exhortations. What is the meaning of this? If it were merely a matter of flattery, we cannot suppose Israelite singers more adept at this than Babylonian or Egyptian; why then is the summons to praise not found outside Israel?

In his discerning *Reflections on the Psalms*, C. S. Lewis offers this interpretation of the praises to God in the psalms in general, and of the summons in particular:

> ... all enjoyment spontaneously overflows into praise.... The world
> rings with praise—lovers praising their mistresses, readers their favor-
> ite poet, walkers praising the countryside.... Praise almost seems to
> be inner health made audible.... Just as men spontaneously praise
> whatever they value, so they spontaneously urge us to join them in
> praising it: "Isn't she lovely? Wasn't it glorious? Don't you think that
> magnificent?" The Psalmists in telling everyone to praise God are
> doing what all men do when they speak of what they care about. (94f.)

This seems to touch the root of the matter, as it accords with the enthusiasm otherwise in evidence in the songs of praise. The Babylonian and Egyptian hymns, showing more deliberation and a greater subservience to form, lack the summons. Its presence in scriptural praises bespeaks the emotion aroused in the authors through consciousness of the divine benefactions. The service of praise has thus the quality of a release of human emotion, an answer to man's need of giving expression to powerful feelings of gratitude, joy, and wonder.

With this we conclude our inquiry into the biblical conception of the service of God. In its biblical refinement, the master-servant figure underwent an essential change: the mutuality of the full-blooded image, in which each party both benefits and derives benefit materially from the other, has been transformed: God is master only in that he sets the terms of his servants' existence; humans are servants only in that they are wholly dependent upon God. But a person's material uselessness to God does not mean that God is indifferent to that person's attitude toward him. On the contrary, God commands that humans worship him, that they recognize their creaturehood and subjection and that they acknowledge God's goodness. This service of God is a value because it has been commanded by him, because it is his pleasure (just as every biblical value derives ultimately from the divine will). Thus, while the material basis of the value of divine service is denied, its spiritual basis is not: humans are a concern of God and their happiness is God's pleasure; hence the condition of their happiness—recognition that they are God's creatures—is a divine desire and command.[18]

Much can be learned about the refinement of the conception of the service of God from the critiques directed against current practice in the prophetic and nonprophetic literature.

The prophetic critique of Israel's worship has often been dealt with, and shall not, therefore, be reviewed here.[19] Its viewpoint is external to the world of worship; it condemns the entire range of Israel's cultic activity, without discriminating between sacrifice and prayer, or between petition and praise—the whole stands under the prophetic judgment that the worship of villains is an abomination to the Lord. Such wholesale rejection, reaching its climax in Micah 6:6–8, where God's requirement of humans is summed up entirely in moral terms, cannot have had much of an effect on the development of sensibility to the issues inherent in the forms of worship. In truth, it is difficult to find prophetic influence on the evolution of sensibility and discrimination in this area; what has been pointed to as such[20] can better be accounted for by internal growth within the institutions of worship.

A remarkable reflex of such internal growth is Psalm 50, a product of critical reflection by one close to the forms of worship. The psalm depicts God's judgment upon two types of worshipers: first, the sacrificer who imagines that he is doing something for God; second, the "reciter of his laws" whose deeds contradict his text. We shall give attention to the reproof directed toward the sacrificer, for here we find a hierarchy of values within the forms of divine service.

> God, the LORD God spoke
> And summoned the world from east to west.
> From Zion, perfect in beauty,
> God appeared ...
> He summoned the heavens above,
> And the earth for the trial of his people. "Bring in my devotees,
> Who made a covenant with me over sacrifice!"
> Then the heavens proclaimed his righteousness,
> For he is a God who judges.
> "Pay heed, my people, and I will speak,
> O Israel, and I will arraign you.
> I am God, your God.
> I censure you not for your sacrifices,
> And your burnt offerings made to me daily;
> I claim no bull from your estate,
> No he-goats from your pens.
> For mine is every animal of the forest,
> The beasts on a thousand mountains,
> I know every bird of the mountains,
> The creatures of the field are subject to me.
> Were I hungry, I would not tell you,
> For mine is the world and all it holds.
> Do I eat the flesh of bulls,
> Or drink the blood of he-goats?
> Sacrifice a thank offering to God,
> And pay your vows to the Most High.
> Call upon me in time of trouble;
> I will rescue you and you shall honor me." (Ps. 50:1–15)

The error of the sacrificer is inferable from the reproof. This is the gist of it: I do not reprove you for slackness in offering the daily animal sacrifices, since all living things are, after all, mine. Even if I hungered, then, I should not look to you for relief. But really, do I eat or drink? Thus far, God has made his points negatively or in rhetorical questions. He addresses those who have "made a covenant with him over sacrifice" (ambiguous: a covenant ratified by/concerned with sacrifice), apparently an ironic title for worshipers whose zeal in making the regular whole and peace offerings was sustained by the notion that in so doing they were doing something for God. Having scolded them more in irony and by indirection than by straightforward condemnation, God turns to exhortation, in which it emerges that what he intends is not a blanket polemic against sacrifice:

> Sacrifice a thank offering to God,
> And pay your vows to the Most High . . .

The next verse, though later in place, is prior in time:

> Call upon me in time of trouble;
> I will rescue you and you shall honor me . . .

The correct temporal order is given, e.g., in Psalm 66:13f.

> I enter your house with burnt offering;
> I pay my vows to you;
> Vows that my lips pronounced,
> That my mouth uttered in my distress . . .

Or in Job 22:27, "Pray to him and he will listen to you, so you shall pay your vows." The thank offering was an occasion for honoring God in that it gave an opportunity to testify publicly to his providential care:

> Because of you I offer praise in the great congregation;
> I pay my vows in the presence of his worshipers.
> Let the lowly eat [viz., of the thank offering] and be satisfied . . .
> (Ps. 22:26f.)

> I will sacrifice a thank offering to you . . .
> I will pay my vows to the LORD
> In the presence of all his people,
> In the courts of the house of the LORD . . . (116:17f.)

In our Psalm 50, the reprover contrasts "your sacrifices and burnt offerings made to me daily"—which he rejects—with the thank offering—which he commands. He rejects the former with a rhetoric aimed against the idea that the sacrificer gives God something he lacks or needs. He sharpens, and perhaps exaggerates polemically, a notion (vague and indeterminate as it might have been) that the daily, regular cult somehow worked to God's benefit. Over against that, the reprover sets the thank offering as an unalloyed honoring of God. How is that? Through the offerer's publishing abroad, incidental to his sacrifice, how he called upon God in distress and how God heard and delivered him.

In the votive thank offering the essence of honoring God—and serving him—is realized: the acknowledgment that one is dependent upon God, that one needs him. The preferred service is that which expresses man's dependence and need for God in unalloyed form. Biblical religion managed to embody this idea even by means of sacrifice. In this psalm, the pagan vestige that adhered to the sacrificial worship—the popular evaluation of the regular cult as doing something for God—was overcome from within the system. The idea of service was purified from inside by discriminating one type of sacrifice from another, in no way like the external, wholesale condemnation of all cult forms by the prophets.

A higher stage of refinement was the preference of the recital of God's saving act to the thank offering. C. Westermann has noted that the undertaking to recite the saving acts of the deity is a motif common to the prayers of Israel, Egypt, and Mesopotamia.[21] In Israel the vow to bring a thank offering must have implied an accompanying recital of God's benefaction. Only so can we understand the formulation of the undertaking as it appears, e.g., in Psalm 27:6:

> I will sacrifice in his tent with shouts of joy,
> Singing and chanting a hymn to the LORD.

or in 54:8:

> Then I will offer you a free-will sacrifice;
> I will acknowledge that your name, LORD, is good.

In many psalms the wish or undertaking to praise God for his benefactions occurs without reference to sacrifice—a regular feature outside Israel as well. For example, Psalm 22:21ff.:

> Save my life from the sword . . .
> Deliver me from a lion's mouth . . .
> Then will I proclaim your fame to my brethren,
> Praise you in the great congregation . . .

And in a petition to Ishtar (ANET, 385b):

> Let my prayers and my supplications come to thee . . .
> As for me, let me glorify thy divinity and thy might before the
>   blackheaded people:
> "Ishtar indeed is exalted, Ishtar indeed is queen . . .
> The valorous daughter of Sin has no rival!"

In Israel, however, this motif underwent a refinement in that from time to time the votive *praise* of God is said to be preferable to the votive *sacrifice* of thanksgiving. The underlying motive seems to be the desire to keep as far as possible from the shadow of suggestion that one is doing something for God; hence sacrifice, even votive sacrifice, is shunned.

> I will extol God's name with song,
> And exalt him with praise.
> That will please the LORD more than oxen.
> Than bulls with horns and hooves. (Ps. 69:31f.)

The very same passage shows a refinement in another direction as well: the aim of the public praise is not merely glorification of God among men (that is a theme of ancient Near Eastern petitions), but more:

> The lowly will see and rejoice;
> You who are mindful of God, take heart!
> For the LORD listens to the needy,
> And does not spurn his captives. (vv. 33f.)

Recital of God's benefactions confirms the faith of hearers in his power and his faithfulness to deliver from distress. This is another aspect of the enthusiasm of the psalmist, noted above in connection with the summons to praise, save that now it is even clearer that the praise is not for the benefit or satisfaction of God, but to encourage his devotees by giving them another testimony to his goodness. At its peak of refinement, the votive praise of biblical prayer not only regards verbal acknowledgment as preferable to sacrifice, but intends to hold up an example to fellows in need. The cry for help is motivated not alone by a private concern, but by the desire to offer an occasion for the fortification of faith among the circle of God's seekers.

That this is so is corroborated by another passage in which the psalmist rejects votive sacrifice:

> You gave me to understand that
> You do not desire sacrifice and meal offering;
> You do not ask for burnt offering and sin offering....[22]
> To do what pleases you, my God, is my desire ...
> I proclaimed your righteousness in a great congregation;
> See, I did not withhold my words ...
> O favor me O LORD, and save me ...
> Let all who seek you be glad and rejoice in you;
> Let those who love your deliverance always say:

Extolled be the Lord. (40:7–11, 14, 17)

The passage appears to say that the psalmist rejects sacrifice as a proper expression of gratitude for God's deliverance (described in vv. 2f.). He was enlightened to understand that God preferred rather that he proclaim his saving deeds in public, and he did so. Now he is again in distress,[23] and he asks for help, not merely for his own sake and for the sake of God's fame, but also to cheer "all those who seek" the Lord. "'Those who seek you,'" comments Kimḥi, "are the same as 'those who love your deliverance,' since they do not seek deliverance from any other source." The poet asks to be saved in order to bring joy to his co-believers, who, like him, resort to God in their distress, and, like him, broadcast God's saving acts to the world. The rescue of the psalmist will thus serve as a source of joy and encouragement to all the faithful.

Yet, a third verification that strengthening the faithful is an additional aim of votive praise comes from the peculiar undertaking of the author of Psalm 51, who likewise rejects the sacrificial thanksgiving:

> You do not want me to bring sacrifices;
> You do not desire burnt offerings.
> True sacrifice to God is a contrite spirit;
> God, you will not despise a contrite and crushed heart. (51:18ff.)

Now, besides his vow to praise—

> Save me from bloodguilt O God, God, my deliverer,
> That I may sing forth your beneficence.

the psalmist undertakes to do more:

> Let me teach transgressors your ways,
> That sinners may return to you.

The request for pardon, the leading motive of this psalm, has here a larger purpose than a merely private one: the pray-er hopes to serve as an example to people of God's merciful ways with sinners, of God's readiness to accept their repentance. Again, the transcendence of the sacrificial mode of thanksgiving coincides with an explicit skewing of the primary aim of the vow (to flatter or propitiate the deity) in the direction of benefit to people, of answering a human spiritual need.

The vow was, as a matter of course, part of a prayer for deliverance, so much so that one psalmist can substitute "vow" for "prayer" in 61:6:

"O God, you hear my vows; grant the plea of those who fear your name." Such prayer is described in a surprising fashion in 66:17:

> I called aloud to him.
> Glorification on my tongue (*romam taḥaṯ l'šoni*).[24]

The meaning is hardly "that under the cry of distress lay already the certainty of God's response. Under the lamenting tongue, the praise of gratitude was already waiting" (H. J. Kraus). The verse speaks of laudation of God as a very component of petition. How is that? We have already noted that, contrary to Mesopotamian petitions, the biblical psalms of petition do not preface their requests by praises of God. Perhaps what our verse refers to is such passages as the following, occurring amidst calls for help:

> Good and upright is the LORD;
> Therefore he shows sinners the way.
> He guides the lowly in the right path,
> And teaches the lowly his way.
> All the LORD's paths are steadfast love
> For those who keep the decrees of his covenant. (25:8ff.)

> For you, my Lord, are good and forgiving,
> Abounding in steadfast love to all who call on you . . .
> There is none among the gods like you, O my Lord,
> And there are no deeds like yours . . .
> For you are great and perform wonders;
> You alone are God. (86:5, 8, 10)

And in a communal petition:

> It was you who drove back the sea with your might,
> Who smashed the heads of the monsters in the waters . . .
> The day is yours, the night also;
> It was you who set in place the orb of the sun;
> You fixed all the boundaries of the earth;
> Summer and winter—you made them. (74:13ff.)

Such allusions to God's wonderful attributes give the ground of the pray-er's confidence in the happy issue of his prayer. They summon God to verify to the pray-er the attributes for which he is famous, by manifesting them in his case. Invoking God's attributes is a source of hope to the pray-er in his hour of need: God need only be himself, and deliverance will come. That is the sense, too, of the repeated phrases, "Do it for your name's sake," or "for the sake of your faithfulness" or "righteousness." Another mode of this line of thought is found in Psalm 143. After relating his despondency in his time of trouble ("My spirit failed within me; my mind was numbed with horror"), the psalmist tells of a turning:

> Then I thought of the days of old;
> I rehearsed all your deeds,
> Recounted the work of your hands.
> I stretched out my hands to you,
> Longing for you like thirsty earth. (143:5–6)

He concludes, appropriately enough, "For the sake of your name, O Lord, preserve me; as you are beneficent, free me from distress. As you are faithful, put an end to my foes; destroy all my mortal enemies, for I am your servant."

For the failing spirit, prayer is possible, the terror can be overcome, because the pray-er can remember that God once before proved able to deliver.[25] Similar are cases in which the pray-er says that he ventured to lay his petition before God only because God had previously assured him with respect to it. Thus Jacob:

> Save me, I beseech you, from the hand of my brother Esau; for I am afraid that he will come and slay me, the mothers with the children. But you promised, "I will be sure to make you prosperous and make your descendants like the sands of the sea, too numerous to count." (Gen. 32:12f.)

Likewise David:

> For you, O Lord of hosts, God of Israel, have revealed to your servant, saying, "I will build you a house"; therefore your servant has found the courage to pray this prayer to you. (2 Sam. 7:27)

Likewise Solomon:

> . . . that your eyes may be open to the supplications of your servant and to the supplication of your people Israel, to give ear to them whenever they cry to you. For you separated them from all the peoples of the earth to be your inheritance, as you promised through Moses your servant, when you brought our fathers out of Egypt, O Lord God. (1 Kings 8:52f.)

In the light of this idea, let us consider the problem of the "precative perfect" in the Psalms. In recent times, M. Buttenweiser has made the most eloquent plea for regarding such passages as the following as containing a perfect that expresses a wish:

3:7   Buttenweiser

Rise, O Lord; help me, O my God,

| *ki hikkita 'et kol 'oyᵉbay lehi*
šinne rᵉša'im šibbarta | Yea, smite all my enemies on the
  cheek;
Break the teeth of the wicked. |

4:2

| When I call, answer me, O God
  my vindicator;
basṣar hirḥabta li
Have mercy on me and hear
  my prayer. | Give thou breadth and freedom to
  me in my distress. |

Buttenweiser rejects the contention that "in the people's present affliction, the Psalmist recalls God's wondrous delivery of them in the past. . . . But is it conceivable," he argues, "that any sane writer, when turning from the gloom of the present to the glory of the past, should fail to indicate the change of scene, and just leave it to his readers to divine his meaning?"[26] Yet it was the custom of supplicators to mention prior benefactions of God in their prayers, and in view of that custom, the shift of scene, especially when accompanied by a shift in tense, can hardly have been problematic.

The ultimate meaning of such expressions is that the capability of prayer arises out of a prior experience of God's turning to men. Such prior experience is of two types: in individual petitions, it may have been a direct private experience whose aftereffect was to keep one from despair in future troubles. When trouble came, his experience fortified him to trust in a repetition of God's turning:

> When I call, answer me, O God my vindicator;
> In trouble you have given me relief;
> Have mercy on me and hear my prayer. (4:2)

In communal petitions, the prior experience may be mediate, through historical tradition that the psalmist has acquired as his own. In distress he is heartened by recalling God's past national deliverances. The capacity to pray is thus conditioned on the hope or trust that what happened once can happen again. That, we suggest, is the meaning of "supplicating God with glorification on one's tongue." If it is, then one who never experienced a saving act of God in his life, or did not adopt the faith in such a divine providence from the experience of a fellow human being, or the traditional history of his people, cannot know the fullness of biblical petitionary prayer, prayer in which praise springs to the lips of the petitioner in the midst of his plea, prayer that has been made possible by grounded hope in the breast of the pray-er.

The dependence of prayer upon God is taken a step further in one or two passages. The author of Psalm 51 pleads:

> Save me from bloodguilt, O God, God my deliverer,
> That my tongue may sing forth your beneficence.
> O Lord, open my lips and let my mouth declare your praise. (vv. 16f.)

Kimḥi glosses this aptly: "Let me have divine assistance in speaking." Another psalmist relates:

> He lifted me out of the miry pit . . .
> And set my feet on a rock . . .
> He put a new song into my mouth,
> A hymn to our God. (40:3f.)

(It is noteworthy that just these two psalms, 40 and 51, contain other, previously noted "peaks.") As one of two alternative explanations Kimḥi gives: "He assisted me in song by means of inspiration, so that a song with fitting words issued from my mouth." The conception that songs of the divine service were inspired appears to have taken root by the end of the biblical age, to such an extent that the verb "prophesy" (*nibba*) served to denote the work of temple singers. We read in 1 Chronicles 25:1: "David and the commanders of the army also set apart for the service certain of the sons of Asaph, Heman and Jeduthun, who should prophesy with lyres, harps and cymbals." For further clarification we read of "Jeduthun, with the lyre, who prophesied, thanking and praising the Lord" (v. 3). Similarly, the capacity to perceive God's working in the world, which, as indicated above, is the basis of trust in petitionary prayer, is also counted as a gift of God:

> O God, you have taught me from my youth,
> And until now I have proclaimed your wondrous deeds. (71:17)

Kimḥi glosses: "You have given me a discerning mind from youth to recognize that all comes from you." Both themes occur in the Scroll of Thanksgiving Hymns from the wilderness of Judah. The author of the hymns counts among the kindnesses of God to him, "You set supplication in the mouth of your servant" (9:11)—i.e., the very formulation of petition. Particularly illuminating is his novel use of *ma'ne lašon*, "utterance of the tongue," a phrase derived from Proverbs 16:1: "A man may arrange his thoughts, but the utterance of the tongue is from the LORD."

> You put into the mouth of your servant thanksgiving, praise and
> supplication,
> Thus creating utterance of the tongue for your creature. (11:34)

> I praise you by the spirits which you have put in me,
> I find utterance of the tongue to recount your beneficences. (17:17)

This is combined with ascription to God of the power to discern his deeds in 11:4f.:

> You make me perceive your wondrous deeds,
> And put thanks into my mouth and on my tongue, praise.

Here are the origins of the idea that the Book of Psalms as a whole is a product of the holy spirit.

Let us sum up this ideational climax with respect to the dependence of the pray-er upon God. Prayer is address to God made possible by a prior turning, or initiative of God to work in the world, in the community, or in the life of an individual. Perception of such divine working is the life-breath of prayer, of petition and praise alike. This is so much the case, that pious souls, whose consciousness of dependence upon God is all-pervasive, regard this precondition of prayer as a favor, a gift of God, a teaching he has taught them. As for the "utterance of the tongue," we understand the idea as follows: In his great concentration and high tension, the pray-er is empowered to frame his sentiments in words marvelously in accord with his need. He perceives this marvelous accord not as a native skill but as an inspiration, a gift of God. Testimonies are forthcoming elsewhere to verify this experience, of which the following description, taken from the eleventh century *Duties of the Heart* by the philosopher Baḥya Ibn Paquda, is a fine example.

> A man should endeavor to do more than was originally in his power, yearn for it with all his heart, rise to it in his thought, and . . . beseech God to help and strengthen him to acquire more knowledge and to serve him more than is at present within his capacity. If he perseveres, the Creator will grant his petitions, will open the gates to him, and strengthen his understanding and physical forces so that . . . he will be enabled to fulfill God's commandments in a higher degree than is now

within his power, as it is said, "I am the LORD your God who teaches you profitably, who leads you in the way you should go" (Isa. 48:17). An analogy is the acquisition of skill in the arts and of proficiency in the sciences. When a person learns an art, he first practices various parts of it and exerts himself according to his understanding to a lesser extent than his capacity. When his comprehension of the art increases, and he is continually engaged with it, the Creator shows him its fundamental principles and general rules. And from these he draws inferences which he did not learn from anyone. The expert in geometry . . . first teaches it to his pupil in the concrete, by means of the figures Euclid placed in his work. . . . When the pupil understands this well, and zealously . . . strives to acquire the knowledge of the deductions that should be drawn from the principles, the Creator teaches him abstraction . . . and he is able to deduce the most difficult figures and make the finest calculations which almost resemble prophecy vouchsafed by God. So it is with the other sciences. For if the pupil studies zealously, he will feel a higher spiritual power which no human being can give him. . . . Elihu said: "But there is a spirit in man, and the inspiration of the Almighty gives them understanding." (Job 32:8)

When the believer strives with heart and soul to fulfill [God's commands] and succeeds as far as is within his power, God will open the gate of spiritual excellences to him, so that he will . . . attain what was beyond his powers. . . . The following illustrates this thought: A man planted trees, broke the ground around them, cleared it of thorns and weeds, watered the trees when necessary and applied fertilizer; then he prays to God that they yield fruit. But if he neglects them, he does not deserve that the Creator give him fruit from them. The same is true of the service of God. If one strives and is keen to do what is within his power, God will aid him to achieve what is beyond his power . . . as our sages say: "Whoso fulfills the Torah amidst poverty will in the end fulfill it amidst riches." (*Ḥeśbon Hannefeš 3, "the 21st way"*)[27]

All that has been said refers to spontaneous prayer that flows from a heart filled with emotion. But it is evident that even in biblical times not all prayers were spontaneous, nor was any prayer wholly original. Form criticism has amply shown the formulaic elements of all prayer, and the very collecting of psalms (the book and the smaller entities that preceded the final collection) attests to a need early felt for a treasury of prayer and praise for the community. Y. Kaufmann has noted the signs of the early fixing of psalm stereotypes:

Every word of prayer is appropriate to the situation in which it is spoken; this is not the case of the psalms whose life context is given. Hannah's prayer (1 Sam. 1:10) accords with her condition, but her hymn of thanksgiving has only one verse (verse 5, "the barren woman gave birth to seven") applicable specifically to her. This one verse was enough for the narrator to have Hannah recite the whole psalm, although verse 10 shows plainly that it is a royal thanksgiving hymn. Jonah's prayer (4:2f.) fits his condition; the hymn of chapter 2, however, is obviously a thanksgiving connected with the payment of vows in the temple. In verses 3ff., the poet employs such figures as "from the belly of Sheol I cried out," and these were enough to justify ascribing the psalm to Jonah in the belly of the fish.... Such instances... of incongruity between a psalm and the occasion in which it is uttered are not editorial mistakes. Once a given psalm has become public property, its application to various situations is obviously considered justified if even a non-essential element can be conceived as relevant. This phenomenon—repeated... through the centuries with the psalms of the Psalter—appearing already in pre-exilic literature testifies to the fixation of psalm stereotypes... in early times.[28]

What is this tendency to use stereotypic psalms (and eventually nonpoetic prayers too)? The answer is implied in what has been said above with respect to the inspiration of prayer. It is not to be supposed that every psalmist, or even most, experienced a divine afflatus guiding his creativity. Nevertheless, the vitality and urgency that emanate from many of the psalms testify to the passion of their authors. True, there is no psalm altogether free of the fixed usages and formulas that belonged to the common stock of ancient Hebrew poetry; on the other hand, there is scarcely a single psalm made up entirely of such formulas. In most, a creative spirit moves, using the formulas in novel combinations and adding original elements. The very difficulty of finding regular structure to psalms of a given category, and the consequent recourse to "mixed categories" in form criticism of the psalms, speaks for the origin of many of them in genuine spiritual excitation. The contrast with the regularity of structure and fixity of elements in Akkadian hymns and prayers is remarkable, and suggests the deliberateness and artifice of the composition of the latter.[29] Every now and then a psalmist betrays a certain consciousness of authorship which points to a sense of originality: in 28:7 the poet says, "I will glorify him *miššīrī*—by one of my songs"; in 45:2 the author of a royal wedding song expressly describes the stages of the creation of his poem.

Now, a person less gifted poetically, agitated by circumstances similar to those that inspired a psalmist but unable to express the turbulence of his or her soul with like aptness, will have recourse to the psalm for an adequate vehicle of his emotion. He or she obtains relief through the record of the emotion of a predecessor. The prepared verses acquire a new, personal significance as they are suffused by the sentiment of the reciter. But there is also a reverse effect: the emotion of the reciter is itself shaped—perhaps even purged and sublimated—by being filtered through the expression of the psalmist. Thus the fixed text becomes an instrument by which the thought of the ancients becomes renewed and enriched through the experience of later generations, while itself working cathartically upon them.

An analogy may be drawn between the power of a fixed prayer text and that of a festival rite to train the spirit. An epoch-making event that altered the course of national life is captured in a festival whose rite is calculated to evoke the event in the consciousness of the celebrants. When the festival is kept afterward, not merely a memory is evoked, but something of the formative effect of the primary event on the souls of those who underwent it. Just as the destiny of the first experiencers was shaped by the event, so destiny of their descendants is by the celebration of the festival. The parallelism with the effect of fixed prayer texts may be spelled out thus:

1. The affecting event generates a festival/a prayer that embodies its emotional charge.
2. Celebration of the festival rite/recital of the prayer as a fixed text arouses and releases emotions similar to those of the primary celebrants/pray-er.
3. Thus the festival/the fixed prayer gives shape to the feelings of later generations, and conserves in them the values of the founders.

There is, of course, the danger of automatism both in the repeated celebration of festivals and the repetition of fixed prayers. That is the object of the divine censure in Isaiah 29:13:

> Because that people has approached me with its mouth and honored me with its lips, but has kept its heart far from me, and its worship of me has been a commandment of men, learned by rote . . .

Nonetheless, neither biblical religion nor any since has been able to dispense altogether with norm and form as vehicles and trainers of spontaneity, and as guarantors of continuity and generational solidarity for the community. What is significant about the fixation of prayer texts in biblical religion is its aim, as described above. It is at the farthest remove from the purpose of the rigorous formulation known from paganism, which served magical and theurgic ends.[30]

This brings us back, by way of conclusion, to the start of our inquiry. Prayer, both in the form of petition and of praise, has as its primitive root the conception that God and man are related as master and servant, king and subject. The need for petition arises originally out of the notion that the knowledge of the gods is limited; praise springs from the desire to propitiate them by flattery. In biblical thought, there was a constant refinement of the idea of worship away from such simple beginnings to the acknowledgment of dependence upon God. Prayer became a vehicle of humility, an expression of un-self-sufficiency, which, in biblical thought, is the proper stance of humans before God. In its highest reaches, biblical prayer remains still the embodiment of the awareness of creaturehood, as much a contrast to theurgic incantation as to the self-containedness of human-centered modernism.

POSTSCRIPT

In a forthcoming study entitled "Ancient Near Eastern Patterns in Prophetic Literature," which he was good enough to show me, my colleague Professor Moshe Weinfeld compares biblical passages preferring praise to sacrifice, to Egyptian material, of which the most striking item is from the end of "The Shipwrecked Sailor" (suggested date, eleventh dynasty, ca. 2000 B.C.E.). Seeking to propitiate the serpent, lord of the island onto which he was cast by the sea, the sailor promises him that, when he is rescued, he will "have brought to you laudanum, *heknu*-oil, *iudeneb*, cassia, and incense. . . . You will be thanked in (my) town in the presence of the magistrates of the entire land. I shall sacrifice to you oxen . . . , and I shall wring the necks of birds for you," etc. The serpent laughs at the sailor, and replies: ". . . Indeed, I am the Prince of Punt; myrrh belongs to me. That *heknu*-oil of which you spoke about bringing me, why it is the main product of this island!" Later, when the sailor is finally rescued, the serpent's parting words are, "Place my good repute in your town; this is all I ask from you." (W. K. Simpson, ed., *The Literature of Ancient Egypt*, New Haven, 1972, 55, lines 139–60)

The similarity with biblical passages discussed above is indeed worthy of note (and I am grateful to Professor Weinfeld for pointing it out to me), but so too are the differences. First, while the serpent disdains the sailor's offer because it is from his island that (part of) the offering comes, God rejects Israel's sacrifice in the comparable Psalm 50:9–12 because, in the last analysis, Israel has failed to adjust its appreciation of sacrifice to the fact that God does not eat or drink (v. 13). The serpent's disdain arises out of an accident of the story (he owns the source of Egypt's spices); there is no inkling of a suggestion that by analogy the cosmic gods take (or could take) a similar view of man's sacrificing at large. Nor do we have evidence elsewhere in Egyptian literature that thinkers developed such an idea on a general, cosmic scale. The psalmist, however, first generalized on the low level of the serpent when he had the cosmic God say, ". . . Were I hungry, I would not tell you, for mine is the world and all it holds" (v. 12); he then immediately advanced to his, and his audience's, peculiarly transcendent level with the question, "Do I eat the flesh of bulls, or drink the blood of he-goats?" (v. 13). Second, while both the serpent and the biblical God are above the material gifts of humans (for different reasons), the substitution therefor of praise to the former is merely to flatter his self-esteem; the substitution of praise to the latter (as, e.g., in Ps. 69:31f.) is in every case more than a matter of flattery, as I have argued above.

Why the serpent in this story should prefer a boost to his reputation over the offer made by the sailor is readily understandable. Why a cosmic God, who stands in no need of humans, should "require" praise or sacrifice, let alone prefer one to the other, cannot be understood by a simple transference of notions from Egypt to Israel. I have tried to penetrate the transvaluations that accompany the adoption in Israel of common Near Eastern language and forms of worship.

NOTES

1. Muffs's essay circulates in mimeographed form as "The Prayer of Prophets." Part Two of his "Introduction to Biblical Religion" lectures at the Jewish Theological Seminary of America, in Hebrew, no date. [See now ch. 1 of his book, *Love and Joy* (New York: Jewish Theological Seminary, 1992), 9–48.] Blank's study appeared in the JBL, 72 (1953):1–14. "Pray-er" (= one who prays) will be so written to distinguish it from "prayer" (= orison).

2. On Honi, see the brief article by Judah Goldin, "On Honi the Circle-Maker: a Demanding Prayer," *HTR*, 61 (1963): 233–37; a more extensive typological survey appears in Gad Ben-Ammi Sarefati's Hebrew study, "Pious Men, Men of Deeds, and the Early Prophets," *Tarbiz*, 26 (1956), 126ff.

3. The most comprehensive and profound study of the phenomena of prayer is still Friedrich Heiler's *Prayer: A Study in the History and Psychology of Religion* (London, New York, and Toronto: Oxford University Press, 1932), translated and edited [and shortened] from the German by S. McComb with the assistance of J. E. Park. My understanding of and approach to the biblical material has been deeply affected by Heiler's study.

A brief survey of the biblical concept of worship is J. Licht's entry *ʿabodat ʾelohim* ("service of God") in EB 6 (Jerusalem: Mosad Bialik, 1971): 37–9; Licht does not include prayer under this rubric.

A painstakingly thorough analysis of biblical prayer outside the psalms and prophets is to be found in A. Wendel, *Das freie Laiengebet im vorexilischen Israel* (Leipzig: Pfeiffer, 1932); illuminating remarks on biblical prayer in general, in Y. Kaufmann, *Toledot Ha-emunah Ha-yisre'elit* II/2 (Tel Aviv: Dvir, 1945):499–506 (abridged in *The Religion of Israel* [Chicago, 1960], 309–11).

In the translation of biblical passages, I have followed, in the psalms, the new Jewish Publication Society version (Philadelphia, 1972); elsewhere *The Old Testament: An American Translation*, ed. J. M. Powis Smith (Chicago: University of Chicago Press, 1927), has served as a guide.

4. "To call upon the name of the LORD" (*qara bᵉšem YHWH*), while properly only the invocation and start of prayer–and as such originally belonging to polytheism, where it is necessary at the outset of prayer to single out by name the deity addressed–is used

here as a synonym of prayer; cf. 1 Kings 18:24ff. In a striking monotheistic skewing of the original sense, the phrase is given the meaning "proclaim the name LORD" = proclaim the attributes to be invoked in prayer, in Exodus 33:19; 34:5 (so rendered in the new Jewish Publication Society version of the Torah [2nd ed., 1967]).

5. S. N. Kramer, *The Sumerians: Their History, Culture, and Character* (Chicago: University of Chicago Press, 1963), 123.

6. The *Enuma Elish* passage and the bilingual cosmogony may be found in A. Heidel, *The Babylonian Genesis*, 2nd ed. (Chicago: University of Chicago Press, 1951), 46, 69f.

7. See note 5.

8. See the story of Gilgamesh and the story of Adapa, ANET 72ff., 101ff.

9. Text and French translation in J. J. A. Van Dijk, *La Sagesse Suméro-Accadienne* (Leiden: Brill, 1953), 13. English translation by T. Jacobsen in H. Frankfort and H. A. Frankfort, et al., *The Intellectual Adventure of Ancient Man* (Chicago: University of Chicago Press, 1946), 205f. Jacobsen's sketch of the Mesopotamian worldview in this volume (republished in paperback [Penguin Books] as *Before Philosophy*) remains one of the best available.

W. W. Hallo has made a full study of letter prayers (Neo-Sumerian), together with classificatory remarks on Sumerian religious poetry and some of its biblical equivalents, in "Individual Prayer in Sumerian: The Continuity of a Tradition," JAOS, 88 (1968), 71ff. (= *Essays in Memory of E. A. Speiser*, ed. by W. W. Hallo, American Oriental Series 53 [New Haven, 1968]).

10. The translation is by E. A. Speiser, "The Case of the Obliging Servant," JCS, 8 (1954):98ff., republished in *Oriental and Biblical Studies: Collected Writings of E. A. Speiser*, edited by J. J. Finkelstein and Moshe Greenberg (Philadelphia: University of Pennsylvania Press, 1967), 344ff.; this stanza is on p. 348. I have not yet seen G. Pettinato, *Das Altorientalische Menschenbild und die sumerischen und akkadischen Schöpfungsmythen* (Heidelberg: Carl Winter, 1971), but J. S. Cooper's detailed review in JAOS, 93 (1973), 581–85 (itself of great interest) indicates that it is a valuable contribution to the understanding of the question here touched upon only cursorily.

11. In spite of the intensive study that has been devoted to the affinities of the covenant between Israel and its God with ancient Near Eastern treaties—and they are important and extensive—the older suggestion that the "royal covenant" establishing the right of a monarch to rule over a given community is the immediate model of Israel's national covenant with God remains attractive (e.g., M. Buber, *Moses* [Oxford: East and West Library, 1947], 103). Of David it is specifically related that upon the recognition by the elders of Israel of his right to reign over them, he "made a covenant for them in Hebron before the LORD" whereupon they anointed him king (2 Sam. 5:1–3). As in the case of Saul's anointing by the people (1 Sam. 11:14f.), acknowledgment of a right to rule is based on some record of service or benefaction to the people. The considerable parallelism between king-subject and God-Israel relationships suggests that the "royal covenant" offered biblical thinkers the model most ready to hand of the establishment of an individual as ruler of an already existent ethnopolity. It has been observed that only in later literature (notably Deuteronomy) does the full treaty form, as it is known from ancient international vassal treaties, appear with respect to Israel's covenant with God; this may well reflect a gradual literary assimilation of vassal treaties with which biblical writers of the Assyrian period came to be familiar through the subjugation of Israel and Judah to Assyria. The earlier covenant documents (e.g., the Decalogue, "the Book of the Covenant") lack essential features of the later treaty form (e.g., blessings and curses); perhaps this is due to their following a different model—the "royal covenant," whose form we do not know, but whose existence is attested at least for David. The essential features of the royal covenant were presumably the acknowledgment of the right of the king to rule on the basis of prior merit, and the obligation of the people to be loyal subjects to him.

12. W. L. Moran, "The Ancient Near Eastern Background of the Love of God in Deuteronomy," CBQ, 25 (1963):77–87.

13. M. Weinfeld, *Deuteronomy and the Deuteronomic School* (Oxford: Clarendon, 1972), 82, continuation of n. 6 from p. 81.

14. So the verbal noun of *hištah«wa*, "bow low," is defined in the tannaitic source adduced in Bab. Tal. Berakot, 34b.

15. J. Milgrom, *Studies in Levitical Terminology, 1: The Encroacher and the Levite; The Term 'Aboda* (Berkeley: University of California Press, 1970), 60ff.

16. Psalm 45, in which the praises of a king are sung incidentally to celebrating his marriage, is the only one of its type. How different it is from extra-biblical hymns of praise to kings can be seen from comparison with the Sumerian examples adduced in A. Falkenstein and W. von Soden, *Sumerische und Akkadische Hymnen und Gebete* (Zürich/ Stuttgart: Artemis, 1953), 115ff., or the Egyptian examples in W. K. Simpson, ed., *The Literature of Ancient Egypt: An Anthology of Stories, Instructions, and Poetry* (New Haven: Yale University Press, 1972), 279ff. Although no examples of such praises to a king exist from ancient Israel, one must be cautious about drawing conclusions from silence. Had not Psalm 45:18 explicitly been found in a royal context, who would have guessed that its reference was to an earthly king?

17. C. Westermann, *The Praise of God in the Psalms*, trans. by K. R. Crim (London: Epworth, 1966), 37, 42, 46f.

18. The observation that the unreined pursuit of human fancies, the desire to carry out whatever can be imagined, to realize to the utmost one's capabilities–that these lead to human self-destruction underlies both the Garden of Eden and the Tower of Babel stories. Recognition of creatureliness, of subservience to God, expressed through a curb upon one's potential activities, is portrayed in these stories as a condition of man's happiness (through showing how their absence led to misfortune). What is in Greece regarded as the jealousy of the gods is in Hebrew Scripture considered simply as the bounds and conditions of human happiness. See my brief note, "On the Meaning of the Garden of Eden Story in Genesis," (Hebrew), *Shedemot*, 33 (Spring 5729 [1969]):10f.

19. For a good, brief, recent statement, with full bibliographic references, see G. Fohrer, *History of Israelite Religion*, trans. by D. E. Green (Nashville: Abingdon, 1972), 276ff.

20. H. Gunkel, J. Begrich, *Einleitung in die Psalmen* (Göttinger Handkommentar zum Alten Testament; Göttingen: Vandenhoeck & Ruprecht, 1933), 366; H. Gunkel, *Die Psalmen* (Fünfte Auflage; Göttingen: Vandenhoeck & Ruprecht, 1968), 216f. Both citations recognize the distinctiveness of the viewpoint of the psalms passages to be discussed below, yet derive it from prophecy. Why?

21. Westermann, *Praise of God*, 38ff., 46. For the Akkadian material, see the examples collected by G. Widengren, *The Accadian and Hebrew Psalms of Lamentation as Religious Documents* (Stockholm: Bökforlags Aktiebolaget Thule, 1937), 311ff. For Northwest Semitic examples, with particularly illuminating remarks on biblical and some Egyptian texts, see H. L. Ginsberg, "Psalms and Inscriptions of Petition and Acknowledgment," *Louis Ginzberg Jubilee Volume*, English Section (New York: American Academy for Jewish Research, 1945), 159ff.

22. A new surmise as to the meaning of verse 8 is contained in the Jewish Publication Society version rendering: "Then I said, 'See, I will bring a scroll recounting what befell me.'" This admittedly speculative effort was inspired by the essay of H. L. Ginsberg mentioned in the previous note.

23. On the (at least secondary) unity of this psalm, evidenced by verbal and ideational connections between its two main parts, see the commentaries of Kissane and Weiser, and the detailed argument of N. H. Ridderbos, *Die Psalmen: stylistische Verfahren und Aufbau . . .* (BZAW, 117, 1972), 289ff.

24. Vocalization of *romam* varies between short and long a; the former, taking the word as a *polal* (passive) "he was glorified," the latter, as a noun, "glorification" (pl cs *rom«mot* from °*romamot*, in Ps. 149:6). *Tahat* with speech organs ("tongue" in Ps. 10:7; "lips" in 140:4) is not different from *'al*, "on" in meaning. H. J. Kraus, *Psalmen* (BK: Neukirchen Kreis Moers, 1961), ad loc., rightly rejects emendations.

25. Cf. B. S. Childs's remarks on memory in the psalms in his *Memory and Tradition in Israel* (London, 1962), 60–5.

26. M. Buttenwieser, "The Importance of the Tenses for the Interpretation of the Psalms," *Hebrew Union College Jubilee Volume* (Cincinnati: Hebrew Union College,

1925), 89ff.; the citation is on 95; the two preceding passages (Pss. 3:7 and 4:1) are interpreted on 99 and 100.

27. With minor alteration, the translation is that of Moses Hyamson, *Duties of the Heart*, etc. (New York: Bloch, 1945), vol. 4, 90ff.

28. Y. Kaufmann, *The Religion of Israel: From Its Beginnings to the Babylonian Exile* (Chicago: University of Chicago, 1960), 310f.

29. See the remarks to this effect in the introduction to Falkenstein and v. Soden, *Sumerische und Akkadische Hymnen und Gebete*, 37ff.

30. The passage from Isaiah just quoted is the clearest evidence of an awareness of the difference between a magical and a religious attitude toward forms of worship. For the people reproved, the form was the essence; prayer was a matter of mouth and lips. For God, prayer must issue from the heart. Another passage to the same effect is Psalm 78:36f.:

> Yet they deceived him with their speech,
> Lied to him with their words;
> Their hearts were inconstant toward him;
> They were untrue to his covenant.

Ibn Ezra glosses verse 37 excellently: "This shows that the essence of prayer is the intention of the heart."

In antiquity, the theurgic notion of prayer was embodied with peculiar force in the Roman liturgy, whose concern over adherence to correct form is notorious. Heiler (*Prayer*, 72) cites Wissowa thus: "[Roman prayer is] the necessary oral explanation of the ritual act which on the mortals' side completes the legal business, and when given in the correct form at the same time compels the divinity to take his part in the juridical relation." Contrast Maimonides' summation of the reason for the adoption of prescribed prayer texts in Judaism, given in his *Code*, Laws of Prayer, 1:4. The exiled Jews spoke a mixture of languages and could not adequately express themselves in Hebrew; hence a fixed liturgy was composed "so that the stammerers might speak as correctly as those who spoke perfectly." This bears a familial similarity to the reason I have proposed.

Additional note:

In a comprehensive critical study entitled "Psalm 50, Its Subject, Form and Place," in *Shnaton: An Annual for Biblical and Ancient Near Eastern Studies* III (1978), 77–106 (in Hebrew), B. Schwartz differs from me in the interpretation of vv. 8–15. Agreeing that the essence of the passage is to ridicule the notion that God benefits from sacrifice, Schwartz paraphrases the verses in question thus: "The whole point of vss. 8–13 was to teach that God does not need sacrifices. . . . Then God says . . . I will prove this to you: Although your sacrifices are acceptable to me [so Schwartz reads v. 8, p. 79], so far as I am concerned you may bring a mere thank-offering (=peace-offering), from which I hardly get any part, yet your worship will be worship, for then you will also call on me in time of trouble," etc. (p. 84). Schwartz claims to follow the interpretation of Ibn Ezra, the gist of which is that God prefers the thank-offering, of which only the fatty parts are burnt on the altar, if it is accompanied by observance of the Torah, to the whole-offering without observance of the Torah.

Neither Ibn Ezra nor Schwartz seem to me to do justice to the contrast between the negations and commands of this passage. That the worth of sacrifice depends on the offerer's observance of the Torah or on some other non-sacrificial factor is not in the text.

The article by M. Weinfeld referred to in the Postscript appeared in VT 27 (1977):178–195.

Religion: Stability and Ferment

1979

THE SOURCES

The biblical sources of our knowledge of Israelite religion during the monarchy may be divided into two classes: those whose pertinence to the period may be assumed more or less confidently—such as the primary materials of the Book of Kings and several of the Prophets, and those of dubious pertinence, such as the Psalms, in which materials from the monarchic and other periods are combined—often, one suspects, indistinguishably.

The Book of Kings draws upon the chronicles of the kings of Israel and Judah; it also contains stories emanating from prophetic circles; the whole is set in a framework that connects and passes judgment upon kings and reigns. The final editing occurred between the latest historical datum in the book—the release of King Jehoiachin from prison in the accession year of Evil-Merodach of Babylon (561 B.C.E.)—and the Restoration, which is beyond its horizon (538). The hybrid religion ascribed to the Samaritans in 2 Kings 17:24–41 also indicates a period anterior to the building of the Second Temple, since at that time the Samaritans were irreproachably YHWH-fearing (otherwise their idolatry would have been cited in the Jews' rebuff of their bid to participate in the building of the Temple).

The contemporary material in the Book of Kings is of the first importance for describing the religion of the age. What makes the book problematic is its tendentious character: it judges the monarchies of Israel and Judah by a late, absolute standard throughout the history. The editor condemns Judah's worship at *bāmōt* from the reign of

Rehoboam to Ahaz, and the entire official cult in Israel from its founding by Jeroboam. Now there is no evidence in the primary sources that such standards obtained throughout the period. The material of north-Israelite provenience—such as the stories of Elijah and Elisha— does not display opposition to the official cult as long as it was free from alien influx. In Judah, no priest or king, be he ever so Godfearing, took exception to the *bāmōt*-worship before the reign of Hezekiah (eighth century). This contrast between the editing and the primary sources can be explained either as reflecting contemporaneous but divergent values, or (which seems more likely) as reflecting different periods. The affinities of the editorial part of Kings to Deuteronomy, both in ideology and language, indicate that it was inspired by that book. The identity of the editor's standard of judgment with the religious policy of the Judahite kings Hezekiah and Josiah (whom he praises unreservedly) suggests that his ideology, while pertaining indeed to the period of the monarchy, probably cannot be dated much before Hezekiah's time.

The primary sources of Kings give the appearance of reliability, if only because of their freedom from the tendency of the editing. Their chief limitation is their narrow purview: excepting the north-Israelite prophetic stories, they deal exclusively with kings. The practices of worship they describe belong to the official cult, founded and maintained by the monarchy. Only in the prophetic stories can one obtain glimpses of popular religion independent of the royal institutions. Thus the Book of Kings gives evidence of the royal policies respecting temples and clergy, in the capitals and the countryside, but tells little about the everyday, popular practice and faith. A pervasive tendency stamps the whole with the character of an indictment of the kingdoms of Israel and Judah.[1]

The Book of Chronicles contains data on the faith and worship of the monarchic period that do not appear in Kings, but the reliability of these data is dubious. The tendency of Chronicles is plain: it wishes to tell the story of the "Israel" that revived in the Persian province of Judah, putting forth those features that bound present to past (while ignoring discontinuities), and drawing lessons for contemporary faith and practice from the fate of the kingdom. To give expression to his ideology, the Chronicler puts speeches in the mouths of historical characters, composed in a distinctive style that cannot be mistaken for that of the Book of Kings. Reports of religious events that accord with this tendency and that are marked by the same style must also be regarded as his inventions (e.g., Manasseh's change of heart, 2 Chron. 33:12–16). Likewise suspect is his ascription to the early monarchy of institutions known to have existed in Second Temple times, but unattested earlier outside of Chronicles (1 Chron. 23–26). Every datum of

the Chronicler requires individual evaluation; no blanket generalization is possible. As a working rule, if that which he ascribes to our periods is attested elsewhere, his evidence can stand; what is not so
attested, had best be left out.[2]

The bulk of the Latter Prophets (Amos, Hosea, Micah, Isaiah
[1–37], Nahum, Zephaniah, Habakkuk, Jeremiah) are placed by their
date-titles in our period. Precisely when these books were edited is
not known; the date of their contents may be conjectured from their
historical horizon. By and large, the writings of the prophets of the
Neo-Assyrian period (Amos, Hosea, Isaiah, Micah) contain no reference to the rise of the Babylonian kingdom; similarly, the writings
of the prophets of the Babylonian period (Nahum, Zephaniah,
Habakkuk, Jeremiah) do not refer to the succeeding empire of the
Persians. Hence it is to be concluded that the prophetic material was
considered sacred close to the time of its publication and was more or
less fixed in the period to which it refers. Verses and even chapters
were interpolated, not only by the prophets' contemporaries, but by
later hands (e.g., Isa. 13 and part of 14), but these are not extensive
and are, on the whole, readily identifiable. Testimony concerning the
religion of the monarchy may therefore, with due criticism, be gathered from most of the prophetic material.[3]

Unlike the Book of Kings, prophecy does not deal only with kings.
The prophets embrace all classes in their purview; those to whom
they address their reproof are "from the smallest to the greatest" (Jer.
8:10). Hence the picture of a given age as drawn in Kings sometimes
differs from that drawn by its contemporary prophets, since many
evils denounced by the prophets were not the fault of the kings and
therefore go unmentioned in the Book of Kings.

The testimony of the prophets is impaired by their tendency to exaggerate and generalize. Their aim was to stir their audience to repentance; to that end, they excoriated sin and sinners without making
nice distinctions. Sins of some were attributed to the whole community. They sometimes failed to discriminate past from present sin, bad
intentions from actual deeds.[4] Prophetic testimony must be search-
ingly examined in order to determine the reality underlying their re-
proofs. The most reliable is the incidental testimony—that which
concerns something not at issue but only mentioned in passing.

Criticism has reached the conclusion that the Torah literature was
not fixed before the age of the monarchy. Among the indications of
this are allusions in the Torah to events from that age, e.g., the struggle between Israel and Edom (Gen. 25:23; 27:40); God's promise to
the patriarchs that kings would descend from them, the climax of divine promises to the patriarchs (Gen. 17:6; 35:11). On the other hand,
the laws of the Torah virtually ignore the monarchy, its institutions

and its values (Deut. 17:14–20 is a notable exception), assuming rather a tribal polity (elders and chiefs) of small farmers and cattle-raisers. The laws do not reflect the economy of merchants and large estate-owners that existed in monarchic times. Tension exists between the wilderness setting of Deuteronomy and its rulings on practices of worship that are not reflected in history before the reigns of Hezekiah and Josiah. It thus appears that while the earliest elements of the Torah literature precede the monarchy, the latest come from its last days. The cultic laws of the Torah are hardest to date. Since they assume a people settled in its land, it is reasonable to date their application to the age of the monarchy. Yet the literature that can most surely be dated to the monarchy makes scant reference to practices regulated by these laws; only in Second Temple literature is the cult law of the Torah clearly reflected. This is explicable in several ways: (1) that the cult laws of the Torah are from late, even post-exilic, times; (2) that the laws existed in the monarchy but were not universally applied until later; (3) that the origin and focus of the datable literature of the monarchy were too remote from the detail of the cult to reflect the laws adequately.

In this quandary, the following rule-of-thumb will be employed: materials of the Torah even partially reflected in literature datable to the monarchic age will be adduced in toto; data not even partially reflected will be left out.

There are no criteria for determining the age of the religious ideas and practices of the Psalms, since ideas and terms known from ancient Ugaritic literature are there juxtaposed to patently Israelite material. Only rarely can a specific historical context be plausibly conjectured for a psalm. References to an earthly king (as in Ps. 2) indicate the period of the monarchy; but allusions to the Babylonian exile (Ps. 137) and a widespread Diaspora (106:47) point to the inclusion in the collection of later material as well. Here, too, the above-mentioned rule will be used: data found only in psalms whose provenience from monarchic times is doubtful will not be adduced unless they are hinted at in material at least probably datable to the monarchy.[5]

The Bible sets forth the conceptions of the spiritual elite of Israel; popular religion is not expressed in it directly at all. The description of the people's sin is the evaluation of the elite, and exaggerates both its extent (as when acts of a limited circle are attributed to the entire people, like the Baal worship of the northern kingdom) and its heinousness (as when an act is condemned according to a standard that was not contemporaneous with it, like the worship at *bāmōt* before the reforms of Hezekiah). And yet one cannot assume an essential gap between the popular religion and that of the authors of the Bible, for the Bible is wholly concerned with the people; its authors address the people and regard their own faith as that of the Israelite people. The elite did not cultivate an esoteric faith, but strove to make the people share in their conceptions. Hence, they portray the popular religion as fundamentally identical with their own, the divergence between the two constituting the people's sin. While such a portrait is of course distorted, the constant orientation of the biblical authors toward the people kept the gap between the two much smaller than, say, the gap separating the religious ideas of the ancient Greek philosophers from those of the Greek masses of their age.

Extra-biblical sources for Israel's religion in the monarchic period are few and of small importance. The earliest extra-biblical attestation of the name of Israel's God occurs in the ninth-century B.C.E. inscription of King Mesha of Moab. According to the probably correct restoration of lines 17–18, Mesha boasts of "dragging the vessels of YHWH (*'[t k]ly yhwh*)" from the (temple of the) captured Israelite town of Nebo "before Chemosh"—that is, into the temple of the Moabite god. The victorious Philistines are said to have done the same with the captured Israelite ark (1 Sam. 5:2).

Many of the names in the seals and documents from eighth century Hazor and Samaria and seventh to sixth century Ophel (Jerusalem), Lachish, and Arad contain the element *yhw/yw*, like the biblical names of the period, and thus attest to belief in YHWH, God of Israel; his epithets *'ēl* and *meleḵ* also appear.[6] There is a noteworthy concentration of names containing the element *ba'al* in the Samaria ostraca (in a ratio of 2:3 to *yhw* names), from the reign of Jeroboam II or Menahem. No such names appear in material of Judahite provenience, hence the supposition that they reflect the imported Baal worship of the northern Omride kings. It is not clear, however, that *ba'al* in these names refers to the Phoenician deity, since the God of Israel probably also bore this title ("master"; cf. the names Meribaal, Eshbaal, Baal Perazim from the times of Saul and David), particularly at the time when ties with Phoenicia were strong.[7]

An oath by the life of YHWH and blessings in his name appear in the Lachish letters.[8] In the Arad ostraca a "house of YHWH" appears, and also the names Pashhur, Meremoth, Kerosi—names of priests, Levites, and Nethinim, according to the Bible.[9]

The testimony of the Elephantine documents deriving from a fifth century Jewish garrison on the southern border of Egypt is problematic. The faith of the soldiers in this remote outpost is glimpsed in the correspondence about their temple (which was destroyed by Egyptians), a temple of YHW (so spelled), where they offered grain, frankincense and whole offerings; in the mention of Passover and Sabbath; and in many *-yhw* names. The religion of these soldiers was probably similar to that of simple folk in the homeland (the erection of a temple outside of Jerusalem has caused astonishment among some scholars, hardly warranted in the light of the analogous second century B.C.E. Jewish temple at Leontopolis in the Delta). To be sure, no trace of sacred scriptures has been found among the Elephantine documents—perhaps because the last inhabitants of the place took them along when they left it. There are allusions to the association of other gods in the worship of the temple and in oaths, and to intermarriage with local non-Jews. But these are subject to various interpretations; moreover, the circumstances of this remote community, surrounded by gentiles, make their religious practice a dubious basis for inferring the state of religion in the kingdom of Judah over a century earlier. Based on the divine epithet *bethel*, found in some names, and the address to Sanballat, governor of Samaria, of the letters concerning the temple, some have thought that the garrison derived ultimately from the north. But *bethel* is an element of Phoenician and Aramaean names, and otherwise too this theory has little to commend it. In sum, no reliance is to be placed on the Elephantine documents as evidence of Israelite religion in biblical times.[10]

In the Arad excavations, a temple from the time of the monarchy, the first such to be laid bare at an ancient Israelite site, was found. The temple has a court, an altar of sacrifice, a holy place, and a raised holy of holies, on the steps of which stood two altars of incense. It thus offers some remarkable parallels to the plan of the Solomonic temple (1 Kings 6). In the holy of holies was a painted *massebah*, and two similar plastered stones. Stones of another altar of sacrifice, including its four "horns," were unearthed in Beersheba, reused in a building of the eighth century B.C.E. On one of the stones the figure of a twisted snake was engraved, recalling the sacred symbol mentioned in Numbers 21:8f., and 2 Kings 18:4. Indirect evidence of yet another Israelite sanctuary is an eighth-century seal belonging to "[ ]*kryw* priest of Dor." Neither the Arad nor the Dor sanctuary is alluded to in the Bible.[11]

Items apparently having to do with the worship from the beginning of the eighth century were found on the Ophel slope: "Two upright stones may have been *massebahs*. On the same site a cave was discovered containing a large hoard of pottery vessels dating from about 800 B.C.E. It may have been a depository for discarded offerings. A square structure, perhaps an altar, was also found there."[12] Diverse cult vessels—not all certainly identified—were found in various excavations, such as the incense altar of Megiddo, and incense ladles from Hazor.

Several types of figurines of naked females have been found in quantity in the land of Israel from the monarchic and other periods. Their relation to known goddesses is problematic, since they often lack specific character. It is commonly assumed that they served as fertility amulets, or as talismans to assure successful childbirth. Very likely they played a role in the popular religion of women (one thinks of the teraphim [housegods?] of Rachel and Michal), but due to the silence of the literary sources our knowledge here is virtually nil.[13]

The sum of testimony outside the Bible regarding Israelite religion during the monarchy does not amount to much. Rather than illuminating, these meager data need themselves to be illuminated. Some confirm the standard belief in YHWH; some indicate "heterodoxy" and perhaps even paganism. At the least, they give color to the biblical condemnations of Israel for deviating from authorized religious practices.

Characteristic of Israelite religion was its dynamic, self-critical component, owing to which it developed a store of ideas and institutions of ultimately universal value. This component flourished in the setting of a popular national religion, whose primary expressions and institutions took shape before the monarchy but like everything spiritual must have changed along with developments in the life of its bearers. Our material, however, does not allow us to follow the shades of change; what comes through is a religious background of considerable stability, which served as the substructure and starting point of ferment in the spiritual elite. From time to time this ferment invaded the substructure and finally worked deep changes in it. In the following sections, the stable and dynamic components of Israelite religion will be, somewhat artificially, distinguished and treated separately for the sake of clarity.

STABLE FACTORS: INSTITUTIONS, PRACTICES, AND BELIEFS

Public Religion

The public worship of God–that which was carried on in the name of the community–took place at public installations: at *bāmōt* and at sanctuaries. The *bāmāh*, usually on a height and apparently roofless (cf. "on every high hill, at the top of every mountain, under every green tree, and under every leafy terebinth" Ezekiel 6:13; cf. Hos. 4:13), stood in cities too (1 Kings 13:32; 2 Kings 23:8). The term *bēt bāmōt* is altogether obscure, and may well be no more than a pejorative turn of the phrase *bēt miqdāš* ("sanctuary house," Solomon's temple [2 Chron. 36:17]), used by the Deuteronomistic narrator to derogate Jeroboam's temples (1 Kings 13:32; 2 Kings 17:29, 32; 23:19). The essence of the *bāmāh* was an altar, alongside which stood a pillar (apparently the sign of God's presence, as appears from the *maṣṣēbōt* in the inner sanctum of the Arad sanctuary; so too outside of Israel),[14] and asherah—i.e., a tree (or wooden pole), whose meaning is obscure, but which served, it seems, as a sign of local sanctity (1 Kings 14:23; 2 Kings 18:4; according to Deut. 16:21, asherah is any tree alongside an altar).[15]

A description of popular (i.e., nonpriestly) sacrifice at a *bāmāh* outside the town of Ramah is given in 1 Samuel 9. Participants were summoned beforehand, doubtless to purify themselves for the occasion, according to 16:5. After the sacrifice they sat down to the sacred meal in an adjoining chamber. The local prophet uttered a blessing over the meat before they ate, then the meal was served by the cook. Since no priest appears at this *bāmāh*, it is doubtful that a regular, daily sacrificial service was performed there.

Kings erected sanctuaries in Jerusalem (David and Solomon), in Bethel and Dan (Jeroboam), and perhaps also in Samaria (the Omrides); cf. "the calf" and "the 'offense' of (*'šmt*) Samaria" (Hos. 8:5f.; Amos 8:14; unless Samaria stands for the northern kingdom and the Bethel calf is meant). In other towns, too (e.g., Hebron and Beersheba), sanctuaries stood.

The founding of temples was a privilege reserved for kings in the ancient east, and a sign of their piety.[15a] That is why David took such pains to found a sanctuary, and, when the project had to be put off, labored to collect the materials for it (the hyperbolic account of 1 Chronicles 22:14 is based on 2 Samuel 8:11). It would seem that sanctuaries were erected at places hallowed by tradition. Those at Hebron and Beersheba could point to legitimation in the time of the patriarchs (e.g., Gen. 13:18; 21:33; 26:23ff.; 46:1). The sanctuary at Arad was built on a site formerly occupied by a *bāmāh*. Several traditions attached themselves to the site of Jerusalem's sanctuary. The etiological note to the story of Isaac's near-sacrifice on Mount Moriah, calling the place "YHWH *yr'h*" (Gen. 22:14), evokes the first element (*yrw-*) of the name Jerusalem; 2 Chronicles 3:1 expressly identifies the Temple Mount with Mount Moriah. Another tradition identified it with the threshing floor of Arawna the Jebusite, at which an angel revealed himself to David in a plague, and where the plague was halted; by order of the prophet Gad, David then bought the site and erected an altar there to commemorate the deliverance (2 Sam. 24:21ff; 2 Chron. 3:1).[16]

The maintenance of the Jerusalem sanctuary fell to the Davidides; they supported it, repaired it, altered its appointments, and disposed of its treasures as they wished (1 Kings 14:26; 15:15, 18; 2 Kings 12; 16:10ff.; 21:4ff.; 22:3–9; 23:6–9). That northern kings did the same is implied by the designation of the Bethel sanctuary as "the king's temple" (Amos 7:13).

The fact of their being royal sanctuaries did not mean that the populace was excluded from them. On the contrary, crowds filled their courts in festive worship (cf. Amos 5:23, presumably of Bethel). The Jerusalem Temple was specifically designed to be a house of prayer for ordinary persons (1 Kings 8:38ff.), and many psalms testify to the people's attachment to it (e.g., 84; 96:8; 100; 116:18f.).

The Jerusalem Temple, like that of Arad, consisted of a court, a porch, the sanctuary proper, and an elevated inner sanctum (the inference of elevation, necessitated by the dimensions given in the text, is now confirmed at Arad). Laity were allowed into the courts, but only consecrated ministers could enter the sanctuary and the inner sanctum (cf. Neh. 6:11, 13). In the court stood a bronze Sea in which the priests washed (2 Chron. 4:6), and an altar for whole offerings, around which the festive throngs marched (Ps. 26:6), and before which the oath-ordeal was administered (1 Kings 8:31). The most sacred spot in the court was the space between the temple porch and the altar, where priests performed sacred offices in the sight of the crowds (Joel 2:17; cf. the blasphemy of Ezek. 8:16). In the porch stood two pillars (in the Jerusalem Temple they were named Jachin and Boaz); their use is unknown. The "Temple vessels" included a table for shewbread (set out weekly; the loaves were consigned to the priests; 1 Samuel 21:7; Leviticus 24:5ff.), lamps, an incense altar to perfume the interior, and basins for purification of the priests at their work. In the windowless inner sanctum ("YHWH has decided to dwell in deep darkness," 1 Kings 8:12) stood the most holy symbol of God's presence: in Jerusalem—the ark of the covenant, over which golden cherubs outspread their wings protectively—replicas of the celestial bearers of "Him who is enthroned upon cherubs" (cf. 2 Sam. 22:11; Ezek. 10:18f.). In accordance with its location under the cherubs (symbolizing the divine throne), the ark was called God's "footstool" (1 Chron. 28:2),[17] while in Jeremiah 3:16f. another epithet of the ark is alluded to, "YHWH's throne." In the inner sanctum of the Arad temple, pillars stood; according to Genesis 28:16ff.; 35:14f., the pillar served to mark God's presence at a site. In the royal sanctuaries of the Northern Kingdom, golden calves took the place of the golden cherubs as pedestals or bearers of God.[18] Hosea's rebuke "they kiss calves" (Hos. 13:2) has given rise to the conjecture that these calves were accessible to the public, perhaps standing in the inner courtyard, rather than the inner sanctum; if so, what stood in the inner sanctum of the northern temples is unknown.

The service at the sanctuary consisted of a priestly, sacrificial rite, conducted in the inner area, and a popular accompaniment of song, dance, procession, and sacred meals that went on outside, particularly at festivals. There was an order of daily service: in Jerusalem, "the morning whole offering and the evening oblation" (2 Kings 16:15) were brought in the name of the king and on behalf of the people too;

the regularity of these offerings made them indicators of the time of day (1 Kings 18:29: "till the time of the oblation"). These are apparently the same as the "regular offering" mentioned in the Torah, consisting of one lamb in the morning and one in the evening, with their flour and wine adjuncts (Num. 28:1ff.). A "regular lamp-lighting" illuminated the temple each night (Lev. 24:1ff.; cf. 1 Sam. 3:3); in Jerusalem there were ten lamps in the Temple (1 Kings 7:49). A "regular incense offering" was made morning and evening (Exod. 30:7f.; cf. the reference to this service in Deut. 33:10; 1 Sam. 2:28),[19] and sets of shewbread appeared weekly on the temple table, to be removed and replaced on the Sabbath by a new set (1 Sam. 21:7; Lev. 24:5ff.). The laity are never mentioned in connection with this regular service; presumably it was the exclusive charge of the priests.

Sacred seasons had two aspects: the sacrificial service and the popular festivity. On the three pilgrimage festivals all males were required to present themselves with gifts before "Lord YHWH" (Lev. 23:17; Exod. 34:23)—apparently, that is, at one of the larger temples (as distinct from a local *bāmāh*).[20] The Torah contains several lists of additional offerings meant for the festivals, of which some are individual obligations (so evidently the first sheaf of the reaping [Lev. 23:9] and the loaves made of the firstfruits of grain [ibid., v. 17]) and others, communal (so evidently the sacrificial animals that accompany the firstfruits [ibid., vv. 18f.] and the whole list of Numbers 28–29). The pilgrims brought with them animals for peace-offerings from which they partook in the sacred meal (cf. 1 Sam. 1:3f.). The large numbers of animals in temple cities on festivals was proverbial: "Like the sacred flocks, like the flocks of Jerusalem on its festivals" (Ezek. 36:38).

The festivals occurred during the two critical agricultural seasons: (1) early spring—the time of grain reaping, the seven weeks between the *maṣṣōt* festival (the start of the barley reaping) and the Feast of Weeks (the festival of reaping [Exod. 23:16], when the firstfruits of the wheat harvest were offered [34:22]; on the weeks, see Leviticus 23:15f.; Deuteronomy 16:9; Jeremiah 5:24: "who keeps for our benefit, the weeks appointed for reaping"); (2) autumn—the end of the threshing season and ingathering of fruit (Exod. 23:16, "when you gather in your produce from the fields"), or *sukkōt* "tabernacles" (Lev. 23:39; Deut. 16:13). Sacred seasons clustered around these pivots of the agricultural year: Just before the spring festival of *maṣṣōt*, the *pesaḥ* ("protection")[21] sacrifice fell; both retain something of the anxiety pertaining to the start of the reaping season, although they were transformed into commemorations of the Exodus.[22] Just before the harvest home festival, "at the outgoing" (or "turn") of the year (Exod. 23:16; 34:22), there occurred two holy days mentioned only in priestly writings. The new moon of the seventh month was "a day of trumpet blasts" (Num. 29:1) or a "commemoration with trumpet blasts" (Lev. 23:24); the tenth of the same month was "a day of atonement" (ibid., vv. 26ff.). "A commemoration with trumpet blasts" recalls on the one hand the blast of horns attending sacrifices "on your days of rejoicing, on your festival days and on your new moon days . . . that they may serve as reminders of you to God" (Num. 10:10). It may be inferred that on the first of the seventh month a supreme effort was made to be remembered for good by God. On the other hand, one recalls the shouts and trumpeting for God so often referred to in psalms describing his kingship (e.g., 47; 95; 98; 100), whence the surmise that this holy day was, like the later Jewish New Year, a celebration of God's kingship and of his deciding the destiny of his creatures.[23] The Day of Atonement, an annual purgation of the sanctuary from its defilement, and atonement for the sins of priests and people, also belongs to the destiny-decision at the turn of the year. The day is described (Lev. 16) as an exclusively priestly celebration, in which the people had no part other than fasting.[24] The seven-day festival of Tabernacles, starting in mid-month, and its contiguous "day of assembly," the joyous harvest-home celebration, culminate this "turn-of-the-year" season. Psalm 81 parallels the new moon day to the full moon day (mid-month) as days of festive horn-blowing, alluding perhaps to the autumn festival season, with its "day of trumpet blasts" on the new moon of the seventh month, and the Feast of Tabernacles at mid-month.[25]

New moon days and Sabbaths had additional offerings (Num. 8:9ff.). Apart from those of the Sabbath, these included whole and sin offerings to atone for the people. New moon and festival sacrifices were accompanied by trumpet blasts, so as "to be remembered by YHWH" (Num. 10:10). The festivals were therefore days of placating God and purgation from sin.

The solemn, and apparently silent, priestly rites were accompanied by joyous popular celebrations. The rejoicing began with the gathering of the pilgrim caravan. "I rejoiced when they said to me: Let us go to the house of YHWH" (Ps. 122:1). As it approached the city, flutes were played (Isa. 30:29). The night of the holy day was filled with song (ibid.), and on its morrow (the holy day itself), the festive throngs ascended to the temple "with shouting and songs of praise" (Ps. 42:5). "First the singers, then the players, amidst maidens drumming" (68:26). Some celebrants walked around the altar, as they told how God dealt wonderfully with them in public fulfillment of their vows of thanksgiving (26:6f.; cf.22:26; 35:18; 40:10). Amos describes the tumult of the singing and the music in the northern sanctuaries (5:23), as well as the merriment of the banqueters there (2:8). Hosea rebukes the license that sometimes accompanied these occasions (4:13f.)[26]

Solemn assemblies were held at the sanctuaries in bad times, such as drought or locust plague, as described in Joel 2:15f.:

> Blow the horn in Zion, declare a sacred fast day, proclaim a solemn assembly! Gather the people; order the congregation to sanctify itself. Collect elders; gather children and sucklings. Let the groom come out of his chamber and the bride from her tent. Between the porch and the altar let the priests, the ministers of YHWH, weep.... [27]

The temple had a special role in the administration of justice: When the plaintiff had no witnesses, he might impose an oath ordeal on the defendant. The ordeal was held at the altar, "before YHWH," and there was enough faith in its effectiveness to deter liars and bring justice to light (1 Kings 8:31f., by which Exodus 22:6ff. is clarified). A reflex of this role is the great vision of Isaiah 2:1ff., where, out of his Temple, God adjudicates among all the nations.

Although the Temple was called "the house of YHWH," the sacrifices "his bread" (Num. 28:2), and the altar his "table" (Ezek. 44:16; Mal. 1:7), it does not seem that the service was understood crassly as fulfilling divine need. David's eagerness to establish a proper and honorable abode for God, instead of the tent in which he dwelt, was answered by an oracle to the effect that God did not want it nor had it been his custom from the time of the Exodus to dwell otherwise (2 Sam. 7:1ff.). Nowhere is there so much as a hint that the Temple service served a need of God (even in the blunt quid pro quo of Malachi 3:10; the food demanded by God is for his temple servitors ["the whole tithe"], not for himself). The people did not give the Temple to God, but he gave it to them (Jer. 7:14). Prophet and audience agreed that "it was not about whole offerings and sacrifice that God commanded Israel when he redeemed them from Egypt" (Jer. 7:22), and that during the forty-year wandering there was no lavish sacrificial service (Amos 5:25). What then did the service mean to Israel?

Altar and sacrifice were the means provided by God to summon his presence to humankind and bring them his blessings (Exod. 20:24). The priestly conception makes the Temple a "dwelling place" (*miškān*), which God commanded "that I may dwell among the Israelites and be a God for them; and they shall know that I, YHWH, am their God, who brought them out of the land of Egypt in order to dwell among them" (Exod. 29:45f.). The visible sign of his indwelling was "the majesty of (*kᵉvōd*) YHWH," in appearance like fire enveloped in a cloud. It filled the desert tabernacle on the day it was set up (Exod. 40:35), its cloud appeared over the lid of the ark (Lev. 16:2), and later filled Solomon's Temple on its inauguration day (1 Kings 8:10f.). Dwelling in the sanctuary, God was able to meet there with

Moses and give him commands for Israel (Exod. 25:22; 29:42f.; Lev. 1:1; Num. 7:89). In this priestly conception, the function of the sanctuary as an oracle-site is dominant. The child Samuel heard God's word in the sanctuary (1 Sam. 3); at the great *bāmāh* in Gibeon, God appeared to Solomon at night in a dream (1 Kings 3:5); Isaiah's vision of the future Zion as the place out of which God's word would go forth to the world (Isa. 2:1–4) is based on the oracular function of the temple. Deuteronomy's analogue to "the indwelling majesty" is God's name: the single authorized sanctuary is the place where YHWH chooses to "set His name," or "cause it to dwell" (Deut. 12:5, 11). According to Solomon's inaugural prayer (a late Deuteronomistic composition) the name of YHWH is "called upon his house," in that he is its owner (cf. 1 Kings 8:43 with vv. 16, 29, etc.). Hence, "YHWH's eyes are ever open" toward that house, and he listens always to prayer offered in it (1 Kings 8:29f.). The sanctuary is a warranty for obtaining justice (through the oath ordeal); a place of public and private prayer (not only for Israelites but for strangers as well); it serves too as a conduit of prayer heavenward from outside the land of Israel. In contrast to the ancient conception of 1 Kings 8:13, where Solomon calls the temple "a princely house for you, a place for your dwelling forever," the prayer stresses that heaven is God's dwelling place, while the temple is only a means for providing for humans. There is no trace of the pagan notion that the temple is a house serving God's needs. More remarkable, this prayer does not even mention sacrifice.[28]

The popular appreciation of sacrifice is far from clear. Even if the sacrifice were not thought of as supplying a need of God—as, say, his food and drink—it was a means of showing him honor and placating him (Proverbs 3:9: "Honor YHWH out of your wealth, out of the best of all your produce"), analogous to gifts and tribute presented to a ruler (cf. the scornful rejection of blemished offerings in Malachi 1:8: "Present it to your governor!"). God's "savoring the pleasant odor" of the gift meant he felt goodwill toward the worshiper (Gen. 8:21; 1 Sam. 26:19). Incense was particularly effective in placating divine wrath and atoning for sin (Num. 17:11). That is why cessation of the sacrificial service might be brandished as a terrible threat—to the people, not to God (Hos. 9:4).[29]

This notion did allow the assessment of sacrifice as a benefit to God, as something done for him. The judgment of God described in Psalms 50:1–14 is directed against such an assessment. It seems to be an inner (priestly?) critique of a popular view from one who (unlike the prophets) does value the service as pleasing to God. God (says the critic) has no complaint against the people concerning their whole and peace offerings—indeed he does not need them. If he did eat and drink (absurd idea!) would he resort to humans, when all the world is at his disposal? Away with the misconception that something is done for God by sacrificing! There is, however, one kind of sacrifice that God does desire, the thanksgiving adjunct to payment of vows. That sacrifice, acknowledging God's favor and manifesting one's dependence upon him, has no trace of the perverse thought that by sacrifice one is benefiting God. "Call upon me in time of trouble; I will rescue you and you will honor me." To turn to God for help in time of trouble, and when help comes, to praise God by thanksgiving sacrifice in payment of vows—that is true honoring of God. Thanksgiving votive offerings are preferable to all other sacrifices, because with them alone there is no room for mistake as to who is doing for whom. It may be going too far to say that this implies a rejection of all other kinds of sacrifice; explicitly, what is rejected is only the mistaken conception that they do something for God.[30]

The royal sanctuaries were supervised by priests who were appointed by kings. David appointed Zadok—whose pedigree is not given in the oldest sources—as priest, along with Abiathar of ancient lineage (Zadok everywhere takes precedence: 2 Samuel 15:24, 29, 35; 19:12; 20:25).[31] Solomon expelled Abiathar, leaving Zadok and his family in sole possession of the Jerusalem office, apparently down to the Exile (cf. Ezekiel 44:15, and the genealogy of 1 Chronicles 5:34–41). In the northern kingdom, too, it was the king who appointed the priests of Bethel and Dan (1 Kings 12:31); Amaziah of Bethel staunchly supported his royal patron against Amos (Amos 7:10–13). It is likely that the country priests were also thought of as royal officers; at any rate, when Josiah saw fit, he abolished the *bāmōt* and their priestly offices at a stroke (2 Kings 23:8, 20).

Who were qualified to be priests? The sources disagree. On the one hand, David's sons are said to have been priests (2 Sam. 8:18), showing how far the king's right to appoint priests went; on the other, the Torah sources limit the priesthood to one tribe (the Levites in Deuteronomy) or one family (Aaron the Levite, in the priestly writings). Hints of the reality that underlay these divergent norms are few and obscure. Since the northern priests are expressly said not to have been Levites, it is to be inferred that their southern rivals were. The polemically inspired similarity between the golden calf stories of Aaron (Exod. 32) and Jeroboam (1 Kings 12) suggests that the northern priesthood had Aaronite origins; and since in the Exodus story the Levites are opposed to Aaron and the calf-worshipers, perhaps Aaron was once not considered a Levite. In early Second Temple times, at any rate, the Jerusalem priesthood did trace its ancestry to Aaron; "sons of Aaron" (not "sons of Zadok") meant legitimacy—in accord with the priestly norm in the Torah. No persuasive historical reconstruction has been offered to account for the conflicts among these fragmentary data. The latest biblical authors, using late priestly traditions, tidied things up through artificial genealogies, deriving all extant lines from Aaron the Levite.

What can be gathered from the evidence is that a definite family-caste crystallization developed. In early times, qualification for sacred office was vague; even laymen might be consecrated (1 Sam. 7:1, with which cf. Deut. 10:8a). But even then, Levites were preferred candidates for priesthood (Judg. 17:13). The ark sanctuary was in control of the Elides, a priestly line that traced its origin to Egypt (1 Sam. 2:27), probably Levite, if not Aaronite (note the Egyptian name Phinehas, common to Aaronites and Elides). The founding of royal temples led to the appointments of new priesthoods by the kings; it is reasonable to suppose that they too preferred pedigreed families—in the first instance Levites and Aaronites (this pleads against the theory that Zadok was a Jebusite). In the countryside, priestly families also took root in newly formed sanctuaries; they naturally tended to regard their privilege as hereditary. Eventually the priestly caste was crystallized as a monopoly of certain families that sought to exclude further accessions to their ranks. An echo of the struggle over qualification is the story of Korah's revolt, in which non-Aaronite Levites are vehemently excluded from priesthood.[32]

The tasks of the priests are listed in the passage on Levi in "Moses' Blessing" (Deut. 33:8–11),[33] and confirmed elsewhere. "They place incense in your nose and whole offerings on your altar" (v. 10) agrees with 1 Samuel 2:28, which states that the Elides were chosen "to ascend onto my altar and offer incense." The altar service was an exclusively priestly domain: it required holiness and ritual purity; service by an unauthorized person was a desecration that imperiled his life.[34] Levi's possession of Urim and Thummim in the Blessing of Moses (v. 8) agrees, again, with the election "to bear the ephod" mentioned in 1 Samuel 2 (cf. also Exod. 28:6–30); these were instruments of divination reserved for priestly use, to which leaders had recourse in early times for state decisions (e.g., concerning warfare, Num. 27:21; 1 Sam. 23:9; 30:7). After David's time, the priestly oracle seems to have been replaced by the prophet. "They teach your judgment (*mišpāṭekā*) to Jacob, and your instructions (*tōrāteka*) to Israel" (Deut. 33:10) refers to priestly instruction concerning what is forbidden and permitted, what is clean and unclean; or, as Leviticus 10:10f. puts it comprehensively, "to distinguish between the sacred and the profane, between the unclean and the clean, and to instruct the Israelites in all the laws which YHWH spoke to them through Moses." Basically, *tōrāh* is "instruction" or "direction" for a specific case; thus, for example, "the *tōrāh* of the leper" (Lev. 14:2) was the set of instructions the Israelites were commanded to observe in a case of "leprosy"—"as the

Levite-priests order you concerning it" (Deut. 24:8). The priest's role in judgment is set out in Deuteronomy 17:8–13 where priests are included in the tribunal of the central sanctuary-town. Ezekiel lays it down that priests "shall be in charge of judgment in litigations; they shall make rulings in accord with my laws" (44:24). Though the earlier sources are silent about the priestly role in justice, these two passages incline scholars to credit the datum of 2 Chronicles 19:8 that King Jehoshaphat of Judah stationed some of the Levites, the priests, and the family heads of Israel in Jerusalem to render God's judgment in litigations.[35] Bearing the main responsibility for maintaining the traditions of civil and ritual law during the monarchy, the priests were called "holders of the *tōrāh*" (Jer. 2:8).

The Jerusalem priests supervised the safety of the Temple: the chief priest (*kōhēn hārōš*; the second-in-rank was titled *kōhēn mišneh* [2 Kings 25:18]) was in charge of the guards at the gates and entrances to the Temple (2 Kings 11). The maintenance of the buildings was a priestly responsibility about which we hear only in connection with their failure to discharge it (2 Kings 12). Theirs was also to keep in check "every madman who played the prophet" on the sacred premises (Jer. 29:26)—a glimpse of the tension between established and enthusiastic religion.

The priests had servitors to assist them at sacrifice, called (in the Shiloh sanctuary) "the priest's boy" (1 Sam. 2:13, 15). The Book of Chronicles lists singers as a significant part of the Temple personnel, and credits David with having founded their guild (1 Chron. 25). There is no reference to Temple singers outside Chronicles, but Israel's worship can hardly have lacked the musical element known in the other oriental cultures (cf. Amos 5:23). Singers appear in the list of immigrants from Babylonia at the Restoration (Ezra 2:41, "Asaphite singers"), and since it is unlikely that such a guild sprang into being after the destruction of the Temple, their existence during the monarchy may safely be assumed. This same argument applies to the other classes of Temple personnel listed in Ezra 2: the gatekeepers (v. 42), the Nethinim, and the sons of Solomon's servants (43–58), some of whom bear foreign-sounding names (Kiros, Meunim, Barkos, Sisera). Indeed, Ezekiel rebukes the Judahites for having brought aliens into the Temple to help in the sacrificial service (Ezek. 44:7). These were presumably descended from captives who were assigned menial tasks in the Temple (cf. the Gibeonite hewers of wood and drawers of water [Josh. 9:27]).[36]

The status of Levites during the monarchy is not clear. From passages in Ezekiel (43:19; 44:15), Jeremiah (33:18–22), 1 Kings (13:31, "Jeroboam made priests . . . who were not Levites") and Deuteronomy (17:9; 18:1, 6ff.), it appears that all Levites were candidates for priesthood even if not all arrived. The lowly Levites of the laws of Deuteronomy, classed with the resident alien, the orphan, and the widow (14:29; 16:14), are probably the nonpriestly sort, who, lacking landholdings, were condemned to penury. If it is assumed that some of these came to serve in temples in inferior capacities, such as gatekeepers and singers, both the inferior status of the Levites in the priestly writings of the Torah and the "Levitization" of the originally non-Levite classes of gatekeepers and singers (cf. Ezra 2:41f. with 1 Chron. 23:5) can be accounted for.[37]

Portions of the people's sacrifices and dedications were assigned to the priests for their maintenance ("I gave to your father's house all the sacrifices of the Israelites" [1 Sam. 2:28]; cf. Num. 18:8–20; Deut. 18:1–5). The sons of Eli wickedly seized their portions indiscriminately and by force, and before the fat (God's portion) was burnt on the altar (1 Sam. 2:13–17). The variety of versions of the priests' lawful dues arises perhaps from differences in custom in various times and places, or from divergent sources. The priestly source has indeed a fuller list of perquisites than others: the skin of the whole offerings, the flesh of sin and guilt offerings (excepting its "token"), the breast and thigh of peace offerings, the firstfruits, devotions, and firstlings (Lev. 6–7, 27; Num. 18:8–20). In Leviticus 27:30ff. even the tithes of beasts and produce are claimed for the priests, though in Numbers 18:21–24 tithes are the Levites' due.[38]

In theory the priests and the Levites did not obtain any tribal possessions in the land; "YHWH is his [Levi's] possession, as he promised him" (Deut. 18:2, referring to Num. 18:20). Their dispersion throughout the country precluded their having a single continuous tribal allotment; but a priest might own fields (1 Kings 2:26; Jer. 32:6ff.), and a city of priests figures in the history (Nob, 1 Sam 22:19). Moreover, the priestly source provides the Levites with 48 cities and surrounding fields; in Joshua 21, these cities are listed. This list (not alluded to anywhere else) has features that make it seem utopian to some scholars, though the existence of priestly towns as such is not denied.[39]

Private Religion

Participation in public worship did not exhaust the religious life of individuals. They had many other opportunities to feel the divine presence, to address and be addressed by God: in birth and death, in eating, in sexual relations, and in their daily occupations.

Ordinary slaughter required an altar on which to dispose of the blood; otherwise, the flesh would be "eaten upon the blood," which was sinful, a "defection" from God (1 Sam. 14:33). According to Leviticus 17:3–7, all slaughter should bear the form of a peace offering; not only the blood but the fat too must be offered up on the altar, to keep the Israelite from sacrificing to the field-demons (the "satyrs").[40] Both sources agree that wholly profane slaughter did not exist. Centralization of worship eventually entailed the notion of profane slaughter, to allow those far from the single sanctuary to slaughter and eat meat (Deut. 12:15–27). In the laws, the ban on eating dead or torn animals applied to all Israel (Exod. 22:30; Deut. 14:21; cf. Lev. 17:15), though in origin it belongs to the priesthood only (Lev. 22:8; Ezek. 44:31). The extent of lay punctiliousness about the laws of uncleanness is unknown, though awareness of them is evident: Samson's mother was warned away from all unclean food during her pregnancy (Judg. 13:7, 14). The main care must have been to stay away from contact with the holy when in an unclean state (e.g., Lev. 12:4). Genital issues were defiling, thus, "sanctification" meant abstinence from sexual activity (Exod. 19:10, 15; 1 Sam. 20:26; 21:5f.). Priestly laws go into much detail on this matter (Lev. 15); evidence for their observance is Bathsheba's washing in order to "sanctify" (i.e., cleanse) herself from her monthly uncleanness (2 Sam. 11:4).

Life crises had their religious rites. A male child was circumcised on the eighth day after birth. The reason for circumcision is given in two versions: the main one connects it with God's covenant with Abraham, and calls circumcision "the sign of the covenant" to be kept by Abraham's descendants forever (Gen. 17). An obscure alternative etiology connects circumcision with Moses, and gives it a protective virtue against supernatural attacks (Exod. 4:24ff.). Though circumcision was practiced among some of Israel's neighbors, its Israelite form was sufficiently peculiar and widespread (especially as an infant rite) to make the epithet "uncircumcised" common to all the gentiles (Gen. 34:14; Exod. 12:48; Judg. 14:3; 1 Sam 14:6; Jer. 9:25).[41] The male firstborn child was considered God's property and had to be redeemed from a priest at the age of one month (Exod. 13:15; Num. 18:15f.).

Marriage and divorce seem not to have been connected with religious ritual. The earliest Jewish documents touching these (at Elephantine) have no religious reference; certain late passages are alleged to represent marriage as involving a covenant and an oath before God, but this is uncertain.[42] The etiological legend of Genesis 2:21ff. does not make God party to or ordainer of the union of Adam and Eve, but all happens naturally; God simply provides the man with a woman to end his loneliness. Their union is not blessed or divinely sanctified. To be sure, unchastity was regarded as an offense against God: Exile was the punishment for sexual immorality (Lev. 18:24–28); to remarry one's divorced wife after she had been married to another was to defile the land (Jer. 3:1; Deut. 24:1ff.).

The sundering of the realm of death from the divine realm in the

Bible is astonishing. In ancient Israel, as elsewhere, death must have been associated with mystery and dread-inspired practices and beliefs. The impurity caused by the dead was severe and highly contagious (Num. 19)—in all likelihood a reflection of fear of the corpse. Mourning customs included self-wounding, rending of clothes, and tearing out of hair (Jer. 16:6; 41:5), although these practices were banned in the laws (Deut. 14:1). They probably originated as protection against ghosts, to judge from extra-Israelite analogues. The obligation of burial lay upon the relatives of the dead—presumably because the ghost had no rest until the body was interred.[43] Gifts of food were made to the dead, apparently as an act of piety (Deut. 26:14). But the dead were cut off from God (Ps. 88:11; 115:17); the pre-exilic literature makes no reference either to reward and punishment in the afterlife, or to prayers on behalf of the dead, or to resurrection as being in store for them. If, nonetheless, the dead were called 'ĕlōhīm "divine beings" (1 Sam. 28:13; Isa. 8:19; and probably Deut. 21:23), one wonders whether the surviving literature has not in fact censored certain popular notions in which the dead played a part in the religious life of the living.[44]

A familial duty embodied in a divine ordinance was the levirate marriage, a means of perpetuating the name of the deceased upon his estate (Deut. 25:5ff.; Ruth 4:5). A certain reluctance is evidenced concerning the performance of levirate (Gen. 38; Ruth 4), doubtless because of the uncompensated expense it entailed: rearing the "son of the deceased" (really the issue of the levir) and managing his property until he was old enough to take over himself.[45]

Everyday piety expressed itself in invocations of God and in various benedictions, such as greeting: "Come in, you blessed of YHWH; why stand outside?" (Gen. 24:31); "YHWH be with you, brave man!" (Judg. 6:12); "YHWH be with you," and its response, "May YHWH bless you" (Ruth 2:4); "The blessing of YHWH be on you," and the response, "We bless you in the name of YHWH" (Ps. 129:8). Particularly common was the oath in God's name or by his "life" (1 Sam. 20:3; Amos 8:14); this was an expression of worship and devotion to him (Deut. 6:13; 10:20; Isa. 65:16; contrast Josh. 23:7). In time of trouble it was customary to take a vow, as did Absalom: "If YHWH will bring me back to Jerusalem, I will worship YHWH" (2 Sam. 15:8). Payment was made by the vower's publicly proclaiming the favor God had bestowed on him at a thanksgiving sacrifice and a sacred meal attended by friends (Ps. 22:26f.; 56:13; 66:13–20; Prov. 7:14). A more refined piety considered the verbal proclamation alone the best form of payment (Ps. 40:7–11; 69:31f.). An attractive conjecture has it that occasionally the thanksgiving was written and deposited as a memorial before God (if that is the meaning of "a written scroll" in Ps. 40:8; cf. Hezekiah's "letter" upon his arising from his sickbed; Isa. 38:9–20).[46]

Prayer also was a significant expression of popular faith. While public prayers usually were offered in a sanctuary ("before YHWH"), and by the clergy (Joel 2:17), an individual might pray anywhere and without mediation (Gen. 24:12; 32:10–13; Judg. 16:28; Jonah 2:2). Although individual prayers were tailored to the need of the moment, they exhibit fixed forms of supplication, thanksgiving, confession, and the like. Patterning is evident also in psalms of the individual— creations, it seems, of temple singers—through which the common man found a voice. An example of the use of ready-to-hand material is "Hannah's Psalm" (1 Sam. 2). Just because this thanksgiving is obviously not tailored to Hannah's case, its attribution to Hannah reflects and thus attests to the custom of utilizing ready-made material by individual worshipers.[47]

The meaning of "detainment before YHWH" (1 Sam. 21:8) and of "dwelling" or "sojourning in his Temple," mentioned in the Psalms (23:6; 27:4; 61:5), is obscure. It may refer to retirement to the Temple precinct as a religious exercise or perhaps to dedication to sacred service.

The Religious Aspect of Warfare

Between the premonarchic and the monarchic period a change came over the religious aspect of warfare. The popular, voluntary character of the armed force disappeared from the time of Saul and David onward with the establishment of a standing army and the employment of mercenaries. Policy was determined by considerations of state that had little to do with religion. The simple "war of YHWH" (last heard of in Saul's time; 1 Sam. 18:17), was replaced by war "on behalf of our people and the cities of our God" (in David's time, 2 Sam. 10:12)—a complex of people, national God, and territory consecrated to him.

Evidently, then, warfare was not altogether separate from religion. God's assurances before and his presence in the camp during the campaign were concerns of the army and its leaders (1 Kings 8:44). Saul placated God with sacrifice before going to war (1 Sam. 13:9–12), consulted the oracle in its course (14:36f.), and kept the ark in the camp to guarantee YHWH's presence there (ibid., 14:18). David made no move without first consulting the oracle; e.g., his ascent to Hebron (2 Sam. 2:1), or his Philistine wars (5:19, 23). From David's time on, prophetic oracles were regularly requested before and sometimes during military campaigns (1 Kings 22; 2 Kings 3:11f.; 19), since a campaign launched with divine backing was regarded as a mission of God (1 Kings 8:44).[48]

Camp life was marked by religious features. As though consecrated, the soldiers kept away from women (1 Sam. 21:6; 2 Sam. 11:11; cf. Deut. 23:10f.), which may provide the background for the biblical idiom "to sanctify [i.e., declare] war" (Mic. 3:5; Jer. 6:4). The army marched out with sacred vessels (the ark, 2 Sam. 11:11), a parallel to the gentile custom of bringing idols into the camp (ibid., 5:21). From Solomon's reign on, the ark indeed appears never to have left the inner sanctum of the temple; but the picture in Numbers 31:6 of the young priest bearing the sacred vessels to the war with Midian— without the ark—may reflect the custom of monarchic times (cf. the military use of trumpets in the regulation of Numbers 10:9; note its setting ["in your land"]). A late source (2 Chron. 13:12, 14; 20:21, 28) describes a battle array including trumpeters and singers.[49] The army was encouraged to believe that YHWH was in the camp, and that he went forth with them into battle (Deut. 20:1–4; 23:10–15; 2 Sam. 5:24; Ps. 44:10). Since victory was of YHWH (1 Sam. 17:47; Ps. 3:9), part of the booty was dedicated to him—i.e., to the temple treasury (2 Sam. 8:11). According to Numbers 31:25–47, set proportions of booty were reserved for the various clergy; there is no corroboration of this custom from the time of the kingdom, though deposit of choice items of the booty in the temple is mentioned (1 Sam. 21:10; cf. the analogous gentile practice, ibid, 5:3; 31:10).

During the monarchy, the ancient practice of proscribing the enemy (*ḥerem*) fell into disuse. The last case recorded is from the time of Saul, who was ordered by Samuel to proscribe the Amalekites; it is significant that Saul's army refused to carry out this stern order, apparently out of self-interest (1 Sam. 15). Later, when the policy of imperial conquest was inaugurated, proscription would only have been self-defeating; instead, the policy of corvée was instituted (1 Kings 9:20f.). Only the prophets clung to the notion of *ḥerem* as an expression of zeal for YHWH, even later ones mentioning it as if it were an extant practice (1 Kings 20:42; Mic. 4:13), when in fact it had long since ceased.[50]

Prophecy
The prophets stood beside the priests as mediators between the people and God; they served both as consultants and as divine messengers. Some of the prophets were men of broad vision, who gave a forward impulse to Israelite religion; these will be described later. Here the role of prophecy as one of the regular means of contact between people and God will be treated (cf. 1 Samuel 28:6: "[God] did not answer [Saul] either by dreams or by Urim or by prophets").

In Saul's time, there were "bands" (*ḥevel, laḥᵃqāh*) of "prophets" whose role and relation to individual prophetic figures (such as Samuel; cf. 1 Sam. 19:20) is unclear. They "prophesied" in a group to the sound of music (1 Sam. 10:5), an apparent reference to ecstatic raving; susceptible persons might be infected with their enthusiasm and behave like them, "madly" (ibid., v. 10; 19:20; 23). Their role is not described; no sermons are ascribed to them.[51] The story of the "prophesying" of the seventy elders of Israel under the impulse of Moses' spirit" (Num. 11:24ff.) shows that the phenomenon was considered worthy; this is also implied by Saul's being counted "among the prophets" after his coming under their spell upon being anointed (1 Sam. 10:12). At the same time, the antics of the "man-of-spirit" were derided; apparently, then, the attitude toward such ecstatics was ambiguous (cf. Hos. 9:7, "The prophet is a fool; the man-of-spirit, mad"). This group phenomenon persisted throughout the monarchy, though its name changed and signs of ecstasy vanished later. From the time of the Omrides, the "sons of the prophets" appear in the north— groups living together under the aegis of a "master," an individual prophetic figure (2 Kings 6:1ff.). The "master" took care of them (ibid., 5:22; 4:38ff.), and they ran errands for him (ibid., 9:1). Such groups appear at times without a master (2 Kings 2, in Bethel and Jericho); on occasion, one of their members might be singled out by "a word of YHWH" for a prophetic mission (1 Kings 20:35ff.). The "sons of prophets" were also the objects of derision, presumably on account of their odd behavior (cf. 2 Kings 9:11). Elisha is the only one of the major figures who resorts to music to induce the prophetic "spirit," thus recalling the practice of "prophetic bands" of earlier times (2 Kings 3:15); unlike those, however, Elisha is inspired by the spirit to give an oracle, not to inarticulate transports.

Alongside this "inspired" figure was the prophet-seer proper, also called "man of God" (sometimes, as in the case of Elisha, the two coincided). The variety of epithets indicates that what were originally separate roles may have merged in the figure of the prophet.

The basic sense of the term *nāvī'*, "prophet" is "mouth of God" (cf. Exod. 4:16 with 7:1; Jer. 15:19), a divinely designated spokesman (Deut. 18:18). According to 1 Samuel 9:9, the prophet was formerly (i.e., in Samuel's time) called "seer," apparently meaning clairvoyant (or perhaps visionary; cf. Balaam, "who saw visions of Shadday, fallen but open eyed" [Num. 24:4, 16], or the non-Mosaic prophet of Numbers 12:6, to whom God reveals himself in visions or speaks in dreams). The prophets were commonly believed to know hidden things, even when not explicitly told by God (see 2 Kings 5:26; 6:9, 12, 17 on Elisha's powers), though "standard" biblical doctrine ascribed such knowledge to a divine revelation (cf. especially 2 Kings 4:27; similarly 1 Sam. 16:7; and 1 Kings 14:5). Such divergence probably reflects different religious levels, the vulgar inclining to a magical conception (the man of God as possessor of a "gift"); the authors of the Bible, to a more "religious" one (the prophet as dependent on the word of God). There is also a middle path—as when the man of God is believed able to issue a decree on his own, with God executing it (Elijah; 1 Kings 17:1).[52]

Both king and commoner resorted to the prophet. He was appealed to as a healer of man and nature (2 Kings 4:22ff.; 2:19ff.; 4:38ff.); he revealed secrets of the present and the future (e.g., the location of lost asses, 1 Samuel 9:6; the fate of a sick person, 1 Kings 14:3; 2 Kings 8:9). A prophet's reputation depended on his reliability: Samuel was famous from Dan to Beersheba as a prophet of YHWH, because "he did not fail to verify all that he said" (i.e., all his responses to inquiries proved true—1 Sam. 3:19; cf.9:6). The success of every important public act was determined in advance by a prophetic oracle: a war campaign (see above); policy under siege (Jer. 37:17); building a temple (2 Sam. 7:2).

As the intimate and confidant of God (cf. Amos 3:7; Jer. 23:18), the prophet was expected to plead the people's cause before him— whether on behalf of an individual or the community (cf. Gen. 20:7; 1 Kings 13:6). Interceding for the public good was so essential a part of the prophet's task that to refuse to do it was deemed a sin (1 Sam. 12:23). Moses and Samuel served as archetypical prophetic intercessors (Jer. 15:1; cf. Ps. 99:6f.; 106:23 with Ezek. 13:5). Many occasions of prophetic prayer on behalf of the people are noted (e.g., 2 Kings 19:4; Jer. 37:3; 42:2).[53]

In addition to their role as respondents and intercessors, prophets served also as messengers of God, coming unasked with a divine message. The messenger-prophet, an early attested but minor figure among the western Semites,[54] became the chief bearer of the idea of God's rule in Israel and the supervisor of God's covenant with Israel. God's rule was embodied in an unbroken line of prophets, acting and speaking in God's service on royal and national issues. It was the prophets who declared the wars of Israel the means of divine self-revelation (1 Kings 20:13f., 28, 35 ff.; 2 Kings 3:18; 14:25). The misdeeds of kings were exposed and condemned by intrepid messengers of God (Nathan, 2 Sam. 12; Elisha, 1 Kings 21). In the northern kingdom, where the original principle of the conditional election of kings was maintained, prophets condemned whole dynasties to perdition; they also took part in, and even initiated conspiracies to depose kings (1 Kings 11:29ff.; 14:5ff.; 16:2ff.; 21:21ff.; 2 Kings 8:12ff.; 9). Theirs was a perilous opposition; the first martyrs for God were prophets of Israel who pursued their anti-monarchic mission to the death (1 Kings 18:4, 13; 19:10; 2 Kings 9:7; Jer. 26). The prophet as messenger and the prophet as respondent are not separate figures; the man who mediated an answer to one who "inquired of YHWH," who did wonders, healed, and told the future, could on occasion be the messenger of God to foretell, warn, or reprove on his behalf. Elijah, eminently God's reproving messenger, champions prophecy's exclusive right to be consulted about the future, condemning Ahaziah's recourse to Baalzebub to learn whether he would recover from his sickness (2 Kings 1). Both roles merge in Elisha's meeting with Hazael (2 Kings 8:7ff.). As respondent, the prophet attested to God's power and control of events. The apogee of this testimony is in the story of Naaman's healing: Though at first the kings of both Aram and Israel ignore Elisha, in the end he makes it manifest "that there is a prophet [i.e., a spokesman of YHWH] in Israel"; and that "there is no God on earth except in Israel" (2 Kings 5). Thus did prophetic interventions express the presence and government of God.

The prophets of the monarchic age mentioned in the Bible were not connected with any institution (Samuel's tie to the Shiloh sanctuary arose from his mother's vow and terminated with the sanctuary's destruction; the priesthood of Jeremiah and Ezekiel was not a factor in their call). How they earned their livelihood is unclear. In exchange for service they received gifts (1 Sam. 9:7; 1 Kings 14:3); mention is once made of firstfruit loaves brought to Elisha (2 Kings 4:42). On new moon and Sabbath, visits were paid to the prophet (2 Kings 4:23) for reasons unknown; perhaps then too gifts were presented. This practice opened the way to corruption; Micah reproaches "the prophets who mislead my people, who predict prosperity when their mouth is filled; but if one does not put something into their mouths, they declare war against him" (3:5). The later literary prophets are not described as rewarded for service.

There are some indications of temple and court prophets. While still a fugitive from Saul, David had Gad as his prophet; when he became king, Gad was "the king's seer" (2 Sam. 24:11). The prophet Nathan, too, appears as a royal adviser. Hundreds of prophets were in the service of the northern kings (1 Kings 22:6; 2 Kings 3:13), and royal officials did not hesitate to instruct them how to prophesy so as to please the king (1 Kings 22:13). Like the Baal prophets (1 Kings 18:19), these must have "eaten at the king's table," that is, served as royal pensioners.[54a]

A connection of prophets with the temple is suggested by the fixed word pair "priest-prophet" (e.g., Isa. 28:7; Jer. 4:9; 14:18), and by passages placing both in the temple (Jer. 23:11; 26:7; Lam. 2:20). In Jeremiah's time, a temple chamber belonged to "the sons of the man of God" (35:4). The use of the verb "prophesy" for the singing of the temple singers in the Book of 1 Chronicles (25:1–5), suggests an institution of prophet-musicians that can only have arisen during the monarchy. A lively picture of the work of such a functionary is given in

2 Chronicles 20:14. After King Jehoshaphat's public prayer in the temple court, a Levite singer was inspired on the spot to deliver a prophecy of victory. The sudden shift from anxious plea to expressions of confidence in several psalms (e.g., 20:7) has been explained by the intervention of a temple prophet with an oracle of deliverance in the course of the prayer.[55]

In Jeremiah's time, prophets were counted among the leading classes, after "kings, officers, priests," and before "the people of the land" (Jer. 8:1; 13:13; 32:32). The "instruction" of priest, the "counsel" of sages, and the "word of YHWH" from the prophet were all state assets (Jer. 18:18; Ezek. 7:26). Prophets participated in shaping policy and advocating it among the people. That is why they were excoriated by the classical prophets in whose writings every "prophet" is of this institutionalized sort.

Popular Belief

Allusions in prophetic literature indicate that the public was generally familiar with tales of God's dealings with the patriarchs, the Egyptian bondage and the Exodus, the wanderings, the expulsion of the Amorites and the settlement of Canaan. God had singled Israel out of the nations and on the basis of his deliverances, had made a covenant with them, obligating them to serve him alone, and to obey his commandments. His blessing would be with those who obeyed him, his curse on those who defied him (Amos 2:4, 10f.; Hosea 8:1, 12; 12:4f., 14; Micah 6:4f.; Jer. 2; Ezek. 33:24).

The idea of the law collections (in the Torah) is that the obligation to keep the terms of the covenant lay on every single Israelite. A ripe formulation of that idea is Exodus 19:6: "You shall be to me a kingdom of priests and a holy nation"; that is, the entire citizenry must observe a level of holiness and nearness to God that is proper to priests.[56] Note, for example, the formulation in Exodus of the ban on eating torn flesh: "You shall be to me holy men; torn flesh in the field you shall not eat" (Exod. 22:30). In origin, this ban applied to priests only, and was designed to keep them in a constant state of purity—i.e., cultic readiness (Lev. 22:8; Ezek. 44:31). In its Exodus form it applies to all Israelites and thus makes the narrow formulation (in Leviticus and Ezekiel) puzzling to exegetes.[57] The bans on cutting the hair at the corners of the head and gashing oneself for the dead apply to all Israel (Lev. 19:27f.), though these too properly belonged only to priests (Lev. 21:4f.). Note the grounding of the law in the holiness and sacred service of priests. The language of the ban in Deuteronomy 14:1–2 likewise applies to the whole nation epithets of holiness proper to priests (Lev. 21:6).

If every Israelite had to fulfill the terms of the covenant, the terms had to be published. Accordingly, tradition had it that the Decalogue was proclaimed in the hearing of all Israel (Exod. 20:18–22; Deut. 5). The rest of the covenantal law collections are set in a narrative framework with Moses proclaiming them to all Israel. The covenant rite described in Exodus 24 includes the public recitation of the terms (the laws) in the hearing of all the people. Deuteronomy provides for the proclamation of the Torah to the assembled people, "men, women, children, and the strangers in your gates," once every seven years, in a reenactment of the great "day of assembly" at the Sinai lawgiving (Deut. 31:10ff.; cf. 4:10).

How far this ideal was realized is unknown. The tradition of the Mosaic covenant-making, with the stipulations proclaimed in the hearing of all, evidently served as a model for the covenant rite in the time of Josiah (2 Kings 23:2), since it is unlikely (and unreported) that the rite was invented by the king. It must therefore be assumed that the tradition of the covenant in Moses' time was transmitted through the centuries in some established, institutionalized form. The enshrining of traditions of the Exodus in cultic forms—such as the paschal sacrifice (Exod. 12:25f.)—suggests the possibility of other regular cultic commemorations of divine interventions in history. Modern scholars have attempted to reconstruct a festival of covenant celebration (or renewal), with the story of the Sinai lawgiving (Exod. 19–24) as its dramatic "script" or ("liturgy"). Verses in Psalm 81, combining trumpet blasts on new moon and at mid-month with verbal reminiscences of the Exodus and lawgiving, are taken as evidence for the connection of the period of the autumn festivals (from the new moon of Tishri to the *Sukkōt* festival starting at mid-month) with commemoration of the covenant. Further support is found in the fact that Deuteronomy's septennial assembly for proclamation of the Torah coincides with the *Sukkōt* festival (Deut. 31:10ff.).[58]

How far did the people as a whole observe the laws of holiness and religion? The biblical histories offer only a few bits of testimony. Saul rigorously enforces among his soldiers the ban of "eating on the blood" (1 Sam. 14:32ff.); this ban is therefore ancient, despite the fact that otherwise it appears only in Leviticus and Ezekiel. Cleansing from menstrual impurity, ordained in Leviticus 15, is practiced by Bathsheba and is the occasion of David's great sin (2 Sam. 11:4). The requirement of purity for a family sacrifice is alluded to in 1 Samuel 20:26; cf. Leviticus 7:20. That Sabbath and new moon were rest-days in the northern kingdom is proven by Amos' rebuke of merchants impatient for them to be over (Amos 8:5), and by the Shunamite husband's amazement at his wife's visit to the prophet "not on Sabbath or new moon" (2 Kings 4:23).

The God of Israel was "the king, YHWH of hosts" (Isa. 6:5); he was hymned as "the king of glory" (Ps. 24:7ff.), "the great king over all the earth (Ps. 47:3, 8), "the great king" (Ps. 48:3). His throne and seat were in heaven (1 Kings 22:19; Isa. 6:1; Ps. 2:4), and he was called "He who sits (is enthroned) upon the cherubs," after his cherubic bearers, who apparently were imagined as forming his throne (2 Sam. 6:2; Ps. 80:2; 99:1; cf. the lions of Solomon's throne, 1 Kings 10:19).[59] He had the suite of a great divine king—seraphim, "the host of heaven" (1 Kings 22:19; Isa. 6:2), "divine beings" (Ps. 29:1), and officers (e.g., "the chief of the army of YHWH" [Josh. 5:14]). The biblical authors distinguished sharply between God and his suite: he alone could be worshiped. The common practice, however, was less discriminating. Psalm 16:3f. indicates that "holy ones" and "mighty ones" were worshiped "in the land." In the seventh century several references are made to the worship of the host of heaven (Zeph. 1:5; Jer. 8:2). That the people should have revered them is no wonder, since even the biblical authors ascribed "dominion" to the sun and the moon (Gen. 1:15). Psalm 82 reflects a protest against the entrenched idea that government of the world was parceled out among the divine beings. Deuteronomy 32:8f. describes this parceling: "He [i.e., the Most High] fixed the bounds of the peoples/According to the number of divine beings" (reading *bny 'l[m?]* with a Qumran fragment and the Septuagint). Divine government thus had two levels: a higher, that of the "God of gods" (Deut. 10:17), who at the beginning reserved Israel for himself (32:9), and a lower, that of his suite, to whom the rest of the peoples were allocated. Now, if the biblical authors themselves assigned dominions to members of the divine suite, simple folk could hardly be blamed for rendering them homage. The point seems long to have been an issue; note the insistence of Deuteronomy 4:19 that sun, moon, and stars have been allotted to the gentiles and must therefore not be worshiped by Israel.

The named gods of the nations (e.g., Ashtoret, Baal) were regarded equivocally. On the one hand, biblical authors dismiss them as "the empty things of the nations" (Jer. 14:22; cf. Deut. 32:21), as manmade idols, as wood and stone (Isa. 37:19). On the other hand, some acknowledgment of their substantiality existed; when, under Israelite-Edomite siege, Mesha, king of Moab, publicly sacrificed his child, there was "great wrath upon Israel" (2 Kings 3:27)—the reference is most naturally to a baleful emanation of the pagan god's power.[60] To call the heathen gods "demons" (Deut. 32:17, and in the late Ps. 106:37) was also to attribute reality to them.

To what extent did alien customs and beliefs affect Israelite religion? When Israelite kings married foreign women, the wives brought their native cults and planted them on Israel's soil. What the covenant laws warned against in this respect (Exod. 34:15; Deut. 7:3f.) was realized in the case of kings Solomon (1 Kings 11:1–6) and Ahab (ibid. 16:31ff.); they were "diverted" from Israel's God by their wives. The intermarriage of commoners must have had similar results, though no direct testimony to this is given. But the exact sense of this "diverting" is unclear: Ahab's sons have names with the theophoric element *ya(hu)*—Ahaziah, Jehoram—and in all the narratives he himself is depicted as a worshiper of Israel's God. The indictment seems therefore a reflection on his building a temple and an altar to Baal in Samaria (or in a particular "town" [quarter?] nearby the king's seat [cf. 2 Kings 10:25]); more precisely, on his allowing and maintaining the Baal worship of his Sidonian wife. In all likelihood this was Solomon's case too: The biblical author, who recognized no shades in idolatry, did not discriminate between Solomon's permitting pagan cults on Israelite soil and maintaining them out of the public treasury, and his outright worship of pagan gods.[61] However that may be, the court was for generations a nest of pagan cults imported with foreign wives (cf. also 1 Kings 15:13).

A Canaanite population, concentrated in the valley of Jezreel and along the coast, was absorbed into the kingdom of Israel when it expanded during the reign of David and Solomon (1 Kings 9:20f.).[62] The assimilation of this alien mass probably affected the character of the popular religion; perhaps this is reflected in the figurines common to early Israelite and Canaanite levels in city-mounds in the land. In Judah, the *qādēš* appeared (1 Kings 14:24; 22:47)—perhaps a male functionary of the fertility cult, alien to biblical religion but known from the customs of western Semites; zealous Judean kings more than once purged the *qādēš* (1 Kings 15:12; 22:47; 2 Kings 23:7). The practice of burning children for the gods is explicitly ascribed to the Canaanites (Deut. 12:31) and the Sepharvites who were settled in the north after the exile of the northern kingdom (2 Kings 17:31). In Jeremiah 7:31; 19:5; 32:35, the Judahites are censured for burning their sons and daughters on *bāmōt* in the valley of Hinnom. According to the latter two passages, this was the worship of Baal or Molech; yet the insistence of the prophet that YHWH "never commanded, or spoke, or imagined it" points to the God of Israel as the object of worship. The Tophet in the valley of Hinnom, where one "passed his son and daughter through the fire to Molech" was among the idolatrous appurtenances that Josiah polluted (2 Kings 23:10). This practice, an imitation of the "abominations of the nations that YHWH drove out before the Israelites," is ascribed to Ahaz (2 Kings 16:3). The passages about Molech in the Torah (Lev. 18:21; 20:2ff.) may be interpreted as meaning dedication to idolatrous service; ancient opinion favored this over the notion of actually burning babies (cf. the summary given in Naḥmanides' commentary to Leviticus 18:21), and latterly some support from Assyrian usage has been adduced for this interpretation. But even if with respect to Molech there is room for doubt, the expression "to burn in fire" is unambiguous evidence of child sacrifice in Judah under foreign influence.[63]

Magical beliefs common to all mankind were current in Israel. This occult realm of knowledge and power was sought directly, without divine mediation. Necromancy, sorcery, and divination were practiced (1 Sam. 28; Isa. 8:19; 2 Kings 21:6; Ezek. 13:17ff.), despite the prohibition in the Torah (e.g. Exod. 22:17; Deut. 18:9ff.); pious kings enforced the ban zealously (1 Sam. 28:3; 2 Kings 23:24), but the practices survived (cf. 1 Sam. 28:7; Isa. 8:19ff.). Ezekiel denounces sorceresses who "for bits of bread and handfuls of barley" condemn to death and decree life (Ezek. 13:17ff.). Few details are recorded, but such "abominations" are counted among the reasons for Israel's fall (2 Kings 17:17; 21:6). The biblical authors, like the common folk, believed in the reality of magic, but precisely for that reason they regarded it as an encroachment on God's prerogatives. The Israelite must be "wholehearted" with God; he must submit himself wholly to him and eschew recourse to magic and all other sources of power and knowledge. God gave Israel prophets, and whatever magicians did for their clients the prophets in Israel could do for those who sought YHWH through him (Deut. 18:14ff.).

DYNAMIC ELEMENTS IN THE RELIGION OF THE MONARCHY: PROPHECY AND REFORM MOVEMENTS

Prophecy and the Monarchy

The critical and innovative element in Israelite religion was prophecy. The religion originated with a man of God: Moses, a messenger of God, who brought tidings of redemption, made the people enter into a covenant with God and fashioned the basic forms of worship. The prophet Samuel established the monarchy, and from then on tension existed between God's word and the command of the king. The monarchy became the focus of prophetic activity because the king was conceived of as the representative of the people before God (largely owing to his responsibility for maintaining the public worship); hence the king was the object of constant prophetic observation and censure.

David was served by two court prophets: "the prophet Gad, the king's seer" (2 Sam. 24:11; cf. 2 Chron. 29:25), and Nathan, who appears as both counselor and censor (2 Sam. 7:1ff.; 12:1–15). Through Nathan the idea of a chosen eternal dynasty arose. God's promise to David—"Your house and your kingship will stand fast forever before me [reading *lᵉfānay*]; your throne will last forever" (7:16)—changed the conditional conception of royal election that originated with Samuel. This was a conscious, deliberate change: "I will not break my faith with him [the Davidide], as I broke it with Saul" (v. 15). This promise came to be called a "covenant," and titles "son" or "firstborn" of God that applied to Israel as God's covenant-partner (Exod. 4:22; Deut. 14:1; 32:6, 19f.; Isa. 1:2) were attached to the Davidic king (Ps. 2:7; 89:27f.). The Davidic dynasty was conceived as the means by which God would fulfill his covenant promises to Israel. Beside Nathan's dynastic oracle, prophecies supported the founding of the Jerusalem Temple. Tradition identified the Temple site with the threshing floor of Arawna the Jebusite (2 Chron. 3:1), where the prophet Gad had directed David to build an altar to commemorate the end of a plague (2 Sam. 24:18, 25). An oracle on the election of Jerusalem as God's seat is found in Psalm 132:13; it accords with the divine promise to David that his son would build a house for God's name (2 Sam. 7:13).[64]

While in the kingdom of Judah the election of the Davidic dynasty was conceived of as permanent, northern prophecy clung to the original conception of Samuel: kingship was conditioned upon obedience to the word of God; disobedience doomed the king and his dynasty. The prime adherent of Samuel's idea, so different from Nathan's oracle to David, was Ahijah the Shilonite, who provoked Jeroboam son of Nebat to rebel against Solomon because of his worship of foreign gods (1 Kings 11:29–40). Ahijah himself later announced to Jeroboam that his house would also be cut off for his sins (14:7–15). To the end, northern prophecy maintained the notion of conditional royal election. In their passionate defense of the God of Israel, northern prophets foretold the end of dynasties and incited rebellion (2 Kings 9:1–10). By so doing they contributed materially to the instability of the northern kingdom, which, in this respect, differed remarkably from the stable Judahite monarchy of Davidides.[65]

According to the Book of Kings, tension between prophet and king almost always arose because of an offense against God's covenant with Israel. There seems to have been a fundamental difference between the rulers and the prophets, though nothing suggests that the rulers intended to do away with the special relation of Israel to its national God. The policy of international cooperation and alliance often involved intermarriage with foreign princesses, who as a matter of course imported their familiar cults, which the Israelite kings were bound to respect and maintain. Solomon showed scruple in erecting the shrines of his wives' gods outside Jerusalem, the city of God, "on the mountain that was opposite Jerusalem, to the south of Mount *Mašḥīt*" (= the southern extension of the Mount of Olives; 1 Kings 11:7; 2 Kings 23:13). Yet the very patronage of these installations by an Israelite king, and the dedication of parcels of the land of Israel and funds out of the public treasury to foreign gods, enraged such zealots as Ahijah. King Asa's mother made "a 'horror' for Asherah" which, with other pagan appurtenances, was purged by Asa and his son Jehoshaphat (1 Kings 15:12f.; 22:47). Prophets are not mentioned in connection with these purges; to judge from the uprising against Athaliah (2 Kings 11), in Judah it was the priesthood that "kept the charge of YHWH," the role played in the northern kingdom by prophets.

The Omrides, who stabilized the northern kingdom, formed ties with neighboring states after the pattern set by David and Solomon. Ahab's marriage to Jezebel, the Sidonian princess, brought the Phoenician Baal into Samaria. A Baal temple was built in Samaria (1 Kings 16:32), and hundreds of "prophets" of Baal and Asherah were pensioners of the queen (18:19). The vehement, protracted opposition of bands of northern prophets, among whom the figures of Elijah and Elisha stand out, indicates that they regarded this cult as dangerous to the faith of the masses (cf. 1 Kings 19:14, 18).

That the foreign cults in Judah never provoked such violence suggest that the danger to the national religion was greater in the north than in the south. Two reasons for this can be conjectured: the proximity of the north to such major centers of alien culture as Aram and Phoenicia with whom close trade and war relations were maintained; and the considerable Canaanite element in the population, particularly of the valleys and coast, only recently annexed to the Israelite kingdom, and as yet hardly assimilated. Queen Jezebel's zealous practice of her Canaanite-Phoenician cult, with the publicity and prominence it must have enjoyed in Samaria, not only checked the process of assimilation by officially endorsing an alien worship, but may well have attracted Israelites. Courtiers and royal merchants who had constant and close relations with the Phoenicians would have favored blurring cultural-religious boundaries, and adopting "the international style," then current, of syncretizing gods and cults.[66] We need not take literally the reproach that only "seven thousand" remained "whose knees had not bent to Baal and whose mouth had not kissed him" (1 Kings 19:18), but its background was probably a considerable spread of Baal worship, especially among the aristocracy.

Since zealotry and persecution are uncharacteristic of paganism, Jezebel's war against the prophets of Israel was probably in reaction to an attack they initiated against her alien cult. If YHWH's altar on Carmel was demolished (1 Kings 18:30), a Baal installation was in all likelihood demolished first. The zealotry of the prophets can be estimated from the way they incited and carried out purges when they were able to do so (1 Kings 18:40; 2 Kings 10:18–28). A religious war broke out between the devotees of YHWH, headed by Elijah, and the worshipers of Baal, protected by the queen. King Ahab himself was hardly involved. Not he, but his wife, threatened Elijah's life; he searched for Elijah "in every nation and kingdom" not to kill him but to make him cancel the famine he decreed (1 Kings 18:1–18). After his victory on Mount Carmel, Elijah was reconciled with the king, and "ran ahead of his chariot." The king never consulted other than prophets of YHWH. What appears as religious equivocation results from differing notions of loyalty to Israel's God. The court permitted itself to enter into alliances with pagan neighbors and practiced the tactful toleration that necessarily accompanied this policy; prophecy, however, took an uncompromising position. The religious state of the mass of people may be inferred from the Elisha-Elijah stories. In them, the rural background does not appear to be pagan; no religious conflict is evident. The countryside worships YHWH loyally and as a matter of course; only in the metropolis, Samaria, and its extensions, are there Baal worshipers and followers.

This is the manifest background of the First Hosea (Hos. 1–3), who denounces Samaria's forsaking her divine husband to follow "Baals." The prophet alludes to a distinction between the people and their rulers: he calls on the "children" (the people) to rebuke their "mother" (the rulers) who played false to her "husband" (God). He foretells a forced return to the desert, where the people would be purged and made fit for a new "wedding" with its God.[67]

Joram, son of Ahab, removed the Baal pillar (2 Kings 3:2), but no basic change was made till Jehu's rebellion that, incited by Elisha, did away with the Omrides and extirpated the Baal cult. Jehu was aided by the Rechabites, a zealot order who withdrew from city life and abstained from wine (2 Kings 10:15, 23; Jer. 35). The custom of the Rechabites was one reaction to the inexorable urbanization that accompanied the advance of material civilization: the conviction that the true Israelite way of life and worship was the simple, pristine manner characteristic of the Wilderness period (cf. Hos. 2:16ff.).[68] According to 2 Kings 10, Jehu did away with the Baal cult at one blow: having gathered the devotees by a ruse into the Baal temple of Samaria, he massacred them, burned down the house, destroyed its appurtenances, and then turned the site into a public toilet. The cult never again appeared in the north; the Second Hosea (4–14) speaks of it only as a phenomenon of the past (11:2; 13:1).

The marriage of Athaliah (daughter of Ahab and Jezebel) to the Judahite Joram, son of Jehoshaphat, brought the Baal cult into Judah. A temple to Baal was built, apparently in Jerusalem, in which one Mattan ministered as priest (2 Kings 11:18). When Jehu assassinated Athaliah's son, King Ahaziah of Judah, the queen mother took over for six years. The priest Jehoiada led an insurrection against her (apparently Judah had as yet no body of active prophets), which ended with her death and the extirpation of the Baal cult. The success was crowned by a three-way covenant between YHWH, the king, and the people, to be "YHWH's people." The reign of the non-Davidide Athaliah and the Baal worship she sponsored were evidently regarded as having broken the covenant that bound the three since the time of David. Operative here is the basic idea of the Davidides that YHWH's covenant with his people is mediated through his covenant with the royal dynasty; when the dynastic covenant is broken, so is the covenant with the people.[69] With this purge, the Baal cult disappeared in Judah till the time of Manasseh.

By the ninth century, the northern prophets had become institutionalized, and the accompanying decay began to show. On the one hand, the prophets respected the king as the mediator of God's blessing to his people, particularly in the military sphere. 1 Kings 20 approvingly depicts prophetic support of a beleaguered king. During an Aramaean attack on Samaria, a prophet approached Ahab with a victory oracle, "that you may know that I am YHWH" (v. 28). The Aramaean king was declared God's "proscribed man" (*'iš hermi*)—the relic of an ancient notion that for centuries had played no part in Israel's warfare with its enemies (v. 42). Thus prophets bestowed religious significance upon acts determined chiefly by political and utilitarian motives. They tried to raise the events of Israel's national life above the mere ambitions of kings. To them, history was the arena in which God's will was manifest—that was the message of Jehu, son of Hanani (1 Kings 16), of Elijah, Elisha, Micaiah, and of Jonah, son of Amittai, the last of the northern prophets mentioned in the Book of Kings (2 Kings 14:25).

On the debit side, however, was the subservience entailed by the prophets' connection with the king, vividly portrayed in 1 Kings 22. Four hundred prophets were collected by the king of Israel to give him an oracle on the eve of his campaign to Ramoth-gilead (1 Kings 22); their victory oracle flattered the king's vanity. Unlike the lone prophet of chapter 20, these did not come on their own, moved by a divine mission, but rather in dutiful response to a royal summons. Their message served to enhance not God's fame, but the king's, "Go up . . . and win, for YHWH will deliver into the hand of the king" (v. 12). The horns that Zedekiah, son of Chenaanah, produced symbolized the strength of the king, not of God, "who has the eminences of a wild ox" (Num. 23:22). These prophets, in all likelihood pensioners of the king, exemplified the objects of Micah's taunt, "The prophets who mislead my people, . . . who predict prosperity when their mouth is filled; but if one does not put something in their mouths, they declare war against him" (Micah 3:5). Their corruption is pointed up by the friendly advice the king's messenger gives to the independent Micaiah ben Imlah: "Let your message be like that of theirs; promise success!" (ibid., v. 13). Even the courtiers assumed the prophet's compliance with the royal wish.

The crisis of prophetic independence came during this period of Aramaean wars. The monarchy's part in international coalitions, intermarriages, and the establishment of alien cults on Israelite soil excited prophetic zealots against the kings. But Israel's struggle for survival was also regarded as a test of its God's power, and roused concern for the fame of YHWH that favored royal enterprises. Two conflicting prophetic styles arose: a prophecy of denunciation and doom directed against the king's breaches of the covenant, and a prophecy of victory over Israel's enemies, with the aim of glorifying Israel's God. The collision of these raised the problem of distinguishing false from true prophecy, first recorded in the story of Micaiah (1 Kings 22). The test of Deuteronomy 18:22 is already applied in this story: "When a prophet speaks in the name of YHWH, and his prediction does not come true—that is what YHWH has not spoken; the prophet spoke it presumptuously, you must not fear him." Accordingly, the king of Israel imprisoned Micaiah, "until my safe return," when, as a manifestly false prophet, he should be put to death.[70]

New ideas emerged from the prophecy of doom. The first martyrs came from these prophets, "servants of God," whose bloodshed God must avenge (1 Kings 18:4, 13; 2 Kings 9:7). They originated the ideas of the "righteous remnant" who should escape the general doom, and of the foreign enemy whom God would appoint to punish the wicked of his people. In tears, Elisha foretold to the Aramaean Hazael the future suffering he would inflict upon Israel (2 Kings 8:12); this only fulfilled the plan of punishment for Baal worship that Elijah had already received (1 Kings 19:15ff.).

It was typical of the northern opposition prophets that they worked to fulfill their oracles. Not content with mere speech, Ahijah the Shilonite, Elijah, and his contemporaries all set actions afoot, not hesitating even to incite insurrection.

Victory prophecy also produced a new idea: the king destined by God to save his people. The aged and ailing Elisha saw in Joash the man destined to deliver Israel from the ravages of the Aramaeans; accordingly, he ordered him to shoot "an arrow of victory" toward Damascus (2 Kings 13:17). Jonah ben Amittai regarded Jeroboam, son of Joash, as the savior of Israel, who would restore the kingdom to its former boundaries (14:25f.). "Messianic" hopes were thus pinned on northern kings before they were pinned on Davidides. A related conception of victory prophecy was "the day of YHWH," a time when

God's judgment would fall upon Israel's enemies, with terrifying signs and portents in heaven and on earth. The description of the "day" in Obadiah may be taken as reflecting the early notion alluded to in Amos 5:18—where, contrary to the peculiar later prophetic skewing, the "day" is a joyous triumph of Israel over its enemies.[71]

Classical Prophecy
The Aramaean wars aggravated the social cleavage caused primarily by the urbanization of Israel. The mass of rural population grew poor and landless as the ruling class grew wealthy and powerful. Natural disasters—drought and agricultural pests (Amos 4:6ff.)—hastened the process of dispossession. God-fearing men saw these as sure signs of God's wrath. But if misfortune chose as its victim the dynasty of Jehu, whose founder purged the land once for all of the Baal cult, its traditional explanation as punishment for worship of alien gods could no longer serve. The author of Kings has recourse to the jejune "sins of Jeroboam" to account for this time of troubles; 2 Kings 10:31f.; 13:2, 6,[72] 11. Out of the crisis of faith, classical prophecy was born, with its new conception of the essence of the covenant, and a new definition of what violation of it meant.

The first of the new prophets was Amos of Judahite Tekoa. "Not a prophet nor a son of a prophet," he was called from his sheep to prophesy in Bethel during the good years of the reign of Jeroboam II. He interpreted the natural disasters that struck at that time as warnings to repent. What sins must be abandoned? Oppression of the poor, the crushing of the needy, wanton and profligate behavior. What value had an ostentatious worship that venerated temples more than God? Morally callous, glorying in their victories, Israel had forgotten God; for that they were doomed to exile and their land to destruction.

In Amos' prophecy, the moral component of the covenant was for the first time given priority over the cultic. The worship tendered by villains was worse than worthless; it was hateful to YHWH.

> I hate, I despise your feasts
> And I take no pleasure in your solemn assemblies.
> Though you offer up to me your whole offerings
> And your meal offerings, I will not accept them . . .
> Take away from me the noise of your songs;
> To the melody of your lyres I will not listen.
> But let justice well forth like water,
> And righteousness, like a perennial stream.
> Did you make sacrifices and meal offerings to me in the
>   Wilderness forty years, O house of Israel? (5:21–25)

Seeking God, which Amos contrasted with resorting to (the temples of) Bethel, Gilgal, and Beersheba, meant: "Seek good and not evil ... Hate evil and love good, and establish justice in the gate" (5:4ff., 14ff.). He predicted that the curses of the covenant—blasting, mildew, plague, exile, and destruction (cf. Deut. 28)—would come upon Israel for violation of the moral laws. Here was a major innovation; the notions then current, deriving from the old covenant documents themselves, singled out apostasy as the sin in whose wake national doom would follow. Amos' revolutionary message, so apt for the circumstances, was not accepted. Amaziah, the priest of Bethel, expelled the prophet from the temple city under indictment for treason since he had prophesied the king's death and his kingdom's exile.[73]

After the death of Jeroboam II, Israel was wracked for years by political turmoil, civil strife, and rapid changes of kings. The kingdom became tributary to Assyria, while subject to native adventurers who battened on its misfortune. The monarchy, emptied of all spiritual content, became an institution dedicated solely to power and exploitation. Against this background, the only classical prophet of the north, the Second Hosea (Hos. 4–14), appeared.

Second Hosea berated his generation for loss of loyalty (*hesed*) and devotion (*da'at*) to God (4:1–6). Authority was gone (10:3); kingship had lost its divine sanction ("they made kings, not from me; made officers, but I knew it not"; 8:4). The people put their trust in human works—in the calf of Samaria, in the numerous altars and pillars, in the multitude of castles and fortified cities (8:14), in Assyria, and in Egypt (5:13; 7:11). Having put God out of mind, their punishment was sure: their cities would be razed, their altars torn down, Egypt and Assyria would be the lands of their exile. There was but one remedy: penitent return to God. The prophet dictated a confession: "Assyria shall not save us; we will not ride on horses, or ever again call the work of our hands 'our god'" (14:4).

Hosea was the first to denounce the power politics of the state, its reliance on weapons and alliances instead of on God. His censure of the north's worship is especially notable. Performed "on mountain tops and on hills," it was polluted with fornication (4:13f.); Ephraim made many altars—"like heaps on the furrows of the fields" (12:12)—for sinning (8:11). Hosea repeatedly condemns the calf-images of the north—"they made a molten image of their silver ... nothing more than a craftsman's work" (13:2), "a no-god" (8:5). No other prophet so sweepingly invalidated the people's worship, not because it was offered to other gods, but because it was Godless; a consecration of places and things instead of devotion to God.[74]

The last king of Israel, Hoshea son of Elah, is said to have done what was evil in the sight of YHWH, "only not like the kings of Israel that preceded him" (2 Kings 17:2). Moreover, Hoshea is the only Israelite king exempted from the censure of having followed the evil ways of Jeroboam, son of Nebat; this may hint at a removal of the golden calves, which so exercised the king's prophetic namesake. Hoshea's revolt against Assyria ended with the final exile of the north. But the literary and prophetic heritage of the northern kingdom was salvaged, transferred to Judah, and there absorbed; the exile of her elder sister bequeathed to Judah a great spiritual reinforcement. Northern influence is to be recognized in the rapid and wonderful quickening of the spiritual life of Judah at the end of the eighth century.

In the first half of the eighth century, under King Uzziah, Judah too had enjoyed prosperity and political success. As in Israel, these were accompanied by corruption and social polarization. Close upon Amos, and remarkably similar in his social message, came the first Judahite prophet, Isaiah, son of Amoz. His first prophecies excoriated the decay of solidarity and social responsibility, rejected the piety of the villainous Jerusalemite aristocracy, and called for repentance on pain of dire punishment.

> Hear the word of YHWH, chiefs of Sodom;
> Give ear to the teaching of our God, O people of Gomorrah.
> What do your many sacrifices mean to me, says YHWH.
> I am sated with offerings of rams and the fat of oxen;
> I have no taste for the blood of bulls and lambs and goats.
> Your newmoons and festivals I abhor; they are a burden to me;
> I cannot stand them.
> When you spread forth your hands, I will close my eyes to you;
> Even though you pray much, I will not listen;
> For your hands are full of blood.
> Wash, purge yourselves, remove your wicked deeds from my sight!
> Stop doing evil; learn to do good;
> Seek justice; defend the right of the deprived;
> Vindicate the orphan; champion the widow!
> If you are agreeable and obedient,
> You will eat the best of the land;
> But if you refuse and rebel,
> You will be eaten by the sword.
> The mouth of YHWH has spoken it. (1:10–20)

The Syro-Ephraimite attack on Judah drove the prophet into the political arena. He demanded trust in God and denounced the plan of King Ahaz to call upon Assyria for help. The king did not listen to him, whereupon the prophet foretold an Assyrian attack upon Judah. Soon Damascus and Samaria bowed before the armies of Assyria, and

Judah followed suit during the reigns of Ahaz and Hezekiah. Assyria's trail of ruthless and irresistible conquest opened the eyes of the prophet to a larger vision: the Assyrian world empire was merely a prelude to the final stage of God's grand design. The culmination would be the redemption forever of Israel and the world from heathen tyranny. For after YHWH had used Assyria to scourge the wicked, he would punish the pride of the haughty king who had far exceeded his commission. Assyria would fall miraculously on the mountains of Judah, and its yoke would be removed from the necks of all the nations. A righteous king would ascend Zion's throne, a shoot from the stock of Jesse, in whose time peace, blessing, and righteousness would prevail in the land. Out of fear of YHWH the nations would throw away their idols and say:

> "Come let us go up to the mountain of YHWH,
>   To the temple of the God of Jacob,
>   That he may instruct us in his ways,
>   And that we might follow his paths.
>   For out of Zion instruction goes forth,
>   And the word of YHWH from Jerusalem."
> Then he will judge between nations,
>   And arbitrate for many peoples;
> So they will beat their swords into plowshares,
>   And their spears into pruninghooks;
> Nation will not lift up sword against nation
> Nor will they experience war any more. (2:3 f.)

The prophet's faith in the eternity of Jerusalem and the Davidic dynasty stood firm when King Hezekiah's rebellion against Sennacherib brought disaster upon Judah. Isaiah deprecated the alliance that Hezekiah made with Egypt in preparation for the rebellion; he deemed it an insult to YHWH (chs. 30–31). When the Assyrian king crushed the rebels, devastated Judah, and laid siege to Jerusalem, the prophet was unshaken in his faith that God would not surrender his city to the blaspheming enemy. He urged Hezekiah not to comply with the Assyrian demand to open the gates, and his faith was repaid.

Three great themes thus run through Isaiah's prophecy: indignation over the moral obtuseness of the upper class of Judah; the vision of God's grand design to turn all men to him and establish his kingdom of peace and righteousness in the world; faith in the role reserved for the dynasty and city of David in the accomplishment of that vision.[75]

Partly contemporary with Isaiah was Micah the Morashtite, whose earliest prophecies precede the fall of Samaria. Micah too denounced the leaders for their cruelty, their corruption, and their refusal to be corrected. But he went beyond Isaiah in foretelling the destruction of Jerusalem for the sins of its inhabitants.

> Hear this you leaders of the house of Jacob,
> You chiefs of the house of Israel,
> Who abhor justice and distort what is straight
> Who build Zion with blood
> And Jerusalem with iniquity—
> Her leaders govern by bribes,
> Her priests instruct for a price,
> Her prophets divine for silver,
> Yet they rely on YHWH, saying
> "Is not YHWH in our midst?
> No evil can befall us."
> So then because of you Zion shall be ploughed up like a field,
> Jerusalem shall become ruins,
> And the temple mount a forested height. (Micah 3:9–12)

A hundred years later, these outspoken words were cited in favor of the prophet Jeremiah, when he was on trial for prophesying in their tenor. At Jeremiah's trial, elders testified that not only did King Hezekiah not harm Micah, but he took his harsh words to heart and propitiated YHWH, and YHWH was pacified (Jer. 26:17ff.). This "propitiation" may be a reference to the reforms Hezekiah made in the official worship of Judah, to be described shortly.

Crises and Movements of Reform
With Judah's participation in international alliances and intrigues during the preceding reigns of kings Uzziah and Ahaz, alien usages had made their way into Jerusalem, as they had earlier into Samaria.

> For you have abandoned your Maker [reading 'ōśekā], O house of
>   Jacob;
> For they have become filled with sorcery [reading miqsám],
> And with divination, like the Philistines,
> And they abound in customs of the aliens. (Isa. 2:6)

Ahaz "caused his son to pass through the fire, like the abominations of the nations which YHWH drove out before Israel" (2 Kings 16:3). He replaced the bronze altar of Solomon's time with a new altar modeled upon "the altar that was in Damascus" (ibid., 10–16). This tendency to imitate the surroundings was checked in Hezekiah's time.

Before Sennacherib's invasion, Hezekiah had put into effect his reforms in the realm of worship. "He removed the *bāmōt* and broke the pillars, and cut down the asherah and ground to pieces the bronze serpent that Moses had made, for up to that time the Israelites had been making burnt offerings to it" (2 Kings 18:4). These practices probably all belonged to the worship of the God of Israel;[76] forms of worship hitherto considered legitimate were henceforth banned. The coincidence of the purged usages with objects of Hosea's denunciation suggests that Hezekiah's policy was affected by Hosea's prophecy (see below with regard to Josiah's reform). In any case, the collapse of the northern kingdom, just before Hezekiah's ascension, must have shaken Judah. The effect could only have been heightened by Micah's foretelling the destruction of Jerusalem. If in Jeremiah's time it was remembered as having caused Hezekiah to propitiate YHWH, an interrelation of the collapse, the prophecy, and the reform seems likely.[77]

Though Sennacherib failed to capture Jerusalem, for the rest of Hezekiah's reign and all through the reign of Manasseh and Amon Judah was a vassal of Assyria. The record condemns the latter two kings for unprecedented religious adulteration—the sponsoring of pagan elements in the official worship of God throughout Judah. Manasseh is blamed for "abominations like those of the nations that YHWH drove out before Israel ... He rebuilt the *bāmōt* that his father Hezekiah had destroyed; he erected altars to Baal, and he made an Asherah as Ahab, King of Israel, had done; he worshiped the whole host of heaven ... and built altars to the whole host of heaven in the two courts of the temple of YHWH. He caused his son to pass through fire; he divined ... practiced necromancy ... He placed the idol of Asherah that he had made in [the temple of YHWH]" (2 Kings 21:2–7). This cultic mixture reflects Canaanite-Phoenician-Aramaean influence; "Horses and chariots to the sun," instituted by the "kings of Judah" (23:11), point to Assyrian influence. Now there is no evidence of an Assyrian policy to coerce vassal kingdoms to practice an Assyrian cult; where such a policy existed—as in annexed provinces—it was not such a mixture, but the cult of the imperial god Ashur that was required. Hence it is necessary to look elsewhere for the origin of the (rather typically Syro-Phoenician) melange of cults transplanted into Judah at this time.

Chapter 1 of the Book of Zephaniah gives an idea of what religion in Judah was like before King Josiah's extensive reforms obliterated the work of Manasseh and Amon. Assimilation to gentile customs was rife among the Jerusalemite aristocracy. Nobles and officers dressed in alien garb; they "skipped over the threshold" (a Philistine custom? Cf. 1 Sam. 5:5). Wealthy merchants pursued gain, doubtless in international trade. In prosperity, the worship of YHWH was halfhearted or indifferent: "YHWH can do neither good nor harm." There was a regular worship of the host of heaven and of Baal (who had priests), besides the worship of YHWH. Archaeological evidence exists for Assyrian influence in architecture and art. Among the primary channels of influence must be counted the obligatory service of units of Judah's army in the forces of Assyria during the campaigns of Ashurbanipal in Egypt, and in the construction works of his predecessor, Esarhaddon. In short, Judah was politically and militarily integrated into the Assyrian empire, a process favored by king and court. Unprecedented commercial opportunities were opened by the forced unification of the states of the region under Assyrian hegemony, and Judahite royal merchants were not slow in exploiting them. This was the setting for the wholesale imitation of gentile customs and the decline of traditional, national religion described in the Book of Kings and in Zephaniah. The impulse to assimilation came from the court–from those ruling and mercantile circles interested in integrating Judah into the lively international scene.

Was there any opposition to the religious effects of this policy? Manasseh is reported to have shed enough innocent blood "to fill Jerusalem from one end to the other" (2 Kings 21:16; 24:4); to be sure, the text does not connect the bloodshed with the religious sin, but seems intent only on portraying the king as a bloody tyrant (cf. the portrayal of Jehoiakim, in Jeremiah 22:17, where no cultic wrongdoing is implied). But Jeremiah, at the very start of his career, expressly condemned that generation for doing away with an opposition: "Your sword devoured your prophets like a ravaging lion" (2:30). Considering the utter absence of prophecy during the nearly six decades of Manasseh and Amon (in an otherwise unbroken succession of prophets), these passages may be taken as indicating a bloody repression of prophetic opposition by the assimilatory kings.[78]

Just as the aftermath of Ahaz was the reform of Hezekiah, so the more extensive "apostasy" of Manasseh brought in its wake the great reform movement of Josiah's time. Josiah's political and military revival kept pace with Assyria's retreat from the west under sustained blows from its hostile neighbors. Hand in hand with political emancipation went the national-religious revival, nourished by a spirit of penitence that demanded far-flung changes in the worship of God. Josiah's purge and reformation of the cult is recorded in two versions, one in 2 Kings 22–23, the other in 2 Chronicles 34–35. A critical combination of the data of both versions yields the following reconstruction of events: In Josiah's eighth regnal year, when he was 16 years old, "he began to seek the God of his father David" (Chron.). This turning came, it may be supposed, under the tutelage of priests and prophets loyal to YHWH (such as are mentioned in 2 Kings 23:2). After four years a great purge of all alien cults was set afoot. It began in Jerusalem and its environs, spread through Judah, and spilled over into Bethel, the cities of Samaria, and Galilee, as the Judahites gained control of the Assyrian province of Samaria. Pagan cult installations were demolished and their priests put to death; worship of heavenly bodies and worship of YHWH at *bāmōt*, with asherim and pillars, was stopped; the *bāmōt* were defiled and their priests gathered in Jerusalem. In the eighteenth year of Josiah's reign, a "scroll of Torah" was found in the temple, incidental to its renovation; perhaps the scroll had been stored away during the terror of Manasseh's reign. When it was brought and read to the king, he was profoundly agitated, and asked the prophetess Huldah for an oracle regarding the fate of the people and the land. She responded that Josiah's penitence as- sured him peace in his time. Then the king assembled the elders, priests, and prophets in the temple court, read out to them the "scroll of the covenant" (= "the Torah scroll"), and pledged them to keep the covenant with their God, after having so long violated it during the reigns of Manasseh and Amon. The Passover season having arrived, it was celebrated with great pomp, in unprecedented fashion, in Jerusalem, "according to what was written in the scroll" (presumably this refers to the concentration of all ceremonies in the Temple of Jerusalem, in contrast to the former countrywide celebration of the festival). Josiah also purged away necromancy and other private cults that had received an impetus from their adoption by Manasseh.[79]

The critical opinion that the "Torah scroll" found and covenanted upon in Josiah's time was a version of Deuteronomy is based on strik- ing similarities between the story of 2 Kings 22–23 and Deuteronomy. Of all the books of the Pentateuch, only Deuteronomy calls itself "this Torah scroll" as well as "the words of the covenant" (29:8, 20; 30:10; cf. 2 Kings 22:8; 23:2). Only Deuteronomy bans the worship of heav- enly bodies, and the worship of YHWH by asherim, pillars, and at many places (contrast Exod. 20:24). The latter prohibitions aim at dis- tinguishing the very forms—not merely the objects—of Israel's wor- ship from those of the gentiles, in line with the Hezekian and Josianic reactions to the assimilatory trend in neo-Assyrian Judah. The old in- junction, "You shall not act as they do" (Exod. 23:24) was meant to ban the worship of foreign gods; in Deuteronomy 12:4, 30–31, it is far-reachingly reinterpreted as "You shall not act thus [as the gentiles do] toward YHWH your God." Worship at many places, a hallmark of the gentiles' cult, is thus excluded, with all its consequences. Celebra- tion of the Passover, as well as all other festivals, is confined to one sanctuary (Deut. 16); country "Levites"—dispossessed by this new ar- rangement—are permitted to serve at that sanctuary "like all their fel- low Levites" (= priests; 18:6–8). Finally, Deuteronomy is the only work explicitly called a "Torah scroll" containing warnings and curses so terrible a king might be shaken by them (ch. 28).

This is not to say that Deuteronomy was composed at the time of Josiah's reform; indeed the narrative of 1 Kings 22 assumes that the secreted Torah scroll had been previously known. The disqualification of *bāmōt* priests from service at the temple altar (2 Kings 23:9), a blatant violation of the magnanimous rule of Deuteronomy 18:6–8, also suggests that the book originated independently of the reform.[80]

Signs of an ultimately northern provenience have been detected in the Book of Deuteronomy: the choice of Shechem as the place where the people are to inscribe and ratify the Torah after they cross the Jordan; some remarkable affinities with the phraseology and views of the prophet Hosea (e.g., the deprecation of pillars and of many altars; a reserved attitude toward kingship). The theory that the core of Deuteronomy was composed in the north, and, after the fall of the north, brought south by fugitive scribes has much to recommend it. Having been adapted to southern conditions, its first recorded effect was Hezekiah's reform. Suppressed during the reigns of Manasseh and Amon, it emerged into the full light of history on the tide of penitence and spiritual revival that rose in the time of Josiah.[81]

By making the Torah scroll the basis of the people's covenant obligation, King Josiah in effect declared it the constitution of his realm. Heretofore no more than a religious document, the product of a creative conservation of ancient traditions, it became the binding law of the kingdom. Conduct "in accord with what was written" became the touchstone of loyalty to both God and king. The covenant made in Josiah's reign was thus the fateful step toward Israel's becoming a "people of the book"—a people defined religiously and politically by adherence to a sacred scripture.[82]

The result of Josiah's reform was to limit the public, sacrificial cult of YHWH to Jerusalem, and thus empty the countryside of all means of public worship. This situation obtained during the score of years remaining before the Exile; nor was public worship renewed among the main body of Judahite exiles in Babylonia. 2 Kings, Lamentations, and Jeremiah say nothing of pagan elements or even of *bāmōt* worship in the official cult after Josiah's reform. To be sure, Jeremiah and Ezekiel refer to *bāmōt* and pagan cults, but it may be supposed that these were private, without official backing.[83]

At first, Josiah enjoyed political success. During his reign the Assyrian empire crumbled before the very eyes of its victims. A cry of relief and revenge sounds in the contemporary prophecy of Nahum. He gloats over the destruction of Nineveh, "the city of blood, the den of lions"; "YHWH has restored the pride of Jacob!" Josiah, full of confidence in his God, sallied to block the passage of Pharaoh Necho's army on its way through Palestine to support the remnant of the Assyrian power in Haran (609 B.C.E.). His plan miscarried, and he was killed at Megiddo. With him died the political and religious impetus he had given to Judah. After a few years of Egyptian dominance, Judah was absorbed into the west-Asiatic domains of the neo-Babylonian empire of Nebuchadnezzar.

Habakkuk's prophecy reflects the Chaldean (= Babylonian) ascendancy, and wrestles with its challenge to faith in divine providence. The Babylonians' conquest might be taken as a divine judgment upon Assyria, but the victimization of smaller nations along the way, and the victor's ascription of his success to his "idols" demanded a response from YHWH. "Why do you look on at the treacherous,/Indifferent, as the guilty destroy the innocent." God replies that the end of the term allotted to the wicked will come; even though it should tarry, wait for it; it must come. In the meanwhile, "the righteous shall live by his faith." Evil will recoil upon the head of the evil ones; the idols will be proven worthless. Then "the land will be filled with knowledge of the majesty of YHWH as waters cover the sea." In this way the prophecy of Isaiah (Isa. 11:9) was adapted to the unexpected rise of the Chaldeans. Like Isaiah, Habakkuk also regarded the success of the cruel conqueror as a universal problem, to which nothing less than a universal revelation of divine power could provide an answer.[84]

Nebuchadnezzar's victory over Pharaoh Necho at Carchemish (605 B.C.E.) decided the fate of Judah; its few remaining years were to be under Babylonian rule.

The last decades of Judah were distinguished by the long, agonized prophecy of Jeremiah son of Hilkiah, of the country priesthood at Anathoth. Even before Josiah's reform, under the pall of Manasseh's "abominations," Jeremiah had foretold the onslaught of an unnamed "nation from the north" to punish Judah's apostasy to "no-gods." Following Hosea, Jeremiah likened Israel to a wife who had broken faith with her husband. Then came Josiah's reforms and successes, and the prophet, apparently in hopes of true repentance and a change of destiny, kept watchfully silent. But Josiah met a sudden, untimely death; the new Babylonian conqueror subjugated the region, and a tyrannical king, Jehoiakim, ascended Judah's throne. The wrath of God toward Judah for Manasseh's sins seemed not to have been assuaged; Jeremiah considered the train of calamities a presage of doom for the kingdom. But the masses, believing in their virtue and in the presence of God within their cleansed temple, refused to credit Jeremiah's warnings. Early in Jehoiakim's reign, Jeremiah prophesied the destruction of the Temple and was nearly condemned to death by the irate crowd (another prophet, Uriah, son of Shemaiah, was actually executed by the king for a similar prophecy [Jer. 26]).[85] Jehoiakim attempted to break loose from Babylonia, but died suddenly; Nebuchadnezzar punished his successor, Jehoiachin, along with Judah's ruling class with exile. The ascension of Zedekiah opened the last phase of Judah's descent. The king was soon involved in an organization of small western states for rebellion against the Babylonian overlord. In Zedekiah's fourth year, Jeremiah announced to a conclave of the conspirators that God had decreed a universal subjection to Nebuchadnezzar, from which no city or nation could escape. But there were other prophetic voices; during that same year Jeremiah collided with Hananiah son of Azur, who prophesied the imminent triumphal return of Jehoiachin's exile. Jeremiah, on the other hand, sent a letter to the exiles that iterated the theme of a seventy-year subjection to Babylonia, but promised them a bright future afterward. For the people of Judah and Jerusalem, however, the prospect was inexorable doom.

The rebels of Jerusalem had faith in the impregnability of the city of YHWH, which they might have grounded on Isaiah's stand and the city's successful defiance of Sennacherib a century before. Under siege, they demonstrated covenant loyalty by emancipating their slaves in exact accord with the law of the "scroll of the covenant" (symbolizing thereby their prayer for liberation from the siege). And relief came; King Apries of Egypt made a sally against the Babylonians and compelled them momentarily to lift the siege (Jer. 34; 37:5). This event indicates the state of religion in Jerusalem's last days. That economic necessity soon forced cancellation of this unprecedented measure does not lessen its significance as a manifestation of religious fervor.

Throughout the siege, Jeremiah called for surrender to the Babylonians. Suspected of intention to defect, he was thrown into prison, whence he continued to prophesy doom, until events bore him out.[86]

Reactions to the Fall
The fall of the kingdom of Judah did not put an end to Israelite-biblical religion. Traditions about the establishment of Israel's covenant with God included threats of misfortunes for breach of it, among which defeat, destruction, and exile figured prominently. The prophets had always warned the people of such misfortunes as punishment for disobedience, so when disaster came it was perceived as the realization of prophetic warnings (which is why so many prophecies of doom have been preserved).[87] A minority of Judahite exiles in Egypt interpreted the fall as the condign vengeance of the Queen of Heaven for the suppression of her cult (apparently by Josiah), and concluded that they must propitiate the goddess by reviving it (Jer. 44). The singularity of their reaction only underlines how differently the disaster was appreciated by the bulk of its victims. The dirges in the book of

Lamentations attribute the fall to God's wrath over Judah's sins. What the sins were, who committed them, and when, were matters on which different views were held. The author of the Book of Kings ascribes the fall of Judah to the sins of Manasseh (2 Kings 23:26; 24:3; cf. Jer. 15:4); the popular saying "Our fathers sinned and are gone; we suffer their punishment" (Lam. 5:7) is, at bottom, in agreement. Cynics expressed the notion differently: "Fathers have eaten unripe grapes; children's teeth are set on edge" (Jer. 31:28; Ezek. 18:1). The exilic prophet Ezekiel reached back to the very origins of Israel in looking for the root of the fall (Ezek. 16; 20; 23). Common to all was the conviction that Israel's evildoing was the cause. All accepted the covenant idea that Israel's destiny was not determined by such "natural" factors as its relative strength, or by some failure of its God, but by the law of retribution embedded in the terms of its covenant with God. This view opened a window to hope in the future, for if indeed sin had caused the disaster, repentance and spiritual regeneration might restore Israel to God's favor and thus to its land. Trust in the efficacy of penitence ultimately rested upon a deep faith that "the covenant with the forefathers" (Lev. 26:44ff.) still stood, in spite of Israel's faithlessness. God remained true to his promise to the patriarchs to be the God of their descendants forever. A prayerful addition to the prophecies of Micah from the time of exile or later ends with an expression of confidence: "You will show constancy to Jacob and loyalty to Abraham,/As you swore to our fathers in olden times" (7:20). Faith in God's unilateral and unconditional covenant loyalty sustained Israel through its fall and Exile and made national revival possible when the opportunity presented itself.

NOTES

1. On the historiography of the Book of Kings, see M. Noth, *Überlieferungsgeschichtliche Studien*, Halle, 1942, 87–110 (includes all the deuteronomistic literature); on the religious standard of judgment, see G. von Rad, *Old Testament Theology*, I (transl. by D. Stalker), Edinburgh & London, 1962, 334–46; F. M. Cross, *Canaanite Myth and Hebrew Epic*, Cambridge, 1973, 274–90 ("The Themes of the Book of Kings and the Structure of the Deuteronomic History").

2. J. Wellhausen's evaluation of the Chronicler's work in *Prolegomena to the History of Israel* (trans. by J. Black and A. Menzies), Edinburgh, 1885, 171–227 is still worth careful study; the religious tendency of the book is characterized by Y. Kaufmann, *Tol°dot*, IV, Tel Aviv, 1957, 451–81. Sara Japhet's *The Ideology of the Book of Chronicles and Its Place in Biblical Thought* (Hebrew), Hebrew University doctoral dissertation, Jerusalem, 1973, a comprehensive and penetrating survey, devotes chapter 2, 209–55 to "Worship of God" (English publication, under the same title, in 1989 [Frankfurt am Main: Peter Lang], ch. 2, 199–265).

3. On the dating of the Latter Prophets, see the detailed analysis of Y. Kaufmann, *Tol°dot*, III: 1–56 (English abridgment by M. Greenberg, *The Religion of Israel*, Chicago,

1960, 347–56; hereafter, E); note the similar (though more cautious) conclusions of D. N. Freedman in "The Law and the Prophets," VTSup, 9 (1963):259–61.

Since throughout these chapters Kaufmann's *Tol'dot* is laid under heavy contribution, the reader may be interested in my assessment and critique of Kaufmann's biblical studies: "Kaufmann on the Bible: An Appreciation," *Judaism*, 13 (1964):78–89.

4. The particularly knotty problem raised by Ezekiel's testimony to the religion of the last age of Judah is a case in point; see my "Prolegomenon" to the re-issue of C. C. Torrey, *Pseudo-Ezekiel and the Original Prophecy* (with the rejoinder of S. Spiegel), in *The Library of Biblical Studies*, ed. H. H. Orlinsky, New York: Ktav, 1970, xviii–xxix.

5. Linguistic criteria for the identification of late psalms are given in A. Hurvitz, *The Transition Period in Biblical Hebrew: A Study in Post-Exilic Hebrew and Its Implications for the Dating of Psalms* (Hebrew), Jerusalem, 1972.

6. Hazor: Y. Yadin, EB, III, 1958, plate 7 (facing 257); Samaria: D. Diringer, *Le iscrizioni antico-ebraiche palestinesi*, Firenze, 1934, 40–79; for dating cf. N. Avigad, *Encyclopaedia of Archaeological Excavations in the Holy Land*, II (Hebrew), Jerusalem, 1971:531–32; Ophel: Diringer, 79; Lachish: N. H. Torczyner, *The Lachish Documents* (Hebrew), Jerusalem, 1940, 230–31; Arad: Y. Aharoni, *Arad Inscriptions* (Hebrew), Jerusalem, 1975, 163f. (Index of Hebrew Names).

7. Hosea 2:18 assumes that YHWH is being called *ba'al*: cf. W. F. Albright, *Archaeology and the Religion of Israel*, Baltimore, 1946, 160–61.

8. Torczyner (n. 6), index, s.v. YHWH; on the oath formula, cf. M. Greenberg, "The Hebrew Oath Particle *ḥay/ḥe*," JBL, 76 (1957):34–9.

9. Aharoni (n. 6), no. 18, 37ff., and 163f.

10. See the comprehensive survey of the question in B. Porten, *Archives from Elephantine*, Berkeley, Los Angeles, 1968, 103–79.

11. Y. Aharoni, "The Israelite Sanctuary at Arad," in D. N. Freedman, J. C. Greenfield, eds., *New Directions in Biblical Archaeology*, New York, 1969, 25–40; idem, "The Horned Altar of Beer-sheba," BA, 37 (1974), 26; N. Avigad, "The Priest of Dor," IEJ, 25 (1975):(101–05).

12. K. Kenyon, *Encyclopaedia of Archaeological Excavations* (see n. 6), I:214 (and the facing illustration) (English, ed. M. Avi-Yonah, vol. II, Jerusalem, 1975:596; illustr., 589, lower left). To such conjectured remains of cult installations must be added the cluster of about twenty tumuli discovered in western Jerusalem, which Ruth Amiran excavated and discussed in *Yediot*, 18 (1954):45–59 (Hebrew). She surmised that these consisted of earth and stone piles artificially heaped upon *bāmōt* of the Judahite monarchy. Y. Elitzur followed with the suggestion that it was at the order of King Josiah that these heaps were raised during his purge of Judah's worship (*Proceedings of the Fifth World Congress of Jewish Studies* [Hebrew; n.d.] 92–97).

13. On the meaning of such figurines, see W. F. Albright, "Astarte Plaques and Figurines from Tell Beit Mirsim," *Mélanges syriens . . . R. Dussaud*, Paris, 1939, I:107–20; idem, *Archaeology and the Religion of Israel*, 114f.

14. A *maṣṣēbāh* of the Arad sanctuary is pictured in the *Encyclopaedia of Archaeological Excavations*, II:475 (English, I:84, lower left); outside Israel: the picture of the pillars symbolizing Ashtoret, standing on her throne (from the Hellenistic period), as interpreted by H. Danthime, *Mélanges . . . Dussaud*, II:857–66.

15. See the assessment of R. de Vaux, *Ancient Israel*, London, 1961, 278f. W. B. Barrick challenges the supposed "funerary character" of the *bāmāh* in VT, 25 (1975), 565–95.

15a. See E. Bickerman, "The Edict of Cyrus . . .," JBL, 65 (1946), 262–68 (reprinted with revisions in Bickerman, *Studies in Jewish and Christian History*, I [Leiden, 1976]: 91–103).

16. The data on Israelite sanctuaries are conveniently summarized by M. Haran in the article "Sanctuaries" (*miqdāš*) EB V, Jerusalem, 1968, cols. 322–28.

17. In Psalms 99:5; 132:7; Lamentations 2:1, the whole Temple is, by extension, called God's footstool; by further extension the whole earth is so called in Isaiah 66:1.

18. For this interpretation of the golden calves, see Kaufmann, *Tol'dot*, II:259–61 (E 271); R. de Vaux, *The Bible and the Ancient Near East* (transl. by D. McHugh), Lon-

don, 1972, 100–03, regards the young bull as an embodiment of the divine attribute of strength and fecundity.

19. On the regular incense offering in First Temple times, cf. M. Haran, "The Uses of Incense in the Ancient Israelite Ritual," VT, 10 (1960):113–29.

20. On the pilgrimage in early Israel, cf. M. Haran, *Ages and Institutions in the Bible* (Hebrew), Tel Aviv, 1973, 77–88.

21. So Mekilta, *Bo'* (*Pasha*, 7); Onkelos at Exodus 12:13; 23:27; Ibn Janah in *The Book of Roots*, s.v. (comparing Isa. 31:5); cf. R. Weiss, *Leshonenu*, 27–28 (1965):127–30, and S. Loewenstamm, *The Tradition of the Exodus and Its Development* (Hebrew), Jerusalem, 1965, 84–8 (English translation by B. J. Schwartz, *The Evolution of the Exodus Tradition* [Jerusalem: Magnes Press, 1992, 197–206]). This interpretation is opposed by J. B. Segal, *The Hebrew Passover*, 1963, 95–101.

22. The anxiety is expressed through ascetic (purificatory) practices: eating unleavened bread, "bread of self-denial" (Deut. 16:3); the ban on eating any new produce until the first sheaf of the reaping was "lifted" (Lev. 23:14). The Jewish customs of counting the days between the festivals of *maṣṣōt* and Pentecost, and quasi-mourning during that interval also reflect the season's anxiety. "Some explain it . . . on the ground that the world is anxious between Passover and Weeks about the crops and the fruit trees . . . Therefore God commanded to count these days, to keep the anxiety of the world in mind and to turn to him in wholehearted repentance, to plead with him to have mercy upon us, on mankind and on the land, so that the crops should turn out well, for they are our life" (*Abudarham haššālēm*, s^efirat ha'omer [ed. Jerusalem, 5719, 241]). See M. P. Nilsson, *Greek Folk Religion* (New York, 1940), 27–29, for parallels, but especially L. H. Silberman, "The Sefirah Season," HUCA, 22 (1949):226–32.

The origin of *pesaḥ* as a nomad festival (L. Rost) may be admitted without prejudicing its meaning for the settled Israelites, our present concern. In the land, *pesaḥ* and the *maṣṣōt* festivals were presumably celebrated as two parts of a single agricultural festival, even as they were fused into a single commemorative one. Neither is mentioned in the narrative between Josh. 5:10f. and 2 Kings 23:21ff., but this does not justify denying their existence during all that period (G. Fohrer, *History of Israelite Religion*, Nashville, 1972, 100f.). No consensus on the origin of the Passover festival has emerged in recent investigations of it; see J. B. Segal, *The Hebrew Passover*, London, etc., 1963; J. Henninger, *Les fêtes de printemps chez les Sémites et la pâque israélite*, Paris, 1975.

23. Kaufmann, *Tol^edot*, II:496–98; H. J. Kraus, *Worship in Israel* (transl. by G. Buswell), Oxford, 1966, 66ff., doubts it.

24. For an analysis of the day's ritual, see J. Milgrom, "Day of Atonement," Enc Jud, V, Jerusalem, 1971, cols. 1384–1387. Milgrom judiciously weighs the doubts about the antiquity of this holy day. (He rebuts the arguments for a late date in *Leviticus 1-16*, Anchor Bible [New York: Doubleday, 1991], 1070–71.)

25. Explicit testimony to the mixture of joy and anxiety that must have accompanied these festivals even in biblical times comes only much later, "R. Akiba (second century C.E.) said: The Torah enjoined you to make an offering of the first sheaf of the barley harvest at the Passover, when the barley ripens, in order that the crops may be blessed; to make an offering of the firstfruits of the wheat at Weeks, when the fruit-trees are ripe, so that the fruit may be blessed; to offer water libations at Tabernacles, so that the rain may be blessed" (Tosefta, *Sukkah*, ch. 3, end). Although the cult laws of the Torah make no connection between the celebration of the festivals and fertility, such a connection is alluded to in Zechariah 14:17f. "Whichever of the families of the earth do not go up to Jerusalem [on the festival of Sukkot; vv. 16, 19] to worship the King, YHWH Sebaoth—no rain shall fall upon them."

A similar clustering of the holy days during the spring is evident in Ezekiel 45:18–20; a two-day purgation of the uncleanness of the Temple (analogous to the Day of Atonement) on the first and seventh of the first (spring) month. See Kaufmann, *Tol^edot*, IV, 492–96 (E, 306–08).

26. A full reconstruction of Israel's festival celebration, combining data of diverse provenience with imagination, is found in Kraus, *Worship* (see n. 23), 208–22.

27. Kraus, 225f.

28. A good account of the priestly and deuteronomic conceptions of the temple is

given in M. Weinfeld, *Deuteronomy and the Deuteronomic School*, Oxford, 1972, 191–209; Weinfeld develops the earlier treatment of G. von Rad, *Studies in Deuteronomy* (transl. by D. Stalker), Chicago, 1953, 37–44.

29. Contrast the pagan view, expressed, for example, in the Egyptian adjuration of the gods threatening to stop their offerings: J. A. Wilson in ANET, 327 (b).

30. Such discrimination between types of sacrifice is not prophetic in spirit; it has nothing to do with the classical prophetic doctrine of the primacy of morality over cult. See my essay, "On the Refinement of the Conception of Prayer in Hebrew Scriptures," AJSR, I (1976):57–92 [reprinted in this volume].

31. There is a theory that Zadok was the native Jebusite priest of pre-Israelite Jerusalem, and that David appointed him to promote syncretism with the conquered Canaanite population (for a brief statement and full bibliography of this theory see H. H. Rowley, *Worship in Ancient Israel*, London, 1967, 72–75); cf. also S. Loewenstamm, "Zadok," in EB, VI, cols. 673–75. Haran, *Ages* (n. 20), 156, plausibly considers Zadok a Levite.

32. For a reconstruction of the history of Israel's priesthood, see Kaufmann, *Tol^edot*, I, 171–84 (E, 193–200). on which cf. my critique in JAOS, 70 (1950):41–47; for a comprehensive treatment, see A. Cody, *A History of Old Testament Priesthood*, Rome 1969; cf. also Haran, *Ages* (above, n. 20), 150–74.

33. Written down during the united monarchy, according to the estimate of F. M. Cross, *Studies in Ancient Yahwistic Poetry*, Baltimore, 1950, 185f., though he dates verses 8–10 later (p. 220). O. Eissfeldt refrains from proposing a date for the Blessing, but regards it as early (*The Old Testament: An Introduction* [trans. by P. Ackroyd], Oxford, 1965, 228f.); Cody (see preceding note) puts the latest elements in the Blessing of Levi (vv. 9ᵇ–10) no later than the eighth century (114–20).

34. See the monograph of Jacob Milgrom, *Studies in Levitical Terminology, I: The Encroacher and the Levite*, Berkeley, Los Angeles, 1970.

35. See W. F. Albright's discussion, with a parallel from ancient Egypt, "The Judicial Reform of Jehoshaphat," *Alexander Marx Jubilee Volume*, English Section, New York, 1950, 76f.

36. On the lower classes of Temple personnel, see R. de Vaux, *Ancient Israel*, 382ff.; Haran, *Ages*, 218–23; on Temple singers, S. Mowinckel, *The Psalms in Israel's Worship*, II, Oxford, 1962, 79–84; on the evidence of names for dating these classes, W. F. Albright, *Archaeology and the Religion of Israel*, 120–27. On the name qrs among the Arad ostraca, see B. Levine, IEJ, 19 (1969):50f.

37. See the literature cited above in n. 32; the view of G. von Rad (*Studies in Deuteronomy*, 14, 66f.) that Levites served as teachers and preachers of Torah during the late monarchy (based in part on their post-exilic role, e.g., in Nehemiah 8) has no support in the sources, and is justly deprecated by Weinfeld, *Deuteronomy*, 54ff. The classical critical view that the inferior status of the Levites came about as a result of the "demotion" of the *bāmōt* priests incidental to Josiah's reform is refuted by Kaufmann (citation in n. 32).

38. On the pre-exilic dating of the passages dealing with the priestly dues, see Kaufmann, *Tol^edot*, I, 143–59 (E, 187–93); Haran offers a convenient summary of the question in the article *matt^enōt k^ehunnah* ("priestly dues"), EB, IV, cols. 39–45; a comprehensive study of the tithe utilizing comparative material, and comparing royal with priestly custom, is M. Weinfeld's "The Tithe in the Bible—Its State and Cultic Background" (Hebrew) in the annual, *Beer-Sheba*, I (1973):122–31.

39. See W. F. Albright, *Archaelogy and the Religion of Israel*, 121–25; M. Haran, "Studies in the Account of the Levitical Cities," JBL, 80 (1961):45–54, 156–65; Y. Kaufmann, *Sefer Yehoshua‘*, Jerusalem, 1959, 270–82; B. Mazar, "The Cities of the Priests and the Levites," VTSup, 7 (1960):193–205.

40. See J. M. Grintz, "Do Not Eat on the Blood," ASTI, 8 (1970–71):78–105, where the prohibition is explained by pagan divination customs.

41. See J. Licht, *mīlāh* ("circumcision"), EB, IV, cols. 894–901; M. Fox examines the meaning of the rite as "the sign of the covenant," in RB, 81 (1974):557–96; he concludes that the sign is to remind God to keep his promise of posterity to Abraham.

42. "After the Babylonian Exile, the conception of marriage changed . . . According

to Ezekiel 16:8 and Malachi 2:13–16, the rite of marriage includes a covenant and an oath that obligates the two parties . . . God serves as witness and judge of violations of the covenant; the rite as a whole gains a religious dimension, and marriage itself acquires increased obligatoriness (Prov. 2:16f.)"—so Z. Falk, *niśśu'im* ("marriage"), EB V, col. 859. But the sense of the passages cited is questionable. The Proverbs passage condemning the adulteress who "forgets the covenant of her God" ("who forsakes the friend of her youth") recalls Ben Sira 23:37 (23): "For first she disdained the teaching of the Most High, next she betrayed her husband." Both passages take adultery as a violation of the divine injunction (in the "Tablets of the Covenant") "Thou shalt not commit adultery."

Malachi 2:14, condemning the betrayal of "the wife of your covenant" (or "your covenant-wife"), must be understood in the light of verse 10: "Why should we be false to one another, thus profaning the covenant of our fathers." This in turn is illuminated by what follows immediately: "For Judah has profaned the holiness of God, which he loved, by taking to wife the daughter of a foreign god." The sanctity of Israel's line of descent from the covenant ancestors was "profaned" by intermarriage with gentile women. The gentile woman–"the daughter of an alien god"–is contrasted to "your companion and the wife of your covenant"–i.e., an Israelite woman, who might well be styled "daughter of your covenant" (viz., "the covenant of our fathers," through which the holy people came into being).

God's "attestation" in verse 14 recalls Genesis 31:50, in which Laban invokes God as witness against Jacob's ever maltreating his daughters or taking other wives besides them. The obscure situation in Malachi 2:11ff. is perhaps analogous: the prophet denounces a current practice of some Jews who took gentile women beside their lawful Jewish wives, and thereby were false to them (since a time-honored view was that such a practice was heinous).

The allegory in Ezekiel 16:8 is no sure ground for asserting that marriage involved a covenant and an oath. The prophet sometimes intrudes the referent into his allegory, e.g., in 17:9b. Since he is allegorizing God's covenant with Israel, which, in his version, involved an oath (20:5f.), it is altogether possible that his allegorical marriage is colored by the reality that God acquired Israel by a covenant oath.

43. T. H. Gaster, *Myth, Legend and Custom in the Old Testament*, New York, 1969, 572; 590–602.

44. Kaufmann, *Tol'dot*, II:544–56 (E, 311–16); Greenberg, "Resurrection," Enc Jud, XIV, cols. 96–98.

45. E. Neufeld, *Ancient Hebrew Marriage Laws*, London, 1944, 23–49; R. Westbrook, "Redemption of Land," *Israel Law Review*, 6 (1971):371–75.

46. H. L. Ginsberg, "Psalms and Inscriptions of Petition and Acknowledgment," *Louis Ginzberg Jubilee Volume*, English Section, New York, 1945, 159–71.

47. Kaufmann, *Tol'dot*, II:499–506 (E, 309–11); A. Wendel, *Das freie Laingebet im vorexilischen Israel*, Leipzig, 1932, a comprehensive study of forms; J. Herrmann, "Prayer in the Old Testament," TDNT, II, Grand Rapids, 1964, 785–800; A. Gonzalez, "Prière," *Supp. Dict. de la Bible*, fasc. 44 (1969):556–85.

48. Divine help in war is asked in several psalms; on Psalms 24, 20, 146, and 46, see S. D. Goitein, *Iyyunim ba-Miqra*, Tel Aviv, 1957, 239–47.

49. Concerning the trumpets, see Y. Yadin, *The Scroll of the War . . .* Oxford, 1962, 87ff., 109ff.

50. See A. Biram, *Mas 'oved, Tarbiz*, 23 (1953):137–42; for the development of the ḥerem, see A. Malamat, "The Ban in Mari and the Bible," *Die Ou-Testamentiese Werkgemeenskap in Suid-Africa: Biblical Essays* (1966), 40–9; Greenberg, "Herem," Enc Jud, VIII: cols. 345–50.

51. W. F. Albright suggested that Samuel employed these enthusiasts in a "revival" movement: *Samuel and the Beginning of the Prophetic Movement*, Cincinnati, 1961.

52. A literary-evolutionary approach to the different depictions of prophetic miracles is found in A. Rofé's "The Classification of the Prophetical Stories," JBL, 89 (1970): 427–40.

53. See the detailed account in F. Hesse, *Die Fürbitte im Alten Testament*, Hamburg,

1951; and Y. Muffs's essay, *Tefillatam šel Nevi'im* ("Prophetic Prayer"), *Molad*, 35–36 (5736):204–10. [Expanded English version in his *Love and Joy* (New York: 1992): 9–48.]

54. See A. Malamat, "Prophetic Revelations in . . . Mari and the Bible," VTSup, 15 (1966):207–27; J. F. Ross, "Prophecy in Hamath, Israel, and Mari," HTR, 63 (1970):1–28.

54a. On the distinction between Nathan's role as prophet and his role as adviser, see Kaufmann, *Mi-kivšonah šel ha-yeṣirah ha-miqra'it*, Tel Aviv, 1966, 180–84; for the possibility that *ḥōzēh* = court prophet, see Z. Zevit, VT, 25 (1975):786–89.

55. See S. R. Johnson, *The Cultic Prophet in Ancient Israel*, Cardiff, 1944.

56. "The essential meaning of this is: Within every community, even among idolaters, there are some pious, ascetical worshipers—such as, nowadays, the priesthood among the Hindus and the Christians—while the rest of the community are abandoned to licentiousness . . . Therefore God said, 'You must all be holy'; that is, 'Among you it must not be that some are pious and ascetical while others are abandoned to license and transgression . . .'" (Commentary to Exod. 19:6 of Abraham, son of Maimonides).

57. See the discussion of the Ezekiel passage in the Talmud, *Menaḥot* 45a, and the forced interpretation reflected by Ibn Ezra in Leviticus 22:8.

58. Comprehensive accounts of these theories are found in H. J. Kraus, *Worship in Israel* (transl. by G. Buswell), Oxford, 1966; W. Beyerlin, *Origins and History of the Oldest Sinaitic Traditions* (transl. by S. Rudman), Oxford, 1965.

59. See the full discussion by M. Haran, "The Ark and the Cherubs" (Hebrew), *Eretz-Israel*, 5 (1958):83–90.

60. Kaufmann, in *Mi-kivšonah šel ha-yeṣirah ha-miqra'it*, Tel Aviv, 1966, 205–07, understands the "wrath" as a reference to some magical effect of the actions of the king's priest-magicians.

61. Regarding the odd language of 2 Kings 10:25, see Y. Yadin's tentative proposal to place Jezebel's Baal temple somewhere in the territory, not the city, of Samaria (*Eretz Shomron* [Jerusalem, 1973], 56–58). As for Solomon, the fourteenth-century commentator Gersonides notes a certain inconsequence in 1 Kings 11:4–8 (the mitigating clauses at the ends of verses 4 and 6), indicating that Solomon's guilt was in allowing his wives to worship foreign gods (so explicitly verse 8) rather than in worshiping them himself.

62. On the ethnic heterogeneity implicit in the differing modes of designating the fiscal districts of Solomon, first suggested by Alt, see the concurring remarks of Z. Kallai, *The Tribes of Israel* (Hebrew), Jerusalem, 1967, 35–38.

63. See A. Soggin, "Der offiziell gefordete Synkretismus in Israel, etc.," ZAW, 78 (1966):179–204; on Molech, M. Cogan, *Imperialism and Religion*, Missoula, Mont. (1974), 77–84; M. Weinfeld, "The Worship of Molech," etc., UF, 4 (1972), 133–54 (criticized by M. Smith, JAOS, 95 [1975]:477–79). For Aramaean influence on Israel's religion, see A. Malamat in D. J. Wiseman, ed., *Peoples of Old Testament Times*, Oxford, 1973, 148–49.

64. The relation on the prose account of the dynastic oracle in 2 Samuel 7 to the poem in Psalm 89 is studied in N. M. Sarna, "Psalm 89: A Study in Inner Biblical Exegesis," in A. Altmann, ed., *Biblical and Other Studies*, Cambridge, Mass., 1963, 29–46. Several passages make the election of the Davidides conditional upon their observance of the covenant laws; e.g., 1 Kings 2:2–4; 8:25; 9:6. The relation of this to the unconditional promise is discussed by A. Šanda, *Die Bücher der Könige*, I, Münster, 1911:224, and M. Weinfeld, "The Covenant of Grant in the OT and in the Ancient Near East," JAOS, 90 (1970):189–96.

65. The contrasting ideologies of royal election in north and south are discussed by A. Alt. *Essays on OT History and Religion* (transl. by R. A. Wilson), Oxford 1966, 239–60. While the basis for later prophetic opposition to the Omrides is clear enough (see below), the reasons for the opposition ascribed to Ahijah (1 Kings 14:9) and Jehu son of Hanani (16:2) seem to reflect the Judahite bias against Jeroboam's calves, rather than the true reason that moved these northern prophets to reject their dynasties (assuming, of course, that the author of Kings correctly depicts them as so doing). Noth conjectures that the northern prophets opposed supplanting Jerusalem, the seat of the ark (see *The Laws in the Pentateuch*, translation, R. Ap-Thomas), Philadelphia, 1967, 136–37).

66. Cf. S. Moscati, *The Face of the Ancient Orient*, Garden City, 1962, 221: ". . . the

Aramaean pantheon has one characteristic feature–none the less significant for being negative–namely, the absence of any god that can definitely be considered as its own."

67. The argument for the separation of Hosea 1–3 from the rest of the book is set forth in Kaufmann, *Tol'dot*, III:93–107 (E, 368–71); further in H. L. Ginsberg, "Hosea, book of," EncJud, VIII, cols. 1010–1017. On the role of the desert, cf. S. Talmon, "The Desert Motif," etc., in A. Altmann, ed., *Biblical Motifs*, Cambridge, Mass., 1966, 50–2.

68. M. Pope, "Rechab," IDB, IV:14–6.

69. J. Gray, in his commentary to Kings, London, 1963, 523f., identifies three sets of relationships in this covenant: God—king, God—people, and people—king. See G. Fohrer, "Der Vertrag zwischen König und Volk in Israel," ZAW, 71 (1959):1–22.

70. The positive and negative features of northern prophecy are assessed in W. Eichrodt, *Theology of the Old Testament*, I, London, 1961, 328–38.

71. On early prophetic eschatology, see Kaufmann, *Tol'dot*, II:249–58, 287–93. (E, 279–82).

72. Verse 6 notes that an asherah stood in Samaria during the reign of Jehoahaz son of Jehu. That neither Jehu nor Elisha took offense at this "heathen symbol" (as it is generally regarded), makes one suspect that its "heathenness" was of the same order as the calves of Jeroboam, to which no northern zealot took exception before Hosea. Deuteronomy 16:21, "You must not plant an asherah—any tree—beside the altar of YHWH your God which you shall make," reads like an equation of all sacred trees, perfectly legitimate through most of Israelite history (cf. Gen. 21:33; Josh. 24:26), with the symbol of the pagan goddess Asherah. This agrees with Deuteronomy's novel, wholesale disqualification of many older usages, which in neo-Assyrian times (see ahead) were associated by puritans with heathen worship (e.g., pillars and *bāmōt*). The deuteronomistic author of Kings shared this evaluation and anachronistically condemned earlier ages for committing those late-born sins. Jehoahaz' asherah probably belongs to this class of sin. Kings, looking for causes of trouble, found one in the sacred tree of Samaria, which he denigratingly (like Deuteronomy) calls an asherah.

73. Kaufmann, *Tol'dot*, III:56–92 (E, 363–68); on the prophetic experience of Amos and his conception of God, see A. J. Heschel, *The Prophets*, New York, 1962, 27–38.

74. Kaufmann, ibid., 107–46 (E 372–77); H. L. Ginsberg, EncJud, VIII, cols. 1017–1022.

75. Kaufmann, ibid, 147–256 (E 378–95); on the prophecies about the nations and on Assyria, see N. K. Gottwald, *All the Kingdoms of the Earth*, New York, 1964, 147–208; for the interweaving of the story of the Assyrian invasion with Isaiah's specific prophecies about it, see B. S. Childs, *Isaiah and the Assyrian Crisis*, London, 1967; see also H. L Ginsberg, "Isaiah in the Light of History," CJ, 22 (1967):1–18, and idem., EncJud, IX:cols 49–60.

76. On the asherah, see note 72, above.

77. Some scholars connect Hezekiah's reforms with his rebellion, as though political subjection to Assyria implied some form of religious subjection as well; e.g., H. H. Rowley, *Men of God*, London, 1963, 126–32; but Cogan (above, n. 63) has shown the error of his view with respect to Judah (ibid., 72–7). The dismantling and profane reuse of the Beersheba stone altar in the eighth century may have been because of Hezekiah's reform (so Aharoni; see above, n. 11).

78. This interpretation of the religio-cultural situation of the reigns of Manasseh and Amon is developed by Cogan, ibid., 65–96. An argument along similar lines was made earlier, by L. E. Fuller, *The Historical and Religious Significance of the Reign of Manasseh*, Leipzig, 1912.

79. For the reconstruction of events, see M. Weinfeld, "Josiah," EncJud, IX:cols. 290–92, and next note.

80. The relation of Deuteronomy to Josiah's reform is reviewed in E. W. Nicholson, *Deuteronomy and Tradition*, Oxford, 1967, 1–12.

81. For a comprehensive survey of opinion on the northern origin of Deuteronomy, see H. Moler-Kodesh, "The Problem of the Northern Sources of Deuteronomy" (Hebrew), *Beth Mikra* 42 (1970):264–97. The theory was first put forward by A. Alt, "Die Heimat des Deuteronomiums," *Kleine Schriften*, II:250–75; on connections between

Deuteronomy and Hosea, see M. Weinfeld, *Deuteronomy and the Deuteronomic School*, Oxford, 1972, 366–70; H. L. Ginsberg, EncJud, VIII:cols. 1022–1025.

82. On the historical-religious significance of Deuteronomy, see Kaufmann, *Tolᵉdot*, I:109–11 (E, 174–75); a rich, comprehensive presentation of Deuteronomic ideology and theology is found in Weinfeld (n. 81).

83. On the problem of the duration of Josiah's measures after his death, see M. Greenberg, "Prolegomenon" (op. cit., n. 4), xviii–xxiii, xxxiii, and n. 47; criticized by M. Smith, "The Veracity of Ezekiel, the Sins of Manasseh, and Jeremiah 44:18," ZAW, 17 (1975):11–6.

84. Kaufmann, *Tolᵉdot*, III:360–68 (E, 398–400).

85. Jeremiah's trial is compared with the trial of Socrates by S. D. Goitein in *'Iyyunim ba-Mikra*, Tel Aviv, 1957, 130–41.

86. The motives of Jeremiah's "Babylonian policy" have long exercised scholars: see Kaufmann, *Tolᵉdot*, III:456–59 (E, 422–24); Goitein, ibid., 142–55; A. C. Welch, *Jeremiah*, Oxford, 1955, 195–212.

87. On the antiquity of the "covenant curses," see D. R. Hillers, *Treaty Curses and the Old Testament Prophets*, Rome, 1964, 82–9.

Additional note:

The most important collection of extrabiblical Israelite data touching on the religion of the monarchic period is Jeffrey H. Tigay's *You Shall Have No Other Gods: Israelite Religion in the Light of Hebrew Inscriptions*, Harvard Semitic Studies, 31 (Atlanta: Scholars Press, 1986). Tigay concludes from his assemblage and evaluation of the evidence (personal names, letter salutations, prayer inscriptions, iconographic evidence—including the much discussed Kuntillet 'Ajrud inscriptions and drawings) that "after the United Monarchy, and perhaps even earlier, the evidence currently available makes it very difficult to suppose that many Israelites worshipped gods other than YHWH" (40). I heartily endorse J.A. Emerton's judgment (in his review in VT 37 [1987] 509f.) that the importance of Tigay's monograph for the study of Israelite religion "is out of all proportion to its modest length."

A fresh examination of the distribution and ideas of the priestly materials of the Pentateuch is Israel Knohl's *The Sanctuary of Silence: A Study of the Priestly Strata in the Pentateuch* (Jerusalem: Magnes Press, 1992 [in Hebrew]). His treatment of the festival laws is available in English, "The Priestly Torah Versus the Holiness School: Sabbath and Festivals," HUCA 58 (1987):65–117. Knohl argues that two schools of priestly ideology are represented in the Pentateuch, distinguished by the nomenclature in the title of his article. The Priestly Torah was originally esoteric; the Holiness School reached out to the people.

The arguments offered in note 42 against the concept of marriage as a covenant are subjected to judicious criticism by Elaine J. Adler in her Berkeley dissertation, *The Background for the Metaphor of Covenant as Marriage in the Hebrew Bible* (1990), 296–308. She concludes that the biblical evidence taken as a whole supports the aptness of the term "covenant" as applied to the marriage relation.

Reflections on Apocalyptic

(unpublished)

To define the apocalyptic literature of early Judaism means distinguishing it on the one hand from pre-apocalyptic and on the other from non-apocalyptic literature that was contemporary with it and with which it must have shared common elements. Typical of the difficulty in arriving at an adequate definition is the omnibus formulation of apocalyptic characteristics made by Lindblom: these are "transcendentalism, mythology, cosmological orientation, pessimistic treatment of history, dualism, division of time into periods, doctrine of two ages, playing with numbers, pseudo-ecstasy, artificial claims to inspiration, pseudonymity, mysteriousness."[1]

There is no doubt that, taken as a whole, apocalyptic literature displays all these features; but they are not found throughout the literature, and, more important, a number of these features are found in literature no one would call apocalyptic (e.g., rabbinic aggada; Qumran Manual of Discipline).

Undisputed apocalypses appear in the Book of Daniel, and that work in its present form cannot be earlier than the Macedonian conquest of the Near East. Another collection of undisputed apocalypses, 1 Enoch, also comes from the Greek period; its earliest portions (chs. 1–36) may antedate Daniel.[2] The state of Judaism at that time is very obscure, owing to the paucity of contemporary sources. But literature that can be dated to the preceding Persian and neo-Babylonian periods allows us to see what trends and notions were already present in pre-Greek times. Their presence in apocalyptic cannot, therefore, be characteristic of that genre.

1. The shock of the political collapse of Judah and the exile had affected some men with an overpowering sense of the transcendent and awful majesty of God. Ezekiel expressed this by his images of God enthroned above the cosmic creatures in resplendent, fiery glory. The Second Isaiah depicts this transcendence in terms of the creator God.

2. The exaltation of God entailed an increase in his entourage: the greater the king, the larger his suite and the more his use of mediaries. Angelic beings appear as regular features of prophetic visions: In Ezekiel, the four creatures bearing God, the six destroyers, the heavenly scribe, the angelic guide through the future Jerusalem; Zechariah regularly has an angelic medium in his visions. For the Chronicler, Satan is a fixed member of the divine court. Angelology thus appeared before the impact of Persian ideas can have been a serious factor, and as an internal Jewish development.

3. The exile and its disappointing aftermath promoted a decidedly pessimistic view of the possibilities of human effectiveness in history. Both Jeremiah and Ezekiel despaired of an unaided human's ability to be reconciled with God. Both look to a divinely effected alteration in human nature to assure the future happiness of Israel. Only the recreation of humans with a new heart and spirit can put an end to the rebelliousness that caused the catastrophe. Ezekiel speaks too of a covenant with nature to ensure the fertility of the land; Zechariah describes drastic topographical changes in Palestine; the Second (Third, or later) Isaiah coined the terms "a new heaven and a new earth" (65:17) for this conception.

4. As for the process that would issue in the golden age, from the time of the First Isaiah, at least, it was postulated that only the direct intervention of God could break the power of the heathen and reconstitute the national integrity of Israel. Assyria would fall by "a sword not of humans" (Isa. 31:8); Gog and his horde would be routed in a God-sent panic (Ezek. 38–39); the Persian empire would go under in earthwide convulsions (Haggai). The prevailing mood was of passive expectancy. In the face of the overwhelming power of empires the Jews could only look to God for the restoration of their fortunes. And in the face of that power, the restoration necessarily had to be envisioned as the product of upheavals, massacres, and the ruin of the heathen empire.

5. The notion that events occur according to a predetermined divine plan is the basis of the First Isaiah's political prophecies (e.g., Isa. 14:26). That the heathen empires had a fixed term was specified by Jeremiah (who set Babylon's at seventy years) and Ezekiel (who implicitly set it at forty). The apocalyptic terms "season" (*mo'ed*), and "term" (*qeṣ*) are creations of Habakkuk. This notion, however, is much older than the classical prophets. Israelite tradition had it that father Abraham was informed in a vision that his descendants would have to wait 400 years before they could take possession of the promised land (Gen. 15:12–16).

6. Revelation of the distant future to an ancient worthy in an ecstatic vision occurs exceptionally in that famous covenant ceremony. Abraham

asks to *know* that his descendants will inherit the land; God answers in a trance vision, sketching the future of Abraham's progeny for some hundreds of years and setting a term to their landlessness. The passage is the closest approach to apocalypse that we have in pre-apocalyptic literature. It is essential that the revelation comes as an answer to a request to know, and that it is not given to be proclaimed as a public message (as prophecies were) but to inform an individual privately.

7. Transportation to distant places is found as a standing feature of Ezekiel's visions. This is an elaboration of a feature ascribed to Elijah, whose mysterious movements gave rise to the belief that he was moved from place to place by the wind (1 Kings 18:12; 2 Kings 2:16). With Ezekiel, the transportation was sometimes in the body (Ezek. 3:12–14), sometimes in vision only (8:1–3; 11:24; 40:1–2). The places to which he was taken were all on earth.

8. Symbolic visions are more frequent and more elaborate in Ezekiel and Zechariah than elsewhere, for no obvious reason. It has been supposed that their baroqueness is peculiarly Babylonian, inspired by the bizarre mixed creatures found sculpted at Babylonian temples and palaces.[3]

Thus, prior to the first undisputedly apocalyptic writings the notions found in them had already formed a part of Israel's sacred traditions: the exalted throne-majesty of God, the multiplication of angelic beings and their use as mediaries; a pessimistic view of human effectiveness, the catastrophic view of the onset of the end-time, a new creation of man and earth, private revelation in a trance, symbolic visions, transportation in spirit. None of these, singly or taken together, are distinctively apocalyptic.

What, then, are the features whose appearance identifies a writing as apocalyptic? Let us consider Daniel and Enoch.

The really new feature of Daniel's visions is what has been called by Kaufmann "perspective vision," that is, a view of a succession of ages, of time planes.[4] The great statue made out of diverse materials, the four beasts, the ram and the buck, the message of the shining angel all disclose the secret of history in stages, usually starting from the age of Daniel and ending with the kingdom of heaven. This differs from all the prophecies concerning the golden age in earlier literature in which there is only the present and the next age that terminates it.

In the Enoch literature a second novel feature is encountered: visionary tours in extraterrestrial regions—heaven and hell, the divine palace, the sources of the winds, the place of reward of the righteous and punishment of the wicked, the storehouse of souls. There is nothing like it in earlier prophecy.

The common denominator of both these new features is, as might have been expected, revelation (Gr. *apokalypsis*) of hidden things. The visionaries are moved by a consuming desire to know what no man can know naturally: the secrets of time, space, and God's management of the political and physical world. Correspondingly God is described in Daniel as "the revealer of things deep and secret, he knows what is in the darkness, and with him dwells the light" (2:22), and Daniel is called a man "equal to any secret" (4:6). Typical of apocalyptic is Enoch's answer to his guide's question as to "why he wishes to learn the truth": "I wish to know about everything" (1 Enoch 25:2).

The fact that Daniel contains only historical revelations while Enoch contains both historical and cosmic ones suggests an unwillingness of the canonizers to publish cosmic revelations. It does not necessarily follow that these two studies were pursued separately—indeed, it is most natural to suppose that the combination of inquiry about time and space found in Enoch is original and reflects an as yet undifferentiated body of esoterica. The historical allusions in the time apocalypses rather clearly reflect the Greek period. In the figure of the four kingdoms an originally Persian idea expressing hostility to the Greeks was taken over by the Jews (as first argued by Swain in 1940).[5] Whether the space apocalypses also made their first appearance at this time is impossible to say. From the onesidedness of the canonical Daniel literature, it appears that from the first such theosophic speculations were regarded by some as unfit for publication. In the Slavonic (=2) Enoch, ignorance (of human nature) is equated with sin (30:16).[6] It is clear that here we are bordering on gnosticism—the peculiarly Jewish form of which took the form of speculation on the divine palaces (*hekalot, maʿaśe merkaba*).

Having defined apocalyptic by its distinctive features—revelatory tours in time and space—and implicitly denied the aptness of this appellation to any literature that lacks these features,[7] I turn to the question of pseudonymity. Why is the hero of every apocalypse an ancient worthy?

It is generally assumed that this is connected with the cessation of prophecy in Israel. But the Jewish phenomena cannot be detached from the orientation toward the past of all the native cultures of the Near East under Persian and Hellenistic rule. In Egypt this orientation had set it even earlier, under the Saite dynasty of the seventh century, and Egypt's meticulous preservation of ancient rites and values impressed Herodotus in the fifth century. Resistance to foreign domination and longing for independence expressed itself in Egypt, as in Israel, through pseudonymous prophecies. The Demotic Chronicle, from Ptolemaic times, represents itself as interpreting oracles from the Persian age—oracles that probably referred to much earlier events, but which went on to speak of the Greeks and, in all likelihood, of the return of native rulers. Under the Ptolemaic or Roman domination, a prophecy made by a lamb living at the time of King Bocchoris (8th c. B.C.E.) was published, predicting troubles for Egypt and, after 900 years, a glorious restoration. "The Apology of the Potter to King Amenophis" preserved a prediction of future calamities under the Greeks. It refers to the city of Alexandria ("it shall be a place where fishermen dry their nets") and ends with a golden age.[8] Another form of resistance to foreigners was the cultivation of legends about ancient heroes: Rameses and Sesostris were favorites. Persian resistance expressed itself, among other ways, in the four kingdom theory, in an oracle (surviving in a later, Roman form) entitled the oracle of Hystaspes—the ancient king who was converted by Zarathustra. Babylonian scholars cultivated their ancient religion and recopied their ancient texts through the Persian and Seleucid periods. Around 275 B.C.E. the priest Berossos published, in Greek, a history of Babylonia and Assyria from creation to his day for the greater glory of his culture. A Nebuchadnezzar legend and a Semiramis legend grew up, competing first with Persian, then with Greek heroes.[9]

Throughout the subjugated Near East, the spirit of the age among the bearers of native cultures was thus deeply conservative and imitative of the past. Incessant warfare had enervated civilizations, and subject peoples were compelled to look to their past for sources of national pride. In Israel the book of Chronicles exemplifies this looking-backward orientation in its exaltation of the monarchy, prophecy, and priesthood of pre-exilic times. There is a strong undertone of messianic yearning in this exaltation, as in the hero-making of past monarchs elsewhere in the Orient. Authority resided in ancient books, in earlier revelations.

It is worth noting, in passing, that contemporary Greek philosophy also displays something of this mood, and with similar literary results. Of Hellenistic philosophy G. F. Moore writes:

Characteristic . . . is the place which the idea of revelation takes in these systems. In the schools the frequent appeal to the authority of the founders tended to a principle of authority which made their teaching decisive; the later Platonists, for example, cite Plato as a canon of truth, even in the act of putting their own ideas into his words by sophistical interpretation. In none of the schools was this more natural than to the Pythagoreans, who had ancient precedent for their deference to the *ipse dixit* of the master. So far one might see in this only a consequence of the decline of originality and intellectual independence. But we must recognize another factor: philosophy had undertaken not only to explain the universe, but to save men's souls . . . Scepticism had thoroughly undermined confidence in the ability of reason to know anything for certain beyond the limits of individual experience . . . On the other hand, the craving for intellectual certitude which scepticism cannot extirpate was reinforced by the demand for religious assurance that the way of salvation in which men are invited to adventure their souls really leads to the goal. What authority but revelation can give this certitude or this assurance. The composite Neopythagorean doctrine was—in all good faith, doubtless—ascribed in its totality to Pythagoras; and the truth Pythagoras taught to men he received from a higher source. In the absence of any authentic old Pythagorean literature, the field was free for apocryphal scriptures under the name of the founder or of his early followers, and a prolific crop of such was produced. Lives of Pythagoras, in which he was represented as the ideal wise man, inspired teacher, and worker of wonders, were also written . . . The wise man . . . now becomes the embodiment of all wisdom and virtue in the person of a Pythagoras or a Plato. Not only was the incontestable verity of revelation accorded to the teachings of these masters, but they themselves were the objects of a religious reverence. Even the Jew, Philo, can speak of the "divine" Plato. Their words carry, in effect, the authority of a supreme personality as well as of inspired scripture.[10]

The key idea for the mood of the times is diffidence, the undermining of spiritual self-confidence. That is why authority required a revealed source, and, equally important, had to come from the past, from the time when God and men were closer. Hence, apocalypses of this age necessarily take the form of ancient books containing inspired predictions about current events. Their literary rather than oral form (the form of pre-exilic prophecy) was dictated by the need of accounting for their survival over the ages.

In Second Temple Judaism, the cessation of prophecy, the predominance of the Torah, and the rise of pseudonymous literature all stem from the same root.[11]

At least since the Josianic reform in Judah, spokesmen of religion taught that observing God's norms as they were found in the Torah of Moses was essential to national well-being. Ezekiel, Jeremiah, and the redactors of Kings are suffused with the language and ideas of major components of the Mosaic Torah. The fall and exile gave monumental proof of the validity of their teachings. The Jews, by and large, accepted the exile as punishment for their failure to keep the covenant as embodied in the Torah. Accordingly, when a measure of national autonomy was renewed under the aegis of Persia, we find a determination on the part of the returnees from Babylonia to do the right thing. In that spirit the reforms of Ezra and Nehemiah were carried out, and the community solemnly pledged itself to a new covenant on the Torah. The Chronicler expresses the spirit of the reformed community in his historiography: as he depicts it, the pre-exilic age was under the rule of the Torah; prophets called for its observance, pious kings observed it; calamity came as the result of disobedience, flagrant and prolonged.

The extent of Torah observance during the Persian and early Hellenistic periods is very hard to gauge. The meager evidence from Palestinian and Greek (Alexandrian) sources indicates that the main religious precepts were kept. Esther, Daniel, Ben-Sira, papyri, Aristeas all show an ethnic community distinguished by a monotheistic religion (the issue of apostasy to foreign gods is dead), peculiar observances— Sabbath, circumcision, food taboos (gradually relaxed in upper social circles)—and institutions (nonsacrificial worship, courts of law). The Persian policy of recognizing and supporting the internal authority of the Torah remained in force under Ptolemaic and Seleucid rulers till the time of Antiochus IV. Everything points to a national mood in which the lesson of the past was taken to heart, and the rule of life was based on the secure foundation of the Mosaic revelation and the admonitions of the ancient prophets.

The great paradox was that precisely during the time when the authority of God's revealed words in Israel was greatest, the sense of the hand of God manifest in national life seems to have been at its lowest ebb. The voice of prophecy, interpreting current events from the standpoint of God's will, and the writing of history as an edifying teaching both peter out. Former students of this phenomenon related the two facts causally: the predominance of the Torah throttled free prophecy. But that is a conflict of which the ancient Israelites living under the Torah were apparently unaware: Classical prophecy flourished for as long *after* the promulgation of Deuteronomy as the rule of national life as *before* that promulgation. Ezekiel and the post-exilic prophets felt no conflict between covenant law and prophecy. And the Chronicler, who writes the history of the pre-exilic age as though it were wholly under the Torah, fills his pages with prophets and oracles, showing that for him, at any rate, the rule of the Torah was fertile soil for the flourishing of prophecy. How then, is the cessation of prophecy in Second Temple times to be explained? It was an aspect of the religious diffidence of the age.

The dedication of the post-exilic community to the Torah was part of a great drama of redemption that was foretold by pre-exilic prophets, felt to be under way by the Second Isaiah, and still believed to be close to consummation for nearly a century thereafter. Israel would return to God and he, in turn, would make a new heaven and a new earth and restore Israel to glory. In the rebuilding of the Temple the Restoration community showed its readiness to do its part; Haggai, Zechariah, and Malachi show what it expected from God. These last prophets are still awaiting the imminent intervention of God, and still blaming the faults of the Jews for its delay. The pledge of allegiance to the Torah taken by the whole community under Nehemiah was the climax of the human effort for redemption. But where was God?

Such a pitch of expectation could not be indefinitely maintained. When decades passed and the glory did not come, it could only be concluded that the age was not worthy, that God's favor had not yet been won, that the dedication to God was not yet sufficient. This at once intensified preoccupation with the Torah and undermined the confidence in the imminence of divine action that had always been an axiom of prophecy. Expectation of the end had been overstrung, and with its ebbing, the prophecy that both fed it and lived on it, ebbed and died. With a sure instinct for the interdependence of the two, Jewish belief held that when the end-time approached, prophecy would be renewed. Every messianic movement in Judaism has been signalled by an upsurge of prophetic manifestations.

In the meanwhile, the religious leaders of Judaism labored to consolidate and conserve, interpret and reapply, and, in so doing, created the social and religious institutions that made the Jews a distinctive, unassimilable entity in the Hellenistic world.

Now, so long as there were no great crises, national life could go on quietly in pious low-keyed expectation of an ultimate redemption. But when the Seleucid administration, with the cooperation of the Hellenized Jewish aristocracy, set afoot the persecution of Judaism, an unprecedented situation for which the ancient revelations offered little solace called forth a new burst of religious vitality. Israel was suffering not for its apostasy, but for its loyalty to God; the apostates were thriving. Nothing in the surface meaning of the ancient prophecies made sense out of this appalling challenge to God's justice. In the conviction that all knowledge of divine things was to be found in the inspired oracles of the past, concerned men immersed themselves in anxious inquiry into their subsurface meaning. And here we note spiritual manifestations that are only beginning to be investigated, let alone understood. If classical prophecy—that is, messages from God of national importance conveyed through human messengers—had ceased, owing to God's disfavor, contact with the divine realm by saintly individuals had not. The belief of the Qumran sectarians and of the rabbis that individuals might be inspired by divine illumination clearly underlies the figure of apocalyptic visionaries. It may have developed directly out of the sort of angelic guide that we find in Zechariah. More mysterious is the manner in which the authors of apocalypses identify themselves with their pseudonyms, for it must be allowed that the authors had genuine visionary experiences that they underwent as somehow identified with an ancient worthy. It is significant that the earliest pseudonyms are Daniel and Enoch: Daniel, saintly sage and interpreter of dreams and enigmatic texts; and Enoch, who walked with God amidst the wickedness that brought on the Flood.

The pseudonymity of apocalypse must thus be taken together with the cessation of prophecy and the predominance of the Torah as an expression of the lasting trauma produced by the failure of the redemption prophecies to come true as they were naïvely understood. The golden age of God's nearness lay in the past, and the present earnestly studied its legacy from that past for clues to understanding God's will and his management of history. No present voice could speak with the authority of a past one.

H. L. Ginsberg has argued persuasively that the circle out of which the apocalypses of Daniel 10–12 emerged regarded itself in the light of the suffering servant of Isaiah.[12] This may serve us as a point of departure for a few final observations on the common opinion that apocalyptic literature was dangerously inflammatory, that it was zealotic and fomented rebellion, and for that reason was suppressed by post–Bar Kochba Judaism.

The fact is that Judaism harbored apocalyptic, both the cosmic and the historical, at least down to the period of the Crusades.[13] The repeated deprecation of historical apocalyptic speculation stemmed not from its inflammatory but its depressive effect: the dashing of messianic expectations inevitably led to despair and crises of faith. Cosmic apocalypses flourished through the first millennium of the Christian era and merged into the mainstream of Jewish mysticism. It was an esoteric doctrine rather than a suppressed one. But these matters go beyond our present concern. What is the evidence that the early apocalypses were inflammatory?

D. S. Russel epitomizes the apocalyptic view of how the end will come thus: "The transformation . . . is not evolutionary but cataclysmic," and "It is brought about not by human or historical (i.e., political and military) forces, but by supernatural powers."[14] The duty of the righteous before the end-time is to hold fast to their righteousness in the face of universal corruption and wait for God to change the world. Daniel, referring apparently to the Maccabean militants, belittles them as "a small help" (11:34); he looks only to God for deliverance. Happily, we have a representative of the other view in the books of the Maccabees, from which we can gather the ideology of the militants. As might be expected, it is anything but passive. Mattathias slays the Jew who would make a pagan sacrifice, "thus showing his zeal for the law, just as Phineas had done in the case of Zimri, son of Salu" (1 Macc. 2:27). On his deathbed he invokes the models not only of the saintly Abraham, Joseph, and Daniel for his sons, but also of Phineas "our father," Joshua, David, and Elijah, "who was taken to heaven because he was exceeding zealous for the Law" (2:49–68). The speeches of Judah are in the idiom of David and Jonathan (3:18–22), and even his final words speak only of "a manful death for our brethren's sake so as not to leave a cause of reproach against our glory" (9:10). Not a word is said of messianic hopes as a motive of Hasmonean activism. Nothing could be more divergent than the motives and expectations of the apocalyptist and the Maccabean rebels.

Nor is there clear evidence associating apocalyptic literature with later manifestations of zealotry. A clear distinction is made by Josephus in his account of the immediate antecedents of the Jewish war between the *sicarii* activists, and the "villains, with purer hands but more impious intentions, who no less than the assassins ruined the peace of the city... Under pretense of divine inspiration.... they persuaded the multitude to act like madmen, and led them out into the desert under the belief that God would there give them tokens of deliverance" (War II:13.4) (cf. the figure of Theudas, Ant. XX:5.1). Activist visionaries must have existed too, and the zeal-inspired Book of Jubilees and the Qumran War Scroll may have been produced in their circle. But neither belongs to the genre of apocalyptic, and it is not useful to obscure the differences.

The essence of the activist is his conviction that it is up to him to bring about a change in his affairs. Nothing in the apocalypses is calculated to foster this notion. The character of this literature has been well sketched by Gerson Cohen:

> As in the case of Daniel of old, so too, in later apocalyptic literature, while the visionary is reassured of Divine vengeance against the Gentiles, he is no less emphatically enjoined to wait for the deliverance of God. In the meantime, he may take comfort in violent and bloody fantasies that will one day become a reality. In other words, far from inciting to riot, apocalyptic literature actually tranquilized and served as a release, a channel by means of which excess emotions were syphoned off. So it was in the case of the Dead Sea sect and the early Christians; so it was in Roman and medieval Palestine.[15]

Therein lies the ambivalence, for us, of apocalyptic. It is the necessary resort of those who have nothing to hope for from human effort. But it is at the same time an opiate for those in a situation in which something can be done. In its first appearance among Jews suffering under Antiochus, the ambivalence is fully seen: for the pious who died passively in maintaining the Torah, it was the only comfort. For the Maccabees, it was a doctrine to be believed in perhaps, but which should not be allowed to hamper finding practical solutions to present problems.

NOTES

1. J. Lindblom, *Die Jesaja-Apokalypse (Jes. 24–27)*, Lund, 1938, 101f.; quoted from H. H. Rowley, *The Relevance of Apocalyptic*, New York, 1963, p. 25, n. 2. But Lindblom himself acknowledged that the essence of apocalyptic was not conveyed by such a list; in his *Prophecy in Ancient Israel*, Philadelphia, 1962, 175, 422, he singles out as its distinctive traits "a system of secret doctrines concerning the cosmos, history, and the age to come."

2. See the summary in H. E. D. Sparks, *The Apocryphal Old Testament*, Oxford, 1984, 173–79.

3. D. S. Russell, *The Method and Message of Jewish Apocalyptic*, Philadelphia, 1964, 90.

4. Y. Kaufmann, *The Religion of Israel*, translated and abridged by M. Greenberg, Chicago, 1962, 348–49. See also his illuminating article, "Apokalyptik," in the German *Encyclopaedia Judaica*, II, Berlin, 1928, cols. 1142–72.

5. J. W. Swain, "The Theory of the Four Monarchies: Opposition History under the Roman Empire," *Classical Philology* 35 (1940):1–21.

6. God speaks: "Whereas I have come to know [Adam's] nature, he does not know his own nature. That is why ignorance is more lamentable than the sin such as it is in him to sin," translated by F. I. Andersen in J. H. Charlesworth, ed., *The Old Testament Pseudepigrapha*, I, Garden City, New York, 1983, 152.

7. Apocalyptic is properly descriptive of a literary type; to use it to describe communities or religious groups is confusing. Usually what seems to be meant by such use is a group with lively eschatological and messianic expectations–chiliasts and the like. Such expectations need not take the literary form of apocalypses; certainly the Qumran War Scroll and the New Jerusalem text, both of which are fiercely eschatological, are not apocalypses. It will be argued at the end of this paper that activist messianic movements could draw on hopes kept alive by apocalyptic, but that the viewpoint of apocalyptic was essentially passive and non-inflammatory. An "apocalyptic religious group" is then a religious group that produces apocalypses. Not every messianic or eschatology-oriented group, however, did so; hence, the label is not coextensive with groups having such an orientation.

8. C. C. McCown, "Hebrew and Egyptian Apocalyptic Literature," HTR 18 (1925):357–411.

9. See S. K. Eddy, *The King Is Dead: Studies in the Near Eastern Resistance to Hellenism, 334–31 B.C.E.*, University of Nebraska, Lincoln, 1961.

10. G. F. Moore, *History of Religions*, I, New York, 1913, 529–30.

11. See Y. Kaufmann, *History of the Religion of Israel, Vol. IV: From the Babylonian Captivity to the End of Prophecy*, translation C. W. Efroymson, New York, Jerusalem, Dallas, 1977, 449–84.

12. "The Oldest Interpretation of the Suffering Servant," VT 3 (1953):400–04.

13. S. W. Baron, *A Social and Religious History of the Jews*, 2nd ed., V, 1957:139–50; the scholarly collection of these medieval apocalypses is Yehuda Ibn Shmuel's *Midreshay Ge'ulla*, 2nd ed., Jerusalem–Tel Aviv, 5714 [1954].

14. Work cited in n. 3, 269.

15. G. D. Cohen, "Messianic Postures of Ashkenazim and Sephardim," *Leo Baeck Memorial Lecture*, 9, New York, 1967:30–31 (= G. D. Cohen, *Studies in the Variety of Rabbinic Cultures*, Philadelphia, 1991, 287).

Additional note:

This essay bears the impression of Y. Kaufmann's definition of apocalyptic literature (see n. 4). A closer relation of apocalyptic to biblical literature is argued by Itamar Gruenwald in his book, *Apocalyptic and Merkavah Mysticism* (Leiden: 1980), 3–72.

Kaufmann on the Bible:
An Appreciation
1964

On October 9, 1963, Yehezkel Kaufmann, the foremost Jewish biblicist of our time and a profound interpreter of Jewish history, died after a long illness. Though all of his life's work is suffused with a devotion to his people, his original grasp of the issues of Jewish existence exploded so many fashionable theories, his views were put forth with such detachment from party, and with such plainspokenness that few of the intellectual and academic establishment in Israel were willing to accord him his due during his lifetime. Never married, a small, ascetic, retiring man, his life was wholly given over to thought, writing, and research. To a request for a curriculum vitae he is said to have replied, "I have no biography, only a bibliography."

The biographical note on Kaufmann in the Hebrew University catalogue reads as follows:

Born Dounaievci (Russia), 1889; Yeshiva of Rabbi C. Tschernowitz; Dr. phil. Berne, 1918; senior teacher of Hebrew subjects, Reali [High] School, Haifa, 1929–49; research scholar, Bible and history of religion; recipient, Israel Prize for Jewish Studies, 1958. Hebrew Univ.: Professor, 1949; Professor Emeritus, 1957.[1]

Kaufmann's Berne dissertation was a philosophic "treatise on the sufficient reason" (*Eine Abhandlung über den Zurreichenden Grund*). Thereafter, although he made a few more contributions to philosophy, his attention focused almost exclusively upon the complex issues making up the riddle of Jewish existence through the ages.[2] His first major work, *Gola ve-Nekar* ("Exile and Alienation"), a four-volume historical-

175

sociological inquiry into Jewish history, dealt chiefly with the post-biblical and Diaspora ages, but one can already find there the germ of the thesis to be developed over the next thirty years in the monumental *Toldot ha-Emuna ha-Yisr'elit* ("History of Israelite Religion," 8 volumes, 1937–1956). Kaufmann believed the singularity of Jewish existence to be determined by the peculiar character of Judaism; but that in turn was rooted in the unique faith of the Bible. Hence, he was inevitably led back to the biblical age in his search for understanding the motives of Jewish history.

Though shy and withdrawn, Kaufmann wrote with vigor and force-fulness. His unorthodoxy (in both the traditional and critical sense), his scope (from the ancient Near East to modern social movements), and his uncompromising self-assurance combined to keep him out of Hebrew University during the best twenty years of his creative life. At the age of sixty, coincident with the retirement of M. Z. Segal in 1949, Kaufmann was suddenly catapulted into a professorship of Bible at the university, which he then held for eight years before retiring. National recognition belatedly followed: the Bialik prize in 1956, the Israel prize in 1958, and in 1961 the highest cultural award, the Bublik prize. It was characteristic of the man that he did not appear at the award-giving ceremonies (once when it was suggested that the ceremony be held at his home, he replied, "If you come for that I will leave for Tiberias"). It was equally characteristic of the award-givers that in the very citation of the Bublik award they expressed reservations about Kaufmann's conclusions in the *Toldot*—for which the award was bestowed (and which, incidentally, was misnamed in the citation).

As time passed, Kaufmann's patience with what he considered the vagaries of biblical criticism grew shorter and shorter. In his final works, the commentaries to Joshua and Judges, his commentatorial virtuosity is spiced with a large dose of pungent criticism and denunciation of the ways of contemporary (especially European) scholarship. In assessing the man's contribution such fulminations must be discounted, but they do help to account for the fact that it took so long to accord him the recognition he richly deserved.

Kaufmann's contribution makes vividly clear how and to what extent the Bible differed from the rest of ancient religious literature, and hence, why its impact on civilization was so much greater. So many parallels between biblical thought and its environment can be shown that the radically different fate of Israel and its religion have become something of an enigma. If, as Wellhausen maintained, "Moab, Ammon, and Edom, Israel's nearest kinsfolk and neighbors, were monotheists in precisely the same sense in which Israel itself was"[3] how account for their divergent destinies? Many attempts, of course, have been made to define the difference: the prophetic doctrine of ethical monotheism; the idea of the covenant; the historical rather than mythological nature of biblical religion. However, not one of these adequately accounts for the others, let alone the rest of the differentia. The ethical emphasis neither requires nor is required by the covenantal idea; the covenantal idea is not necessarily anti-mythological or monotheistic. Zoroastrianism was highly ethical–and polytheistic; the Sumerians knew the concept of a covenant between a deity and a king or state; Hittites and Mesopotamians saw theological significance in history. What was it that made for the combination of these and other elements into the unique configuration of biblical thought?

Kaufmann answers: a new intuition of the meaning of reality based on the revolutionary idea that the ground of all is a single Divine Will, transcendent–above fate and magic, outside the continuum of creation–who ordained the world order and revealed his will to men. Breaking the grip of necessity that encloses all pagan views of the world, liberating divinity from fatality, this new intuition infused everything with a radically new meaning. Old forms were largely retained–hence, the many formal parallels between biblical and nonbiblical religion; but they were filled with such new content that (as Kaufmann argues) the bearers of biblical religion no longer understood the pagan conceptions that underlay the practices of their neighbors.

Sacrifice, for example, was no longer regarded as a need of the gods (or God)–a mysterious-magical participation in and maintenance of the cosmic order. It became instead a token of obeisance, a ritual of homage given to men by the grace of God. That is why the prophets could threaten Israel with a stoppage of the cult as a divine punishment for their sin–in utter contrast to pagans who may threaten to stop serving their gods if they fail them. How far biblical writers were from pagan conceptions can be seen in the story of the Philistine "guilt offering" (1 Sam. 5–6). Seeking to rid themselves of a plague of tumors and mice that followed the captured Ark as it moved from town to town, the Philistines make golden images of tumors and mice and, loading them with the Ark on a wagon, send them back to Israelite territory. The modern student recognizes in this a familiar sympathetic magic rite of expulsion; the biblical writer, however, regards the golden images as a guilt offering to God–the only means he knew of getting relief from a plague.

This freedom of the deity from fate and necessity has important consequences in the moral sphere. Human freedom acquires a ground in the ultimate reality–in God. This lends meaning to human choices and justifies human responsibility. A new kind of cosmic drama comes into being, whose protagonists are God and humans, and whose motive is the tension between the free wills of the two. History displaces myth as the tale of significant events.

But God is not only the author of the material world; he authors the world of values as well. Law and morality both stem from the will of God, unlike the pagan conception in which these are impersonal, primordial elements of the universe, which of themselves do not address or make demands upon persons. The biblical God communicates laws and moral injunctions–expressions of his will–to people directly through revelation. Such an address of one will to another is the only way in which this God can be conceived as relating himself to humans. Since there is no genetic connection, no substantial continuity between God and humans, relationships based on such a connection are precluded. Only the bond created by the meeting of wills remains; therefore, the relation of covenant between God and humans is the only one to which the biblical idea of God was amenable. The covenant idea, argues Kaufmann, was the outcome, not the condition of the distinctive biblical idea of God.

In a comparative morphology that embraces the major manifestations of religious thought, Kaufmann argues with a wealth of detail the distinctiveness of biblical conceptions of cosmogony, cultic ordinances, magic, divination and prophecy, sin and atonement. He shows all of them have been transmuted by the monotheistic idea. Moreover, Kaufmann insists, the non-pagan character of biblical religion is visible in every stratum of the Bible. Hence, he concludes, it is true of every stage of Israel's religion. From its beginning it parted ways with the mythological polytheism of the environment. Living in relative isolation from its neighbors, Israel was able to preserve the distinctive character of its religion throughout the pre-exilic period.

This theory necessitates the detailed arguing of the following major premises:

1. The sources of the Pentateuch, in which the monotheistic viewpoint is generally conceded by all hands, are pre-exilic—including and especially the Priestly Code. Indeed, they belong to a stage of development prior to literary prophecy. Thus, the documents of the earliest stage of Israelite religion already exhibit its essential features.

2. The conditions of the Conquest and Settlement enabled Israel to live relatively insulated from contact with the Canaanites. Kaufmann regarded this as such a crucial matter that instead of completing his *Toldot* he devoted the last ten years of his life to a study of the books of Joshua and Judges.[4]

> I see [he wrote me in 1960] that you too are unhappy about my preoc-
> cupation with commenting these books. Your view is the same as that
> of all my good friends, but I cannot agree.... These books recount the
> beginnings of the people of Israel, and so their testimony is decisive for
> the beginnings of Israel's faith as well.... There are pre-monarchic
> narratives here, though biblical criticism refuses to acknowledge the
> fact, since that would demolish its position.

The generally accepted view, based in part on what seems to be
the biblical evidence, is that after the Israelites entered Canaan (the
manner of that entry being in dispute) an amalgamation of populations
occurred, with the inevitable coloration of Israelite religion by
Canaanite. Indeed, the two must at times have been hardly distin-
guishable. Kaufmann rejects this view in its entirety. He seeks to demonstrate the historicity of the representation of the invasion in the
book of Joshua as a unified attack upon Canaan, carried out with ruthless terror. The highlands of Palestine were cleared of natives, except
for a few clearly defined enclaves; only in the coastal and lowlands
could the Canaanites hold out for a time owing to their superior chariotry. There was no peaceful settling of Israel among the Canaanites,
and hence no basis for a syncresis of their religions.

3. This brings us to the most radical and fundamental part of
Kaufmann's argument: the insistence that pre-exilic Israel was not a
pagan people; that the biblical indictment of Israel as a backsliding,
apostate, "stiffnecked" people is tendentious and exaggerated.

For Kaufmann is not content with arguing the monotheistic character of biblical literature. In his view, that literature is a faithful reflection of the religion of the folk as well. Kaufmann has felt with peculiar
sensibility the popular nature of biblical religion. It does not have the
character of an esoteric doctrine held by a spiritual elite. This was a
folk religion; its leaders sprang from the folk, addressed themselves to
the folk, and built their teachings upon the faith of the folk. Israel's
prophets introduced no new God, taught no new theology or history.
They shared with the folk the same paradigmatic stories about the
mighty acts of God in Israel and elsewhere. To be sure, they deduced
consequences from this God-belief with a consistency and rigor that
the folk could not follow, but this cannot obscure the fundamental
unity of their faith with that of the folk.

Another line of argument takes its departure from the consistent misrepresentation of pagan religion as fetishism. A remarkable fact which
Kaufmann never tires of reiterating is that throughout the Bible,
pagan worship is depicted as the adoration of wood and stone, gold

and silver, of gods that see not and hear not and speak not and eat not. Not a word is said about the living gods and goddesses of which the idols (as we know) were but symbols. The biblical writers seem ignorant of the world of mythology that described the lives and actions of these living gods. To real pagans such jeering at the images would have been wholly irrelevant. Kaufmann accounts for this strange misrepresentation by assuming that Israel was no longer aware of the real nature of paganism. The belief they ascribe to the pagans was, in fact, nothing else than the vestigial idolatry that survived in Israel after genuine mythological polytheism had died—a fetishistic veneration of charmed objects; a superstitious, unofficial, private cult of figurines without benefit of clergy and temple. It was not a culturally productive part of national life at all.

Kaufmann allows that there were occurrences of genuine pagan beliefs. But these turn out, upon examination, to have been importations, not a native product: such phenomena as the chapels built by Solomon for his foreign wives outside of Jerusalem, or the company of Baal prophets and priests that Jezebel brought with her from Tyre to Samaria, or the unique case of Manasseh, the servile vassal of Assyria who paganized Judah forcibly, "filling Jerusalem with blood from one end to the other." It is typical and indicative of the foreignness of these phenomena that they come and go in bloody strife. And what further differentiates them from Israel's vestigial idolatry is their cultic accoutrements: these gods have sanctuaries, priests, and prophets.

For Kaufmann, then, what the Bible calls idolatry is just that: the worship of images, fetishes, nothing more. This mythless, magical adoration of images was indeed practiced by the vulgar throughout the pre-exilic age, and beyond it (cf. 2 Macc. 12:40ff.). Essentially it posed no rival to Israel's God; nonetheless, the zealots of YHWH regarded it as apostasy, and branded it as vicious folly.

Again, the biblical writers brand as idolatrous customs belonging to earlier stages of Israelite religion—customs in themselves not essentially polytheistic—that were later outlawed, e.g., the use of sacred commemorative pillars in the cult of YHWH. To interpret idolatry as "the way of the nations roundabout Israel" as we know it to have been rather than as it is depicted in the Bible itself is an egregious error. The gentile cults that the Bible attributes to Israel are utterly different from the mythological polytheism we know gentile religion to have been from its own sources. Gentile religion according to the Bible is fetishism; that, argues Kaufmann, is but a projection of Israel's own peculiar idolatry on its neighbors. Pagan beliefs had died so long before that the earliest records of Israel already misunderstand them.

The currently regnant opinion that pre-exilic Israel was ridden through with pagan beliefs makes Israel's survival through the Babylonian Exile and its restoration a great riddle. Had Israel worshiped the pagan gods while in its homeland, what reason had it to abandon them in favor of YHWH, whose temple lay in ruins and whose king and army had fallen, when it went into exile? If with virtually no trace of struggle the exiled folk accepted the prophetic interpretation of the exile as punishment for violating the covenant (though, as Jeremiah 44 shows, an alternative pagan interpretation was available to a handful of Judeans); if in Persian times tens of thousands returned to Judea to rebuild it (with the support of those who remained behind)–this can mean only that those who went into exile were, in their vast bulk, worshipers of YHWH.

Kaufmann thus has grave reservations regarding the validity of the biblical denunciation of Israel's apostasy. For he regards this denunciation as flowing from a theological postulate that tended to distort reality: the need of theodicy. Justification of God's judgment upon Israel is a leading motif of biblical thought. The whole historical narrative serves as an explanation for the failure of God's covenant with Israel. In accord with biblical doctrine, that failure must be blamed on human dereliction—hence, the necessity of amassing an overwhelming, decisive indictment against Israel which would leave no doubt about the justice of its fate. This led, Kaufmann argues, to the generalization of guilt from the few to the many; to an exaggeration, and even an invention of guilt. And the guilt had to be idolatry, for that was the one national sin that would entail exile according to the oldest, most widely accepted view of the terms of the covenant. Whereas in other matters the theological postulates of the Bible tend to bolster our confidence in the record (e.g., the absence of self-glorification derived from the insistence that the power of God is behind all success), here a postulate acts to distort it. Israel's apostasy is a need of theodicy, hence its assertion cannot be taken at face value.

Criticism of Kaufmann's work since it has come to the attention of Western scholars[5] has focused upon his sharp differentiation of Israelite religion from paganism on the one hand, and his "cavalier," "arbitrary" rejection of the biblical indictment of Israel's idolatry on the other. The two amount to the same thing. For the tendency of modern biblical scholarship is to assimilate the phenomenon of Israel to the rest of the ancient Near East. Leaning on analogy, elements of Israelite religion are interpreted as similar in meaning to parallels elsewhere. What Kaufmann takes to be fossils of pre-Israelite conceptions embedded in a later context, and requiring interpretation in the light of that context, others take to be clues to an earlier stage of Israel's religion itself. Certain Psalms call the king the "son of God": Kaufmann insists that this cliché of Near Eastern court style must be qualified on every side by the absence elsewhere of any trace of deification of kings in Israel. Others, however, consider such a phrase to be a clue to an attitude toward kings that has otherwise been obscured by later editing of the Bible. Kaufmann, they say, here and in similar cases, bases his views on the weakest of foundations: an argument from silence. To this Kaufmann replies: silence here is eloquent, for if such pagan usages really obtained, the biblical authors, intent as they were upon scraping together every bit of sin to damn Israel, would never have omitted it!

There is a serious methodological issue at stake here. How is one to interpret fossils in religion? No scholar will deny that biblical religion, like all religions, shows stratification. The question is whether such stratification betrays stages in the history of biblical religion, or, since it is characteristic of religion to conserve the old alongside the new, and since Israelite religion came into being late, stratification here may not simply be the effect of incorporating older bodies whole into the new Israelite context–with the new determining (for the Israelite) the meaning of the old. In view of the overwhelmingly monotheistic context of biblical thought, the burden would seem to rest on those who claim that fossils are more than memorials to a stage that is prehistoric, so far as Israel is concerned.

Kaufmann's inclination to interpret the atypical in the light of the typical has resulted in the charge that he is anti-evolutionary, that he sees without perspective.

It is true that Kaufmann denies an evolution from the pagan to the Israelite conception of deity. The biblical monotheistic idea is, for him, a new intuition of reality, not an arithmetic matter of diminishing the number of the gods. Even if all the pagan gods were rolled into one, this one would still be far from the God of Israel–an utterly transcendent being, free from necessity and fate, beyond magic, etc. But in tracing the evolution of the monotheistic idea itself in Israel, Kaufmann has outdone his critics. He shows how in its early stage (Torah and histories) few of the far-reaching implications of monotheism for the cult and eschatology were realized. Not until classical prophecy, Kaufmann shows, was the primacy of morality over the cult expounded, or the ideal of the reunification of mankind envisioned. Not before apocalypse was the full-blown historical determinism incipient in the prophets manifest. Kaufmann traces the development of the idea that idolatry is counted a sin against the gentiles through Isaiah, Habakkuk, Jeremiah, and postbiblical writings. There is a beautiful chapter (on Jonah) showing the evolution of the idea of repentance.

No one has done more than Kaufmann to give a perspective vision of the unfolding of the monotheistic idea in Israel.

Why, then, does he appear to so many to be anti-evolutionary? Because of the gross misconception that the only terms in which evolution may be spoken of in biblical religion is from polytheism to monotheism. Insensitive to the record of evolution of the monotheistic idea itself, stages in it have been apportioned between polytheism and monotheism. Before the Babylonian period, for example, the idolatry of the nations was not only condoned by Israel's thinkers, but believed by them to have been divinely appointed. Habakkuk and Jeremiah are the first to open an attack on the idolatry of the nations. Accordingly it is asserted by some that Jeremiah, or the Second Isaiah, were the first *real* monotheists–as though *real* monotheism were incapable of conceiving that the one God had chosen to make Himself known only to a portion of mankind, leaving the rest in ignorance.

Kaufmann's critique of the biblical condemnation of Israel for idolatry has come under heavy fire. He himself believed that fire to have a theological animus.

> Christians are especially incapable [he wrote me in 1962] of reconciling themselves to the idea that Israel was not a sinful nation, a people weighted with iniquity; for didn't they crucify Jesus and reject Christianity? And yet . . . !

The truth of the matter is that modern chroniclers of the history of Israelite religion have not always managed to disengage their views from the judgments of faith made by the biblical authors. Thus, modern accounts of the last years of Judah regularly depict in lurid colors borrowed chiefly from Ezekiel the syncretism and debased religious practices that flourished in Jerusalem before the Fall. But this picture of Judah's spiritual decay depends on the biblical conviction that Israel's destiny was determined by a special divine providence, governed by a unique standard, the standard of covenant obligation of loyalty to God. The terrible calamity that befell Israel meant a terrible burden of guilt. The tale of that guilt included murder, fornication, bribe-taking, stealing, as well as apostasy, and it went back to the beginning of Israel's history in order to fill the measure. The modern historian who takes such catalogues of sin at face value is naïve; only a sober, nontheological criticism, balancing the evidence of Ezekiel against that of Kings, Jeremiah, and Lamentations, can hope to arrive at an approximation of the true state of affairs. Kaufmann maintains that such a sober criticism reveals that much of Israel's sin is the result of the special standard to which the prophets hold Israel, much else the result of generalization. This is not chauvinism or special pleading;

it is simply an attempt to separate empirical history from theological judgments made about history. In the field of biblical scholarship such attempts have been all too few.

A word concerning Kaufmann's "rationalistic" bias may be said here. In the Joshua commentary particularly, the rationalistic presuppositions are much in evidence as Kaufmann declares legendary one after another of the many miraculous embellishments of the Conquest narrative. Yet it is not the shallow rationalism that believes every phenomenon capable of explanation. In particular, it refuses to undertake to account for the birth of a new idea.

> The birth of an original, genial creation, of an individual or of a society, is not susceptible of "explanation." The rise of every new and original idea is a marvel, any "explanation" of which is bound to be specious and superficial. True, a historian is obligated to explain the phenomena, but this obligation involves too the determination of what he is unable to explain. . . .
>
> Why and how the new religious idea of a transcendent divine will was born in the mind of Moses cannot be known. It could not be known even if more had come down to us concerning that revelation than a beautiful and wondrous fabric of legend. Only with regard to the social-historical background of that revelation is it possible to say something on the basis of the biblical evidence. . . . (*Toldot*, II, 41, 45)

Thus, though himself not a man of faith, Kaufmann leaves room for the answer of faith to the phenomenon of the Bible.[6]

Kaufmann's great strength lay unquestionably in the philosophic-analytic sphere–in the discrimination, interrelation, and development of ideas. His strictly historical and philological contributions, though often containing valuable and suggestive insights, generally lack the same creative brilliance. Here the critic comes to the fore, exposing the weakness in the theories of his predecessors, rather than the master-builder. His historical and exegetical work is similar in that both aim to make sense out of the given data with a minimum of recourse to extrinsic sources. Kaufmann endeavors to show the given in the most plausible light, and while he does not hesitate to emend, rearrange, or excise texts when he feels it necessary, he has done more than most modern scholars to make the biblical text cohere without such recourse. His historical inquiries too contrast with those of the Alt (and even the Albright) school in their restraint. They hew much more closely to the data in their present form, showing little of the imaginative and detective-like approach advocated, say, by Collingwood in the reconstruction of history from documents.

In any historical narrative there must be a good measure of speculation [he wrote me in 1962]. But Collingwood's "detective" theory is too ingenuous. The historian cannot play the detective. Moreover, we know that lawmen investigate and judge and sentence and–fail, clearing the guilty and condemning the innocent.

If at times the guiding principle of biblical criticism appears to be "since the text says so it must be otherwise," the net effect of Kaufmann's approach is to make him (save in the case of Israel's indictment for idolatry, as explained earlier) the advocate of the text. And this tendency grew to its fullest expression in the commentaries to Judges and Joshua.

Countering this tendency at certain points was the pressure of Kaufmann's system, forcing recalcitrant material into the desired mold against the plain sense. As is true with all great synthesists, Kaufmann seemed unable to appreciate fairly data that did not fit readily into the grand pattern. Gideon's battle with Baal is a case in point. Here is one instance, at least, of an Israelite cult of a Canaanite deity that calls into question Kaufmann's insistence upon the absence of contamination of early Israelite religion by Canaanite. So Kaufmann tried, for a time, to deny the plain sense by interpreting the battle as raging over the proper epithets of YHWH (*Toldot*, II: 143). Only later, in his commentary to Judges, did he allow that "perhaps there were some Canaanite vestiges in Ophrah." More revealing is his refusal to acknowledge the presence of vicarious suffering and atonement in Isaiah 53. To my expression of disagreement with his handling of the subject he replied:

It is true, as you say, that the idea is rabbinic; but is that not a Christian influence? . . . The conception of justice and mercy is Jewish. But the conception of vicarious suffering is rooted in that of the avenging Erinyes, who require satisfaction. That is something fundamentally pagan. I cannot believe that an Israelite prophet conceived such an idea.

There were more things in ancient Israel than are dreamed of even in Kaufmann's philosophy. The biblical record is too true to life to be encompassed by a single system, be it ever so complex, ramified and marvelously integrated. The varieties of contemporary religious expression that Kaufmann convincingly pleads for, in opposition to the naïve rectilinear systems of his predecessors, were in fact more various than he was willing to admit.

Since Kaufmann's categorical language has been a stumbling block, a word of exegesis is here in order. It is part of classical Hebrew style to favor hyperbole and picturesque imagery that, if translated literally into English, must seem barbarous. A familiar Talmudic dictum, "No reliance is to be placed upon categorical statements" takes this penchant into account and to a considerable extent must be applied to Kaufmann's style for a proper reading of him. Amidst the many categorical statements one must be on the lookout for the qualification, which usually makes its appearance sooner or later, and which must be extended to all further occurrences of that statement. A crucial example is Kaufmann's oft-repeated assertion that the biblical writers are ignorant of mythological polytheism, from which he proceeds to infer that Israel's world was free from myth. In one passage the following significant qualification is made:

> A psychological consideration rebels against adopting in its extreme form the conclusion . . . that the biblical age was not only ignorant of pagan myths but also of the gentile's belief in living gods. For how is it possible that Israel, between whom and the gentiles there was always constant intercourse, and in whose midst, as it seems, zealous and loyal pagans lived, was not aware that the gentiles believed in living gods, not in fetishes alone? We do not, in fact, mean to assert that there were no circles in Israel who knew paganism better than the authors of the Bible. After all, no pagan-Israelite sources have come down to us, hence we cannot make a sweeping categorical judgment. However, the fact that in the Bible no myth concerning a foreign deity is ever mentioned or alluded to, and that the Bible was able to base its antiidolatry polemic solely on the argument of fetishism teaches us, at least, that the chief influence of foreign paganism upon Israel was not in the realm of mythology; and that in essence the struggle of the faith of YHWH against foreign cults was not a struggle against foreign myths. (I:283)

To my recollection Kaufmann never again mentions "pagan-Israelite sources"; indeed, he endeavors to minimize their presence to the vanishing point. What interests him is the mainstream of Israel's culture, and that, he is convinced, is to be found in the biblical record.

One may be convinced, after Kaufmann, that the phenomenology of biblical faith is indeed as he has portrayed it and yet be haunted by the doubt that it so wholly dominated the scene in ancient Israel. It is true that the Bible says virtually nothing about a native Israelite magic, or demonology, or illegitimate YHWH-divination—yet these all existed in postbiblical and rabbinic times. Is it not more plausible to interpret such later phenomena as survivals rather than as later importations? Perhaps the biblical silence on these matters is not as decisive as Kaufmann would have it. It is true, again, that the polemic against idolatry consistently misrepresents pagan worship as fetishism–an argument that could not convince a theologically informed pagan. But what do we know of the level of belief of the pagan, let alone the Israelite, masses? How much of a mythological basis had the vulgar religion? Again, what assurance is there that the polemic has not distorted the opposed beliefs in the light of the polemicists' own views? Consider the alternative that Elijah puts to his audience at Mount Carmel: Either YHWH or Baal, you cannot have both. That is certainly not a pagan way of looking at things, and, to the extent that the audience were informed Baal worshipers, the alternative would not have appeared a real one. The formulation is addressed to wavering *monotheists*, presupposes the monotheistic viewpoint, and chooses to disregard the pagan one. And yet it is hard to doubt that there were real pagans present. Whether Elijah actually spoke as reported or the narrator has recast his speech, a pagan viewpoint that seems likely to have been present has gone unnoticed in the biblical record; when pagans are addressed a viewpoint of the writer is ascribed to them.

It seems clear that, as has been maintained vigorously by modern criticism, ancient Israel had more than one religion. Where criticism appears to have erred is in assuming that we can form a picture of Israel's nonbiblical religion(s) from the biblical evidence. Israel's nonbiblical religion(s) can no more be known from the biblical evidence than can the religions of Israel's neighbors. For the true objects of the biblical polemic are either faults of monotheism (e.g., the overvaluation of the cult) or a caricature or vestige of true paganism called idolatry. Kaufmann contends that this proves the absence of real polytheists in Israel, but all it proves is that the biblical writers never addressed themselves to such persons, though it seems certain that they existed. Biblical literature grew in and spoke to the monotheistic actuality and potentiality of ancient Israel. Ideally (to these writers) all Israel was included, but what proportion of the population was really involved can hardly be known. That this was the official public religion of Israel in pre-exilic times may be granted. By post-exilic times it was the sole surviving form of ancient Israel's faith.

Of this religion, then, Kaufmann has given a magnificent account, in which the parts cohere in a remarkably integrated whole. That he has found a key to the phenomena cannot be doubted, for otherwise so much could not be illuminated by his fundamental thesis on the nature of the monotheistic idea. Kaufmann's philosophic grasp of the elements of the biblical worldview makes it possible to comprehend it with a new clarity as one of the perennially relevant expressions of the quest for meaning. This perhaps is Kaufmann's greatest contribution: that he has elevated the discussion of biblical thought above ecclesiastical dogma and partisanship into the realm of the eternally significant ideas.

NOTES

1. 1960 edition; for further information see the obituary notices and appreciations in *Davar*, 11 October 1963; *Haaretz*, 11 October 1963; *Yediʿot Aharonot*, 18 October 1963; but especially Israeli President Shazar's memoir in *Hadoar*, 13 Kislev 5724, and Nahum Glatzer's in *Bitzaron* 49/1 (October 1963):1–5, and the editorial notice, ibid., 47.

2. A full bibliography of Kaufmann's writings appeared in the *Yehezkel Kaufmann Jubilee Volume*, ed. Menahem Haran (Jerusalem 1960), א–י.

3. J. Wellhausen, article, "Israel," reprinted from the *EncBrit* (ninth ed., 1880, XIII, 396–420) in the English translation of *Prolegomena to the History of Israel* (Edinburgh, 1885), 440.

4. Kaufmann's full-dress Hebrew commentaries on these works appeared in 1959 and 1961, respectively. A preliminary study, *The Biblical Account of the Conquest of Palestine*, appeared in English in 1953 (cf. the reaction of John Bright in *Early Israel in Recent History Writing* [Chicago, 1956], 56–78). (Reissued as *The Biblical Account of the Conquest of Canaan* in 1985, with a preface by me and maps by Shmuel Aḥituv.)

5. In the present writer's English abridgment, *The Religion of Israel* (second corrected printing, Chicago, 1963); cf. representative reviews by J. P. Hyatt, JBR, January, 1961; D. R. Dumm, CBQ, January 1961; (London) *Times Literary Supplement*, June 16, 1961; G. E. Mendenhall, *The Lutheran*, August 9, 1961; D. N. Freedman, JBL, March 1962; W. Harrelson, Int, October 1962.

6. On the question of Kaufmann's "faith," the reference to Providence on page 39 of the Preface to the 1960 printing of the *Toldot* is noteworthy.

Additional note:

An intellectual biography of Kaufmann has now appeared: Thomas M. Krapf, *Yehezkel Kaufmann: Ein Lebens-und Erkenntnisweg zur Theologie der Hebräischen Bibel* (Berlin: Institut Kirche und Judentum, 1990). Krapf has also produced a comprehensive account of Kaufmann's thesis concerning the antiquity of the priestly source of the Pentateuch, its neglect by Christian biblical scholarship and its Jewish-Israeli advocates: *Die Priesterschrift und die vorexilische Zeit: Yehezkel Kaufmanns vernachlässigter Beitrag zur Geschichte der biblischen Religion* (Freiburg, Schweiz: Universitätsverlag/Göttingen: Vandenhoeck & Ruprecht, 1992).

Kaufmann's argument that the biblical depiction of pagan religion misrepresents it as fetishism ("worship of wood and stone") is contested by J. Faur, "The Biblical Idea of Idolatry," JQR 69 (1978):1–15. Faur adduces much evidence for the pagan conception of the god-image as divine in itself. On the other hand, J.D. Levenson, "Yehezkel Kaufmann and Mythology," *Conservative Judaism* 36 (1982):36–43 discounts the fetishistic representation as a distorting reductionism by biblical polemicists (cf. my argument from the story of Elijah on Mount Carmel). Levenson further criticizes Kaufmann for adopting too narrow a definition of mythology—after the correcting of which Levenson finds allusions to myths about YHWH. Yet Levenson admits that the Bible, so far alone in the ancient Near East, exhibits a "disjunction from" and a "restriction of" the world of myth.

THE BIBLICAL TEXT AND ITS INTERPRETATION

The Stabilization of the Text of the Hebrew Bible, Reviewed in the Light of the Biblical Materials from the Judean Desert*

1956

The remarkable caches of ancient documents discovered in the Wilderness of Judah enable us for the first time to see what the text of the Hebrew Bible looked like at about the turn of the Era. What was formerly a matter largely of inference from early translations and the testimony of rabbinic literature can now be controlled by manuscript evidence. The material is extensive and will take years to publish, yet a sufficient amount has already been made available to make some tentative judgments possible, and, indeed, necessary. The following is an attempt to sketch the effect of the new material on our understanding of the old, and to outline some major stages in the formation of the received Hebrew text from the early Hellenistic period onward.

The text of the Hebrew Bible is made up of three historically distinct elements: in order of antiquity and stability they are the consonants, the vowel letters, and the system of diacritical marks for vowels and cantillation. The present system of diacritical marks was developed by the Masoretes (the preservers of the text tradition) of the Palestinian

*A paper presented to the Oriental Club of Philadelphia. In the course of revision I had the benefit of discussing the major points with Professor Harry M. Orlinsky. He also made available to me his as yet unpublished contribution to the Irwin *Festschrift*. I wish to acknowledge here his courtesy and valuable criticism. [Orlinsky's "Notes on the Present State of Textual Criticism of the Judaean Biblical Cave Scrolls" appeared in E. C. Hobbs, ed., *A Stubborn Faith* ... to honor W. A. Irwin (Dallas: 1956), 117–131.]

school at Tiberias in the ninth century. It is the product of two centuries of intensive text-critical work in the schools of Palestine and Babylonia, whose object was the establishment of the correct pronunciation and text.[1] The Masoretic ideal remained, however, unachieved. For in the consonantal text–let alone the diacritical marks–thousands of minute differences touching the vowel letters, particles, the copula, singular and plural, and the like, remained. Masoretic manuals listed many of these differences but did not resolve them. The text of our Western Bibles is substantially that of Jacob ben Ḥayyim, the editor of the second Rabbinic Bible published by Daniel Bomberg at Venice in 1524–25. His harmonizing efforts were supplemented by others; later editions, for example, have incorporated the text-critical commentary of Jedidiah Solomon Norzi (*Minḥat Shay,* 1626). The difficulties these men faced can be gathered from their prefatory remarks. Jacob ben Ḥayyim writes:

> [Bomberg] bent every effort, sending throughout all these countries to search out what could be found of Massoretic manuals . . . After I saw these manuals and examined them I discovered that they were extremely confused and corrupt . . . In places where there was an omission . . . I searched the manuals and corrected accordingly: where I found them mutually contradictory I have recorded the conflicting statements . . . Where one book was self-contradictory, or in error, I investigated until I found what appeared to me to be the truth; at times, however, I left the matter unsettled . . . God knows how I labored on this.[2]

Jedidiah Solomon recounts the types of dissensions the books of his time contained:

> Conflicts are legion; the Torah has become, not two Torot, but numberless Torot owing to the great number of variations found in our local books–old and new alike–throughout the entire Bible. There is not a passage which is clear of confusion and errors in the vowel letters, in accents and vowel signs, in the *qrē* and *k̲tīb̲* in *dāgēš* and *rāfe* . . . Nor have the Massoretic manuals escaped the same fate in several places . . . so that if a man undertake to write a Torah scroll according to law, he must necessarily err in respect of the vowel letters, and be like a blind man groping in pitch darkness.[3]

It is owing to the energy of Paul Kahle in publishing great quantities of early manuscripts, primarily from the Cairo Genizah, that we have today a clearer picture of the work of the Palestinian and Babylonian Masoretes of the seventh to ninth centuries. We now see that the bewildering variety of Masoretic notes confronting the later editors had its roots in the differences among and within these schools.[4] Thanks to Kahle a Leningrad manuscript dated to 1008–09 copied from a codex made by Aaron ben Moses ben Asher–the last of the Tiberian Masoretes–was published as the text of the third and subsequent editions of Kittel's *Biblia Hebraica.* Thus for the first time a genuine Masoretic text (not *the* Masoretic text, which is now recognized as a will-o'-the-wisp, but the text of one famous Masorete) was made available. If Kahle is right against Cassuto, this is a copy of the very ben Asher text utilized and recommended by Maimonides.[5]

The Genizah manuscripts, like those confronting the later editors, show many small disagreements in vowel letters, diacritical marks, particles, and the like. After discounting copyists' errors and unwitting alterations, the real variants are negligible. To regard the Masoretes as having created a new recension is true only insofar as their fixing of certain orthographic and diacritical details.[6] It is perfectly plain that all the Genizah manuscripts belong to the same consonantal recension, and that this was made long before the Masoretes. For the history of that recension we must look to our early sources and the newly discovered manuscripts.

Jewish tradition attributes several types of textual activity to the *sōfrīm*–the "bookmen" of the Persian and Hellenistic period–and especially to the archetypal *sōfēr* Ezra. The change from paleo-Hebrew to the so-called square script in writing the Torah is dated to the time of Ezra.[7] Text-critical activity of a sort is also ascribed to him:

> There are ten dotted places in the Torah ... For Ezra thought, "If Elijah should come and ask, 'Why did you write these?' I can answer, 'I have already marked them with dots'; and if he should say, 'You did well in so writing' I shall remove the dots."[8]

This is a picturesque way of saying that the text in ten places was suspect, and, following a practice which was common to the Alexandrian Greek grammarians, these doubtful passages were marked with dots. It was doubtless on the evidence of other manuscripts that they were so marked; in four cases out of the ten the dotted matter is lacking in the Septuagint or the Samaritan Pentateuch.[9]

Another parallel to Greek text-critical marks are the *sīmāniyyōt* "marks" (Hebraized from Greek *sēmeia*) placed before and after Numbers 10:35–6.[10] From the recorded forms of these signs Lieberman has argued to identify them with the Alexandrian *antisigma;* like the latter the *sīmāniyyōt* were understood to mark a transposition of verses.[11] Tradition ascribes the introduction of the *sīmāniyyōt* into the text to God himself; at any rate it is clear that they must have been found in Torah scrolls at a very early date.

Two other types of text-critical activity by the *sōfrīm* are specified: they are termed *tiqqūn sōfrīm* "emendation of the bookmen" and *'iṭṭūr sōfrīm* "deletion of the bookmen." Some rabbinic sources list eleven, others eighteen, cases of "emendation" in the Bible.[12] In all but one case the alteration of a single letter is involved–the one exception involves a change in the word order–in passages which unemended would have been theologically offensive. Lieberman has suggested that the principle behind this procedure lurks in an expression now found only as a figure of speech in rabbinic texts: "Better that one letter be removed from the Torah than that the Divine Name be publicly profaned."[13]

Five examples of "deletion" are given, drawn from the Torah and Psalms; in each case the copula *waw* is deleted, thus creating an asyndeton.[14] An eleventh century Talmudic thesaurus gives this interesting explanation of the deletions:

> It would appear that anciently the village people were not careful in their Bibles, and read [the copula in each of these cases] ... They fell into error at these places in that time, thinking that they were right because it made good sense ... And when the bookmen saw this they removed these *waws*, and called these instances "deletions of the bookmen"... And until quite recently people were similarly erring and reading (in Ex. 23:13) "*and* it shall not be heard in thy mouth"...[15]

That is to say, the readings with the copula were popular smoothing of the text. Such vulgar readings were recognized by the bookmen as they were by the eleventh-century lexicographer, and, accordingly, expunged from authoritative manuscripts.

Rabbinic literature reserves the name *sōfrīm* for scholars of the period between Ezra and Simon the Just, i.e., from about the middle of the fifth to the beginning of the second century B.C.E. At what time the editorial activity ascribed to them took place we cannot say. But it is implied that by Maccabean times the text had been largely stabilized–at least that of the Torah, Prophets, and Psalms. To be sure, since Lagarde the fixing of the text has been placed in the first part of the second century C.E., as if it was inspired by Rabbi Aqiba's minute exegesis, which involves every jot and tittle of the text.[16] But it has been pointed out several times–most recently by Segal[17]–that Aqiba was not the innovator of this method. He learned it from his teacher, Naḥum of Gimzo, and as early as the time of Herod Hillel the Elder was already utilizing hermeneutical methods that presuppose a text verbally stable.[18] Moreover, Josephus, writing toward the end of the first century C.E., writes of the Scriptures that

> during so many ages as have already passed, no one has been so bold as either to add anything to them, to take anything from them or to make any change in them.[19]

Literary sources, then, suggest a date well before the end of the first Christian century for the stabilization of the Bible text. Now this was the period of the Hasmonean dynasty, whose rise gave birth to a cultural as well as a political renascence among the Jews. The literature and architecture of the period testify to the flourishing of Hebraic arts, and there is good reason to look for the origins of Mishnaic Hebrew in the legal and chancery style of the Hasmonean palace.[20] Hasmonean interest in reestablishing the Temple archives, which had been destroyed during the Syrian persecution (cf. 1 Macc. 1:56), is reflected in an incidental notice in the "Hanukka letter" sent by the Jerusalem community to the Jews of Alexandria in 143 B.C.E.:

> Even so did Judah the Maccabee collect for us all the writings which had been scattered owing to the outbreak of war, and they are with us still.[21]

For Pseudo-Aristeas, writing perhaps a decade later,[22] the authority of the Septuagint rests, in the first place, on its having been translated from a copy of the Torah sent from Jerusalem by the High Priest himself;[23] and Josephus likewise appeals to "books deposited in the Temple" for confirmation of his biblical history.[24] The existence of a Temple library in which official copies of sacred documents were preserved is common in the ancient Near East; indeed, it would have been odd had the Jews not had such an archive at Jerusalem. Several scholars have plausibly suggested that the stabilizing of the biblical text is to be associated with this renovation of the Temple library made after the success of Maccabean arms.[25] As we shall see, there may be other signs that point the same way.

Rabbinic sources also make mention of the "book of the Temple Court," apparently a standard scroll used for public reading on holy days. Books of the Prophets–possibly including some of the Hagiographa as well–are likewise mentioned as belonging to the Temple Court.[26] We are warned, however, against considering the text even of the Temple books as finally fixed in every detail by two circumstances: There were "correctors of the book of the Temple Court" maintained out of the public treasury.[27] These were not merely correctors of exemplars made from the Temple book, for one passage explicitly speaks of correcting the Temple scroll itself.[28] What such correction might have entailed is related elsewhere thus:

> Three scrolls were found in the Temple Court: the scroll *m'wny,* the scroll *z'twty* and the scroll *hy'*. In one scroll they found written *m'wn* (in Deut. 33:27), in the other two *m'wnh;* the sages discarded the reading of the one and adopted the reading of the two. In one they found written *z'twty,* in the other two *n'ry* (in Ex. 24:5) . . . In one they found nine occurrences of *hy',* in the other two eleven; they discarded the reading of the one and adopted the reading of the two.[29]

There thus appear to have been several authoritative Torah scrolls in the archives, and the editorial activity on them was a continuing process. The Bibles of the people and even of the local synagogues could hardly have kept pace with the continuing refinement of the standard scrolls,[30] and it should occasion no surprise that evidence is at hand to show that deviations in detail were current even in synagogue manuscripts at the turn of the Era. An interesting case in point is the so-called Codex Severus referred to in an eleventh-century midrash as "having been captured in Jerusalem and brought to Rome, and there stored away in the Synagogue of Severus." The midrash lists 29 variant readings contained in this scroll, presumably taken as part of Titus' plunder in 70 C.E. These variants consist of scribal errors, orthographic peculiarities reflecting earlier practice, Aramaized spellings, and a few altered readings–smoothings or expansions on the basis of parallel passages.[31] The midrash states that this scroll was "stored away" (*gnūzā ūstūmā*), meaning that it was later withdrawn from public use because of its deviations. This withdrawal reflects the increased weight of rabbinic authority among Jews after the fall of Jerusalem, when the economy of crisis forced Judaism into a more rigid mold in which there was no room for deviations. Thus Aqiba exhorts his disciple from prison, "When you teach your son, teach only from a corrected text,"[32] and a later authority applies Job 11:13 "Let not evil dwell in thy tents" to the retention beyond thirty days of uncorrected books in one's home.[33] But the presence of vulgata containing small deviations is demonstrable from citations throughout rabbinic literature; it has even been suggested that these deviant citations point to the use of the vulgata by the rabbis in their preaching, in spite of their differing from the standard text.[34]

The final stage in the fixing of the Bible text seems thus to have been arrived at gradually by the successive refinement of a selected recension during the last pre-Christian centuries. The impetus to this may well have been the reorganization of the Temple library following the Maccabean victory. The editorial work of the bookmen did not immediately affect the Bibles in the hands of the people. Only after the consolidation of rabbinic Judaism between the two revolts (70–132 C.E.) did a more thorough supervision of the text on the basis of the standard became possible. But while the standard was made to prevail at this time, vulgar readings cropping up throughout rabbinic literature testify to the tenacity of the popular texts.

The received text is the end result of work on one recension. Two other recensions of the Torah attest to the type of text that was set aside by that of the bookmen: the Samaritan Pentateuch and the Hebrew *Vorlage* of the Septuagint.

The Samaritan Pentateuch has been made available in an eclectic edition by von Gall.[35] Although von Gall failed to utilize the earliest manuscripts, and conformed his text to the Jewish Torah in some ways,[36] we can still utilize his work to get a reasonably good conception of the distinctive features of this recension. The Samaritan Pentateuch is less asyndetic than the Jewish. Those passages of the Torah which the Talmud enumerates as bearing "deletions of the bookmen" show up here with the copula. Unusual expressions are replaced by more common ones. Archaic grammatical forms found in the Jewish text are replaced with later forms. Words and phrases are added, drawn as a rule from similar or parallel passages. The effect is to make the text smoother and more repetitive without altering the meaning. A good instance is the account of the theophany at Sinai in Exodus 20. Deuteronomy 5 contains a different version of the event; in the Samaritan, however, the accounts of Exodus and Deuteronomy are neatly combined, giving a fully harmonized story. Here and there an explanatory remark is found; e.g., following the prohibition of cooking a kid in its mother's milk in Exodus 23:19, we read, "Whoever does this is like one who sacrifices a *škḥ* (?); it is sin to the God of Jacob."

These features are typical of later Jewish popular translations of the Bible, such as the Aramaic Targums or Saadya's Arabic Bible. The antiquity of the Samaritan text has, accordingly, been questioned. The Samaritans broke away from the Jews during the fifth to fourth centuries B.C.E., before the change from paleo-Hebrew to the square character was made. Accordingly their Torah is still written in a form of paleo-Hebrew, and separates words by dots–the custom of very early times. The oldest manuscript is in Nablus and has been seen by few scholars. Moses Gaster, who was an enthusiastic advocate of Samaritan tradition, saw it and dated it no later than the first Christian century;[37] his date has not been generally accepted though few, indeed, are qualified to speak on the matter. Support for the Samaritan, however, is forthcoming from a source of undisputed antiquity, the Septuagint. Cases of agreement between the Septuagint and the Samaritan against the received Hebrew in their additions and divergent readings are so numerous as to require the assumption of some relationship. In earlier days this agreement served the ends of theological polemic: the Catholic Church sought to discredit the received Hebrew on the basis of the Septuagint and Samaritan; the Protestants defended the Hebrew, denigrating the value of the other two. Bizarre theories have been spun to explain this agreement: One held that the Samaritan and the Septuagint were translations of an Aramaic version of the original Hebrew. Another was that the Samaritan was a Hebrew rendering of the Septuagint. The first sober verdict was given by Gesenius in 1815, who maintained that the two must have originated in a Hebrew text earlier than the fixing of our Masoretic text.[38]

The matter is more complicated, however. For in spite of their many agreements the Septuagint is not nearly as full as the Samaritan. None of the large-scale harmonizing and transposing of verses of the Samaritan appears in the Greek. Does this mean that, as suspected, the Samaritan is a later conflation?

We are indebted to Kahle for pointing to the indications that the Septuagint as we have it may not have been the first Greek translation of the Torah, but a revision of earlier translations. Pseudo-Aristeas explicitly refers to earlier translations of the Law, made before the Seventy.[39] Inquiring after possible remains and reflexes of these superseded translations Kahle noted that some Torah citations in the New Testament which conflict with our Septuagint agree with the readings of the Samaritan Pentateuch. Moreover, he noted that readings of certain Septuagintal manuscripts agreed with the Samaritan not only in their similar readings, but even in their having that fuller text so characteristically Samaritan and unlike our Septuagint.[40]

We are thus led to think that–allowing for certain obvious dogmatic changes–the Samaritan represents an early Hebrew text type. Its fullness, its harmonizations and levelings will be part of its popular character, as a text in circulation from times before the text-criticism of the bookmen provoked the search for better, less expanded (and therefore less popular) recensions.[41] There seems to be no reason to exclude the origin of this text type from as early as the fourth century B.C.E. Remains of early Greek translations preserved in out-of-the-way places appear to reflect a Samaritan-like Hebrew *Vorlage*. At some time toward the middle of the second century B.C.E. before Pseudo-Aristeas, a new Greek translation of the Torah was produced. It is reasonable to suppose that one of the purposes of this undertaking was to adapt the Greek version in accordance with the best Hebrew text of the time; hence, Pseudo-Aristeas' stress on the fact that the scroll from which the translation was made came from Jerusalem's High Priest. Interestingly enough the early Hasmonean Hebrew text reflected in the Septuagint *Vorlage* shows, in relation to the Samaritan, a considerable amount of pruning and editing. This accords with the view set forth above that the final phase of the fixing of the text had begun by early Hasmonean times. Thus, the Septuagint *Vorlage* will represent an intermediate stage between the full Samaritan and the pruned received Hebrew. In the Septuagint *Vorlage* we will probably see an early product of the text-critical endeavors of the *sōfrīm* to establish an authentic Torah on the basis of older, less edited manuscripts than those in circulation among the people.

The materials from the Wilderness of Judah now enable us to see at first hand some of the types of biblical texts that were current in Palestine in the centuries just before and after the turn of the Era.

The settlement at Khirbet Qumran belonged to a community that had broken with the authorities in Jerusalem. It was a religious order organized along communistic lines, with a rigidly graded structure: priests, Levites, and lay members with various further subdivisions involving seniority. It saw itself as Israel in miniature, as true Israel, and looked for the day when God would lead its army in successful battle against the heathens and apostate Jews.[42] The abandonment of the settlement has been dated to the period of the First Revolt (66–70) on the basis of dated coins, pottery, and the type of manuscript remains found: the latter consist of biblical, apocryphal-eschatological, and liturgical works written on skins; some papyrus fragments were found too, but no paper and no codices. Ten caves have thus far been found to contain manuscript fragments; those of Cave I have recently been published, while specimens of the far richer store of Cave IV had been published previously.[43]

The biblical fragments in square script have been examined by F. M. Cross with a view to their paleography. His conclusions are that the vast majority fall in the Hasmonean period, especially the latter half, and the Herodian period, again especially the latter part; a few are dated to the end of the third century B.C.E.[44] Fragments in paleo-Hebrew were also found, including an Exodus manuscript, largely intact. These have been variously dated from the fifth to the first centuries B.C.E.[45] It is best, therefore, to await further publication of this material and refrain at present from drawing the far-reaching conclusions that an early date would permit.

There is a great variety in the orthography of the fragments. Some are written with a profusion of vowel letters–although it must be stressed that this fullness is essentially different from that of medieval Jewish manuscripts.[46] Manuscript fragments of this type of orthography may be considered as vulgata. In the case of Isaiah *a*[47] we are dealing with a careless copyist (or copyists); the scroll abounds in errors, smoothings, paraphrases, and conjectural filling-in.[48] Orlinsky, who has published the only detailed studies of individual variants in the scroll, characterizes its text as "an oral variation on the theme of the text tradition which came to be known . . . as Masoretic." "Its text is worthless to the student who wishes to get behind the Masoretic text or to recover the Hebrew *Vorlage* of the ancient primary versions; it is a vulgar text, largely, if not wholly, orally contrived."[49] This severe judgment is stated in perhaps overly drastic terms; it is justifiable as a much needed corrective to the text-critical conclusions which have been drawn from hasty and unmethodical work.[50] But that even vulgar texts may on occasion preserve more original readings is a possibility that must be allowed.[51]

To this category belongs also Deuteronomy *a*, a fragment containing some inferior variants and a misspelling due to the current pronunciation of Hebrew in which laryngeals appear to have lost their distinctive pronunciation. It is of interest to note that the practice of crossing out errors rather than erasing them–a practice not permitted in the writing of authorized texts–has been found so far only in this type of text.[52]

The orthographic and grammatical peculiarities of the vulgata reflect a type of Hebrew strongly influenced by Aramaic and similar in several respects to the Hebrew known from Samaritan sources. This is significant support for the authenticity of the Samaritan tradition: it now appears to have retained features of early popular Hebrew that were modified in later development.[53]

Another series of fragments have an orthography generally similar to, occasionally slightly fuller than, that of late biblical books. These have readings now like the Septuagint, now like the Samaritan (in the Pentateuch), now like the Masoretic text against them both, and sometimes a reading otherwise unattested. Of particular interest is an Exodus manuscript having throughout additional verses and expansions often identical with those of the Samaritan Pentateuch.[54] Fragments of Samuel and Deuteronomy from the same cave (IV) show variations and additions with Septuagintal affinities.[55]

Finally, there are some manuscripts with the standard biblical orthography. The Isaiah scroll *b* is such a text,[56] as are the fragments of Psalter *a*. To be sure, there are many slight deviations from the Masoretic text, but these are almost always of the type that keep occurring throughout the history of biblical manuscripts.

Thus the Qumran material witnesses to a variety of text types all current contemporaneously. This is an important point. It is not possible to set up a line of development of text forms from this material, so that the form closest to our Hebrew be the latest. Three Psalter fragments that do not appear to have been written at any considerable interval run the orthographic gamut from exceptional fullness to Masoretic leanness. Of the two Deuteronomy fragments the one whose orthography is closest to Masoretic shows two variants with Septuagint parallels.

It would thus appear that the forerunner of our received text was extant and current during the last pre-Christian centuries. The Isaiah *b* scroll and Psalter *a* testify to that. But in the Qumran community other texts were also current: the Samaritan type of Torah, and manuscripts with Septuagint-like readings in the Torah and Prophets. There is no standard text at Qumran. While this at first may seem strange it is not really so. Piety is not always accompanied by a critical sense. To the devout reader, a text giving the substance of the sacred message is not invalidated by slight verbal divergences from other texts. It must be also kept in mind that no binding laws were derived at Qumran from the letters of Scripture. Examples are ready at hand of pious indifferences to textual considerations among Jews of later ages. The position of the "received" Talmud text studied in the yeshiva has not been affected to any large degree by the great corpus of variant readings collected by Rabbinovicz over seventy years ago. Nor has the impetus to publish critical texts of rabbinic writings always come from circles marked by piety. Kahle's resuscitation of a genuine ben Asher manuscript of the Bible has not been met by acclamation outside of academic circles, despite the endorsement given it by Maimonides (if Kahle's identification be correct). Just so the verbal and orthographic divergences, which rarely affected the meaning, the additional phrases and verses, which were based on parallels or traditional interpretations–these need not have troubled the Qumran pietists any more than they do those of a later day.

What is exceedingly valuable in these manuscripts and fragments is their evidence for the antiquity and reality of variants whose existence, attested to heretofore only by the versions, had been questionable. The Greek Samuel, so different at times from our Hebrew, seems now to have a relative in the Samuel manuscript of Cave IV. The antiquity of the Samaritan Pentateuch, whose extraordinary conflateness had been taken as a sign of lateness, is now supported by a Qumran Exodus manuscript. At the same time, the received Hebrew is shown to have had early representatives, although at Qumran at least, it had not gained dominance.

But the peculiar nature of the Qumran community prohibits us from drawing conclusions confidently as to the state of affairs in Jerusalem. What the official priesthood and bookmen had achieved in stabilizing the text need not have been reflected in this community that had cut itself off from the rest of Judea, and was irreconcilably hostile to Jerusalem and its authority. Hence we must consider the possibility that just as the Samaritan tradition froze the Torah in a relatively unedited and uncritical form, and did not share in the successive refinement that resulted in the received text, so too the Qumran manuscripts may show an uncritical acceptance of all types of texts. But their attitude need not have reflected the state of affairs in official Jewish circles.

The state of the text in the first and second Christian centuries can be seen from the finds in Wadi Murabba'āt, some twenty kilometers south of Qumran. Here several dated documents show the main post-exilic settlement to have been that of a Jewish military post in the mid-second century, followed by some decades of Roman occupation. The Jews appear to have been an outpost of Bar-Kochba's rebel army. Now, since the spiritual leaders of this Second Revolt against Rome (132–35 C.E.) were some of the most eminent rabbis, there is no question as to the orthodoxy of this group. Accordingly, we do not find any heterodox literature at Murabba'āt as was found at Qumran. Moreover, the biblical fragments–remnants of the Torah and Isaiah–agree in every detail with our text.[57] Equally interesting is what Barthelemy regards as a Jewish-Greek prototype of Aquila, Symmachus, and Theodotian dating from the first century–i.e., from approximately the same time as the latest Qumran materials. In six out of eight cases where comparison with Qumran texts is possible the Murabba'āt Greek agrees with the Masoretic text where the Qumran text agrees with the Septuagint.[58] This is, to be sure, not much to go by, but it may be a hint that the Qumran community showed a lag in its textual level as compared with the Jewish orthodoxy.

To summarize, it would appear that at the beginning of the Hellenistic period biblical texts were extant in two main types, a fuller and a shorter text. The longer texts were the popular ones; in the Torah they are represented by the Samaritan tradition, which broke away from the line of further evolution at this time. During the Ptolemaic period the text-critical work of the *sōfrīm* began and accelerated, probably, under the Hasmonean renascence. Their effort was directed toward selecting the manuscripts reflecting the oldest tradition, and to make them standard. In the case of the Torah it was the shorter text, with its earlier orthography and older linguistic forms, that was made the norm.[59] The editing was a continuing process that reached its end by the first Christian century, well before the First Revolt. The standard became all prevalent, however, only after the fall of Jerusalem, when rabbinic Judaism came into exclusive hegemony. Previously the various stages of the text work coexisted in the Bibles of the people. While types modeled after the evolving standard trickled down from Jerusalem, they had to compete with older, less edited texts, and with such as were written in a fuller, vulgar orthography. The prevalence of the standard, not its creation, came after 70 C.E., and is the necessary precondition of the highly literal exegesis that flourished in the Tannaitic academies. Such an exegesis, undertaken in all seriousness by earnest men, is inconceivable had the text not been hallowed in its letter well beforehand.

It is instructive to compare the evolution of the biblical text with that of the Greek classics as we now see it, thanks to the discovery of the papyri.

With the aid of the papyri it is possible to get behind the text of the tenth- to fifteenth-century vellums to as early as the third century B.C. It can be seen that by the first century C.E. the texts of the chief prose authors, without being altogether uniform, were, by and large, in the form they appear in the medieval manuscripts. But the Homer and Plato fragments of the early Ptolemaic period reveal a text in a decidedly unsettled condition. The Homeric fragments contain a striking amount of additional matter, consisting chiefly of tags from parallel passages. Kenyon observed that "with hardly an exception they add nothing substantial to the poem, but are just such additions as a rhapsodist might make who was anxious to extend the bulk of his recitation." (One might say, a "Samaritan recension" of Homer.) It was during the second century B.C.E. that the shorter, esthetically superior text came to prevail, the outcome, it would appear, of the text-critical work of the Alexandrians. During this time many transition forms are found side by side (much as our Qumran material reflects the contemporaneous currency of various text types during this very period in Judea.)[60]

The concurrence of Jewish textual activity with the work of the Alexandrian grammarians is suggestive. That the *sōfrīm* utilized critical marks strikingly similar to those of the Greeks lends plausibility to the assumption of a connection between the two. To be sure, the methods of the Greeks and their attitude toward their classics differed fundamentally from the methods and attitudes of the Jews.[61] Nonetheless, it would appear likely that some of the techniques of criticism, if not the very stimulus to undertake it, came to Judea from abroad. The editing and standardization of the biblical text thus has a claim to be regarded among the several phenomena that, while thoroughly Judaized, had their roots at least in part in the Hellenistic world.[62]

NOTES

1. A concise survey of the work of the Masoretes is B. J. Roberts, "The Emergence of the Tiberian Masoretic Text," JTS, XLIX (1948):8ff.

2. C. D. Ginsburg, *Jacob ben Chajim ben Adonijah's Introduction . . .*[2] London, 1867, 77f. On ben Ḥayyim's eclectic method, see also Sperber, "Problems of the Masora," HUCA, XVII (1943):370ff. It is important to note that ben Ḥayyim's editorial activity does not go beyond selecting one of the given variants. He does not invent readings; in this he may well serve as a representative of Massoretic conservatism.

3. Introduction to *Minḥaṭ Shay*, reprinted in Shulsinger's *Pentateuch* (Hebrew), VI:8f.

4. Kahle has summarized this aspect of his life work in his *The Cairo Genizah* (hereafter cited as CG) (London, 1947), 36ff.

5. Maimonides, *Code, Sefer Torah* 8, 4; cf. Kahle, "The Hebrew ben Asher Bible Manuscripts," VT, 1 (1951):161ff. [The debate over which Ben Asher text (Leningrad, Cairo, or Aleppo) Maimonides recommended as a model text was settled by Moshe Goshen-Gottstein's decisive study, "The Authenticity of the Aleppo Codex," *Textus* I (1960):17–58. D. S. Loewinger's conclusion that the Aleppo codex "shows the maximum concentration of Tiberian criteria" (ibid., 94) has been borne out by further study. That codex (despite its having suffered the destruction of most of the Pentateuch) is the textual basis of the Hebrew University Bible Project, directed until his death by Goshen-Gottstein; of Bar-Ilan University's *Mikra'ot Gedolot 'Haketer'* edited by Menachem Cohen; and of the *Tanakh* edited by M. Breuer. However, A. Dotan's edition of the *Tanakh*, and the *Biblia Hebraica Stuttgartensia*, the standard critical version of the Hebrew text, are based on the Leningrad manuscript, still the oldest dated manuscript of the complete Hebrew Bible (1008/9 C.E.).

A fine survey of the issues confronting an editor of "the Masoretic text" is Menachem Cohen's "Introduction to the 'Haketer' Edition" (in Hebrew).]

6. See Orlinsky's remarks in JAOS LXI (1941):84ff., and compare the more detailed treatment of Roberts in JJS, I (1949):147ff., where, on page 152, the same conclusion is reached regarding the single consonantal recession.

7. *Tosefta Sanhedrin* 4, 7; *Bab. Sanhedrin* 22a.

8. *Aboth de Rabbi Nathan* I 34, II:37 (translated by J. Goldin, *The Fathers According to Rabbi Nathan, Yale Judaica Series* X:138f.). On these and other critical marks discussed below see the fundamental study by S. Lieberman, *Hellenism in Jewish Palestine* (New York, 1950), 38ff.

9. The second *y* of *wbynyk* (Gen. 16:5) lacking in Samaritan; *wyśqhw* (Gen. 33:4) lacking in Septuagint; *w'hrn* (Num. 3:39) lacking in Samaritan; *r* of *'śr* (Num. 21:30) lacking in both Samaritan and Septuagint.

10. *Sifre* I:84; *Aboth de R. Nathan* I:34 (tr. Goldin 137).

11. See Lieberman's discussion, op. cit. 39ff.

12. Ibid. 28ff.

13. Ibid. 35f.

14. *Bab. Nedarim* 37b.

15. Nathan ben Yeḥiel, *Sefer he'ārūk*, s. v. *'āṭar*; cited by Jacob ben Ḥayyim in *Introduction*, ed. Ginsburg 66f.

16. Cf. e.g., Pfeiffer, *Introduction to the Old Testament* (New York, 1948), 76f.

17. M. H. Segal, "The Promulgation of the Authoritative Text of the Hebrew Bible," JBL, LXXII (1953):36f.

18. See, e.g., the two Talmuds to *Pesaḥim* 6, 1 where Hillel argues from a *gzērā šāwā* (verbal analogy, on which cf. Lieberman, op. cit. 58ff.), a hermeneutic that could not have developed before the fixing of the text.

19. *Against Apion*, I:42.

20. J. Klausner, *The Second Temple at Its Height* (Hebrew). Tel-Aviv, 1930, 148ff. M. H. Segal (*Grammar of Mishnaic Hebrew* [Hebrew], TelAviv, 1936, 13) argues for an earlier origin but agrees that the Hasmonean period saw the "expansion and enrichment" of Mishnaic.

21. 2 Maccabees 2:14; on this letter cf. Bickermann, *Zeitschrift f. d. neutest. Wissenschaft*, XXXII (1933):254.

22. For the most recent discussion of the date of Ps.-Aristeas see M. Hadas, *Aristeas to Philocrates*, New York, 1951. On page 54 he decides for the approximate date 130

B.C.E. For an earlier date (before 170 B.C.E.) cf. Orlinsky, *Crozer Quarterly,* XXIX (1952):202ff.

23. *Ps.-Aristeas* 176; see Bickerman, JBL., LXIII (1944):343.

24. *Antiquities* V:1, 17: III:1, 7; see also *War* VII:5, 5.

25. M. Gaster, *The Samaritans* (London, 1925), 132; Segal, JBL, LXXII (1953):40.

26. References to the books of the Temple Court are collected and fully discussed in L. Blau, *Studien zum althebräischen Buchwesen* (Budapest, 1902), 107ff. That Hagiographia may be included under the rubric Prophets in Jewish sources is shown ibid., 63.

27. *Pal. Sheqalim* 48a; Blau, op. cit. 107.

28. *Mishna Mo'ed Qatan* 3, 4. The verb *higgī^ah*, which elsewhere means "correct (a manuscript)," "proofread," is sometimes taken to mean "re-ink" in this one passage (Jastrow, *Dictionary* 872: Segal, ibid. 43). But "re-ink" is expressed otherwise (*he'ebïr qulmus 'al, ḥiddēš* cf. Rashi, *Bab. Shabbat* 104b, s.v. *kātab al gab hakktāb*): as for instances of correcting the Temple scroll, see ahead in the text.

29. *Sifre* II: 356, *Aboth de R. Nathan* II: 46, *Soferim* 4, 4: see Lieberman, op. cit. 21f. and references there.

30. Note the allegation by Ps.-Aristeas (30) that the Hebrew copies of the Torah current in Alexandria were corrupt; for this meaning cf. Bickerman, JBL, LXIII (1944): 343, n. 24.

31. Published and discussed by A. Epstein in *Chwolson Festschrift* 49f.; Sperber gives the variants, op. cit. 333f., as does Segal, op. cit. 46f. See also Lieberman, op. cit. 23f.

32. *Bab. Pesaḥim,* 112a.

33. *Bab. Kethubboth,* 19b.

34. Lieberman, op. cit., 26. The most thorough collection of biblical variants found in rabbinic literature is by V. Aptowitzer, *Das Schriftwort in der Rabbinischen Literatur* (Vienna, 1906–15). His material covers only Joshua, Judges, and Samuel. Despite Aptowitzer's care much of it cannot be said to reflect real text variants, but is rather to be explained by the rabbinic practice of citing memoriter or in paraphrase. Aptowitzer has set forth the rabbinic methods of citation in excellent summary in Part I of his work, 21ff.

35. August Freiherr von Gall, *Der Hebräische Pentateuch der Samaritaner* (Giessen, 1914–18).

36. On manuscripts see CG 50 n. 1; on von Gall's editorial method, see his *Vorwort* lxviii.

37. *The Samaritans,* 108.

38. A survey of the shifting opinions concerning the value of the Samaritan Torah is found in Geiger, *Urschrift und Übersetzungen der Bibel* (Breslau, 1857), 14ff.; Montgomery, *The Samaritans* (Philadelphia, 1907), 286ff.

39. The clear statement of Ps.-Aristeas 314, where the writer tells us that Theopompus (early fourth century B.C.E.) "had been driven out of his mind for more than thirty days because he intended to insert in his history some of the incidents from the earlier and somewhat unreliable translations of the law" (so rendered by Andrews in Charles, *Apocrypha* II: 121). It is true that *episphalesteron* may be taken rather with *prosistorein* (see Andrews's note), and the passage rendered ". . . when he was too rashly intending to introduce into his history some of the incidents of the law which had been previously translated" (Thackery *apud* Andrews, similarly Hadas). But even so the fact of previous translation still stands, although the need to *revise* "somewhat unreliable translations" is more obvious. Yet even following Thackery and Hadas the necessity for making a new translation is best explained as due to the desire to revise previously existing efforts. Thus even if Kahle's argument from paragraph 30 is rejected–and it would appear from Orlinsky, *Crozer Quarterly,* XXIX (1952): 205 that it must be–the evidence of paragraph 314 is clearly in favor of a pre-Septuagint Greek translation.

40. CG 132ff., and especially 144ff.

41. Ibid., 147f., but so already Gaster, *The Samaritans,* 123ff. On the popular character of the Samaritan, see S. Talmon, JJS II (1951):144ff.

42. The ideology of the community is set forth well in their various writings, for a

provisional translation of which see the selection in Burrows, *The Dead Sea Scrolls* (New York, 1955).

43. The materials of Cave I have been published by D. Barthelemy and J. T. Milik, with contributions by R. de Vaux et al. in *Discoveries in the Judaean Desert I. Qumran Cave I* (Oxford, 1955). References to Qumran material are to this publication unless otherwise noted.

The following have been published from Cave IV:

a. F. M. Cross, Jr., "A New Qumran Biblical Fragment Related to the Original Hebrew Underlying the Septuagint," BASOR, CXXXII (1953):15ff.

b. J. Muilenberg, "A Qoheleth Scroll from Qumran," BASOR, CXXXV (1954): 20ff.

c. Idem, "Fragments of Another Qumran Isaiah Scroll," ibid., 28ff.

d. P. W. Skehan, "A Fragment of the 'Song of Moses' . . . ," BASOR (1954):12ff.

e. F. M. Cross, Jr., "The Oldest Manuscripts from Qumran," JBL, LXXIV (1955):165ff.

f. P. W. Skehan, "Exodus in the Samaritan Recension from Qumran," ibid., 182ff.

The latest comprehensive report of the work being done on the Qumran finds at the Palestine Archaeological Museum is in RB, LXIII (1956):49ff.; a brief survey is given by Cross in BASOR, CXLI (1956):9ff.

44. See e in the preceding note.

45. The Leviticus fragments of Cave I have been dated to the second half of the fifth century (Birnbaum, BASOR CXVIII [1950]: 27); late fourth to early third centuries (Diringer, BA, XIII [1950]: 93ff.); fourth century (de Vaux, RB LVI [1949]:600ff.); second to first centuries (Yeivin, BASOR CXVIII [1950]: 28 ff., Cross, JBL, LXXIV [1955]: 147, n. 1 ["archaizing," so too Albright, BASOR CXL (1955): 33, n. 29]). The Samaritan-type Exodus manuscript, and with it all other paleo-Hebrew fragments, are dated to "the normal period of Qumran cursive documents" by Skehan, RB, LXIII (1956): 58; cf. JBL, LXXIV: 182f.

46. As shown by H. Yalon in *Kirjath Sepher*, XXVII (1951): 164f., from which I quote the following "This fullness involves only *he* and *waw* . . . *yod* is treated as it is in Massoretic orthography, never occurring before strong *dāgēš* or before quiescent *šwā* [in contrast to medieval orthography where it frequently does occur in these positions] . . . In the Isaiah *a* scroll there is not a single instance of a double consonantal *waw*, which is the normal way of indicating consonantal *waw* in medieval writing." Cf. also *Kirjath Sepher*, XXVIII (1952):65.

47. Published in *The Dead Sea Scrolls of St. Mark's Monastery*, Vol. I, ed. M. Burrows (New Haven, 1950).

48. Listed by Burrows in BASOR, CXI (1948): 16ff.; CXIII (1949): 24ff.

49. These judgments will be found respectively in his "Studies in the St. Mark's Isaiah Scroll," JBL, LXIX (1950): 157; JQR, XLIII (1952–53): 338. Further installments of Orlinsky's studies are in JJS, II (1951): 151ff.; JNES, XI (1952): 153ff., IEJ, IV (1954): 5ff., *Tarbiz*, XXIV (1954): 4ff. See the full English summary, i–ii, HUCA, XXV (1954): 85ff.

50. See Orlinsky's strong critique, "Notes on the Present State of the Textual Criticism of the Judean Biblical Cave Scrolls" (*A Stubborn Faith*, ed. E. C. Hobbs [Dallas, 1956], 117–31) to appear in the forthcoming Irwin *Festschrift*. The especial merit of his studies lies in the painstaking care and rigorous method with which they are pursued, and of which they are indeed models.

51. That Orlinsky may have overstated the case against the textual value of the Isaiah *a* scroll appears to be indicated by the occasional, rare reading that is original and seems superior both to the received Hebrew and the Greek. One such is *ymrw* (*yimrū*) "they shall feed" for received *wmry* (*ūmrī'*) "and a fatling" at 11:6; the Greek here is conflate and in disorder (cf. Gray, *Isaiah* in ICC *ad loc.*). Another case occurs at 37:27b–28a, where the scroll's *hnšdfl lfny qdym; qwmkh* (*hanniśdāf lifnē qādīm; qūmkā*) "which is parched by the east-wind: thy rising," etc., makes original good sense out of unintelligible Hebrew. The Greek had the same Hebrew before it. On this passage, cf. Burrows, BASOR, CXI (1948): 23 and CXIII (1949): 28 (toward the bottom).

As to the scroll's reflecting the Greek's Hebrew *Vorlage*, two instances may be cited: 51:23a where the scroll's plus *wm'ynk*, and 53:11a where its plus *'wr* are both represented in the Greek (the latter plus is found even in Isaiah *b*, which hews so closely to our received text).

52. In Isaiah *a* (see list on p. xv, bottom), and the Qoheleth fragment (note 43b, above) at 6:4.

53. Yalon, *Kirjath Sepher*, XXVII (1951): 170f. Gaster's feeling that the language of the "Zadokite Documents"–seven manuscripts of which have now been found at Qumran (see Milik's report in RB, LXIII [1956]: 61)–had its closest affinities with Samaritan Hebrew (*Samaritans* 100) is thus strikingly borne out.

54. See note 43f.

55. See note 43d e.

56. The bulk of Isaiah *b* was published in *Ōṣar hammgillōt haggnūzōt* (*Treasury of Cached Scrolls*), ed. Sukenik (Jerusalem, 1954). Some additional bits are published in Barthelemy-Milik, *Discoveries*.

57. See the preliminary report of de Vaux, RB, LX (1953):245ff.

58. D. Barthélemy, "Redécouverte d'un chainon manquant de l'histoire de la Septante," ibid., 18ff.

59. In other cases, however, it was not the shorter text that was finally adopted. The Greek Job, for example, seems to reflect a *Vorlage* shorter by at least one-sixth than the received Hebrew (see Gray in the ICC on Job, lxxiv, n. 1). But the nature of the Greek's omissions supports the overall priority of the Hebrew; e.g., in many cases the omission destroys the poetic parallelism (ibid.). The Greek Jeremiah is one-eighth shorter than the Hebrew, and has, in addition, some considerable transpositions. "The variations of the LXX are in part 'recensional,' i.e., they are due to the fact that the Hebrew text used by the translators deviated in some particulars from that which we at present possess; but in part, also, they are due to the faulty manner in which the translators executed their work ... *on the whole* the Massoretic text deserves the preference: but it is impossible to uphold the unconditional superiority of either" (Driver, *Introduction to the Literature of the OT*[9] 270).

In those frequent cases in which the translators appear merely to have condensed the Hebrew, there is the likelihood that they were adjusting the text to Greek taste. Similarly, the contemporary Alexandrian grammarians appear to have eliminated a considerable amount of the repetitions found in the early Ptolemaic text of Homer. See the next note.

60. The value of the papyri for the text-criticism of Greek literature presents several relevant considerations to the student of the Judean Desert material. See the following surveys: F. G. Kenyon, *Proceedings of the British Academy* 1903–04, 141ff.: B. P. Grenfell, *Journal of Hellenic Studies*, XXXIX (1919): 16ff.; W. Schubart, *Einführung in die Papyruskunde* (Berlin, 1918), Ch. V.

Whether the received, shorter Homer text is older and closer to the original than the longer, early Ptolemaic text is discussed by Grenfell, who tended to doubt it. If the Alexandrians had a hand in creating the received text we have here an example of the differing approaches of Greek and Jewish criticism: The Greeks worked on their text creatively, making it meet criteria of reason and taste (see the next note); the Jews refined their text on the basis of what they judged to be the best available manuscripts and the best attested readings. Aside from the recognized "emendations of the bookmen" there is no objective evidence of deliberate text alteration by the *sōfrīm*. That this has not stood in the way of scholarly conjecture can be seen in Pfeiffer, *Introduction to the OT*, 86ff. Ancient cacophemisms (the substitution of *bōšet* for *ba'al* in proper names, already attested to in the Greek); ancient euphemisms (substituting "bless" for "curse God," already in the Greek), and changes to be made in recitation–not in the body of the text–are here combined and ascribed to the history of the text during the period 135–500 C.E.

61. See Lieberman, op. cit., 27, especially n. 34.

62. On the Hellenistic infiltration of Judaism during the Hasmonean period see the suggestive remarks of Bickerman in *The Maccabees* (New York, 1947), 83ff., 113ff., and *The Jews*, ed. L. Finkelstein, 109f.

Additional note:

This article, published in 1956, reflects the state of knowledge then available to the public on biblical materials from the Wilderness of Judah (see notes 43–45 for a listing of these materials). What remains of value in the article is its presentation of "pre-Qumran" sources, and its integration of the new textual data into the body of earlier knowledge. The article also sets out a classification of the data that can still serve as a primary orientation. The basic thesis—that the earliest evidence points to an original multiplicity of text forms (I would not today use the term "text types") remains valid in my opinion. This has consequences for the theory that at first there was one original text from which all the rest sprang—consequences that are drawn out in my later article "The Use of the Ancient Versions for Interpreting the Hebrew Text." The focus on the Pentateuch and Isaiah tends to create the impression—false—that what is valid for the Torah and Isaiah holds true in general: namely, that the Masoretic form of the text was already present at the turn of the era and that it was superior to its contemporary variant text forms. The evidence in fact differs from book to book. For example, there is a Qumran text of Samuel better preserved than that of the Masoretic text, and the text of some Jeremiah manuscripts agrees with the *Vorlage* of the Septuagint in terseness that may well be primary as against the turgidity of the Masoretic Jeremiah.

The present state of the evidence is set out comprehensively in Emanuel Tov's *Textual Criticism of the Hebrew Bible* (Minneapolis: Fortress Press and Assen/Maastrich: Van Gorcum, 1992).

The Use of the Ancient Versions
for Interpreting the Hebrew Text:
A Sampling from Ezekiel 2:1–3:11
1978

I feel honored by the invitation of our President, Professor Walther Zimmerli, to deliver a paper to this learned audience. I wish to acknowledge this feeling at the outset because the argument I shall put forward, though critical of much that is being done in textual work today, is yet one that only colleagues in scholarly training and endeavor can judge; the opportunity of presenting it to such an audience is therefore precious to me. Since my argument originated in work on a commentary to the Book of Ezekiel, I wish further to acknowledge my special debt to Professor Zimmerli for his monumental contribution to the understanding of every facet of that difficult book. If I seem to be directing an inordinate measure of criticism at Zimmerli, it is only that no one else since Cornill has stated his reasoning in text-critical and exegetical matters in comparable detail. Through his careful justification of his decisions, it is possible to study the axioms of Old Testament criticism at large. If I believe that in some matters I can move beyond the point reached by the present consensus, it is only because I have started from the advance positions won by the patient and erudite labors of such predecessors.

Modern scholarly interpretation of Ezekiel[1]—as of all biblical books—works with a text restored as far as possible to the form of "the lost original"; as Eichrodt writes, "Exegetical work during the last few decades ... displays increasing certainty in penetrating to the original text ..." (p. 11). The method of restoration has been to collate the ancient versions—among which G(reek) has chief importance—with the

209

Hebrew, and (1) when the Hebrew is unintelligible or looks corrupt or awkward, to correct it by recourse to the versions or conjecture; (2) where the Hebrew is different from or not represented in the versions, to decide in each case which reading is closer to the original, or make a conjecture based on the divergence. (3) On the assumption that the M(asoretic) T(ext) is considerably removed from the original, the work of restoration continues even where it and the versions agree; e.g., on theoretical grounds, matter may be deleted that is attested in all or most witnesses—repetitions, synonymous or explanatory phrases may be declared secondary or editorial. The necessity of step 1 is here granted; the legitimacy of steps 2 and 3 as now practiced must be questioned, on the ground that the stated goal of textual criticism is, in reality, obscure.

Consider the treatment of Ezekiel's commissioning (2:1–3:11) in three recent commentaries—those of Fohrer (1955), Eichrodt (1965–66), and Zimmerli (1955–69). The wording of G differs from that of MT, mostly by minuses, in 10 percent of the passage. F(ohrer) reconstructs a text diverging from MT by over 20 percent, mostly in minuses; the texts of E(ichrodt) and Z(immerli), though not identical, diverge similarly from MT by 14 percent. "Restoration of the original text" is manifestly more an art than a science; let us study the state of the art as displayed in our specimen. See the Hebrew text.

Our critics are unanimous in deleting, in 2:2 *ka^ašer dibber ʾelay;* in 2:4a *w^ehabbanim q^eše panim w^eḥizqe leb;* in 3:1 *ʾet ʾ^ašer timṣa ʾ^ekol* and in 3:6 *lo*—all these are not in G. However, though *ʾ^ašer ʾ^ani* in 2:8 is likewise not in G, not one of our critics proposes to delete it. On the other hand, several items evidenced in G are nonetheless deleted by all of them: in 3:5 *ʾel bet yiśraʾel,* and in 3:5–6 *kibde lašon* twice and *ʿimqe śapa* once. A theoretical model of a short "original" evidently exists, although this is not followed absolutely. For not only is G's minus in 2:8 *ʾ^ašer ʾ^ani* not adopted, but all our critics insert G's plus *(bet)* in 2:7, and add the copula with G and other versions to *lo* in 3:6. We must proceed to cases in order to learn what guiding principles are at work.

The most extensive divergence between MT and the restored text is the deletion, with G, of 2:4a. Here is the reasoning: F and E regard it as a gloss "quoted" from 3:7 [*ḥizqe meṣaḥ uq^eše leb*]; Z takes it as a secondary explanation of the text: *banim* is not used anywhere else in Ezekiel for the status of the people vis-à-vis YHWH, while it is a favorite expression of Isaiah and Jeremiah. On the other hand, *q^eše panim* will be a free variation of the formula found in 3:7f. 2:4b attaches best to 2:3.

Beside the basic fact of G's not evidencing these words, two or three reasons are offered for disregarding them. First, their similarity

EZEKIEL 2:1–3:11

[ii] 1 ויאמר אלי בן אדם עמד על־רגליך ואדבר אתך   2 ותבא בי רוח כאשר דבר
אלי ותעמדני על־רגלי ואשמע את מדבר אלי   3 ויאמר אלי בן־אדם שולח אני
אותך אל־בני ישראל אל־גוים המורדים אשר מרדו־בי המה ואבותם פשעו בי עד
עצם היום הזה   4 והבנים קשי פנים וחזקי־לב אני שולח אותך אליהם ואמרת אליהם
כה אמר אדני ה'   5 והמה אם־ישמעו ואם־יחדלו כי בית מרי המה וידעו כי נביא
היה בתוכם   6 ואתה בן־אדם אל־תירא מהם ומדבריהם אל־תירא כי סרבים
וסלונים אותך ואל־עקרבים אתה יושב מדבריהם אל־תירא ומפניהם אל־תחת כי
בית מרי המה   7 ודברת את־דברי אליהם אם־ישמעו ואם יחדלו כי מרי המה
8 ואתה בן־אדם שמע את אשר־אני מדבר אליך אל־תהי־מרי כבית המרי פצה
פיך ואכל את אשר־אני נתן אליך   9 ואראה והנה יד שלוחה אלי והנה־בו
מגלת־ספר   10 ויפרש אותה לפני והיא כתובה פנים ואחור וכתוב אליה קנים והגה
והי   1 [iii] ויאמר אלי בן־אדם את אשר־תמצא אכול אכול את־המגלה הזאת ולך
דבר אל־בית ישראל   2 ואפתח את־פי ויאכלני את המגלה הזאת   3 ויאמר אלי
בן־אדם בטנך תאכל ומעיך תמלא את המגלה הזאת אשר אני נתן אליך ותהי
בפי כדבש למתוק   4 ויאמר אלי בן־אדם לך־בא אל־בית ישראל ודברת בדברי
אליהם   5 כי לא אל־עם עמקי שפה וכבדי לשון אתה שלוח אל־בית ישראל
6 לא אל עמים רבים עמקי שפה וכבדי לשון אשר לא־תשמע דבריהם אם־לא
אליהם שלחתיך המה ישמעו אליך   7 ובית ישראל לא יאבו לשמע אליך כי־אינם
אבים לשמע אלי כי כל־בית ישראל חזקי־מצח וקשי־לב המה   8 הנה נתתי
את־פניך חזקים לעמת פניהם ואת־מצחך חזק לעמת מצחם   9 כשמיר חזק מצר
נתתי מצחך לא־תירא אותם ולא־תחת מפניהם כי בית־מרי המה   10 ויאמר אלי
בן־אדם את כל דברי אשר אדבר אליך קח בלבבך ובאזניך שמע   11 ולך בא אל
הגולה אל־בני עמך ודברת אליהם ואמרת אליהם כה אמר אדני ה' אם־ישמעו
ואם־יחדלו

e +בית ZEF LXX	a אתו Z	not in LXX ————	
f בה ZF (LXX)	b בית ZE (LXX)	'' Fohrer —— ——	
g קינה F (LXX)	c-c ואל תחת מפניהם Z (LXX)	[] Eichrodt _ _ _ _ _	
h ולא ZEF (LXX)	d-d סבבים וסולים EF	[] Zimmerli _ _ _ _ _	
	סלונים סבבים Z		

to phrases in 3:7 which, though not identical, are close enough to be judged as their inspiration. F (followed by E) uses "gloss" here not in the normal sense of "a brief explanation of a difficult or obscure word or expression," but—as Z puts it better—an explanatory expansion. But what needed explanation? In the end our critics mean only that 4a is an expansion suspiciously similar to words found in 3:7; as repetitious and lacking in G, it is adjudged unoriginal. Indeed, many repetitions and parallelisms have suffered at the hand of our critics, whether attested to in G or not; see the various fates of *mar'du/paš'u* (2:3), *'al tira/ 'al tira* (2:6), *middibrehem 'al tira umipp'nehem 'al tehat* (2:6), *'ekol, 'ekol 'ekol* (2:8, 3:1), *hamm'gilla hazzot, hamm'gilla hazzot, hamm'gilla hazzot 'ašer 'ani noten 'eleka* (3:1–3), *'imqe šapa w'kibde lašon* [twice] (3:5–6). On the other hand, others have survived: the repetitions of *'im yišm'u w'im yehdalu* (2:5, 7, 3:11), *ki bet m'ri hemma* (2:5, 7; but not unanimously in 2:6, 3:9); the parallelisms *bitn'ka ta'akel ume'eka t'malle* (3:3), all of 3:8, and *qah bil'bab'ka ub'ozneka š'ma'* in 3:10. A criterion for deleting does not emerge.

Before leaving this matter, it is worth noting that *q'še panim* in 2:4a is not merely a "free variation of the formula of 3:7f." It is unique. It does not mean "hard, unyielding" (Ges.-Buhl), but in the light of 3:7's *hizqe mesaḥ* must be comprehended as an original play on *q'še 'orep* (which does mean "unyielding"), with *panim* substituted for *'orep* and a consequent shift in sense to "impudent" (if anything had to be glossed, it was *q'še panim* itself!).

A second reason for disregarding 2:4a is given by Z: *banim* is not used anywhere else in Ezekiel to represent Israel's status vis-à-vis God. That is true, but it applies here as well. For *banim* in 2:4a means "the sons"—the present generation of Israelites. Cornill, who likewise rejected these phrases, argued better when he asserted that "the whole [of 2:4a] is spun out of the simple *hemma wa'abotam* [of the preceding verse]"; for Cornill, it was only "the striking vacillation in the existing mss. of G [with respect to MT's 2:4a that] shows it to be unoriginal."

Thirdly and last is Z's observation that the words are not missed, since 2:3 is best followed by 2:4b.

The judgment that the words *w'habbanim q'še panim w'hizqe leb* are unoriginal rests then on the following grounds: foremost, their absence in G; then their repetitiveness, the uncommon usage of *w'habbanim* (a ground that fails here), and their dispensability.

Before weighing these grounds, we must give our attention to a small item in 2:3: for MT *b'ne yiśra'el* G reflects *bet yiśra'el*. F renders *Israeliten*, staying with MT, but E and Z choose G. Z defends the choice: *bet yiśra'el* agrees with the dominant usage of Ezekiel; moreover, it is the point of departure for the following *bet mᵉri* (v. 5). MT is a pale [i.e., commonplace] substitute, the fault of a copyist.

At first glance, this divergence seems to be a meaningless variant.[2] On second thought a question arises: is it meaningless that G which reads *bet yiśraʾel* in 2:3 does not read *wᵉhabbanim* etc. in verse 4a, while MT which reads *bᵉne yiśraʾel* in verse 3 does read *wᵉhabbanim* etc., in verse 4a? Considering these correlations, has the divergence no exegetical import? Is MT merely more verbose? G and MT certainly agree on the gist of God's speech: Ezekiel is sent to a hard audience. But what is only hinted at in *hemma waʾᵃbotam* of verse 3 (which G has) is a veritable subtheme of the paragraph in MT. Israel's evil character is hereditary and hence hopeless. The prophet is forewarned that he is sent not to "vinegar son of wine"—to use a Talmudic phrase—but to "vinegar son of vinegar." The impudence and unyieldingness of his audience is the product of a generations-long blemish. Moses called his generation of Israelites *bᵉne meri* "sons of rebelliousness" (Num. 17:25); Ezekiel's generation, descendants of these, are called by God in the next verse *bet meri* a "house"—that is, a dynasty and a line[3]—of rebelliousness. The correlation in MT of *habbanim/bᵉne* has a consequence for translation. *bᵉne yiśraʾel* must be rendered not "Israelites" (*Israeliten*) but precisely "sons of Israel" so that one can pick up the point of verse 4, "And the sons, impudent and stubborn," etc.

It is an acute observation of Z that G's *bet yiśraʾel* is, in its context, a point of departure for *bet meri*—a pejorative twist of the name. But it turns out, upon an alert reading, that MT has its own message, conveyed precisely by its differences from G; in its context of *habbanim/bᵉne*, *bet meri* evokes *bᵉne meri*, which it converts into a hereditary line, fully in accord with a view taken elsewhere in Ezekiel of Israel's ingrained sinfulness (e.g., chs. 16, 20). The two versions thus convey different messages in this paragraph, for which their distinctive formulations are the necessary vehicles. Can one message be made a criterion for the other? Which one is more original? On what ground will the decision be made?

Two features of the MT of this passage have been mentioned that now may be enlarged upon. First, the variety of double expressions that permeate the passage: (a) apposition—"to the sons of Israel, to the rebellious nations" (2:3) at the opening of the speech; "to the exiles, to the sons of your people" (3:11) at its end; (b) synonymy and parallelism—"rebelled/transgressed" (2:3), "do not be afraid of them / of their words do not be afraid" (2:6), "hard-faced/tough-hearted" (2:4), "feed your belly / fill your stomach" (3:3), "of obscure speech/ of unintelligible language" (3:5–6), "tough browed / hard-hearted" (3:7), "do not be afraid of them / do not be dismayed by their faces"

(3:9), "take in to your heart / hear with your ears" (3:10). Chiastic alternation occurs frequently, always indicating interrelation, often resumption: in 2:3–4 *šole^ah* *^{ɔa}ni/^{ɔa}ni šole^ah;* in 2:6 *ɔal tira mehem umiddibrehem ɔal tira;* in 2:8, 3:1 *^{ɔe}kol ɔet ^{ɔa}šer ^{ɔa}ni noten / ɔet ^{ɔa}šer timṣa ^{ɔe}kol / ^{ɔe}kol ɔet hamm^egilla;* in 2:4, 3:7 *q^eše . . . w^ehizqe/ḥizqe . . . uq^eše;* in 2:3, 3:11 *ɔel b^ene yiśra^ɔel ɔel goyim hammor^edim / ɔel haggola ɔel b^ene ʿammeka* (these last two, at the beginning and the end of the passage, call attention to the interrelation of these separated phrases); and finally, *qaḥ bil^ebab^eka ub^{eɔ}ozneka š^ema^ʿ* (3:10). A feature of the parallel expressions is that one member almost invariably displays a semantic innovation or is unique while the other is commonplace: *q^eše panim w^ehizqe leb;* *ʿimqe śapa w^ekibde lašon*—the second phrase means, uniquely, "of unintelligible speech," *ḥizqe meṣaḥ uq^eše leb*, *bitn^eka ta^{ɔa}kel ume^ʿeka t^emalle*—on the first, unique phrase, see ahead; *qaḥ bil^ebab^eka ub^{eɔ}ozneka š^ema^ʿ*—the first phrase has the unique sense "take into your heart."

This feature of repetition and parallelism, occurring throughout MT, is exhibited in several items which have been deleted by one critic or another, although most have versional support. If MT exhibits such a uniform texture, on what ground other than arbitrary canons of taste can some of these items be retained, others deleted?

The second feature of the commissioning scene, which has been in a way observed by critics who supposed that 2:4a was an outgrowth of 3:7, is the close interrelation of its parts. The chiastic reversal of the adjectival parts of the phrases in 2:4a and 3:7 shows that the two are indeed interrelated, and that the interrelation was intended to be felt. A survey of the entire passage shows that such interrelation extends over the whole, and the key to the overall design is precisely the two adjectival phrases of 2:4a—*q^eše panim*—an exterior figure, and *hizqe leb*—an interior one. These play a thematic role in the sequel.

In the paragraph following immediately (2:6–7), the exterior image is taken up by *umipp^enehem ɔal tehat*, which must be rendered, not by the conventional "do not be dismayed by them," but "do not be dismayed by their faces"—so as to bring out the connection with *q^eše panim*. But the main burden of this paragraph is indicated by the threefold *ɔal tira* and the threefold occurrence of *d^ebarīm*: It is the fortification of the prophet against the stinging speech of his audience. This is directly related to the interior image *hizqe leb*, since *leb* means not only "heart" but also "source of speech" (i.e., chest), as in Proverbs 23:33 *ʿeneka yir^ɔu zarot w^elibb^eka y^edabber tahpukot* which, with H. L. Ginsberg (*EncJud*, s.v. "Heart") is to be rendered "Your eyes will see strange things and your throat will utter garbled things."

In the next paragraphs the prophet is equipped for his hard task interiorly and exteriorly. In 2:8–3:3 he is fed a scroll in order to fill his inside with messages of doom. In 3:4ff. the theme of speech leads into the exterior image: the prophet is equipped to *outface* his impudent audience. Note that the final exhortation in 3:9 differs from the similar ones in 2:6 in that *dibrehem* (which belongs to the interior image) is missing; only *mipp^enehem* is mentioned, in accord with the reference to the exterior figure.

The alternation of exterior and interior themes, the stylistic effects (chiasm) employed to interrelate the parts of the passage—these add to the impression of the integralness of MT. By deleting entire elements or altering them to accord with G, the integral effect is diminished when not destroyed. On what ground? In 2:6a MT has a monotonous but emphatic parallelism *'al tira mehem umiddibrehem 'al tira;* the second monotonous clause is deleted by F ("a variant gloss, after 6b") and replaced by Z with G's commonplace *w^e'al tehat mipp^enehem.* Why is G's commonplace variant preferable to MT's monotonous emphasis on the—for it—key elements *'al tira* and *d^ebarim*? Is one text explicable as a corruption of the other, or do we have simply variants spontaneously arising, unconnected with each other and creating different effects?

We turn now to another plus of MT over G, unanimously judged to be secondary: *'et ^ašer timṣa ^ekol* of 3:1. F, who takes out all of 3:1 as "an explanatory gloss to 2:9b," regards this clause as even more derivative—"a more closely defining gloss to the scroll"; E declares it a gloss, after Jeremiah 15:16, a point enlarged upon by Z, who reasons as follows: "The clause overloads the verse, and, materially, it is unsuitable; the scroll has already been shown to Ezekiel, so he has nothing more to find [this argument comes from Cornill]. At this juncture, we expect a command regarding the object just shown, and it appears in the second half of the verse—*^ekol 'et hamm^egilla hazzot.* The gloss is valuable because it is obviously spun out of Jeremiah 15:16 *nimṣ^e'u d^ebareka wa'ok^elem;* Ezekiel's act was thus explicitly illuminated from Jeremiah . . ."

We begin our discussion of this passage with the observation that *maṣa* means not only "find" but "find there" (BDB, 593a; cf. F *vorfindest*). The command of MT means, then, "What you find (= see) there, eat!" (NEB "eat what is in front of you"). In this clause *maṣa* has nothing to do with discovery.

As for G's minus, it is important, again, to see how the data of MT and G correlate. In MT, *'et ^ašer timṣa ^ekol* correlates with two prior clauses of identical construction: in 2:8 *š^ema^ 'et ^ašer ^ani m^edabber 'eleka* and *p^eṣe pika we^ekol 'et ^ašer ^ani noten 'eleka.* Each of these three clauses subjects the prophet to an ever more defined command of

God. First, a comprehensive demand for unconditional obedience expressly contrasted with the disobedience of Israel: "Listen to *'et ᵃšer* I speak to you! Do not be rebellious like the rebellious house! Open your mouth and eat *'et ᵃser* I give you!" Then, after the display of the object to be eaten (a scroll!), a chiastic, resumptive command, "*'et ᵃšer* you find there, eat!" One wonders whether *'et ᵃšer* here does not carry a meaning particularly fit for expressing unconditional submission to a command, namely "all that, whatever." A survey of its usage, consulting other translations to preclude self-serving, idiosyncratic interpretation, turns up evidence for just this meaning. TJ at Numbers 32:31 (*'et ᵃšer dibber YHWH 'el ᶜᵃbadeka ken naᶜᵃśe*) and Deuteronomy 29:14 (*'et ᵃšer yešno . . . wᵉᵉt ᵃšer 'enenu*) renders the combination *yat kol di*, and NEB at the last verse and at Genesis 18:19, 34:28, and Exodus 24:34 renders "all that, everything that." The Ezekiel passages may be interpreted accordingly: in all three commands the object is left vague in order to express the unconditional submission of the prophet (Z understands the idea well but does not perceive how the formulation of the sentences expresses it). After "Listen to whatever I speak to you" comes the command, "Eat whatever I give you"; the prophet had, of course, no notion of what was to be offered. He (and the reader) might well expect some kind of food. Then the scroll is displayed, and we can imagine the prophet's amazement. God's third command answers the prophet's unspoken, incredulous question, "Am I supposed to eat that?" to which God's retort is, "Whatever you find there, eat!" and then, with complete specificity, "Eat this scroll."

In 3:2 the narrative continues: "I opened my mouth (showing myself ready to obey) and he offered me the scroll to eat, saying 'Feed your belly [a strange, unique expression] and fill your stomach. . . .'" Kimḥi aptly glosses, "so as not to vomit it out of your mouth." The unusual terms of the fresh command answer the apprehension of the prophet that, though he take the scroll into his mouth and even chew it, he will never be able to swallow the indigestible mass. Accordingly God commands, "Feed your belly," that is, get it down there. Thereupon, "I ate it"—meaning I chewed it and gulped it down—"and (a miracle!) in my mouth it turned sweet as honey" (Kimḥi: "and so I fed my belly and did not vomit it").

MT thus has a graduated series of interlaced commands and acts, revealing by means of interrupted monologue the unexpressed reactions of the prophet to the strange demands of God. The gradation from a blanket demand of absolute obedience to the specific, outrageous imposition upon Ezekiel's alimentary system is skillfully drawn in MT; essential elements in it are the three commands with *'et ᵃšer* in 2:8 and 3:1.

Turning to G, we note that the absence of *'et ᵃšer timṣa ᵉkol* in 3:1

correlates with the absence of the first *ʾᵃšer* *ʾᵃni* in 2:8. The beginning of 2:8 in G reads "Hear the one talking to you"—exactly the way G renders the end of 2:2, "I heard the one talking to me." For G, 2:8 echoes as it were the beginning of the audition; not obedience is called for in G's rendition but attention: "Hear what the speaker is to say." Nothing of the graduated series of commands in MT is reflected in G, though, to be sure, it gives a perfectly intelligible, if flatter text. Once again, we have two versions, each with its own quality and its own coherence. Is a decision to be made between them? How?

Let us recapitulate: We have tried to show through a study of two examples that divergences between MT and G in Ezekiel (and by implication elsewhere) may constitute alternative messages, each with its own validity. Exegetical rewards came, in each case, by asking not which reading was the original one, but what effect did the divergence work on the messages of the respective versions. That question alerted us to correlations between divergences within each version, and stimulated a more thorough investigation of the content and language of each, particularly of MT, whose divergences were largely pluses. That question focused exegetical work where it belongs, on the working out of the meaning of the texts. Instead of hurrying to decide which of two readings is original, we tarried at the threshold of an anterior question: What does each reading mean in its own context? Experience has taught us that every divergence must be approached as possibly significant. Of course, not every one may in fact be so; but unless one is predisposed to find significance, one cannot hope to discover it if it should be there. In this way, divergences between the versions and the MT can be turned into a powerful heuristic resource; scarcely one has proven sterile in our labors on the commissioning scene.

Suppose, then, that the versional messages have each been worked out. Is it not now necessary to press on and ask which of these comes closest to the original? Several preliminary questions arise: What is meant by "the original" and what are the criteria for recognizing it? What is the likelihood that, given the present state of evidence, the quest for "the original" can meet with any measure of success?

E. Würthwein (*The Text of the Old Testament* [Oxford, 1957], 70) defines the aim of textual criticism thus: ". . . to restore the oldest text which can be recovered. This does not mean the recovery of the actual form in which the individual sentences were first conceived, but the form of the text which the OT books had when they had already attained their present shape, as regards extent and content, and were becoming canonical, which happened . . . from the fourth century B.C. onwards." In a similar vein, M. Noth writes (*The Old Testament World* [London and Philadelphia, 1966], 359): "By 'Original Text' . . . we have in mind . . the hypothetical textual form of the OT which the Palestinian canon produced as it was taking shape . . . from about the fourth century B.C." The features of this hypothetical text are unknown, but that is not a fatal obstacle to inquiry, as we read on: "It must be definitely assumed that the 'Original Text' of the OT has been corrupted . . . at a time to which no remaining textual witness extends, not even the Septuagint translation which came into being very early; furthermore we must assume that a number of original readings which had been maintained for some time were not assimilated either in M[T] or in any of the translations. Therefore, there is basically the right of free conjecture . . . , which means an assumption about the original wording which is not supported by any available old textual witness" (p. 361).

This conception of the task of textual criticism will not stand up under scrutiny. The notion of "the hypothetical textual form" (in the singular) that existed at the time of canonization posits an identity between canonization and text standardization that is flatly contradicted by all the evidence we have.[4] The only part of Hebrew Scriptures about which anything of the process of text standardization is known is the Pentateuch. An informed scholarly guess is that at some time during the Hasmonean period the Pentateuchal text was subjected to critical sifting, and that in the subsequent century or so until the destruction of the Temple a "Scroll of the Temple Court," described by tannaitic sources as a model-text, was in existence. Not only did such standardization of the text occur centuries after the Pentateuch became canonical, it occurred (according to our best guess) after the Septuagint was made. Now if scholars aimed their textual criticism at the recovery of the standard text of the Temple Court, they at least could claim to be aiming at a target known to have existed, and thus, in theory at least, attainable. But no scholar I know makes that his goal; all unhesitatingly use the Septuagint to emend and improve on MT, without knowing—indeed without caring—whether such restorations reflect the Scroll of the Temple Court or not. To what "Original Text" of the Pentateuch are they then aspiring? To the one Ezra may have brought with him from Persia? But for that early age there is absolutely no evidence of standardization! Presumably, several text forms circulated simultaneously. The Septuagint, though it may have originated before the Scroll of the Temple Court, does not, ipso facto, reflect an "older" text form. The age of text forms is not determined by the time their vehicles were produced, but by their lineage and characteristics. Judging by these, the MT—in all probability a lineal descendant of the Scroll of the Temple Court—has less vulgar characteristics than the Septuagint, despite its lateness, and thus represents a text form at least as old as that of the *Vorlage* of the Septuagint. But this means that in the third century B.C.E., when the Septuagint was made, several text forms were extant and considered authoritative.[5] Which of these is the "Original Text" that criticism aims to restore?

In the rest of the Hebrew Scriptures the situation is worse. For the Prophets and Hagiographa, evidence of text standardization does not antedate the second century C.E., when revision of the Septuagint was undertaken (e.g., by Aquila) to bring the old G into line with the recently established Hebrew standard. Tannaitic literature (to the end of the third century) attests massively to a standard text of all of Scriptures (not fully made to prevail, but the ideal was there). However, no scholar aims at recovering the standard text of tannaitic times when he applies text criticism to the MT—despite the at least theoretical possibility of attaining such a goal. Instead, we hear of "the text form when the books became canonical" as the goal, though as a criterion this is meaningless. Even according to the conventional (and improbable) view that Prophets and Hagiographa attained to canonical status only at the end of the first century, canonization and standardization were still not simultaneous in the Prophets and Hagiographa any more than in the Pentateuch. It is virtually certain, however, that canonization of the rest of Scripture occurred well before the Christian era[6]; the authority of Scripture in the intertestamental literature is warrant enough for that. Qumran fragments and G make it equally certain that before the end of the Second Temple, centuries before, variant versions of canonical books were extant. Not a scrap of evidence exists for a standardization of Prophets and Hagiographa before the second century C.E.[7] What, then, is the "Original Text" which textual criticism aims at here? Suppose we had, not the G of the commissioning scene in Ezekiel, but the Hebrew *Vorlage* of G (which, let us grant, we have correctly reconstituted in the preceding discussion); suppose it was datable to the mid-second century B.C.E. How much better off would we be than now? By what criterion would the shorter *Vorlage*, which, in chronological terms, would be older than MT, be recognizable as more "original"? To be sure, it would be a shorter text, but a poorer one too in literary values. Mere oldness is no sign of originality unless it is joined by other features known to be associated with the original. Do we know enough about the original to decide between shortness and literary richness as its hallmark? It is affirmed that shortness is a feature of originality (see Wevers, p. 35), and on that basis the minuses of the versions are combined, other subtractions ("glosses") are proposed, and a text shorter than any in evidence is "restored" as "original to the prophet". But even if the prophet spoke tersely (and there is no evidence that this was the rule), we are, after all, working with written texts. Is there any reason to think that the first written form of prophecies, whether at the dictation of the prophet or by deposition from the memory of his devotees, was also terse? Considering the pallor of the written word relative to the rich color of the spoken, it is intrinsically probable that reduction to writing entailed from the first compensatory verbal elaboration. Do we know that there was, from the first, just one collection of the prophet's speeches, from which all others descended? Was a collection completed at once, or were new finds and variants added, so that by the time it was completed it contained "authenticated" variants that diverged from and mutually contaminated each other? Were the several collections themselves sealed off from influencing one another? Is it not possible, nay probable, that within a couple of generations of the prophet's death there were already in existence not only the ancestors of the various text forms of Jeremiah and Ezekiel that underlie our MT and G, but other texts and mixed forms? Does not this probability militate against the working assumption of "the (single) hypothetical original" from the fourth century onward from which all our witnesses derive and toward the reconstruction of which all text criticism must aspire? If we further admit, with Noth and all others, that this hypothetical original was already corrupt; if we license, accordingly, free conjectural restorations, we end up in pursuit of a chimera—"the original words of the prophet" for whose identification not a single objective criterion is available.[8]

What, then, should be the object of text criticism and of exegesis based on it? We recall the facts: Extensive manuscripts of Hebrew Scripture start only from the ninth century C.E., and they all represent a single text-form, MT, though with many very minor variations which scarcely affect the sense. Before then, only very partial manuscripts and scraps fill the interval to the Qumran fragments from the turn of the era. Excepting the Samaritan Pentateuch, these all show the standard text attested in the Talmud and Midrash, again with insignificant variations. Contemporary with this fragmentary Hebrew evidence of, basically, a single text type, and a few centuries earlier, are translations of varying fidelity, the earliest parts of G reaching back to the third century B.C.E. The study of the early translations in order to reconstruct their Hebrew *Vorlagen*, though over a century old, has still far to go until its principles are worked out systematically and extensively enough to command confidence.[9] What is clear today, owing to the agreement of Qumran fragments with the Samaritan Hebrew Pentateuch and the G, is the existence in pre-Christian times of text forms of biblical books diverging from contemporary ancestors of MT. The evidence is still too meager for constructing stemmata, for at best we have (for Isaiah and Samuel) only another one or two extensive texts with which to compare a single book of MT.[10] But it is enough for assuming that not all versional divergences from MT derive from the translators; some demonstrably go back to ancient non-MT types.

Such meager resources make the task of the Hebrew text critic fundamentally different from that of the NT, the Septuagintal, or the classical text critic. For all practical purposes, the first operation of those critics lies outside his scope—the operation called "recension" (*recensio*). "Unless the manuscript tradition depends on a single witness, the function of recension is to establish the relationships of the surviving manuscripts to each other, to eliminate from consideration those which are derived exclusively from other existing manuscripts and therefore have no independent value . . . and to use this stemma or family tree to reconstruct the lost manuscript (or manuscripts) from which the surviving witnesses descend" (L. D. Reynolds and N. G. Wilson, *Scribes and Scholars* [Oxford, 1968], 137). The Hebrew text critic starts, for the greatest part of the literature, by examining the relation of the MT—the single text form in which the Hebrew has reached us—to the reconstituted *Vorlagen* of the early translations, in order to test its authenticity. Where MT shows corruption, emendation by reference to the versional *Vorlagen* and conjecture is surely a task of text criticism. It is where the Hebrew is perfectly intelligible that the present practice is, as I see it, in need of revision. If the *Vorlagen* show a divergence, too often critics have supplanted the Hebrew by it without realizing that what is at stake is not an isolated reading, but an entire context and message, or without awareness that they may be contaminating the text of one edition by that of another.[11] Elsewhere, even without versional evidence, the Hebrew has been tailored to fit a literary theory before its message has been adequately deciphered. How much may be missed by such license I have tried to show in a small specimen.

To avoid premature text alteration, exegesis and text criticism must proceed together, each illuminating the other. The exegete, whose task is to interpret text in hand, must work on the hypothesis that every element in his texts has significance—that it contributes to the meaning of its context. Only such a hypothesis keeps him alert to discover significance and design if it is there, and he will cling to it until he is baffled (at which point he may be inclined to think that some flaw exists in the text). While he notes the particulars of the versions, his focus is the MT, not because it is the best or oldest, but because it is the only complete text of the Hebrew Bible, and only through it can sound exegesis, interpreting the Hebrew by the Hebrew, be achieved.

But for illuminating the MT, no external help comes near the ancient versions, correctly used. Every divergence from the MT in a translation made from the Hebrew (like the Greek, Syriac, or Targum) calls for explanation, whether or not it is adjudged a reflection of a differing *Vorlage*. Where MT is degenerate, the value of *Vorlage* variants of the versions is undisputed. But even where MT is sound—indeed especially there—the versions are a cardinal help. For where MT is sound, the exegete glides easily onward, often without noticing hidden problems (contradictions with far and near passages), interrelations, verbal assonance and other devices that are of the essence of ancient composition. Here the versions offer a powerful stimulus: A substitution, a small omission or addition may point up a carrier of meaning that would otherwise go unobserved. Wider divergences may suggest differences in conception (of the translators or the *Vorlage*) that illuminate the Hebrew by their very contrast with it. The first question to be asked when a divergence appears is, What is its effect on the respective messages of each version? This often entails laborious lexical, syntactic, and stylistic inquiry, sometimes over new ground, but here is where discovery and excitement reward the patient exegete. Nor can he content himself with isolated readings, but he must seek correlations within each of the versions of divergences that add up to a pattern of meaning. After seeking the sense of each version in its own terms he will end up in each case with or without design, integrality, and regularity. With such results in hand, he is qualified to ask the final question: in cases of versional divergences that seem to reflect a different *Vorlage*, which reading is the best?

Given the problems of our evidence, what is a useful definition of "the best reading"? I submit: that reading by which the other(s) can be explained. If the critic can identify (or reconstruct) the reading from which the variant(s) in the other witness(es) can be derived, and if he can indicate how the variant(s) came into being according to the documented ways in which texts become corrupted or altered, he will have established the best reading that the extant witnesses make available. This is, to be sure, a relative gain only, and it leaves the "lost original" beyond the scope of text-critical inquiry, where it belongs. Sometimes (as I believe is the case in the examples shown above from Ezekiel), the critic will not be able to derive one version from the other(s). He must then be content with having reached the limit of his understanding of the witnesses—a praiseworthy, if limited, result. But to recognize and stay within one's limitations is a sign of responsibility, and it is as a call for responsibility in text-critical and exegetical work, for abandoning illusory goals in favor of the proper tasks that summon us, that my argument is advanced.

NOTES

1. Modern works on Ezekiel referred to in this article are, in alphabetic order: C. H. Cornill, *Das Buch des Propheten Ezechiel* (Leipzig, 1886); and the commentaries of W. Eichrodt (ATD Göttingen, 1965–66; English translation OTL London, 1970); G. Fohrer (HAT, Tübingen, 1955); J. W. Wevers (Century Bible, NS, London, 1969); W. Zimmerli (BK, Neukirchen Kreis Moers, 1955–69).

The commentary of (R. David) Kimḥi is cited as printed in standard rabbinic Bibles (*Miqra'ot G^edolot*).

2. As seem to be, at first glance, the five other cases of G reflecting *bet* where MT has *b^ne* listed in the *Biblia Hebraica Stuttgartensia* (K. Elliger, ed., 1971) at 2:3 note a (cf. 3:1 note b, where MT *bet* corresponds to a G reflection of *b^ne*, and BHS note b thereto listing four other such cases). The following argument for the meaningfulness of this particular variation is based on correlations uniquely present in the passages under discussion. This argument is without prejudice to the other listed cases in which the variation may or may not turn out to be meaningful.

3. That this is the nuance of *bayit* here was suggested to me by Professor Jacob Milgrom.

4. See the fine summary by Sh. Talmon, in P. R. Ackroyd and C. F. Evans (ed.), *The Cambridge History of the Bible* I (Cambridge, 1970):159–99 ("The Old Testament Text"); reprinted in F. Cross and Sh. Talmon (ed.), *Qumran and History of the Biblical Text* (Cambridge, Mass., 1975):1–43.

5. See the studies by M. H. Segal (JBL 72 [1959]:35–47), M. Greenberg (JAOS 76 [1956]: pp. 157–67), and Sh. Talmon (*Textus* 2 [1962]:14–27); reprinted in S. Leiman, *The Canon and Masorah of the Hebrew Bible* (New York, 1974):285–326, 455–68. Though old, the positions put forward in these articles respecting the Pentateuch still merit attention.

6. The carefully reasoned conclusion of S. Leiman, *The Canonization of Hebrew Scripture* (Hamden, 1976), is that the mid-second century B.C.E. is the time of the closing of the biblical canon (131ff.).

7. L. Blau, *Studien zum althebräischen Buchwesen* (Budapest, 1902), 110f., thought that Tosefta Kelim II:5.8 (584[10]) alluded to a standard Temple text of the Prophets. The passage is wholly obscure; see Leiman, *Canonization,* 104f., and notes thereto.

The fundamental difference between the Torah and the rest of Scripture with respect to text-stabilization has not hitherto been adequately noticed. It was Professor Elias Bickerman who called it to my attention, observing that since the Torah was the constitution of the Jewish polity, the fountainhead of law of the religious community, there was a special urgency in establishing its text and standardizing it for the entire people. This will account for the evidence that only for the Torah was any editing work done, as well as for the decided superiority of the MT of the Torah (presumably a direct descendant of the Scroll of the Temple Court) over the other ancient versions. As is known, outside the Torah, MT often has no such superiority (as in the text of Samuel).

8. Talmon (in the article cited above, note 3) raised the possibility, on the basis of the correlation of antiquity and variety in the textual evidence that "individual variants, and also groups or even types of variants, which have been preserved in the ancient versions both in Hebrew and in translations, may derive from divergent pristine textual traditions" (162). Accordingly, at the end of his study, "the investigator may carefully conclude that with the available evidence no 'first' text form can be established. Or else, . . . he may attempt to reconstitute the presumed pristine texts of each of the major versions individually. It then still remains to be debated whether these proto-texts of the extant versions can be reduced to one common stem, or whether, at least in part, they must be considered to represent intrinsically independent textual traditions . . ." (163). Since the situation varies from book to book, generalization is not very useful except for alerting one to alternatives. I am pleading against the working hypothesis of an "original" where available evidence runs against it, as seems to me to be the case in many of the variants between MT and G I have so far found in Ezekiel. This hypothesis here has simply short-circuited the exegetical process.

224 : The Biblical Text and Its Interpretation

It may be noted, incidentally, that F. M. Cross's conviction that the rise of divergent text types requires geographic dispersion and local isolation is not well grounded: some random counterexamples from ancient Near Eastern literature have been adduced by M. Tsevat in "Common Sense and Hypothesis in OT Study," VTSup 28 (1975): 225f. For a recent reiteration by Cross of his conviction see *Qumran and the History of the Biblical Text,* 309.

The question of "original texts" takes on an altered aspect in light of the inner-biblical variant, synonymous and double readings (see Talmon's latest, suggestive contribution to the understanding of these phenomena in the just-cited work, 321–400), but especially in the light of the theory of an oral substratum that underlies them. Perhaps the earliest grappling with the problem is Ibn Ezra's (d. 1164), in his comment at Exodus 20:1 on the double tradition of the Decalogue: "It was the custom of speakers of Hebrew sometimes to speak at length, sometimes to say what they had to tersely, but so as to enable the hearer to grasp their meaning. Understand that words are like bodies and meanings like souls, and the body is to the soul like a vessel; hence it is the custom of all wise men in speaking any language to preserve the meanings while not being concerned over changing the words, so long as their meaning is the same." R. B. Coote ("The Application of Oral Theory to Biblical Hebrew Literature," *Semeia* 5 [1976:51–64) proposes that oral theory suggests a way to account for "hyparchetypical, or irreducible variants (zero variants, parallel variants, synonymous readings and the like)." "It can be argued that there must have been a first writing down of a composition, somewhere, some time. But if the tradition of its transmission accepted or produced reformulations and preserved its multiforms, why should greater importance be imputed to the hypothetical original than the ancients thought it had? Their indifference to verbatim fidelity to an original makes the recovery of a single original text an elusive and possibly mistaken goal" (60–1). Postbiblical Jewish literature offers a large field for observing the practice of written transmission of an originally oral literature; particularly relevant is J. Heinemann's discussion of "The development of prayers and the problem of 'the original text,'" chapter 2 of his *Prayer in the Talmud* (Berlin, 1977).

I am aware that the argument for multiple "originals" can be turned against me: if the transcribers and transmitters exercised such freedom as long as it did not alter the meaning, what justifies poring over their products in order to extract significance from their variations? The answer is that "meaning" is a broad term. There are several ways to "say" something, and their effects may not be the same. It is precisely the exegete's task to determine whether the various ways of saying a given thing all have the same significance. His results will gain in persuasiveness to the extent that they are based on combination and correlation of several items in a given version, as I have tried to show in the examples from Ezekiel.

9. See the excellent cautions of J. Barr, *Comparative Philology and the Text of the Old Testament* (Oxford, 1968): 238–72; much new light on the nature of the Peshitta as a translation, and, hence, on how to judge it as a reflection of a Hebrew *Vorlage* is contained in Y. Maori, *The Peshitta Version of the Pentateuch in Its Relation to the Sources of Jewish Exegesis* (Jerusalem [Heb. Univ. diss.], 1975). For a detailed illustration of the extreme care taken by the editor of the Hebrew University Bible Project to avoid pitfalls in retroversion, see M. Goshen-Gottstein, "Theory and Practice of Textual Criticism," *Textus* 3 (1963):130–58.

10. L'Abbé Jean Carmignac informs me that for the Book of Chronicles he has been able to construct a stemma, combining the evidence of the Hebrew (Chronicles and Kings) and the Greek, going back to a single archetype. It is much to be desired that at least samples of chapter length be published for the inspection and edification of fellow workers in the field.

11. On the latter danger, see the sober strictures of E. Tov in his "Studies in the methods and limitations of biblical text criticism" (Heb.), to appear in the Loewenstamm *Festschrift*; in that article (whose proofs Dr. Tov kindly allowed me to read) he develops some points summarized in his entry "Septuagint. Contribution to OT Scholarship," in the *Supplementary Volume* of the IDB (Nashville, 1976):807–11. Tov recognizes recensions of biblical books, identifiable by systematic stylistic or doctrinal characteristics (e.g., the short and long recensions of Jeremiah, the divergent chronological sys-

tems of the G and MT of Kings); he regards recensions as lineally related. He does not consider the possibility of irreducible variants going back to plural primary versions.

Additional note:

The view that the early Jewish liturgy was loosely formulated and liable to various realizations has been powerfully challenged by Ezra Fleischer in "On the Beginnings of the Obligatory Prayers in Judaism," *Tarbiz* 59 (5750 [1990]), 397–441 (in Hebrew).

Reflections on Interpretation*
1979

Two opposed axioms have served, historically, for the interpretation of the Bible, one theological, the other historical-analogical. The theological axiom maintains that without insight gained from faith in the divine origin of Scripture, its message cannot be understood. Faith is rewarded by grace whose light illumines the meaning of Scripture. A modern Catholic states the axiom as follows:

> ... the Church has always maintained ... that ... all natural knowledge, even the maximum of natural knowledge, will never succeed in understanding the Word of God as it should be understood ... if the light of grace and the holy desire for what is good, inspired by grace, do not enlighten and animate the reader of the Bible. The vitally essential ... content of the divine message can be ... more clearly perceived by a simple and upright soul responding to God's call ... than by a very erudite and, humanly speaking, very acute scholar who is impervious to the things of God.[1]

Historically, the product of this axiom has usually been an exegesis that puts into Scripture what ought to be believed rather than attending to what it says. The reaction, which reached fullest articulation in Chapter vii of Spinoza's *Theological-Political Tractate* (first printing, 1670), insisted that nothing but what Scripture itself revealed of its sense might be used in interpreting it. The ordinary process of induction, so fruitful in arriving at an understanding of nature, was adequate for—was indeed the only legitimate basis of—interpreting the Bible.

*Bibliog. 140, first part

> . . . the method of interpreting Scripture does not differ from the
> method of interpreting nature . . . For as the interpretation of nature
> consists in drawing up a history (= a systematic account of the data) of
> nature and therefrom inferring definitions of natural phenomena, so
> Scriptural interpretation necessarily proceeds by drawing up a true
> history of Scripture and from it . . . to infer correctly the intentions of
> the authors of Scripture . . . Everyone will advance without danger of
> error . . . if they admit no principles for interpreting Scripture . . . save
> such as they find in Scripture itself.[2]

This program promised a universe of discourse transcending partisanship by adopting for Scripture interpretation the universally accepted
canons of natural science. For scholars, the prospect of getting beyond
dogmatic particularity and disagreement to scientific universality and
consensus was the value that outweighed whatever spiritual treasure
accrued from treating Scripture differently from all other literature as
a special language of divine truths. Having voted for scientific universality, the interpretation of Scripture became linked in the nineteenth
century to the career of literary-historical interpretation at large. The
analogy of the latter was decisive for the former.

> The main conclusions of critics . . . rest upon reasonings the cogency of
> which cannot be denied without denying the ordinary principles by
> which history is judged and evidence estimated.
>
> The character of a particular part of the OT cannot be decided by
> an *a priori* argument as regards what it *must* be; it can only be deter-
> mined by an application of the canons of evidence and probability uni-
> versally employed in historical or literary investigation.[3]

As it is often put: the Bible must be interpreted like any other ancient
book.

Western critics approach biblical literature with expectations
formed from familiarity with Western literature and literary criticism.
Biblical narrative, history, legal writing, prophetic sermons, and
poems are judged by their presumed Western counterparts. Order,
progression, (con)sequentiality, regularity, consistency, and coherence
are the features of good Western models of each of these genres. If
flaws in these attributes occur they may signal corruption, tampering,
or multiple authorship. Critical training of biblicists sharpens the perception of these attributes or the lack of them in the biblical texts and
accounts for the predominance of criticism based on such criteria in
biblical scholarship. It is axiomatic that any other estimate of a literary
piece follow upon a literary-historical analysis and depend on it. Before assessing the meaning of a prophetic sermon, one must give an

account of its integrity—the criteria of this account having been drawn from elsewhere than prophetic literature.

One notes an increasing dissatisfaction with such a method of criticism; its standards are drawn from too narrow a range of literature and lack the support of extensive descriptions of biblical literature in its own terms. Despite the large amount of poetry in the Bible, the process and products of Hebrew poetic creativity aside from such structural matters as form, meter, and parallelism have been slighted. (The application to biblical poetry of "canons universally employed in literary investigation" by earlier critics led to conclusions about meter and parallelism justifying wholesale rewriting of psalms; the enlarged horizon of post-Ugaritic scholarship makes that earlier criticism appear hopelessly parochial.) In the course of analyzing and describing the poetry and poetic devices of the Song of Songs, a scholarly poet has recently shown up the failures of modern scholarly commentary to the Song, due to a simple ignorance of what poetry is.[4] Since biblicists have so seldom produced systematic accounts of Hebrew rhetoric and storytelling, linguists, folklorists, comparativists, and the like have ranged uninhibitedly up and down the Bible, often to the justified chagrin of biblicists.

We know so little about the principles of composition of the various genres of Hebrew literature that it behooves us to stay our hands until we open our ears. It is observed in the Midrash that "Scripture disregards chronological order";[5] modern criticism has also noted that, and proceeds to rearrange text-material according to chronology. But if native Hebrew narrative (or editing) valued historical order less than we do, such a procedure only highlights the gap in values between us and them, without shedding light on their values. Standard critical procedure yields an analysis of the text that points up its tensions— according to history-oriented canons. The tension is resolved by separating the material into kernels and accretions whose combination allegedly produced the tension. But it is never demonstrated (it cannot be) that the tension was not there from the start, so that the tensionless reconstruction may be an answer to a modern critical, but no proven ancient, canon of composition. By such a procedure one can hardly be led to other principles of composition, compared to which the chronological might be subordinate (a corollary of the above-mentioned midrashic observation, for example, is the legitimacy of inference from juxtaposition; i.e., propinquity is exegetically significant).[6]

As an alternative to both the foregoing, we propose a holistic interpretation, "emphasizing the organic or functional relation between parts and wholes" (Webster).[7] As the religious person approaches the text open to God's call, so must the interpreter come "all ears" to hear what the text is saying. One must subjugate one's habits of thought and expression to the words before him or her and become actively passive—full of initiatives to heighten receptivity. For an axiom, one has the working hypothesis that the text as is has been designed to convey a message, a meaning. For if it does have design and meaning, that design and meaning will be discovered only by effort expended to justify such an assumption. Readiness to find evidence of design and significance is the exegete's analogue to openness to hear God's word on the part of the faithful reader.

How can such an approach be guarded against uncritical accept- ance of things as they are, and against reading in ad hoc explanations or making fanciful connections? Here it appropriates something of the historical-analogical, namely, the inference from the text itself of prin- ciples of its interpretation. Being "all ears" means to lend a general attentiveness to the text given normally today only to poetry. One must be ready to find signifiers on several levels and of several types. Since one cannot know a priori where the clues lie, one's attention must include vocabulary, grammatical forms, phonology, and asso- nance. The following battery of questions is calculated to discover the pattern(s) of significance of a passage from inside it. (No mind is paid to overlapping.)

Is the unit that is delimited formally (by, say, opening and closing formulas)[8] shown to be a unit through its structure (a recognized pat- tern?), its content, its figures, or its verbal devices?

How much interrelation and reference occurs among its parts?

How much repetition (if with variations, are they significant)?

How much irregularity occurs (in grammar, in length of lines, etc.), and how much regularity?

In the event of nonsequentiality, is another ground of collocation evident (e.g., thematic, or verbal association)?

Are affective elements present besides the plain sense of senten- ces, such as alliteration, punning, or chiasm? To what do they call attention?[9]

How much ambiguity is present; what are its causes and effects?

Are elements that seem opaque illuminated by considering their placement (significance through juxtaposition)?

To what extent are themes, peculiarities, or difficulties recurrent elsewhere? in identical or variant form? if not in the Bible, then out- side it?

How far is one's perception of the main message of a unit corrobo- rated by later readers (postbiblical literature, medieval commentar- ies); if there is a difference, why?

After submitting the text to such a battery and patiently pursuing all leads to significance, one may end up with intractable intrusions, anachronisms, opaque matter, which defy integration into a single (temporal, thematic) pattern. With respect to such matter, the working hypothesis will have failed; the alternatives of corruption, accident, or secondary, clumsy addition may be invoked. But these are last resorts, and there must always lurk in the back of one's mind the possibility that one has missed a point.

Was there a historical time in which the text was (or might have been) understood in accord with our holistic interpretation of it? To clarify this, we must put the same question to the theological and the historical-analogical methods. It seems that involved in the answer of each is a presupposition, a prejudice of a kind that casts doubt on the historical validity of any exegesis on the one hand, while, on the other, it justifies the (even contemporaneous) variety of interpretations of a text regarded as a cultural heritage.

Theological exegesis takes the text at face value—it is the inspired words of the prophet. Though the prophet spoke in particular circumstances, his message contains teaching for the godly of all ages, since the meaning of God's words is inexhaustible. The audience of the prophet caught his meaning according to the variety of their capacities, but even the prophet himself may not necessarily have plumbed the sense of what he spoke. Theological interpretation is ultimately uninterested in the historical question we posed above; its concern is to educe the timeless truths of the divine message. In all cases these truths are couched in the intellectual idiom of the exegete; if he is a midrashist, the prophet is made to speak the idiom and values of midrash; if an Aristotelian, of Aristotle, if a kabbalist, of the Kabbala. The explicit intention of theological exegesis is to illuminate the text by the light of the best and deepest comprehension of divine matters known to the exegete. Theoretically, such a comprehension might have existed at any time; in the view of the exegete, it is not time-bound. That is the necessary implication of the theological prejudice concerning the inexhaustibility of God's word.

Historical-analogical exegesis aims at a perspective view of the biblical text: an original core having a meaning conditioned by time and place, with subsequent reworkings and additions—all portrayed as a process of development. As presently practiced, this method lacks empirically established criteria and therefore yields results too divergent to inspire confidence. That nevertheless it has been almost universally adopted as a criterion for scholarship in the field means that it answers some overriding need or prejudice. Two such may readily be identified. The triumphs of evolutionism in natural science have made it the hallmark of intellectual modernity. Over against the essentially medieval unconcern (and unawareness) of history, so characteristic of theological exegesis, current critical exegesis opposes its perspective, developmental view of the text as its chief qualification for intellectual respectability in our time. Hence, any proposal of literary development is better than none—better in that it demonstrates sophistication, that is, advancement beyond medieval, dogmatic prejudices and naïveté.

A second need for the historical-analogical method arises from the situation of the Christian faith community that is its matrix. First, that community must justify its retention of the Old Testament alongside the New, and does so by showing that light is shed upon the New by viewing the Old as a series of steps leading up to it. The more fully this can be worked out, the greater the value set on the Old Testament. Second (though less articulated), that community, though buffeted by change and modernity, affirms the validity of its ancient Scripture in the present. This affirmation is accomplished by showing that the biblical text itself incorporates a record of reinterpretation, adjustment to change and supplementation by later hands. Given the community's overriding need for validating constant reinterpretation, any proposal that roots that process in the biblical text itself will have a bias in its favor.

The validity of the historical outlook and the need of faith-communities to justify change is not impugned when one suggests that prejudices rooted in these underlie the academic encouragement of ever new and divergent analyses of literary development. Such prejudices make scholars tolerate the narrow, inadequately tested assumptions on which these analyses are based and the divergences that must undermine their claims to reflect the stages of textual development.

Our holistic interpretation seeks to reconstitute the perception of the text by an ideal reader living at a time when it had reached its present disposition. "Ideal reader" is a personified realization of the possibilities inherent in the text at that moment. In the case of Ezekiel, for example, the context of densest significance for that ideal reader will have been the canonical book. As he read it the first time, each encounter with a fresh passage, a repetition, a variation on a phrase or theme will have affected him according to his growing experience of the book. On the second reading, these will have complexified as later elements now seemed foreshadowed, and as early elements resonated in later reminiscences. Our ideal reader will have been sensible of such resonances, echoes and allusions, and the holistic interpreter will attempt to reproduce those sensibilities. The ideal reader will also have been familiar with the literary, the historical, and the environmental allusions in the book; the exegete must resort to the rest of biblical literature (preferably, but not exclusively, to works that might have been known to the prophet), and, where relevant, to extrabiblical literature for such information. The ideal reader treats the book as full of significance (it offers a key to his people's destiny in the past and future); the interpreter will strain to discover this significance through the battery of questions listed above. Where he fails, he will consider, beside his own shortcomings, the possibility of faults or intrusions of various kinds in the text; in this he will use the early witness to the Hebrew, conscious of the limitations of such use. Evident compositeness of a literary unit will be duly noted, but not taken to release the interpreter from the obligation to see the interrelation of the components; for all he knows such interrelation as he may discover was already in the mind of whoever collocated these components, perhaps the prophet himself. Palpable accretions or intrusions, such as contradictions and anachronisms, the interpreter does not undertake, of course, to integrate into the surrounding material; but he will try to explain their presence and consider their (confusing) effect on the ideal reader (aided by the makeshifts of translators and early commentators).

In his quest for significance—necessarily, significance for him— the holistic interpreter partially resembles the theological exegete seeking timeless truth. In the historical controls he imposes on himself, he resembles partly the historical-analogical exegete. Because he resembles both, he compounds his risks. He must beware of reading into his texts private or modern significances on the one hand, and of overrating his historical-literary judgment on the other. What lures him into this double jeopardy? The chance that he may discover the cause of (and thus corroborate) the initial veneration of the Scriptures; that he may experience the editor-canonizer as a fellow intelligence, whose product became a classic not (perversely) in spite of its character but (deservedly) because of it. Ultimately, the holistic interpreter is animated by a respect for his cultural heritage that takes the form of a prejudice in favor of the ancient biblical author-editors and their transmitters. He requires more than a theoretical cause before discounting and disintegrating their products. He sees himself not so different from them as to be unable to appreciate what they did in terms at once native to them and meaningful to him. The holistic interpreter is prepared to risk failure in order to establish the claim of his cultural heritage on its heirs.[10]

NOTES

1. J. Levie, S.J., *The Bible, Word of God in Words of Men* (English translation from French by S. H. Treman), New York: Kenedy, n.d. (imprimatur, 1961), 130f.

2. The Elwes translation (reprinted New York: Dover, 1951), 99, adjusted to Wirzubski's (Hebrew, Jerusalem: Magnes, 1961), 79.

3. S. R. Driver, *An Introduction to the Literature of the Old Testament*, 9th ed. (Edinburgh: Clark, 1913) viif., x. On the "omnicompetence of analogy" for criticism, see the citation from Tröltsch in G. von Rad, *Old Testament Theology*, vol. I (English translation from German by D. M. G. Stalker; Edinburgh and London: Oliver and Boyd, 1962):107, n. 3.

4. M. Falk, *The Song of Songs: a verse translation with exposition*, Stanford University dissertation, 1976; see especially 133ff. on the *wasf* [published as *The Song of Songs: A New Translation and Interpretation*, HarperSanFrancisco, 1990; the *wasf* is treated on pages 127ff].

5. Mechilta to Exodus 15:9, "The enemy said"; see comments of J. Goldin, *The Song at the Sea* (New Haven and London: Yale, 1971), 174ff.

6. Sifre, Numbers to 25:1; see W. Bacher, *Die exegetische Terminologie der jüdischen Traditionsliteratur*, 2 vols. (Leipzig 1899, 1905; reprinted Darmstadt: Wissenschaftliche Buchgesellschaft, 1965), I:133; II:143.

7. Many have followed a similar method in studies of individual pieces of biblical literature, without much effect on modern Bible commentators. I have learned much from M. Weiss, who describes and illustrates his "Total-Interpretation" in VTSup 22 (*Congress Volume Uppsala*, Leiden: Brill, 1972):88–112 (see p. 90, n. 1 for earlier items) and in his book *Hammiqra kid‛muto*[2] (Jerusalem: Bialik, 1967 [revised and augmented in English, *The Bible from Within*, Jerusalem: Magnes Press, 1984]). A recent contribution full of interest is Alan M. Cooper, *Biblical Poetics: a Linguistic Approach*, Yale University dissertation, 1976.

8. This characteristic of Ezekiel is, of course, not shared by all other prophetic books.

9. Although commentators are increasingly alert to the presence of such elements, they are notably remiss in interpreting them; a lesson in the interpretation of alliteration and chiasm is the luminous study of the Tower of Babel story in J. P. Fokkelman, *Narrative Art in Genesis: specimens of stylistic and structural analysis* (Amsterdam/Assen: Van Gorcum, 1975).

10. An important appeal for serious consideration of the exegetical and theological significance of the canonized form of biblical literature—heightened by awareness of its probable antecedent stages—is made by B. S. Childs, in "The Exegetical Significance of Canon for the Study of the Old Testament," *Congress Volume: Göttingen 1977* (VTSup, xxix, Leiden: Brill, 1978), 66–80.

To Whom and for What Should a Bible Commentator Be Responsible?
1990

The following remarks result from long consideration of the question: What should be the nature of a modern scholarly Hebrew Bible commentary aimed at the broad readership of the Bible in Israel?[1]

The readership I have in view has graduated from a local high school, and hence has gained a rudimentary knowledge of the Bible from the years' long public school Bible curriculum. It respects the Bible as a national treasure and as the foundation document of the people—a component of its identity. But the bulk of this readership is not committed to religious observances and does not subscribe to traditional doctrines. It is theologically naive, with little idea of the complexity of religious thought or the issues of interpretation of literature in general, and of the Bible in particular. Though defining itself predominantly as secular, it has at least a residual spiritual faculty that seeks activation. This faculty is the potential point of contact between the broad Israeli public and the Bible commentator, since one of its expressions is an interest in the meaning and significance of the Bible for its time and for ours.[2] How can the commentator engage such a readership? What can he or she offer it? More pointedly, what should be offered?

For today's orthodox readership, a Hebrew Bible commentary is well under way: the series *Da'at Mikra* published by Mossad Harav Kook. The volumes of that series bring current philological, archaeological, and historical findings to the attention of the reader as long as they do not challenge traditional positions.[3] Their religious sophistication is at a level roughly equivalent to that of medieval theology, and the bounds of their interpretational liberty are in principle those set by mainstream plain-sense medieval exegetes. Particularly simplistic and conservative is *Da'at Mikra*'s handling of questions of literary history: It does not challenge traditional ascriptions of authorship or investigate the arguments against such ascriptions. It does not discuss literary history and evidences of stages of composition, alteration, or corruption. The idea of development and change—among the components of biblical literature, or between the Bible and normative Talmudic Judaism—is repugnant to orthodoxy, and hence to its Bible commentary. Such curbs on curiosity and research are alien to modern secular worldviews and scholarship: they limit the acceptability and usefulness of *Da'at Mikra* to circles of orthodoxy.

What the modern Israeli scholarly Bible commentator can offer the general reader need not coincide with what he or she should offer; I address my further remarks to the distinction.

A scholarly commentator is first (chronologically) a scholar; and unless he or she is unusually reflective, the notion of this task is determined by a scholar's method and agenda. The method is historical-philological, and the agenda consists in the main of analysis: on the historical side, sorting out the history of the text—what lies behind the finished text, what elements constitute it, and how they came together; on the philological side, the study of lexicography and grammar, stylistics, and poetics. The latter study too is historically oriented; e.g., early and late linguistic elements, and developmental poetics. Attention is paid to the history of ideas as it is reflected in the divergent elements of the text. In Israeli Bible scholarship the significance of the texts—their bearing on life, their universal or timeless value—whether it be revealed through form criticism or religious phenomenology, is secondary and slighted. This is perhaps due to sheer exhaustion: When the historical-philological inquiry is finished, there's no energy left for the inquiry into the significance. Such inquiry may be avoided also out of fear of its seeming to be apologetic. Moreover, it seems less objective, more liable to emotional or valuational bias. As to form criticism, it is too conjectural, lacking hard evidence for its reconstructed occasions and life-settings. I suspect too that in reaction to premodern confusion of theology and interpretation, paralleled by modern confusion of ideology and interpretation, current Israeli Bible scholars play it safe by avoiding inquiry into the significance of the texts they study. Little wonder, then, that the academic study of the Bible is perceived as irrelevant by the bulk of the Israeli public.[4]

Recently, under the impact of general literary criticism, the meaning of the finished composition has become a legitimate academic study—the synthesizing task of understanding the text in hand as a coherent artifact, a carrier of a message through the very manner by which its elements have been fashioned and combined. But the way in which meaning is achieved, the esthetic appeal, and the power of the text, are not usually related to larger, existential issues of moral, religious, political, or social significance even for the biblical age.

Such then are the tasks that the scholarly method and agenda of Israel biblical scholarship enable the scholar to perform as a commentator. Do they answer to the purposes for which the public turns to a commentary? What might be those purposes?

1. To satisfy curiosity or dispel perplexity about the facts of the text (e.g., historical, geographical) or its meaning (e.g., textual or lexical puzzles, literary or mythical allusions).
2. To answer questions about the moral level of Scripture (does the "fellow" [*re'aka*] of Leviticus 19:18 whom you must love as yourself include the non-Israelite? What does the answer imply regarding the universality of biblical law?); to explain (not excuse) its morally embarrassing and offensive passages and concepts (e.g., the genocidal *herem* law).
3. To understand concepts alien to modern secularity (holiness/profaneness and purity/impurity; miracles).
4. Ultimately, to get some idea of the importance of the Bible—why it was and remains the basis of Jewish culture.

If the scope of historical-philology is bounded by the linguistic aspect of the document and the history of its composition, only the first questions will be treated in the commentary. But if elucidating the cultural cargo of the document is included in the commentator's task, then such general concepts as are included in questions 2, 3, and 4 will be addressed as well. But for these, a certain philosophical outlook is needed, at least a modest habit of conceptualization and generalization, and a minimal interest in cultural comparisons and anthropology.

Narrow construction of the commentator's task is exemplified in Martin Noth's treatment of the passages regulating sexual relations in his commentary to Leviticus.[5] He dwells on the form of the list of prohibited relations, from which he deduces the kernel of the list and its later accretions. He seeks some order in the prohibited relations. The reader will not find anything about the ground of these prohibitions, their purpose or function, the values underlying them or their connection with other biblical values—let alone what distinctiveness, if any, the biblical prohibitions have in their ancient setting. Not all commentators have laid such constraints on their curiosity and that of their readers. Some Iberian-Jewish medievals who were philosophically trained (e.g., Joseph Ibn Caspi; Abravanel) sought psychological and social grounds for the incest rules. A modern commentator should probably prefer to render an account more in anthropological terms. If Noth's curiosity was ever stirred by the question of the motives and purposes of the sexual prohibitions of Leviticus, he hid the fact from his readers. But surely that is what might relate the dry list to the modern reader's life and concerns.

Perhaps the greatest need of the Israeli public, with respect to its reading of the Bible, is to be emancipated from the simple positivistic appreciation of the historical narratives as either truth or fabrications. One either accepts or strives to show that the events related happened as told, or that nothing or little in reality corresponds to the narrative. A secular fundamentalism prevails that misses the purpose of the narrative to express a religious perception of events. The categorization of the conquest stories in the book of Joshua as either true or false representations of the course of Israel's occupation of Canaan is the primary task of a military historian. It cannot be the primary task of a commentator to the book of Joshua. The historian's first task is to render a judgment about the reliability and accuracy of witnesses. The commentator is called on to do something else: to be the voice and mediator to a modern reader of the ancient witness—its worldview, and its meaning and significance. The message conveyed by the stories of the book of Joshua is that the conquest of the land of Canaan by ancient Israel was a train of divine interventions on behalf of Israel. The Psalmist expressed it with poetic economy:

> It was not by their sword that they took the land, their arm did not give them victory, but your right hand, your arm, and your goodwill, for you favored them. (44:4)

The events themselves are mere vehicles of this message. The best current archaeological conjecture concerning the Israelite occupation of Canaan, if substituted for the biblical data, would not convey the essential feature of the biblical narrative, which is not a specific sequence of events, but the presentation of those events as the working of God in Israel's history. Taken on positivistic terms, the Book of Joshua will be judged inferior to any modern history of ancient Israel's land-taking.[6] As a religious perception of that epoch, the conquest story serves as a precedent and a model for God's faithfulness to his covenant promise, and for the connection of Israel's fate to its faith and conduct. To be sure, the commentator has a responsibility to the reader to indicate (perhaps in an appendix) what is thought today to be the relation of the biblical story to the story historians and archaeologists tell. But the first task is to interpret the biblical story as the foundation of Israel's understanding the terms on which it took possession of its land, and retains possession of it—terms that shaped

Judaism's vision of its ultimate reoccupation of the promised land as well. The rhetoric of that foundation document is the proper object of commentatorial exposition: What is the cause of the persuasive power the foundation story exercised on generations of readers? The positivistic alternatives—historical/unhistorical—simply do not do justice to the text of Joshua. They miss the essence of the document, why it was received into the sacred canon and why it was transmitted for the ages. They also make it easy to ignore the moral issue raised in the mind of any unspoiled reader by the genocidal policy ascribed to Joshua—as though a modern Jew could or should be indifferent toward it![7]

This leads us to another aspect of the commentator's task that is absent from the conventional agenda of the philological-historical method: taking notice of the effect produced by the biblical text on later readers.

According to the tenets of the historical-philological method, the meaning of a text is determined by its historical setting. Properly understood, this tenet includes the work of the historical philologists: their understanding is conditioned by their historical setting as well. Awareness of this basic condition of interpretation must recommend diffidence in deciding the meaning of the text. It must especially open the mind to one crippling stricture the historical-philological tenet tends to impose: the neglect of later readings of the biblical text. It is not merely that later readers might and often do supply interpretations that illuminate the primary sense—which so often transcends its specific setting. It is that the meaning and significance of a passage (an event, an utterance) may not be realized until activated by later circumstances or contemplation.[8] Given that the primary task of a commentator is to set forth the first meaning of a text—that which may be supposed to have been understood by its first hearers or readers, this does not settle the status of understandings not documented till post-biblical times, but that, once discovered, cast a vivid light on the biblical text. Should not profound implications of a passage, realized only later, also be considered within the scope of a commentary whose aim is to show how and why the Bible became the formative document of Judaism?

From the fact that in the creation story Adam was the sole exemplar of humanity while other species were created in plurality, nothing is inferred in the Bible. Later Jewish sages, impressed by the teleology of the story—the whole world seems designed for humans—were struck by the disproportion: heaven and earth and all therein created for one human (or human pair)! They drew the inspired inference from this that each human being, a copy of Adam or Eve, is worth the world; hence, to destroy any human is tantamount to destroying an

Adam or an Eve, i.e., tantamount to overturning God's purpose in creating the world. Another inference: all humankind, being descendants of the same parents, are of equal rank and value; none can claim superior pedigree. And another lesson: how glorious the creator is who can produce endless copies of the first pair without ever repeating himself! The irreducible individuality of each human reflects glory on God (all the above, Mishnah Sanhedrin, 4:5). None of these value concepts are to be found or even alluded to in the Bible, yet they are of the very essence of Jewish anthropology. In an exposition of the biblical story of creation can the author of a Jewish commentary justifiably omit informing the reader of these profound outworkings of the biblical story?

An example of a passage whose later interpretation has a claim to be considered a first meaning, because later events seem to confirm it, is the universalistic spiritual reading of the divine assurance or prediction to Abraham, "All the families of the earth will be blessed (or: will bless themselves) in/by you" (Gen. 12:3). Jewish interpretations cluster around two poles:

a) People will bless each other by (citing) you: "May He who blessed Abraham bless you" (Abraham and his progeny will be models of well-being so that no better blessing can be imagined than, "May God bless you as he blessed Abraham" [Tanḥuma; Rashi]).

b) "You will mediate God's blessing to all mankind." This was early on interpreted materially—"Rain through your virtue; dew through your virtue" (the general welfare of mankind will be protected because of you—i.e., Abraham and his offspring will justify the world to God and earn by their merit his care and provision [Genesis Rabba]). Centuries later it was interpreted spiritually by Abravanel: "All the families of the earth will be blessed, provided for and benefitted on his account, for the world will become aware of God through Abraham and his offspring. Blessing and providence will adhere to any people that adopt his discipline and his faith."

The thoughtful commentator will not rush to decide what was the "original meaning" of this passage. How paltry a reading results from a deliberate skewing of the universal one appears in the comment offered by an outstanding modern Jewish commentator, U. Cassuto: "(Abraham) will have the merit of being a source of blessing to all the peoples of the land—his virtue and prayers working on their behalf with the heavenly court."[9] Cassuto has Abraham's intercessory role on behalf of Abimelech and Sodom and Gomorrah in mind. Does such specificity give the full scope of mediation attributed to the patriarch? This example raises the question of interpretational adequacy.

As we said at the outset, the Bible has a special status in the eyes of all Israeli Jews (as for Jews in general). How ought that fact to influence its exegesis? By recommending to the commentator the principle that, all things being equal, the adequate reading of the text is the one that gets the best meaning out of it. If the choice is between an interpretation that posits incoherence and one that posits coherence, the commentator ought to choose the latter. If one reading posits a pedestrian writer, and another reveals an artist, he or she should choose the latter. This bias in favor of the text is justified by the enormous power it has exercised on the history of culture. Weak readings simply fail as explicators of the text's effect. One has to admit that there is a risk of overinterpretation, but erroneous overinterpretation will come closer to historical truth than erroneous underinterpretation. The Bible has through all the ages excited admiration, inspired profound contemplation of the human condition, and aroused people to great acts. The commentator who wishes to do justice to such a text ought to fear belittling it more than he or she fears overestimating it. What timidity and meanness of spirit those biblical scholars reveal who spend their energies on deadening dissection, gaze unmarveling at literary artistry, and resolutely avoid admiration. If those who are in the best position to judge the Bible's distinctiveness refuse to share their judgment with the public, refuse indeed to make such judgments, out of a distorted ideal of objectivity, is it any wonder that their place is taken by enthusiasts and fanatics who have no philological and historical controls over their misperception of the biblical message?[10]

I have pleaded for a hierarchy of commentatorial tasks, each, after the first, based on the foregoing, and together tracing something of the path taken by the literature through time to produce:

1. a nondogmatic commentary that will inform the reader of the *realia* of the Bible (history, geography, linguistics, textual history) and describe the thought and literary creativity of the biblical writers;

2. a commentary that will not stop at analysis of components but will aim at synthesis, describing not only what produced the work but also the character of the synthesized product;

3. a commentary that will seek an answer to the question: Why was this work incorporated into the foundation document of ancient Israel? Why was it valued by the ancients; what was the source of its vitality that made it worth not only reading, but re-reading again and again?

4. a commentary that will take some notice of the fresh readings of the text by later members of the believing community, not only be-

cause the meaning of dense texts, such as the Bible, cannot be fully illuminated, indeed in many instances cannot even be seen, by the light
of their initial settings, but because there is no better way for the
modern reader, largely ignorant of cultural history, to understand the
role filled by the Bible as a foundation document. A commentary that
aims to represent the nature and stature of any classical work must describe not only how the work came into being and its significance for
its original milieu, but how it interacted with subsequent milieux
through the witness of later readings: how, in other words, it retained
its vitality and meaningfulness through its conversation with the
ages.[11] Only by undertaking such a task can a commentary have a
chance to become one more bridge between the foundation text and
the generations whose identity was shaped by it.

NOTES

1. An earlier, briefer attempt to answer this question is to be found in the prospectus to *Mikra Le Yisra'el Commentary,* editors Moshe Greenberg and Shmuel Ahituv, Tel
Aviv: Am Oved Publishers, 1985 (Hebrew and English). The present essay is effectively
a commentary to this wishful sentence in the prospectus: ". . . all [the contributors]
share the aim of helping the reader appreciate the Bible's centrality in Jewish culture."

2. Cf. E. D. Hirsch, *The Aims of Interpretation,* Chicago: University of Chicago
Press, 1976, 2–3: ". . . 'meaning' refers to the whole verbal meaning of a text, and 'significance' to textual meaning in relation to a larger context, i.e., another mind, another
era, a wider subject matter, an alien system of values, and so on. In other words, 'significance' is textual meaning as related to some context, indeed any context, beside itself."

3. This material is taken from the jacket blurb of the series.

4. "It is notable that among the general public critical [= historical-philological]
Bible scholarship is absolutely ignored. The two programs of the Broadcasting Authority, 'Daily Bible Reading' on radio, and 'Foundation Passages' on television . . . convey
only traditional-harmonistic interpretation," M. Inbar, review of A. Rofé, *Introduction to
Deuteronomy* in *Beth Mikra* 108 (April–June 1989), 260 (in Hebrew).

5. In the Old Testament Library series; Philadelphia: Westminster Press, 1965,
134–36.

6. "Most biblical archaeologists and historians agree that [the account of] . . . the
Conquest of Canaan and the Israelite Settlement requires to be told in a different version," Magen Broshi, *Jerusalem Post Magazine,* 5 May 1989, 13.

7. I have struggled with some of the educational issues in the Book of Joshua in *Ha-
segulla ve-ha-koah,* Tel Aviv: Sifriat Poalim, 1985, 11–27.

8. James D. Smart, *The Interpretation of Scripture,* Philadelphia: Westminster Press,
1961, 117.

9. *From Noah to Abraham* (Hebrew), Jerusalem: Magnes Press, 1959, 215.

10. Far the most outspoken portrayal of the distinctiveness of biblical religion over
against its pagan setting is Yehezkel Kaufmann's *Toldot ha-emuna ha-yisr'elit,* 4 vols. Tel
Aviv: Dvir, 1937–1956 (English abridgment of the first three volumes by M. Greenberg,
The Religion of Israel, Chicago: University of Chicago, 1960; vol. 4 by Clarence W.
Efroymson, *History of the Religion of Israel,* vol. iv, New York: Ktav, 1977). Characteristically, Kaufmann's successors at the Hebrew University prescind from his comparisons
with paganism, considering them apologetic. I myself was reproached by a great classical historian, Elias Bickerman, for this failure. Of an effort of mine at describing the religion of the monarchy Bickerman wrote to me (5 July 1980):

> You deal with the Hebrew religion in isolation and thus leave the reader asking: what was the singularity of the Mosaic faith? Your essay describes one essential difference ... the kingdom of priests. But precisely for the general reader this topic should have been treated more fully. I think also ... *creatio ex nihilo* ... the asexuality of the Deity. You surely could find several other singularities of Hebrew religion.

Thus "objectivity" that is governed by fear of apologetics ends by failing to do justice to the phenomena.

11. This is the main point of Wilfred Cantwell Smith's essay, "The Study of Religion and the Study of the Bible," in *Journal of the American Academy of Religion* 39 (1971) 1:31–40 (reprinted with minor alterations in W. G. Oxtoby, ed. *Religious Diversity: Essays by Wilfred Cantwell Smith*, New York: Harper and Row, 1976, 41–58).

The New Torah Translation
1963

In January, 1962, The Jewish Publication Society of America brought out a new translation of the Torah,[1] the first part of a work that is planned to embrace the whole Bible. The range of sentiments that greeted this volume was predictable—the matter touching so intimately upon individual habits and sensibilities. Yet it would be a misfortune if, in the heat and noise of public debate, the qualities of this monumental undertaking went unappreciated.

What did the translators[2] set out to do? As stated in their Preface, the general aim was to produce a translation as accurate and as intelligible as present-day knowledge permits. While the old JPS Bible[3] followed the style of the classic King James Version of 1611, being in essence but a revision of it, the new translation is a wholly fresh rendering of the Hebrew. Obsolete words and grammatical constructions were avoided. Idioms were transposed as far as possible into their normal English equivalents. "You" was employed even when referring to God, in contrast to the RSV,° which retained "Thou" in such cases (in spite of its general modernization)–a reverential mannerism foreign to the Hebrew, which uses no distinctive grammatical forms in addressing God. The common Hebrew particle *waw*, whose usual rendering "and" gives biblical English its peculiar quality, was translated "however," "yet," "when," and the like, as the sense required, or left untranslated when its force could be indicated otherwise (e.g., by subordination of clauses) or not at all.

°Hereafter the old JPS Bible will be referred to as the OJPS: the new Torah translation, as the NJPS. The King James Version of 1611 will be referred to as KJV; its latest American revision, the Revised Standard Version of 1952, as the RSV.

The radical break with the KJV tradition means that the reader must expect to meet a text different from all former official English versions, which have uniformly endeavored to preserve the flavor of the 1611 classic.[4] If the archaic language of the older versions has, through years of habituation, become charged with special meaning for the reader, he or she will, of course, balk at giving up a familiar and beloved text for a new and, to the reader, "flat" one. Indeed, it would be presumptuous to ask one to do so. But even such readers are well advised to have, alongside their old Bibles, this edifying variation on its theme for the fresh, surprising insights it will constantly afford them. With perhaps the majority of present-day readers, however, such habituation to the style of the KJV is not the rule. The rejection of that style holds out to them the promise that the biblical text will be a continuously intelligible, coherent whole, instead of a sea of blurred meaning with islands of beautiful and familiar phrases.

The first thing that strikes one about this work is its format: the normal format of a book, with the lines running straight across the page. Only the small verse numerals and the occasional chapter numbers indicate that anything but an ordinary book is in hand. Habit dictates that a Bible be double-columned, not "like a novel." But this habit has no basis in Jewish custom; the Hebrew Bible is set up just like any other book; homeliness is its hallmark.

Concern for lucidity is shown in the typographical layout. Poetry is indented and centered–and more passages are identified as poetry than heretofore. The description of the desert encampment, with its four divisions and subdivisions, is paragraphed and indented so as to set forth with admirable clarity the structure of the account (Num. 2). Complex sentences are made clear through imaginative paragraphing. Here, for example, is the structure of Leviticus 5:1–5:

> If a person incurs guilt:
>> When he has heard a public imprecation . . . ;
>> Or when a person touches any unclean thing . . . ;
>> Or when he touches human uncleanness . . . ;
>> Or when a person utters an oath . . . —
> when he realizes his guilt in any of these matters, he shall confess that wherein he has sinned.

Large numbers are written as figures; compare in Numbers 2:9:

OJPS: . . . all that were numbered of the camp of Judah being a hundred thousand and fourscore thousand and six thousand and four hundred . . .

NJPS: The total enrolled in the division of Judah: 186,400 . . .

There is a variety and a quantity of footnotes greater than anything available in comparable works. One value of these notes is that they permit the reader to enter into the mind of the translators and to appreciate somewhat the ambiguities and uncertainties that confronted them at every turn. The notices "Heb. obscure," "Heb. uncertain" occur with a frequency that will astonish the uninitiate. "The eighth day of solemn assembly" being a familiar holy day (*Shemini Atzereth*) it will doubtless come as a surprise to learn that the meaning of *'aṣereth* [NJPS: "solemn gathering"] is uncertain. Yet a glance even at the traditional commentaries will reveal a divergence of opinion masked by the unanimity of all the English versions that render "solemn assembly" with no trace of doubt. More such notes would have been entirely in order.

Alternative renderings are given in notes with the rubric "Or." At Exodus 34:6 (The LORD passed before him and proclaimed: "The LORD! the LORD! a God compassionate . . .") a note reads:

> Or "and the LORD proclaimed: The LORD! a God compassionate," etc.; cf. Num. 14.17–18.[5]

"A passover offering" of Exodus 12:11 is footnoted "Or 'protective offering,'" an interpretation of *pesah* found in the *Mechilta.*

Another class of notes, with the rubric "others," records old renderings no longer retained but so well known they were likely to be missed (Preface). Thus at Genesis 1:2: "a wind from God," a note reads: "Others 'the spirit of.'"

Interpretative notes supply cross-references and explain points likely to prove troublesome. Typical of their excellence is the note to Genesis 5:29:

> And he named him Noah, saying, "This one will provide us relief[a] from our work and from the toil of our hands, out of the very soil which the Lord placed under a curse."
>
> [a]Connecting Noah with Heb. niham "to comfort"; cf. 9.20 ff.

The cross-reference indicates nicely how Noah fulfilled the expectations of his father:

Noah, the tiller of the soil, was the first to plant a vineyard . . .

For the first time in a Jewish translation significant variants from Hebrew manuscripts and ancient Bible versions are noted (Church Bibles, from KJV on, have contained such notes). The sum of the Kohathites in Numbers 3:28 is given in the received Hebrew text as 8,600, while in the Septuagint, as 8,300. The note recording this variant goes on to suggest its significance by referring to verse 39, where the grand total of all the clans of Levi exceeds the sum of the individuals by just 300. The traditional text is thus preserved intact in the translation, while the reader is frankly informed of evidence of a smoother reading elsewhere. As we shall see later, this exemplary procedure was not always followed.

Turning now to the text itself, the first impression is of graceful simplicity and clarity. Indeed, for clarity this translation has no peer. Passage after passage, obscure in the older versions, has been elucidated here for the first time. Take Numbers 23:23 for example:

OJPS: For there is no enchantment with Jacob,
Neither is there any divination with Israel;
Now is it said of Jacob and of Israel:
"What hath God wrought!"

NJPS: Lo, there is no augury in Jacob,
No divining in Israel:
Jacob is told at once,
Yea Israel, what God has planned.

The verse coheres only in the NJPS, and only here has the complementary structure of the last two lines been caught. Graceful expression has been given to the meaning understood already by Ibn Ezra: "They have no need of a diviner, for at all times they are told, without recourse to divination, what God intends to do."

Here now are a few of the hundreds of improvements that have been embodied in the NJPS—neglected insights of earlier scholars[6] as well as new contributions of the translators themselves:

Senu'a, when opposed to *'ahuva*—"loved" (in Gen. 29:31, Deut. 21:15), is "unloved" (OJPS: "hated").

Zimrath is "might" in Exodus 15:2, in accord with comparative Semitic evidence[7] (OJPS: "song").

Shevet in Numbers 24:17, paralleling "star," is "meteor" (OJPS: "sceptre"), suggested by Babylonian Aramaic.

'Eduth, in "ark of the *'eduth,*" "tablets of the *'eduth*" is "Pact" (OJPS: "testimony")—a synonym of *berith* ("covenant") as shown by new comparative Semitic evidence.

Better appreciation of ancient idiom and custom yields "all who sat on the council of his town" (Gen. 23:10) for the meaningless OJPS "all that went in at the gate of his city"; and, in 34:24, "all the fighting men in his community" instead of OJPS "all that went out of the gate of his city." Reflection on how learning was accomplished in antiquity will commend "recite them" in Deuteronomy 6:7 for the traditional (OJPS) "talk of them."

The long-lost distinction between *neshekh* and *tarbith*[8] (Lev. 25:36; OJPS: "interest and increase") has been recovered as "advance or accrued interest," "i.e., interest deducted in advance, or interest added at the time of repayment"– in accord with ancient Near Eastern custom.

Word-for-word literalism has virtually been done away with. The common *'amar,* regularly "say" in the older versions, here has its sense determined by the context: "shout," "warn," "foretell," "demand," and so forth. The nuances of *qarav 'el* (in OJPS virtually always "draw nigh unto") have been finely sorted out: the circumcised stranger "shall be admitted" to offer the paschal sacrifice (Exod. 12:48); the maimed priest is not "qualified" to make offerings (Lev. 21:17ff.); the Levites "must not have any contact with" the sanctuary furnishings; outsiders must not "intrude upon" the officiating clerics; any outsider who "encroaches" shall be put to death (Num. 18:3–7).[9] For the sexual sense, "approach" has been retained (e.g., Deut. 22:14).

The various senses of *lifne* (OJPS: "before") are similarly discriminated: Nimrod is a mighty hunter "by the grace of" the LORD (Gen. 10:9); Ishmael is to live "by [the LORD's] favor" (Gen. 17:18); Nadab and Abihu die "at the instance" of the LORD (Lev. 10:2); the spies "by [His] will" (Num. 14:37); God places the land "at the disposal" of the Israelites (Deut. 1:8). Only in Numbers 32:20ff. does the handling seem a bit wooden: The repeated "at the instance of the Lord" is not more perspicuous than the old "before the Lord"; in a few instances at least "in the sight of" (AT) or "under the eyes of" (Moffat) appears preferable.

The problem of rendering the root *qn'* has been particularly well handled. The standard rendering "jealous" both obscures and distorts: In the KJV tradition the Lord is a "jealous" God (Exod. 20:5); He praises Phinehas for being "very jealous" for his sake (Num. 25:11); no-gods provoke him to "jealousy" (Deut.32:21). Similarly, Joshua is "jealous" for Moses' sake (Num. 11:29). But the essential meaning of *qn',* as beautifully defined by Rashi, is [the feeling of] one who gives his whole heart to something to vindicate or promote it . . .; most deeply concerned in a matter [at Num. 11:29]. *Qin'a* is ascribed to one who gets worked up over his cause or the cause of another [Gittin 7a].

Now, in defense of KJV's "jealous" it ought to be said that in the seventeenth century the word still carried the meaning "vehement in wrath, desire, or devotion," and so conformed far better to the Hebrew than it does at present. For today's reader the sensitive handling of the NJPS rather closely approximates the nuances of the Hebrew. Joshua is "wrought up on [Moses'] account"; God is "incensed" at no-gods, and lauds Phinehas for "displaying among [the Israelites] his passion for Me." The LORD is an "impassioned God," one who becomes wrought up—at affronts to him, at the sight of Jerusalem's desolation (Zech. 1:14), at the sound of his people's cries (Isa. 63:15). The epithet expresses, in short, God's profound concern with the world.

A common feature of Hebrew little noticed in the standard translations is hendiadys: the expression of a complex idea by two words connected with "and." The pair *hesed we'emeth* was recognized as a hendiadys as early as Talmudic times (*Midrash Rabba* to Genesis 47:29); all the more surprising, then, that the NJPS is the first English version to incorporate this recognition: "[pledge me] your steadfast loyalty," says Jacob to Joseph (ibid., OJPS: "deal kindly and truly with me"; AT: "kindly and faithfully"; RSV: "loyally and faithfully"). Further examples: "his talk about his dreams" (Gen. 37:8; OJPS: "his dreams and . . . his words"); "the cattle they own" (Num. 35:3; OJPS: "their cattle and . . . their substance"); "hereditary share" (Deut. 10:9; OJPS: "portion [and] inheritance"); "disputed case of assault" (Deut. 21:5; OJPS: "controversy and . . . stroke"). Some of the cases construed as hendiadys are debatable, but even after allowance for them has been made the number of convincing cases establishes beyond doubt that this is a feature of Hebrew never before accorded adequate recognition.

The rendering of round numbers is a typical problem of idiom. Rashbam at Genesis 31:7 (OJPS: "your father hath . . . changed my wages ten times") remarks that "ten" can mean simply "many"; NJPS translates here "time and again," giving the literal translation in a note. But in Leviticus 26:26 it renders "ten women shall bake . . . in a single oven" (Ibn Ezra: "a round number"; Rashbam: "many"). The inconsistency may be defended, and in any case hardly affects the sense. "Five" might serve as a round number for "a few" (e.g., in Isa. 30:17), but here doubts arise. The likelihood is that such a usage had a reflex in practice: things were done in fives much as we do things in threes. Can one be sure, with the NJPS, that Benjamin's portion was meant to be vaguely "several times" larger than his brothers' (Gen. 43:34), or that Joseph selected "a few" of his brothers to present to Pharaoh (47:2) when the Hebrew reads "five"? When it is embedded among other numbers it seems almost perverse to round it off: "three hundred . . . several . . . ten" (45:22–23). Might not the better course have been to translate literally, leaving it to the commentator to interpret this nuance of Semitic idiom?

However that may be, one can have no argument with the fundamental principle of the translators, that the translation be a self-contained, immediately intelligible whole. To this end they have not hesitated to make unobtrusive additions that make the difference between meaning and unmeaning. Compare the following renderings of Exodus 24:1–2:

> OJPS: And unto Moses He said: 'Come up unto the LORD, thou, and Aaron, Nadab, and Abihu, and seventy of the elders of Israel; and worship ye afar off; and Moses alone shall come near unto the LORD; but they shall not come near; neither shall the people go up with him.'

> NJPS: Then He said to Moses, "Come up to the LORD, you and Aaron, Nadab and Abihu, and seventy elders of Israel, and bow low from afar. Only Moses shall come near the LORD, but they shall not come near; and the people shall not come up with him at all."

The chances that the old version will convey to the reader the three-fold gradation of nearness to God implied in these instructions are slim; the chances that the new will do so are pretty good, owing to the inspired "at all" at the end.

Again, the plain sense of the famous "not by bread alone" passage in Deuteronomy 8:3 is conveyed in the new translation by a few crucial improvements. The sermonic sense ("man does not live by material food alone but also by spiritual nourishment") is virtually dictated by the old rendering–which characteristically obscures the connection of the two parts of the verse:

> OJPS: And He afflicted thee, and suffered thee to hunger, and fed thee with manna, which thou knewest not, neither did thy fathers know; that He might make thee know that man doth not live by bread only [so KJV; RSV: alone], but by everything that proceedeth out of the mouth of the LORD doth man live.

> NJPS: He subjected you to the hardship of hunger and then gave you manna to eat, which neither you nor your fathers had ever known, in

order to teach you that man does not live on bread alone, but that man may live on anything that the Lord decrees.

The lesson of the manna is now crystal clear: With God man is liberated from bondage to nature; even bread is dispensable, for the Israelites lived forty years in the wilderness without it.

In concluding this appreciation of the achievement of the translators a few of their more exquisite turns of expression may be noted: the perfect rendering of Moses' five-word prayer for Miriam, *el na refa na lah*—"O God, pray heal her" (Num. 12:13; OJPS: "Heal her now, O God, I beseech Thee"); the rendering "token portion" for *azkara* (others: "memorial-part" and the like); the idiomatic analogues "turn tail" for *nathan 'oref* (Exod. 23:27; OJPS: "turn their backs") and "let us head back" for *nittena rosh* (Num. 14:4; OJPS: "Let us make a captain"–but cf. Neh. 9:17). And, finally, a brief taste of Moses' Song (*Ha'azinu*, Deut. 32), to illustrate the triumphs scored in rendering the poetry. Bear in mind that the Hebrew of this poem shows lines of three beats each:

Verses 10–12
He found him in a desert region,
In an empty howling waste.
He engirded him, watched over him,
Guarded him as the pupil of His eye.
Like an eagle who rouses his nestlings,
Gliding down to his young,
So spread He His wings and took him,
Bore him along on His pinions;
The Lord alone did guide him,
No alien god at his side.

Verses 30–35
"How could one have routed a thousand
Or two put ten thousand to flight,
Unless their Rock had sold them,
The Lord had given them up?"
For their rock is not like our Rock,
In our enemies' own estimation.
Ah! The vine for them is from Sodom,
From the vineyards of Gomorrah;
The grapes for them are poison,
A bitter growth their clusters.
Their wine is the venom of asps,
The pitiless poison of vipers.
Lo, I have it all put away,
Sealed up in My storehouses,

To be My vengeance and recompense,
At the time their foot falters.
Yea, their day of disaster is near,
And destiny rushes upon them.

What is the relation of the NJPS to Jewish tradition?

Popular misconception has it that "tradition" contains a monolithic, approved view of the meaning of the Bible. The fact is that the authoritative teachers of Judaism never confined the text of Scripture to a single meaning.

> "My word is like fire," says the Lord, "like a hammer that shatters rock" (Jer. 23:29)—just as a hammer strikes many sparks so a single passage yields many senses. (Sanhedrin 34a)

Moreover, no matter how many applications a given passage has, "Scripture never loses its plain sense" (Shabbat 63a). From Talmudic times on the distinction between the plain sense and the applied law, the Halakhah, has always been recognized, and so long as the authority of Halakhah was accepted, biblical exegetes were free to state the truth of the plain sense as they saw it. The charter of independent Jewish exegesis was the doctrine that while the practical implications of the Torah were defined by Halakhah, the plain sense was not—indeed it might even contradict it. The most trenchant expression of this liberty is found in Rashbam's introductory remarks to his commentary on *parashat Mishpatim:*

> Let the intelligent reader take note that I do not regard it my task to expound *halachoth*, even though they are the essential part [of Judaism], for as I have explained (at Gen. 1:1) the *haggadoth* and the *halachoth* are derived from redundancies of Scripture ... My task is to expound the plain sense of Scripture; thus, I shall explain the laws and norms in the light of common experience [*derekh 'eres*]. Nonetheless, the *halachoth* remain the essential part, as our Rabbis say, "*Halachah* supplants Scripture."[10] (*Sotah* 16a)

The NJPS has carried on in this tradition of scholarly independence. That the translators consulted medieval Jewish exegesis regularly is evident from the unique renderings—some of which have already been noted—that derive exclusively from that inexhaustible reservoir. At times a significant innovation is supported by explicitly citing medieval authority for it. Thus a footnote to Deuteronomy 6:4 refers the reader to Ibn Ezra and Rashbam for this rendering of the *Shema:*

Hear, O Israel! The LORD is our God, the LORD alone.

Not uncommonly, rabbinic interpretation has here entered an English version for the first time because, in the judgment of the translators, it has caught the plain sense best. This has occurred, for example, in Leviticus 18:17: *Do not uncover the nakedness of your wife's daughter,* which conforms to the Talmudic view, while OJPS's . . . "of a woman and her daughter" does not. Or contrast the explicit NJPS at Deuteronomy 29:28:

> Concealed acts concern the Lord our God; but with overt acts, it is for us and our children ever to apply all the provisions of this Teaching.

which follows the rabbis, in contrast to the cloudy language of the KJV that the OJPS perpetuated:

> The secret things belong unto the Lord our God; but the things that are revealed belong unto us and to our children for ever, that we may do all the words of this law.

Departures from rabbinic interpretation are, of course, numerous, since "*Halachah* supplants Scripture." But characteristically, many of these departures can themselves be traced to a commentator lodged in rabbinic Bibles. One example must suffice: According to the rabbinic view of Deuteronomy 25:3, the penalty of flogging consisted in all cases of a fixed sum of lashes—one less than the prescribed forty. The NJPS, alone of all versions, inserts two words whose effect is explicitly to exclude taking the number forty as a fixed amount:

> [the culprit is to be flogged] as his guilt warrants. He may be given up to forty lashes, but not more . . .

Compare now Ibn Ezra's astute comment here:

> The apparent sense is that a given offense may warrant ten lashes, or twenty, or more or less—witness the phrase "as his guilt warrants"—only never more than forty. So it would appear, were it not for the tradition, which alone is true.

As for the traditional divisions of the text, the translators have at their discretion ignored both the Christian-originated chapters as well as the older Jewish verse division. This is no radical break with the past. Rashi himself saw fit to combine the first three verses of Genesis into a single sentence, so that here the NJPS but follows in his tracks:

> When God began to create the heaven and the earth—the earth being
> unformed and void . . . —God said. . .

The authority of the accents (*te'amim*) is also overridden from time to
time, with some striking effects. By attaching the latter half of Genesis
2:4 alone to the sequel, the opening of the Garden of Eden story is
made structurally parallel to that of Genesis 1:

> When the LORD God made heaven and earth—no shrub of the field
> being yet in the earth . . . —the Lord God formed man. . .

And a shift in the location of the mid-verse in Deuteronomy 28:24 restores symmetry to an otherwise unbalanced verse:

> The Lord will make the rain of your land dust, and sand shall drop on
> you from the sky. . .

(Contrast OJPS: ". . . powder and dust; from heaven shall it come down
upon thee.")

By and large the translators have stood by their undertaking "faithfully to follow the traditional (Masoretic) text" (Preface). How variant
readings have been brought to the reader's attention by footnotes has
been noted previously. The usual policy in places where the received
Hebrew is difficult or in apparent disorder was to render the traditional text as gracefully as possible[11] while giving any evidence for a
better reading in a note. Issue might be taken with the notes proffer-
ing conjectural emendations where the received text is, on the face
of it, smooth. Why the place name Calneh (Gen. 10:10) should be:
"better vocalized *we-khullanah* 'all of them being,'" will not be clear
to one reader in a thousand and had better been left to a commentator to argue. The dubious propriety of a translator correcting mistakes of the original (if this is a mistake), as well as considerations of
tact, plead against this procedure where, superficially, emendation
seems gratuitous.

Here and there an emendation, tacit or explicit, has been adopted
in the body of the translation. In Genesis 49:10 the cryptic *'ad ki yavo
shilo* (OJPS: "as long as men come to Shiloh") has been rendered:

> So that tribute shall come to him[b]
>
> [b]*Shiloh, understood as* shai loh *"tribute to him," following Midrash;* . . .
> Heb. *uncertain.* . . .

The peculiar *'ayil ahar* (OJPS: "behind him a ram") of Genesis 22:13 is
translated "a ram," as though the second word were *ehad* ("one"), with

"many Heb. mss. and ancient versions," as the note says.[12] Conjectural restorations are made in Genesis 10:5 and Numbers 21:24–though these passages are no more difficult than others that have been handled without such recourse. A few emendations have been concealed behind misleading "lit." or "others" notes, e.g., at Numbers 25:1:

> ª-profaned themselves by whoring-ª
>
> ª-ªOthers *"began to commit harlotry."*

The difference rests, in fact, on changing the Masoretic vowels of the verb so as to derive it from another root altogether; the "others" rendering is that of the received Hebrew; the one adopted in the text follows the Septuagint.

The independence which the translators have used to such good advantage entails hazards of its own. In their endeavor to avoid wooden literalism they have sometimes fallen into unwarranted inconsistency and paraphrase. There is a gain in elegance with no injury to the sense in varying the English of *'akhal dam* from "consume," to "eat," to "partake of blood" (Lev. 7:26f.; 17:14). But to render the same word once as "the outrage of" and once "the outcry (against)" Sodom and Gomorrah (Gen. 18:20f.; 19:13) in identical contexts looks like straddling. Such instances are not uncommon: *miqra (qodesh)* is once "(sacred) convocation"—as though from *qr'*, "call," but elsewhere "occasion"—as though from *qr'*, "happen" (Exod. 12:16; Lev. 23:2); *yissar* in similar contexts is now "flog," now "discipline" (Deut. 21:18; 22:18). Whether to render *'ani Adonay* at the clause-end as "I am the Lord" or "Mine the Lord's/Me the Lord" seems to be an arbitrary choice (contrast Leviticus. 21:12 with 19:12; 26:2 with 19:3; Numbers 3:41 with Leviticus 22:3). The various renderings of *'ah* in the ethical injunctions could well have been avoided:

> lest . . . your *brother* be degraded before your eyes. (Deut. 25:3)
>
> If you see your *fellow's* ox or sheep gone astray. . . . (Deut. 22:1)
>
> You shall not hate your *kinsman* in your heart. (Lev. 19:17)

One must "love" the stranger in Leviticus 19:34, "befriend" him in Deuteronomy 10:19—but the Hebrew has the same verb. "We ask only for passage on foot" (Num. 20:19) is quoted verbatim in Deuteronomy 2:28, though one would never know it from the NJPS "just let me pass through."

Undue liberties have been taken with the text in such examples as the following: "he reverted to his guilty ways" (Exod. 9:34), where the Hebrew says "he went on sinning, hardening his heart." The distinctive title of the holy day of the first of Tishri has been obliterated in the NJPS paraphrase of Leviticus 23:24: "a sacred occasion commemorated with loud blasts," with which contrast the literal OJPS: "a memorial proclaimed with the blast of the horns [*zikhron teru'a*], a holy convocation."

Certain paraphrases have what can only be termed a harmonistic or apologetic cast. Consider the startling divergence between the old and new renderings of Genesis 1:26:

> OJPS: And God said: 'Let us make man in our image, after our likeness ...
>
> NJPS: ... "I will make man in My image, after My likeness...

The Talmud relates (*Megilla 9a*) how, in the third century B.C.E., the first translators of the Bible into Greek substituted "I will make man," etc., for the embarrassing Hebrew plural expressions in this verse. What the Talmud admits was an apologetic rendering is in the NJPS defended as the plain sense: the plurals, argues a footnote, are "plurals of majesty." But since the language of Genesis 3:22—"man [says God] has become like one of us"—conclusively points to a divine company with God, the unforced, plural sense of 1:26 has to be retained.

Lack of evidence for Egyptian cavalry (as opposed to abundant evidence for chariotry) at the time of the Exodus probably accounts for the following divergence in Exodus 15:1:

> OJPS: The horse and his rider
>
> NJPS: Horse and driver

But in Genesis 49:17, where the apparent anachronism is less palpable, NJPS renders the identical Hebrew terms "horse" and "its rider."

The treatment of the term *sara'ath* ("leprosy" in the older versions) is at once too sophisticated and inconsistent. Today we realize that the Bible lumps under *sara'ath* various conditions other than and in addition to true leprosy. Accordingly, the translator's stated policy was to render the term "scaly affection" or the like, except where a human being is declared unclean by reason of *sara'ath* where "leprosy" has been retained (note to Lev. 13:2). But this policy was not, in fact, followed (see, e.g., Lev. 13:30; 22:4); even when Miriam had to be expelled from the camp—like the person with a "leprous affection" (Lev. 13:45)—she is said merely to have been "stricken with scales" (Num. 12:10). When houses and clothes are involved, *sara'ath* is always rendered "malignant eruption" and the like. Such nice discriminations satisfy our desire to be scientifically correct, but do they faithfully convey the sense of the original, which regarded ṣara'ath as a single malady that could affect humans, clothing, and houses alike? Only the consistent rendering by a single English equivalent would have conveyed the naive viewpoint of the Hebrew. Since during the medieval period the term "leprosy" signified almost any cutaneous disease that erupted in scaly patches, it might have been fittingly retained, with an appropriate note, as a monument to the primitive science of a bygone age.

A similar problem—namely, the likelihood of an incongruence of ancient and modern terminology—underlies the coinage "Sea of Reeds" that has everywhere replaced the traditional "Red Sea." A theory especially prevalent among American scholars locates the body of water crossed by the Israelites at the Exodus (Hebrew *Yam Suf* in Exodus 13:18 and elsewhere) far to the north of the Red Sea, at an unidentified site in the eastern Nile Delta called in an Egyptian text "Lake of Reeds" (for which *Yam Suf* would be a good Hebrew translation). At the same time another series of references (Exod. 23:31; Num. 21:4; Deut. 2:1; 1 Kings 9:26) identify *Yam Suf* with what can only be the eastern arm of the Red Sea (Gulf of Akaba). This is not the place to consider the avenues by which scholars attempt to extricate themselves from their own dilemma. But it must be pointed out that the certainties are (a) that an arm of the Red Sea was called *Yam Suf*; (b) that by the third century B.C.E. (the time of the Septuagint) Jews in Egypt located the historic crossing of the Exodus at the Red Sea. Would it not have been sounder, in the circumstances, to keep "Red Sea," with an explanatory note in Exodus 13 indicating doubt, rather than to coin a "Sea of Reeds" that "clarifies" what is really obscure (the site of the crossing) while obscuring what is really clear (the Red Sea of Exodus 23, Numbers 21, etc.)?

Outright errors are gratifyingly few.[13] But here and there idiosyncratic renderings crop up that few persons outside the committee of translators will cheerfully espouse. To judge which scholarly inspirations are likely to win a consensus is admittedly a most delicate matter, yet I venture to suggest that such renderings as the following do not belong in that class:

"Pilgrimage" for *ḥag* ("festival") in Exodus 10:9—an Arabism with scant basis in Hebrew usage.

"Repudiate" for *qillel* in Exodus 21:17. While calling attention to the ineptness of the standard rendering "curse" (cf. "insult" in the parallel Deuteronomy 27:16, and the content of the act in 2 Samuel 16:5–13), it is itself too narrowly specific. Mesopotamian references to repudiating parents may illustrate an aspect, but hardly cover all the ground, of Hebrew *qillel* "treat with contempt," "revile," "curse."

"On the new moon" rather than "in the month" of Abib as the time of celebrating the Passover. This curious speculation touching at best upon the prehistory of the festival, since it contradicts the express terms of Exodus 12:6 and Numbers 9:5, keeps appearing in the notes (cf. the references collected at Deuteronomy 16:1). The translators' flirtation with this notion finally distracted them into the hybrid rendering that appears in Deuteronomy 16:1: . . . *for it was* on [!] *the month of Abib* . . .

Much more can and ought to be said about this grand work. The public at large will measure its stature by the meaning and insight that it pours into every corner of the Torah, and by the ease and pleasure with which it is read. The student and scholar will find delight, surprise, and provocation to deeper study in virtually every chapter. The very failings of the work are edifying. All in all this translation has done more to open the Torah to the comprehension of the present-day reader than any other work of our time. Its sensitivity to idiom, the wide learning that it embodies, and its concern for lucidity raise it at once to the forefront of English versions.

NOTES

1. *The Torah: The Five Books of Moses. A new translation of The Holy Scriptures according to the Masoretic text: First Section*, Philadelphia, 1962.

2. The committee of translators was composed of Dr. Harry M. Orlinsky, professor of Bible at Hebrew Union College–Jewish Institute of Religion, editor-in-chief; Dr. H. L. Ginsberg, professor of Bible at the Jewish Theological Seminary, and Dr. E. A. Speiser, head of the Department of Semitic and Oriental Languages at the University of Pennsylvania, co-editors. With them were associated Rabbis Max Arzt, Bernard J. Bamberger, and Harry Freedman, belonging to the three sections of organized Jewish religious life. Dr. Solomon Grayzel, editor of The Jewish Publication Society, was secretary of the committee.

3. *The Holy Scriptures according to the Masoretic text: A new translation*, Philadelphia, 1917. This has become the standard Jewish version of the Bible in English. It was incorporated by Chief Rabbi Hertz in his widely used *The Pentateuch and Haftorahs*.

4. Two earlier modern English versions are worthy of mention: James Moffatt's *The Old Testament, A New Translation*, published in 1924, and *The Old Testament, an American Translation*, edited by J. M. P. Smith and published in 1927. Both are quite readable, though Moffatt is very periphrastic and the *American Translation* (hereafter AT) is at times diffuse. Neither is committed to the traditional Hebrew text.

5. In Numbers 14 this passage is quoted with only one "the LORD."

6. One past scholar has been so heavily drawn upon as to make him seem, in effect, an invisible presence among the committee of translators. Arnold B. Ehrlich's multivolumed Hebrew and German notes on the Bible, published between 1899 and 1914, have left their mark throughout the NJPS. Ehrlich is unfailingly brilliant (if not always convincing), and NJPS's constant attention to him has contributed to its verve and pointedness.

7. With *zimrath ha'areṣ* (Gen. 43:11) "the choice products [lit. might] of the land" compare the *koaḥ* ("strength") of the earth in Genesis 4:12.

8. Known to Eliezer of Beaugency (twelfth century) and found in his commentary to Ezekiel at 18:8.

9. In Leviticus 22:3 *qarav 'el* is paraphrased "partake of (a sacred donation)" in line with Rashbam and Rashi. How periphrastic this is comes out in Rashi's comment that the Talmud could not infer that eating was involved except by means of *gezera shawa*!

10. Our printings unaccountably have "Mishnah."

11. With the result that the NJPS is smooth and intelligible where the Hebrew may not be.

12. Interestingly enough, neither AT nor RSV, given as both are to emendation, emend here.

13. Hebrew words have been left out in Genesis 31:50; 50:15; Numbers 19:12. Mistranslations (the corrected reading is after the slash): Leviticus 25:55 "their"/"your"; Deuteronomy 9:28 "them"/"us"; Genesis 41:56 "grain"/"food"; v. 57 "buy grain"/"get rations"; 43:2 "grain"/"food"; Leviticus 21:23 "enter behind"/"approach"; Numbers 2:9–31 past tenses should be future; Deuteronomy 22:28 "is not"/"has never been." There is some error in Genesis 42:3; Exodus 18:19, and 30:16. Deuteronomy 23:14 should probably read "have [to] squat." Typos occur in the note to Genesis 4:7 (*rabiṣu*), and at Leviticus 13:55; Numbers 11:28; Numbers 22:37 "to meet me"/"to me."

Additional note:

There are differences between the first, 1962 edition of the Torah—which is the subject of this review—and the version published by the JPS in the complete TANAKH (1985). Here are some examples of changes made in the 1985 version from renderings commented upon in my article: The reference to the Septuagint at Numbers 3:28 is omitted. At Numbers 24:17 old "scepter" replaces "meteor" (cf. H.M. Orlinsky, *Notes on the New Translation of the Torah* [Philadelphia: Jewish Publication Society, 1969], 238). In Genesis 23:10 "entered the gate" and in 34:24 "went out of the gate" are revived (Orlinsky, 100). Deuteronomy 21:5 does not contain a hendiadys (Orlinsky, 253). What I called "the inspired 'at all' " at the end of Exodus 24:2 has disappeared in the wake of an inferior recasting of the sentence (Orlinsky, 184–85). The agreement with Talmudic tradition in translating "your wife's daughter" in Leviticus 18:17 has likewise disappeared (Orlinsky, 216, who defends "a woman and her daughter" by citing Lev. 20:14—which may be invoked contrariwise to support the Talmudic view since it bans "*marrying* a woman and her daughter"). The apologetic "I will make man in My image . . ." (Gen. 1:26) has been replaced by the literal, "Let us make man in our image . . ." (Orlinsky, 58). Idiosyncratic "pilgrimage" (Exod. 10:9) yields to traditional "festival"; "repudiate" (21:17) to "insult." On the whole the revisions tend to more conventional, safer renditions.

Thoughtful discussions of the issues raised by translations of the Bible are E.L. Greenstein, "Theories of Modern Bible Translation," in *Prooftexts* 3 (1985), 9–39 (reprinted in his *Essays on Biblical Method and Translation*, Brown Judaic Studies 92 [Atlanta: Scholars Press, 1989], 85–118) and Gerald Hammond, "English Translations of the Bible," in Robert Alter and Frank Kermode, eds., *The Literary Guide to the Bible*, Cambridge, Mass.: Belknap Press of Harvard University Press, 1987, 647–66.

Another Look at Rachel's Theft of the Teraphim*

1961

In the long history of exegesis, Rachel's unexplained theft of Laban's teraphim-gods on the eve of Jacob's secret departure from Laban (Gen. 31:19) has received many and curious interpretations. Josephus[1] supposed that Rachel wanted them so as "to have recourse to them to obtain pardon" in case Laban overtook them. Genesis Rabba (ad loc.) credits the matriarch with the noble desire to purge old Laban of his idolatry. Later midrash[2] suggests more plausibly that she stole them to prevent their revealing to Laban that Jacob's household had fled—for teraphim do speak, according to Zechariah 10:2.[3] Frazer[4] thought the theft was motivated by fear lest the gods might resent and punish the injury done to their owner. Other modern scholars suggest that Rachel wished to enjoy the protection of her hearth gods away from home.[5] Gunkel elaborates: "It was the business of such teraphim to help the protégé in home and farm, to bless his family and flocks. Rachel believed that in stealing this image she was thus carrying along the Fortune of the house; and Laban would sooner have given up anything rather than this house-fetish of his, which he himself must have inherited from his father." For comparison Gunkel cites the story of the abduction of Micah's priest and teraphim by the migrating Danites (Judg. 18), though, to be sure, there the divinatory value of the teraphim appears to be uppermost in the minds of the abductors.

While this view is certainly plausible, it must be admitted that no material, biblical or extrabiblical, has yet been adduced in support of it, closely paralleling the tale in Genesis. Something more common-

°Dedicated to Professor E. A. Speiser in his sixtieth year.

place than the Danite abduction, more a matter of family custom, seems to be involved in Rachel's act.

Just such material, as is now well known, has been made available by the Nuzi tablets. The most important document for our discussion is Gadd 51, published in 1926 and immediately seized upon as highly significant of the relations between Jacob and Laban.[6] Gadd 51 is an adoption document: The adopter states that at his death the adoptee shall become his *ewuru* (heir by irregular succession). Should a natural son be born to the adopter beforehand, that son and the adoptee shall inherit equally, but only the son shall receive the household gods. If there is no son, the gods are to be taken by the adoptee.

The reconstruction of the relations between Jacob and Laban and the motive for Rachel's theft that have been proposed on the basis of this tablet have by now entered all up-to-date handbooks. H. H. Rowley[7] summarized them as follows: "It has been conjectured that Laban had no sons at the time of Jacob's marriage of Leah, but that he subsequently became the father of sons, who were therefore now superior in legal standing to Jacob. By carrying off the teraphim, however, Rachel preserved for Jacob the chief title to Laban's estate." J. Bright[8] writes more simply of "Rachel's theft of Laban's gods (tantamount to title to the inheritance)."

The persuasiveness of this interpretation rests not only on the skill with which it has been argued and the authority of its advocates—among whom are the cuneiformists S. Smith,[9] E. A. Speiser,[10] T. J. Meek,[11] C. H. Gordon,[12] and most recently A. Draffkorn[13]—but on the coherence it lends to the total picture of the Jacob-Laban dealings. A key that opens so many doors can hardly be the wrong one!

The main object of this paper is to call attention to a passage in Josephus which, to my knowledge, has never been brought into modern discussions of Rachel's theft. This neglected passage is important for the simple and unsophisticated explanation it suggests in an altogether incidental remark. But while weighing the relative merits of Josephus and Nuzi as aids to understanding Rachel's mind, it appeared to me that the Nuzi material would bear a closer analysis. Have our cuneiform colleagues drawn the correct conclusion from the documents in question? I do not wish to be misunderstood: The strictures made in the following remarks are queries to the cuneiformist. It seems to me that there are some difficulties in their theory insofar as it touches upon Rachel's theft of the teraphim that have not been faced. Without prejudice to the interpretation of the Jacob-Laban relationship as a whole, the effect of these difficulties seems to impair the usefulness of the Nuzi material for explaining Rachel's act.

The crucial lines of Gadd 51 read:

When Nashwi [the adopter] dies, Wullu [the adoptee] shall become the *ewuru* [irregular heir]. If Nashwi should have a son of his own, he shall divide the estate equally with Wullu, but the son of Nashwi shall take the (house) gods of Nashwi. And if Nashwi has no son of his own, then Wullu shall take the (house) gods of Nashwi. Furthermore, he gave his daughter Nuḥuya to Wullu in marriage. (11. 7–19)

These lines are said to mean that "transfer of the father's household gods was a prerequisite in certain cases where property was to pass to a daughter's husband."[14] Or, again, that when property is to pass to other than normal heirs "the house gods, as the protectors and symbols of family holdings, are thus drawn in, as it were, to safeguard and to render legitimate—not only the property, but also the person in relation to the property—against possible future claims."[15] This is not a precise statement of the import of our document. For even if Nashwi should have a natural son who gets the gods, Wullu remains an equal heir with him. No gods must be produced by Wullu to safeguard his right to share in the estate, despite his being an irregular heir. Applying this to Jacob's situation: If Jacob were regarded as an *ewuru*, he did not need to have Laban's gods to ensure his title to a share in Laban's estate. All he needed was Laban's statement that he was entitled to a share. Having that, his title was secure. But what if he did not have that, or if Laban wished to cut him off from a previously promised share? Would his possession of the house gods defeat Laban's purpose? To answer that we must first clarify the place of house gods in inheritance.

What is determined by bequeathal of the gods is not title to an inheritance share but rather who is to carry on as paterfamilias. That determination is separate from the matter of dividing up shares in the estate, in this document as well as in others. One document cited by Draffkorn (HSS XIV, 108) appears to equalize the several shares, and then goes on to stipulate that the eldest son is to get the gods. In other words, while all are heirs regardless of who gets the gods, only the eldest is designated paterfamilias.[16]

Hence Rachel's desire to possess the gods of Laban, if it meant anything in this connection, could mean only that she wished Jacob to be recognized as paterfamilias after Laban's death—assuming, of course, that such a claim could be urged on the strength of possessing the gods. If she really meant only to ensure an inheritance share for Jacob, she went too far—much too far, as we shall see.

The question is: In Nuzi law could a person in Jacob's circumstances have made a credible claim to be paterfamilias of Laban's family on the ground of possessing his house gods? If he could, the Nuzian interpretation of Rachel's act is colorable. If not, the interpretation has to assume that Rachel acted irrationally or futilely. Since no Nuzi text speaks to the point directly, we are reduced to speculation to answer our question. What, then, does reasonable inference suggest would have been the effect of Rachel's act relative to the end she is supposed to have had in view?

Taking the circumstances of Gadd 51 as a model, Laban will have drawn up his will disposing of his property and appointing his successor as paterfamilias prior to the theft. Some cuneiformists[17] have assumed that it was just such a will—whereby Jacob, formerly chief heir, was now reduced in status owing to the birth of Laban's own sons—that Rachel sought to defeat by her act. But if Laban had already designated a son of his as paterfamilias, anyone else who came forward with the gods must surely have ipso facto stood condemned as a thief. We must bear in mind that it was not the gods that made the paterfamilias, but the father's act of bequeathing them. And where bequeathal could be shown to be to another than the possessor of the gods, such possession was no more than self-condemnation.

For there to be any point in stealing the gods we must suppose a situation in which the father died intestate, without designating the paterfamilias. Might not seizure of the gods then create a presumption in favor of the seizer?[18] We may best judge the strength of such a presumption from an analogy. The coronet and armband of Saul (cf. 2 Sam. 1:10) symbolized his royalty; they belonged by right only to the crown prince after his father's death. After the death of Saul, did the kingship go to the first man to reach the dead king and seize his insignia? Was a presumption of kingship enjoyed by the Amalekite who did so? Was David's claim bolstered when the insignia came into his possession? Did he advance a claim on the strength of possessing them? Was Ishbaal's position jeopardized by his not possessing the insignia? Does possession of the insignia play any part at all in the rivalry of the two camps? The negative answer to these questions suggests—what common sense itself dictates—that mere possession of symbolic objects was not enough to establish a claim to the office they symbolized. The question turned entirely upon *who* possessed these symbols and *how* he possessed them. To the extent that circumstances worked in favor of the presumption that the possessor received them in bequest, to that extent was possession presumptive of designation as chief heir. But if circumstances were suspicious, no such presumption in favor of the possessor could have existed. Now, what sort of presumption could have existed in the case of Jacob, not a natural son of Laban, who had, after all, abandoned the family estate to flee to Canaan?[19]

All these interesting problems are raised in connection with a father who died intestate. But the circumstances of Rachel's theft are entirely different: Laban was still alive. Whatever the situation was after the death of the father, an adoptee had nothing to gain and everything to lose by making off with the family gods during the adopter's lifetime. That would have been as foolish as the theft, by a king's son, of the crown while his father still lived, in the expectation that possession of the crown would safeguard his claim to the throne. Just as the crown belonged to the king until his death, so the household gods belong to the paterfamilias until his death. We may well imagine a father's outrage if any son—let alone an adoptee!—dared to run off with them during his lifetime. The father-adopter had various means of punishing such trespass, up to and including disherison.[20] In any event, such an appropriation could hardly have had any legal validity against the express will of a still-living father. If Rachel was really interested in safeguarding Jacob's primacy, was this the way to go about it?

Finally we must ask: Does anything in the story suggest that, now or ever after, Rachel (through Jacob) pressed a claim against Laban on the strength of having these gods? What was the mood of Jacob's household when they fled? All of them appear to have had quite enough of Laban and family. Their chief desire was quickly to put as large a distance between them and him as possible. Later Jacob and Laban agree to set up a permanent boundary between them, and we never again hear that they had anything to do with each other afterward. Is all this consistent with the supposition that Jacob's family had designs on Laban's estate?[21]

Human motives are, of course, too complex and mysterious for us to rule out categorically a given possibility. Perhaps the regnant view of Rachel's motive, despite its apparent unreasonableness, is right. In her embitterment against Laban, Rachel may have acted irrationally, or under a gross misapprehension of the legal effect of her act. Is there any other way the "Nuzian" interpretation of Rachel's theft can be maintained except by making it an unreasonable or a mistaken act?[22]

Let us now consider what Josephus has to offer by way of help.

It is most remarkable that the passage in question, *Ant.* 18.9.5, has been overlooked in all modern treatments of our problem despite its universal accessibility. The passage is part of the account of the adventures of the brothers Asinaeus and Anilaeus, Babylonian Jewish soldiers of fortune, who, with a band of desperadoes, terrorized the Babylonian countryside for some fifteen years (about 18–33 c.e.). The brothers eventually fell out over a woman. Here is the beginning of that story:[23]

The trouble arose when they met a certain Parthian, who had arrived as commander in those regions. . . . He was accompanied by his wife, whose praises were sung beyond all other women for other qualities, yet it was her marvelous beauty that gave her most effective control over him. . . . [Anilaeus] became at once her lover. . . . Therefore, her husband was at once declared an enemy and a "dead man" forced into a battle, in which he fell. After he had been slain, his widow was captured and became the wife of her passionate wooer. Nevertheless, she did not enter the family without a train of great disasters, of one such I shall relate the occasion. . . . When after the death of her husband she had been taken captive, she took along the ancestral images of the gods belonging to her husband and to herself—for it is the custom among all the people in that country to have objects of worship in their house and to take them along when going abroad. She too therefore secretly carried them off in observance of her national custom in these matters.

It appears that the only man to have seen the relevance of this passage to our problem was the venerable William Whiston (1677–1752), who appended this note to his translation: "This custom of the Mesopotamians to carry their household-gods along with them wherever they travelled is as old as the days of Jacob, when Rachel his wife did the same."

This passage not only supplies a simple explanation for Rachel's act—that much Gunkel already gave us—but the welcome information that a millennium and a half after her Near Eastern women were still in the habit of taking along their house gods when going into a foreign land—concealed if need be. Rachel was about to depart for a far-off land from which, to all appearances, she had no thought of returning. In the normal course of events, we may suppose, she would have had made, or her father would have given her, replicas of her hearth gods, to accompany and protect her. But the decision of Jacob and his wives to flee was taken secretly, and Laban had to be kept in the dark about it. So Rachel resorted to a desperate device: she absconded with the original images themselves. That was reason enough for Laban to light out after them. The original images were the most sacred heirloom of the family; they must never leave their consecrated niche in the home.[24] Rachel's particular concern to have the teraphim may be illuminated by the fact that, in common with the one other biblical woman whom we know to have had teraphim—Michal, wife of David (1 Sam. 19:13; cf. 2 Sam. 6:23)—Rachel was anxious for children (cf. her desperate rivalry with Leah in Genesis 30). For that the hearth god must have been particularly vital—note Jacob's "Can I take the place of God who has denied you fruit of the womb?" (Gen. 30:2).

Further on in Genesis (35:2ff.) we read that, after being charged by God to fulfill his vow at Bethel, Jacob said to his household: "Re-

move the foreign gods that are among you and purify yourselves. . . .
So they gave Jacob all the foreign gods they had with them, and their
earrings, and Jacob hid them under the oak which was at Shechem."
We see then that Rachel was but one among several persons in Jacob's
household who carried along their gods from the old country. Are we
justified in looking for a special reason for Rachel's act if it was dupli-
cated by others among her compatriots? Or were all of them actuated
by a misconceived purpose to stake out an absentee claim to family
headship?[25]

Josephus suggests a single, simple explanation for the transportation of all these gods: ". . . it is the custom among all the people in that
country to have objects of worship in their house and to take them
along when going abroad." The passage is, to be sure, late; it deals
anecdotally with a foreign (apparently Parthian[26]) custom. Yet this
unique oriental parallel to Rachel's act has, at least, the merit of not
being encumbered by difficulties. It is not easy to forgo a theory
based (as is the Nuzi theory) on material coming almost from the same
time and place as the patriarchs themselves. But in view of the problematic assumptions that theory entails, one may well ask whether the
straightforward motive suggested by the Josephus passage is not, on
balance, more attractive.[27]

The same mail that brought the galleys of this article also brought a
letter from Dr. Hildegard Lewy kindly calling my attention to several
new mentions of house gods in recently and about-to-be published
Nuzi texts. The argument of this article is not affected thereby, but it
seems that in at least one of these texts bequeathal of certain gods
means something other than designation as paterfamilias. That there
were several kinds of domestic gods at Nuzi and that they served various functions comes as no surprise. The same is true for the domestic
gods of classical antiquity.

NOTES

1. *Antt.* 1, 19, 8.
2. *Tanhuma, Wayyese,* §12; Palestinian Targum to Genesis 31:19. (With the grue-
some necromancy there described, compare the method of divination used by the witch
Erichtho in Lucan, *Pharsalia,* translated by Robert Graves, 143f.) Most of the major
medieval Hebrew commentators (RŠBM, Ibn Ezra, Kimhi, Nahmanides) adopt this explanation; Răsi follows Genesis Rabba.
3. For the Greco-Roman notion that house gods utter oracles *on their own* (which
seems to underlie the midrash: It is the *fact* of the flight that Rachel fears the teraphim
will reveal, before Laban discovers it!), cf. *Aeneid* iii, 148ff., in which an oracle volun-
teered by Aeneas' house gods is described.
4. *Folklore in the Old Testament,* abr. ed., 244.

5. E.g., Skinner, *Genesis*, 396 (the Aeneid reference in note 3 [above] is cited); Gunkel, *Genesis*, 344f.; cf. also Kaufmann, *The Religion of Israel*, 145 (the teraphim were stolen "surely for their religious value").

6. Original publication by C. J. Gadd in RA, 23 (1926: 126f.; cf. S. Smith's note on 127. This tablet is translated in ANET, 219f.

7. In "Recent Discovery and the Patriarchal Age," *The Servant of the Lord and Other Essays on the Old Testament*, 302.

8. *A History of Israel*, 71. See also B. Mazar et al., *Views of the Biblical World* (Israel, 1959):1, 85: "[The Nuzi] documents show that the teraphim . . . carried with them the right of inheritance. Thus Rachel was perhaps endeavoring to preserve this right for herself at the moment of Jacob's final departure from Laban's household. . . ." Interpreters differ as to whose title—Jacob's or Rachel's—was involved; see (ahead) n. 19.

9. JThS, 33 (1932):33–36.

10. AASOR, 13 (1933): 44; IEJ, 7 (1957): 213. I wish to record here my gratitude to my mentor and colleague, Professor E. A. Speiser, whose searching critique of this article (which diverges from his own view of the matter) has compelled me to refine my thought and take into consideration aspects of the question I should not have seen otherwise.

11. *Hebrew Origins*, 15; cf. ANET, 220, n. 51.

12. BASOR, 66 (1937):25–7; BA, 3 (1940): 5–6. Professor Gordon has kindly called my attention by letter to the latest formulation of his view on the subject. On page 129 of his *The World of the Old Testament* he writes: "Since they were bound for Canaan and were leaving Mesopotamia for good, it is not likely that the gods conveyed valuable property rights. The possession of the gods may rather have betokened clan leadership and spiritual power to an extent that made possessing them of paramount importance." This is reiterated in the second revised edition of his *Geschichtliche Grundlagen des AT* (Zürich, 1961), 123.

13. JBL, 76 (1957): 219f.

14. Speiser, IEJ, ibid.

15. Draffkorn, op. cit., 222.

16. Cf. Gordon: "The possession of these gods . . . may have implied leadership of the family" (BA, ibid.)—a position to which he has now returned (n. 12, above). In BASOR, ibid., he writes: "The gods apparently constituted the title to the chief inheritance portion and leadership of the family." Similarly Draffkorn speaks at one point of the gods safeguarding inheritance rights (222; cf. 220, on Rachel), at another, of them determining who was to be the head of the family (221). Title to an inheritance share and family headship must be rigorously distinguished; the clauses regarding disposition of the household gods have reference only to the latter.

Another source of confusion has been the repeated assertion that *possession* of the household gods constituted title, safeguarded rights, etc. What Gadd 51 (and related documents) signifies is that *bequeathal* of the household gods determines something— namely, the paterfamilias. Possession is legally significant only to the extent that it may create a presumption in favor of the possessor that he has gotten the gods by bequest; but that presumption would appear to depend entirely on the circumstances of the possession. See page 000.

The precise connection of the gods with the paterfamilias is not stated in our documents. It is reasonable to suppose that, as in classical antiquity, the paterfamilias was the head of the domestic cult; hence it was he who "took"—i.e., was charged with the service of—the house gods. To be sure this is never said in our sources, but that may be due to the socioeconomic and legal character of the Nuzi texts; they shed only oblique light (as here) on the inner religious life of the Nuzians.

It is worthwhile to dwell a moment on some of the striking agreements between classical and Nuzian interpenetration of religion and economics to see how far one is entitled to import Greco-Roman practices to illuminate obscurities at Nuzi. The classical situation is presented with brilliant insight by Fustel de Coulanges in *The Ancient City* (English translation, New York, 1956). Fustel shows that "the ancient family was a religious rather than a natural association; . . . the son was no longer counted in it when he had renounced the worship or had been emancipated; . . . on the other hand, an adopted son was counted a real son, because, though he had not the ties of blood, he had something better—a community of worship; . . . finally . . . relationship and the right of inheritance were governed not by birth, but the rights of participation in the worship . . . " (42). On the relation of the house gods to the family estate he has this to say: "Every domain was under the eyes of household divinities who watched over it [citation in n. *Lares agri custodes*]" (67). "Property was so inherent in the domestic religion that a family could not renounce one without renouncing the other. The house and the field were—so to speak—incorporated in it, and it could neither lose them nor dispose of them" (70). This inseparability determined the law of succession: "The rule for the worship is, that it shall be transmitted from male to male; the rule for the inheritance is, that it shall follow the worship" (74); hence, daughters could not inherit. But if a man had no sons, "the law decided that the daughter should marry the heir" so as to be able to enjoy her father's estate (76). If a man died childless, "to know who the heir of his estate was we have only to learn who was qualified to continue his worship" (77).

Childlessness was the chief, when not the sole, ground for adoption (54–5). "When a son was adopted, it was necessary, first of all, that he should be initiated into a form of worship 'introduced into a domestic religion, brought into the presence of new Penates.' . . . Gods, sacred objects, rites, prayers, all became common between him and his adopted father. They said of him, *In sacra transiit*—He has passed to the worship of the new family" (55). On the economic effect of emancipation and adoption we read: "The son who had been excluded from the paternal worship by emancipation was also excluded from the inheritance. On the other hand, the stranger who had been associated in the worship of a family by adoption became a son there; he continued its worship, and inherited the estate" (79). Finally, on the connection of the house gods with the chief heir: "[In the time of Demosthenes] at Athens there existed the privilege of the elder. It consisted in retaining, above his proportion, the paternal dwelling—an advantage which was materially considerable, and which was still more considerable in a religious point of view; for the paternal house contained the ancient hearth of the family. While the younger sons, in the time of Demosthenes, left home to light new fires, the oldest, the true heir, remained in possession of the paternal hearth and of the tomb of his ancestors" (84).

Draffkorn has already indicated that at Nuzi too the house gods "are, above all, the protectors of the family stake as a whole" (223). Making all due allowances for differences in civilization, it does seem that the bond of gods, family, and estate at Nuzi and in classical antiquity is grounded on fundamentally the same conception. It is possible to interpret all the material adduced by Draffkorn consistently in the light of the principle of the basically religious constitution of the ancient family. Exactly parallel to the status of the emancipated Roman son, who is excluded at once from family worship and property, is that of the Nuzi son whose clump of clay has been broken (JEN 478; [cf. Draffkorn, 221]): the act of dissociation is performed before the AN.ZAB figurines (analogously to the act of Roman adoption, done in the presences of the Penates). As a result, the son "may not have access to the gods, to the family spirits, and (its) fields and houses" *(ana ilāni ū ana etemmē [ū] eqlāti ū bītāti lā ilakka).* Similarly, it is a fundamental distinction between real and sale adoptions at Nuzi that, while in real adoptions the adoptee both inherits and participates in the family worship so far that he may be bequeathed the gods (as in Gadd 51), in sale adoptions, the merely formal adoptee is expressly excluded both from family rights to the feudal holdings as well as to the family gods *(ana irwisse ū ana ilāni lā iqerreb* [JEN 89:10ff.; 216:14f.]). Draffkorn interprets this to refer to unauthorized appropriation of the house gods (221); but does it not rather mean to exclude the persons in question from normal rights enjoyed by all members of the family in the family estate and its domestic cult? (On the exclusive and private character of the Roman domestic cult see Fustel, 37.)

In view of the foregoing it appears reasonable to suppose that in the Nuzi bequeathal of gods there was involved, in the first place, the designation of that son who, as paterfamilias, was charged with the maintenance of the family cult.

17. E.g., Gordon (see n. 12 above) and Smith (n. 9).

18. Smith, loc. cit.: "Rachel's desire to possess them [depended] on the fact that the possessor of them was presumptive heir" (34).

19. To be sure, Draffkorn (220) has Rachel concerned over her own rights, not Jacob's (and see above, n. 8, end); yet this may be simply loose phrasing, for just before (219, n. 16) Jacob is said to have been viewed as an *ewuru* by his wives—making him the heir. The observation (Draffkorn, 220) that when there are no sons a daughter may inherit, while important in itself, is irrelevant here, since *ex hypothesi* there was a male heir (either the *ewuru* Jacob, or Laban's own sons).

20. On disherison, cf. Cod. Hamm. 168–9, Driver-Miles, *The Babylonian Laws*, I, 348ff. Whether Hammurabi's law of disherison was followed in Nuzi practice is unknown; even if it was, it is unlikely that in such a case as is here postulated the requirement of a second offense would have been insisted upon. That disherison was practiced at Nuzi is known from JEN 478 (cf. Draffkorn, 221).

21. See Gordon's reasoning in n. 12 above.

22. A question of method seems to be involved: The Nuzian interpretation of Rachel's act grounds it on a motive that, as far as we can tell, would not have moved a reasonable person. But if we assume that Rachel acted irrationally, have we not undercut all efforts to understand her, since who can say what the ground of an irrational act might have been?

23. This translation was kindly communicated to me by Dr. Louis Feldman, whose completion of the *Antiquities* in the Loeb Classical Library [is] published [as vol. IX in the Loeb *Josephus* (1965), 194–95].

24. Draffkorn, 223, correctly asserts that the firstborn, the normal chief heir, retained the original house gods—a sacred patrimony that belonged solely to the paterfamilias.

25. If the same motive actuated Rachel and her compatriots, why then is she alone said to have *stolen* the gods? The answer may be simply that only in her case was the breakup of a family unit involved. The rest of Jacob's entourage—his domestics and servants–came along as whole families; in their case there was no need to provide for a member of the family who was leaving the protection of the household deity.

26. Professor Richard N. Frye has been good enough to inform me (by letter, March 8, 1962) that, on the strength of archaeological evidence from Iraq and Central Asia, and from meager literary indications, the existence of household cults among the Parthians in which idols figured may be reasonably inferred. "There is no reason," he writes, "to doubt Josephus' information."

27. Why is the narrator of Genesis 31 silent about the motive of Rachel's theft? If the motive suggested by the Josephus passage is correct, probably because the narrator regarded it as self-evident to his readers. For only her theft distinguished Rachel from countless other foreign women who, when they married Israelites, imported their native gods into their new homes as a matter of course. The idolatrous importations of Solomon's foreign queens, of Jezebel and her daughter Athaliah, possibly also of the Geshurite Maachah and her granddaughter (1 Kings 15:13), are notorious. But the female commoner was no less devoted to her gods than were queens, whence the peculiar formulation of the ban on intermarriage: "... and you take of their daughters for your sons, and their daughters play the harlot after their gods and make your sons play the harlot after their gods" (Exod. 34:16; see also Deut. 7:4; Judg. 3:6). Biblical writers are aware of the general custom of persons compelled to leave their homeland carrying along their gods: 2 Kings 17:29; Amos 5:26f.; Isa. 46:1f. It is not surprising, then, that our narrator did not think it necessary to explain why Rachel took Laban's gods.

Additional note:

This article, dedicated to E.A. Speiser, my teacher, colleague, and department head at the University of Pennsylvania, takes issue with one of his cherished theses—see note 10 and his *Genesis* (Anchor Bible, 1964), 250–51. The atmosphere that he fostered in Penn's department of Oriental Studies was such that it never occurred to me to suppress my differences with him in scholarly matters. In fact, he would cite this article in his class on Genesis as wrongheaded but with pride in the testimony it rendered to the freedom of scholarly expression that prevailed in his department. Subsequent life experience taught me how rare such magnanimity is.

With the passage of time, additional data and analyses have increased doubt about the direct light that Nuzi texts can shed on details of the patriarchal narrative. In 1989, Barry Eichler's "Nuzi and the Bible: A Retrospective," appeared in H. Behrens, et al., eds., *DUMU-E₂-DUB-BA-A: Studies in honor of Aake W. Sjoeberg,* (Philadelphia: University [of Pennsylvania] Museum), 107–121. On the subject of this article Eichler writes: "[T]he assertion that the Nuzi house gods functioned as tokens of the possessor's right to inherit ancestral property has not been substantiated by more recently published documents. . . . [T]here is no evidence that the house gods served to legitimate one's inheritance rights since they are not given exclusively to the chief heir nor are they consistently given to all the heirs. . . . The only explicit references to their function in the texts . . . remain closely associated with cultic matters" (113–14).

Hebrew *s^egullā*: Akkadian *sikiltu*
1951

A glance at the more recent translations of the Code of Hammurabi, paragraph 141, will suffice to indicate that a further attempt at interpreting this law is not unwarranted. The difficulty lies in the protasis, in which the actions of a wife bent on leaving her husband are described:

> *šumma aššat awēlim ša ina bīt awēlim wašbat ana waṣēm paniša*
> *ištakanma sikiltam isakkil bītsa usappaḫ musa ušamṭā* ... "If a married
> woman who was living in the house of her husband has made up her
> mind to leave and... ..., ruined her home, and humiliated her
> husband ..."

The crux of the passage is the phrase *sikiltam isakkil;* translators have followed two lines in its interpretation. One view would connect the phrase with the familiar Hebrew root *sākal* and render "stulte egerit" (Deimel), "playing the fool" (Luckenbill), or "a l'habitude de faire des folies" (Cruveilhier).[1] Others, seeing here an Akkadian *sakālu* "to acquire"[2] give the phrase a more mercenary flavor; "das Wirtschaftsgeld beiseite schafft" (Eilers), and "in order that she may engage in business" (Meek).[3]

The error of the association with Hebrew *sākal* can be shown from Akkadian usage itself. A Nuzi tablet parallels *sikiltu* with *mānaḫātu/i* "earnings through toil,"[4] thus clearly indicating that the former is an economic term. But I believe that we can arrive at a more precise understanding of *sikiltam sakālu* from certain usages in rabbinic literature. The recognized influence of Babylonian legal terminology on

Talmudic terminology (e.g. *nudunnū-nᵉdunyā, mulūgu-mᵉlōg*) obviates any surprise that these two sources should be mutually enlightening. Such mutual clarification, I feel, can be found in our present case by consideration of the rabbinic usage of *sᵉgullā* and its denominative verb *siggēl*. The equation of *sikiltu-sᵉgullā* is not a new one: as early as 1921 S. Smith compared the two words to support his view that the *k* of the Akkadian was really a *q;*[5] more recently F. Zorell in his *Lexicon Hebraicum* has compared both Akkadian *sakālu* as well as Akkadian *sugullu* in discussing the etymology of *sᵉgullā*[6]—a good instance of linguistic fence-straddling. This confusion justifies a reexamination of the pertinent material on both sides and a statement of the morphological questions involved. We shall consider first a few rabbinic passages.

> This is like a shepherd who began with only a staff and turban. He bestirred himself, *siggēl* and bought sheep. One day wolves entered his flock and tore them to pieces; whereupon he said, "I had better return to my staff and turban."[7]
>
> R. Ammi said: In the case of a son who appears to be independent while his father is still alive, whatever he *siggēl* belongs to him (i.e., it cannot be claimed by the rest of the family upon the father's death as part of the common inheritance).[8]

From these passages it appears that *siggēl* may be defined as "to accumulate for oneself," "to save up (money, or the like)." The noun shows a similar connotation:

> This is like one who has a very precious *sᵉgullā* which he counts repeatedly to know its sum, rejoicing at each count.[9]
>
> Deposits for safekeeping are not accepted from women, bondsmen, and children ... If one has accepted such from a minor, he must set it up for him as a *sᵉgullā*.[10]

Sᵉgullā, then, will denote "a private accumulation, or hoard"; in the second passage, it is used in the specialized sense of "trust fund."

These meanings, when applied to Akkadian *sikiltam sakālu*, fit rather well, as will be evident from the following instances. First, from the account of Sennacherib's first campaign:[11]

> ... *ezib nišē imērē gamālē alpē ū ṣēnē iš* ... [*ša*] *ummāniya ebukūnimma ana ramānišunu iskilū sikiltu.* "... aside from people, asses, camels, cattle and sheep ... which my soldiers took for themselves and made themselves private accumulations."

Or again, from the account of Sargon's eighth campaign:[12]

... ultu ulla ana ruppuš mātišunu iskilū šar pani ālikūt maḫrēšu.
". . . (cities which) from days of yore early kings who had gone before
him had accumulated to broaden their land."

Far more instructive for our present purpose, however, is the connotation which attaches to *siggēl s^egullā* in rabbinic sources when the
agents are of inferior legal status, such as women, bondsmen, and
minors.

> This is like two brothers who were *m^esagg^elīn* money from their father:
> the one had no sooner collected two denarii than he spent them, while
> the other, who collected and laid aside, became rich in time.[13]
>   This is like a good wife whose husband allotted her a few articles
> and expenses. Afterwards, when her husband returned, she said, "See
> what you allotted me and what I *siggaltī* for you, even adding to what
> you gave me!"[14]
>   "And ye shall be to me a *s^egullā* (Exod. 19:5)": Just as precious as a
> person's *s^egullā* to him will you be to me. R. Joshua b. Qarḥa said: This
> figure was employed only for vividness (i.e., is not to be taken liter-
> ally). And lest you conceive the meaning really to be "as the wife
> *m^esaggelet* from her husband, the son from his father, the bondsman
> from his master, and the bondswoman from her mistress—so you are
> *m^esuggalīn* to me from others," Scripture follows with the explicit
> statement "for the whole earth is mine!"[15]

We see, then, that with classes legally inferior *s^egullōt* were commonly accumulated[16] from the property of others upon whom they
were dependent. It could scarcely have been otherwise, since rabbinic
law did not ordinarily permit such classes to acquire property outright. This is precisely the situation that obtains in our Hammurabi
passage, and if we apply this significance to *sikiltam isakkil* the entire
law may be seen in a new light:

> If a married woman who was living in the house of her husband has
> made up her mind to leave, and has accumulated (out of her husband's
> property) a private fund, ruined her home, etc.

Thus the woman first assured her financial sufficiency by carefully
amassing a private fund, consisting probably of whatever odds and
ends of her husband's property she could spirit away unobserved—
even diverting part of the allotted household expenses to her savings,
to judge from the disruption of her home (cf. Eilers' interpretation).
Then she set about disgracing her husband so as to instigate him to
begin divorce proceedings against her. If such machinations could be
proved against her, the law goes on to state, the husband may divorce

his wife, but is exempted from adding to her hoard by paying the divorce settlement and traveling expenses; or he may reduce her to the status of a maidservant.

Another mention of a wife's *sikiltu* is found in a Nuzi tablet—a will detailing the division of a man's property between his wife and son—the pertinent part of which runs as follows:

> *minummē šamnū ū erū sikiltaša ša ᶠKiraše ana ᶠKiraše nadnū.* "Whatever oils and copper which Kiraše [the wife] has privately accumulated, are given to her."[17]

This passage is doubly instructive. In the first place it affords us a glimpse of the type of objects that a woman would want to collect for her *sikiltu*—in this case, indeed with no ulterior intent. But it also suggests an answer to a question that might be raised from our Hammurabi law; namely, why did the legislator not require the wife to restore the property she had surreptitiously accumulated from her husband? From this Nuzi passage it appears that a woman's *sikiltu* was actually recognized in some sense as her own private property; in the division of the deceased's inheritance, therefore, her *sikiltu* did not revert to the common property of the husband to be distributed among the various inheritors. If this be a permissible inference from the slender evidence, it suggests that likewise in the Code of Hammurabi a woman's *sikiltu* was actually legally acquired by her, so that notwithstanding the circumstances attendant upon her acquisition, and despite her being divorced or reduced to servitude, her *sikiltu* remained her own property.

Considering now the relation of Hebrew *segullā* to Akkadian *sikiltu*, it would appear that Akkadian √*skl* is related to Hebrew √*sgl* as, say, Akkadian √*nkp* to Hebrew √*ngp*; that is to say, the two are cognates. That voiceless explosives of Akkadian may appear in Hebrew as voiced (and vice versa) is a well-known phenomenon (cf. Akk. *gapšu*, Heb. *gabiš*; Akk. *abatu*, Heb. *abad*; Akk. *Šarrukēn*, Heb. *Sargōn*). While there is no apparent morphological connection between the two nominal forms, they have much in common semantically. Just as Akkadian *qitiltu* serves commonly to form abstracts of *qatālu* (*raḥāṣu* "inundate," *riḥiṣtu* "inundation"; *saḥāru* "turn around," *siḥirtu* "environs"; *batāqu* "cut through," *bitiqtu* "loss"; *naṣāru* "guard," *niṣirtu* "treasure"; and the like), so is Hebrew *qᵉtullā* a relatively frequent abstract for *qātal* (*gᵉ'ullā* "redemption," *ḥᵃnukkā* "dedication," *ᵃhuzzā* "possession," *ᵃlummā* "sheaf," *kᵉtubbā* "marriage document" [Mishnaic]). Hence, cognates in these parallel nominal forms may also correspond semantically; e.g., *piqittu—p^equddā* "order." In this last category we may also place the cognates *sikiltu—s^egullā*, representing abstracts of the simple stem in a passive sense: "that which is accumulated," "hoard," and the like. That Hebrew *s^egullā* should be construed with a *pi"ēl* verb, *siggēl*, is no more unusual than that *'alummā* should appear with *'illem* or *k^ehunna* with *kih (h) en;* the denominative nature of these three verbs is vouched for by the fact that the regular abstract to *pi"ēl* is *qattālā* (e.g., *baqqāšā* "request") or *qittūl* (e.g., *šillūm* "requital"). Of course, the present interpretation necessitates the rejection of the usual connection of *s^egullā* with Akkadian *sugullu* "herd," with the consequent loss of another semantic parallel to *pecu–pecunia, cattle–chattel.*

A final word on the use of *s^egullā* in the Bible. In 1 Chronicles 29:3 we have a usage identical with what has been shown:

> Furthermore [says David] because of my ardent interest in the house of my God, my own private accumulation (*yēš lī s^egullā*) of gold and silver I have given over to the house of my God, over and above what I had prepared for the holy house.

But besides this literal usage (also found in Ecclesiastes 2:8) a more spiritual connotation became attached to the word. The material aspect of "private savings" gave way to the spiritual attachment to objects diligently and patiently acquired. Thus *s^egullā* comes to mean a dear personal possession, a "treasure" only in the sense of that which is treasured or cherished. This is its meaning on the numerous passages in which Israel is called the *s^egullā* of God, as the Midrashic commentary on Exodus 19:5, which we saw above, was at such pains to point out.[18]

NOTES

1. A. Deimel, *Codex Hammurabi: transcriptio et translatio latina* 26 (Rome, 1930); D. D. Luckenbill and E. Chiera in J. M. P. Smith, *The Origin and History of Hebrew Law* 201 (Chicago, 1931); P. Cruveilhier, *Commentaire du Code d'Hammourabi* 141 (Paris, 1938).

2. So defined, e.g., in Bezold, *Babylonisch-Assyrisches Glossar* 212 (Heidelberg, 1926). For earlier discussions, see Thureau-Dangin, *Huitième campagne de Sargon* 38, n. 1 (TCL III, 1912); S. Smith, *First Campaign of Sennacherib* 82, n. to line 61 (London, 1921); G. R. Driver, *Early Babylonian Letters* 55, letter 81, n. to line 12 (in OECT III, 1924).

3. W. Eilers, *Die Gesetzesstele Chammurabis,* Der alte Orient XXXI, Heft 3/4, 35 (1931); T. J. Meek, ANET 172.

4. HSS V 74: 8; cf. E.A. Speiser, AASOR X 56 (1930).

5. S. Smith, loc. cit.

6. F. Zorell, *Lexicon Hebraicum et Aramaicum* 546 (Rome, 1946[–1954]).

7. 'Ēkā Rabbā, ed. Buber 79; cf. n. 390 in which Buber explains his deletion (unnecessary now) of qānā "bought," which appears in the earliest printings.

8. Talmūd Yerūšalmī, Bābā Batrā IX:17a, top; cf. P'nē Mošē ad loc.

9. Bemidbar Rabbā 37b, end.

10. Talmūd Bablī Bābā Batrā 52a; cf. Rashi ad loc.

11. D. D. Luckenbill, Annals of Sennacherib 55, line 61 (OIP II, 1924); S. Smith, op. cit. 44. [Transcription follows the Chicago Assyrian Dictionary 15.69 (1984).]

12. Thureau-Dangin, op. cit., plate XII, line 234.

13. Yalqūṭ Shim'ōnī, Deut. 873.

14. Šir Haššīrīm Rabbā VII:14.

15. Mekīltā, Baḥodes 2, ed. Horovitz-Rabin 208; cf. variants and note ad loc. The point of this passage is: Israel is God's s'gullā only insofar as its dearness to God may be compared to the dearness of a s'gullā to its human owner; it must not be supposed, however, that God, like the woman, the minor, etc., had to scrape his s'gullā together from the property of others, for, indeed, there are no proprietors on earth other than he.

16. The use of the preposition 'aḥar, mē'aḥar after the verb siggēl in these passages recalls such phrases as liqqeṭ aḥ'rē, 'āsap aḥ'rē (both illustrated in Ruth 2:7), referring specifically to gleaning. One is strongly tempted, therefore, to render siggēl (mē) 'aḥar "accumulate the leftovers of—," "scrape together the small change of—." Such a meaning would describe well the accumulation of these propertyless classes.

17. HSS V:71:17ff.; cf. E. A. Speiser, op. cit., 49. Note also the occurrence of sakālu in the Idrimi Stela, cf. A. Goetze, JCS 4 (1950): 227.

18. Perhaps a parallel Akkadian development underlies the name Sikilti-Adad (K. Tallqvist, Assyrian Personal Names 195), meaning "cherished possession of Adad"? Cf. also the Alalaḫ) occurrence, for which see Goetze, loc. cit.

Additional note:

The equation proposed in this article has been accepted both by Assyriologists (see, e.g., the Chicago Assyrian Dictionary 15 (1984), 69, 245) and Hebraists (e.g., Theologisches Handwoerterbuch zum Alten Testament II (1976), 142). Accepting the equation, Moshe Held noted "some problems [that] remain unsolved" in JCS 15 (1961): 11–12.

The Decalogue Tradition
Critically Examined
1989

This essay surveys traditions about the Ten Commandments in the Bible as well as in the literature of commentary that has grown up around them. My intention is to examine the biblical texts as they stand, noting the difficulties that they present, unprejudiced by the aura of sanctity that surrounds them. Such a clear-eyed approach will reveal both the uncertainties and the ambiguities attached to these few short sentences that have given rise to so much thought and discussion through the ages.

THE HEBREW NAME "THE TEN UTTERANCES"
('ASERETH HA-DIBBEROTH)

When Moses repeats the Ten Commandments (Deut. 5:6–18) he calls them "these words (*devarim*) which the LORD spoke . . . to your whole congregation at the mountain (Horeb) with a mighty voice out of the fire" (5:19). Earlier, he had introduced these Commandments as "the ten words" (i.e., utterances): ('*asereth ha-devarim*, 4:13),[1] the same expression used in Exodus 34:28 for the text inscribed on the second set of tablets that he had hewed, "He wrote down on the tablets the terms of the covenant, the ten words." According to Deuteronomy (10:4) these were the same Commandments as those written on the first tablets, although this is not made entirely clear in Exodus 34 (see below); and in the original account of the giving of the Commandments (Exod. 20), the name "ten words" does not appear at all.

Later on, Mishnaic Hebrew replaced *devarim* with *dibberoth*, the plural of *dibber*, the term specialized for divine speech.[2] This rabbinic theological term is cognate with the Aramaic *'asartei dibberaya* of the Palestinian Targumim (including the Neofiti), and corresponds to the phrase *'asra pithgamin* used by Onkelos (Exod. 34:28; Deut. 4:13).

THE NARRATIVE SETTING

The Torah does not provide a single, clear, consistent account of the giving of the Ten Commandments. In Exodus 19:9 we read that before their proclamation, God told Moses on Mount Sinai: "I will come to you in a thick cloud, in order that the people may hear when I speak with you and so trust you ever after." To what does this refer? Ibn Ezra writes:

> In my opinion this verse alludes to the Sinaitic revelation when God spoke the words of the covenant, i.e., the Ten Commandments . . . and the "trust" refers to the fact that many Israelites said that it is impossible that an incorporeal being speak with a man of flesh and that he remain alive. Proof of this is [the people's confession] "We have seen this day that man may live though God has spoken to him." (Deut. 5:21)

And indeed Exodus 19:19 does mention a kind of dialogue between God and Moses, with Mount Sinai covered in smoke because the LORD had descended upon it; amidst the blare of the horn "Moses spoke, and God answered him in thunder (lit. 'in voice')." Rashi understands this verse too as an allusion to the proclamation of the Decalogue: "When Moses was speaking and proclaiming the Commandments to Israel . . . the LORD helped him by granting him strength so that his voice would be powerful and audible."

Rabbi Meyuhas b. Elijah (fourteenth–fifteenth centuries) makes an explicit connection between Exodus 19:9 and 19:19:

> The LORD would dictate to Moses, and Moses would repeat the words to Israel, like one who reads from the Torah, and Israel would hear both of them—as it is said earlier, "that the people may hear when I speak with you" (v. 9), and further on, "I stood between the LORD and you at that time to convey the LORD's words to you." (Deut. 5:5)

However, it is not universally accepted that verse 19 refers to the giving of the Decalogue. Nahmanides links it to the adjacent verses 20–24, in which the LORD descends to Mount Sinai before the proclamation and calls Moses to Him:

> And he [Moses] spoke with the Israelites to instruct them what to do, and Israel heard the LORD's voice which answered Moses and com-

manded him, but they did not understand what He said to him. God gave Moses the instructions listed in the paragraph "Go down, warn the people." (19:21)

Then, after Moses goes down to the people (Exod. 19:25), God speaks "all these words," i.e., the Ten Commandments. It is not, however, clear to whom he spoke. The Alexandrinus manuscript of the Septuagint adds "to Moses" (verse 20:1), a reading that is consistent with the above explanations. Yet verse 20:19[22] reads, "You yourselves saw that I spoke to you [plural] from the very heavens," which implies that God spoke to all of the Israelites. The people are frightened and they ask Moses to be an intermediary between them and God, "Let not God speak to us, lest we die" (Exod. 20:16[19]). Here we learn for the first time that God is to speak directly to the people. Moses reassures the people, and then, in order to receive the rest of the covenant stipulations, he approaches the cloud enshrouding God (vv. 17–18[20–21]). Despite the appropriateness of verses 15–18[18–21] to the context, Nahmanides claims (at 20:15[18]) that these verses should precede the giving of the Decalogue and that the people's fear and their request to Moses should immediately follow the preparatory events of 19:18–19ᵃ. After all, verses 20:15–16[18–19] do not mention that the people were afraid of the divine voice, nor do the people request that "God not speak to us *any more.*

Deuteronomy relates that God commanded Moses to gather the people at Mount Horeb so that they might hear his words and learn to revere him forever (Deut. 4:10; cf. Exod. 20:17[20]). He spoke to them face to face from the fire (Deut. 5:4), while Moses stood between the LORD and the people to convey His words, as the people were afraid of the fire and would not go up the mountain (Deut. 5:5).[3] After they heard the Ten Commandments, they were afraid that "if we hear the voice of the LORD our God any longer, we shall die" (5:22), so they request that Moses serve as the intermediary.

Unless we manipulate them, these details do not add up to a continuous, consistent story. Nahmanides' approach, for example, forces him to assume that the people drew back twice, and that they twice requested Moses to act as intermediary—once prior to the proclamation of the Decalogue (Exod. 20) and once subsequent to it (Deut. 5). The tension between Deuteronomy 5:4 and 5:5 is resolved by the explanation that God gave the two Commandments "I the LORD am your God," and "You shall have no other gods" (Commandments in which he speaks in the first person), to the people "face to face," whereas Moses "stood between the LORD and you . . . to convey" the rest of the Commandments. (Hizzequni accordingly claims that Exodus 20:15–17[18–20], which relates the people's fear and request for mediation, "should actually follow 'keep my commandments' (20:6), but the Torah did not want to interrupt the recitation of the Decalogue.")

An unbiased reading of these narratives reveals that differing conceptions of the event have been interwoven: (a) God spoke with Moses, and the people overheard; (b) he spoke with Moses, and then Moses transmitted His words to the people; (c) God spoke to the people directly.[4] Common to them is the idea that all the people experienced the revelation at Mount Sinai; they differ only concerning the manner in which the Decalogue was received—whether from God directly or via Moses.[5]

What is the significance of this public theophany? Both Exodus 20:17[20] and Deuteronomy 4:10 say that it was intended to instill the fear of God in the hearts of the people. Another purpose was to cause the people to believe in Moses' prophecy, and to have them accept his mediation between them and God (Exod. 19:9; 20:16[19]; Deut. 5:21–24).[6] Medieval theologians perceived the latter as the main purpose:

> The Jews did not believe in Moses despite the miracles he had performed. . . . What then did inspire belief in him? The event at Mount Sinai. Because we heard with our own ears and saw with our own eyes the fire and the thunder and lightning. We saw Moses enter the dark cloud and heard the Voice telling him "Moses, Moses, go and tell the people thus and so." This too is the purpose of the passage (Deut. 5:4) "Face to face the LORD spoke to you on the mountain"; likewise (v. 3) "It was not with our fathers that the LORD made this covenant but with us." Now, whence do we know that it was the revelation at Sinai that confirmed Moses as a prophet? . . . from the passage (Exod. 19:9) "I will come to you in a thick cloud, in order that the people may hear when I speak with you and so trust you ever after." The implication is that beforehand they had not had implicit faith in him, of the unshakeable kind. Their belief in him was conditional, clouded by doubts. (Maimonides, *Mishneh Torah, Yesodei Torah*, 8:1)[7]

That the Decalogue was written by the finger of God on two stone tablets, and that it comprised the terms of the covenant between God and Israel, is the concept clearly expressed in the book of Deuteronomy (4:12–13; 9:10). Hence the significance of the term "the Tablets of the Covenant," used in Deuteronomy (9:9, 11, 15). The Exodus account is more obscure: one must combine several verses: 24:12 ("Come up to Me on the mountain . . . and I will give you the stone tablets . . . which I have inscribed to instruct them"); 31:18 ("When He finished speaking to him . . . , He gave Moses the two tablets of the

Pact, stone tablets inscribed with the finger of God"); 32:15, 19 (the two tablets of the Pact that Moses broke when he saw the golden calf); 34:1 (carving two more tablets like the first); and 34:28 ("and he wrote down on the tablets the terms of the covenant, the Ten Commandments"). Even after combining these verses, there is still no definite identification of the Commandments in Exodus 20 with the contents of the first and second sets of stone tablets (see below for discussion on Exodus 34:28). Only by turning to Deuteronomy do we find a connecting link, for the Exodus traditions are less crystallized and shaped than the tradition in Deuteronomy.

Likewise, the epithet "tablets of the Pact" (*luḥoth ha'eduth*) is obscure: early exegetes interpreted *'eduth* as from *'ed*, i.e., "testimony" (Onkelos, *sahadutha*): "an eternal reminder testifying to the covenant between God and Israel" (see Cassuto, *Commentary on Exodus*, 30–31:18). This explanation is supported by the custom of making covenants in the ancient Near East (see below). Other commentators rely on the parallel phrase "tablets of the covenant" (*luḥoth ha-berith*) and regard *'eduth* as coming from the root *'dy*, as in the ancient Aramaic term *'dy* (plural construct) or *'dy'* (plural definite), meaning "covenant."[8]

Moses breaks the first tablets in anger over the golden calf, and after conciliating God, is ordered to engrave a second set of tablets just like the first. On these latter tablets is inscribed exactly what had been written on the first (Exod. 32:19; 34:1, 4, 28[b]; Deut. 9:17; 10:1–4). At God's bidding a wooden ark is made for the tablets, an ark called the "Ark of the Pact" (*"'aron ha-'eduth,"* Exod. 25:21–22) or the "Ark of the Covenant" (*"'aron ha-berith,"* Josh. 3:6); "Ark of the LORD's Covenant" (*"'aron berith YHWH,"* Num. 10:33; Deut. 10: 8). In the desert the Ark was housed in the "tent sanctuary of the Pact" (Exod. 40:20–21; Num. 1:50; 9:15; 17:22); then later in Shiloh (1 Sam. 4:3–4), and in Kiriath-jearim (1 Sam. 7:1), until David brought it to Jerusalem and placed it in the tent he pitched for it (2 Sam. 6). Finally, the priests placed the Ark in the sanctuary of Solomon's Temple. The last mention of the tablets appears in this context: "There was nothing inside the Ark but the two tablets of stone which Moses placed there at Horeb" (1 Kings 8:9). If the cherubs above the Ark are God's chair, since He is styled "Enthroned on the Cherubim" (1 Chron. 13:6), then the Ark itself is the "footstool of our LORD" (1 Chron. 28:2). Accordingly, storing the tablets inside the Ark is parallel to the ancient Egyptian custom of depositing important documents beneath statues of the gods as evidence of the solemn commitment of the owners of the documents in the presence of the gods (a custom that supports the view that the "tablets of the Pact" testify to the covenant).[9]

To what does the expression "the terms of the Covenant, the Ten

Commandments" in Exodus 34:28 refer? Verses 10–26 present a short series of commandments, opening with God's declaration, "I hereby make a covenant." About this covenant, God says to Moses (v. 27): "Write down these commandments, for in accordance with these commandments I make a covenant with you and with Israel." This series includes: (1) forbidding alliances with the Canaanites; (2) forbidding molten gods; (3) enjoining the Festival of Unleavened Bread; (4) firstlings; (5) the Sabbath; (6) the Festival of Weeks; (7) the Ingathering Festival; (8) pilgrimages; (9) statutes concerning the Passover sacrifice; (10) first fruits; and (11) a ban on cooking a kid in its mother's milk. After noting that Moses spent forty days and nights fasting before the LORD, the text reports that "he inscribed on the tablets the terms of the Covenant, the Ten Commandments" (v. 28).

In context Moses is apparently the one who inscribed, and what he inscribed is the preceding series of commandments.[10] Yet if this is indeed the case, then we have before us another series called the "Ten Words" ('*asereth ha-devarim*)! However, since it is improbable that one designation should cover two such different series of injunctions, it appears that the end of verse 28 refers to verse 1 ("I will inscribe upon the tablets the words that were on the first tablets") and is to be detached from its adjacent context. Hence, an independent series of covenant injunctions appears between verses 1 and 28b, which is not called the "Ten Words."[11] The relationship of these two series to each other, and of both to the "record of the covenant" (Exod. 24:7) containing "all these commands" with reference to which the Sinai covenant was made according to Exodus 24:8, is unclear. Evidently several documents called the "Words of the Covenant" were preserved by ancient tradition; the biblical narrator integrated them all into the story of the giving of the Torah, and he was unable (or did not want) to smooth over the problems caused by his conservative method—an outcome of the awe in which he held these traditions.

VERSIONS OF THE DECALOGUE*

In addition to the two versions of the Decalogue found in the Masoretic text of the Pentateuch (Exod. 20:2–17 and Deut. 5:6–19); the Samaritan Pentateuch preserves slightly differing Hebrew texts.

*See the detailed table on the following pages.

The Samaritan text tends to reduce the differences between the versions in Exodus and Deuteronomy. For example:

Masoretic Version	*Samaritan Version, Both Books*
Exod.: Remember	Observe
Deut.: Observe	
Exod.: You shall not covet your neighbor's house	You shall not covet your neighbor's house
Deut.: And you shall not covet your neighbor's wife	
Exod.: You shall not covet your neighbor's wife	And you shall not covet your neighbor's wife
Deut.: And you shall not crave your neighbor's house	
Exod.: his male or his female slave, or his ox, or his ass	
Deut.: his field, or his male or his female slave, or his ox, or his ass	his field, his male or his female slave, his ox, or his ass
Exod.: after "you shall not murder," five "you-shall-not" 's	four "you-shall-not" 's
Deut.: five "and you-shall-not" 's	the fifth: "*and* you-shall-not"

The major difference between the Masoretic and the Samaritan versions is the Samaritan addition of a Commandment considered the Tenth, according to their numbering (their First Commandment is "You shall have no other gods . . . "). This comprises the injunction to publish the Decalogue on Mount Gerizim and to build an altar there. The Samaritan Exodus and Deuteronomy both contain the passage:

> And it will come to pass when the Lord brings you to Canaan and you possess the land (cf. Deut. 11:29), then you shall raise up large stones and coat them with plaster and write on the stones all the words of this Torah. (Deut. 27:2b–3:1a)

> And when you cross the Jordan you will raise these stones which I command you this day on MountGerizim (it appears thus, as one word; cf. Deut. 27:4a in the Masoretic version: "Mount Ebal") and you shall build an altar there to the Lord your God, a stone altar, etc. (27:5–7), that mountain west of the Jordan, by the terebinth of Moreh, opposite Shechem (Deut. 11:30 in the Samaritan version).

VERSIONS OF THE DECALOGUE

EXODUS (E)   DEUTERONOMY (D)

(The superscript numbers refer to the variants listed below)

I the LORD am your God who brought you out of the land of Egypt, the house of bondage: You shall have no other gods beside Me. You shall not make for yourself a sculptured image, or any (D: any)[1] likeness of what is in the heavens above, or on the earth below, or in the waters under the earth. You shall not bow down to them or serve them. For I the LORD your God am an impassioned[2] God, visiting the guilt of the fathers upon the children, (D: and)[3] upon the third and upon the fourth generations of those who reject Me, but showing kindness to the thousandth generation of those who love Me and keep My commandments (D: *ktiv* His commandments).

You shall not swear falsely by the name of the LORD your God, for the LORD will not clear one who swears falsely by his name.[4]

Remember[5] the sabbath day and keep it holy. Six days you shall labor and do all your work, but[6] the seventh day is a sabbath of the LORD your God: you shall not do any work[7] — you, your son or daughter, your male or female slave,[8] or[9] your cattle, or the stranger who is within your settlements. **For in six days the LORD made heaven and earth, sea and all that is in them, and He rested on the seventh day; therefore the LORD blessed the sabbath day and hallowed it.**[10]

Observe the sabbath day and keep it holy, **as the LORD your God has commanded you**. Six days you shall labor and do all[11] your work, but[6] the seventh day is a sabbath of the LORD your God: you shall not do any work[7] — you, your son or your daughter, **and**[12] your male or female slave, and[13] **your ox or your ass,**[14] **or any of your** cattle,[14] or the stranger who is within your settlements, **so that your male and female slave may rest as you do. Remember that your were a slave in the land of Egypt and the LORD your God freed you from there with a mighty hand and an out-stretched arm; therefore the LORD your God has commanded you to make**[15] **the sabbath day.**[16]

Honor your father and your mother,[17] that you may long endure on the[18] land which the LORD your God is giving you.

Honor your father and your mother, **as the LORD your God has commanded you,**[19] that you may long endure, **and that you may fare well,**[19] in the land that the LORD your God is giving you.

[20]You shall not murder.

(D: And)[21] You shall not commit adultery.

(D: And)[21] You shall not steal.[20]

(D: And)[21] You shall not bear false (E: *šeqer*; D: *šaw*) witness against your neighbor.

You shall not covet your neighbor's **house;**[22] **you shall not covet**[22a] **your neighbor's**[24] **wife,**[23] or[25] his male or female slave, **or**[26] his ox or his ass,[27] or anything that is your neighbor's.

And[21] You shall not covet your neighbor's **wife.**[28] **And**[28a] **you shall not crave**[29] **your neighbor's house,**[30] **or his field,**[31] or his male[32] or female slave,[33] or his ox,[34] or his ass,[35] or anything that is your neighbor's.

VARIANTS

1	Q, Ds, Dg: +any	17	+ that you may fare well and N, Eg
2	N: (q n w')	18	+ good Eg
3	Q, Ds, Dg: upon	19	that you may fare well and
4	N: [š]mh		that you may long endure Dg
5	Observe Es	20	adultery, theft, murder Eg;
6	+on N, Q		adultery, murder, theft N, Dg (Philo)
7	+ on it (*bh*) N; (*bw*) Q, Eg, Dg; =Es, Ds	21	> Q, Ds, Dg
		22	wife [N], Eg
8	+ your ox and your ass and all your N, Eg	22a	*ttm ?wh* N
		23	house N, Eg
9	> Es	23	house N, Eg
10	N: *vyqdsyw*	24	N, Es, Eg + his field
11	Q: + *eth*	25	> Es
12	> Q, Ds, Dg	26	Es: his cattle
13	> Q, Ds, Dg	27	+ or all his cattle Eg
14	Q: and your cattle	28	house(hold) Ds
15	observe Q,	28a	> Q, Dg
16	+ and to hallow it Dg; + to hallow it, for in six days YHWH made heaven and earth, the sea all that is in them, and He rested on the seventh day; therefore YHWH blessed the sabbath day to hallow it Q	29	covet Q, Sd, Dg
		30	wife Ds
		31	+or Dg
		32	> Q, Ds
		33	> Q
		34	or Dg
		35	+ or all his cattle Dg

KEY TO VARIANTS

Dg = Greek Deut. (LXX) (ed. Rahlfs)

Ds = Samaritan Deut. (ed. von Gall)

Eg = Greek Exod.

Es = Samaritan Exod.

N = Nash Papyrus

Q = 4Q Deut.$_m$ (in "Scrolls from the Wilderness of the Dead Sea: A Catalogue of the Exhibition", *The Dead Sea Scrolls of Jordan*, University of California, 1965).

+ = added matter in source(s) indicated

> = "is missing in"

This Commandment reflects, on the one hand, the Samaritan belief in the holiness of Mount Gerizim,[12] and on the other hand the notion, first attested in Hellenistic-Jewish literature, that the Decalogue contains "all the words of the Torah." The Nash Papyrus discovered in Egypt, and dating from about the second century B.C.E. to the first century C.E., contains yet another version of the Decalogue. Because the passage *Shema' Yisra'el* follows, it has been postulated that the Nash text had a liturgical use (i.e., it reflects the order of reciting the portions during prayer, see below). The Nash Papyrus version of the Decalogue is close to the Septuagint translation of Exodus, and it is likely that it was copied from the Hebrew version underlying the Greek translation.[13]

There is a marked tendency among non-Masoretic texts to assimilate the Exodus and the Deuteronomy version of the Decalogue and to combine them. Thus, itemization of property in the Sabbath Commandment and in "Thou shall not covet" are brought more closely into line. The differentiated Masoretic version is evidently the older one and the others are dependent on it.

Most of the differences between the Masoretic readings of Exodus and those of Deuteronomy can be attributed to the Deuteronomic context, and should be viewed as secondary to the Exodus Decalogue. The essence of the Sabbath Commandment in Exodus (God's hallowing the seventh day on which he rested after the six days of Creation) is related to the initial clause of the Commandment ("Remember . . . to hallow it"), inasmuch as God's rest is the sole basis for the holiness of the day ("therefore the Lord hallowed it").[14] In contrast, Deuteronomy's explanation, "so that your male and female slave may rest as you do" (cf. Exod. 23:12), is more appropriate to that book's humanitarian attitude.[15] "Remember that you were a slave in the land of Egypt," which appears in the sequel, is one of many similar mentions of the Egyptian bondage found throughout Deuteronomy's legal material (e.g., 15:15; 16:12; 24:18–22). The rhetorical expansions "that you may long endure" and "as the Lord your God has commanded you," which appear in Deuteronomy's Commandments on the Sabbath and on parental honor, are typically Deuteronomic; see Deuteronomy 5:26; 6:18; 12:25ff.; 4:23; and 20:17. The addition of ox and ass in the list of a man's property in the Deuteronomic Sabbath Commandment is apparently taken from the Commandment "You shall not crave." Exodus begins the list of objects which "You shall not covet" with the general "house" = all the members of your neighbor's household (cf. Gen. 18:19; Deut. 25:9), and then proceeds to detail human and animal members in descending order of value omitting real property, reflecting perhaps a setting in nomadic life. Deuteronomy, which does include real property, places the wife first (as in Exodus) and joins house (here meaning the building) to field (a common pair, cf. Gen. 39:5; 2 Kings 8:3, 5). In these cases, the Deuteronomic reading is obviously secondary. Ibn Ezra's note (in the introduction to the Decalogue, in his long commentary on Exodus) applies to the other changes in wording:

> The custom of the speakers of the sacred tongue (Hebrew) is sometimes to explicate matters at length and sometimes to use only so many words as are needed to make their meaning plain. Words are like bodies, their meaning is like the soul; the body is like a vessel for the soul. Hence the custom of the wise to use language that preserves the sense, and not to be concerned about changes in the words so long as their meaning stays the same.

THE DIVISION INTO TEN COMMANDMENTS

The tradition governing the division of the Decalogue into paragraphs (*parashiyot*) does not conform to the tradition of its division into Ten Commandments (see *Minḥat Shai* on Exodus 20:4, the end). The long section in which God speaks in the first person (verses 1–6, "I the LORD ... My commandments") is one paragraph–as opposed to its usual division into two Commandments, as for example, in the *Mekhilta Baḥodesh*, chapter 8 (ed. Lauterbach, vol. II: 262), which counts "I the LORD" as the First and "You shall have no other gods ... My commandments" as the Second Commandment.[16] On the other hand, it was apparently in order to arrive at ten paragraphs that the prohibition of coveting in Exodus 20:14[17] was broken into two *parashiyot*, each beginning with "You shall not covet" (in Deuteronomy 5:18 it is "You shall not covet" and "You shall not crave"); this, even though the accepted reckoning (e.g., the *Mekhilta*) considers them to be one Commandment.[17]

There are two sets of cantillations for the Decalogue; Hizzequni explains them as follows (at the end of his commentary on the Exodus Decalogue):

> Most of the Ten Commandments have two sets of cantillation signs. To wit: on Shavuot, which is a representation of the giving of the Torah, and the Commandments are accompanied by the [explanatory] Targum,[18] we chant the whole Commandment, "You shall have no other gods," and the whole Commandment, "Remember the Sabbath," with the "enlarging" cantillation, which treats each one as a single verse since each is an individual Commandment. The Commandments "You shall not murder," "You shall not commit adultery," "You shall not steal," and "You shall not bear false witness," are chanted with the "shortening" cantillation, which breaks them into four verses, for they are four individual Commandments. In the month of Shevat, however, when one

290 : *The Biblical Text and Its Interpretation*

reads the Torah portion "Jethro" as a regular weekly portion, one chants "You shall have no other gods" and "Remember" in the "shortening" cantillation, so that each of them becomes four verses, while the Commandments "You shall not murder," "You shall not commit adultery," "You shall not steal," and "You shall not bear false witness," are chanted with the "enlarging" cantillation, so that they all become one verse, since nowhere else in the Bible is there a verse consisting of only two words. Only on Shavuot as I said above, are the Commandments "I the LORD," and "You shall have no other gods," chanted according to the "enlarging" cantillation, making them one verse in order to remind us that they were proclaimed in a single utterance.

The gist of this is that on the Feast of Shavuot one chants the Commandments in a versification that represents the way in which Israel heard the Ten Commandments at Mount Sinai–some very long utterances and some very short utterances. On the Sabbath for which "Jethro" (Exod. 18:1–20:23[26]) is the Torah portion, one chants the Commandments according to a normalizing cantillation that breaks the passage into verses of usual length. The system that lengthens or shortens the verses is called the "upper cantillation," and the system that normalizes the verses is called "lower cantillation."[19] (*Minḥat Shai* asserts that the upper cantillation is for public reading of the Decalogue and that the lower cantillation is for private reading.)

The chief difficulty and the focus of disagreement is the first paragraph ("I the LORD ... My commandments"), which is stylistically uniform–entirely in the first person–yet diverse in its content.[20] Philo defines the content of the First Commandment: "to acknowledge and honour the God Who is above all" (*On the Decalogue*, 65); he describes the Second Commandment as dealing with "idols of stone and wood and images in general made by human hands" (ibid., 51).[21] Josephus too defines the First Commandment as teaching, "that God is one and that He only must be worshipped," and the Second Commandment as "a commandment to make no image of any living creature for adoration."[22] Apparently both Philo and Josephus considered "You shall not make for yourself a sculptured image" as beginning the Second Commandment. A similar division is made by Rabbi Ishmael in *Sifre Numbers* (112) commenting on "he has spurned the word of the Lord" (Num. 15:31):

> R. Ishmael says: the Torah refers here to idolatry, as it is written, "He spurned the word of the LORD" (that is, "God's utterance"). He spurned the first utterance God made to Moses: "I the LORD am your God. You shall have no other gods beside me."

We called this "a similar division," because it is not clear whether

Philo and Josephus considered "I the Lord" as part of the First Commandment. The Samaritans do not count it in, nor do most Christians.[23] However, the link between "I the LORD" and "You shall have no other gods," can be seen in the sequence of ideas in the following verses:

> I brought you up out of Egypt and freed you from the house of bondage . . . And I said to you, "I the LORD am your God: you must not worship the gods of the Amorites in whose land you dwell." . . . (Judg. 6:8–10)

> You shall have no foreign god, / you shall not bow to an alien god. / I the LORD am your God / who brought you out of the land of Egypt. . . . (Ps. 81:10–11)

We see here that the mention of the Exodus from Egypt serves as a motive for the Commandment adjacent to (either preceding or following) it; i.e., "because I the LORD am your God, you must not worship the gods of the Amorites"; "you shall have no foreign god . . . because I the LORD am your God who brought you . . ." According to these parallels, and following Philo, Josephus, and Rabbi Ishmael, for whom the First Commandment ends with verse 3 ("You shall have no other gods beside Me"), the First Commandment should be defined as the imperative to recognize the LORD as the sole God because he revealed himself as "your God (= your shield and your saviour) who brought you out of the land of Egypt." Compare this verse with Hosea 13:4: "Only I the LORD have been your God / Ever since the land of Egypt; / You have never known a [true] God but Me, / You have never had a helper other than Me." (The parallel between "God" and "helper" shows that the first half of the verse means: "Only I the LORD have been your God [who revealed himself as your helper] since the land of Egypt"; just so we must understand the beginning of the First Commandment.)[24]

The Second Commandment begins "You shall not make for yourself,"[25] and prohibits any sculptured images for worship. Artistic renderings for decoration (e.g., plant forms, figures of various animals for the Temple) are not forbidden, nor is the making of image of God's entourage, such as cherubim. What is prohibited is the making of images of the Deity. No distinction is made between the Israelite God and pagan gods; indeed no distinction is made between the image and the deity. That the image is a symbolic rendering of a (usually) invisible deity is not recognized. Every sculptured image is equally forbidden, since it is perceived as a deity itself. The sculptured image is "other gods," and the idol worshiper arouses God's passion by transgressing the (first) Commandment "You shall have no other gods beside me."[26]

This prohibition is explained in Deuteronomy 4:15–18: "since you saw no shape when the LORD your God spoke to you at Horeb out of the fire." One is forbidden to create an image (or sculpture) of the LORD because no one knows how he looks; any picture that one may draw will be false. It is implied that an idol represents (albeit here falsely) an invisible being. A distinction between the symbol and the symbolized emerges here for the first time, even though this distinction is quite infrequent in the Bible, and is absent in the Decalogue. It appears to be the product of reflection, of an attempt to find a rational explanation, overly simplistic, for the Decalogue's ancient prohibition.

This lack of distinction between the image and the deity is neither a mistake (Kaufmann's view) nor a polemical exaggeration. For the idol worshiper, the line between the invisible deity and the image was truly blurred. By a prescribed ritual he was able to "animate" the idol, and all worship, all acceptance of worship, and all of the deity's relationship with the worshipers were accomplished through the idol.[27] The "fetishistic" version of the prohibition found in the Decalogue is directed at a widespread and psychologically deep-rooted conception that was common among idol worshipers in the ancient world. The Second Commandment was right on the mark when it ignored the difference between the symbol and the thing symbolized. The polemic against idolatry, depicting it as man worshiping his own handiwork in wood or stone, is likewise well founded (e.g., 2 Kings 19:18; Isa. 2:8; Ps. 115:3–7).

Deuteronomy's innovative explanation ("since you saw no shape") may not have a precedent, but it certainly has derivatives. Isaiah 40:18 expands this idea to express the incomparability of God: "To whom, then, can you liken God, / What form compare to Him?"–as the introduction to the mockery of idolatry (cf. 46:5), an idea adopted later by many to explain the Second Commandment (cf. Buber: "He should not be imagined, that is, limited to any one definite form; nor should He be equated to one or other of the 'figures' in nature, that is, restricted to any one definite manifestation").[28] This is an attractive rationalization, but it does not reach the psychological ground of the original ancient Commandment.

The Third Commandment is ambiguous. It reads literally "You shall not bear the name of the LORD your God in vain." "Bear" is interpreted according to the fuller phrase of Psalm 16:4 "I will not bear their names on my lips" = utter their names[29] (cf. also Ps. 50:16). The Hebrew word *la-šaw'* can refer to lying or deceit (Ps. 144:8, 11; cf. the substitution for *'ed šeqer* in the Exodus Decalogue,

by '*ed šaw*' in the Deuteronomy Decalogue, both meaning "false witness"). It can also mean "for naught," or "in vain" (Jer. 2:30; 4:30;
6:29). The complete phrase can be understood as "Do not utter the
name of the LORD falsely/in vain"–still ambiguous. The parallelism
found in Psalm 24:4 (literally "who has not borne my life in vain or
sworn deceitfully"[30]) leads one to understand that the Third Commandment forbids using the name of the LORD in a false oath, as in
Leviticus 19:12: "You shall not swear falsely by my name, profaning
the name of your God."

According to the other meaning of *la-šaw*', however, the ancients
understood the prohibition to forbid the name of the LORD in unnecessary oaths. Philo understood it in both senses: a prohibition against
false oaths, as well as the habit of "some who without even any gain in
prospect have an evil habit of swearing incessantly and thoughtlessly
about ordinary matters . . . for from much swearing springs false
swearing and impiety" (*On the Decalogue*, 84–91). Onkelos includes
both interpretations: "You shall not swear by the name of the LORD
your God frivolously, for the LORD will not clear one who swears
falsely by His name." There are still other possibilities since the Hebrew verb here, *nś*' means "utter," "express" (not necessarily in an
oath). The Sages expanded the scope of the Commandment to include
the prohibition of any idle use of God's name; for example "Whoever
says a blessing that is superfluous transgresses the Third Commandment" (Ber. 33a).

The Fourth Commandment ordains the sanctification of the Sabbath by ceasing from all work. This cessation is explained in Exodus as
honoring the day because God blessed and hallowed it by resting from
Creation. We can compare this reason to the one given in Isaiah
58:13: "If you call the sabbath 'delight', / The LORD's holy day 'honored'; / And if you honor it and go not your ways / Nor look to your affairs, nor strike bargains. . . ." The motive for the Sabbath in Exodus
depends on the Creation story in Genesis 1–2, and is similar to it as
well in ascribing an anthropomorphic attribute (resting) to God. Deuteronomy substitutes a humanitarian ground, one that actually refers
only to a man's household, without giving a reason for his own rest:
"so that your male and female slave may rest as you do" (cf. Exod.
23:12).

Deuteronomy also adds another reason for observing this Commandment: "Remember that you were a slave in the land of Egypt and
the Lord your God freed you from there. . . ." This motive recurs frequently in Deuteronomy, and is a comprehensive one that may be
compared to the opening of the First Commandment ("I the LORD").
Compare Deuteronomy 6:21–24, where observing all of the LORD's
commandments is grounded on loyalty to him, and gratitude for his

many benefactions. As Ibn Ezra puts it: "The LORD redeemed us from the house of bondage and bestowed on us this good; therefore we are obliged to revere Him."[31]

The Fifth Commandment enjoins honoring one's father and mother. As here, the other laws dealing with parent-child relations treat both parents as equals: striking or cursing a parent (Exod. 21:15, 17; Lev. 20:9; Deut. 27:16), and the wayward or defiant son "who does not heed his father or mother" (Deut. 21:18ff.). In Leviticus (19:3) also the commandment to honor one's parents appears next to the commandment to honor the Sabbath. It bridges the first set of Commandments, which deal with the relations between man and God, and the later Commandments dealing with the relations between man and man. The ancients explained the transitional position of this Commandment in this way: "The three of them–God, one's father and one's mother–are partners in every person" (*Mekhilta de R. Simeon b. Yoḥai*, ed. E. Z. Melammed, p. 152).[32] Compare this interpretation to Genesis 4:1 and Rashi's interpretation thereof: "I have gained a male child with the help of the LORD." Rashi explains: "When He created me and my husband He created us by Himself, but in the case of this one we are copartners with Him." (Compare *Nid.* 31a: "In every person's life there are three partners: God, his father and his mother.")

The Sixth Commandment prohibits shedding innocent blood. Joseph Bekhor Shor (France, twelfth century) comments:

> In the vernacular, *mwrtr*,[33] that is to say, the unlawful taking of life. The verb applies only to such an act, whereas the terms *mithah* and *haregah* refer to any taking of life, lawful or otherwise. Note that when the Bible refers to execution by law, as in Deut. 13:10, it says, "You shall take his life" (*harog tahargennu*); or in Lev. 20:9 "He shall be put to death" (*moth yumath*). Hence there is no need for the Commandment to describe the circumstances at this point; the use of the word *rṣḥ* shows that only unlawful homicide is meant.[34]

This Commandment affirms the sanctity of human life, in the spirit of Genesis 9:6: "For in His image did God make man."

The Seventh Commandment prohibits adultery, defined as sexual relations between a man and a married woman. This is the usual sense in the Bible of the verb *n'f*: "If a man commits adultery with a married woman, committing adultery with his fellow's wife" (Lev. 20:10); "committing adultery with the wives of their fellows" (Jer. 29:23); "the adulterous wife who welcomes strangers instead of her husband" (Ezek. 16:32).[35] When a married woman willingly has sexual relations with a man other than her husband, she, too, is called "adulterer"

(Lev. 20:10). Later commentators expanded the scope of the prohibition to include all illicit sex (Joseph Bekhor Shor comments: "An adulterer is one who has relations with any of those on the forbidden list" (Lev. 18:6–20; 20:10–21; see *Meor ha-Afelah*).[36] Saadiah went so far as to identify six levels of sex forbidden under this prohibition. (Ibn Ezra cites them in his long commentary.) This Commandment is necessary for the preservation of a patrilineal society. Philo describes at length the damage to society that results from violating this Commandment (*On the Decalogue*, 121–31).

The Eighth Commandment "You shall not steal" has undergone an interesting process of interpretation. According to its ordinary usage, "steal" in this Commandment means "to take property by stealth" (Ibn Ezra)–that is, without the owner's knowledge and consent–since the biblical verb *gnb* refers, in the vast majority of instances, to theft of property, possessions. However, the Sages interpret this Commandment as referring to the theft of persons–kidnapping:

> This is a case where we derive the meaning from the context. And what is the context here? It is *nefashot*, "persons" (or "lives"). Consequently, this Commandment, too, deals with *nefashot*. (Sanh. 86a)

(If *nefashot* means "persons" then the scriptural context is, "*Do not murder*"—a person; "*Do not commit adultery*"—with a person; therefore "*Do not steal*"–a person. Alternatively, if it means "lives," as in *dinei nefashot* = "cases involving lives" = capital crimes, then the context is: *murder,* a capital crime; *adultery,* a capital crime; therefore *stealing* = the capital crime of kidnapping.

Although this logic is not compelling (since the immediately following Commandment dealing with false witness is not necessarily a capital crime, and has an equal claim to serve as the context of "You shall not steal") some contemporary scholars have concluded that the Eighth Commandment really does refer to kidnapping.[37] However, it seems doubtful that the meaning of this Commandment should be determined by the penalty prescribed elsewhere for its violation, since it appears in a document that makes no mention at all of sanctions. It is more reasonable to take *gnb* in its usual sense as "theft of property," though in certain circumstances, it may refer to theft of persons. This Commandment affirms the principle that every person has the right to his possessions.

The Ninth Commandment forbids testifying "against your fellow" as a "false witness."[38] The setting is a court of law, whose verdict derives its legitimacy from the reliability of the evidence. When, in the absence of other proof, witnesses support or contradict the claims of the litigants, it becomes possible to arrive at the truth–providing the witnesses are trustworthy.

This Commandment is not the same as the talionic law of the "scheming witnesses" (Deut. 19:16–19). That deals exclusively with cases of injury to the person.[39] The scope of this Commandment is much wider, since witnesses also play a role in civil matters (e.g., transfer of property, as in Jer. 32:12). The thrust of this Commandment is to protect the validity and reliability of the judicial process, on which the social order depends.

The meaning of the Tenth Commandment has been, and still is, the subject of controversy, on account of the ambiguity of the verb *ḥmd* (modern scholars are often unaware that they are repeating the arguments of the ancients).[40] Thus, the *Mekhilta de R. Simeon Bar Yoḥai* (ed. Epstein-Melammed, Jerusalem 1955, 153):

> Here it says "You shall not covet," but further on it says "You shall not crave" (Deut. 5:18) . . . What is craving? When one says (text breaks off). . . . And what is coveting? When one exerts pressure to obtain possession.

The *Mekhilta de R. Ishmael* (ed. Horovitz-Rabin, Jerusalem 1960, 235; cf. ed. Lauterbach, II, 266) reads:

> Perhaps even the mere verbal expression of coveting is banned? No; for it says (Deut. 7:25): "You shall not covet the silver and gold on them and take it for yourself." Just as there, only acting [on one's desire] is forbidden, so also here what is forbidden is only to act [on one's desire].

Levi ben Gershon (1288–1344) reinforced this interpretation with the following argument:

> The meaning of "covet" is to attempt to obtain something from one's neighbor, for example, to offer him money to divorce his wife so that he can marry her, or to sell him his male or female slave or his ox or his ass . . . for this is a very evil characteristic, to attempt to take away the possessions of one's neighbor. We know that coveting is not just in one's heart but that it entails some action from what is said in the Torah "You shall not covet . . . and *take* it for yourselves" (Deut. 7:25). Moreover, it says "no one will covet your land" (Exod. 34:24), which means that no one will attempt to take your land when you make a pilgrimage; and it is also said "They covet fields, and seize them" (Mic. 2:2). Hence we infer that one does not violate the prohibition if one does not actually do something in order to obtain the coveted object.[41]

Ibn Ezra presents a more balanced explanation in his commentary on Deut. 5:18:

> The word "covet" in the Bible has two meanings. The first is to seize or to extort or to take from others forcibly, as in "no one will covet your land" (Exod. 34:24), for if this is not the meaning, then the land would be bad–but the Torah means to praise it. The second meaning is to crave in one's heart without acting on that desire, as we see in "You shall not covet your neighbor's house" in the Ninth Commandment (in the Exodus Decalogue, not counting "I the Lord" as a commandment) and "You shall not covet your neighbor's wife" in the Tenth Commandment. . . . The proof [that "covet" here means "crave"] is that in Deuteronomy, where Moses explains the Torah, he substitutes for "You shall not covet" the words "You shall not crave."

It appears that the principles of halakhic interpretation are at work in these commentaries, e.g., the principle that there is no superfluity or redundancy in the Torah, so that there must be two separate meanings for "You shall not covet" and "You shall not crave." It further appears that the guiding principle is that the Ten Commandments have the status of enforceable laws so that it is desirable to consider "covet" as an overt act, removing it from the internal realm of thought and from the problematic area of speech. However, if we confine ourselves to the linguistic evidence, it does not, in fact, support the definition of "covet" as "take," etc. (The opposite is true–the texts indicate that one must complement "covet" with another verb like "take" or "seize," because the former does *not* include this sense.) The substitution of "You shall not crave" for "You shall not covet" indicates that "covet" = "crave."

In Micah 2:2, the verb "covet" (*ḥmd*) is complemented by the verb "seize." In Proverbs 31:16 a similar sequence uses the verb "resolve" (*zmm*) followed by "acquire." Both are instances of planning followed by action, yielding the equation *ḥmd:gzl = zmm:lqh*. "To covet," therefore, means "to have thoughts (= *zmm*) of acquiring someone else's possessions." As for the idiom "covet in one's heart" (Prov. 6:25) it probably differs from ordinary coveting in the same way that "say in one's heart" differs from ordinary saying; namely, in that the former denotes coveting in thought only while the latter denotes coveting overtly, in speech or behavior. From there it is but a short step to "attempt" or "exert pressure."

One way or the other, this is the most scrupulous of the Commandments. It aims at preventing the flagrantly evil acts enumerated in the preceding Commandments, by mastering those impulses that drive people to commit such acts.

A CRITICAL VIEW OF THE ORIGINAL VERSION OF THE DECALOGUE

Modern critics try to reconstruct a primary form of the Decalogue, on the assumption that originally the Commandments constituted a series uniform in both form and style, similar to the list of "curses" in Deuteronomy 27:15–26 or to the list of virtues in Psalm 15. The fact that motive clauses appear only in the first Commandments, and that divergent grounds for the Sabbath are presented in Exodus and Deuteronomy, raises doubts about the originality of both. Likewise, the surprising shift in the motive clauses from first to third person with reference to God[42] and the shifts from "thou shalt not" to "thou shalt" run counter to the assumption of unity of style. Therefore, critics suggest terse, monotonous reconstructions. Below are two examples:

I

Thou shalt not bow down before any other god.
Thou shalt not make to thyself any idol.
Thou shalt not take the name of Yahweh in vain.
Thou shalt not do any work on the Sabbath day.
Thou shalt not despise thy father or thy mother.
Thou shalt not commit adultery with thy neighbour's wife.
Thou shalt not pour out the blood of thy neighbour.
Thou shalt not steal any man from thy neighbour.
Thou shalt not bear false witness against thy neighbour.
Thou shalt not covet thy neighbour's house.[43]

II

There shall not be to thee (or: Thou shalt not have) other gods.
Thou shalt not make for thyself an idol.
Thou shalt not lift up the name of Yahweh for mischief.
Thou shalt not despise (or treat with contempt) the sabbath day.
Thou shalt not curse thy father or thy mother.
Thou shalt not kill (or take the life of) thy neighbor.
Thou shalt not commit adultery with the wife of thy neighbor.
Thou shalt not steal anything that is thy neighbor's.
Thou shalt not answer thy neighbour as a false witness.
Thou shalt not covet the household of thy neighbor.[44]

There are two separate questions involved in dating the Decalogue: 1) what is the date of the text in its present form, including all of the "expansions" which are clearly tied to other parts of the Torah? (e.g., the Exodus motive for the Sabbath, tying it to the Creation story attributed to the Priestly source, Genesis chapters 1–2; or special idioms in the Deuteronomic Decalogue also appearing throughout the Book of

Deuteronomy); 2) what is the date of the original as reconstructed, free of any such literary influences?

The answer to the first question depends on the dating of the assumed sources, but at any rate it is certainly not early. As for the reconstructed original version, scholars today favor a very early date, as there is nothing in it that necessitates a late one. The obligations to worship only the LORD and not to make sculptured images are as old as, and inseparable from, biblical faith. The concept of the Sabbath as a day of rest is already present in the parts of the manna story (Exod. 16) attributed to the ancient sources JE. The ethical level of the interpersonal Commandments is also reflected in ancient Near Eastern texts as early as, or even earlier than, the time of Moses. One such example is the "Protestation of Guiltlessness" of the dead, an Egyptian text from the New Kingdom (16th century B.C.E.). The deceased addresses his divine judges, each with a special declaration (the names of the deities are omitted here). The first ten lines of this declaration read:[45]

  1. I have not committed evil.
  2. I have not stolen.
  3. I have not been covetous.
  4. I have not robbed.
  5. I have not killed men.
  6. I have not damaged the grain measure.
  7. I have not caused crookedness.
  8. I have not stolen the property of a god.
  9. I have not told lies.
 10. I have not taken away food.
(19.) I have not committed adultery.

The Decalogue does not reflect the prophetic ethic which would have necessitated dating it as late as the classical prophetic period. Placing first the obligations to God and balancing them with one's obligations to one's fellow is not typical of the prophetic message, which prefers the latter and deemphasizes the former. Furthermore, the main prophetic themes are absent from the Decalogue: saving the oppressed from the hand of the oppressor, aiding the poor, executing justice at the gate, etc. Therefore, neither the religious nor the ethical content of the Ten Commandments points to a late date, nor do they negate the possibility of a date as early as the birth of the nation. It seems that the expanded version of the first five Commandments, which express values specific to Israel (including the connection between living long in the land and honoring one's father and mother), bear the impress of those of the Torah's sources that were not formulated before the monarchy (P and D). Literary traces of the Decalogue in the rest of the Bible tend to confirm the early date of at least a terse form. The Commandments are echoed in the words of Hosea: "[False] swearing, dishonesty, and murder, / And theft and adultery are rife" (Hos. 4:2); "I the LORD have been your God / Ever since the land of Egypt" (Hos. 12:10; see also 13:4). We also see a trace in Jeremiah: "Will you steal and murder and commit adultery and swear falsely, and sacrifice to Baal, and follow other gods whom you have not experienced?" (Jer. 7:9).

A clear echo is Psalms 81:9–11 (which is difficult to date):

> Hear, My people, and I will admonish you;
>   Israel, if you would but listen to Me!
> You shall have no foreign god,
>   you shall not bow to an alien god.
> I the LORD am your God
>   who brought you out of the land of Egypt. . . .

THE STRUCTURE OF THE DECALOGUE

The ancients already sensed that the Decalogue had a significant structure and arrangement. Thus, Philo:

> "The superior set of five . . . the first set of enactments begins with God the Father and Maker of all, and ends with parents who copy His nature by begetting particular persons. The other set of five contains all the prohibitions. . . ." (*On the Decalogue*, 51)

The first five Commandments deal with matters "between a person and the Creator" (Ibn Ezra's introduction to the short commentary), and the second group of five deals with matters between a person and his fellow. The first group, furthermore, expresses special Israelite values, and therefore all its items are motivated by invoking the authority of the God of Israel. God is not mentioned in the second group, which codifies universally recognized values that do not require any grounding. The inclusion of the Commandment on honoring parents among the first five Commandments points to the special value assigned to parental authority, an authority that is affirmed and supported by God's blessing for those who honor it.[46] The distinction between the two groups of five is aptly expressed in the following, attributed to the Roman Emperor Hadrian: "The first five Commandments that the Lord gave to Israel all bear his name, while the last five Commandments that he gave to all the nations of the world do not bear his name" (*Pesikta Rabbati*, 21, ed. Ish-shalom, p. 99a; the Midrash rejects this explanation).

The Ten Commandments are said to have been engraved on two stone tablets (Exod. 31:18; Deut. 9:10): ". . . tablets inscribed on both their surfaces: they were inscribed on the one side and on the other" (Exod. 32:15). Rectangular writing tablets made of wood and ivory have been found in Mesopotamia, including two or three diptychs and triptychs.[47] Yet the meaning of "on both their surfaces" has not yet been clarified. The widely accepted traditional explanation is that there were five Commandments written on each side (in a diptych), without consideration for the resulting quantitative imbalance. This explanation is included in an ingenious homily on the correlation of the Commandments from the two sets of five:

> How were the Ten Commandments arranged? Five on the one tablet and five on the other. On the one tablet was written: "I am the Lord thy God," and opposite it on the other tablet was written: "Thou shalt not murder." This tells us that if one sheds blood it is accounted to him as though he diminished the divine image. . . . On the one tablet was written: "Thou shalt have no other god," and opposite it on the other tablet was written: "Thou shalt not commit adultery." This tells us that if one worships idols it is accounted to him as though he committed adultery, breaking his covenant with God. . . . On the one tablet was written: "Thou shalt not swear falsely," and opposite it on the other tablet was written: "Thou shalt not steal." This tells us that he who steals will in the end also swear falsely. On the one tablet was written: "Remember the sabbath day to keep it holy," and opposite it on the other tablet was written: "Thou shalt not bear false witness." This tells us that if one profanes the Sabbath it is as though he testified in the presence of him by whose word the world came into being, that he did not create the world in six days and did not rest on the seventh day. . . . On the one tablet was written: "Honor thy father and thy mother," etc., and opposite it on the other tablet was written: "Thou shalt not covet thy neighbor's wife." This tells us that he who covets will in the end beget a son who may curse his real father while giving filial honor to one who is not his father. (*Mekhilta de R. Ismael*, Horovitz-Rabin, 234; Lauterbach, vol. II, 262f.)

By correlating the "parallel" Commandments, this homily signals how the relation of man to God is linked to the relation of man to man. By shifting the point of departure for each correlation back and forth between the two series their equal value is emphasized. (At the same time, it is noteworthy that the homily starts its correlation more often from the second set, the social one, than from the first, including the opening and closing.)

The Commandments are arranged in a clearly hierarchical order: matters between man and God precede matters between man and man. Even within each set of five there is specific hierarchy: the obligation to worship God precedes the duty to honor his name, and both of these injunctions precede honoring his holy day. Finally in the first set, one must also honor one's parents. There is also a hierarchy among the five ethical Commandments: the value of life, the marriage bond (in the Masoretic version), the right to possession, reliability of public testimony, and finally the prohibition of guilty desires, which aims at safeguarding the previous four superior values.[48]

ORIGIN AND FUNCTION

The Rabbis interpreted the verse, "So Moses declared to the Israelites the set times of the LORD" (Lev. 23:44) to mean that "each paragraph [dealing with a particular holy day] in that chapter shall be read in its due season" (Mishnah *Megillah* 3:6). In the Talmud to that Mishnah (*Megillah* 31a), the view of "others" is that on Shavuot, which is the anniversary of the giving of the Torah,[49] the prescribed public reading begins at Exodus 19:1–"In the third new moon"; according to Abudarham (fourteenth-century Spanish authority on the liturgy) the reading continues to the end of chapter 20, encompassing the Decalogue and its narrative setting. This is the prevailing practice today, and it lends some credence to the modern theory that in ancient Israel there existed a festival of "covenant renewal" whose liturgy included the recitation of the Decalogue.

This theory draws support from the ceremonial public reading of the Torah appointed for the "assembly" to be convoked during the Feast of Sukkot of the sabbatical fallow year (Deut. 31:10–11). Moreover, Psalm 81 hints at a connection between the first Commandments (vv. 9–11) and a holiday accompanied by horn blasts that occurred between the new moon and the *keseh* (the full moon; v. 4)[50]–evidently during the first two weeks of the seventh month. These data and their implications provide the basis for the theory of a covenant renewal festival, which was also the Feast of the Ingathering and the New Year. Such a central holiday was, it is hypothesized, an opportunity for an annual reaffirmation of the principles of the covenant, and the main means for transmitting the Decalogue–which is the essence of the terms of the covenant–to the people throughout the generations.[51]

This theory touches mainly on the transmission of the Ten Commandments and their dissemination, but it does not offer any satisfactory suggestion concerning their origin. A helpful analogy might be found in the formal similarity between the Decalogue and the Rechabite regimen recorded in Jeremiah 35:6–7:

... for our ancestor, Jonadab son of Rechab, commanded us:
"You shall never drink wine, either you or your children.
Nor shall you build houses ˙
or sow fields
or plant vineyards, nor shall you own such things;
but you shall live in tents all your days,
so that you may live long upon the land where you sojourn."

The "sons of Rechab" know the "five commandments" (most but
not all negative) given them by their ancestor, the founder of the
order. These "commandments" define the order's way of life, and accepting them is a condition of belonging to the order. The Ten Commandments constitute a collection similar in purpose: They are the
Commandments of the founder of the "order" of the children of Israel
as "the LORD's nation," as "his holy people," the founder being God
himself. This compilation is just one of several scattered throughout
the Torah having the character of a list of stipulations—most but not
all of them negative—that the Israelites must fulfill in order to meet
the obligations of their consecration to God.

It is especially enlightening to compare the Decalogue to the collection found in Leviticus 19:1–18, which opens: "... Speak to the
whole Israelite community[52].... You shall be holy, for I, the LORD your
God, am holy," and continues with a detailed list of the terms of consecration, with "You shall" and "You shall not" commandments, reminiscent of much of the Decalogue. Common to both collections is that
they were proclaimed before the entire nation; they served as the
basis for the making of the covenant, or they were included in a
broader document that was the basis for the covenant between God
and his people. This covenantal ceremony is depicted as including a
solemn obligation on the part of the nation to observe the injunctions
presented to them. Such ceremonies appear several times in the history of the Israelites: during the days of Joshua (Josh. 24), Josiah (2
Kings 23), and Ezra (Neh. 8–10). They are all patterned after the
Sinai ceremony, a sort of imitation of it. It is reasonable to assume that
the origin of the ceremony really does go back to the dawn of the nation (Mosaic times), and that its central point was a collection of "Constituent Rules of the Order." There is no reason to dismiss the
possibility that the kernel of the Decalogue was this very collection,
even though we cannot reconstruct a "mundane" account of the proclamation of the Decalogue that can serve as a "historical" replacement
for the legendary versions found in Exodus and Deuteronomy.[53]

Of all such lists and collections, the Decalogue is outstanding for
its scope and its suggestiveness. Its terms are general and even ambiguous; it does not prescribe penalties (which would have defined and

limited the scope of each Commandment); it invites explication, clarification, or even expansion. The Decalogue is further distinctive because it evenly balances obligations to God and to man and because its choice of subjects comes close to reflecting the Torah's most important concerns.

As a result, Jewish thinkers have often regarded the Ten Commandments as the essence of the Torah. Philo's essay is entitled: "About the Decalogue, Being the Principal Laws of Moses," and in it he itemizes the individual laws of the Torah as deriving from each of the Commandments. For example:

> Under the Third he includes directions as to all the cases when swearing is forbidden, and as to the time, place, matters, persons, state of soul and body which justify the taking of an oath. . . . The Fourth, which treats of the seventh day, must be regarded as nothing less than a gathering under one head of the feasts and the purifications ordained for each feast . . . and the acceptable prayer and the flawless sacrifices, with which the ritual was carried out (*Decalogue*, 157–158). In the Fifth Commandment, on honouring one's parents, we have a suggestion of many necessary laws drawn up to deal with the relations of old to young, rulers to subjects, benefactors to benefited, slaves to masters. . . . (*Decalogue*, 165)

And so he continues: the Sixth Commandment covers all matters concerning sexual morality; the Seventh covers laws of bodily injury; the Eighth deals with property damages; the Ninth concerns matters of breach of trust (see *On the Decalogue*, 157–172).

This perception evidently underlies the Second Temple period liturgical practice of reciting the Ten Commandments before the *Shema*, thereby enumerating the principles of the Torah before reciting the formula for accepting the obligation to observe them (M. *Tamid* 5:1). The Nash papyrus offers external evidence of the combination of these texts, apparently reflecting Jewish prayer in Egypt.

That the Decalogue was joined to the *Shema* is also evidenced by *tefillin* found at Qumran; it has been supposed that the ancient order of biblical passages in the *tefillin* corresponded to the liturgy in the Second Temple, as described in the Mishnah.[54] Because of the conflict with heretics during the first centuries of Christianity, the recitation of the Decalogue was discontinued, as related in the Palestinian Talmud:

> R. Matna and R. Samuel b. Nahman [Amoraim at the end of the third century c.e.] both say: the Ten Commandments should properly be recited every day; but now they are not read because of the zeal of the

heretics, in order that they not be able to say that these [command-ments] alone were given to Moses at Mount Sinai. (*Yer. Ber.* I. 5, 3c)[55]

By way of compensation for removing the Decalogue, the idea arose that it is in fact entirely incorporated in the Shema; moreover, for that reason we recite the *Shema* (*Yer.*, ibid.)! Despite the Rabbis' ban, the Jews of Egypt continued their daily public recitation of the Ten Commandments for many generations, and Babylonian Jews continued to write the Decalogue in their *tefillin* until the end of the fourth century.[56]

No doubt because of this polemic, rabbinic writings retain but few references to the centrality of the Decalogue. Nevertheless, there do remain vestiges of the ancient view that the Ten Commandments are the essence of the Torah, or that they include all of the Torah.[57] At the end of the Gaonic period, and toward the beginning of medieval times, this view resurfaced. An outstanding expression of it is the composition of *Azharot, piyyutim* in honor of Shavuot in which the entire canon of 613 commandments is spun out of the Decalogue. An excellent example of this genre was composed by Saadiah Gaon, and appears in his *Siddur* (ed. Israel Davidson, et al., Jerusalem 1941, 191–216; see also Ismar M. Elbogen, *Der jüdisch Gottesdienst usw.*, Frankfurt-on-Main 1931, 218).

Jewish thinkers of the Middle Ages had no hesitation in exalting the Ten Commandments, much like Philo, as befits philosophers who seek general principles from which particulars may be derived.[58]

Translated from the Hebrew by "In Other Words,"
Moshav Shorashim

NOTES

1. The term recurs in 10:4, where the Septuagint translates it into Greek: *deka logoi* (so too in Exodus 34:28); the origin of the English "Decalogue."
2. In Jeremiah 5:13, the wicked say of the prophets of God, that "the Word (*ha-dibber*) is not in them" (so Radak, correctly, for verses 12–13 are a single utterance and God's response begins only afterwards). Rashi explains: *dibber* is "the sacred word that they tell us in the Lord's name"; Radak concurs: "i.e., the holy spirit"; likewise, the Septuagint translates it *logos Kyriou* (= the word of God). Jonah ibn Janah (*Sefer ha-Shorashim*, translated from Arabic to Hebrew by Judah ibn Tibbon, ed. W. Bacher, Berlin 1896, 104) adds the example: "The beginning of the word (*dibber*) of the Lᴏʀᴅ to Hosea" (Hos. 1.2; Septuagint translates *arche logou Kyriou*, like Targum Jonathan: "The beginning of the word of God"). "The form of this noun," says Ibn Janah, "is the same as that of *qitter* 'offering by fire' in Jeremiah 44:21." Another example of this noun form is: "Mine are vengeance and *shillem* ('recompense')" (Deut. 32:35). All of these are verbal nouns, properly–"speaking," "offering," "avenging." In rabbinic Hebrew, the noun *dibber* came to refer specifically to prophecy, but due to its rarity in the Bible, and the frequency of the word *dibbur* (= "speech") in rabbinic Hebrew, copyists miswrote it

until *dibber* was almost consistently replaced by *dibbur* in printed texts. With the help of manuscripts we can verify the existence of the theological term *dibber* in rabbinic Hebrew. See, for example, *Torat Kohanim*, manuscript Rome, vocalized text, ed. Louis Finkelstein, New York, 1957, top of page 6); D. Goldschmidt, ed., *The Passover Haggadah, Sources and History* (Hebrew), Jerusalem 1960, top of page 80; where a Genizah manuscript of the Haggadah reads *'anūs al pi ha-dibber* (see note there); *Mekhilta de R. Simeon bar Yoḥai*, ed. Epstein-Melammed, Jerusalem 1955, 7, lines 14–15. Concerning the plural form, *dibberoth*, see M. Z. Segal, *Mishnaic Grammar* (Hebrew), Tel Aviv 1936, page 94. The form *middabber* appears in the *Mekhilta de R. Simeon bar Yoḥai*, page 7, line 17. *Niddabber* (the base form of the verb) refers only to prophetic speech in rabbinic usage, and it is that usage that underlies the peculiar vocalization *middabber* that occurs three times in the Bible (Num. 7:89; Ezek. 2:2; 43:6)–all dealing with the word of God to the prophets. See Rashi on these verses.

3. Isaac Abrabanel enumerates the problems in these verses: If God spoke to them "face to face," then why does Moses say, "I stood between the Lord and you at that time to convey the Lord's words to you"? Another difficulty is the implicit accusation in Moses' words "for you . . . did not go up the mountain"; according to the narrative in Exodus 19:12, he warned them from the outset not to go up the mountain.

4. Is (b) perhaps a compromise between (a) and (c)? For a detailed analysis of this problem, see Arie Toeg, *Lawgiving at Sinai* (Hebrew), Jerusalem: Magnes 1977, 46–59.

5. Another divergence, concerning the place where the Decalogue was proclaimed, may be concealed in this complex of traditions. Cf. the apparent inner contradiction in Nehemiah 9:13, "You came down on Mount Sinai and spoke to them from heaven." Compare also the *Baraita of Rabbi Ishmael*, at the beginning of the *Sifra*, where Exodus 19:20 ("The Lord came down upon Mount Sinai, on the top of the mountain") and Deuteronomy 4:36 ("From the heavens He let you hear His voice to discipline you") are said to be an example of two verses that contradict one another. For the difference of opinion about this in rabbinic thought, see A. J. Heschel, *Theology of Ancient Judaism* (Hebrew), London 1965, II, chapters 2, 3.

6. M. Greenberg, "נסה in Exodus 20:20 and the Purpose of the Sinaitic Theophany," JBL, 79 (1960):273–76.

7. Cf. Judah Halevi, *The Kuzari*, 1:87.

8. See M. Parnes, "*'Eduth, 'Edoth, and 'Edvoth* in the Bible in the Light of External Evidence" (Hebrew), *Shnaton, Annual of Biblical and Near Eastern Studies*, I (1976):235–46.

9. See N. H. Tur-Sinai, in *Language and Book* (Hebrew), 3, *Beliefs and Concepts*, Jerusalem: Bialik Institute 1956, 60–1; M. Haran, "The Holy Ark and the Cherubim" (Hebrew), in *Eretz Yisrael*, 5 (Mazar Volume) (1958):87–8; R. de Vaux, *The Bible and the Ancient Near East*, London: Darton, Longman & Todd 1972, 147f. However, S. Japhet maintains that the idea of the ark as God's footstool is an innovation of the Chronicler and is not an ancient concept; see her *The Ideology of the Book of Chronicles* (Hebrew), Jerusalem: Mosad Bialik 1977, 71–3. (English translation, 76–79.)

10. It is difficult to determine exactly the number of commandments in this series, but it is equally difficult to determine the number of commandments in the Decalogue in Exodus 20 (see below). The connection between the series of commandments in Exodus 34 and the foregoing story of the Golden Calf is pointed out in Joseph Bekhor Shor's commentary on verses 14, 18.

11. It is a widely held scholarly theory that Exodus 34:10–26 comprises a deca- (or dodeca-)logue. This is called the "cultic decalogue" (because it deals only with the relationship between Israel and God), and is assumed to be more primitive religiously than the Ten Commandments (Exod. 20) which is designated the "ethical decalogue." The religion of Israel is supposed to have undergone a far-reaching evolution from a level at which cultic-commandments were central to a culmination in classical prophecy when ethics became primary. Critics of this theory point, among other things, to the fact that the ethical stance of our Decalogue is far from unique. It can be found not only in pre-prophetic parts of the Bible, but also in extrabiblical literature (see an example below). One of the first scholars to reject this theory was H. Gressmann, *Mose und seine Zeit*, Göttingen: Vandenhoeck & Ruprecht, 1913, pp. 473ff.

12. See Y. Ben Zvi, *The Book of the Samaritans* (Hebrew), Jerusalem: Yad Ben-Zvi 1970, 140–41.

13. See M. Z. Segal, *Tradition and Criticism* (Hebrew), Jerusalem: Kiryat-Sefer 1956, 227–36.

14. It is difficult to find a reason for Deuteronomy's substitution of "observe" for Exodus' "remember," since "remember" goes with "day" in Deuteronomy (16:3) just as "observe" goes with "day" in Exodus (12:17), and neither book shows any preference for one or the other term. Concerning the free substitution of synonyms in parallel expressions, see S. Talmon, "Synonymous Readings in . . . the Old Testament," *Scripta Hierosolymitana*, 8 (1961):335–83.

15. M. Weinfeld describes the humanitarian nature of Deuteronomy in his book, *Deuteronomy and the Deuteronomic School*, Oxford: Clarendon Press, 1972, 282ff. On the differences in the Sabbath Commandment, see ibid., 222 (for an opinion different from mine).

16. Cf. Hizzequni on Exodus 20:14: "The Commandments 'I the Lord' and 'You shall have no other gods' also carry 'large' cantillation accents combining them into one verse, as a reminder that they were given as one utterance." Concerning the cantillation, see below.

17. Ibn Ezra, in his introduction to the Ten Commandments (the long commentary) deprecates the separation of these clauses. *Minḥat Shai* surmises that the division into paragraphs caused this "error."

18. In Germany and France there were only two especially solemn occasions when the prescribed Torah reading was accompanied by an Aramaic translation [Targum]. These were the Seventh Day of Passover, when the story of the Exodus is read (Exod. 13:17–15:26), and Shavuot, when the scriptural portion describes the revelation at Sinai (Exod. 19 and 20). For these two days, Mahzor Vitry (twelfth century) provides a peculiar translation, a combination of Onkelos with the "Fragment-Targum." Ismar Elbogen, *Der jüdischen Gottesdienst in seiner geschichtlichen Entwicklung*, Frankfurt am Main 1931, 191.

19. See the example of the two systems of cantillation in the EB, s.v. "*ṭe'amim*," Vol. 3:403–04. Based on manuscript evidence, S. Pinsker suggested that the origin of the term "upper cantillation" was the Babylonian supralinear vocalization system by contrast with the Tiberian system, which is mainly under the letters. See *Liquṭe Qadmoniot*, Vienna 1860, 33–37, and *Mavo el hanniqud ha-ashuri*, Vienna 1863, 19ff.

20. On the division of the Commandments, see essays in G. Levi, ed., *The Ten Commandments in History and Tradition* (Jerusalem: 1989) by Mordechai Breuer, "The Division of the Decalogue into Verses and Commandments," and Gad B. Sarfatti, "The Tablets of the Covenant as a Symbol of Judaism" (= *Tarbiẓ*, 29 [1960], especially 386f.).

21. *Philo*, The Loeb Classical Library, translation, F. H. Colson, Cambridge–Harvard University Press 1968; VII, 38 and 31; see also Yehoshua Amir, "The Decalogue According to the Teachings of Philo," in *The Ten Commandments in History and Tradition* (see n. 20).

22. Josephus, *Antiquities*, III: 91.

23. See W. Harrelson's convenient chart in *The Ten Commandments and Human Rights*, Philadelphia: Fortress Press 1980, 47. Compare Ibn Ezra's position in his introduction to the Decalogue.

24. Note the punctuation in *Tanakh*, Philadelphia: JPS, 1985:115: "I the Lord am your God who brought you out of the land of Egypt, the house of bondage: You shall have no other gods beside me."

The rabbinic Sages, who called the Commandment "I the Lord" (v. 2 alone) "Acceptance of God's Sovereignty," counted it as the First Commandment (see n. 16 above, and the text to which it is attached; also *Mekhilta Bahodesh*, 6). The commentators disagreed over the question whether verse 2, the self-description of God, is actually a commandment, or is the basis of belief from which the other commandments derive. See, for example, Maimonides, *Sefer Ha-Mitzvoth*, positive commandment number 1, and Nahmanides' critique thereof.

25. Sarfatti in his article in *The Ten Commandments in History and Tradition* (above, n. 20) notes that on some representations of the Tablets of the Covenant in Italian Syna-

gogues, the Second Commandment is "You shall not make for yourself a sculptured image."

26. That the Second Commandment is not a prohibition against art is argued by C. Konikoff, *The Second Commandment and Its Interpretation in the Art of Ancient Israel*, Genève: Imprimerie du Journal de Genève, 1973, 26. On the lack of distinction between the sculptured image and the deity itself throughout the Bible, and especially in biblical legislation, see Y. Kaufmann, "The Bible and Mythological Polytheism," JBL, 70 (1951):179–97; specifically on the Decalogue, ibid., 188–89. My reservations about his comments on Deuteronomy 4:15–18, and about his judgment that the biblical polemic distorts idolatry, appear below.

27. A. L. Oppenheim, *Ancient Mesopotamia: Portrait of a Dead Civilization*, Chicago, 1977, 183–93; H. Frankfort, *Kingship and the Gods*, Chicago: University of Chicago, 1948, 302–06; E. Bevan, *Holy Images*, London: Allen & Unwin, 1940, Lecture 1, 13–45. A critique of Kaufmann's view, richly illustrated from ancient texts, is J. Faur, "The Biblical Idea of Idolatry," JQR 69 (1978):1–15.

28. M. Buber, *Moses*, translated into English, New York: Harper and Row 1958, 127. Josephus comes closer to the Deuteronomic idea with his explanation of the prohibition against making a sculptured image of God: "By His works and His bounties He is plainly seen, indeed more manifest than aught else, but His form and magnitude surpass our powers of description. No materials, however costly, are fit to make an image of Him, no art has skill to conceive and represent it. The like of Him we have never seen, we do not imagine and it is impious to conjecture" (*Apion*, II:190–91).

29. The phrase "bear on one's lips," parallel to "rise on one's heart" (= come to mind) occurs in the Sefire Inscription III:14–15, with the same meaning as "utter"; see J. C. Greenfield, "Stylistic Aspects of the Sefire Treaty Inscriptions," *Acta Orientalia*, 29 (1965):5.

30. David Kimhi in his commentary on Psalms says of this verse, "The words 'by my life,' are spoken by God himself . . . 'His life' means 'his Name,' as in Amos 6:8: 'The LORD God has sworn by himself (literally "by his life").'" It is noteworthy that swearing truthfully by God's name not only permitted, it is considered an expression of commendable reverence for God: Deuteronomy 6:13; Jeremiah 12:16, Psalms 63:12.

31. Cf. my comments in *Studies in Jeremiah* (Hebrew), B. Z. Luria ed., Part II, the Society for Biblical Research in Israel (1971), 32–3. On the anthropomorphism in the conception of the holiness of the Sabbath in Genesis 1–2, and in the relevant Commandment, see M. Weinfeld, "God the Creator in Genesis 1 and in Deutero-Isaiah" (Hebrew), *Tarbiz*, 37 (1968), 105–12. I have already referred to Weinfeld's description of the humanitarian character of Deuteronomy. In his discussion of the motives for the Sabbath in the Decalogue (*Deuteronomy, etc.*, [above, n. 15] 222) he does not consider the possibility that the replacement of an anthropomorphic by a humanitarian ground conforms to Deuteronomy's ideology—which he himself fully documents, 191ff.

32. Nahmanides develops this idea in his commentary on the Commandment, but unlike his sources, he relates to the father alone!

33. The medieval French equivalent of modern *meurtre* = "murder."

34. The use of the term *rṣḥ* for accidental homicide (Num. 35:11; Deut. 4:42) does not disprove this sound observation, since it, too, is illegal.

35. There is a semantic difference between the root used here—*n'f*—and the verb *znh*. The latter means properly "to participate willingly in sexual intercourse with a man not one's husband," the subject being nearly always a woman, single or married. (When used metaphorically, the subject is usually the Israelites, and the offense–idolatry.) Hence, there is a measure of correspondence between the two verbs (see Amos 7:17), but also a decisive difference, as when Ezekiel (23:2–3) uses *znh* for fornication on the part of two (figurative) girls who are unmarried. The distinction is made even clearer by the parallelism in Hosea (4:13): "Your daughters [unmarried] fornicate / and your daughters-in-law [obviously married] commit adultery." Ibn Ezra attempts to prove that *ni'uf* and *zenuth* are synonymous, on the basis of Jeremiah 3:9: "She committed adultery with stone and wood." But that verse merely proves that the verb *n'f* can have as its subject a woman as well as a man (a married woman who voluntarily has intercourse with anyone beside her husband). Jeremiah's use of the word is precise: he is comparing Is-

rael to a married woman. Thus every act of adultery is fornication, but not every act of fornication is adultery.

36. Nethanel ben Isaiah, *Me'or ha-'Afelah* (Hebrew), translated from the Arabic by Y. Kafaḥ, Jerusalem: The Society for Preserving Yemenite Documents 1957.

37. A. Alt, "Das Verbot des Diebstahls im Dekalog," *Kleine Schriften zür Geschichte des Volkes Israel*, Vol. 1, München: Beck, 1953:330–40; A. Phillips, *Ancient Israel's Criminal Law*, New York: Schocken 1970, 130ff.

38. Exodus has *'ed šeqer;* Deuteronomy, *'ed šaw'*, but they mean the same thing. Grammatically *'ed šeqer* "(as a) false witness" expresses a state of being; cf. "fell *ḥᵃlalim*—slain," lit. "as slain men" (1 Sam. 31:1); "went out *gᵉdudim*—in bands," lit. "as bands" (2 Kings 5:2).

39. The *Mekhilta* combines these verses, and Phillips (above, n. 37, 143) infers from their juxtaposition that the Commandment deals with a capital case.

40. Compare the citations given below with Alt's argument (above, n. 37) that "covet" entails action, making it almost the equivalent of "steal." See also W. Kessler, "Problematic des Dekalogs," *VT*, 7 (1957), 13.

41. Maimonides, in his *Book of Commandments*, negative commandment no. 266 (cf. translation by C. B. Chavel, London–New York 1967, vol. II:250ff.) writes as follows: "If you see something desirable in the possession of someone else, and you can't stop thinking about it and craving it, you have violated the Commandment in Deuteronomy 'You shall not crave.' But if your desire for the object is so strong that you take measures to acquire it, and you don't stop importuning the owner and exerting pressure on him [compare the terminology in the *Mekhilta de R. Simeon*] to sell it to you or to exchange it for something of greater value . . . and you achieve your purpose, you have also violated 'You shall not covet.'"

42. This shift led to the traditional view that the Commandments, "I the Lᴏʀᴅ" and "You shalt have no other" were heard directly from God (*Mak.* 24a), whereas the rest of the Commandments were mediated to the people by Moses. See the detailed explanation by Joseph B. Simeon Kara (France, eleventh to twelfth century) quoted in the commentary of Joseph Bekhor Shor on this verse. To be sure, such a change of person occurs in other places as well (e.g., Exod. 23:13–19; 34:11–26), and there, too, the change serves critics as a basis for stratifying the text.

43. E. Neilsen, *The Ten Commandments in New Perspective*, Studies in Biblical Theology, 2/7, Naperville: Allenson 1968, 84f.

44. Harrelson (above n. 23), 42, 207.

45. ANET, 35 (the B list).

46. Because parental authority is upheld by a death sentence for those who violate it (Exod. 21:15, 17; Lev. 20:9; Deut. 21:18–21), there is substance to the homily of Rabbi Judah the Patriarch: "The honor of father and mother is very dear in the sight of Him by whose word the world came into being, for He declared their honor to be equal to His own" (*Mekhilta, Ba-Ḥodesh*, Horovitz-Rabin, 231; cf. Lauterbach, II, 257). Note the sequence of maledictions in Deuteronomy 27:15, 16. In the Code of Hammurabi (parag. 195, which corresponds to Exod. 21:15), one who strikes his parents is punished by having his hand amputated. In the same Code, parag. 192 and 193, dealing with an adopted son who rejects his adoptive parents, prescribe cutting out his tongue or his eye; in the Bible the rebellious son is punished by death.

47. A photograph of three hinged ivory tablets from Assyria is found in ANEP, 348, no. 803.

48. The commentators discuss the meaning of the sequence of the Commandments: see, e.g., Ibn Ezra, who quotes Saadiah Gaon's explanations along with his own. Joseph Bekhor Shor provides entirely different explanations.

49. According to Jubilees, 6:17–22, the festival in the third month has celebrated the renewal of the covenant since the time of Noah.

50. For this meaning of *keseh*, see W. Baumgartner, *Hebräisches und Aramäisches Lexicon zum Alten Testament*, 3te Auflage, Lieferung II, Leiden: Brill 1974, 463–64.

51. The principal fathers of this theory are S. Mowinckel and Albrecht Alt. A convenient summary of its development and critique of the thesis can be found in J. J.

Stamm and M. E. Andrew, *The Ten Commandments in Recent Research*, Studies in Biblical Theology, 2/2, Naperville: Allenson, 1967, 22–75.

52. Based on this expression, R. Ḥiyya drew an analogy between the nineteenth chapter of Leviticus and the Ten Commandments: "R Ḥiyya taught: From this we conclude that this section was proclaimed to the entire assembly of Israel [like the Decalogue; see Deut. 4:10].... R. Levi said: Because this section includes the Ten Commandments."

53. On the origin of the Decalogue as a set of rules binding a community of believers and on its subsequent role, see the instructive article by M. Weinfeld: "The Decalogue: Its Meaning and Evolution in Jewish Tradition," in *Reflections on the Bible: Studies in Memory of Yishai Ron* (Hebrew), II, Jerusalem, 1977, 109–21. See also Weinfeld's essay in *The Ten Commandments in History and Tradition:* "The Uniqueness of the Decalogue and Its Place in Jewish Tradition."

54. A. M. Haberman, "*Tefillin* in Ancient Times" (Hebrew), *Eretz Israel*, 3 (Cassuto Volume), Jerusalem: Israel Exploration Society, and the Bialik Institute, 1954, 174. For *tefillin* containing both the Decalogue and the *Shema*, see R. de Vaux, J. T. Milik, *Qumran Grotte 4*, II, *Discoveries in the Judaean Desert*, VI, Oxford: Clarendon Press 1977:52, 59–62, 74–75. Other examples of Qumran *tefillin* containing the Decalogue (without the *Shema*) are found in Y. Yadin, "*Tefillin* for the Head from Qumran" (Hebrew), *Eretz Israel*, 9 (Albright Volume) Jerusalem: Israel Exploration Society, 1969:60–85.

55. For interpreting *ṭinnath* in the sense of "zeal" (cf. the Syriac *ṭnn* "be zealous") so that the passage would mean "because of their strict devotion to their false belief," see L. Ginzberg, *A Commentary on the Palestinian Talmud* (Hebrew), New York: Jewish Theological Seminary 1951, 1, 166. Ginzberg identifies these heretics as "the Christians and their like, who taught that their Savior had promulgated a new religion, according to which a person had only to believe in the Creator, in reward and punishment and similar fundamentals of faith, and to abide by the socio-ethical Commandments of the Decalogue, but not by the ritual mitzvot of Judaism." See Ber. 12a, and Rashi ad loc. In *Maḥzor Vitry*, ed. S. H. Horovitz, Nuremberg 1923, Part I:12, the reading is " . . . so that the disciples [*of Jesus*] should not say: the rest of the Torah is not true, and the proof is that we recite only that which the LORD Himself spoke, and which the Israelites heard at Mt. Sinai." This formulation has been couched in terms of the ongoing polemic between Jews and Christians in the Middle Ages. In this connection see Elazar Touitou, "Plain Sense and Apologetics in the Commentary of Samuel ben Meir on the Biblical Moses Stories" (Hebrew), *Tarbiz*, 51 (1982):230, 234, and n. 45. On the problem of identifying the *Minim* mentioned in the Talmud, see G. F. Moore, *Judaism*, Harvard University Press, Cambridge 1945, III:95f., n. 64; R. Kimmelman, "*Birkat Ha-Minim* . . . ," in: E. P. Sanders et al., eds., *Jewish and Christian Self-Definition*, II, Philadelphia: Fortress Press, 1981:226–44.

56. On the recitation of the Ten Commandments in Egypt, see J. Mann, "Genizah Fragments of the Palestinian Order of Service," HUCA, 2 (1925):283; on the Decalogue in Babylonian Tefillin, see Haberman, above, n. 54, 175.

57. See A. J. Heschel, *Theology of Ancient Judaism* (Hebrew), London–New York: Soncino 1965, 2, 108–10; but this interesting material must be treated critically with due regard to variations in dating. E. E. Urbach strongly denies that the Sages elevated the value of the Decalogue above the other commandments; see his *The Sages*, Jerusalem: Magnes Press 1975, 360–5; but perhaps this very fact reflects an ongoing polemic on the matter.

58. A clear example is provided by Joseph Albo, *Sefer ha-Ikkarim*, III, chapter 66.

Additional Note:

This essay was translated from my Hebrew, which appeared in the original Hebrew collection of essays on the Decalogue, *'Aseret ha-dibb-rot bi-r-'i ha-dorot*, ed. Ben-Zion Segal (Jerusalem: Magnes Press, 1986).

In notes 20, 21, 25, and 53 reference is made to other articles in the English translation of the collection: *The Ten Commandments in History and Tradition*, ed. Gershon Levi (Jerusalem: Magnes Press, 1990).

The Qumran text in which the Decalogue appears—referred to in the Table of versions as 4QDeut$_m$—has been published in a critical edition by Esther Eshel, "4QDeut^n—A Text That Has Undergone Harmonistic Editing," HUCA 72 (1991), 117–54.

Idealism and Practicality in Numbers 35:4-5 and Ezekiel 48

1968

To one familiar with the sometimes cavalier operation of biblical criticism, the salient feature of E. A. Speiser's approach to the Bible was his predisposition to regard everything carefully, even material that seemed on the face of it to be the product of error or fantasy. With his profound understanding of the Near East this predisposition resulted time and again in evoking new information from hitherto uncommunicative texts. The priestly writings of Israel were particular beneficiaries of his attention: repeatedly they were shown to harbor genuinely ancient, even pre-Israelite practices and terminology. The following study of two problematic passages in that literature is inspired by his example and dedicated in gratitude to his memory.[1]

THE PASTURE LANDS OF THE LEVITES

> In framing an ideal we may assume what we wish, but should avoid impossibilities.—Aristotle, Politics, Book II: Chapter 6 (1265a)

The penchant for schematizing, so evident in the priestly writings of ancient Israel, has been felt to bespeak a visionary mentality distant from mundane realities. It has been invoked as evidence for an exilic provenance. On the scheme of Levitical cities (Num. 35; Josh. 21) Wellhausen wrote:

> It would hardly have occurred to an author living in the monarchical period, when the continuity of the older history was still unbroken, to look so completely away from all the conditions of the then existing re-

313

ality; had he done so, he would have produced upon his contemporaries the impression merely that he had scarcely all his wits about him. But after the exile had annihilated the ancient Israel, and violently and completely broken the old connection with the ancient conditions, there was nothing to hinder from planting and partitioning the *tabula rasa* in thought at pleasure, just as geographers are wont to do with their map as long as the countries are unknown.[2]

Since Wellhausen, Palestinologists have made notable progress in finding a historical-geographical anchorage for this scheme,[3] although they, along with others who regard it as an early element in Israelite tradition,[4] concede the utopian character of a good part of it. To the historian, the unreal aspect is annoying; he deprecates it as unhelpful for his quest. To the exegete, however, it poses the question, How did the author intend to be understood? Nowhere is this question more pressing than at Numbers 35:4–5—a passage admitted on all hands to be "utopian" (i.e., fantastic)—the rule allocating pasture lands to the Levitical cities:

> [4]The town pasture that you are to assign to the Levites shall extend a thousand cubits outside the town wall all around.
> [5]You shall measure off two thousand cubits outside the town on the east side, two thousand on the south side, two thousand on the west side, and two thousand on the north side, with the town in the center.[5]

As Gray and others have pointed out, the only interpretation that this allows without forcing is a figure of this shape:

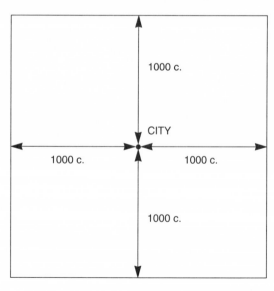

"It necessarily follows that the writer . . . forgot to allow for the dimensions of the city."[6] Wellhausen set forth trenchantly the objections to our passage.

> The regulation that a rectangular territory of two thousand ells square should be measured off as pasture for the Levites around each city (which at the same time is itself regarded only as a point . . .) might, to speak with Graf, be very well carried out perhaps in a South Russian steppe or in newly founded townships in the western States of America, but not in a mountainous country like Palestine, where territory that can be thus geometrically portioned off does not exist, and where it is by no means left to arbitrary legal enactments to determine what pieces of ground are adapted for pasturage and what for tillage and gardening; there too, the cities were already in existence, the land was already under cultivation, as the Israelites slowly conquered it in the course of centuries.[7]

Such scoffing appears less in place today, or at least will have to be extended to a far larger field, in the light of the liberal doses of theory that appear sprinkled throughout ancient Near Eastern law collections. Impractically rigid and merely paradigmatic formulations are not infrequently found there alongside what seems to be case law. What, for example, could be more impracticable than the codification in Hammurabi and Eshnunna of prices and wages, as though these items might be eternally fixed through all time?[8] The rules of talion in Hammurabi and the Pentateuch must similarly be regarded as theoretical.[9] Especially significant for our purpose is the implicitly paradigmatic nature of some laws—valid as formulated in specific circumstances only, though their limited applicability is not expressly stated. Such a law is that of the goring ox in Eshnunna 53 and Exodus 21:35: if an ox not known to be a gorer gores another ox, the owners must divide between themselves the worth of the living and of the dead ox. Goetze has seen the principle behind this ruling: in view of the unforeseeability of the accident and the risk assumed by the victim's owner when he let his ox mingle with others, the owner of the gorer is not made to bear the entire loss. "It is the intention of the legislator to divide the loss as evenly as possible."[10] As was anciently noticed, however, the ruling achieves its intention only when the two live oxen are of equal worth; should there be a disparity in their values, the procedure indicated by the law cannot result in an evenly shared loss (indeed if the victim is, say, half the value of the gorer its owner will actually be enhanced).[11] This law, then, is strictly applicable in one case only; in all others the principle derivable from this paradigm must be applied; namely, that when an innocent ox gores another, the two owners divide the loss equally—or, in other words, the gorer's owner is liable only to half-damages.[12]

Now the provision of a rectangular strip of pasture land around each Levitical city appears to belong to paradigmatic law. What is important is the principle that the landless class of Levites (e.g., Num. 18:23f.) be furnished such a strip of ground around each of its towns on which to graze its animals. How to deal with natural obstructions and the like that might interfere with laying out the area as prescribed is no business of this statement, whose purpose is to formulate the principle. Yet there is this difference between the goring ox paradigm and that of the pasture land: in the former, one case, at any rate, exists in which the paradigm is applicable as stated, but in the latter no case can be imagined in which the town in the center is a mere mathematical point. Did the author "forget" the dimensions of the town? How can his paradigm be generalized?

The earliest explication of Numbers 35:4–5 is found in the Tannaitic regulations about the Sabbath limit (2000 cubits from the place a man lives, beyond which he was forbidden to go on the Sabbath).

> ... R. Akiba expounded it thus: "You shall measure off two thousand cubits outside the town on the east side, etc." (vs. 5)—but the other verse (vs. 4) says, "a thousand cubits outside the town wall all around"! ... How are the two to be harmonized? One thousand cubits defines the pasture land; two thousand, the Sabbath limit [i.e. the town limit with respect to Sabbath movement]. R. Eliezer, son of R. Yose the Galileean, says: One thousand cubits for pasture, the second thousand for farmland and vineyards [both, then, refer to the Levite's territory, and there is no reference here to the Sabbath limit]. (Mishna, Soṭa 5.3)

Both regard the total depth of the strip prescribed in Numbers 35:4–5 as 2000 cubits (erroneously, it seems to us).[13] Moreover, though a difference appears between R. Akiba and R. Eliezer concerning the grounding of the Sabbath limit on that passage, all authorities agreed that the limit was in fact 2000 cubits deep. In view of the relatedness of these two topics, it is of interest to us to inquire how the Tannaim drew the Sabbath limit around a town, for presumably that will represent as well how they understood the drawing of the Levites' pasture land:

> How is the shape of a town regularized [so as to facilitate drawing its Sabbath limits]? If the town is oblong, it is left as is [and the limit is measured from its real boundaries]. If it is a circle, it is squared. If it is square [but its sides do not parallel true north, south, east and west] it is not squared again [to make it so]. If it is wide on one side and narrow

on the other, both sides are made equal [i.e. it is turned into a rectangle]. If a house projected like a stage, or two houses [on different sides of the town] projected like a stage, a straight line is drawn including them and the 2000 cubits are measured from that line outward. If the town was shaped like a bow or a gamma [the interior] is considered full of houses and courtyards and the 2000 cubits are measured from these [imaginary boundaries] outward.[14]

When a circular city is to be squared, it is turned into the shape of a square tablet (ABCD). The Sabbath limits are then drawn square like another square tablet (EFGH). When the depth of the Sabbath limit is measured, one does not measure 2000 cubits diagonally from an angle of the town square to an angle of the Sabbath limit square (BK), for that would reduce the corners of the Sabbath limit. But the corners are drawn by laying a tablet 2000 cubits square diagonally from the angle of the town square (IFJB).[15]

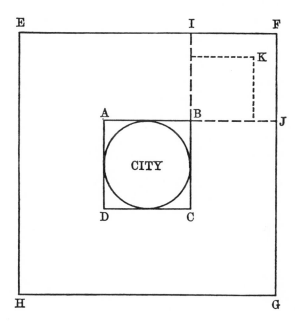

The Tannaim thus regarded the Sabbath limit area as a rectangle whose sides were preferably lined up with the compass points; its depth was 2000 cubits from the extreme limits of the town on each of its four compass points—expressed by the squaring or rectangling of the town. Now, since the Sabbath limit took its reference from the pasture land of the Levitical cities,[16] this discussion provides, in fact,

the earliest detailed commentary on the biblical passage. Its agreement with the modern view of the shape intended by Numbers 35:4–
5—a square with the town in the center—encourages one to ask
whether it has any light to shed on our question: why the biblical author treated the town as a point. Indeed it does.

The first lesson of the Tannaitic discussion (and only a sampling has
been given here) is how very complicated the description of this area
becomes once the town at its center is given dimensions and treated as
a changeable quantity. The simplicity of the expedient adopted in
Numbers 35:4–5 to describe the relation of the area to the town is
highlighted by comparison. The depth of the pasture land, say the
verses, is to be 1000 cubits from the town limits on all sides, laid out
in such a way that, given a town of 0 dimensions it would form a 2000
cubit square around it. What if the city had dimensions and was irregular to boot? Then an analogous procedure was to be followed: from
the easternmost point of the town extend a line due east for 1000 cubits, and from the extreme points of the town's south, west, and north
extend corresponding lines of 1000 cubits toward the other compass
points. Then draw a square (or rectangle) whose sides would be per-
pendicular to these lines at their end point; thus[17]

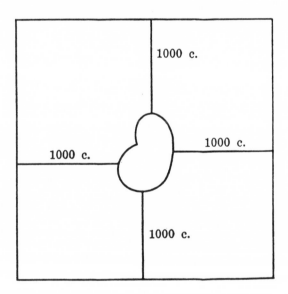

As in the goring ox paradigm, the specific terms in which the law is
formulated are inapplicable to any other situation, but from them a
principle may be extracted and generalized. The principles here are as

follows: a depth of 1000 cubits from the town limits in each direction; a square (or rectangular) area whose sides are aligned with each of the compass points. (The 2000 cubit measurement of the four sides is paradigmatic and given only to bring home the square shape. Without it, the direction to extend the pasture "a thousand cubits outside the town wall all around" could have been misconstrued to mean a circular area.) The complicated Tannaitic prescriptions for the Sabbath limit furnish the answer to our question; far from having "forgotten" the dimensions of the town, the biblical author will be seen to have omitted them as an unnecessarily complicating factor. His postulation of a town of 0 size turns out to be the most economical way of giving directions for the layout of the pasture land.

At the same time it is the most practical. His purpose was to provide a strip of land around each town with a constant measurement. Had he been truly an impractical visionary, he might have prescribed following the contours of the town at a depth of 1000 cubits all around it. But the difficulty of carrying out such a prescription for an irregularly shaped town (as many, if not most are) would effectively preclude its ever having been carried out by the Israelite peasantry. It must have been practicality that urged on the Tannaim as well the rectangular conception of the Levite pastures and the Sabbath limit area, in contrast to the strange shapes concocted by more recent commentators to the biblical text.[18]

Since the Tannaim were prescribing boundaries in Palestine, not in South Russia or the western United States, they gave thought to dealing with intervening mountains, gullies, houses, graves, and the like.[19] What occurred to them on this head was not beyond the imagination of the priestly author of Numbers 35. To be sure, there is no evidence that the early author ever worked matters out so finely for the Levitical pasture lands. But in view of the later discussion, critics' dismissal of Numbers 35:4–5 as fantastic for having failed to spell out such details does little justice to the inventiveness of legalists. It is having it both ways to reproach a man for fantasy and deny him the capacity to work out his problem imaginatively.

Finally, it is of interest that Old Babylonian geometrical texts have been found posing problems similar to those we have been discussing. Questions of enclosing square fields within larger squares or enlarging circular cities by larger concentric circles are treated, at times with drawings. Thus neither the idea of treating territory as abstract geometric shapes nor the knowledge of the requisite mathematical operations was absent from Near Eastern antiquity.[20] That abstract shapes were applied in reality to settlements will be shown later.

EZEKIEL'S ALLOCATIONS OF TRIBAL TERRITORY

> The allocation of land in the age to come will be different from the al-
> location in this age. In this age, if one has a grain field, he has no or-
> chard; if an orchard, he has no grain field. But in the age to come
> everyone will have holdings in the highlands, in the foothills, and in
> the valleys.—*Bab. Talmud, Baba Batra*, 122a

Gray (*Numbers*, p. 466) considered the geometrical treatment of
the Levitical cities, "impossible in the actual land, [paralleled] in
Ezekiel's ideal division of W. Palestine into a series of exact parallelo-
grams (Ezek. 48)." On that scheme Julius Bewer wrote, "It takes no
account of the physical and topographical realities. Parallel lines are
drawn at equal intervals (cf. 47:14) between the N. and S. borders
from E. to W. to mark the territory of each tribe without regard to the
contour of the land and its widening toward the S., or to the territorial
needs of different tribes." The overall shape is thought to be a paral-
lelogram, wholly unrealistic.[21]

Now it is true that the oracle fills Palestine from north to south
with strips running across it from its eastern to its western borders,
and that the tribes are thereby to divide the land "equally" (47:14).
But nothing is said of the width of each tribal portion, so that
Davidson's more circumspect judgment is to be preferred that "[there
is no] indication whether the greater or lesser breadth of the country
from the Jordan to the sea was taken into account."[22] Apart from that
qualification, however, Bewer's comment represents the current opinion on the scheme. Is it justified?

The vagueness about the dimensions of the tribal portions contrasts
with the precision regarding both the disposition of the holy district
(45:1–8; 48:8–22) and—what is relevant to our present interest—the
location of each tribe. Allowance is made for Jerusalem's eccentric position: seven tribes are ranged north of it, five to its south. To that extent, then, as even critics admit, the scheme accords with reality.[23]

At this point, it is necessary to consider the tendency of the larger
unit of which Ezekiel 47–48 forms the climax. Kaufmann[24] has aptly
called chapters 40 to 48 "a messianic Priestly Code," designed to
bring up to date provisions of the Torah that had by then become obsolete, and (we may add) to set aright wrongs in Israel's past life. With
regard to the land, significant new rulings are laid down. Land tenure,
for example, is to be based (as it was originally) on inalienable tribal
allotments. These are to be made, not by lot and human surveyors (cf.
Josh. 18:1–10), but by the explicit decree of God (47:13f.; 48:29).
The resident alien's landlessness, a long-standing disability that en-
croached seriously on the old ideal "the same rule shall apply to you

and to the alien resident in your midst" (Num. 15:16), is remedied by allowing him to obtain holdings in the territory of his host tribe (47:22–23). Special provision is made for the king's property and for lands he might distribute to his sons and servants: formerly, the king confiscated private property for such purposes; in the future, crown lands—part of a special thirteenth portion, over and above the twelve tribal portions—will be at his disposal, "and he shall not take any of the inheritance of the people, thrusting them out of their property" (46:18; cf. vv. 16f. and 45:8). The boundaries of the future settlement will accord with the ancient oracle promising only cisjordan to the patriarchs. The transjordan tribes will be resettled on the west bank, the northern boundary of settlement extended into southern Syria.

Concord and unity will reign among the tribes. Ezekiel envisioned the end of the dual kingdoms of Judah and Israel: "I will make them one nation in the land . . . and one king shall be king over them all; and they shall no longer be two nations, and no longer be divided into two kingdoms (37:22)." Perhaps to promote integration, the tribe of Judah is relocated north of Jerusalem, in the heartland of the former northern kingdom. Benjamin, on the other hand, is moved south to adjoin Simeon. Unequal shares in the land might sow resentment, and so it is laid down (47:14) that the tribes shall take possession of the land "equally" (literally, "each like his brother").

So far, then, the provisions of the land apportionment can be seen to stem from a realistic view of political, geographical, and religious determinants. In the provision for equal shares an important assumption is made: the equal size of the tribal populations and their similar needs in land. But inasmuch as the makeup of the future restored tribes was entirely unknown, since the bulk of them had scattered beyond recall, such a convenient assumption is hardly censurable as a working basis for a theory of restoration. Where the scheme seems to take flight from reality is in the astonishing north-to-south array of tribes in strips across the country, so different from the historical tribal division recorded in the book of Joshua, and so apparently heedless of the terrain of Palestine. This array gives the whole a fantastic appearance. Has it a grounding in some reality?

Let us look more closely at what is implied in the notion that the tribes will have equal shares in the land. Tradition recorded an apportionment made in Joshua's time; was there a lesson to be learned from it for the future? Joshua 17:14–18 tells how the Josephides complained to Joshua of their share: It was wooded highlands and therefore inadequate for a tribe of their size. Joshua advised them to clear the land and it would suffice for them, but more or different land is what the tribe wanted. How could such cause for complaint be averted in the future?

The tenth century Palestinian Arab geographer Al Muqaddasi ("the Jerusalemite") gives what in all essentials has remained to this day the standard gross geographic description of Palestine and Syria:

> The country, physically, may be divided into four zones. The first zone is that on the border of the Mediterranean Sea. It is the plain-country, the sandy tracts following one another, and alternating with the culti-vated land. Of towns situated herein are Ar-Ramlah, and also all the cities of the sea-coast. The second zone is the mountain-country, well wooded, and possessing many springs, with frequent villages and culti-vated fields. Of the cities that are situated in this part are: Bait Jibrîl, Jerusalem, Nâbulus, Al-Lajjûn, Kâbul, Kadas, the towns of the Bikâʿ and Antioch. The third zone is that of the valleys of the (Jordan) Ghaur, wherein are found many villages and streams, also palm-trees, well cultivated fields, and indigo plantations. Among the towns in this part are Wailah, Tabûk, Sughar, Jericho, Baisân, Tiberias. Bâniyâs. The fourth zone is that bordering on the Desert. The mountains here are high and bleak, and the climate resembles that of the Waste; but it has many villages, with springs of water and forest trees. Of the towns therein are Maâb, ʿAmmân, Adhraʿâh, Damascus, Hims, Tadmur, and Aleppo.[25]

In a word, Palestine–Syria may be described as comprising four longi-tudinal zones, of which three are included in cisjordan: the coastal plain, the western highlands, and the central (Jordan) valley.[26]

Now if one wished to apportion the country from southern Syria to the tip of the Dead Sea into equal shares, the only way to do it would be to take cuts across the three longitudinal zones, thus providing each share with a bit of coastal plain, a bit of highlands, and a bit of the central valley. To be sure, the equalization would be only approxi-mate, but it would be closer by this than by any other ready method. Far from disregarding reality, then, the scheme of Ezekiel 48 adopts the only way the topography of Palestine allows to parcel the land into roughly similar shares.

ARTIFICIALITY IN TERRITORIAL ARRANGEMENTS IN ANTIQUITY

The passages we have studied in Numbers and Ezekiel are designs for the future, according to their plain sense. Schematization and idealiza-tion are to be expected in them. How far from reality such schemati-zation was depends on the amount of abstraction in topographical layouts that the Israelite found about him, and that is virtually un-known to us. Evidence of city planning has become available in recent decades. "Macalister could still write that the typical Israelite settlement from the age of the monarchy was built without rational order and plan. It is now clear that this notion was based on the spotty work of early archeologists. Wherever connected areas of considerable size have been exposed, a latticework of streets intersecting at right angles, or nearly at right angles, has been found."[27]

From all over the Near East evidence exists for the patterned shape of ancient cities.

> Normally the wall of a Mesopotamian city is arranged in wide curves or in rectilinear, mostly quadrilateral, and often symmetrical designs.... Square, rectangular, and round cities are typically new foundations; these forms clearly represent abstractions, natural only in planned cities.... It has been repeatedly asserted that both rectangular and round city plans have as their prototype such military encampments as those represented on Assyrian reliefs.... In fact, symmetrical enclosures forming simple geometric figures are the customary way in which migrating tribes or armies arrange their camps.[28]

A remote yet intriguing analogue to the tribal reapportionment of Ezekiel 47–48 can be found in Athens, a generation after Ezekiel, among the reforms of Cleisthenes. Aiming to abolish undue local and family influence on politics, and to enfranchise new citizens, many of whom were resident aliens (cf. Ezek. 47:22f.), Cleisthenes revolutionized the tribal system in a way that evokes the wonder of modern historians: "A system more artificial than the tribes and trittyes of Cleisthenes it might well pass the wit of man to devise."[29]

> Taking the map of Attica as he found it, consisting of between one and two hundred demes or small districts, Cleisthenes distinguished three regions: the region of the city, the region of the coast, and the inland. In each of these regions he divided the demes into ten groups called *trittyes,* so that there were thirty such trittyes in all.... Out of the thirty trittyes he then formed ten groups of three, in such a way that no group contained two trittyes from the same region. Each of these groups constituted a tribe, and the citizens of all the demes contained in its three trittyes were fellow tribesmen.... The ten new tribes, based on artificial geography, took the place of the four old tribes, based on birth.... And the deme, a local unit, replaced the social unit of the clan. This scheme of Cleisthenes ... might seem almost too artificial to last. The secret of its permanence lay in the fact that the demes, the units on which it was built up, were natural divisions, which he did not attempt to reduce to a round number.[30]

The reform of Cleisthenes and Ezekiel's resettlement scheme have in common: tribes, geographical regions whose nature (if we have interpreted Ezekiel rightly) is crucial for the scheme, and resident aliens that must be integrated. How differently each dealt with these variables is most instructive. The Athenian had a democratic ideal before him, the Judahite, an ideal of concord and justice, ultimately based on religion. The motive for integrating the resident alien illustrates the difference. For the former, it was a matter of reshaping the balance of political power; for the latter, the fulfillment of an ideal of equal treatment under the law. Even more characteristic: For the Athenian, the locality was fundamental, the tribe an artificial, political creation. For the Judahite, the tribe was fundamental and the locality artificially molded to serve it.[31] On the score of artificiality, however, Cleisthenes' historically attested reform makes the visionary tribal apportionment of Ezekiel seem the essence of simplicity and naturalness.

The priestly writers, like the legislators, were fond of ideal formulations. But to understand them it is necessary to credit them with more than extravagant imagination, reckless of reality. "In framing an ideal we may assume what we wish, but should avoid impossibilities." In the two items we have studied the priestly writers have hewn to Aristotle's injunction.

NOTES

1. A representative offering of Speiser's biblical studies will be found in the section so entitled of *Oriental and Biblical Studies: Collected Writings of E. A. Speiser*, edited by J. J. Finkelstein and Moshe Greenberg (Philadelphia: University of Pennsylvania, 1967).

2. J. Wellhausen, *Prolegomena*, translated by Black and Menzies, 161.

3. ש. קליין. ערי הכהנים והלויים וערי מקלט, קובץ החברה העברית לחקירת ארץ־ישראל ועתיקותיה, לזכר א. מ. מזיא, ירושלים, תרצ"ה, 81–94. W. F. Albright, "The List of Levitic Cities," in *Louis Ginzberg Jubilee Volume: English Section* (New York, 1945), 49–73; A. Alt, *Kleine Schriften*, II (München, 1953):294–315; B. Mazar, "The Cities of the Priests and the Levites," *Congress Volume, Oxford 1959* (VTSup, VII [Leiden, 1960]):193–205.

4. M. Haran, "The Levitical Cities: Utopia and Historical Reality" (Hebrew), *Tarbiz* 27 (1958):421–39; cf. JBL 80 (1961):45–54; Y. Kaufmann, *The Book of Joshua* (Hebrew) (Jerusalem, 1959), 270–82.

5. The translation is that of *The Torah . . . A New Translation* (Philadelphia: The Jewish Publication Society of America, 1962). On the philological problems, cf. G. B. Gray, *Numbers* (ICC) ad loc., and Haran, *Tarbiz*, 430, n. 15. the LXX "2000" in verse 4 is a harmonistic, inferior reading; cf. S. D. Luzzatto, *Commentary to the Pentateuch* (Hebrew), ed. P. Schlesinger (Tel Aviv, 1965), 493f., *sabib* means "on every side" as in Ezekiel 45:2b. A summary of various interpretations is in J. Greenstone, *Numbers* (Philadelphia, 1939), 353f.

6. Gray, 468. Haran's conception (*Tarbiz*, 430, n. 15) allows for a city in the center of the area. He takes *qir ha'ir* to mean the built-up part of the town, since *qir* never means "town wall" (Heb. *homa*). He then makes the starting point of the 1000 cubit lines the center of this built-up part. Thus the city area would consume part of the 1000 cubits on every side; but since Israelite towns were small [see details in Noth, *The Old*

Testament World, English translation, 147], free space would always remain around the town in the 2000 cubit square for pasture land. Haran's idea is plausible in itself, but a starting point in the center of the built-up part is hardly consonant with the expression *miqqir ha'ir wahusa*, which sounds as though the starting point of measurement is at the limit of the town's *qir*, not its center. Perhaps *qir ha'ir* is an ellipsis for *qir homat ha'ir* (cf. Josh. 2:15) "the (outer) side of the city wall"; Ben-Yehuda's *Thesaurus* properly defines *qir* as "the side (or surface) of a wall (*homa*)." So we are still faced with the problem of the legislator's having "forgotten" the dimensions of the city.

7. *Prolegomena*, 159. Similarly A. Bentzen, *Introduction to the OT*, II (Copenhagen, 1948):70: "The descriptions are given quite theoretically. The town is regarded as a mathematical point without any idea of concrete geographical situations. This is presumably best understood as the work of an 'author' living outside Palestine."

8. J. Miles (*The Babylonian Laws*, I [Oxford, 1952]:474) found that, where controls are available, the rents for boats in Hammurabi appear to be "not compulsory, but exemplary."

9. Ibid., 408, 426; "Crimes and Punishments," in *Interpreters' Dictionary of the Bible*, 742. B. Landsberger cast doubts on the validity and seriousness of some of Hammurabi's laws in his "Die babylonischen Termini für Gesetz und Recht," *Symbolae . . . Koschaker* (Stud. et Doc. ad Iura Or. Ant. Pert. [Leiden, 1939]), 219–34; especially relevant are the rulings listed there in note 11 (221) that "make the impression of theory."

10. *The Laws of Eshnunna* (AASOR 31 [1956]), 138; almost the same is Doughty's formulation in *Arabia Deserta* I:351 (reference from Driver, *Exodus*): "The custom of the desert is that of Moses, 'If any man's beast hurt the beast of another man, the loss shall be divided.'"

11. Consider the following examples:

Gorer's worth (owned by A)	Victim's worth (owned by B)	Cadaver's worth; victim's depreciation	Proceeds of sales to each owner	A's Loss	B's Loss
100	200	20; −180	60	40	140
200	200	20; −180	110	90	90
200	100	10; −90	105	95	gain of 5

12. See Mekhilta to Exodus 21:35 (ed. Lauterbach, III:95f.) and Rashi ad loc. The formulation of the law (reminiscent of Solomon's judgment) evidently intends to underscore the idea that both parties are to contribute to the settlement equally.

13. Like the LXX, the Tannaim took the cubit measurement of both verses 4 and 5 to refer to the depth of the strip outside the town walls. Unlike the LXX, they did not harmonize the difference between the measurements.

By a singular exegesis of R. Eliezer's opinion, Maimonides (*Code, Laws of the Sabbatical and Jubilee Year*, 13.2) concluded that the Pentateuchal law prescribed a strip of land 3000 cubits deep for the Levites' pasture!

14. Baraita in *Bab. Erubin*, 55a; with variants in *Tosefta Erubin* 4.1–6 (on which see S. Lieberman, *Tosefta Kifshuta*, III:366f.). Cf. Soncino Talmud, ad loc. for drawings.

15. Baraita in *Bab. Erubin*, 56b.

16. Hence the discussion of the former merges into a discussion of the latter (ibid.; cf. *Tosefta, Arakin*, 5.19).

17. This solution to the practical question of generalizing the prescription of Numbers 35:4–5 was suggested to me some years ago by my brother, Daniel A. Greenberg.

18. E.g., J. L. Saalschütz, *Das mosaische Recht*, I (Berlin, 1846):101. Saalschütz raises the question of the size of the city in relation to the pasture around it, pertinently observing that the lawgiver must have had regard for the relation of the grazing area to the needs of its inhabitants. In our discussion, we have postulated that, while the 2000

cubits are exemplary, the 1000 are meant to be the fixed depth of the pasture strip everywhere. It may be supposed than the lawgiver had in view a town of average size, for which he reckoned this to be adequate grazing land.

19. *Mishna, Erubin,* 5.4; *Gemara,* ad loc.

20. See Anne D. Kilmer, "The Use of Akkadian *DKŠ* in Old Babylonian Geometry Texts," in *Studies Presented to A. Leo Oppenheim* (Chicago, 1964), 140–46.

21. Bewer, *Ezekiel (Harper's Annotated Bible Series,* No. 9), II, 80, at 48:1–7; Cooke, *Ezekiel* (ICC), II:524; Fohrer, *Ezechiel* (HAT), 260; May, in IB VI:332.

22. *Ezekiel* (CB), 387; note too May's "apparently."

23. Smend, *Ezechiel* (KHAT), 392.

24. *Toldot ha'emuna,* VII:566ff.; *The Religion of Israel,* 443ff.

25. M. J. de Goeje, *Bibliotheca Geographorum Arabicorum* (Leiden, 1870, 1873), vol. III:186: cited by G. Le Strange, *Palestine under the Moslems* (reprinted Beirut, 1965), 15, whence the above translation is taken.

26. D. Baly, *The Geography of the Bible* (London, 1957), 8f.; see the graphic map in *Eretz Israel* 2 (Jerusalem, 1953), facing page 25; cf., finally, the lucid exposition of G. A. Smith, *Historical Geography of the Holy Land*[25] (London, 1931), 46–54, which includes the biblical terminology for geographical divisions of the country, attesting to native awareness of these areas.

27. Avi-yonah and Yeivin, *The Antiquities of Israel* (Hebrew) (Tel Aviv, 1955), 99; cf. the more qualified opinion by McCown, in article "City," IDB I, 636a; a contrary opinion in G. E. Wright, *Biblical Archaeology,* 186—but the town plan in Avi-yonah, 99 (Megiddo) and the remarks of Kenyon, *Archaeology in the Holy Land,* 252f. (on Beth-Shemesh) and 254 (Tell el Far'ah) speak for at least some planning.

28. A. L. Oppenheim, *Ancient Mesopotamia* (Chicago, 1964), 133ff.

29. E. M. Walker in *CAH,* IV:143; I am grateful to my teacher and colleague Lloyd W. Daly for bringing Cleisthenes' reform to my attention.

30. J. B. Bury, *A History of Greece*[3] (London, 1951), 211f.

31. On the significance and persistence of familial groupings in Israel, cf. E. A. Speiser, "'People' and 'Nation' of Israel," JBL 79 (1960):157–63.

Additional note:

Jacob Milgrom shows how the solution proposed here to the riddle of Numbers 35:4–5 allows for growth of the pasture area as the size of the town grows; see his *The JPS Torah Commentary: Numbers* (Philadelphia: Jewish Publication Society, 1990), 502–4.

Reflections on Job's Theology
1980

Job is a book not so much about God's justice as about the transformation of a man whose piety and view of the world were formed in a setting of wealth and happiness, and into whose life burst calamities that put an end to both. How can piety nurtured in prosperity prove truly deep-rooted and disinterested, and not merely a spiritual adjunct of good fortune ("God has been good to me so I am faithful to Him")? Can a man pious in prosperity remain pious when he is cut down by anarchical events that belie his orderly view of the world? The Book of Job tells how one man suddenly awakened to the anarchy rampant in the world, yet his attachment to God outlived the ruin of his tidy system.

Job is a pious believer who is struck by misfortune so great that it cannot be explained in the usual way as a prompting to repentance, a warning, let alone a punishment (the arguments later addressed to him by his friends). His piety is great enough to accept the misfortune without rebelling against God: "Should we accept only good from God and not accept evil?" (2:10). But his inability, during seven days of grief in the company of his silent friends, to find a reasonable relation between the misfortune and the moral state of its victims (himself and his children) opens Job's eyes to the fact that in the world at large the same lack of relation prevails (9:22–24; 12:6–9; 21:7–34). Until then, the crying contradiction between the idea of a just order and the reality of individual destinies had, because of his prosperity, hardly been visible to Job. He may not have been as simple as his friends, but neither was he more perceptive than Elihu, who, at the end (chs. 32–37), offers those above-mentioned explanations of misfortune. But Job now

327

knows their absurdity and their inadequacy to save a reasonable divine order according to human standards of morality.

The prologue of the book, telling of Satan's wager and the subsequent disaster that befell Job, has been a scandal to many readers. But the prologue is necessary, first of all, to establish Job's righteousness. To depict the effect of dire misfortune that demolishes the faith of a perfectly blameless man in a just divine order is the author's purpose. The book is not merely an exposition of ideas, a theological argument, but the portrayal of a spiritual journey from simple piety to the sudden painful awareness and eventual acceptance of the fact that inexplicable misfortune is the lot of man. Without the prologue we should lack the essential knowledge that Job's misfortune really made no sense; without the prologue the friends' arguments that misfortune indicates sin would be plausible, and Job's resistance to them liable to be construed as moral arrogance. The prologue convinces us from the outset of Job's integrity; hence, we can never side with the friends. For Job is a paradigm ("He never was or existed," says a Talmudic rabbi, "except as an example" [*Baba Batra*, 15a]). He personifies every pious man who, when confronted with an absurd disaster, is too honest to lie in order to justify God. The author must convince his readers that Job's self-estimation is correct, and that therefore his view of moral disorder in God's management of the world is warranted. That is one purpose of the prologue.

Satan's wager and God's assent to it dramatize a terrible quandary of faith: a pious man whose life has always been placid can never know whether his faith in God is more than an interested bargain—a convenience that has worked to his benefit—unless it is tested by events that defy the postulate of a divine moral order. Only when unreasonable misfortune erupts into a man's life can he come to know the basis of his relation to God, thus allaying doubts (personified here by Satan) that both he and others must harbor toward his faith. To conquer these doubts by demonstrating that disinterested devotion to God can indeed exist is necessary for man's spiritual well-being; God's acquiescence in Satan's wager expresses this necessity. The terrible paradox is that no righteous man can measure his love of God unless he suffers a fate befitting the wicked.

The speeches of Job reveal the collapse of his former outlook. For the first time in his life he has become aware of the prevalence of disorder in the government of the world. In his former state of well-being, Job would hardly have countenanced in himself or in others a death wish; in his misfortune, however, he expresses it vehemently (3:11–23). Could Job, in his prosperity, have appreciated the anguish of victims of senseless misfortune, or have regarded God as an enemy of man (7:17–21; 9:13–24; 16:9–14)? Job would previously have responded to despair of God as his friends and Elihu responded to him in his misery and despair. For Job's friends were his peers ideologically no less than socially; he belonged to their circle both in deed and in creed. A chasm opened between him and them only because of a disaster that Job alone knew to be undeserved.

Job's pathetic appeals for a bill of indictment (10:2; 13:18ff.; 23:1ff.; 31:35f.) belong to the context of the neat, orderly system in which he had once believed. One wonders whether such repeated affirmations of his innocence are not aimed as much toward his friends as toward God, in an effort to break down their complacency. But since his friends neither have undergone his suffering nor share his confidence in his own righteousness, they will not question the validity or give up the security of their system.

Though Job never tires of denouncing the inadequacy of his former concept of the divine government (a concept that his friends still adhere to), his complaints are addressed to God. The orderly fabric of his life has been irreparably rent, yet his relation to God persists. We shall soon consider how that could be.

The outcome of the drama is that the collapse of a complacent view of the divine economy can be overcome. For Job this came about through a sudden overwhelming awareness of the complexity of God's manifestation in reasonless phenomena of nature. Job's flood of insight comes in a storm (סערה)—we may suppose, through the experience of its awesomeness. One may compare and contrast the midrashic wordplay that has Job hearing God's answer out of a "hair" (שערה), from contemplation of a microcosm. The grand vista of nature opens before Job, and it reveals the working of God in a realm other than man's moral order. Job responds to, and thus gets a response from, the numinous presence underlying the whole panorama; he hears God's voice in the storm. The fault in the moral order—the plane on which God and man interact—is subsumed under the totality of God's work, not all of which is reasonable. Senseless calamity loses some of its demoralizing effect when morale does not depend entirely on the comprehensibility of the phenomena but, rather, on the conviction that they are pervaded by the presence of God. As nature shows, this does not necessarily mean that they are sensible and intelligible.

It has been objected that God's speeches (chs. 38–41) are irrelevant to Job's challenge. God—the objection runs—asserts his power in reply to a challenge to his moral government. But this sets up a false dichotomy. To be sure, God's examples from nature are exhibitions of his power, but they are also exhibitions of his wisdom and his providence for his creatures (38:27; 39:1–4, 26). Through nature, God reveals himself to Job as both purposive and nonpurposive, playful and uncanny, as evidenced by the monsters he created. To study nature is to perceive the complexity, the unity of contraries, in God's attributes, and the inadequacy of human reason to explain his behavior, not the least in his dealings with man.

For it may be inferred that in God's dealings with man, this complexity is also present—a unity of opposites: reasonability, justice, playfulness, uncanniness (the latter appearing demonic in the short view). When Job recognizes in the God of nature, with his fullness of attributes, the very same God revealed in his own individual destiny, the tumult in his soul is stilled. He has fathomed the truth concerning God's character; he is no longer tortured by a concept that fails to account for the phenomena, as did his former notion of God's orderly working (42:1–6).

If God is a combination of divergent attributes, and is a cause of misfortune, why does Job not reject him?

What had Job known of God in his former happy state? He had known him as one who confers order and good. Basking in his light, Job's life had been suffused with blessings (29:2–5). No later evidence to the contrary could wipe out Job's knowledge of God's benignity gained from personal experience. Job calls that former knowledge of God a "hearing," while his latter knowledge, earned through suffering, is a "seeing" (42:5); that is, the latter knowledge gained about God is to the former as seeing is to hearing—far more comprehensive and adequate. Formerly, Job had only a limited notion of God's nature—as a benign, constructive factor in his life, "good" in terms of human morality. At that time, any evidence that ran against this conception of God was peripheral: it lay outside Job's focus. He assumed that it too could somehow be contained in his view of the divine moral order, but nothing pressed him to look the uncongenial facts in the face.

But misfortune moved the periphery into the center, and the perplexity that ensued is a testimony to Job's piety, for he was not transformed by senseless misfortune into a scoffer—a denier of God—but, instead, thrown into confusion. His experience of God in good times had left on him an indelible conviction of God's goodness that clashed with the new, equally strong evidence of God's enmity. Though one contradicted the other, Job experienced both as the work of God, and did not forget the first (as did his wife) when the second overtook him.

The author of Job had a dedication to theological honesty and a passion to teach the reality of God's relation to man that are unique in the Bible.° Job cannot rest after the collapse of his old outlook until he

---

°Kohelet shares with Job the clear-eyed vision of a flawed moral governance of the world, yet he has none of Job's anguished perplexity. That is because Kohelet, to all appearances, never had Job's experience of the goodness of God, with which the anarchy in the world might clash. Job might well have turned cynical had he never "heard" God in his earlier days.

has come to a better one, more congruent with the facts of experience. How highly the author prizes right knowledge of God is revealed by his final estimate of Job's friends. Although they argued in evident good faith, in the epilogue God is angry at them and declares them in need of forgiveness (42:7–8). Wrong thinking about God is reprehensible. One might say that an aim of the author of Job is to warn men away from such culpable misconceptions. After Job, God is not willing to be conceived of in the friends' terms; after Job, such views are abhorrent to him.

To the very end, Job remains ignorant of the true cause of his misfortunes, for he never learns of Satan's wager. Job appears to have found consolation in his realization of the complexity of God, but the reader knows more: he knows that Job's suffering was the result of a divine bet on Job's disinterested piety.

Why couldn't Job, like Abraham, have been told at the end that the entire event was a trial, and have heard, as did Abraham, "Now I know that you fear God" (Gen. 22:12)?

From the epilogue, it is clear that God's vindication of Job's honesty, proven in his passionate recriminations against God and against his friends' simplistic theories, is more important for Job than knowing the reason for his suffering. The epilogue shows Job satisfied by the divine assurance that his friends' arguments were specious, as he had always asserted (13:7–10; 19:22–29; 42:7–9). Beyond that God does not go in revealing to Job the cause of his suffering.

Abraham's case is not identical to Job's, for, in the end, Abraham did not sacrifice Isaac, while Job lost all his children and his possessions. It was dreadful enough for Abraham to learn that his God was capable of subjecting his followers to trials that brought them to the verge of disaster, even though he rescued them at the last moment. For Job to have learned that his family and his possessions had been annihilated because of a mere wager with Satan—that he had been a pawn in a celestial game—would have been far harder to accept than was the mystery of a God part known, part hidden, whose overall work is nevertheless good. For it is easier to bear a mixture of benignity and enmity, with their ultimate meaning clouded in mystery, than to accept a cold-blooded toying with the fortunes and lives of men.

Nonetheless, the framework story says that one reason for senseless suffering is to test the motives of a pious man. This is stated only as the particular circumstance of this case and not as a general principle: One pious man, famous for his integrity, was visited with calamity for no reason other than to prove his character. That the same reason may apply to other pious men on whom senseless calamity falls is not said. But it is a possibility, one which lends a potentially heroic dimension to every such case; that is the exemplary value of the book.

Job ends up a wiser man, for he sees better the nature of God's work in the world and recognizes the limitations of his former viewpoint. The manifestation of his peace with God, of his renewed spiritual vigor, is that he reconstitutes his life. He is a vessel into which blessings can be poured; he who wished to have died at birth now fathers new sons and daughters. That, in addition to answering the demands of simple justice, is the significance of the epilogue (which many critics have belittled as crass).

This concept of God contradicts not only that of the wisdom of the Book of Proverbs (in which the principle of just individual retribution is iterated in its simplest form) but that of the Torah and the Prophets as well. These writings bear the imprint of God's saving acts, the Exodus and the Conquest; they represent God as the maintainer of the moral order, and interpret events in terms of reward and punishment. But the Torah and the Prophets refer to the nation more than to the individual, and in their time no situation arose in which that concept failed. On the national level, Israel could always be regarded as falling short of righteousness and integrity; there were always elements within it that could rightly be reproached as deserving of punishment and, under the principle of collective responsibility established by the public covenant, of tainting the people at large with their guilt.

The later inability to find an explanation for national destiny in the Torah and the Prophets is reflected, not in Job, but in the apocalyptic literature that arose in the Hellenistic period. There was no explanation in the tradition for the persecution by Antiochus IV, which singled out those loyal to God while leaving the apostates in peace. The faithful were reconciled to their suffering only because they saw it as the preordained prelude to an eventual spiritual domination of the world by the Saints of the Most High (Dan. 7:27). Taking his cue from hints in the Suffering Servant passages of Isaiah (also a response to those perplexed by a topsy-turvy world in which the heathen prospered and the devotees of the Lord were humiliated), the apocalyptic visionary of Daniel perceived the suffering of the righteous as a necessary phase in a determined sequence of universal salvation. Thus he lent a significance to the reasonless suffering of his community which was outside the categories of ordinary justice.

Is the retention in the biblical canon of Proverbs alongside Job, or the Torah and the Prophets alongside the apocalypses of Daniel, just thoughtless conservatism?

The religious sensibility apparently absorbs or even affirms the contradictions embodied in these books. That may be because these contradictions are perceived to exist in reality. One can see in individ-

ual life as in collective life a moral causality (which the religious regard as divinely maintained; indeed, as a reflection of God's attributes): Evil recoils upon the evildoers, whether individual or collective; goodness brings blessings. At the same time, the manifestation of
this causality can be so erratic or so delayed as to cast doubt on its validity as the single key to the destiny of people and nations. Hence the
sober believer does not pin his or her faith solely on a simple axiom of
the divine maintenance of moral causality, but neither will he or she
altogether deny its force. No single key unlocks the mystery of destiny: "Within our ken is neither the tranquillity of the wicked nor the
suffering of the righteous" (Abot 4:17), but, for all that, the sober believer does not endorse nihilism. Wisdom, Torah, and Prophets continue to represent for him one aspect of causality in events that he can
confirm in his own private experience. But this is one aspect only. The
other stands beyond his moral judgment, though it is still under God:
namely, the mysterious or preordained decree of God, toward which
the proper attitude is "Though he slay me, yet will I trust in him" (Job
13:15, *qere*).

NOTES

   That the apocalyptic visionary of Daniel identified the victims of Antiochus IV's
persecution with the Suffering Servant of Isaiah is a brilliant discovery of H.L.
Ginsberg. See his "The Oldest Interpretation of the Suffering Servant," VT 3 (1953),
400–4 and the addendum to his article "Daniel" in EB 2:949–52.

Job

1987

The prophet Ezekiel mentions Job alongside Noah and Daniel as a paragon of righteousness (Ezek. 14:12–20); from this we know that Job was a byword among the sixth-century B.C.E. Judahite exiles whom the prophet addressed. But from Ezekiel and from the late passing reference to Job's patience (or perseverance) in James 5:10–11, one would never guess the complexity of the character set forth in the book that bears his name. Indeed the book's representation of Job seems to some modern scholars so disharmonious as to warrant the hypothesis that two characters have been fused in it: "Job the patient," the hero of the prose frame of the book; and "Job the impatient," the central figure of the poetic dialogue. In the prose story, Job the patient withstands all the calamities inflicted on him to test the sincerity of his piety and is finally rewarded by redoubled prosperity. The moral is: Piety for its own sake is true virtue and in the end is requited. It is this old story—often called a folktale—that is supposed to have been known to Ezekiel's audience. Later, the hypothesis continues, a far more profound thinker (perhaps a survivor of the Babylonian Exile and its crisis of faith) used the temporary misfortune of the hero as the setting for his poem, in which the conventional wisdom of the tale is radically challenged.

This theory is based on expectations of simplicity, consistency, and linearity that are confuted by the whole tenor of the book. Reversal and subversion prevail throughout—in sudden shifts of mood and role and in a rhetoric of sarcasm and irony. The dialogue contains much response and reaction but no predictable or consistent course of argument. When to these disconcerting features are added the exotic language (loaded with Aramaisms and Arabisms) and the uncertain state of the text in many places—from apparent corruption of words to unintelligible sequences of verses—the confidence of some critics in their ability to reconstitute the original text by rewriting and rearrangement seems exaggerated. This essay discusses the book as we have it.

The chief literary (as distinct from theological or literary-historical) problem of Job is its coherence: Do the prose and the poetry or the speeches of Job and his Friends hang together? How are they related? We must gain an awareness of the complexities of interplay among the elements of the book. The truncation of the third round of speeches and the integrality to the book of Elihu's speeches have been treated by most critics as problems to be solved by a theory of textual dislocation or adulteration. I shall try to describe how these elements in their present shape work upon the reader. This is not to assert the infallibility of the text in hand, but rather to confess our inability to justify on grounds other than individual predilection the alternatives proposed to it. It also reflects a conviction that the literary complexity of the book is consistent with and appropriate to the nature of the issues with which it deals.

The background of the dialogue is established in chapters 1 and 2 in five movements. The first movement introduces the magnate Job, one of the "dwellers in the east" (1:3)[1]—that is, east of the Land of Israel—in the uncertainly located country of Uz (connected with Aram to the north in Genesis 10:23, but with Edom to the south in Lamentations 4:21). He is a "blameless and upright man, one who fears God and shuns evil" (1:1). His wealth and family are described in numbers typifying abundance—seven sons and three daughters, seven thousand small cattle and three thousand camels, and so forth. The happiness of the family is epitomized in the constant round of banquets held by the children; Job's scrupulousness is shown by his sacrifices on their behalf, lest in a careless moment they "bless" (euphemism for "blaspheme") God in their hearts (1:5).

In the second movement, the action that shatters this idyll starts. "One day," at a periodic assembly of the divine court (1:6), God singles out Job for praise to the Adversary (the antecedent of the later Satan and anachronistically so called in the King James Version; in Hebrew Scriptures an angel whose task is to roam the earth and expose human wrongdoing). This commendation virtually invites the Adversary to suggest that since God has built a protective hedge around Job, his piety may not be disinterested ("for nothing," 1:9): only deprive him of his possessions and see whether he won't "bless" God to his face! God accepts the challenge and empowers the Adversary to carry out the test.

The third movement takes place "one day" as a round of the children's banquets begins and they are gathered in the house of the eldest son (1:13). A terrible chain of calamities befalls Job: one messenger after another arrives to report the destruction of every component of Job's fortune, culminating in the death of his children. Job goes into mourning, but with a blessing of God on his lips (the Adversary is thwarted, but his expectation is literally realized!). The movement concludes, "In all this Job did not sin or impute anything unsavory to God" (1:22).

The scene of the fourth movement is heaven again. "One day," at the periodic assembly of the divine court (2:1), God repeats his praise of Job to the Adversary, adding, "and he still holds on to his integrity, so you incited me to destroy him for nothing" (2:3). The Adversary proposes the ultimate test: afflict Job's own body and see whether he won't "bless" God. God agrees, with the proviso that Job's life be preserved, and the Adversary hurries off to inflict a loathsome skin disease on Job, driving him to constant scratching with a sherd as he sits in the dust (the Greek translation reads, "on the dungheap far from the city"). His wife protests: "Do you still hold on to your integrity? 'Bless' God, and die" (2:9). Job remonstrates with her: "Should we then accept the good from God and not accept the bad?" (2:10). The question is rhetorical, but in every rhetorical question lurks the possible affirmation of what is ostensibly denied. Moreover, by bluntly calling what he has received from God "bad," Job has moved from his nonjudgmental blessing of God after the first stage of his ruin. The movement concludes with a variant of the preceding conclusion: "In all this Job did not sin with his lips." Is "with his lips" a mere equivalent of "did not impute anything unsavory to God," or did the Talmudic sage correctly perceive in it a reservation: with his lips he sinned not, but in his heart he did![2] Is the impatient Job of the poem already foreshadowed in the closing stage of the narrative?

The last movement brings the three Friends of Job (also of Abrahamitic, extra-Israelite stock) into the picture. Coming from afar to comfort Job, they assume his condition—they sit on the ground with him, having torn their clothes and thrown dust on their heads. They keep him company in silence for seven days until he starts to speak.

The contrast between the simple folktale and the artful poem must not be overdrawn. In fact the artistry in the narrative is considerable. The representation of time in the first to the fourth movements progresses from duration to instant. In movement one, the regularity of happy, uneventful lives is expressed by verbs in the durational mode: "would go and would make a banquet," "would send word," "always used to do." The decision in heaven to test Job and its earthly realization in calamities (the second and third movements) occur each on separate days. Moreover, temporal disjunction is accompanied by disjunction of agent: Although the Adversary is empowered to ruin Job, he is not mentioned in the subsequent story of disasters. But in the climactic fourth movement, the pace is stepped up and the events are concentrated. Events in heaven and their effect on earth occur on one and the same day; God licenses the Adversary to afflict Job's body, and the Adversary sets to work immediately and in person, as though eager to win his wager. The parallelism of the second stage of Job's trial to the first is expressed with the intensification and focusing that are characteristic of the second verset of poetic parallelism.

Dialogue and elements of poetic diction permeate the prose tale, further diminishing the contrast between the frame and the poem. Only the last movement of the story is speechless—owing to the courteous silence of the Friends. The first movement ends with Job's internal dialogue of concern lest his children blaspheme in secret. The second movement and the corresponding first half of the fourth movement consist almost entirely of dialogue between God and the Adversary, with the latter employing markedly elevated speech: parallelism ("roaming the land and walking about in it," 1:7; "the work of his hands you blessed, and his cattle abound in the land," 1:10); proverbs ("Skin for skin; all a man has he will give for his life," 2:4), emphatic repetition ("a hedge about him and about his household and about all he has," 1:10). The chain of calamities in the third movement is conveyed entirely through reports of messengers, all of which exhibit the same pattern. The details of the accounts of disaster are artfully disposed: Human and natural destroyers alternate, and the loss of Job's children is delayed to the end. Job's acquiescence in God's decree, with its parallelism, its compression, and its balanced lines, is poetry proper:

> Naked came I forth from the belly of my mother
> and naked shall I return thither:
> The Lord gave, and the Lord took away;
> blessed be the name of the Lord. (1:21)

The terrestrial scene of the fourth movement is dominated by the sharp exchange between Job and his wife in which an ironic touch is visible. Job's wife unwittingly advocates the Adversary's cause to Job ("'Bless' God, and die") while expressing her exasperation with her husband in the very terms used by God to praise him ("still hold on to your integrity"). Such reuse by one character of the language of another is a constant feature of the poem; its occurrence here in the narrative is another bond between the two parts of the book.

The preliminary narrative establishes Job's virtuous character and so provides us with inside information known to heaven and Job alone. Our judgment on what Job and his Friends will say about his character must be determined by this information. We also know—what neither Job nor his Friends do—that Job's sufferings are designed to test him. These circumstances are fertile ground for irony; their impact on our reception of the arguments put forward in the poetic dialogue is an open and intriguing issue. If we now follow the debate step by step, we will get a clearer sense of the artful interplay between statements and positions, of the elements of progression in the arguments, and of the overarching ironies of the book as a whole.

After brooding over his fate for seven days, Job breaks his silence with a bitter diatribe against his life and its symbol, light (ch. 3). He wishes that the day of his birth would be reclaimed by primeval darkness and imagines the peace he would have enjoyed in Sheol had he been still-born. Why does God give life to the wretched, whom he has "hedged about" (that is, obstructed—a reversal of the meaning of the very phrase used by the Adversary to describe Job's security)? He recollects his lifelong fear of calamity (one thinks of his anxious sacrificing on behalf of his children), which did not avail to prevent it.

This outburst takes the Friends by surprise. They had come to commiserate and encourage, not to participate in a rebellion against God's judgment. Their first spokesman, Eliphaz, opens softly (chs. 4–5), reminding Job of his custom of cheering victims of misfortune, and gently chiding him for breaking down under his own calamities. He preaches the doctrine of distributive justice: no innocent man was ever wiped out, while the wicked reap their deserts. He reports a revelation made to him "in thought-filled visions of the night" (4:13); man is by nature too base to be innocent before God—even the angels are not trusted by him! Short-lived as he is ("cut down from morning to evening," 4:20), man cannot acquire the wisdom to comprehend his fate. Will Job seek vindication from some (other) divine being? Only fools let vexation kill them; "taking root" for a moment, they suddenly lose everything they own through their blindness to the truth that "man is to misery born as the sparks fly upward" (5:7). In Job's place, Eliphaz would turn to God, who works wonders and benefactions and who constantly reverses the fortunes of men. It is a lucky man whom God disciplines, for if the man—here Job—accepts it and repents, he has good hope of being healed and of living prosperous and happy to a ripe old age. All this has been proved by experience.

In this first exchange, each party starts from advanced positions. Job vents his death wish with untempered passion, becoming the spokesman of all the wretched of the earth. Eliphaz's carefully modulated reply sets the pattern for all subsequent speeches of the Friends: a prologue, demurring to Job, followed by a multithematic advocacy of the conventional view of God's distributive justice. Most of the themes of the Friends' argument are included in Eliphaz's speech: man's worthlessness before God, man's ephemerality and (consequent) ignorance, a call to turn to God in penitence, praise of God, the disciplinary purpose of misfortune, the happiness of the penitent, the claim to possess wisdom greater than Job's.

The rhetoric of debate pervades the speech of Eliphaz and all that follow. Themes are introduced by expressions of interrogation ("Is/ Does not . . ."), demonstration ("look, behold"), exhortation ("Remember! Consider! Know!"), and exception ("but, however"). Among the rhetorical questions peppering Eliphaz's speech, one exhibits the unconscious irony typical of many in the Friends' speeches: "Call now, will anyone answer you;/to which of the divine beings will you turn?" (5:1). Eliphaz is scoffing, but in the event Job will not only call upon a heavenly witness, arbitrator and vindicator; he will ultimately be answered by the greatest and holiest of them all.

A constant difference between the general and particular observations of Job and the Friends is already evident in this first exchange. Both parties pass back and forth from the particular case of Job to the general condition of mankind. But in Job's speeches his particular misfortune governs his vision of the general; his unmerited suffering opens his eyes to the injustice rampant in society at large. In the Friends' speeches, on the other hand, the general doctrine of distributive justice governs their judgment of Job's case: He must be wicked in order to fit into their scheme of things. Job's empirically based generalities reflect reality; the Friends' perception of the particular is as fictive as the general doctrine from which it springs.

Echoes of Job's speech may be heard in that of Eliphaz. Job's "roarings" (3:24) reflect his anguish; Eliphaz speaks of the "lion's roar" (4:10). Birth and misery figure prominently in Job's speech; Eliphaz combines them in his epigrammatic "man is born to misery." Countering Job's wish for a direct passage from birth to grave, Eliphaz holds out hope of a penitent Job reaching the grave happy and in ripe old age. Such echoes and allusions pervade the dialogue, arguing against a commonly held opinion that the poem of Job consists of a series of disconnected monologues.

Job begins his reply to Eliphaz (chs. 6–7) with a reference to *ka'as,* "vexation" (which Eliphaz warned kills fools, 5:2); overwhelming vexation has caused Job to speak so intemperately (6:2–3). He is the victim of God's terrors; to hold out hope to him is mockery, for his only wish is to be speedily dispatched ("crushed" he says in 6:9, using Eliphaz's language in 5:4). He is not made of stone so as to be able to tolerate his suffering any longer (6:12; in 5:17–18 Eliphaz called it God's benign discipline). He is disappointed that his Friends have deserted him. As when thirsty travelers seek out a wadi and find it has run dry in summer heat, so now when Job looks to his Friends for support they fail him. All he asks of them is to pay attention to his case, show him his fault, and stop producing vapid arguments. Job turns Eliphaz's theme of man's ephemerality to his own use: Man's life is like a hireling's term of service; his only relief is night and wages. But Job's life is a hopeless agony; night brings him only the terrors of his dreams and night visions (a bitter echo of Eliphaz). Since human life is so brief, it is a wonder that God fills it with such suffering. Job parodies a verse in Psalms: "What is man, that you are mindful of him,/mortal man, that you take note of him?" (Ps. 8:5; cf. 144:3: "Lord, what is man, that you should care about him, / mortal man, that you should think of him?"). This is skewed sardonically into:

> What is man, that you make much of him,
>   that you fix your attention upon him—
> inspect him every morning,
>   examine him every minute? (7:17–18)

If only the "watcher of men" would look away for a while and let Job live out his few remaining days in peace!

Establishing here the pattern for the following dialogues, Job's answer is longer than his predecessor's. He has been goaded by Eliphaz's pious generalities and oblique rebuke into itemizing his experience of God's enmity and its universal implications. In this way all the replies of the Friends arouse Job to ever-new perceptions of his condition and of the divine governance of the world.

Job's complaint scandalizes Bildad, the new interlocutor (ch. 8). "Will the Almighty pervert justice?" he asks rhetorically (v. 3), and proceeds to ascribe the death of Job's children to their sins. Thus, Bildad lays bare the implications of the speeches of both his predecessors. Job ought to supplicate God contritely rather than assert a claim against him. Since we are so short-lived, it behooves us to consult the ancient sages; they teach that as it is nature's law that plants wither without water, so the course of the godless leads to perdition (the moral law). God will not repudiate the blameless or support the wicked; hence, if Job repents, a joyous future, better than his past, is in store for him.

In his reply (chs. 9–10), Job exploits the forensic metaphor in the rhetorical questions of Eliphaz and Bildad ("Can mortals be acquitted by God?" 4:17; "Will the Almighty pervert justice?" 8:3). It expresses the covenantal-legal postulate of ancient piety with its doctrine of distributive justice, shared by all the characters in the dialogue. God refuses to follow the rules, Job asserts: "Man cannot win a suit against God!" (9:2). God indeed works wonders (echoing Eliphaz)—mainly in displays of his destructive power in nature (a parody of Eliphaz's doxology). Such aggression he directs against any who seek redress from him for calamity inflicted on them undeservedly. In language suffused with legal terms, Job denounces God's disregard of his right: He terrorizes Job into confusion; even if Job could plead, his own words would be twisted against him. Contrary to Bildad's assertion, God indiscriminately destroys the innocent and the guilty, for "he wounds me much for nothing" (9:17; ironically, Job has unwittingly stumbled on the true reason for his suffering). If God would allow him, Job would demand of him a bill of indictment. He would charge him with unworthy conduct: he spurns his creature while smiling on the wicked; he searches for Job's sin, though he knows Job is not guilty. He carefully fashioned Job and sustained him through the years—only to hunt him down with a wondrous display of power (themes of Psalm 139 are sarcastically reused here).

It is now Zophar's turn (ch. 11). After denouncing Job's mockery and self-righteousness, he speaks as one privy to God's counsels: if God would answer Job, he'd show him his ignorance; the fact is that God has treated Job better than he deserves. God's purpose is unfathomable:

> higher than heaven,
>   deeper than Sheol,—
> longer than the earth,
>   broader than the sea. (vv. 8–9)

Job should pray to God and remove his iniquity; then he will enjoy the hope, the light, the peace and the sound sleep of the righteous.

Each of the three Friends having had his say, Job now delivers his longest answer yet (chs. 12–14). Goaded by Bildad, he mockingly acknowledges their monopoly of wisdom, but claims he is no less wise. A shower of irony and sarcasm follows. Borrowing terms from Bildad's invocation of the ancient sages and Zophar's celebration of God's boundless wisdom, Job grotesquely invokes the dumb creatures of sky, sea, and earth to teach the commonplace. "With him [God] are wisdom and power; his are counsel and insight" (12:13), followed by another parodic doxology depicting divine power exercised with sheerly destructive results in the social realm. In this context the stock praise of God that he "uncovers deep things out of darkness, brings deep gloom to light" (12:22; cf. Dan. 2:22) suggests that he tears the lid off submerged forces of death and chaos, allowing them to surface and overcome order.³ As for the Friends, they are quacksalvers, liars, obsequiously partial to God; they ascribe false principles to him and ought to be in dread of his ever subjecting them to scrutiny. Job, despite his ruined state, will stand up to God, convinced God must recognize integrity.

> Let him slay me; I have no [*or* in him I will] hope;
>   yet I will argue my cause before him.
> Through this shall I gain victory:
>   that no godless man can come into his presence. (13:15–16)

This burst of confidence collapses into the mournful realization of his vulnerability to God's terrors. Again he asks to be allowed to converse with God, to be informed of his sin (13:20–23; cf. 6:24, 10:2). Again he complains of God's enmity, wonders at his petty keeping of accounts and his persecution of "a driven leaf" (13:25). Again he implores God to let him live out his term of service in peace, for, unlike a tree, which after being felled can still renew itself from its roots, man once cut down sleeps eternally in Sheol.

But must containment in Sheol be final? Might it not be a temporary shelter from God's wrath? "If a man dies, can he revive?" (14:14) —hope wells up in the question, and the fantasy of reversal continues: When wrath subsides, God would call and Job would answer, God would long for his creature. But this anticipation of a doctrine whose time was not yet ripe, this flight of a mind liberated by the collapse of its concept of order, is a momentary flash. Job falls back into despondency.

When the first round of dialogue began, Job rejected life; by its conclusion, he is clinging to it and longing for renewed intimacy with God. Lamentation, anger, despair, and hope succeed each other in waves, but a clear gathering of energy is visible in his speeches. The Friends, hurt by Job's challenge to their concept of the moral order, have turned from comforters to scolds, each harsher than his predecessor. Eliphaz only implies that Job is a sinner; Bildad openly proposes that his children have died for their sins; Zophar assures Job that his suffering is less than he deserves. Yet each ends with a promise of a bright future if Job will only acknowledge his guilt and implore God's forgiveness. Though they provide no direct comfort to Job, by blackening his character they rouse him out of the torpor of despair and kindle in him the desire to assert himself.

Eliphaz opens the second round (chs. 15–21), deploring Job's mockery of his Friends' counsel. His pernicious arguments undermine piety. Is Job Wisdom personified ("Were you born before the moun-

344 : The Biblical Text and Its Interpretation

tains?" at 15:7 evokes Proverbs 8:25 in reference to Dame Wisdom); does *he* have a monopoly of it (cf. 12:2–3)? Job's ridicule of sapiential tradition rankles with Bildad and Zophar as well ("Why are we thought of as brutes?" 18:3; "reproof that insults me," 20:3). One would think Job had listened in on God's council when in fact it was to Eliphaz that insight into man's true condition was vouchsafed in a night vision (15:14–16 repeats with slight variation the oracle on man's baseness in Eliphaz's first speech, 4:17–21). Eliphaz proceeds to depict the life and exemplary fate of the wicked as taught by the sages. This theme, briefly touched upon previously, is elaborated at length throughout the second round of the Friends' speeches. Since they cannot persuade Job to withdraw his arraignment of God, his very perseverance in his claims appears to them to convict him of sin. Hence they endeavor, in this round, to frighten him into recanting by describing in detail the punishment of the wicked. That these descriptions, ostensibly generic, contain items identical with Job's misfortunes, is of course not accidental. The poet exhibits virtuosity in playing variations on this single theme. He has Eliphaz focus on the tormented person of the wicked man (ch. 15); here the most blatant allusions to Job's condition occur. Bildad concentrates on the destruction of his "tent" and progeny:

> Light has darkened in his tent;
>   his lamp fails him . . .
> Generations to come will be appalled at his fate [and say],
>   "These were the dwellings of the wicked;
>   here was the place of him who knew not God." (18:6, 20–21)

Zophar (ch. 20) develops an alimentary figure: the ill-got gain of the wicked are sweets he tries to swallow but must vomit, or they will turn to poison in him and kill him.

Job answers the monitory descriptions of the fate of the wicked with pathetic descriptions of his misery (ch. 16). In response to Eliphaz he figures God as an enemy rushing at him like a hero, setting him up as his target—inverting Eliphaz's picture of the wicked playing the hero and running defiantly at God (15:25–26). He has been afflicted despite his innocence, and this very thought moves him to plead that the wrong done to him not be forgotten ("Earth, do not cover my blood," 16:18). In a transport of faith he avers he has a witness in heaven who will arbitrate between him and God, then descends again into despair.

Responding to Bildad's depiction of the wicked man's loss of home and kin, Job relates (ch. 19) how God has stripped him of honor; how friends, wife, and servants have abandoned him till only his flesh and bones remain attached to him. He implores the compassion of his Friends, wishes for a permanent record of his arguments, and consoles himself with the assurance that although he is forsaken in the present, his redeemer-kinsman (*go'el*) lives and will in the end appear to vindicate him.

In his reply to Zophar (ch. 21), concluding the second round of dialogue, Job bids his Friends be silent and listen to something truly appalling (Job spurns as specious the horror over the pretended destruction of the wicked described by Bildad, 18:20), namely the real situation of the wicked. Contrary to the Friends' doctrine, the wicked live long and prosper, surrounded by frolicking children; they die without pangs. They flaunt their indifference toward God with impunity. How often is their light extinguished (contrary to Bildad's claim)? Their children will pay for their sins?—why doesn't God pay *them* back! The Friends have reproached Job with insolence toward God: "Can God be instructed in knowledge—/he who judges from the heights?" (21:22; the verse seems to cite the Friends, but it is a pseudo-citation since in fact they never said this; in the heat of debate Job ascribes to the Friends what can at most have been implied in their speeches). Job answers: What sort of judge distributes well-being and misfortune according to no standard? The Friends have admonished: "Where is the tent in which the wicked dwelled?" (see the end of Bildad's speech, 18:21). Job retorts: every traveler (that is, worldly wise person, not necessarily old) knows that even in death the wicked are honored.

In the second round the Friends dwelt one-sidedly on the punishment of the wicked, intending Job to see in the wicked a mirror of himself. What they succeeded in doing is to move him to particularize his own suffering and—equally one-sidedly—the success of the wicked, thus at once proving he is not one of them and confirming again God's perversity. In this round, too, Job experiences sporadic moments of hopefulness and intimations of vindication. Significant of things to come in round three is the frequency (especially in Job's last speech) with which Job cites the Friends or anticipates their responses to him. In the first speech of this round he says that were he in their place he would mouth the same sort of platitudes (16:4); in his last speech he begins to show he can do it.

Eliphaz returns to the arena yet a third time (ch. 22). Is your righteousness of any interest to God? he asks Job (v. 3); the implication seems to be that Job's clamor for a hearing is arrant presumption (Eliphaz cannot know that God indeed has a stake in Job's righteousness). In fact, he continues, you are very wicked—behaving in a cruel and callous manner toward the weak and defenseless. Eliphaz has been driven to this extreme by his tenacious adherence to the doctrine of distributive justice, the threat to which may be gauged by his incredible accusation. In the sequel, Eliphaz misconstrues Job's pseudo-citation (21:22) to mean that God cannot see through the cloud-cover to judge mankind; but, he affirms, the wicked are punished. Job must return to God, give up his trust in gold (another fabricated charge), and pray to God; reformed, he will be God's favorite, capable of interceding with him on behalf of the guilty. Once again Eliphaz suggests he knows God's counsels; he cannot know that in the end his prediction will come true when Job prays to avert God's wrath from Eliphaz and his companions!

Job replies in a soliloquy (chs. 23–24) indirectly relating to Eliphaz. He would like to find God, not in order to repent, but to argue his case before him, for he is sure he would be cleared; but he finds him nowhere. He would emerge as pure gold from a test, and God knows it, yet the deity capriciously harasses him. A list of crimes committed by the wicked now appears, intertwined with a description of the downtrodden, and ending with the cutting reproach "Yet God does not regard it unseemly!" (24:12). After describing a trio of "rebels against the light"—murderer, thief, and adulterer, who shun the light of day—the speech becomes unintelligible till its last defiant line: "Surely no one can give me the lie/or set my words at naught" (24:25).

Bildad's third speech (ch. 25) is a mere six verses, a doxology consisting chiefly of a repetition (for the second time; see 15:14–16) of Eliphaz's threadbare oracle (cf. 4:17–21). The following speech of Job contains a doxology that might well continue this one (26:5–14); indeed many critics have taken it for the misplaced end of Bildad's speech. But an alternative interpretation is commendable for its piquancy: "Bildad's speech is short and sounds like what Job says in reply precisely because Job cuts him off and finishes the speech for him."[4] Such mimicry accords with the tenor of the beginning of Job's speech, in which he derides Bildad's rhetorical impotence and suggests that even his banalities are not his own ("Whose breath issued from you?" 26:4). Job demonstrates with great flourish that he can better anything Bildad does. When the Friends are reduced to repeating one another and Job can say their pieces for them, we know that the dialogue has ended.

And indeed Zophar has nothing to say in this third round. To be sure, critics have identified his "lost speech" in the next speech of Job: 27:13 is a variant of the conclusion of Zophar's last speech (20:29)—picking up as it were where he ended—and the subsequent description of the doom of the wicked continues Zophar's specific theme of dispossession. That these two passages are connected can hardly be in doubt, but is the latter an alien intrusion into Job's speech? Its context permits another explanation.

After waiting in vain for Zophar to speak, Job (ch. 27) resumes his address (aptly not called a reply) with an oath invoking (paradoxically) "God who has deprived me of justice" (v. 2). He affirms his blamelessness against his Friends' vilification. He will hold on to his integrity (an echo of 2:3, 9) as long as he lives, for God destroys the impious who contend with him. He offers to teach his Friends "what is with the Almighty" (27:11)—perhaps a reference to wisdom (cf. "it is not with me," 28:14, and "[What do] you understand that is not with us?" 15:9), in respect of which the Friends held themselves superior to Job (15:9–10). For now, they must stop talking the nonsense that their own experience contradicts (27:12). As an example of such nonsense Job then offers what Zophar might have said had he spoken, in a second display of expert mimicry.

Still formally part of Job's speech is the sublime poem on wisdom that follows (ch. 28)—the wisdom by which the world is governed, by which the meaning of events is unlocked. Man knows how to ferret precious ores out of the earth; he conquers the most daunting natural obstacles in order to obtain treasure. But he does not have a map to the sources of wisdom. The primeval waters, Tehom and the sea, do not contain it; farsighted birds of the sky do not know its place; Death (the realm next to divinity) has heard only a rumor of it. God alone, whose control of the elements of weather exemplifies his wide-ranging power, comprehends it. For man he has appointed, as its functional equivalent, the obligation to fear God and shun evil—wherewith he adjusts himself to the divine order.

The topic of this poem and its serene resignation seem out of place at this juncture. Critics generally excise the poem from its context, though some ascribe it nonetheless to the author of the dialogue. It is a self-contained piece having only tangential connections with its environment, but these may account for its location. The mention of silver in the first line links the poem to the preceding description of the wicked man's loss of his silver (27:16–17). More substantial is the possible connection with Job's undertaking to teach his Friends "what is with the Almighty" (27:11), preparatory to which they should stop talking nonsense. If, as was suggested above, this is a reference to wisdom, which is with God alone, then the Friends' parade of assurance that they know the reason for Job's suffering is sheer presumption. As the medieval exegete Naḥmanides put it, "He instructed them to say, 'I don't know.'"[5] A closer paraphrase might be: abandon your futile doctrine; it is a reproach to you and will not gain you God's favor. This is Job's last word to his Friends.

Job's speech in chapters 27 and 28 is framed by phrases that echo his initial characterization in the prose tale. At the beginning, the expressions "I will maintain my integrity/I will hold on to my righteousness" (27:5–6) recall God's praise: "he still holds on to his integrity" (2:3). At the end, the human equivalent of wisdom is "to fear the Lord and shun evil" (28:28), the very traits of which, according to the story, Job was a paragon. Between these appears Job's arraignment of God and his friends, and the denial that wisdom is accessible to man. Taken together, these evince the sheer heroism of a naked man, forsaken by his God and his friends and bereft of a clue to understand his suffering, still maintaining faith in the value of his virtue and in the absolute duty of man to be virtuous. The universe has turned its back on him, yet Job persists in the affirmation of his own worth and the transcendent worth of unrewarded good. Perhaps this is the sense of the difficult passage in 17:8–9:

> The upright are appalled at this [Job's fate];
> The innocent man is aroused against the impious [Job's Friends];
> The righteous man holds to his way [despite it all];
> He whose hands are pure grows stronger.

If such is the gist of this complex speech, it marks a stage in Job's reconciliation with God, undercutting the climax in chapter 42. But did the ancient poet share our predilection for the single climax? He has depicted Job attaining to peaks of confidence several times, only to relapse into despondency. The same may hold true for Job's making his peace with his fate and with God.

Job's final speech, a long soliloquy (chs. 29–31), reverts even more explicitly to his former state as "the greatest of all the dwellers in the east." He recollects pathetically his past glory, the awe in which he was held, his regal patronage of the needy and helpless (a pointed refutation of Eliphaz's gratuitous accusations); how he looked forward to living out his days in happiness, surrounded by his family and honored by society "like a king among his troop, as one who comforts mourners" (29:25). Instead he now drinks bitter drafts of insult from a rabble "whose fathers I would have disdained to put among my sheepdogs" (30:1). Once again he describes his suffering—God's cruel enmity toward him—ending his lament with a line contrasting with the conclusion of the previous picture: "My lyre is given to mourning,/my pipe to accompany weepers" (30:31).

In the last section of the soliloquy (ch. 31), Job forcefully affirms his blamelessness in a form derived from the terminal curse-sanctions of covenants. The biblical models are Leviticus 26 and Deuteronomy 28: If Israel obeys the stipulations of the Covenant, it will prosper, if not, it will suffer disaster upon disaster. Attention is directed to this traditional pattern by allusion to a "covenant" Job made with his eyes not to gaze on a maiden (31:1). In the immediate sequel he spells out the classic covenantal doctrine by which he has guided his steps: "Surely disaster is appointed for the iniquitous:/trouble for the wrongdoer" (31:3). (In the retrospective light of this conception, all of Job's speeches assume the character of a "covenant lawsuit" in reverse: man accusing God, instead of God accusing man [Israel] as in the books of the Prophets.) In the thin guise of self-curses Job recites a catalogue of his virtues—the code of a nobleman who does not allow his status to weaken his solidarity with the unfortunate. The virtues come in bundles and are interrupted by an only occasional self-curse ("If I did not practice such and such a virtue, may this or that calamity overtake me"), indicating that the pattern (in which normally the curses are prominent) is more form than substance—a vehicle serving the double purpose of marking a conclusion (the function of covenant curses) and of manifesting the unbroken spirit of Job. The latter is underlined by Job's wish that his Litigant produce a bill of indictment: he would display it as an ornament, so sure is he that it would prove him righteous!

Having played out their parts, the Friends fell silent; now Job falls silent, and the scene assumes the form it had before the dialogue began. But there is a tension in the air: will the Litigant respond?

Resolution of the tension is delayed by the sudden appearance of a new character: angry at the Friends for their inability to answer Job otherwise than by declaring him a sinner, and at Job for justifying himself against God, brash young Elihu the Buzite takes possession of the stage (chs. 32–37). He excuses his intervention by citing the impotence of his elders and delivers himself of three highly wrought speeches, full of obscure language and not always to the point. Though insisting he will not repeat what has been said (32:14), he does go over familiar ground; new are the grandiloquence and the occasional argument in favor of positions already taken. Thus to Job's charge that God does not answer, Elihu replies (off the point) that God speaks to man through dreams and illness designed to humble man's pride and turn him from his bad course (Eliphaz said as much in 5:17–18, but without elaborating the suffering and later confession and thanksgiving of the penitent). He counters Job's complaint of God's injustice by affirming, tautologically, that the sole ruler of the earth cannot do wrong, since it is of the essence of rulership to be just. From the transcendence of God Eliphaz had argued that man's works cannot interest him (22:2–3); Job had reasoned from the same fact of transcendence that even if he sinned, it could scarcely matter to God (7:20); Elihu advances the thought that the good and evil that men do cannot affect God, but only other men. Hence—if we understand 35:9

rightly—human misery has its cause in human evil; yet God is not indifferent, and in the end he punishes the guilty. Elihu's last speech opens with an interpretation of the suffering of the virtuous as disciplinary, and concludes with a rhapsodic paean to God's greatness as evidenced in the phenomena of rain, thunder, and lightning.

Elihu has indeed championed God's cause without condemning Job (except in 34:8: Job makes common cause with the wicked); his ornate eloquence has contributed color but little substance to the debate. Critics consider his speeches redundant and hence from another hand or at least outside the original plan of the book. But if repetition is an indication of unoriginality, considerable tracts of the dialogue of Job and his Friends would have to be declared secondary. The pattern of alternating dialogue is absent in Elihu's section, but it has already lapsed in the last spell of Job's oratory. Elihu's style is different from that of his predecessors, but might not that difference be intentional, to distinguish impetuous youthfulness from more deliberative age? Our author may simply have sought another character through which to display rhetorical invention. Indeed, can a better reason be given for the extension of the dialogue for three rounds than the delight of the poet in the exercise of his gift? This very motive animates the ancient Egyptian composition called "The Eloquent Peasant," whose thematic similarity to Job has been observed: A peasant who has been robbed pleads his cause before the governor; the king, who is told of the peasant's eloquence, deliberately delays judgment of the case so as to enjoy more and more of it. By this device the author gains scope for exercising his skill in playing variations on a few themes. (A modern editor's evaluation of the piece recalls evaluations of Elihu's speeches: "The peasant's speeches are, to modern taste, unduly repetitive, with high-flown language and constant harping on a few metaphors.")[6] Be that as it may, the unconventional representation of youth outdoing age bespeaks the author of the rest of the poem, whose hallmark is subversion of tradition. Elihu has marginally surpassed the Friends in affirming that God does speak to man, that not all suffering is punitive, and that contemplation of nature's elements opens the mind to God's greatness—a line of apology for God that does not entail blackening Job's character. We are on the way to God's answer from the storm.

The chief problem raised by God's answer to Job (chs. 38–41) is to relate the panorama it paints of God's amazing creativity to the issues the interlocutors have been wrestling with.

In opening his speech (chs. 38–39), God exchanges roles with Job: Till now, Job has demanded answers from God; now God sets unanswerable questions to Job about the foundations of the universe. Does Job know anything about the fashioning and operation of the cosmic

elements—earth, sea, the underworld, and darkness? Has he knowledge of, can he control, the celestial phenomena of snow, hail, thunder, and lightning, or the constellations? From these spectacles of
nature God turns to wilderness animals and their provisioning: the
lions, who lie in ambush for their prey; the raven, whose young cry to
God for food; the mountain goats, whose birth only God attends; the
wild ass, who roams far from civilization; the wild ox, who mocks
man's attempt to subjugate him; the silly ostrich; the war horse, with
his uncanny lust for battle; the soaring falcon and eagle, who sight
their prey from afar. None owe man anything; the ways of none are
comprehended by him.

How different this survey of creation is from that of Genesis 1 or
the hymn to nature of Psalm 104. Here man is incidental—mainly an
impotent foil to God. In Genesis 1 (and its echo, Ps. 8) teleology pervades a process of creation whose goal and crown is man. All is directed to his benefit; the earth and its creatures are his to rule. In
Psalm 104 nature exhibits a providential harmony of which man is an
integral part. But the God of Job celebrates each act and product of
his creation for itself, an independent value attesting his power and
grace. Job, representing mankind, stands outside the picture, displaced from its center to a remote periphery. He who would form a
proper judgment of God cannot confine himself to his relations with
man, who is, after all, only one of an astonishing panoply of creatures
created and sustained in ways unfathomable to the human mind.

Instead of confessing his ignorance and, by implication, his
presumptuousness, in judging God, Job replies (40:3–5) that he is too
insignificant to reply; that he can say no more. This response, as
Saadya Gaon observed in the tenth century, is ambiguous: "When one
interlocutor says to his partner, 'I can't answer you,' it may mean that
he acquiesces in the other's position, equivalent to 'I can't gainsay the
truth'; or it may mean he feels overborne by his partner, equivalent to
'How can I answer you when you have the upper hand?'"[7] In order to
elicit an unequivocal response, God speaks again.

In language identical with that of the first speech, God declares he
will put questions to Job: "Would you impugn my justice,/condemn
me, that you may be right?" (40:8). Job has dwelt on the prosperity of
the wicked, attributing it to divine indifference or cruelty. God invites
Job to try his hand at righting wrongs, if he has the hand to do it:
"Have you an arm like God's?/Can you thunder with a voice like
him?" (40:9). If he can do better, God will sing his praises. Once
again, Job's ignorance and impotence are invoked to disqualify him
from arraigning God; only one who comprehends the vastness and
complexity of God's work can pass judgment on his performance. To
drive home Job's powerlessness, two monstrous animals are described

that mock the Genesis notion of man's rule of terrestrial and sea creatures. Behemoth, a land animal, is briefly described: his muscles are
powerful, his bones like metal bars. Leviathan, a denizen of the waters, is a living fortress, whose parts evoke shields and military forma-
tions; flames and smoke issue from him; no weapon avails against him;
his tracks are supernally luminous; he lords it over the arrogant.

The effect of this parade of wonders is to excite amazement at the
grandeur and exotic character of divine creativity. By disregarding
man, the author rejects the anthropocentrism of all the rest of Scripture. God's governance cannot be judged by its manifestations in
human society alone. Had the moral disarray evident in society been
tolerated by a mere human ruler, other humans of like nature and motives would have been entitled to judge him as vicious. But no man can
comprehend God whose works defy teleological and rational categories; hence, to condemn his supervision of human events because it
does not conform to human conceptions of reason and justice is
improper.

Man's capacity to respond with amazement to God's mysterious
creativity, and to admire even those manifestations of it that are of no
use or benefit to him, enables him to affirm God's work despite its deficiencies in the moral realm. Such deficiencies, like so much else in
the amazing cosmos, stand outside human judgment. Chapter 28 has
already anticipated the conclusion at which Job must arrive in face of
God's wonders: for mankind wisdom consists of fearing God and shun-
ning evil; more than that he cannot know.

Job now submits unequivocally (42:2–6). He confesses his ignorance and his presumptuousness in speaking of matters beyond his
knowledge. Now that he has not merely "heard of" God–that is,
known of him by tradition—but also "seen" him—that is, gained direct cognition of his nature—he rejects what he formerly maintained
and "is consoled for [being mere] dust and ashes" (v. 6). Lowly creature that he is, he has yet been granted understanding of the inscruta-
bility of God; this has liberated him from the false expectations raised
by the old covenant concept, so misleading to him and his interlocutors.

The Adversary has lost his wager. Throughout his trial Job has neither rejected God (he has clung to him even in despair) nor ever expressed regret for having lived righteously (cf. Ps. 73:13–14). He thus
gave the lie to the Adversary's insinuation that his uprightness was
contingent on reward. Yet this last word of the poet does not pull all
things together. God's answer does not relate to the issues raised in
the dialogue; it seeks rather to submerge them under higher considerations. Although the poet rejects the covenant relation between God
and man with its sanctions of distributive justice, he offers no alterna-

tive. In effect, he puts the relation entirely on a footing of faith—in the language of the Adversary, "fearing God for nothing" (1:9).

The narrative epilogue (42:7–17) relates Job's rehabilitation. God reproaches Eliphaz, the chief and representative of the Friends, for not having spoken rightly about him as Job did. God thus seconds Job's protest in 13:7–10:

> Will you speak unjustly on God's behalf?
> Will you speak deceitfully for him? . . .
> He will surely reprove you
> if in your heart you are partial toward him.

God forbids a conception of himself as a moral accountant, according to which the Friends interpreted Job's suffering as punishment and Job ascribed injustice to God. Since the prayer of the injured on behalf of those who injured him is the most effective intercession (cf. Abraham's intercession for Abimelech, Gen. 20:7, 17), God orders the Friends to seek Job's intervention with him on their behalf (ironically, Eliphaz promised Job this power, 22:30). With this act of mutual reconciliation, Job is restored to his material and social position: His possessions are doubled (cf. Bildad's promise, 8:7), and he has children equal to the number of those reported dead by the messenger. Unlike 1:2, 42:13 does not state that the children "were born to him"; Nahmanides infers from this difference that the original children were restored, having been only spirited away by the Adversary[8]—a laudably humane, if unpersuasive, piece of exegesis. The story pays unusual regard to Job's daughters, noting their incomparable beauty, their exotic names—which may be rendered "Day-bright" (so ancient tradition understood *Yemima*), "Cassia" (a perfume-herb), and "Horn of Eye-Cosmetic"—and their equalization with their brothers as heirs, an egalitarian touch worthy of our unconventional author. Job dies at a ripe old age surrounded by four generations of his family (42:16; cf. 5:26, 29:18).

Critics have deemed this conclusion, yielding as it does to the instinct of natural justice, anticlimactic and a vulgar capitulation to convention; the common reader, on the other hand, has found this righting of a terribly disturbed balance wholly appropriate. In its reversal, the conclusion is of a piece with the rest of the book, so consistently subverting expectations and traditional values. Thus the story is set in motion by the Adversary's undermining the value of convenant-keeping piety, casting doubt on its disinterestedness. This instigates the immoral exercise of dealing the deserts of the wicked to pious Job in order to try his mettle—a perverse measure that cannot be avoided if doubts about his motives are to be allayed. Job, true to his character, blesses God even in adversity; however, soon thereafter he awakens to the moral disarray in the world and comes near blasphemy by accusing God of indiscriminate cruelty. Job despairs, yet continues to look to God for vindication. The Friends come to console, but exhaust themselves in vexatious arguments with Job; seeking his repentance, they incite him to ever bolder protest. They propose to teach him traditional wisdom; he ends by teaching them the inaccessibility of true wisdom. Job calls on God to present his bill of indictment, believing and not believing he will respond, and eager to present his defense. God does actually respond, but not to Job's questions; and Job has no answer at all. God rebukes Job for presumptuousness, but he also rebukes the Friends for misrepresenting him. Finally, when Job has resigned himself to being dust and ashes in the face of the cosmic grandeur revealed to him, God reverses his misfortune and smiles on him to the end of his life. The piquancy of these incessant turns of plot, mood, and character is heightened by the overarching ironies resulting from the union of the frame story and the dialogue. We see a handful of men striving vainly to penetrate the secret of God's providence, guessing futilely at the meaning of what they see, while we know that behind this specific case of suffering is a celestial wager. The effect of keeping the background setting and the foreground dialogue simultaneously in mind is almost vertiginous. For example, the Friends appear so far right in insisting, and Job so far wrong in denying, that God discriminates in his visitations—for a reason none can know. All are wrong in asserting that whether Job (man) sins or not is of no account to God. Job's sardonic charge that he is persecuted just because he is righteous is truer than any of the human characters can know. At the same time, the surface meaning of the dialogue is not invalidated: appearances do support Job's contention that God is indifferent to those who cling to him and smiles on the wicked; the Friends' depiction of society as a perfectly realized moral order is really nonsense. The beacon of the righteous is not hope of reward but the conviction that, for man, cosmic wisdom is summed up in the duty to fear God and shun evil, whether or not these virtues bear fruit. The misfortunes of the righteous ought not to imply a condemnation of God, in view of the grandeur and mystery of God's creative work at large.

Vacillating between the "truth" of the story and the arguments of the dialogue, the reader may be inclined to harmonize the two: The suffering of the righteous is, or may be, a test of the disinterestedness of their virtue. This of course can never be known to the sufferers or their neighbors; the case of Job is a stern warning never to infer sin from suffering (the error of the Friends), or the enmity of God toward the sufferer (the error of Job). Although such a harmonization may offer some consolation to Job-like suffering, it is not spelled out in the book. With its ironies and surprises, its claims and arguments in unresolved tension, the Book of Job remains the classic expression in world literature of the irrepressible yearning for divine order, baffled but never stifled by the disarray of reality.

THE POETRY OF JOB

The poetry of Job is a sustained manifestation of the sublime, in the classical sense of "exhibit[ing] great objects with a magnificent display of imagery and diction" and having "that force of composition . . . which strikes and overpowers the mind, which excites the passions, and which expresses ideas at once with perspicuity and elevation,"[9] It embraces an extraordinary range of objects of universal interest: emotions of serenity and terror, hope and despair; the contrasting characters of men; doubts about and affirmations of cosmic justice; the splendors and wonders of animate and inanimate nature. To be sure, these appear elsewhere in biblical literature, but only in the Book of Job are these themes expressed with such concentration, such invention and vivid imagery.

The poet makes use of the various genres of biblical lyric and sapiential poetry: the personal complaint of Psalms in Job's self-descriptions; the moral character portraits of Proverbs (the lazybones, the drunkard) in the depictions of the righteous and the wicked; the psalmic hymns in the doxologies, which in Job are sometimes straightforward and sometimes parodic. However, Job's brilliant descriptions of weather and animal phenomena and the evocation of man's exploration and exploitation of earth's resources have only rudimentary antecedents in earlier biblical poetry.

Innovative imagery pervades the book: the tree cut down that renews itself from its roots (14:7–9) as a metaphoric foil for man's irrevocable death; humanity's kinship with maggots (17:14) and jackals (30:29) as an image of alienation and isolation; the congealing of milk (10:10) as a figure for the formation of the embryo; the movement of a weaver's shuttle (7:6), of a runner in flight, or of the swooping eagle (9:25–26) as similes for the speedy passage of a lifetime; God's hostility figured as an attacking army (19:12); God's absence represented in the image of a traveler's unfound goal in every direction (23:8; a striking reversal of the expression of God's ubiquity in Psalm 139:7–10).

The diction of the poems is distinguished by lexical richness, with many unique, unusual, and "foreign" expressions, lending color to the non-Israelite setting and characters. For example, *'or*, besides its normal Hebrew sense of "light," seems to bear dialectical Aramaic senses of "evening" (24:14) and "west wind" (38:24); and there are many other terms that occur only in this book. There is much expressive repetition of sound (alliteration, assonance); the explosive *p* sound, for instance, dominates 16:9–14, a passage in which Job pictures himself as a battered and shattered object of God's pitiless assaults. Verbal ambiguity is abundantly exploited: *be'efes tiqwah* in the weaving image of 7:6 can mean "without hope" or "till the thread runs out"; in 9:30–31, the opposites *bor*, "soap," and *shahat*, "muck," are homonyms of two synonyms meaning "pit," thus conveying the suggestion "out of one pit into another." Contrariwise, the same expression recurs in different contexts, effecting cohesion while at the same time producing variety: The pair "vision/dream" serves as the vehicle of oracular experience (33:15), nightmares (7:14), or a figure of ephemerality (20:8); the pair "dust (dirt)/clay" expresses the qualities of insubstantiality (4:19), lifeless malleability (10:9), worthlessness (13:12), and multitude (27:16).

What quality in poetry makes it the preferred vehicle for this author's vision? Poetry was the form taken by sapiential observation and speculation throughout the ancient Near East. With its engagement of the emotions and the imagination, it was the usual mode of persuasive discourse. Through its compression, poetry allows stark, untempered expression that, while powerful in impact, awakens the kind of careful reflection that leads to the fuller apprehension of a subject. Moreover, the density of poetic language, compelling the reader to complement, to fill in gaps, fits it peculiarly for representing impassioned discourse, which by nature proceeds in associative leaps rather than by logical development. Spontaneous debate, too, is characterized by zigzag, repetitive, and spiral movement in which sequence is determined more by word and thought association than by linearity. Someone listening in to debate must supply the connections in a manner not very different from the complementing required for the comprehension of poetry. Such passionate argument is precisely reflected in the poetry of Job, as each interlocutor links theme to theme without troubling to arrange them according to logical sequentiallity, and by that very liberty enriching the connotations and multiplying the facets of the argument.

The poetry of Job is continually astonishing in its power and inventiveness. Its compression allows multiple possibilities of interpretation, corresponding to the open, unresolved tensions in the author's vision of reality. It is a beautifully appropriate vehicle for a writer bent on compelling us to see things in new ways.

NOTES

References

1. All translations in this essay are my own.
2. Rava, in Babylonian Talmud, Bava Batra, 16a.

3. Based on an interpretation of 12:22 in J. Gerald Janzen, *Job* (Atlanta, 1985), 104–05.

4. P. W. Skehan, "Strophic Patterns in the Book of Job," CBQ, 23 (1961):141.

5. Charles Chavel, ed., *Kitve Rabbenu Moshe ben Naḥman*, I (Jerusalem, 1964):86 (comment to 27:14).

6. W. K. Simpson, ed., *The Literature of Ancient Egypt* (New Haven, 1972), 31.

7. Yosef Kafaḥ, ed., *'Iyyov 'im Targum u-Ferush Ha-gaon Rabbenu Saadya* ... (Jerusalem, 1973), 198–99.

8. Chavel, *Kitve ... Naḥman*, I, 128.

9. Robert Lowth, *Lectures on the Sacred Poetry of the Hebrews*, translated by G. Gregory (London, 1847), 155.

Bibliography

L. L. Besserman, *The Legend of Job in the Middle Ages* (Cambridge, 1979).

Eugene Goodheart, "Job and the Modern World," *Judaism*, 10 (1961):21–28.

J. Gerald Janzen, *Job* (Atlanta, 1985).

Jack Kahn, *Job's Illness: Loss, Grief and Integration* (Oxford, 1975).

R. B. Sewall, *The Vision of Tragedy* (New Haven, 1956), 1–24.

Meir Weiss, *The Story of Job's Beginning, Job 1–2: A Literary Analysis* (Jerusalem, 1983).

J. W. Whedbee, "The Comedy of Job," *Semeia*, 7 (1977):1–39.

Additional note:

"Job the Patient and Job the Impatient" is the title of an analysis and reallocation of the material in the book presented by H.L. Ginsberg in *Conservative Judaism* 21 (1967), 12–28.

THE BIBLE IN JEWISH THOUGHT

Exegesis

1987

Jewish exegesis works with a canon, or a set of inspired books, subject to the following conditions: (1) the number and the text of these books are fixed and may not be added to or brought up to date; (2) the books are authoritative—that is, they bind the Jews to a certain world-view and way of life; (3) they are perceived as a harmonious whole, conveying a coherent divine message for the guidance of the individual and the community. Since the Jews have clung to this canon through the ages and amid the most diverse circumstances, an unbridgeable gap in understanding and perceived relevance might well have interposed between them and these books were it not for the succession of exegetes whose ever-renewing interpretation of the Bible maintained its vitality for the faith community. The continuing sacred status of the Bible among the Jews is due entirely to their faithful work.

The concerns of Jewish Bible exegesis arise from the aforesaid conditions: they include (1) how to enlarge the content of the closed canon so as to apply it to new topics; (2) how to render the fixed text pliable and subject to change in accord with arising cultural and intellectual needs; (3) how to relate to the original sense of Scripture after exegesis had departed from it; and (4) in modern times, how to maintain the sacred (or at least the special) status of the canonical literature in the face of scientific and historical challenges to the traditional conceptions of its truth and validity.

Among the earliest aims of exegesis was the application of prophecy to current events. In the mid-second century B.C.E., when the canon of the Prophets had long been closed, the Seleucid persecution of pious Jews in Judea awakened interest in the ancient prophecies of consolation. Daniel 9 records the solution of a contemporary visionary to the riddle of the delayed fulfillment of God's promise revealed to Jeremiah (in the sixth century B.C.E.) to restore Jerusalem's glory in seventy years: Seventy Sabbaths of years—that is, 490—were meant. The sectarians of the Qumran commune in the Judean desert read into the ancient prophecies allusions to their situation in the second or first centuries B.C.E. Thus, their commentary to Habakkuk 2:15 reads: "Its interpretation concerns the Wicked Priest [the archenemy of the sect] who pursued the Righteous Teacher [the inspired leader of the sect], to destroy him . . . in his exile abode, and at the appointed time of the rest-day of atonement appeared to them to destroy them and make them stumble [= err] on the Sabbath-day fast of their rest."

Legal exegesis derived new laws from the old scriptural ones, and connected traditional and innovated unwritten laws to biblical verses. For example, Hillel, in the first century B.C.E., once used three modes of interpretation in order to decide that the paschal sacrifice might be slaughtered even if it fell due on the Sabbath, when ordinary slaughter is forbidden. These were (1) analogy: since the regular daily offering is a public sacrifice and so is the paschal offering, the latter overrides Sabbath prohibitions, as does the former; (2) argument *a fortiori:* if the regular daily offering, for whose omission there is no penalty of excision, overrides the Sabbath prohibitions, the paschal offering, for whose omission that penalty is exacted, surely overrides it; and (3) argument from identical phrases: in both offerings the expression "in its appointed time" appears, hence rules governing the time of each are the same (PT Pesaḥim 33a). Seven hermeneutical principles or modes (*middot*) are ascribed to Hillel; Rabbi Ishmael, a second-century C.E. sage, is purported to be the author of an expanded list of thirteen.[1] Reference to these modes is surprisingly infrequent in Talmudic literature; in effect the constructive work of the legists proceeded very freely.

During this age of exuberant creativity, a period extending from the second century B.C.E. to the sixth century C.E., no preference was given to the plain (contextual) sense of the text over any other sense derived from or based on it, however fancifully. Indeed, it was a cardinal Talmudic principle that every biblical utterance was polysemous: alongside its contextual sense it might yield many others when taken in isolation. The principle was "heard" in a prophetic passage, itself treated as polysemous: "Behold, My word is like fire—declares the Lord—and like a hammer that shatters rock" (Jer. 23:29). Contextually, this means that overwhelming power and penetrating impact characterize genuine, as opposed to spurious, prophecy; isolated and interpreted as expressing an exegetical axiom, the passage is heard to say, "As a hammer[stroke] scatters many slivers (or sparks) so a single Scriptural passage yields many senses" (BT Sanh. 34a). A psalm text displaying a commonplace parallelistic number pattern (x / x + 1) when taken by itself serves as another proof-text for this axiom: " 'One thing God has spoken; two things have I heard' (Ps. 62:12)—a single Scriptural passage yields several senses, but one and the same sense cannot be derived from several passages" (ibid.). This axiom lies at the heart of the proliferation of Talmudic midrash, that searching (*darash*) of scripture for its latent meanings, its suggestions, and associations.

The danger to recognition of the plain sense posed by the prevalence of midrash is reflected in the warning principle: "The plain sense of a Scriptural passage is never superseded." An example of its operation is the following (BT Shab. 63a): Rabbi Eliezer ruled that a sword was an ornamental part of male attire, and hence might be worn on the Sabbath without violating the Sabbath ban on carriage, on the basis of the verse, "Gird your sword upon your thigh, O hero, in your splendor and your glory" (Ps. 45:4). Another sage protested: It was common knowledge that the verse had been interpreted allegorically, "sword" being Torah learning (and "hero" being the Talmudic sage; hence the verse could not serve to decide the status of a real sword). To this came the reply, "The plain sense of a Scriptural passage is never superseded"; that is, midrashic, "second" meanings—here the allegory—add to the primary one but never annul it (hence the Psalm verse may be invoked to prove that a sword is an ornament for a man). This assertion of the permanent validity of the primary, contextual sense, despite all hermeneutical reinterpretation, was repeatedly resorted to during the Middle Ages to defend the plain (historical) sense against subversion by Christian spiritualization and allegorization.

The luxuriance of Talmudic-midrashic exegesis turned the Bible into a treasury of meaning that has proven to be inexhaustible. Jewish interpreters through the ages have been shaped by it—some adopting it or continuing to create in imitation of it, some opposing its whimsicality in favor of a single, true sense of Scripture, and some simply reveling noncommittally and eclectically in its wealth.

Methodic Jewish Bible interpretation arose during the conflict between Talmudic Judaism and its adversaries during the early centuries of Islam, the seventh to tenth centuries C.E. Jews participated in the cultural ferment caused by the challenge of an Islam that was soon fortified by the best minds and philosophies of the age and that posed a threat to all traditional faiths and authorities. The most serious manifestation of dissolution among Jewry was the Karaite schism, inaugurated by Anan ben David during the eighth century; rejecting Talmudism in the name of rationalism and individualism, it sought legitimation by an independent and often capricious interpretation of

Scripture. For example, Anan rejected the Talmudic ban on eating meat with milk products by interpreting the proof-text, "You shall not boil a kid (*gedi*) in its mother's milk" (Exod. 23:19)—so greatly extended by the Talmud—to mean "Do not cause fruit (*meged*) to ripen by [daubing it with] sap of its tree."[2] By boldly metaphorizing the verb and the prepositional phrase, Anan obtained a meaning that related the clause to what precedes it, namely, the admonition to bring first-fruits to the temple. Furthermore, freethinkers both inside and outside of Jewry subjected all revealed Scripture to rationalistic criticism, ridiculing their anthropomorphism, their fabulous tales, and such theological scandals as sacrificial worship. Talmudism, at first helpless, eventually found its champion in Saadiah ben Joseph, Gaon of Sura (ninth to tenth centuries), who met these challenges by devising a methodic exegesis. The need, as Saadiah saw it, was to define the conditions in which the language of Scripture could or must be metaphorized, so that, on the one hand, the caprices of the Karaites might be controlled and, on the other, objections to the literal sense of Scripture might be parried. Saadiah formulated the following grand rule: the common, prevalent sense of words must determine the meaning of a passage, except when it would yield a meaning that conflicted with one of the four sources of knowledge: (1) the senses (that Eve was "the mother of all the living" [Gen. 3:20] cannot be taken literally); (2) reason ("the Lord your God is a consuming fire" [Deut. 4:24] cannot be taken literally, for while fire is a created thing, reason dictates that God is not); (3) a clear passage ("Do not try the Lord your God" [Deut. 6:16] is a clear passage that requires giving some kind of a figurative interpretation to Malachi 3:10, "Bring the full tithe ... and thus put me to the test"); (4) the oral (Talmudic) tradition ("You shall not boil a kid in its mother's milk" must be metaphorized so as to signify a ban on eating meat with milk). In other words, as revealed truth, the Bible must be reconcilable with the highest attainments of the human mind. The equation of the truths of reason and revelation asserted by Saadiah remained a governing principle of Jewish exegesis until its overthrow in the seventeenth century by Baruch Spinoza, who insisted that the meaning of Scripture could not be prejudged by the antecedent conviction that it was equivalent to the truth as determined through reason.

Subsequent Jewish exegesis is characterized by (1) its incorporation of the advances of Judeo-Spanish Hebrew philology—for example, the discovery of the triconsonantal nature of Hebrew roots, making possible a scientific grammar, etymology, and lexicography; utilization of Arabic, Aramaic, and postbiblical Hebrew to clarify obscurities in biblical Hebrew; (2) ever-increasing skill in, and preference for, ascertaining the plain sense—based on context and on parallel and analogous passages—and an awareness of the invalidity of midrashic interpretations as an exegetical resource (most impressive strides toward emancipation from midrash were made in the school of Rashi, eleventh to twelfth centuries); (3) a growing interest— particularly in reaction to Christian spiritualizing exegesis—in the historical context of prophecies, curbing Christological reference by setting the prophecies in a specific time frame (for example, David Kimhi).

From the vantage point of an exegete whose aim is to ascertain the primary sense of Scripture, premodern Jewish exegesis suffers from two disabilities. First, in matters legal and normative for religious practice, it submits to the authority of the Talmud, interpreting the Bible according to the pertinent Talmudic view (including the dogma of the supremacy of Moses' prophecy, which necessitated conforming all the rest of the Bible to it). This submission was, first of all, a response to Karaism, and then a reflection of the role of law as the bond of the Diaspora—the guarantor of unity and survival despite scattering and the temptations of heresy, apostasy, and freethinking. Its effect on the interpretation of biblical passages having legal implications is harmonizing and often enough distorting. It is the unusual commentator—for example, Samuel ben Meir, a grandson of Rashi— who shows independence of Talmudic authority in interpreting legal texts, although it is not clear, in most such cases, what motivates this merely academic exercise. On the other hand, in treating matter that has no normative implications, the outstanding commentators, such as Rashi, ibn Ezra, Nahmanides, and Abrabanel, have no compunctions about differing from the Talmud and among themselves. From time to time, in an entirely sporadic manner, a non-Talmudic interpretation of a legal topic may occur in the writings of one of these commentators, but its rarity only proves the rule.

The second disability of premodern exegesis is that in identifying the teaching of Scripture with the best current thought, most exegetes interpreted passages of ethical and theological import in accord with their favorite philosophical or mystical system. An example of the consequences is the particularly powerful effect of Bahya's *Hovot ha-Levavot* (*Duties of the Heart*) and Maimonides' *Guide of the Perplexed* on the exegesis of Psalms and the wisdom books (Proverbs, Ecclesiastes), markedly diminishing the medieval Jewish contribution to the understanding of the plain sense of these biblical books.

The issues of modern exegesis were posed by Baruch Spinoza in his *Theological Political Tractate*, published in 1670, in which he sought to dethrone Scripture and its traditional interpreters by separating the question of meaning from truth. Judgment of the truth content of the Bible, Spinoza declared, must follow upon the determination of what it means. That determination can rest only on a philological method analogous to the method of natural science: collection of data, classification, and, finally, generalization. In no way may information from outside the text of the Bible be imported into the determination of what its words mean. Knowledge of the historical context of the various books and their authors is also needed for ascertaining their sense. Since the intended audience of the prophets consisted of sinners and common folk, it was wrong to suppose that any sort of philosophic sophistication was requisite for understanding their message. On the contrary, Scripture addresses the imagination and the passions rather than reason; much of it is "unintelligible," that is, irrational. (The Jewish medieval commentators would not have disagreed with Spinoza about the method of ascertaining the plain sense of Scripture; they would have insisted, however, that it is but a cloak for higher ideas.)

With the advance of empirical sciences, modern exegesis did in fact relinquish the medieval claim that the Bible was a source of scientific and philosophic knowledge. Instead, it came to be appreciated for other virtues. In the eighteenth century, the aesthetic and poetic qualities of the Scriptures were discovered and carefully delineated by gentile and Jewish scholars such as Robert Lowth, Johann Gottfried Herder, Moses Hayyim Luzzatto, and Moses Mendelssohn. The ethical and moral excellence of the law and the prophets was stressed by Samuel David Luzzatto in the nineteenth century.

As biblical criticism broke down the integrity of the books of the Bible, assigning their composition to various hands and times, and as comparative data revealed more and more similarities between it and the literatures of neighboring peoples from which the Israelites most likely borrowed, Jewish exegesis of the twentieth century has developed along the following lines: (1) The Bible is approached as a "special" book whose divine origin is reflected in the spiritual riches it yields to the careful, reverent reader. While not assuming that the received text is perfect, the exegete, aware of the trail of discredited emendations of suspected corruptions made by earlier critics, is wary of adding to them by making further conjectural emendations of his own. And while not denying the genetic heterogeneity of any given book, he is chiefly concerned with its finally redacted, canonical form—whether because that alone is a fact of historical import, or because, with Franz Rosenzweig, he resolves the critical siglum R (for redactor) as *rabbenu* (our teacher), "For whoever he was and whatever material he had at his disposal, he is our Teacher, his theology, our Teaching."[3] Modern Jewish exegetes such as Benno Jacob, Franz Rosenzweig, Martin Buber, and Moses David Cassuto have concentrated their efforts on showing the design in the composition of biblical books and the leading motifs, key words, and ideas that link complexes into unities. In the wake of these efforts, a new appreciation of the art of storytelling and poetry is being gained, as in the work of Meir Weiss. Talmudic-midrashic literature is receiving new attention for the light it sheds on the principles of biblical composition (for example, association of ideas) and its illustration of exegetical processes that can be discerned as already present within the Bible itself (later texts building on earlier ones). (2) The comparative resources of ancient Near Eastern culture are exploited for showing not only what Israel held in common with its neighbors, but wherein it differed from them. This need not be (though it often is) motivated by apologetics, but by a sincere, scholarly pursuit of the individual character of biblical creativity.

Thus, the modern substitute for finding in Scripture the highest and best truths is to find in it design that bespeaks subtle intelligence, and an artful observation of and reflection on a reality that can still speak to the contemporary reader. Furthermore, the peculiarly Israelite character of the Bible, demonstrable by comparison, enables us to discern in it the origin of the ethos and the values comprising the Jewish expression through the ages. Jewish exegesis thus continues to serve the faith community by providing it access to its basic document that both edifies the community and enables it to retain its identity through continuity with its past.

NOTES

References

1. See W. S. Towner, "Hermeneutical Systems of Hillel and the Tannaim: A Fresh Look," in HUCA 53 (1982).
2. A. Harkavy, *Aus den ältesten Käraischen Gesetzbüchern* (1903), 151–52.
3. Franz Rosenzweig, "Die Einheit der Bibel," in Martin Buber and Franz Rosenzweig, *Die Schrift und ihre Verdeutschung* (1936), 47.

Additional note:

The earliest stage of biblical exegesis—"inner biblical–exegesis" (for the term, see Nahum Sarna, "Psalm 89: A Study in Inner Biblical Exegesis," in A. Altmann, ed., *Biblical and Other Studies* [Cambridge, Mass.: Harvard University Press, 1963], 29–46) is comprehensively treated in Michael Fishbane's *Biblical Interpretation in Ancient Israel* (Oxford: Clarendon Press, 1985).

A novel approach to the mentality of the Talmudists as exhibited in their biblical exegesis is David Weiss Halivni's *Peshat and Derash: Plain and Applied Meaning in Rabbinic Exegesis* (New York and Oxford: Oxford University Press, 1991).

Bibliography

Salo Baron, *A Social and Religious History of the Jews* 6 (1958), 253–313.
W. Bacher, "Bible Exegesis," in *Jewish Encyclopaedia* 3 (1902).
Moshe Greenberg, ed., *Parshanut ha-Mikra ha-Yehudit: Pirkei Mavo* (1983). Contains extensive bibliography.

Simon Rawidowicz, "On Interpretation," in Nahum N. Glatzer, ed., *Studies in Jewish Thought* (1974).

E. I. J. Rosenthal, "The Study of the Bible in Medieval Judaism," in G. W. H. Lampe, ed., *The Cambridge History of the Bible* 2 (1969), 252–79.

Franz Rosenzweig, "Die Einheit der Bibel," in Martin Buber and Franz Rosenzweig, *Die Schrift und ihre Verdeutschung* (1936), 46–54.

W. S. Towner, "Hermeneutical Systems of Hillel and the Tannaim: A Fresh Look," in HUCA 53 (1982).

Geza Vermes, *The Dead Sea Scrolls in English* (1962), 214–47.

Meir Weiss, *The Bible from Within* (1984).

Mankind, Israel, and the Nations
in the Hebraic Heritage
1971

If the needs of the hour seem to have outrun the resources of venerable religious bodies, this is due at least in part to a pious reluctance to sift critically the accumulated traditions they have received in order to distinguish the timeless and needful from the ephemeral and dispensable. The configuration of rites, ideas, and attitudes taught to the common people by today's religions often reflects a level of civilization and human interconnection long since past. Robert Redfield has described well the interaction of the moral and the technical orders and their relative progress:

> The unit of political life tends to become identified with a people who share a common moral life ... So the tribe, the city-state, the nation are such approximate identifications of equivalent units of society, peoples that are both a technical and a moral unit. Yet as one looks at any one of these politico-moral societal types ... one sees that the technical order, in the form of exchange of goods and in the conflict of war, has already gone beyond the politico-moral unit ... ; and one begins to look forward to the extension of the moral order to larger societal units, which will in turn call for political inventions. Today, some people, recognizing that the technical order has gone far beyond the national state, and that its destructive power threatens everyone, begin to argue that the peace of the world must be planned by all the peoples of the world ... and then, looking at the fact that these visions have come and begin to be transmuted into plans for action, one is required to admit that the fact that people speak as if world order and world peace must and will come about is itself influential in history... The idea that a world community is necessary is an idea created by devel-

opments in the technical order. This idea in turn influences the actual moral order to develop in its direction, and helps to bring about political inventions ... that would both express and create the enlarging moral order.[1]

The heritage of Judaism from biblical times onward contains a series of adjustments to change: of enlargements and contractions of outlook in accord with the experiences of Jews in the world. The latest formulations of that heritage are now centuries old.[2] They presuppose compact, internally autonomous Diaspora communities with no sense of a common destiny with the rest of pre-Messianic-age mankind. Attempts of eighteenth and nineteenth century European Jews to integrate their communities into the new nation-states by surrendering aspects of their distinctiveness injured their integrity without achieving the hoped-for results.[3] In the light of their twentieth century experience, Jews are torn between a deep doubt of the Gentiles' capacity to feel solidarity with them, and a need and desire greater than ever for harmonious relations with the rest of mankind. In this dilemma, work on the ecumenical front is promoted chiefly with the defensive aim of disposing Gentiles favorably toward Jews. However, as important as that effort is, it is equally necessary to consider what Jews as a religious community envisage as the ideal attitude toward the Gentiles. Unless Jews are aware of the terms on which, without loss of spiritual integrity, they can be at one with the world, such a union can hardly come about. These terms can be found in the received traditions of Judaism, but they must be highlighted and emphasized among the mass of inherited materials, while opposing conceptions must be recognized for what they are, and denied equal authority.

This essay attempts to delineate the Jewish conceptions of the unity of mankind and the postulates of Judaism's integration in the world. It draws upon the classic Hebraic sources: Scriptures and the rabbinic literature. The presentation is more conceptual than historical, and selective of what shows a constructive concern with the issue. Not an apology, it foregoes explaining (away) the anti-gentile elements of the tradition;[4] just enough of them as are needful for understanding the positive elements are adduced. By the same token, singular universalistic expressions are unnoticed except such as are attached directly to basic and pervasive notions. In sum, the testimonies offered here are believed representative of the essential Jewish teachings on our theme.[5]

ADAMITES (*BENE 'ADAM*)

Hebrew history begins not with the patriarch Abraham, but with the father of the human race, Adam. Its proper subject is man as the self-conscious creature and subject of God; Israel arrives on the scene late, after several fruitless experiments with previous generations of men.

The Hebrew valuation of man grew out of reflection upon the implications of the story of his creation as told in Genesis 1:26–27 and 5:1–2. The first couple—Adam ("man," popularly connected with *'adama* "earth"; i.e. "earthling") and Eve (*ḥawwa*, popularly connected with *ḥay* "living thing")—generated all mankind. Having a typical patriarchal viewpoint, the Bible depicts the entire human race as a family descended from a single father, and names it accordingly "Adamites" (children/sons of Adam/man; e.g., Ps. 115:16).[6]

The belief that man is in God's image serves as the rationale for regarding homicide as a capital offense. As the family of Noah started a new life after the Flood, God admonished them:

> Whoever sheds the blood of man
> By man shall his blood be shed;
> For in his image
> Did God make man. (Gen. 9:6)

It must be borne in mind that this appreciation of man extends to all men; it attaches to the ancestor of the race, not to Israelites alone, who have not yet come upon the stage of history. The creation story inspired the Psalmist to wonder at God's favor toward man:

> What is man that you have been mindful of him,
> Mortal man that you have taken note of him,
> That you have made him little less than divine,
> And adorned him with glory and majesty;
> You have made him master over your handiwork,
> Laying the world at his feet . . . (8:5–7)

God-like attributes attach to all human beings; they are not a specifically Israelite property.

Humans are the objects of God's special care. The earth was designed as their home; Eden was to be their abode. Even after their offense, and having condemned them to expulsion from Eden, "the Lord God made garments of skins for Adam and his wife, and clothed them" (Gen. 3:21). After the Flood, he renewed his gracious relationship to mankind, promising never again to destroy the world and confirming his goodwill by the token of the rainbow. Ever since creation God has sustained the world faithfully:

> The Lord is good to all
> And has compassion for all he has made . . .

You open your hand graciously
And give every living thing his fill. (Ps. 145:9, 16)

The point of the book of Jonah is God's impartial concern for the well-being of all his creatures: "Should I not care about Nineveh, that great city, in which there are more than a hundred and twenty thousand persons who do not yet know their right hand from their left, and many beasts as well!" (4:11). That the repentant Ninevites remain pagans matters not.

Being his creatures, all humans have access to God. Adam, Cain, Enoch, Noah were intimate with God. Abraham's contemporary, Melchizedek, was a priest of the Most High God (Gen. 14:18); king Abimelech of Gerar conversed with God in a night vision (20:4f.). The Mesopotamian wizard Balaam conversed with God and his angel (Num. 22:9ff., 31ff.). Jethro, the Midianite priest, sacrificed to God (Exod. 18:12); Solomon's temple was open to foreigners (1 Kings 8:41ff.); and the Aramaean officer Naaman undertook to worship God alone in his homeland (2 Kings 5:17). The law allowed the Gentile to sacrifice in an Israelite sanctuary (Leviticus 22:25 as understood by the Talmud, Temurah 7a), or—as the Talmud later put it explicitly— "to build himself a private altar and offer up whatever he wished on it" (Zebaḥim 116b).[7] That this actually occurred is the plain sense of the debated passage Malachi 1:11: "For from the rising of the sun to its setting my name is great among the nations, and in every place incense is offered to my name and a pure offering: for my name is great among the nations, says the Lord of hosts."[8] In this spirit, a late midrash affirms the impartial outpouring of the Holy Spirit upon any and all deserving mortals:

> I call heaven and earth to witness that whether it be Gentile or Jew, man or woman, slave or handmaid, according to the deeds that they do, so will the Holy Spirit rest on them. (Tanna deBe Eliyahu, 9 [p. 48])

The most profound expressions of the value of humans are found in Tannaitic reflections upon the creation story.

> [Rabbi Akiba] used to say: Beloved is man for he was created in the Image; extraordinary is the love in that it was made known to him that he was created in the Image, as it is said, "For in his image did God make man." (Gen. 9:6). (Abot 3.14[9])

In the course of admonishing witnesses in capital cases to tell the truth, the infinite worth of each human being was emphasized in this striking homily:

> For this reason was one single man created: to teach you that anyone who destroys a single life is as though he destroyed the whole of mankind, and anyone who preserves a single life is as though he preserved the whole of mankind;
>
> (and to foster harmony among men: that none might claim, "My ancestry is nobler than yours" ... ;)
>
> (and to show the greatness of God: for when man stamps many coins in one die they are all alike; but God stamped all men in the die of Adam, yet no two are alike);
>
> Therefore [since each of us is an Adam] everyone must say, "For my sake the world was created." (Sanhedrin 4.5)[10]

The implications drawn from the creation story with respect to humans are these: Man is dear to God, as his image; moreover, every man is equivalent to Adam, for whose sake the whole world was made; the multiplication of Adam's exemplars in no way diminishes the Adam-like worth of each exemplar. Hence arises the dignity of all human beings and the sanctity of their lives. Since all are descendants of father Adam, no people can claim to be racially superior to others, or essentially alien to or heterogeneous with their fellows. On this is founded the potentiality and the obligation of harmony among humans. Individual differences are esteemed as testimonies to the creative greatness of God.

The essentials of a comprehensive doctrine of the unity of humankind are to be found in this passage. We proceed to inquire into its ramifications in classical Hebrew thought.

NOACHITES AND RIGHTEOUS GENTILES

After the Flood, God laid down to Noah and his sons the terms of a new order. Taking note of changed conditions, he now permitted them to eat animals (who owed their very existence to humans)—on condition that flesh with its lifeblood still in it not be eaten. To take human life—cheap before the Flood and depreciated by it—was declared a capital offense, to be punished by a human agency; courts were thus authorized to execute killers (Gen. 9:1–7). The descendants of Noah—all mankind (Gen. 10)—were thus held accountable to a minimal number of divine commands.[11]

However, later divine punishments are neither justified by reference to these commands, nor are they inflicted for violations of them only (cf. the offense of the Sodomites [Gen. 19:5ff.]). Throughout biblical literature, the Gentiles are required to answer for breaking elementary moral laws, though nowhere is the ground for their responsibility set out. The moral impulse of Gentiles, what we might call their conscience, derives in the biblical conception from "god-fearing" (*yir'at 'elohim*)—a common human virtue that has no reference to knowledge of or revelations from the true God. It keeps them from murder (Gen. 20:11), adultery (39:9), and breach of faith (39:8f.; 42:18); lack of it accounts for Amalek's dastardly attack on Israel's stragglers (Deut. 25:18). Evidently this common property of all people is enough to make them accountable for wrongdoing despite their ignorance of God's laws (Ps. 147:20).

That the Gentiles' worship of "false gods" was a sin came to be a common doctrine only in Second Temple times. Deuteronomy 4:19 and 29:25 reflect the notion that the misdirected worship of the pagans was a divine ordinance. The first hints of a new attitude occur in Jeremiah 10:11, a polemical fragment against idolatry addressed to the pagans in Aramaic; in 50:38 idolatry appears to be held against a Gentile nation.[12] From here it is but a step to making the renunciation of false gods one of the minimal obligations of all people. This step was taken in the later formulation of the "Noachite laws."

Second Temple and rabbinic literature recognize universal standards of righteousness apart from the peculiar obligations of Judaism. The notion of Noachite laws binding upon all people becomes formalized while the "fear of God" is credited to a broad class of non-Jews who gave up belief in the pagan gods, inspired by Jewish example.

The Book of Jubilees, dated variously between the third and first centuries B.C.E., depicts Noah teaching his sons "the ordinances and commandments and all the judgments that he knew":

> and he exhorted his sons to observe righteousness,
> and to cover the shame of their flesh,
> and to bless their Creator,
> and to honor father and mother,
> and love their neighbor,
> and guard their souls from fornication
>   and uncleanness and all iniquity . . .
> Whoso sheddeth man's blood, and whoso
>   eateth the blood of any flesh,
> Shall be destroyed from the earth . . . (7:20–39)

The Talmud and Midrash canonized this notion in lists of commandments believed to have been given to Adam and supplemented in a new revelation to Noah. The generally accepted list consists of seven items, with respect to (1) idolatry, (2) blasphemy, (3) homicide, (4) incest and adultery, (5) robbery, (6) eating the flesh of a live creature, (7) establishing a system of justice.[13] Although in theory these commandments were explicitly revealed to Adam and Noah, what they prohibited was thought to be self-evident to any human mind and conscience:

> *"You must keep my rulings"* (Lev. 18:5): This refers to injunctions of the Torah which, had they not been written in it, by right should have been written, such as (prohibition of) robbery, incest, idolatry, blasphemy, and homicide. (Sifra, Aḥare Mot, *ad loc.*)

During Hellenistic-Roman times there were many Gentiles who, disillusioned with paganism and attracted by the faith and mode of living of Jews, renounced the gods and adopted rudiments of Jewish observance. While in no sense regarded as Jews, such persons were esteemed as "fearers of God" (*yir'e šamayim*); they were held beloved by God and assured of their ultimate reward.[14]

> *The Lord loves the righteous* (Ps. 146:8): Says the Holy One, blessed be he: *I love those who love me* (Prov. 8:17) . . . Why does the Holy One, blessed be he, love the righteous? Because they are not what they are through heredity or lineage. You find that priests are a family, Levites are a family—*O house of Aaron, bless the Lord! O house of Levi, bless the Lord* (Ps. 135:19f.). If someone wants to become a priest or Levite, he cannot, since his father was not of their family. But if a man wants to be righteous, even being a Gentile he can be, since the righteous are not a family. Hence it says, *O you fearers of the Lord, bless the Lord!* not, "O house of fearers of the Lord," but simply "fearers," since they are not a family, but came by their own impulse to love the Holy One, blessed be he. That is why he loves them . . . (Numbers Rabba, 8.2)

> R. Eliezer says: Gentiles have no place in the world to come; it says, *Let the wicked go back to Sheol, all nations who have forgotten God* (Ps. 9:18) . . . R. Joshua replied: Had it said, "Let the wicked go back to Sheol, all nations" and stopped, I should agree. But since it adds "who have forgotten God," I infer that there are righteous among the nations who have a place in the world to come. (Tosefta Sanhedrin, 13,2).

These ideas were synthesized in the definition of the resident alien (*ger tošab*)—the Gentile who may live in Jewish territory. Of various theoretical definitions (theoretical because formulated after loss of Jewish independence) the most widely accepted was: the Gentile who observes the seven Noachite laws (e.g., Aboda Zara 64b, 65a). An eighth century midrash sums up the discussion:

> The difference between the righteous Jew and the righteous Gentile is this: a Jew is not considered righteous unless he observes the whole Torah. But a Gentile is considered righteous if he keeps the seven commandments laid upon the Noachites—them and their ramifications,[15]

and on condition that they understand their obligation to stem, through their ancestor Noah, from the command of God. If they keep them in this spirit, they have a share in the world to come just like Jews—despite their non-observance of Sabbaths and holydays, which they were never commanded to keep. If, however, they kept the seven commandments because they believed them instituted by some human authority, or as a dictate of reason; or if they ascribed a partner to God, they receive a reward in this world only.[16] (Mishnat R. Eliezer, vi [Enelow, 121])

Thus not only are all humans as Adamites a single family, precious in God's sight, but by observance of the universal moral laws laid upon the Noachites they may be perfectly reconciled with God and enjoy the ultimate bliss. The consequence of the classical Jewish doctrine of man was that for his salvation neither Israel nor the Torah were, strictly speaking, necessary.

Historically, however, the Noachites had refused to accept their obligations; the nations were ignorant of the true God and barbaric in their conduct (cf. Aboda Zara 2bff.). While the individual Noachite might be a Godfearer, for the salvation of the race a catalytic became necessary. That role was assigned to Israel.

ISRAELITES

The effort of the builders of the Tower to defy God ended with the division of humankind into many nations and tongues; since henceforth the nations are depicted as idolatrous, a general falling away from God seems to have ensued. As the remedy to this frustration of his design, God chose Abraham to father a special nation "to instruct his . . . posterity to keep the way of the Lord by doing what is just and right" (Gen. 18:19).[17] The special relation of Israel to God was announced to the assemblage of the people just before the Sinaitic theophany:

> You have seen what I did to the Egyptians,
> How I bore you on eagles' wings and brought you to me.
> Now then, if you will obey me faithfully
> And keep my covenant,
> You shall be my treasured possession among all the peoples;
> Indeed all the earth is mine,
> But you shall be to me
> A kingdom of priests
> And a holy nation. (Exod. 19:4–6)

Comparison of the covenant laws of Israel with other law collections of antiquity reveals the sense of the phrases "kingdom of priests and holy nation."

> Religious laws are . . . rare in the Hittite law collection and altogether missing in the Mesopotamian ones. In contrast to Israel, these peoples did not consider themselves "kingdoms of priests and holy nations." The individual among them addressed the gods through the king, who was the chief priest, or through his priests, who served as his deputies. The community at large had only a small part to play in the public worship. A body of cult rules that bound every man did not exist among them, hence they saw no need to set out the details of such rules in legislation.[18]

In Israel, on the other hand, the very purpose of the covenant was to draw the whole people near to God—as he had intended all of the human race to have been. Both the standard of conduct and ritual obligations elsewhere pertaining to priests were laid in Israel upon everyone. Priestly food taboos (Lev. 22:8; Ezek. 44:31) were extended to all Israelites (Exod. 22:30; Deut. 14:21), with the same rationale: you must be consecrated to me. Mourning rites banned to priests (Lev. 21:5f.) were forbidden to the laity (19:28) for the same reason: "You are a people holy to the Lord" (Deut. 14:2).

A high moral standard of holiness was also imposed on Israel. Leviticus 19 opens with the charge: "You shall be holy, for I, the Lord your God, am holy"; this was later understood as a call to imitate God:

> Abba Saul said: What is the duty of the king's retinue? To do what the king does. (Sifra, *ad loc.*)

The chapter proceeds to spell out the meaning of holiness in moral and ceremonial terms: observance of the Sabbath, reverence of parents, rejection of idolatry, leaving the due of the poor in field and vineyard, not lying or stealing or perjuring oneself, loving one's fellow as oneself, loving the stranger as oneself, and more.

What were the limits of the covenant group? Despite its name "Israel(ites)" the group in fact included anyone who wished to be included in it. The Exodus story mentions a "mixed multitude" (Exod. 12:38) who accompanied the Israelites; the Passover regulations anticipate the presence of non-Israelites in the future community, and allow for their taking part in the celebration (vv. 43–49).

"There shall be one law for the citizen and for the stranger (*ger*) who dwells among you" (Exod. 12:49; Num. 9:14) is a recurrent injunction of the corpus of priestly laws (just where we might have expected the rigorous exclusion of aliens!). In Leviticus 24:22 it concludes rules of civil and criminal responsibility; it recurs thrice in the sacrificial ordinances of Numbers 15:15f., 29. Equation of citizen and resident alien occurs in Leviticus 17:8, 10, regarding sacrifice and the ban on blood; in 20:2, prohibiting Molech worship; in Numbers 35:15, regarding the privilege of asylum in the cities of refuge.

The protection of the resident alien (*ger*) along with the native weak and needy is frequently commanded (e.g., Lev. 19:10, 33f.; Deut. 16:11ff.; 24:14f., 17, 19, 20, 21; 26:11f.; 27:19; or Exod. 22:20–23). Peak expressions of solicitude are Leviticus 19:33f.:

> When a stranger resides with you in your land, you shall not wrong him. The stranger who resides with you shall be as one of your citizens; you shall love him as yourself, for you were strangers in the land of Egypt; I the Lord am your God.

And Deuteronomy 10:17f.:

> For the Lord your God ... shows no favor and takes no bribe, but upholds the cause of the fatherless and the widow, and loves the stranger, providing him with food and clothing. You too must love the stranger, for you were strangers in the land of Egypt.

Prophetic denunciation of social wrongs often includes the stranger among the native oppressed (Jer. 7:6; Ezek. 22:7; Zech. 7:10; Mal. 3:5).

According to Deuteronomy the strangers in Israel actually took part in the covenant ceremony concluded just before Moses' death (Deut. 29:10). As a consequence, in the septennial public recitation of the Torah, the stranger must be present alongside the native "to learn to fear the Lord, your God" (31:12).

Thus the covenant community of Israel was open to non-Israelites from the start. Doubtless, the resident alien suffered disabilities owing to lack of family and precarious economic circumstances. He had no share in tribal land—an inequity which Ezekiel took care to remove in his ideal legislation for the future commonwealth (47:22f.). Nonetheless, Leviticus 25:47 contemplates a stranger's rising above Israelites, and the historical books show that foreigners were particularly welcome in the royal courts and received high offices.[19]

Living within the community, the stranger gradually assimilated to it. Ruth's declaration of fidelity to Naomi epitomizes the process: "Your people shall be my people and your God my God" (Ruth 1:16). The discrepancy between Deuteronomy 14:21 and Leviticus 17:15 respecting the stranger's obligation to observe a food taboo bespeaks some vacillation with regard to the extent he was required to follow the finer points of the law. Yet there can be little doubt that within a generation or two his family was indistinguishable from native-born Israelites.

Even the exiled community of Judahites in Babylonia remained open to foreigners who wished to join it, and—what is more remarkable—there were foreigners who, in spite of the Judahites' low fortunes, actually entered the exilic community. We know this from Isaiah 56:2–8, the germane parts of which merit full citation:

Happy the man who does this,
The Adamite who holds it fast—
Who keeps the sabbath unprofaned
And keeps his hand from doing any evil.
Let not the alien who has attached himself to the Lord say
"The Lord will separate me from his people (when he restores
  them to their land)" . . .
The aliens who attach themselves to the Lord, to minister to him,
To love the name of the Lord and be his servants—
  Everyone who keeps the sabbath unprofaned
And holds my covenant fast—
I will bring them to my holy mountain,
And make them joyful in my house of prayer;
Their burnt offerings and their sacrifices shall be welcome upon my
  altar,
For my house shall be called a house of prayer for all the peoples.
This is the oracle of the Lord God,
Who gathers the outcasts of Israel;
I will yet gather to them others beside their own gathered ones!

The readiness of strangers to join this politically crushed community is not more astonishing than its accepting them; in the very midst of a profound existential crisis, it would have been natural for the exiles to have closed ranks tightly. That this did not happen testifies to the radical hospitality of Israel to foreigners—a hospitality ultimately grounded on a self-conscious representation of God's interest among men.

PROSELYTES[20]

Even the earliest traditions ascribe to Israel's history a significance transcending its national boundaries. Israel being the arena of activity of the one, universal God, what happened in it had worldwide repercussions and determined the reputation of the true God among all men (Exod. 15:14ff.; Josh. 2:8ff.; 1 Sam. 4:8). On that basis Moses appealed to God to renounce his plans to destroy Israel in the desert (Exod. 32:12; Num. 14:13–16), the Psalmists pleaded for help (e.g., 83:19; 115:1ff.), and Ezekiel assured his hearers that God must restore his shattered people in their land (36:22–36).

The greater the devotion to God, the more intense the desire to see his fame spread among men—in rabbinic terminology, "to sanctify God's name." Foreigners were encouraged to "try" Israel's God, to learn his power and responsiveness. A passage in Solomon's temple prayer concerning the alien expresses this pious sentiment and its ramifications perfectly:

> Then also as to the alien, who is not of your people Israel, but comes from a far country for your name's sake—for they shall hear of your great name, and your mighty hand and of your outstretched arm—when he shall come and pray toward this house, may you hear in the heaven your dwelling-place and do according to whatever the alien petitions you, that all the peoples of the earth may know your name, to fear you as do your people Israel ... (1 Kings 8:41–43)

The spirit in which Elisha undertook to cure the Aramaean Naaman's leprosy was the same ("Let him know that there is a prophet in Israel!" [2 Kings 5:8]); while Naaman's confession upon being cured ("Truly I know now that there is no God in all the earth but in Israel!" [v. 15]) and his conversion to the sole worship of Israel's God (v. 17) are models of the desired effect of such a trial.

As long as it was necessary to journey to the land of Israel to try Israel's God, conversions of outsiders to his worship must remain few. With the creation of the Diaspora, Gentile contact with Jews became much more common; Isaiah 56 shows what effects the ardent faith of even a band of exiles could have on their surroundings. Accessibility of Jewish teaching was much furthered in Second Temple times by the canonization of the Torah (5th century B.C.E.), and the constitutional function of the Torah resulted in a definition of the Jewish nation as that whose life was directed by its teaching. Add to this the increase in individualism within as well as without Judaism in the Hellenistic period, and the ingredients of a new phenomenon, religious conversion (as opposed to ethnic-cultural assimilation) are all at hand.

The success of Judaism in winning converts during the centuries just before and after the turn of the era resulted from the propaganda efforts of considerable numbers of Jews—the Hellenistic-Jewish work produced in Egypt being the parade example[21]—and the receptivity of the Jews toward the newcomers. That propaganda for God was a duty is the message of a homily applying to Israel, as God's witness, the injunction not to suppress testimony (Lev. 5:1).

> *Though he is a witness* (Lev. 5:1)—"And you are my witness, says the Lord, and I am God" (Isa. 43:12);
> *whether he has seen*—"To you it was shown, that you might know" (Deut. 4:35);

or come to know the matter—"Know, therefore, and lay it to your
heart [that the Lord is God ... there is none else]" (Deut. 4:39);
yet he does not speak, he shall bear his iniquity—Said the Holy
One, blessed be he, to Israel: "If you will not speak my
Godhood among the nations of the world I will punish you for
it" ... (Lev. Rabba 6.6)

Attracting Gentiles to God was a manifestation of love of fellow humans. Hillel urged to "love mankind and draw them to the Torah"
(Abot 1.12). Abraham exemplified Hillel's saying:

This teaches that one should bend men to and lead them under the
wings of the Shekinah the way Abraham our father used to bend men
to and lead them under the wings of the Shekinah. And not Abraham
alone did this, but Sarah as well; for it is said, *And Abram took Sarai his
wife and Lot his brother's son, and all their substance that they had
gathered, and the souls that they had made in Haran* (Gen. 12:5). Now,
not all the inhabitants of the world together can create even a single
gnat! How then does the verse say, *And the souls that they had made in
Haran?* This teaches that the Holy One, blessed be he, accounted [the
converting of Gentiles] to Abraham and Sarah as though they had made
them. (Abot de Rabbi Nathan A, 12 [trans. Goldin, 68])

Since the Septuagint renders *ger* mostly by "proselyte" (incidentally attesting the institution of religious conversion as early as the
third pre-Christian century), it is clear that all the ordinances favoring
aliens and equating them to the native Israelite were applied to proselytes. Philo emphasizes the welcome given proselytes by the Torah:

[The lawgiver] holds that the incomers too should be accorded every
favor and consideration as their due, because, abandoning their kinsfolk by blood, their country, their customs, and the temples and images
of their gods, and the tributes and honors paid to them, they have
taken the journey to a better home ... He commands all members of
the nation to love the incomer, not only as friends and kinsfolk but as
themselves both in body and soul: in bodily matters, by acting as far as
may be for their common interest; in mental, by having the same griefs
and joys, so that they may seem to be the separate parts of a single living being ... (*On Virtues*, 102–103)

Rabbinic homilies dwell upon the proselyte's merits:

Dearer to God is the proselyte, who has come to him of his own accord, than all the crowd of Israelites who stood at Mount Sinai! For had
the Israelites not witnessed the thunders and lightnings, the quaking
mountain and the blaring trumpet, they would not have accepted the

Torah. But the proselyte without having seen any of these things comes and gives himself to the Holy One, blessed be he, and takes upon himself the yoke of Heaven. Can anyone be dearer to God than this man? (Tanhuma Buber, Lek Leka, 6)

On the basis of Deuteronomy 29:14 it was affirmed that all future converts were present with Israel and entered the covenant from the first (Shebuot 39a).

The regnant view was that all were welcome as converts: "The Holy One, blessed be he, disqualifies no one; he receives everyone. The gates are always open, and whoever wishes to enter may do so" (Exod. Rabba, 19.4). Biblical exclusions of certain peoples from marrying into the Jewish community were circumvented in behalf of proselytes. The test case and its landmark decision appear in Mishnah Yadayim 4.4:

Judah the Ammonite proselyte appeared before [the scholars] in the academy and asked them: Am I permitted to marry a Jewess? [lit. "to enter the congregation"]. R. Gamliel replied, "You are not." R. Joshua replied, "You are."

R. Gamliel retorted: "Scripture says, 'No Ammonite or Moabite shall enter the congregation of the Lord; even to the tenth generation, etc.' (Deut. 23:4)."

R. Joshua said to him: "And are Ammonites and Moabites still in their homelands? Long ago Sennacherib king of Assyria came up and mixed all the peoples, as it says, 'I have removed the boundaries of peoples' [Isa. 10:13]."

R. Gamliel retorted: "But Scripture says 'But afterwards I will restore the fortunes of the Ammonites' (Jer. 49:6), and they have long since returned."

R. Joshua said to him: "Scripture also says, 'I will restore the fortunes of my people Israel' (Amos 9:14), and they have not yet returned."

So they permitted him to marry.[22]

Desirous of making the spiritual kinship of the proselyte supersede his genetic foreignness, the Rabbis also interpret the term "your brother" in the laws of the Torah as including the proselyte "since he is one of our brothers in the Torah and the commandments" (Midrash Tannaim, Deut. 24:7 [156]).[23] The institution of proselytism thus reflects a conception of Israel as a potentially universal people. By an act of will, any Gentile could be initiated into Judaism, and immediately be considered a Jew. The privileges (and obligations) of the Torah, with the promises held out by prophecy to Israel, were thrown open to all who wished to share them.

Jewish hospitality to proselytes fluctuated with the political status of the Jews: pagan Rome sporadically, Christian Rome persistently persecuted Jews, forbidding proselytizing on pain of death.[24] Hard times impelled some converts to relapse, and some of these betrayed the resistance and disobedience of the Jews to their hostile governments. Such conditions advised careful screening of would-be converts and their initial discouragement (Yebamot 47a,b); they also account for the notorious adage of R. Helbo (first half of the fourth century, c.e.) that "Proselytes are as bad as the scab for the Jews" (Yebamot 109b).[25] Nevertheless, Jews continued to accept sincere converts, and even facilitated the acceptance of those who wished to marry into their community.[26]

The zeal for bringing the Gentiles under the wings of the Shekinah shown in the Second Temple and Tannaitic ages passed, and with it the eagerness of outsiders to join Israel's ranks. The misfortunes of the Jews had much to do with this, as did also the contraction of the field of proselyting endeavor due to the spread of Christianity and Islam. Jewish proselyting had never been motivated by the notion that outside of Judaism there was no access to God; hence the dwindling number of converts was not regarded a failure of Judaism to discharge its duty. Jews continued to believe that their primary task was to be a holy nation, sanctifying the name of God. If for the moment they were shunned and despised, vindication would surely come in the Messianic age.

JEWS AND GENTILES

To be a holy nation meant, in the first place, to be separated from the pollution of the nations. In biblical terms this pollution consisted of idolatry and its concomitant moral corruption—the two being indissolubly bound in biblical thought (cf. Lev. 18:24; Deut. 12:31). Accordingly, the territory in which Israel lived must be purged clean of idolatry and idolaters (pagan and Israelite alike; e.g., Deut. 7:1–6; 13:13–19). Not even the private pagan cults of the foreign wives of kings were to be tolerated (1 Kings 11:1ff.; 15:13; 16:31–33; 21:25). The dissolute character of the pagans is exemplified in the patriarchal contacts with them (Gen. 19:5–9 [Sodomites]; 39 [Potiphar's wife]), by the vicious Phoenician queen Jezebel (1 Kings 21 [Naboth's vineyard]), and by the corruption of Israelites who apostatized (e.g., Ahaz [2 Kings 16:3]; Manasseh [21:16]). To give sufferance to such persons was to risk learning from them (Exod. 23:32f.; Deut. 20:18).

Intolerance of idolatry in territory controlled by Jews marked the policy of the Hasmonean kings. Where they could, these kings forcibly converted subject populations or destroyed them for resisting con-

version (Josephus, *Antiquities*, 13.9.1; 11.3; 15.4). Later discussion of
the subject was academic, since the Jews nowhere could impose their
will on Gentiles. It is nonetheless of interest to note the final formulation of these discussions by Maimonides; it proves to be more moder-
ate than ancient practice:

> When Jews are in control we may not tolerate an idolater in our midst.
> Even if he is a transient or a travelling merchant, he may not pass
> through our land until he accepts the seven Noachite commandments
> ... If he accepts them, he is then a resident alien (*ger tošab*). (Code,
> Idolatry, 10.6)

> Our teacher Moses bequeathed the Torah and commandments as the
> heritage of Israel and proselytes alone.... If anyone else refuses them,
> he is not to be coerced into accepting them. Moses, at God's behest,
> also commanded us to coerce all the inhabitants of the world to accept
> the seven Noachite commandments. Whoever refuses to accept them is
> to be put to death; whoever accepts them has the status of a resident
> alien ... (Ibid., Kings 8.9)

Having pre-empted for the proselyte all the favorable rulings of
biblical law concerning the *ger* ([resident] alien), the Rabbis appropriated the relatively infrequent and undefined biblical term *ger tošab* to
denote the Gentile who may reside in Jewish territory. His status was
based on the principle that the Jewish community was obliged to provide him with sustenance (derived artificially from Lev. 25:35; cf.
Pesaḥim 21b). From this, Naḥmanides decided that he must be cared
for when sick, and aided when in mortal danger (Supp. to Maimonides, *Book of Commandments*, Pos. Comm. 16), and Maimonides
sweepingly equated him with a Jew in all matters ethical and charita-
ble (Code, Kings, 10.12).

To sum up the academic discussion of the alien resident in Jewish
controlled territory: He is to be subject to the Noachite laws inasmuch
as it is the duty of all men to obey those laws. But since observance of
those laws entitled the Gentile to be called righteous (see above), it
also creates an obligation of solidarity between Jews and such a righteous Gentile.

Relations with external Gentiles are hardly alluded to in the Torah,
leaving them, in effect, subject to custom and prudential arrangements. Deuteronomy 15:3 and 23:21 exclude the nonresident for-
eigner (*nokri*) from the benefit of the internal Israelite institutions of
sabbatical cancellation of debt and interest-free loans. These aids to
the poor were the expression of solidarity among Israelites; outsiders
could neither be expected to share such obligations, nor expect to
enjoy their benefits. A similar reciprocity is (according to some au-

thorities) the reason for the Tannaitic exemption of a Jew from liability if his ox gored a Gentile's (Mishnah Baba Qama 4.3)—"because the Gentiles do not hold a man liable for the damages of his beast, and we judge them by their own laws" (Maimonides' Code, Property Damages 8.5).

Other rulings however are frankly discriminatory, and reflect the mutual alienation and hostility of Jews and Gentiles. We may leave out of account the body of encumbrances to free intercourse with pagans, based on a repugnance toward promoting or participating in idolatry in any way (cf. Tractate Aboda Zara); these, after all, spring from the sensibilities of monotheistic faith. More typical of hostile rulings is the exemption of a Jew from obligation to restore a Gentile's lost property, or to advise him of a business error he made in a Jew's favor (Baba Qama, 113b). Collections of these records of enmity have been made and repeatedly discussed in anti-Jewish and apologetic literature.

Our interest lies in the principles by which law and conduct rose above such enmity. The very ruling cited above regarding lost property is supplemented by the admonition that "in a case where God's name would be dishonored the Gentile's lost article is not forfeit." An exemplary tale goes further and shows how such a situation is an opportunity for sanctifying the name of God among the Gentiles.

Simon ben Shaṭaḥ [1st century B.C.E.] was a flax-merchant. Once his disciples said to him, "Master, take it easy! Let us buy you a donkey so you will not have to work so hard." They went and bought him a donkey from an Arab, on which a jewel was hanging. Then they came and said to him, "Now you will not have to work!" He asked, "Why not?" They replied, "Because we bought you a donkey from an Arab on which a jewel was hanging!" He asked them, "Was its owner aware of it?" They replied, "No." He said, "Then take it back to him—

(But didn't R. Huna say . . . in the name of Rab: ". . . granted that robbing a gentile is forbidden; his lost article may, in everyone's opinion, be appropriated"?)

—What do you think, that Simon ben Shaṭaḥ is a barbarian? Why, he would rather hear 'Blessed be the God of the Jews!' [from the mouth of the grateful Arab] than have all the rewards of this world!" (Pal. Talmud, Baba Meṣiʿa 2.2)

Another consideration that bridged the gap between Jew and Gentile was obedience to the "ways of harmony" (*darke šalom*).

The Gentile poor are not to be prevented from gleaning in [Jewish fields] and vineyards on account of the ways of harmony . . . The Gentile poor are supported along with the Jewish, their sick visited along with the Jewish, their dead buried along with the Jewish, on account of the ways of harmony. (Gittin 61a)

The sense of this phrase is illuminated by Maimonides' enlargement upon it: "It is said, 'The Lord is good to all and has compassion for all his works' (Ps. 145:9); it is further said, 'Its ways are ways of pleasantness and all its paths, harmony'" (Prov. 3:17). Abaye's statement may also be compared: "The entire Torah too is 'on account of the ways of harmony.'" (Gittin 59b). The proper aim of the Torah is to establish harmony among men; being the word of the universal God who cares for all his creatures, the scope of the Torah is no less than all men. Hence when a situation arises in which harmony between Jew and Gentile can be furthered, to do so becomes a dictate of the Torah.

Thus even when intercommunal hostility alienated Jews from Gentiles, Jewish thinkers and legists applied the grand principles of sanctification of God's name, imitation of God, and harmony among men to create unilateral obligations toward the Gentiles—obligations that did not depend upon reciprocity.

The Gentile of whom the classical Hebrew sources (Bible and Talmud) speak is a pagan, whose idolatry and immorality were an almost impassable barrier to feelings of solidarity.[27] The traditional image of the Gentile, however, became more and more incongruous with reality as Christianity and Islam spread in the lands of the Jewish Diaspora. The grounds for encumbering free intercourse with non-Jews and discriminating against them became inapplicable; actual relations with Christians and Moslems diverged from the Talmudic prescriptions. At the end of the thirteenth century, an authority appeared in south France who cleared away the multitude of ad hoc harmonizations between law and life by stating a revolutionary hermeneutical principle. Rabbi Menaham HaMeiri laid it down flatly that the Gentiles of his time were not to be equated with those of the Bible and Talmud:

> [Biblical and Talmudic rulings] apply to those times, and concern those nations who were idolatrous, filthy in their deeds and depraved in their character [he refers to Lev. 18:3] . . . But other nations who are disciplined by religion, and unsullied by those depravities—who indeed penalize them—are without question outside the purview of such rulings . . . (Commentary to Aboda Zara 22a)

> No discrimination may be practiced against such nations in ethical matters: It is forbidden to rob even idolaters and persons undisciplined by religion . . . Yet one is not obligated to take the trouble to restore their lost articles . . . since finding gives some title and restoring is an act of solidarity—and we are not obligated to show solidarity with godless

barbarians . . . Still if he is aware of the facts, we must restore it . . . and so too in any situation where not to restore would result in a dishonoring of God's name.

Hence you may infer that anyone belonging to a nation disciplined by religion, who worships God in any fashion—be it ever so different from our faith—is not in the above category. As regards these matters, he is entirely like a Jew—in respect to his lost articles or errors [made in a Jew's favor] or anything else—no distinction at all being made [between Jew and Gentile]. (Commentary to Baba Qama, 113b)

Elsewhere HaMeiri compares the religious Gentiles of his time to observers of the Noachite laws, yet clearly distinguishing between them (ibid. to 37b). Indeed, HaMeiri has broken with that traditional category of righteous gentiles in freeing his religious Gentiles from any dependence upon biblical revelation. Their religio-ethical virtue alone, whatever be its source, entitles them to fair and equitable treatment.[28] A source of value independent of Judaism and its Torah is acknowledged—a mediaeval version of the Gentile "fear of God" known to Scripture.

Under the impact of the European Enlightenment this tendency culminated in the elimination of every criterion but the ethical in the definition of the Gentile to whom the Jew owes solidarity. The development is highlighted by comparing an ancient and an eighteenth century treatment of the biblical admonition, "You shall love your neighbor as yourself" (Lev. 19:18). First, a Tannaitic discussion of the verse:

One should not think, "Love the sages but hate the disciples," or "Love the disciples but hate the ignorant," but love all of these and hate the sectarians, apostates and informers. So David said, *"Do I not hate them, O Lord, who hate you?"* (Ps. 139:21)

But does it not say, *You shall love your neighbor as yourself: I am the Lord:* What is the sense? Because I (the Lord) have created him. Indeed! If he acts as your people do, you shall love him; but if not, you shall not love him (as though the sense were "you shall love your neighbor when he is as yourself"). (The Fathers according to Rabbi Nathan A 16, in the translation of J. Goldin, p. 86)

And now a taste of the interpretation of Pinhas Eliah Hurwitz, a pious mystic of the eighteenth century, whose *Sefer Ha-Berit*—a scientific religio-ethical encyclopedia from which the following is taken—enjoyed great popularity among European and North African Jews.

The essence of neighborly love consists in loving all mankind, all who walk on two legs, of whatever people and whatever tongue, by virtue of their identical humanity, and their civilization—builders, farmers, merchants, artisans . . . each serving the needs of men in his own way . . . Human society is to be conceived of as a single individual composed of many organs and parts; each person is like an organ or a part of this individual . . . All are interdependent and interconnected like the links of a chain . . . The meaning of the scripture "You shall love your neighbor as yourself" is not confined to Jews only, but the sense is "your neighbor who is a human being as yourself"—people of all nations are included, any fellow humans . . . (*Sefer Ha-Berit* [Bruenn, 1797] II:13)[29]

While the Tannaitic criterion is ethical (for by "acting as your people do" is meant observing the Torah), it does not apply the law of love beyond the bounds of Israel (although within Israel too it explicitly excludes heretics, etc.).[30] The later statement, however, with universalistic humanism typical of the age, conditions love of fellows only on their being civilized human beings, contributors to the common wealth. For this Jewish son of the Enlightenment the biblical admonition of neighborly love knew no boundaries short of the whole human race.

A UNIFIED HUMANITY

The kinship of all people as the descendants of one father and the creatures of one Creator impressed itself upon the Hebrew imagination. How could I ignore the rightful claim of my servant, cries Job, "Did not he who made me in the belly make him? Did not One fashion us both in the womb?" (Job 31:15) This passage so worked upon the Palestinian sage, R. Yohanan, that "whatever food he partook of he shared with his servant" (Pal. Talmud Ketubbot, 5.5). Ben Azzai and Rabbi Akiba argued over the most overarching principle of the Torah; the latter put forward "You must love your neighbor as yourself," the former, "This is the account of the generations of man" (Gen. 5:1). A late commentator explains: "While 'You shall love your neighbor' obligates one to love on the basis of fellowship, 'This is the account' bases the duty on brotherhood—a more absolute ground."[31]

The myth of one mankind under one God in primeval times—from Adam to the Tower-builders—pressed for a complementary vision of a reunited mankind under God at the end of time. The author of that vision was the prophet Isaiah. The imperial success of Assyria in imposing its yoke on the necks of all the nations on Israel's horizon seems to have fired Isaiah's imagination to conceive of a deeper unification of men under one greater than Assyria. The pagan empire was a preparation for God's universal kingdom; when Assyria had performed its allotted task, it would be broken on the mountains of Israel. The ensuing worldwide shock would be followed by a general renunciation of trust in human handiwork—in chariots, ships, towers, and idols; men would turn to Zion's hill for divine instruction. Wars would cease, for God would

> . . . judge among the nations
> and arbitrate for the many peoples;
> and they shall beat their swords into plowshares
> and their spears into pruning hooks:
> nation shall not lift up sword against nation
> neither shall they experience war any more. (Isa. 2:4)

Then Egypt and Assyria, converted to the worship of God, would be joined with Israel as a blessed triad, acknowledged by God as equally his own:

> In that day, Israel shall be a third
> with Egypt and Assyria
> as a standard of blessedness throughout the world,
> which the Lord of hosts will have established,
> saying, "Blessed be my people Egypt,
> my handiwork Assyria,
> and my heritage Israel." (19:24–25)[32]

Isaiah's prediction that the nations would be converted to the worship of the one God was taken up by Zephaniah; annulling the punishment of the Tower-builders, God would "transform the speech of all the peoples into a clear language, that they may all invoke the name of the Lord and worship him in unison" (3:9). The idea recurs in Jeremiah (e.g., 3:17) and Habakkuk (2:14). It is a major theme of the second Isaiah:

> By myself I have sworn,
> From my mouth there has issued, triumphant,
> A word that shall not be thwarted:
> "To me every knee shall bow,
> Every tongue swear allegiance." (45:23)

Zechariah envisions a veritable frenzy of the nations to adhere to the God of the Jews (8:20–23; cf. 14:9, 16ff.).

These visions animated the messianic dreams of Judaism. Their promise of a glorious dénouement to human history, in which Israel's faith and steadfastness to its covenant would be vindicated and all men would join hands with it in subservience to their common Creator, were a beacon of hope in the vale of gloom and tears through which Israel walked for centuries. Some forms of this hope mirrored the animosity of the Gentiles by depicting the prelude to the messianic age as the destruction of the Gentile nations. But the form that entered the daily liturgy of the Jews was inspired by the noble vision of Isaiah. Originally composed for the New Year's liturgy, the following has, since about 1300, closed each of the three daily services of Judaism:

> We therefore hope in you, O Lord our God,
> that we may soon behold your glorious might
> when you remove the abominations from the earth,
> and the idols disappear;
> when the world will be perfected under the kingship of the Almighty,
> and all flesh invoke your name;
> when all the wicked of the earth will be turned to you.
> Let all the inhabitants of the world acknowledge and know
> that to you every knee must bend,
> every tongue swear allegiance;
> before you O Lord our God let them kneel and fall,
> and give honor to your glorious name.
> Let them all accept the yoke of your kingship,
> and may you reign over them soon for ever and ever.
> For kingship is yours
> and may you reign in glory to all eternity,
> As it is said, "The Lord shall reign for ever and ever" (Exod. 15:19);
> And again, "The Lord shall be king over all the earth; in that day the Lord shall be one, and his name one." (Zech. 14:9)

Classical Hebrew thought affirmed the basic unity of humankind in its creation myth, and complemented that myth with its messianic vision of a united humanity under God. It recognized access to God and saving virtue outside of Judaism, since its own covenant with God bound the covenant-community only. The rest of humankind was justified by observance of the Noachite laws or the discipline of religion. As for Israel, its task was to keep itself holy and sanctify God's name on earth. Israel's relation to its neighbors was never merely reciprocal; something of its calling to witness the effect of God's word always tempered its external dealings. Its messianic fervor, never entirely cooled, has repeatedly flared up in one form or another at any suggestion of a movement to realize the brotherhood of all peoples.

NOTES

1. Robert Redfield, *The Primitive World and Its Transformations* (Ithaca, 1953), 74ff.
2. See Louis Ginzberg, *On Jewish Law and Lore* (Philadelphia, 1955), 180–83.
3. See Salo W. Baron's summary in ed. Leo W. Schwarz, *Great Ages and Ideas of the Jewish People* (New York, 1956), 315–90.
4. Extensive, competent discussions of these elements are to be found in Michael Guttmann, *Das Judentum und seine Umwelt* (Berlin, 1927) and Joseph S. Bloch, *Israel and the Nations* (Berlin-Vienna, 1927).
5. Important reflections on our theme are embodied in Isidore Twersky's "One World—One Ethics?: Judaism's Approach to Ethical Universalism," an unpublished paper of the 1959 Meeting of Fellows of the Conference on Science, Philosophy and Religion. I thank the Conference office, at the Jewish Theological Seminary of America, for allowing me to use Professor Twersky's paper.
6. The variety of the races of men was later ascribed to environmental factors (e.g., climate); cf. the nineteenth century Mishnah commentary *Tif'eret Yisra'el* at Sanhedrin 4.5, note 38.
7. Cf. E. J. Bickerman, "The Altars of the Gentiles: A Note on the Jewish 'ius sacrum,'" *Revue International des Droits de l'antiquité*, V (1958):137–64.
8. This testimony to the effect of the Jewish Diaspora on its pagan environment is preceded by a still earlier testimony in Isaiah 56:3ff.
9. Following Maimonides; cf. J. Goldin, *The Wisdom of the Talmud* (Chicago, 1957), 140.
10. Printed editions read, in the first paragraph, "destroys/preserves a single life in Israel"; I follow the manuscripts and Albeck's note in his edition of the Mishnah. The significance of this passage is elaborated in my essay "The Biblical Grounding of Human Value," in *The Samuel Friedland Lectures, 1960–1966* (New York: The Jewish Theological Seminary of America), 47–52.

Additional note:

See the thorough text history of this passage by E. E. Urbach, "'Whoever preserves a single life . . .'—Transformations of a Text, Perversities of the Censor, and Printers' Business," *Tarbiz* 40 (5731=1971), 268–84 (in Hebrew).

That Mishnah Sanhedrin 4.5 is reflected in the Koran (5 ["The Table]:35) was noticed by Abraham Geiger, *Was hat Mohammed aus dem Judenthume aufgenommen?* (Leipzig: Kaufmann Verlag, 1902), 102-3. The Koran passage is as follows:

"Therefore We prescribed for the Children of Israel
that whoso slays a soul not to retaliate
for a soul slain, nor for corruption
done in the land, shall be as if he had
slain mankind altogether; and whoso
gives life to a soul, shall be as if he had
given life to mankind altogether.
(A.J. Arberry, *The Koran Interpreted*, 105)

The limiting phrase "in Israel" is not reflected here, another indication that it is not original in the Mishnah.

11. See the insightful comments of Gerhard von Rad in his *Genesis* commentary *ad loc.* (Philadelphia, 1961), 126–29.
12. Yehezkel Kaufmann, *The Religion of Israel* (Chicago, 1963), 424f.
13. Sanhedrin 56a and parallels; Gen. Rabba 16.16 and 34.19 (ed. Theodor-Albeck, 149f., 316f., with important notes). For the relation of the Noachite laws to Christian "natural law," see N. Isaacs in ed. E. R. Bevan and C. Singer, *The Legacy of Israel* (Oxford, 1928), 383–87; to the Roman *ius gentium*, Boaz Cohen, *Jewish and Roman Law*, 2 vols. (New York, 1966), Index, s.v. Noachian laws.

14. See Bernard J. Bamberger, *Proselytism in the Talmudic Period* (Cincinnati, 1939), 134ff.; Saul Lieberman, *Greek in Jewish Palestine* (New York, 1942), 77ff.

15. Some of which are given in the article "Laws, Noachian" in *The Jewish Encyclopaedia*, VII:648ff.; comprehensively set out in the article *ben noah* in *Enṣiqlopedia Talmudit*, III:348–62.

16. M. Guttmann ("Maimonides sur l'universalité de la morale religieuse," *Revue des études juives*, LXXXIX [1935]:34–35) observed that this passage was one of the sources of Maimonides' formulation in Code, Kings 8.11. That Maimonides requires the gentile to acknowledge Moses' agency in revelation of the Noachite laws accords with his exaltation of the prophet.

17. G. von Rad, *The Problem of the Hexateuch and Other Essays*, trans. E. W. T. Dicken (Edinburgh and London, 1966), 64–66; M. Buber, "The Mission of Abraham" (Heb.) in *Darko šel Miqra (The Way of the Bible)* (Jerusalem, 1964), 65–81, esp. 68–71.

18. J. J. Finkelstein, "Law, Ancient Near Eastern" (Heb.), in EB, V (Jerusalem, 1968): 614.

19. Cf. Alfred Bertholet, *Die Stellung der Israeliten und Juden zu den Fremden* (Freiburg und Leipzig, 1896), 37–45.

20. On the subject at large, see Bamberger (n. 14, above); W. G. Braude, *Jewish Proselytizing in the First Five Centuries of the Common Era* (Providence, R.I., 1940). Briefer treatments: G. F. Moore, *Judaism* (Cambridge 1950), I:323–53; S. W. Baron, *A Social and Religious History of the Jews*, I (New York, 1952):165–211. The classic discussion of the distinction between ethnic assimilation of resident aliens and religious conversion is by Yehezkel Kaufmann, *Gola veNekar* (Tel Aviv, 1934), I:227–56.

21. Cf. Bickerman (n. 7, above); R. H. Pfeiffer, *History of New Testament Times* (New York, 1949), 197–230.

22. Cf. Maimonides, Code, Prohibited Connexions 12.25: "When Sennacherib King of Assyria came up, he thoroughly mixed the nations and exiled them from their homelands. The Egyptians now living in Egypt are a different people, so too the Edomites in the Field of Edom. And since the four banned nations [cf. Deut. 23:4, 8] have been mixed up among the rest of the nations, who are permitted, all are permitted. For anyone who separates himself from them to convert to Judaism is presumed to have come from the majority. Hence anyone who converts nowadays from anywhere, be he an Edomite, an Egyptian, an Ammonite or a Moabite, an Ethiopian or any other nationality, male or female, is allowed to intermarry with us immediately."

23. But not enough of a "brother" to qualify for kingship (cf. Deut. 17:15) or any other public office (Maim. Code, Kings 1.4). The Mishnaic disallowance of the proselyte to use "our fathers" in prayer was contradicted by the tanna R. Judah on the ground that Abraham was expressly called "father of a multitude of nations/gentiles" (*goyim*); thus the proselyte may claim Abraham as his father. The law was decided according to R. Judah against the Mishnah (Pal. Talmud, Bikkurim 1.4 end). Maimonides passionately defended the right of the proselyte Obadaiah to pray exactly as every other Jew, without changing a word; *Responsa*, ed. Blau, no. 293 [ed. Freimann, no. 42].

24. James Parkes, *The Conflict of the Church and the Synagogue* (Cleveland and New York, 1961), Index, s.v. Conversion to Judaism: prohibited.

25. See Braude (n. 20 above), 42ff., 48.

26. "If a man had intercourse with a Gentile woman . . . once she has converted and accepted Judaism we presume that pressure of necessity made her conversion sincere; for we have a rule that a man who converted to Judaism for the sake of a woman, or a woman who converted for the sake of a man are considered proselytes in all respects." (*Nimuqe Yosef* [Habiba (fifteenth century)], to Yebamot 24b).

27. Yet the Rabbis recognized and esteemed virtuous pagans; cf. Lieberman (n. 14 above), 68–90.

28. See Jacob Katz's analysis of HaMeiri's position in chapter 10 of his illuminating survey, *Exclusiveness and Tolerance, Studies in Jewish-Gentile Relations* (London, 1961). A later version of HaMeiri's redefinition, designed specifically to bring Christians within the bounds of those to whom Jews owed ethical obligations, made biblical faith the determining factor: "These nations among whom we . . . are scattered . . . believe in the Creation and the Exodus, and in several basic articles of faith, and have in mind the

Maker of heaven and earth . . . We are duty-bound to pray for their welfare." (R. Moses Ribkas [17th c.] *Be'er HaGola* at *Šulḥan 'Aruk, Oraḥ Ḥayyim* 425).

29. Cited from I. Zinberg, *History of Jewish Literature* (Hebrew) III:323. My attention was originally directed to Hurwitz's *Sefer Ha-Berit* by note 6 of J. Z. Lauterbach's "The Attitude of the Jew toward the Non-Jew," *Yearbook of the Central Conference of American Rabbis*, XXXI (1921):186–233.

30. Still valuable is the balanced discussion of the Rabbinic and Gospel statements on love and hate in C. G. Montefiore, *Rabbinic Literature and Gospel Teachings* (London, 1930), 85–104. The writings of the Qumran sectarians now enable us to see the matter in a new light; see D. Flusser, "A New Sensitivity in Judaism and the Christian Message," HTR, LXI (1968):107–27.

31. Aaron ben Haim of Morocco (seventeenth century), cited from Lauterbach (n. 29 above).

32. See H. L. Ginsberg, "Isaiah in the Light of History," *Conservative Judaism*, XXII (1967):1–18; for an appreciation of Isaiah's vision of peace, cf. Y. Kaufmann, *The Religion of Israel* (Chicago, 1963), 386–95.

Rabbinic Reflections on Defying Illegal Orders: Amasa, Abner, and Joab*

1970

It has always been recognized that the Israelite king of biblical times was not accorded unlimited power. The base subterfuges used by David to do away with Uriah and by Ahab to do away with Naboth are oblique tributes to the subjection of Israel's kings to custom and law. The strong censure that Nathan and Elijah directed at these kings, the rebukes that kings generally received for their misdeeds from the mouths of prophets show a common acknowledgment of royal accountability to a higher law. The idea was legally formulated in Deuteronomy 17:14–20—the only ordinance concerning kings in the Torah—where the king is bound by various strictures and admonished to be humble and Godfearing, and to keep the Torah all his life.

Nevertheless, the powers of the king were broad and only vaguely delimited. Samuel's catalogue of despotic privileges (1 Sam. 8:11–18), Saul's whimsical massacre of the priests of Nob, and the free hand kings had in exterminating rivals and their families illustrate the lack of effective checks against arbitrary exercise of royal authority. While the laws of the Torah define insubordination to parents and to the high court (Deut: 17:8–13; 21:18–21) their predominantly premonarchic orientation excludes treatment either of the rights of the king or their limitations. For the conception of treason we are dependent on occasional notices in the historical books; of justified defiance of royal authority we scarcely have a clue.[1]

This lack was partly made up by the Talmudists, whose elaboration

---

*These remarks were presented to a gathering at the Jewish Theological Seminary of America marking the Vietnam Moratorium, 15 October 1969.

of biblical law and ethics included such topics, even though they were no longer practical issues. Their views on the limitations of royal authority were not set forth in legal exegesis, since no relevant biblical laws exist. Instead, incidents in the books of Samuel and Kings were used as points of departure. The army chiefs Abner, Amasa, and Joab, endowed with the requisite authority to make their words and deeds legally significant,[2] became representative of opposed courses of action in the face of a conflict between the king's orders and higher law. Although the treatment is far from systematic, the scattered rabbinic observations reflect a coherent underlying doctrine, which eventually found statutory expression in Maimonides' Code (see below).

The legal-constitutional principle in the rabbinic discussion facilitates comparing it with other systems and applying it to other situations. The king's authority to coerce obedience on pain of death (as opposed to his election) is not regarded as divinely ordained, nor are his opponents divinely appointed prophets, as in the Bible. On the contrary, the royal authority is derived from the people, and the opponents of the king are courageous, morally sensitive men who take their stand on a constitutional ground.

The basic text relates an episode in Solomon's trial of Joab for treason. The entire passage is a typical rhetorical exercise, in which arguments are put forward for and against historical figures. But these arguments are not improvised just for the occasion; they recur in other contexts, as we shall see, and thus have a claim to be taken seriously.

It is significant, at the outset, that the summary execution described in 1 Kings 2:31ff. is here preceded by a trial; even in the case of treason the king must act through the proper judicial procedure.[2a] Joab is required to answer the charge that he slew Abner and Amasa unlawfully (cf. 1 Kings 2:5). He defends himself successfully in the case of Abner: Abner had needlessly killed Joab's brother, Asael, so Joab was only doing his duty as a redeemer of blood.

Then Solomon said to him, "What warrant had you to kill Amasa?" He replied, "Amasa defied the king, as the record shows:

> The King said to Amasa, "Go call up the men of Judah for me in three days, and be here yourself." Amasa went to call up the Judahites, but he delayed beyond the time that the king had set for him. (2 Sam. 20:4f.)

Solomon retorted, "Amasa construed *buts* and *onlys* in the law. He found the Israelites engaged in studying a tractate and reasoned thus: It is written,

> Whoever defies your order and disobeys your command, whatever it
> may be, shall be put to death. (Josh. 1:18)
>
> Can this apply even if it conflicts with a matter of the Torah? The
> end of the verse indicates that it does not:
> *Only* be sure and resolute. (Sanhedrin 49a)

This elliptical repartee needs explanation. The king's right to execute defiant subjects arises out of the people's solemn asseveration to
Joshua that anyone who disobeyed him would be put to death. It was
conferred by the people upon their leader, and is not a divinely ordained rule of the Torah.[3] The conferral was made in a war camp and
was particularly necessary for military discipline. General Joab under-
standably took the language of the conferral literally: any infringe-
ment whatever of the king's order was a capital offense. Thus he
justified slaying Amasa for having transgressed the king's deadline.
Such rigor accords with Joab's character and devotion to David. External warrants can also be adduced for Joab's severity. Amasa had been
the commander of the rebel forces of Absalom, and had yet to prove
his loyalty to David. Moreover, David himself had stressed the importance of speed in nipping Sheba's new revolt in the bud (2 Sam. 20:6).
Amasa's delay was therefore suspicious and in the circumstances,
downright injurious to the king. There was some color to Joab's judgment that Amasa was in defiance of the king.

But Solomon rejects Joab's argument and exculpates Amasa, citing
with approval his reason for the delay. When Amasa undertook to mo-
bilize the people, he found them busy in the study of a tractate (the
reference is to the semi-annual *kalla* sessions, in which a prean-
nounced tractate was publicly taught for a month to thousands of students). Should he interrupt the session—an implementation of God's
command to study and teach the Torah—for the sake of meeting the
king's deadline? He reasoned his way out of the dilemma thus: The
people (in Josh. 1:18) could not have meant to confer upon their
leader authority higher than God's. A formal indication that they did
not is the *only*-clause that they appended to their conferral, "only be
sure and resolute." "*Onlys* and *buts* are restrictive," runs the
hermeneutical rule used by Amasa; they limit the application of the
law to which they are attached. The nature of the limitation here was
doubtless suggested by an identical "only" clause a few verses earlier
(v. 7), in which God admonishes Joshua "Only be sure and resolute in
carefully observing all of the Torah that my servant Moses commanded..." The people's exhortation echoed God's admonition,
thereby implying that the authority they granted their leader was subject to God's Torah.

Amasa then went on to decide that public study of the Torah was a matter that superseded royal authority. For this further step he adduced no scriptural authority; it appears as his own, innovative decision. By such bold reasoning Amasa felt authorized to delay the mobilization briefly to allow the study session to run its course (we are evidently to understand that it was nearing its end anyway).

Joab was thus wrong in regarding Amasa as a rebel and killing him. Yet the trial goes on and a new charge is brought against him—of being himself a rebel (cf. 1 Kings 2:28)—and of that he is apparently convicted. One must conclude that although he was morally guilty of Amasa's death, he was not legally culpable. This distinction will be enlarged upon later.

The model for defying illegal orders is found by the Rabbis in 1 Samuel 22. Suspecting the priests of Nob of having conspired with outlawed David, Saul commanded his men to

> Go round and put the priests of the Lord to death, for they too are David's partisans. But the king's servants were unwilling to lift their hand to harm the priests of the Lord. (v. 17)

The Palestinian Talmud asks:

> Who were those servants? R. Samuel son of R. Isaac said: they were Abner and Amasa. They replied to Saul, "Do we owe you anything beyond this belt and mantle (insignia of office)? Here, take them back!" (Sanhedrin 29a)

They would rather resign the high position held by them than accede to the king's demand.[4] As we shall see, the Babylonian Talmud grounds their defiance on their "construing *buts* and *onlys*." In the event it proved inadequate to prevent execution of the king's orders; he found another instrument to carry out his will. This raised the question as to whether Abner and Amasa had really done all they could to stave off the massacre. There is one opinion that they did not.

> R. Judah said in the name of Rab: Why did Abner meet an untimely death? Because he might have made a stand against Saul but did not. R. Isaac said: He did make a stand but was overruled. (Sanhedrin 20a)

Both rabbis agree that by merely refusing to carry out an illegal order Abner did not discharge his full moral responsibility. It is not enough to dissociate oneself from wrongdoing—even at the price of demotion;[5] one must actively oppose it, even if one is eventually overruled. Not to do so is a moral dereliction, guilty in the sight of God.

R. Zera once said to R. Simon, "You must censure the Exilarch's court!" He replied, "They won't listen to me." R. Zera retorted, "You must censure them all the same," and that accords with R. Aḥa's homily:

The only time God ever reversed himself with regard to a benign decision was when he said to his scribe,

"Go through the city, through Jerusalem, and put a mark upon the foreheads of the men who sigh and groan over all the abominations that are committed in it." (Ezek. 9:4)

The Holy One said to Gabriel: "Go mark the foreheads of the righteous with an X of ink so that the angels of death do not harm them, and the foreheads of the wicked with an X of blood so that the angels of death do harm them."[6] Hearing that, Justice spoke up and said, "Lord of the Universe, what's the difference between them?" God answered, "Why, these are wholly righteous and those wholly wicked!" She replied, "Lord of the Universe, they could have protested but did not." Said He, "But I know that even if they had protested no one would have listened to them." Said she, "Lord of the Universe, you knew it but did they?" Now God had at first said, "Pass through the city and smite it ... but touch no one who bears a mark" (Ezek. 9:5f). But then we read, "and begin with my sanctuary (*miqdaši*)." R. Joseph taught, "Read it 'begin with my holy ones' (*mᵉquddašay*)—those who kept my Torah from A to Z." (Shabbat 55a)

The first to be punished in an evil society, says the homily (with typical hyperbole), are those who could have taken a stand against the evil but did not—regardless of the fact that they kept themselves apart from it.[7]

The example of insensitivity to the demands of the higher law is Joab—who received David's letter ordering him to contrive the death of Uriah in battle and complied with it unhesitatingly.[7a] An unfavorable comparison of Joab with Abner and Amasa occurs in a rabbinic comment on Solomon's condemnation of Joab,

Now the Lord has brought his bloodguilt down upon his head, for having struck down two men more righteous and better than he [Abner and Amasa]. (1 Kings 2:32)

Better—in that they construed *buts* and *onlys*, while he did not. More righteous—in that they received their command from [the king's] mouth yet defied it, while his came by letter and he obeyed it. (Sanhedrin 49a)

The two men were better than Joab because they showed awareness of the moral problem posed by the king's illegal order, and a capacity to authorize refusal to obey it. As Maharsha suggests, their goodness saved the goodness of the law. Had the king's right been absolutized (as Joab was inclined to do), it would have been destructive of the value-context that law aims to preserve. Only by making the larger context determine the construction of particular laws can the Torah be kept from dissolving in a welter of incoherent rulings, adding up to no intelligible pattern of goodness.

The righteousness of Abner and Amasa consisted in their readiness to act on their interpretation, novel and risky as it was. And they acted in the most difficult of situations—confronting the king in person and having received the order from his mouth. Thus, they were superior in theory and more righteous in practice than Joab.

The rabbis' disapproval of Joab is so obvious that the question must now be posed, How is it that they failed to reprobate Joab's compliance with David's criminal order concerning Uriah in their story of Joab's trial? Did they clear him of culpability in the matter? The issue is raised in connection with the law of agency.

> If a man says to his agent, "Go kill so and so," and he does it, the agent is culpable and the principal is exempt. Shammai the elder said in the name of the prophet Haggai: the principal is culpable, as it says, "And him (Uriah) you (David) killed by the sword of the Ammonites" (2 Sam. 12:9: David the principal is blamed for the murder, not Joab the agent). (Qiddušin 43a)

The rule is that "there is no agency for wrongdoing": An agent who commits a wrong cannot defend himself on the ground that he was merely executing orders; his moral autonomy is not cancelled by his agency and he remains responsible for his acts. The rule is eminently just; "when a master's orders conflict with a servant's (here, God's with man's), whose should be obeyed?" (Qiddušin, 42b). Hence an agent-killer is regarded as autonomous and culpable for his crime. Yet the prophet blames David for Uriah's death, not Joab; whence Shammai inferred a contrary ruling: In a murder by proxy, the principal is culpable.[7b]

But Shammai's inference is problematic. Murder by proxy under orders of a king is too special a case to serve as a basis for a general rule.

> Even though it is always the case that "there is no agency for wrongdoing," and the principal is exempt and the agent culpable, the case of Uriah is different; the text calls David the killer. The reason is, that since he was a king and nobody disobeyed him he is the killer. Simi-

larly with Saul, who ordered the massacre of the Nob priests—it is as though he killed them (1 Sam. 22:21). Now it is true that in such a situation one should not execute the king's orders [reference is made to construing *buts* and *onlys*] . . . but since not everyone is aware of this or knows how to construe *buts* and *onlys*, punishment falls on the king. (Kimḥi at 2 Sam. 12:9)

The king's right to obedience on pain of death was an established, notorious right, which the people were conditioned to respect. Knowledge of its limits and discernment to know when its limits were transgressed could not be presupposed in everyone. The right was recorded in writing; the limitation was a bold construction of morally sensitive men. A good soldier like Joab could very well have been ignorant of his obligation to refuse an illegal order; or, having heard of the notion, might have (mistakenly) argued that it was a dangerous policy to adopt. He might be condemned as morally obtuse; he might be held guilty in the eyes of God. He cannot be held legally culpable for a wrong committed under royal orders.[8]

Amasa and Abner had to depend on their insight to set limits to the king's authority: later ages did not. For what was earlier the property only of those who knew how to construe *buts* and *onlys* became the property of all Jews who could read the law. The great Code of Maimonides, aimed at the common man, incorporated the limitation of royal power in a statute and published it to the world.

Whoever disregards a royal order because he is busy with God's commandments—even the slightest commandments—is exempt (from blame of defying the king). If the master's orders conflict with the servant's, the master's take precedence. And it goes without saying, that if a king ordered violation of God's commandments, he is not to be obeyed. (Laws of Kings, 3:9)

This spare statement of the principle leaves unsaid what the subject *is* to do with that illegal order, or what penalty he incurs if he obeys it. Joab's compliance went unpunished because he was excusably ignorant or mistaken. Now that the obligation to disobey has been published, everyone is on notice that an illegal order of the king is to be defied. He who receives such an order now is therefore on a different footing from Joab; he is in one respect like Abner and Amasa who knew that a royal order could be illegal and must then be defied. But if he is an ordinary Jew he suffers a crucial disadvantage: the lack of that learning and insight that those ancient worthies had (by rabbinic convention), and that authorized them to decide rightly when to defy the king. He is, to be sure, competent enough to decide that to massacre a townful of priests is a crime, but he may puzzle over the postponement of a mobilization order for the sake of finishing a public lecture series on Torah. He will want to take advice from an authority before deciding on action—and exposing himself to risk of death for defying a legal order of the king.[8a]

But if, when all is done, he finds himself with an order he knows to be illegal, what is his duty? On the basis of the Talmudic material here assembled we can sum it up in three propositions:

1. He must refuse to carry out the order even if it means a fall in rank and status.

2. He must actively oppose the order and try to prevent its execution: otherwise he will be guilty before God.[9]

3. If he voluntarily obeys the order, he is not only guilty before God, but legally culpable as well. He cannot exempt himself on the ground of being merely the king's agent, for there is no agency for wrongdoing—and, unlike Joab, he can no longer plead ignorance of the limitations on royal authority.

NOTES

1. See I. Benzinger, in *Encyclopaedia Biblica* (ed. Cheyne and Black), Vol. II, art. "Government," sec. 22–23, col. 1909–10; T. H. Robinson, *A History of Israel*, Vol I:225, 228ff.; S. W. Baron, *A Social and Religious History of the Jews* I/1:91–93; D. J. Silver, "Monarchy," in D. J. Silver, ed., *In Time of Harvest: Essays in Honor of Abba Hillel Silver*... (New York, 1963), 421–32; G. Fohrer, "Der Vertrag zwischen König und Volk in Israel," ZAW 71 (1950):1–22 (studies such passages as 2 Sam. 3:21; 5:3; 2 Kings 11:17). On the concept of treason, cf. M. Greenberg, in *Interpreters Dictionary of the Bible*, "Crimes and Punishments," 740b.

2. Abner and Amasa were "lions in the Torah" (Pal. Tal. Peah 16a); Joab was the president of the Sanhedrin (Pesikta Rabbati 11 [ed. Friedman, 43b]); cf. Louis Ginzberg, *Legends of the Jews* VI:240[91], 258[76].

2a. Tosafot to Sanhedrin 36a (s.v., *Rabba bar bar Ḥanna*) resolves conflicting views on the subject thus: Treason cases must be heard by the Sanhedrin, but some of its rigid procedural requirements may be relaxed. See further, Zevi Hirsch Chajes, "*Din Melek B'yisra'el*," in *Kol Sifre Mahraṣ Chajes* I:43–49. I am indebted to Sid Leiman of Yale University for calling my attention to this interesting study.

3. The Meiri in his commentary (*Bet Habb'ḥira*, ed. Sofer, p. 204) says expressly that the king's authority to put rebels to death is not derived from the Torah (*'en b'din tora ken*). Chajes develops the theory that the royal prerogatives flow from a contract (*k'tav hitqaśś'rut*) between the people and the king: The people surrender some of their rights in property and life to a single leader who will lead them in battle and provide for the general welfare (46–47). Cf. Fohrer's article (n. 1), 17ff.

4. Ginzberg, *Legends* VI:240[92].

5. Assuming, for the sake of a systematic presentation, that R. Judah (Rab) held the view of R. Samuel son of R. Isaac that Abner had at least refused to carry out Saul's order with an offer of resignation.

6. On these two X's (originally one an X canceling debts—a mark of freedom, the other a Greek *theta* (Θ) for *thanatos* "death"–a sign of death), see S. Lieberman, *Greek in Jewish Palestine*, 185–91.

7. The complexity of the injunction to protest wrongs actively is only suggested by the Tosafot *ad loc.*, who absolve one from the duty when it is certain to be futile; and cf.

Yebamot 65b "Just as one is enjoined to speak out when he will be listened to, so he is enjoined not to speak out when he will not be listened to." *Sefer Haḥinuk*, sec. 218 (ed. Chavel) offers a convenient summary of the injunction with some indications of its limits.

7a. Though, for practical reasons, and in order to conceal the plot, he did not execute the king's orders literally; cf. U. Simon, "The Poor Man's Ewe-Lamb," *Biblica* 148 (1967), 216f.; M. Perry and M. Sternberg, "The King Through Ironic Eyes: The Narrator's Devices in the Biblical Story of David and Bathsheba . . . ," *Hasifrut* I (Tel Aviv University, 1968), 278f (in Hebrew).

7b. That Shammai's ruling reflects a patrician viewpoint is plausibly argued by L. Finkelstein, *The Pharisees* (Philadelphia, 1962), 285.

8. Compare the formulation of the U.S. Department of the Army, Field Manual: The Law of Land Warfare, 182, which admonishes military courts "to take into consideration the fact that obedience to lawful orders is the duty of every member of the armed forces; that the latter cannot be expected, in conditions of war discipline, to weigh scrupulously the legal merits of the orders received . . ." The American Law Institute's Model Penal Code (from which the above is cited, p. 41) has the following to say on military orders (Section 2.10, 41): "It is an affirmative defense that the actor, in engaging in the conduct charged to constitute an offense, does no more than execute an order of his superior in the armed services which he does not know to be unlawful." I owe this to Stephen R. Goldstein of the University of Pennsylvania Law School.

8a. The complexity of this question is suggested by the juxtaposition in Maimonides' Code, Kings 3.8,10; 5.3 of extraordinary rights (e.g., capital punishment for crimes evidenced only circumstantially; right of expropriating to build the king's highway) alongside prohibitions against unlawful actions (e.g., confiscation without compensation). Chajes looks to the principle of the general welfare for an explanation of the apparent inconsistency: The people have relinquished their rights to the king for the common good; but where a royal law violates Torah-given rights for the private good of the king only, it falls outside the contract with the king and is illegal. Regrettably, Chajes did not inquire at all into the right of the people to defy an illegal royal command.

9. These two propositions assume that the king will not unlawfully coerce his subject to execute his illegal order on pain of death. If he does apply such duress, the compliance of the subject cannot be legally culpable. See Maimonides, Code, Yᶜsode Ha-Tora 5.4 and 'Ensiqlopedia Talmudit, s.v., 'ones.

Additional note:

A much more elaborate and ramified treatment of this subject is Aaron Kirschenbaum's "A Cog in the Wheel: The Defence of 'Obedience to Superior Orders' in Jewish Law," *Israel Yearbook on Human Rights* 3 (1974), 168–93.

Jewish Conceptions of the Human Factor in Biblical Prophecy

1989

Fellow-feeling with Walter Harrelson grew out of our meetings and conversations in Jerusalem, attendant upon his reconciling director-ship of the Ecumenical Institute at Tantur. This essay in Jewish theology is offered to him in appreciation of his manifold contributions to biblical thought, hermeneutics, and interfaith understanding.

Modern critical study of Hebrew Scriptures by Jews has seldom been conducted in the light of any theological principle.[1] Its proponents have either ignored the tenets of traditional religion in philological-historical inquiries that avoid engagement with theology or existential issues, or have focused on different objects of inquiry, such as poetics, in which the historical factor is muted.[2] By orthodoxy, biblical criticism is generally regarded as incompatible with the foundations of Jewish belief.[3]

This situation differs from that obtaining in Christianity. Both the Protestant and Roman Catholic churches have accommodated them-selves to the practice and main findings of criticism: Theological seminaries are today the academic berths of most biblical critics. This was not accomplished without overcoming opposition, but the battles fought in the churches in the nineteenth and twentieth centuries and the conceptual refinement and clarification resulting therefrom have had no counterparts in the synagogue.[4] It is in order to contribute to the assessment of the relation of critical principles to Judaism and to the practice of Jewish exegetes that this essay is undertaken. It focuses on one aspect of the critical stance: the supposition that in the formu-

405

lation of prophetic writings (and most of Scripture is ascribed by Jews
to prophets) a human factor was present to such an extent that no account of them can overlook the personal circumstances and particular
situation of their human authors.[5]

That this supposition is not in itself a denial of divine inspiration or
revelation has been affirmed vigorously by modern Christian critics.
Canon S. R. Driver stated in the preface to the eighth edition of his
Introduction to the Literature of the Old Testament (Edinburgh, 1909):

> It is not the case that critical conclusions, such as those expressed in
> the present volume, are in conflict either with the Christian creeds or
> with the articles of the Christian faith. Those conclusions affect not the
> *fact* of revelation, but only its *form*. . . . That both the religion of Israel
> itself, and the record of its history embodied in the Old Testament, are
> the work of men whose hearts have been touched and minds illumined,
> in different degree, by the Spirit of God, is manifest: but the recogni-
> tion of this truth does not decide the question of the author by whom,
> or the date at which, particular parts of the Old Testament were com-
> mitted to writing. . . . There is a human factor in the Bible, which,
> though quickened and sustained by the informing Spirit, is never
> wholly absorbed or neutralized by it; and the limits of its operation
> cannot be ascertained by an arbitrary *a priori* determination of the
> methods of inspiration; the only means by which they can be ascer-
> tained is by an assiduous and comprehensive study of the facts pre-
> sented by the Old Testament itself. (pp. viii, ix, xi)

Such a latitudinarian approach to Scripture would seem to have no
place in Judaism. Certainly Maimonides' formulation of the eighth of
his thirteen principles of faith (a byword among orthodox Jews) leaves
little room for it:

> [The] Torah from Heaven. To wit: we believe that the whole of this
> Torah that we have today is the selfsame that was given to Moses; and
> all of it is from the Power [= God]; that is, it came to him, all of it did,
> from God—a coming called metaphorically speech, but whose manner
> is unknown to all but him (peace be to him) to whom it came; and that
> he was in the capacity [lit. degree] of a scribe to whom one dictates,
> and he wrote it all down—dates, stories, and commandments.[6]

This rigorous formulation is directed against Moslem attacks on the integrity of the Torah, and the charge or the suspicion that Moses, independently of God, invented it.[7] A glance at Talmudic antecedents
shows that Maimonides chose the language of the most uncompromising of several views found in that treasury of classical (and wellspring
of all subsequent) Jewish thought.

It was a jealously guarded dogma of early Judaism that "[the] Torah was from Heaven," meaning that not a word of the Pentateuch was—as charged by anti-Jewish writers of Hellenistic-Roman times[8]—an invention of Moses:

> And these have no portion in the world to come: Whoever says . . . [the] Torah is not from Heaven. (*m. Sanhedrin* 10.1)

Another Tannaitic dictum:

> "Because he has spurned the world of the Lord" (Numbers 15:31)— this refers to whoever says, "[the] Torah is not from Heaven"; and even if he said, "The whole Torah is from Heaven excepting a given verse, which the Holy One—blessed be He—did not utter, but Moses, on his own [lit. from his own mouth]," he is one who "has spurned the word of the Lord." (*b. Sanhedrin* 99a)

This dogma had to be adjusted to evidence contrary to several scriptural passages. For example, the final verses of the Pentateuch tell of Moses' death and burial.

> "There died Moses, the servant of the Lord" (Deut. 34:5): Is it possible that Moses wrote "There died Moses" while he was still alive? Rather, up to that verse Moses wrote, but from that verse onward Joshua wrote; so Rabbi Judah. Simon bar Yohai retorted: Is it possible that the Torah scroll [that Moses delivered into the custody of the Levite-priests] was missing even a letter? Yet it is written, "Take this Torah scroll" (Deut. 31:26, the account of the delivery)! Rather, up to that verse ["There died Moses"] the Holy One—blessed be he—was speaking and Moses was writing; from that verse on, the Holy One—blessed be he—was speaking and Moses was writing with tears, as it is written [of a similar procedure], "Baruch said to them, 'He [Jeremiah] recited aloud [lit. from his mouth] to me all these things while I wrote in a scroll with ink.'" (*b. Menahot* 30a)

Other difficulties arise, perhaps the foremost being the style of Deuteronomy in which Moses speaks in the first person and appears to gloss freely, on his own, quotations of God's utterances (e.g., the insert, "as the Lord your God commanded you," in the Sabbath commandment of the Decalogue, 5:12). The Rabbis described the difference between the curses at the end of Leviticus (26:14ff.) and the curses at the end of Deuteronomy (28:15ff.) as follows:

> Those [of Leviticus] are couched in the plural and Moses said them from the mouth of the Power, while these [of Deuteronomy] are

couched in the singular and Moses said them on his own [lit. from his own mouth]. (b. Megillah 31b)[9]

This blatant contravention of the Sanhedrin passages troubled commentators. The Tosaphists took the edge off the *Megillah* statement by qualifying "Moses said on his own" with the explanation "and by the Holy Spirit [of prophecy]," which at least derives Moses' speech from divine inspiration. Abarbanel made a distinction.

> Moses . . . said these things and expounded the commandments mentioned here to Israel under the necessity of his taking leave of them, and the Holy One wished that after he finished saying them . . . all should be written down in the Torah scroll just as Moses said it. . . . Hence, while the saying of these things to Israel was of Moses . . . the writing of it in the Torah scroll was not . . . for how could he write down anything on his own in God's Torah? . . . So this book is included among the divine books just like the others. Whoever says that Moses wrote down any given verse of them on his own—he is one who has "spurned the word of the Lord. . . ." That is why they said in *Megillah*, "The curses in Deuteronomy . . . Moses said them on his own"—said them, not wrote them. . . . Similarly Moses prayed on behalf of the people at the incident of the Golden Calf on his own, for he was not commanded to do so by God—indeed to the contrary, he demanded that Moses desist from him. . . . But the writing down of all such in the Torah was from the mouth of the Power . . . and whoever says . . . about the writing of the Torah that he [Moses] wrote anything that God did not say [= dictate] to him, he is one who has "spurned the word of the Lord." (Commentary, Introduction to Deuteronomy)

The pietistic commentator Ḥayyim ben Atar did not hesitate to emphasize the Mosaic provenience of Deuteronomy in his comment to the book's first verse:

> "These are the words"—these and not the preceding ones—"that Moses spoke"—these are his own words, for the whole book is Moses' warning and admonition directed against any who would transgress God's words. . . . Even when he resumed God's words in order to explain them it was not because he was ordered to do so but on his own.

Ben Atar calls the reference to the Egyptian bondage in Deuteronomy's version of the Sabbath commandment of the Decalogue (it is missing from Exodus) "the words of Moses" (at 5:15). He regards the speech beginning in 8:1 as displaying Moses' psychological insight.[10]

Such attributions to Moses do not deprive Deuteronomy of divine sanction (or even dictation); that is a dogmatic necessity no medieval believer would have challenged. What is notable is the latitude permitted within the scope of the dogma for human creativity. The literary (stylistic) facts point to Moses as the author of most of the book of Deuteronomy; the book's authority derived from the dogma that Moses' language was adopted by God and dictated back to him at the time the book was written down.

Quite surprising is the latitude shown in the interpretation of the prophetic message-formula, *kōh-'āmar YHWH* "thus said the Lord," used by Moses in the narrative of Exodus. In Exodus 32:27 Moses cites a divine command to slay the worshipers of the calf; but where is that command? The *Mekhilta*[11] finds it in Exodus 22:19, "Whoever sacrifices to a god other than the Lord alone shall be proscribed." A midrash puts it thus:

> Where did the Holy One—blessed be he—tell him to slay his fellows?
> He intimated to him at Sinai that anyone who worshiped an alien deity
> is subject to the death penalty; as it is said, "Whoever sacrifices to a
> god, etc." When he descended and found them worshiping an alien
> deity ... he thought, "These are subject to the death penalty."[12]

It is clearly implied that the message-formula need not always be taken literally; a prophet's inference from an earlier utterance of God may be couched in the language of a direct citation, when in fact the prophet tailored it for the occasion.[13]

An obscure passage in Sifre to Numbers 30:2 was understood by later interpreters to refer to this latitude:

> "This is the word that the Lord spoke" (Num. 30:2). This tells that just
> as Moses prophesied with [the formula] "Thus said [the Lord]" so the
> other prophets prophesied with "Thus said"; but Moses exceeded them
> in that of him it is said, "This is the word, etc."[14]

The fifteenth-century philologist, Profiat Duran, interpreted this passage in the course of explaining the Hebrew particle *kōh*, which he called "a term of comparison":

> "Thus shall you say to my lord [Esau]" (Gen. 32:5) means "the likes of
> these words," for Jacob did not care about the wording, only that they
> kept to the purport. I take similarly every "thus said the Lord" found
> in the sayings of the prophets. They mean by it the purport of God's
> speech to them, what is to be understood by his words. They do not
> scruple to make some verbal changes in it so long as the purport is kept
> unchanged. Hence "thus said the Lord" means "the likes of these
> words said the Lord." Now, when the sages said [that Moses used this
> common prophetic formula, yet exceeded the other prophets in using

"This is the word"] they meant that what Moses relates [after the preface, "this is the word"] is the very speech that God uttered, without any verbal change. By saying, "This" it is not enough to retain the purport—the general idea—as did the other prophets. That much may be inferred from the sense of *kōh*. But a better case can be made from the substance of the matter: Since the other prophets were foretellers only, not having been sent to give commandments but to admonish and warn concerning the observance of the Torah, while Moses alone (peace be to him) was sent to give commandments and Torah, therefore they said that "all the prophets prophesied with 'Thus said'— referring to the foretelling and the admonitions; but Moses our teacher (peace be to him) . . . exceeded them in that he gave commandments and Torah, and that is what is conveyed by 'This is the word that the Lord commanded.'"[15]

As lawgiver, Moses had to be precise in communicating the divine statutes.

Rashi, at Numbers 30:2, cites the enigmatic midrash without explanation; a supercommentary to Rashi fills the lack, offering a variation of Duran's view:

"Thus" refers to the purport of some verbal matter while "this" refers to the matter itself. Since all the prophets prophesied through an "unclear mirror," being incapable of receiving more than the purport of the matter communicated to them, they had to use the formula, "thus said the Lord." . . . But since the prophecy of our teacher Moses (peace be to him) was through a "clear mirror," and he was capable of receiving what was communicated to him just as it was, in his case "this is the word" was used, meaning this very matter, without any alteration. But because at the start of his mission our teacher Moses (peace be to him) had not yet attained to the degree that he enjoyed at its end, he had also to use to formula "thus said the Lord" on several occasions . . . namely, at the start of his career.[16]

The application to Moses of varying degrees of prophecy[17] recurs in another way in Abarbanel's comment to Moses' Song at the Sea (Exod. 15). How is it that the song is attributed to Moses (and, similarly, Deborah's Song to her and Barak, and Solomon's Song to him)? Because, Abarbanel answers, what is called song (*šîr[āh]*) is produced by a human whose ability has been heightened by the Holy Spirit:

The Holy Spirit is not [like a full-fledged prophecy], for it does not produce visions of forms and parables, and its appearance is not marked by deep sleep and loss of senses. Rather the prophet voluntarily chooses to speak wise sayings, or hymns, or admonitions, etc. And because the divine spirit joins itself to him and helps him shape his speech, his degree is called the Holy Spirit. . . . For just as a prophet does not prophesy continuously, but starts and stops, so he may prophesy at one time in the form of the highest degree and at another in a lower degree, or through the Holy Spirit.

. . . Every song found among the sayings of the prophets is an utterance they themselves formulated through the Holy Spirit. . . . When they are not prophesying they can speak through the Holy Spirit in beautiful figures and in high style. . . . Jeremiah wrote his book and the Book of Kings through prophecy, which is why they are included in the second division of Scripture, the Prophets; Lamentations he composed through the Holy Spirit, which is why it is in the Hagiographa. And because songs are produced and formulated by the prophet . . . they are always attributed to the one who made them. . . . To be sure, all those songs were written down in the Torah and the Prophets because they were approved by God and ordered by him to be written there. . . . Thus the formulation of the Song at the Sea was by our teacher Moses, but its having been written down in the Torah was from the mouth of the Power.[18]

In summary, the prevailing dogma was that every word in the Torah was dictated by God. This dogma was the necessary support of a hermeneutic that ascribed significance not only to the contextual sense, but to subcontextual units—clauses, phrases, even individual words torn out of context. Extreme hermeneutical freedom had to be counterbalanced by absolute assurance that the groundtext was perfect and supercharged with significance—in other words, that it was divine through and through. This formal ascription of the final form of the text to divine dictation did not blind exegetes to the varied styles of the Torah and the exigencies that indicated a human (Mosaic) origin for many passages. Room was left for a natural attribution to humans, even of prophetic speech introduced by the formula, "thus said the Lord."

In dealing with the rest of the prophets, tradition readily conceded the presence of a human factor, in accord with the literary evidence. The fundamental observation was made by a late third-century Talmudic sage:

Rabbi Isaac said: The same communication (*signôn*, from Latin *signum* "watchword") occurs to several prophets, yet no two prophets prophesy the same communication. [The prophet] Obadiah said, "Your arrogant heart has seduced you" (1:3), while Jeremiah said, "Your horrible nature has seduced you, your arrogant heart" (49:16). (*b. Sanhedrin* 89a)

Meiri glossed this as follows: "Prophets do not prophesy in the same language even when their prophecy is the same communication. For example: Obadiah and Jeremiah [have identical communications] in their prophecies against Edom, yet the language differs."[19] By this criterion the Talmud discovers the sign by which King Jehoshaphat of Judah judged the four hundred prophets of the Israelite king false: they all predicted victory at Ramoth Gilead in identical language (1 Kings 22:6).

How did Jewish thinkers explain this diversity in unity? By variations in the vehicles of prophecy. Here are excerpts from the account given by Joseph Albo, a fifteenth-century theologian:

> Since prophecy springs from a single active cause—God, may he be blessed, and its end is forever the same—to lead mankind to happiness, why do the words of the prophets differ from one another even when they treat of the same topic? . . . Our sages suggest an explanation in *Bereshit Rabba* (4.4): "A Cuthean (= gentile) once asked Rabbi Meir, 'Is it possible that he of whom it is said, "Do I not fill heaven and earth" (Jer. 23:24), should have spoken to Moses from between the staves of the Ark' (cf. Exod. 25:22)? He replied, 'Bring me a large (= magnifying) mirror'; and he brought it. He said, 'Look at your reflection'; he looked and saw it large. Then he said, 'Bring me a small (= reducing) mirror'; and he brought it. He said, 'Look at your reflection'; he looked and saw it small. Then he said to him: 'If you, mere flesh and blood, can change yourself into several forms at will, how much more so he who spoke and the world came into being!'" Apparently the Cuthean meant to deny that prophecy was an emanation from God. He thought that it was rather a mere work of the imagination, as is the opinion of the philosophers and their followers . . . because it is impossible that he, being one, should be seen by prophets under so many different forms. For that conduces to thinking that if it comes from the deity, the divine active cause must be plural and changing in nature. . . . Rabbi Meir confuted this notion through the analogy of mirrors. As an object appears in different forms . . . according to the shape of the mirror in which it is reflected . . . though the object is unchanging, so God, be he blessed, appears to the prophets in many forms according to the clarity and purity of the media [e.g., the imaginative faculty], though he . . . is neither plural nor changing. . . . In the same manner, the object seen changes in accord with change in the seers: if the seer . . . has clear vision he will see the reflection one way, but if he is weak-visioned he will see it in another. . . . (*Ikkarim* iii.9)[20]

As Albo himself summarizes at the start of the discussion, "Different effects may arise from the same agent, depending on the nature of the recipients." This medieval theory states abstractly the assumption of a Talmudic comparison of the throne visions of Isaiah (ch. 6) and Ezekiel (ch. 1):

> Rava said: All that Ezekiel saw Isaiah saw [only he did not go into detail]. To whom may Ezekiel be likened? To a country bumpkin who saw the king. To whom may Isaiah be likened? To a dweller in the [capital-] city who saw the king [and does not trouble to tell about it] (*b. Hagigah* 13b).

Thus the human factor is regarded as decisive in explaining divergences between prophetic descriptions of one and the same object of vision.

The most developed conception of human conditioning of prophecy is found in Abarbanel's commentary. We have already noted how he ascribed "songs" to prophets freely composing under the Holy Spirit, and how near contemporaries—Duran and Mizrahi—affirmed that the prophetic formula "Thus said the Lord" introduces the gist of a divine communication whose wording belongs to the prophet. Evidently the humanism of Christian Europe, with its renewed emphasis on the individual and self-expression, affected Jewish conceptions of prophecy. Here is how Abarbanel elaborated the Talmudic observation of prophetic diversity in unity in accounting for the similar eschatological visions of the Temple Mount in Isaiah 2 and Micah 4:

> [Rabbi Isaac asserted] that it is possible that the matter perceived by [two prophets] will be identical but the wording divergent. When I saw that Isaiah and Micah both prophesied the same communication, I thought: Isaiah prophesied this first, wherefore it is said here, "The word that Isaiah visioned," since he indeed was the one who had the vision. When Micah perceived the same general matter in the course of his prophesying he couched it in Isaiah's very words. That is to say: Micah received from God ... the matter of the prophecy, while the wording of the communication he took from Isaiah. Hence [the vision] is not introduced in Micah with the formula, "Thus said the Lord" or "The word of the Lord that came to Micah," like other prophecies of his. For this speech came from God first to Isaiah, not to Micah who took it from Isaiah's words and inserted into it some explanatory additions.
>
> Likewise ... our lord Moses himself said in the *Ha'ăzînû* song (Deut. 32:36), "For the Lord will vindicate His people, and get satisfaction for His servants," and David repeated this very verse in Psalm 135[:14] .... Surely David did not prophesy the very same communication as did [Moses] ... rather, he took that verse from the words of his teacher.... Frequently we find ... that one prophet says what another prophet already said in the very same words. (Comment to Isa. 2:1)

Abarbanel reverts to the subject in his comment to Jeremiah 49:16, further developing his understanding of Rabbi Isaac's dictum:

The prophets [other than Moses] perceived the general purport of the matter communicated to them by the Holy One—blessed be he—and then related and wrote it down in their own language. Hence when they perceived similar matters, they sometimes couched them in the very words that they saw in the prophecies of other prophets, with which they were familiar.... Isaiah said, "For my strength and my song is Yah, the Lord; and he has been my deliverance,"—a line derived from [Moses'] Song at the Sea (Exod. 15:2).... Not that prophecies came to [later prophets] in the same wording as to Moses our teacher and in his degree; rather they perceived matters [in a general sense] and on their own couched them in the language of verses with which they were familiar. So [is the case of] this prophecy of Jeremiah, which he couched in the language of Obadiah.

Abarbanel has virtually anticipated the modern notion of the literary education of prophets, and on the same ground: evidence within the oracles of familiarity with antecedent Israelite traditions.

Albo ascribed the differences among the prophets to divergences in their faculties; his younger contemporary Abarbanel applied this general principle to specific cases—for example, in this comparison of Jeremiah with Isaiah:

I am of the opinion that Jeremiah was not very expert either at composition or rhetoric, as was Isaiah or other prophets. Hence you find in his speeches many verses ... missing a word or two ... very, very frequent use of *'al* [properly "on"] for *'el* [properly "to"], masculine for feminine ... singular for plural and vice versa, past for future and vice versa, and shifts of second to third person in a single sentence. Moreover, there is chronological disorder in his speeches.

I believe that the cause of this was the youth of Jeremiah when he was called to prophesy.... Indeed he protested, "I do not know how to speak, for I am but a youth" (1:6). Isaiah, of royal blood and raised in the court of the king, spoke with eloquence; the other prophets were called after they attained to maturity in worldly matters and gained experience in dealing with people; so they knew how to arrange their sermons. Jeremiah, on the other hand, was of the priests of Anathoth [a class apart and a villager to boot]; while still young, being called to prophesy ... he was constrained to proclaim what the Lord commanded in language he was accustomed to. (Introduction to the Jeremiah commentary)

Abarbanel thus assigns to the human factor a predominant role in the verbal formulation and arrangement of a prophetic collection of oracles. He holds the modern hermeneutical principle that the language of prophecy is conditioned by the personal circumstances and talent of the prophet—his biography, his experience, and his education.[21]

Jewish exegesis of late antiquity and medieval times thus recognized that the prophet had a hand in the shaping of his prophecy. Did it also recognize an effect of the audience on prophecy? The one area in which early Jewish thinkers delved into the reception-factor in prophecy was anthropomorphism and related theological scandals such as the sacrificial cult. The exigency of adjusting naive biblical conceptions to sensibilities arising from theological reflection resulted in tacit criticism of aspects of biblical language about God. Rudimentary in Talmudic literature, such criticism reaches full expression under the impact of Islamic polemics. In defense, Jewish exegesis seized upon a Talmudic dictum, "The Torah spoke in the language of humankind," originally meaning that biblical language is to be interpreted according to ordinary usage, and gave it the new sense, "Biblical speech about God employs language drawn from human experience." By this adroit hermeneutical move all the vivid imagery of scriptural speech about God became metaphoric. The reason offered by Jewish thinkers and exegetes for the Bible's use of such scandalous language was the ignorant and brutish state of the Israelites who received the Torah: they had to be spoken to in the gross terms suitable to their understanding. The wise, however, realize the necessity of translating the picturesque God-language of the Bible into appropriate philosophic conceptions.

This vast topic—in theological terms, "the condescendence of God"—has been systematically treated by every major medieval Jewish thinker, and so will not be further discussed here. But to forestall misunderstanding the following important caution is cited from a recent survey: Unlike the idea that the prophetic message was conditioned by human factors in which premoderns and moderns agree, the idea of divine condescendence differs in a crucial point from its apparent modern counterpart:

> We are not dealing here with an evolutionary mentality, which sees Jewish history as moving from a primitive state (in need of such condescendence on the part of the divine) to a more perfect one. Such a view was virtually unknown in antiquity. . . . We are dealing here with a synchronic view; at all times there are both learned and simple people, but God places himself within reach of the simple.[22]

In summary: From the Talmud to the Renaissance classical Jewish thought and exegesis invests the prophetic writings with divine authority: all were inspired by the Holy Spirit—in the case of the Torah (the prophecy of Moses), the text was ultimately dictated by God. This formal, dogmatic predication of divine inspiration and authorship did not hinder acknowledgment of the literary evidence of human shaping of the text. Even the Torah contains extensive tracts formulated by Moses; their inclusion in the Torah means that they were ultimately sanctioned (dictated) by God, but the personal touch of Moses is there to this day. Apart from the Torah it is freely posited that prophecy is conditioned by the personality and the capacity of the prophet: His age, his spiritual level, his education, all affect his message. This alone accounts for the variety of styles and formulations that distinguish the prophets from one another, even when—and particularly when—they communicate similar messages. Hence, the introductory prophetic formula, "thus said the Lord," signifies no more than, "this is the substance of the Lord's communication to me, couched in my own language." It also happens that one prophet adopts the wording of his predecessor, with which he was familiar by education, when that wording seemed to him a suitable vehicle for the word of God that came to him. The personal factor may be so dominant that the inexperience and unlearnedness of a prophet result in faulty language and a disordered text.

Classical Jewish exegetes acknowledged these literary facts in the face of the great temptation to absolutize the authority of Scripture and silence the incessant challenges to its integrity and validity by categorically asserting that all is simply divine dictation. To modern Jewish critics they are a model of reverence toward the source of religion that does not entail blindness to the complexity of that source or the adoption of farfetched cloaking of that complexity. The tradition of honest and sober reasoning, accommodating articles of faith to (literary) facts, stands the critics in good stead as they confront a wave of simplistic dogmatic piety that seeks to impose itself on the entire community, stifling curiosity and independence of judgment.

NOTES

1. For rare exceptions see the prefaces of S. D. Luzzatto to his commentaries to the Pentateuch (1829) and Isaiah (1855), available in S. D. Luzzatto, *Ketavim* [Selected Writings] (ed. M. E. Artom; Jerusalem: Bialik Institute, 1976) 2:97–134, 206–16. Also consult Franz Rosenzweig's letter to J. Rosenheim, in F. Rosenzweig and M. Buber, *Die Schrift und ihre Verdeutschung* (Berlin: Schocken, 1936):46–54, disproportionately famous owing to the scarcity of theological deliberation by Jewish scholars with critical sophistication.

2. Examples of the first category: Y. Kaufmann, H. L. Ginsberg, H. M. Orlinsky, E. A. Speiser; of the second, U. Cassuto, M. Weiss. For brief surveys of modern Jewish critical exegesis, see M. Waxman, *A History of Jewish Literature* (New York: Bloch, 1947) 4:633–70; EncJud (Jerusalem: Keter, 1971) 4:899–903.

3. See S. Shaw, "Orthodox Reactions to the Challenge of Biblical Criticism," *Tradition* 10 (1969):61–85 (with bibliography); Sh. Rosenberg, "Biblical Criticism in Modern

Jewish Religious Thought" (in Hebrew), in *Ha-miqra va'anahnu* [We and the Bible] (ed. U. Simon; Tel Aviv: Dvir, 1979) 86–110 (extensive bibliographic survey). A good exposition of theological reactions to criticism is R. J. Z. Werblowski, "Biblical Criticism as a Religious Problem" (in Hebrew), *Molad* 18 (1960):162–68.

4. The distinction certain rabbis made between allowed and prohibited criticism (Hirschensohn) or the metaphysical accommodation of it to faith (Kook) described by Rosenberg (see previous note) remained private musings for all practical purposes. Decades later M. Kapustin ("Biblical Criticism: A Traditionalist View," *Tradition* 3 [1960]: 25–33) could still crudely characterize and reject "Biblical criticism [for which] the Torah is not word for word and letter for letter direct divine revelation. Neither are the writings of the *Nevi'im* (Prophets) or the *Ketuvim* (Hagiographa) divinely inspired, products of the *ruach ha-kodesh* (holy spirit). For the critics [they are] the works of certain individual personalities representing the 'Hebraic genius.'" Contrast the position of S. R. Driver—an eminent British critic—adduced ahead in the body of this article.

5. The question is this: When the prophet says, "Thus said YHWH," and proceeds to deliver a speech, what is the relation of his speech to what God said to him? I shall not deal with the question of how the prophet receives revelation or what form the divine communication to him takes, but only with the question of the immediate origin of the speech issuing from the prophet, and which he commonly prefaces by the formula, "Thus said YHWH" or the like. How precise is "thus"?

The views presented in this essay are chiefly those arising from explication of scriptural data, whether by exegetes or others. They are not such as are primarily grounded in a theology, in which extra-scriptural (often extra-Jewish) systematic thinking is determinative. (Even the citation of the theologian Joseph Albo—see note 20—bases itself on scriptural phenomena.) I seek to document the acknowledgment of literary facts, particularly those that resist easy accommodation to dogma. It is notable that when Abarbanel writes as a philosophic critic his position is more doctrinaire than when he writes as an exegete; see note 21.

For the following selection of sources I have drawn heavily on the monumental collection of A. J. Heschel, *Torah min ha-shamayim be-aspaklaria shel ha-dorot* [Torah from Heaven in the perspective of the ages] (London: Soncino, 1965) 2:123–298; and on the treatise on "The order in which the Torah was written," in *Torah Shelemah* (ed. M. Kasher; New York: American Biblical Encyclopedia Co., 1959) 19:328–79. Selection, arrangement, and interpretation are my own.

6. Maimonides, Commentary to Mishnah Sanhedrin 10.1; *Mishnah 'im Perush Rabbenu Moshe ben Maimon, Seder Neziqin* (ed. J. Kafah; Jerusalem: Mossad Harav Kook, 1964), 214.

7. See, for example, *Samau'al al-Maghribi: Ifham al-Yahud* (Silencing the Jews), ed. M. Perlmann, PAAJR 32 (1964):53–57.

K. P. Bland ("Moses and the Law according to Maimonides," in *Mystics, Philosophers, and Politicians* [ed. D. Swetschinski; Durham: Duke University, 1982], 49–66) argues that Maimonides "does not believe that Moses ever received the particulars of his law in revelation," but rather "considered Moses to have been the direct author of the Law" (63)—despite "the obvious efforts [in the thirteen principles] to find language that emphasizes the divine origin of the Law while minimizing the creative role of Moses in its promulgation" (65). Bland's argument has cogency for Maimonides' esoteric doctrine; however, no reading of the eighth principle will yield a "minimizing" of Moses' "creative role" but a forceful denial of it: Moses is figured as a scribe taking dictation. That is how believers through the ages have understood the principle, and Maimonides' choice of language and figure indicates that is how he intended to be understood by the masses.

I am grateful to Alfred Ivri for calling my attention to Bland's stimulating article.

8. See M. Stern, *Greek and Latin Authors on Jews and Judaism*, III Indexes (Jerusalem: Israel Academy of Sciences and Humanities, 1984):137, s.v. Moses: legislator of Jews.

9. "'Moses said those [of Leviticus] from the mouth of the Power'—having been commissioned by Him to say, . . . 'I shall set [such a curse], I shall visit [you with such a bane], I shall let loose [such a scourge]'—He who has the ability to do speaks so. But in

Deuteronomy... Moses speaks on his own, 'He will visit [you with such a bane]' "
(Rashi). Rashi's comment to Deuteronomy 28:23: "[Moses] mitigated his curses compared with those of God [in Leviticus]."

10. See E. Touito, *Rabbi Ḥayyim ben 'Atar u-Ferusho Or ha-ḥayyim 'al ha-Torah*
[Rabbi Ḥayyim ben Atar and his Commentary to the Torah "Or ha-ḥayyim"] (Jerusalem:
Ministry of Education, 1982) 33–34.

11. *Masseket de-Pisḥa, parasha* 12; restored from early quotations, see H. S.
Horovitz and I. A. Rabin, *Mechilta D'Rabbi Ishmael* (Jerusalem: Bamberger & Wahrman,
1960) 40, lines 9f.

12. L. Ginzberg, *Genizah Studies in Memory of ... Schechter* (New York: Jewish
Theological Seminary of America, 1928) 1:74f. (reference from Heschel, *Torah*, 145
[above, note 5]).

13. Or even invented it deliberately; see the following midrash aggadah from *Seder
Eliahu Rabba* (ed. M. Friedmann; Vienna: Verlag der israelitisch theologischen
Lehranstalt, 1900) 17:

> I call heaven and earth to witness that the Holy One—blessed be he—never
> said to Moses to stand in the gate of the camp and say, "Who is for the
> Lord—to me!" (Exod. 32:26), or to say, "Thus said the Lord ... 'Each of you ...
> slay brother, neighbor, and kin'" (v. 27). Rather, righteous Moses reasoned: "If I
> say to the Israelites, 'Each of you slay his brother, etc.,' they will say, 'Did you
> not teach us that a court that condemns to death one person in a sabbatical
> cycle is called murderous' [*Mishnah, Makkot* 1.10]? How come you put three
> thousand to death in one day (v. 28)?'" So he ascribed [the order] to the Heav-
> enly Glory, as it is said, "Thus said the Lord, etc." What follows? "The Levites
> did [as Moses had bidden]" (v. 28).

14. *Seder Mattot, pisqa* 153: *Siphre D'be Rab* (ed. H. S. Horovitz; Lipsiae:
Gustav Fock, 1917) 198.

15. *Maase Efod* (ed. J. Friedlaender and J. Kohn; Vienna: Holzwarth, 1865)
170.

16. Eliyahu Mizraḥi printed in *'Arba'a Perushim 'al ... Rashi* (Jerusalem: Divre
Ḥakamim, 1958) part 4 [Numbers], 54b. On "(un)clear mirror" see I. Gruenwald,
Apocalyptic and Merkavah Mysticism (Leiden: Brill, 1980) 135.

17. See Maimonides, *The Guide of the Perplexed*, II:45; in the translation of Sh.
Pines (Chicago: University of Chicago, 1963) 395ff.

18. Don Isaac Abarbanel, *Perush 'al Ha-torah* (Jerusalem: Bne Arb'el, 1964)
2:124f.

19. R. Menaḥem Meiri, *Sefer Bet Ha-beḥira 'al ... Sanhedrin* (ed. A. Sofer
[Schreiber]; Frankfort: Hermon [no date]) 323.

20. For the full text, see *Sefer Ha-'ikkarim* [*Book of Principles*] by Joseph Albo
(edited and translated by I. Husik; Philadelphia: Jewish Publication Society, 1946)
3:76–84.

21. These citations from Abarbanel's commentary to the Prophets give much
more scope to the human element in the formulation of prophecy than appears in
his *Commentary to Maimonides' Guide of the Perplexed*—as the latter's position is
summarized in A. J. Reines, *Maimonides and Abrabanel on Prophecy* (Cincinnati:
Hebrew Union College, 1970); see, e.g., Reines's summary statement:
"... prophecy is miraculously communicated as a finished creation from God to the
prophet, who is merely a passive recipient and produces nothing of the prophecy he
apprehends" (lxxv).

22. F. Dreyfus, O.P., "Divine Condescendence (synkatabasis) as a Hermeneutic
Principle of the Old Testament in Jewish and Christian Tradition," *Immanuel* 19
(Winter 1984/85):74–86; citation on page 83. The original French version of this
article appears in *Congress Volume, Salamanca 1983* (VTSup 36; ed. J. A. Emerton;
Leiden: Brill, 1985):96–107.

A more extensive treatment is S. D. Benin, "The 'Cunning of God' and Divine
Accommodation," *Journal of the History of Ideas* 45/2 (1984):179–91. On page 189
Benin cites Yehuda ha-Levi's *Kuzari* (I:98; Hirschfeld translation, 67) to the effect

that even if all persons at the time of Israel's beginnings had been philosophers, "discoursing on the unity and government of God, they would have been unable to dispense with images, and would have taught the masses that a divine influence hovered over this image, which was distinguished by some miraculous feature" (*Kuzari*, ibid.). This seems to conflict with Dreyfus's rejection of an evolutionary view. And yet it may be harmonized with Dreyfus as follows: The masses do gradually move from crude to more refined ideas, through divine pedagogy and condescendence, so one may speak of an evolution of refinement among masses. Philosophers (like Moses and the prophets) knew better from the first. Ha-Levi's assertion that even the philosophers of antiquity would have been unable to dispense with images is connected with what they "would have taught the masses"—suggesting that their teaching was an accommodation to a level of understanding lower than their own.

I am grateful to Mr. Benin for calling my attention to his illuminating article.

Additional note:

On the disinclination of modern Jewish Bible scholars to theologize, see the trenchant essay by Jon D. Levenson, "Why Jews Are Not Interested in Biblical Theology," in J. Neusner, et al., eds,., *Judaic Perspectives on Ancient Israel* (Philadelphia: Fortress Press, 1987), 281–307.

Bible Interpretation as Exhibited in the First Book of Maimonides' *Code*

1989

In the cultural tradition of the West the Jews are the oldest extant example of a people constituted throughout most of its history by allegiance to a written document—the Torah (in its larger sense, all of Hebrew Scripture and its authorized interpretation). The canonical Scripture defined Israel, prescribed its norms of conduct, and described its place in the past and future of mankind. Two factors made the Torah effective in society: (1) its popular base—rudimentary means of mass education prescribed in the Torah had been elaborated by the start of the Christian era; and (2) a vigorous growing body of exegesis, as old as the canon, that assured its constant adjustment to contemporary needs.

Both factors are exemplified in the great digest of Jewish law and theology composed by Maimonides (1135–1204) for popular edification, the *Mishneh Torah* (English: the *Code*). This work sums up the beliefs and practices of Judaism topically, in categorical nonargumentative form, as they may be gathered from Talmudic-midrashic-gaonic (= post-Talmudic legal) literature. But it also incorporates a large amount of Bible interpretation, in the guise of proof-texts, most of them taken from the sources, but some (especially on theological matters) original with Maimonides. By noting the gap between the meaning of the proof-text in its primary scriptural context and its use in the *Code*, a hermeneutical operation is revealed, and by adding instance to instance one can survey the full range of hermeneutics at the disposal of classical Judaism in its maturity. This essay analyzes the use of proof-texts in *Sefer ha-madda* ("The Book of Knowledge"), the first and most theological part of the *Code*.[1]

In his introduction to the *Code,* Maimonides explains the name which he gave it—*Mishneh Torah,* "a second to the Torah"—as follows:

> A person who will first read the Written Torah and afterwards this work, through which he will learn the Oral Law entire, will not need to read another book besides.

Now the *Mishneh Torah* is itself full of citations of Scripture ("the Written Torah"), much more so than the Mishnah of R. Judah the Prince, which it ostensibly imitates. *Sefer ha-madda* for example, comprising 455 paragraphs, contains about 400 citations, or a citation for approximately every one and one-eighth paragraphs. The highest density of citation occurs in *Teshuvah,* averaging two citations per paragraph; the lowest occurs in *'Avodah Zarah* (treatise on idolatry), averaging one citation in every one and three-quarters paragraphs. But even this is higher than the corresponding mishnaic tractate *'Avodah Zarah* with its one citation for every five and a half paragraphs, or—an even closer analogy to *Sefer ha-madda*—the ethical and pedagogic Mishnah treatise *'Abot,* with one citation for every three paragraphs. Thus the *Mishneh Torah* not only seconds or complements Scripture but through its constant incorporation of citations from Scripture provides abundant illustration of its authoritative interpretation. Most of the citations embody Talmudic-midrashic understanding; they are not used by Maimonides in an original and innovative sense, and so cannot serve as a window to his distinctive Bible interpretation (an exception is the whole body of deanthropomorphizing interpretation, which is pointedly nonTalmudic, if not always original with Maimonides—Saadiah did precede him).[2] But our purpose is to ascertain not the originality of the scriptural interpretation found in *Sefer ha-madda* but rather the range and extent of the modes of interpretation that Maimonides' "ideal reader" (the person who read only Scripture and *Mishneh Torah* and no other book besides) would learn. Here is a ready source from which to gather how an enlightened thirteenth-century Jewish reader might perceive "the senses of Scripture," not as theoretical possibilities but as living and binding interpretation.

Before entering into the details of interpretational modes, it may be of interest to tabulate Maimonides' selections from Scripture.

Biblical Book	No. of Citations	Distribution in Sefer ha-madda *(partial data)*
Deuteronomy	112	48 in *'Avodah Zarah* 31 in *Yesode Torah*
Leviticus	35	13 in *'Avodah Zarah*

Exodus	33	10 in *Yesode Torah*
		14 in *ʿAvodah Zarah*
Isaiah	31	22 in *Teshuvah*
Proverbs	30	10 in *Deʿot*
		7 in *Talmud Torah*
Psalms	29	16 in *Teshuvah*
Numbers	23	Evenly distributed in all treatises except *Deʿot*
Ecclesiastes	15	Mostly in *Teshuvah* and *Deʿot*
Jeremiah	15	Mostly in *Teshuvah* and *Deʿot*
Genesis	13	Mostly in *Yesode Torah* and *Teshuvah*
Samuel	11	Mostly in discussion of prophecy in *Yesode Torah*
Other books	72	Six or less citations per book

The distribution of biblical books from which Maimonides drew citations correlates well with the ethical and theological concerns of this first book of his *Code*.

What modes of Scripture interpretation does the reader of *Sefer ha-maddaʿ* encounter? What are the hermeneutical operations he can observe? They are many; I shall list them and then illustrate each with examples.

A. Plain sense–the sense determined by the biblical context;

B. Generalization—what is true for a particular case (the cited passage) is true for others;

C. Specification—a generality is concretized in a particular;

D. Rubrication or "proverbization"—the citation (sometimes a fragment of a verse) is abstracted from its context and serves as a rubric (a title, a name) or as a proverb, in that it encapsulates a value or a principle;

E. Use of a story to illustrate a rule—as an example to emulate or to shun (the story may be adjusted to fit the rule).

The scriptural text is assumed to be supercharged with meaning; manifestations of this are:

F. Multiple meanings in a given passage—the overload of the text being, as it were, repeatedly discharged. This is often connected with

G. Decontextualization and atomization—the ascription of meaning to fragments of sentences or to expressions abstracted from their context;

424 : *The Bible in Jewish Thought*

H. Inference from juxtaposition—the adjacency of passages is significant;

I. Alternative lexical and syntactic options—exploitation of other meanings of words and of innovative syntactic constructions (usually accompanied by decontextualization and abstraction of a segment of text);

J. Maximization—drawing implications or consequences beyond the primary sense. This may be effected by

K. Literalization or prosification—taking figures of speech at face value, or restricting words to a sense other or narrower than that required by the context.

The assumption of the intellectual and spiritual excellence of the Bible governs exegesis—it is assumed that the Bible agrees with the best thought of the age. Accordingly we find:

L. Rationalization, spiritualization, and refinement of the primary sense of Scripture;

M. Importation of philosophical ideas, especially through metaphorization of the primary sense.

The assumption of the timeless validity of Scripture is highlighted in

N. Contemporization—the application to current circumstances of notations and ordinances predicated on different (obsolete) arrangements.

Virtually all of the citations in *Sefer ha-maddaᶜ* are embraced in these hermeneutical categories; many fall into several at once; very few are mere embellishments, and fewer still are enigmatic.

We proceed to illustrate these categories with a couple of examples of each. Where appropriate, a comment appears explicating the gap between the primary sense of the citation—its sense in its biblical context—and the sense in which it serves Maimonides as a proof-text. Although that sense is usually found in his rabbinic sources, Maimonides will, in the sequel, be conventionally called its author. Bracketed matter is paraphrase.

A. Plain sense: Maimonides cites a verse according to its contextual sense, at times supplying a commentary.

A.1 The sage does not run in public or behave in a frenzied manner . . . but walks equably, like one preoccupied. Even from one's manner of walking it is manifest whether he is a sage or a fool, as Solomon said, "On the road also, when a fool walks, his mind is absent, and he says to all that he is a fool" (Eccles. 10:3)—he proclaims to everyone concerning himself that he is a fool (*Deᶜot* 5.8).

A.2 [God did not determine what every individual would do when he foretold how the Egyptians or the Israelites would behave in the future: He only described in general terms how people customarily act, as in the verse, "For the poor shall not cease being in the land" (Deut. 15:11), which is not a decree of fate but a description of the way things are (*minhago shel ʿolam*)] (*Teshuvah* 6.5).

Comment: Maimonides observes correctly that Deuteronomy 15:11, though it sounds like a prediction of what has been determined to be, merely predicates the habitual presence of the poor in society as the ground of an exhortation to be openhanded. This serves Maimonides as a warrant to interpret similarly other passages in which God predicts human behavior, and thus avoid the conflict between determinism and human responsibility. Knowing how things are, God predicts the general course of events; this puts no constraint on the conduct of any individual, leaving him free to choose his actions.

B. Generalization—what is true for a particular case is also true for others or generally; this includes stereotyping, and may entail abstraction from the context.

B.1 Whoever transgresses willfully any one of the commandments . . . desecrates God's name; that is why we read, in the case of false oath, "You must not swear falsely by My name and thus desecrate the name of your God; I am the Lord" (Lev. 19:12; *Yesode Torah* 5.10).

Comment: The citation refers only to a false oath by God's name, where the resulting desecration of the name is obvious; Maimonides generalizes this to apply to every case of willful transgression of a commandment.

B.2 Gentiles, coarse in nature, nurse their anger forever, as the text says of the Gibeonites, inasmuch as they refused to forgive and be conciliated, and demanded the death of Saul's sons, "Now the Gibeonites were not of the Israelites" (2 Sam. 21:2; *Teshuvah* 2.10).

Comment: The clause cited is part of a parenthetic statement that supplies the background of Saul's massacre of the Gibeonites, a remnant of the indigenous Amorites. It recalls the oath of protection that the Israelites swore to them at the time of the conquest of the Holy Land, which Saul violated. Maimonides abstracts the clause, and construes it as a deliberate contrast between Gibeonites and Israelites in order to explain the former's ruthlessness. This trait is then generalized to all Gentiles.

C. Specification—a generality is concretized in a particular, or a general admonition is institutionalized.

C.1 Our sages forbade self-affliction by fasting; concerning such practices Solomon commanded, "Do not be excessively righteous; and do not be over-clever, lest you destroy yourself" (Eccles. 7:16; De'ot 3.1).

C.2 Everyone is obligated to love each and every fellow-Jew like oneself, as it is said, "You shall love your fellow as yourself" (Lev. 19:18). Accordingly, one must speak well of his fellow and care for his property as one cares for one's own property and is solicitous of one's own honor (De'ot 3.3).

C.3 Repentance is always in order, but during the ten days between the New Year holy day and the Day of Atonement it is most appropriate and is immediately accepted, as it is said, "Seek the Lord when he makes himself available; call on him when he is near" (Isa. 55:6; Teshuvah 2.6).

Comment: The biblical context is a prophecy of redemption from exile; the prophet's admonition is couched in general terms of seasons of special grace; Maimonides applies it in particular to the annual Ten Days of Repentance.

D. Rubrication or proverbization—a citation (often a fragment of a verse) is abstracted to serve as rubric (title, name) for a value or a principle, or as a proverb.

D.1 If a sage behaved scrupulously, spoke pleasantly to people, acted in a conciliatory manner, received people graciously, did not answer insult with insult . . . conducted his business honestly . . . went beyond the letter of the law . . . so that everybody praised him, loved him, and tried to emulate him, such a person sanctified the name of God; of him Scripture says, "You are my servant, Israel, in whom I will be glorified" (Isa. 49:3; Yesode Torah 5.11).

Comment: In its scriptural context this is a quotation by "the servant of the Lord" of God's declaration to him; the quotation climaxes a brief account of the servant's preparation from birth to be an instrument in God's hand for returning Israel to him and to bring his salvation to the ends of the earth (vv. 5–6). In Maimonides the verse-fragment is abstracted from the context and is employed to express a relationship between man and God whereby man is an instrument of God's glorification. Specifically, through the Torah-sage's exemplary conduct, the Torah and God who gave it are praised. The scriptural citation acts as a proverb defining a value embodied in a specific situation, or as a rubric of that value.

D.2 An elementary school teacher who leaves his pupils, or does other work while he is with them, or is careless about their learning, is in the category of "Cursed be whoever does the work of the Lord slackly" (Jer. 48:10; Talmud Torah 2.3).

Comment: The continuation of the verse, of which this is the first half, is, "Cursed be whoever withholds his sword from shedding blood"; the context is a prophecy of Moab's devastation by divinely appointed executioners. The verse lays a curse on any of them who does God's bloody work slackly. In Maimonides the verse-fragment is abstracted from its scriptural context and its essence is extracted, to wit: Damnable is the person who executes a sacred task incumbent on him in a slovenly manner. This essence defines, as a rubric or as a proverb, a category of behavior; as such Maimonides applies it to the specific case of the unreliable teacher.[3]

E. Use of a story to illustrate a rule or principle; this may entail adjusting the story to suit the rule or principle.

E.1 When one has offended his fellow, the offended party must not harbor hatred silently, as it is said of a villain, "Absalom did not speak hostilely or amicably to Amnon, for Absalom hated Amnon" (2 Sam. 13:22); rather he is commanded to advise the offender, saying to him, "Why did you do thus and so to me?" ... And if the offender repents and begs his pardon, he must pardon. Nor may the pardoner be hardhearted, as it is said, "Abraham prayed to God, and God healed Abimelech" (Gen. 20:17; *De'ot* 6:6).

Comment: In the first citation Absalom's silent hatred is an explicit scriptural illustration of condemned behavior (cf. F.1 below); the citation is used according to its plain sense (cf. A above). The second citation (Gen. 20:17) is a problem. In the story Abimelech, a Philistine king, told by Abraham that Sarah is his sister (a device to protect Abraham's life), takes her to wife, only to be stricken for it by God with a plague. God reveals to Abimelech his offense, and he is told to return Sarah to Abraham, at which time Abraham will pray in his behalf to cure him. The king complies, and Abraham intercedes on behalf of the king, illustrating the principle that a pardoner should not be hardhearted, but should accept graciously the relenting offender's plea for pardon.

The difficulty with the proof-text is the typing of Abimelech as the offender and of Abraham as the offended, who, in the role of the reprover, when begged to pardon, graciously accedes. In the biblical story Abimelech appears more offended than offending, and far from begging pardon remonstrates with Abraham almost in the very words that Maimonides prescribes that an offended person use for reproof: "What have you done to us, and how have I sinned against you, that you have involved me and my kingdom in a grievous sin?" (Gen. 20:9). Maimonides reads the story in the light of a ready-made pattern of behavior posited by the rules of conciliation, namely, the sequence of offense, open reproof, repentant plea for pardon, gracious acceptance of the plea. This pattern is imposed on a different sequence in our story: Abimelech's unwitting sin of near-adultery owing to Abraham's deceit, according to Maimonides' pattern, is construed as Abimelech's offense against Abraham; God's reproof of Abimelech, as Abraham's reproof; Abimelech's coerced return of Sarah, as his bid for pardon. Maimonides' view has, to be sure, a scriptural basis: God does treat the king as an offender, and the king's retreat is answered by a favor from Abraham. This is a good example of a hermeneutical maneuver, the result of which reacts on our perception of the original text.

E.2 One may not practice divination as do the Gentiles . . . What constitutes divination? . . . Also the setting up of signs: "If such and such a thing happens to me, I will do this or that, and if it does not happen, I won't do it"—as Eliezer the servant of Abraham did (Gen. 24:12–24; *'Avodah Zarah* 11.4).

Comment: The sign set by Abraham's servant (identified with Eliezer of Gen. 15:2) to identify Isaac's future wife is represented in the biblical story as legitimate (God signals his choice through it). Maimonides' rejection of it illustrates the occasional tension between the values of Scripture and those of rabbinic Judaism.

F. Ascription of multiple meanings to a given text, out of conviction that the biblical text is supercharged.

F.1 When a person has been offended, he must not harbor hatred silently . . . but is commanded to reprove the offender by saying to him, "Why did you do thus and so to me, and why did you sin against me in such and such a matter?", as it is said, ("You shall not hate your brother in your heart), you shall surely reprove your comrade" (Lev. 19:17; *De'ot* 6.6).

If one sees his fellow sinning, or following an evil course, he is obligated to set him aright and warn him that he is sinning against himself by his evil deeds, as it is said, "You shall surely reprove your comrade" (ibid., 6.7).

Comment: The clause "You shall surely reprove your comrade" is interpreted twice: once in connection with the preceding clause, "You shall not hate your brother in your heart, rather (*waw* adversative) you shall surely reprove your comrade," and once as independent of it, a discrete injunction to intervene when seeing one's fellow behave in a reprobate manner.

F.2 God has commanded us not to read such books (composed by idolaters describing their worship) . . . concerning this it is said, "Lest you inquire after their gods, saying, 'How do these nations worship?'" (Deut. 12:30). You must not inquire about the manner of idol-worship, even though you do not practice it, for this will cause you to turn your mind to it, and to do as they do, as the verse continues, "I would do so too" (*'Avodah Zarah* 2.2).

(Different idols have differing modes of worship; Jews are forbidden to worship an idol according to its proper mode), as it is said, "How do these nations worship their gods? I would do so too" (*'Avodah Zarah* 3.2).

Comment: The same text yields two meanings: One must not study the idolaters' manner of worship by asking how they do it, for that might lead to imitating them. Nor must one worship the idol according to its proper mode, for that is prohibited by the same language; indeed Scripture defines culpable idol-worship as only that which is performed according to the proper ritual of the particular idol.

Neither interpretation accords with the plain sense of Deuteronomy 12:30, whose concern is to ban the study of idol worship in order to imitate it in the worship of Israel's God—i.e., to introduce idolatrous ways of worship (such as child sacrifice) into the Jewish worship of God (see v. 31).

A pervasive hermeneutical operation reflecting the conviction that the text is supercharged is

G. Atomization—interpretation of a verse-fragment apart from its context, and recombining such fragments into new wholes.

G.1 Whoever obliterates one of the sacred pure names by which God is called incurs the penalty of flogging. In connection with idolatry it is said, "You must obliterate their (= the idols') names from that place (of idol-worship). You must not do so to the Lord your God" (Deut. 12:3–4; *Yesode Torah* 6.1).

Comment: The full text of these verses prohibits worshiping the God of Israel at many sites, as the pagans worship their gods; rather, Israelites must confine their worship to a single site to be chosen by God: "²You must obliterate all the places at which the nations whom you are dispossessing worshiped their gods, on high mountains, and on hills, and under every leafy tree. ³You must demolish their altars and break their pillars . . . and obliterate their names from that place. ⁴You must not do so to the Lord your God; but to the place where the Lord your God shall choose out of all your tribes to set his name there—to his dwelling you shall resort and come there" (Deut. 12:2–5). Maimonides combines the final clause of verse 3 with the initial clause of verse 4—both abstracted from their context—thus creating the new interdiction and commandment to "obliterate the names of the pagan gods"—i.e., to erase their names, and a ban on "doing so to/for the Lord your God," namely erasing his name. This hermeneutic maneuver raises to a symbolic level (dealing with names) the coarser physical injunctions of the biblical text to separate Israel from pagan ways (cf. L below).

G.2 It is written in the Torah, "It (= the Torah) is not in heaven, nor is it across the sea" (Deut. 30:12–13): "it is not in heaven"—it is not to be found in the haughty; "nor is it across the sea"—not in those who traverse the sea (in pursuit of commercial gain) (*Talmud Torah* 3:8).

Comment: In their original setting these clauses belong to a discourse on the accessibility of the Torah: "It is not in heaven that you need say, 'Who will go up for us to heaven and take it for us and let us hear it, that we may observe it?' Nor is it across the sea, that you need say 'Who will go for us across the sea and take it for us and let us hear, that we may observe it?'" Maimonides adopts an atomizing hermeneutic that also metaphorizes "heaven" and "across the sea" (see below, M) into the haughty and the merchants, in order to find a pedagogic lesson in these phrases. Again, there is a common concern conjoining the plain sense with that evoked through atomization (conditions of acquiring Torah).

It must be stressed that the results of such hermeneutical operations are additional senses, alongside the plain contextual sense. They do not supplant the primary sense but add to it; thus they reflect the conviction that the text is supercharged.

H. Inference from juxtaposition—the adjacency of passages is significant.

H.1 It is the custom of sensible people to acquire a gainful occupation first, then to buy a home, and then to take a wife, as it is said, "What man has planted a vineyard but has not yet desacralized it . . . has built a house but has not yet dedicated it . . . has betrothed a woman but has not yet taken her to wife?" (Deut. 20:5–7). But the fool marries first, and afterward, if he can afford it, he buys a house, and later yet, when he is along in years, he tries to acquire a trade or lives off the dole; and so we read in the [covenant-]curses, "You will betroth a woman, you will build a house, you will plant a vineyard" (Deut. 28:30); i.e., your actions will run backward, so that you will not prosper in your efforts (*De'ot* 5.11).

Comment: The first trio comprises three classes of conscripts declared exempt from military service by the priest who accompanies the army; the order seems hierarchical, with marriage the highest value. For Maimonides the collocation of items in the series has an additional meaning: It suggests the recommended sequence of adult life stations. Maimonides has inverted the first two items in the citation—the scriptural order being "built a house" then "planted a vineyard"—to suit his didactic purpose. Probably he was also influenced by the (reverse) order in the curse passage, for there (Deut. 28) the items of Deuteronomy 20 appear in the sequence "take a wife, build a house, plant a vineyard." The ominous context—punishment for breach of covenant—dictates that the added significance be negative: This is the sequence of a fool's life-stations.

Maimonides' manipulation of the order of items in the first series is an interesting display of hermeneutical liberty.

H.2 If a woman has shaved her sidelocks she is not liable, since it is said, "You shall not cut the sidelocks of your heads, and you shall not destroy the edges of your beard" (Lev. 19:27). Only he who is liable for transgressing "You shall not destroy" may be held liable for "You shall not cut," and a woman is not liable for "You shall not destroy," for she has no beard ('Avodah Zarah 12.2).

Comment: In addition to the specific prohibitions in this verse, conveyed by the two clauses, information on those who are subject to them is conveyed by their juxtaposition. Both men and women have sidelocks, but only men have beards; by ascribing significance to the conjoining of these two prohibitions new information is elicited from the text, limiting the scope of the former to those affected by the latter. Collocational meaning is a supercharge on the verbal meaning of the verse.

I. Exploitation of alternative lexical and syntactical options, usually with abstraction from context and fragmentation.

I.1 One who lives off his own labor is highly meritorious. . . . Thereby he earns all honor and good in this world and in the world to come, as it is said, "When (*ki*) you eat of the toil of your hands, you are happy, and it shall be good for you (Ps. 128:2)—"you are happy" in this world, "and it shall be good for you" in the world that is wholly good (*Talmud Torah* 3.11).

Comment: The Psalm details the happiness of "all who fear the Lord, who walk in His ways" (v. 1) Hence our verse 2 can no more be conditional (*ki* = "when") than the rest of the verses in the Psalm that assert categorically the blessings of the Godfearer. The *ki* of verse 2 is asseverative, "indeed" (as in Lamentations 3:23: "The kindnesses of the Lord have indeed (*ki*) not ceased, His mercies have indeed (*ki*) not ended"), and the verse means: "[as a Godfearer], you shall indeed eat the products of your toil, you shall be happy," etc. This contrasts with the wicked, who are cursed thus: "The yield of your soil and the produce of all your toil shall be consumed by a people whom you do not know" (Deut. 28:33).

In Maimonides the verse is abstracted and interpreted according to the temporal/conditional sense of *ki*, namely "if, when": When are you happy? when you eat what your own hands, not another's, have produced. Moreover, the parallelism of the clauses, "you are happy and it shall be good for you," is suppressed in favor of maximal distinction between them—the first a reference to this world, the second, to the next.[4] By alternative lexical and syntactical construction the abstracted verse serves as the scriptural peg on which to hang a Talmudic value—the virtue of being gainfully employed—a biblical verse is enriched with a second meaning, and a nonbiblical concept is naturalized into Torah. In effect, the abstracted verse has been rubricized (see D), i.e., turned into a proverbial embodiment of a value concept.

I.2 Those who cause a town in Israel to apostatize are subject to the penalty of stoning, even if they themselves did not apostatize but merely incited their fellow townsmen to apostatize and worship (an alien deity) . . . What passage warns against inciting to apostasy (without stating its penalty)? "[The name of another god] shall not be sounded by [*al*] your mouth" (Exod. 23:13; *'Avodah Zarah* 4.1).

Comment: The full verse reads, "You shall not mention the name of another god; it shall not be heard in [*al*] your mouth"; the two clauses are parallel and prohibit uttering the name of an alien god (e.g., in a prayer or in an oath). Maimonides cites the second clause only, and by means of an alternative sense of *'al pi-*, "at the bidding of," arrives at the sense "the name of an alien god must not be heard at your instigation"—a warning without penalty against incitement to idolatry. This answers the requirement of rabbinic legal exegesis that every penal law (here Deut. 13:13–19) must have a nonpenal warning in a scriptural passage corresponding to it.

J. Maximization—drawing extreme consequences, beyond the normal range of meaning.

J.1 If one's neighbors are scoundrels and sinners who would not let him dwell in the town unless he become like them and follow their evil conduct, he should depart for the caves, the brambles, and the deserts rather than lead the life of a sinner, according to the tenor of "Would that I were in the desert, in a wayfarer's lodge, that I might leave my people and go away from them; for they are all adulterers, a band of faithless men" (Jer. 9:1; *De'ot* 6.1).

Comment: The prophet conjures up a state he is not in and a course he did not follow, namely, to remove himself from civilization in order to separate himself from his sinful neighbors. Maimonides regards the passage as a recommendation—indeed a model—for proper behavior, which means, however, not to wish to withdraw to the desert but so to act. What the prophet yearned for but did not do becomes maximized into a mandate for action.

J.2 But when the Jews control the Gentiles, we are prohibited from allowing an idolatrous Gentile among us. Even if he is only a temporary resident or a transient for the purpose of trade, he may not pass through our country until he has accepted the seven Noachite commandments (minimal religio-moral precepts of humanity), as it is said, "They shall not dwell in your land" (Exod. 23:33); [he may not stay] even for a moment (*ʿAvodah Zarah* 10.6).

> *Comment:* The citation is taken from a warning not to come to terms with the inhabitants of Canaan: "They shall not dwell in your land, lest they lead you to sin against me when you worship their gods, for that will ensnare you." The sense is to rid the country of its settled population of idolaters. Maimonides maximizes the ban by investing the durative "dwell" with the momentary meaning "stay for a moment," thus excluding even transients whose commerce requires them to pass through the Holy Land and who can hardly be in a position to lead Jews into error. Fear of temptation warrants an extreme exegesis that cuts Jews off from any contact with idolaters in their Holy Land. Note the same purpose in the following example.

J.3 We are not to follow the customs of the Gentiles, we are not to assimilate with them either in costume or in hair-style, or the like, as it is written, "And you shall not conduct yourselves according to the norms of the nation(s)" (Lev. 20:23), and it is also said, "And by their norms you shall not conduct yourselves" (Lev. 18:3), and, "Be careful not to be ensnared by them" (Deut. 12:30; *ʿAvodah Zarah* 11.1).

> *Comment:* All the above-cited passages deal with the natives of Canaan, from whose immorality and idolatry Israel is warned to keep away. Maimonides extends the prohibition to external cultural features (costume and hair-style) of all Gentiles. Fear of assimilation (conversion to the religion of the Gentiles) commands a policy of total cultural separation, supported by maximizing exegesis.

K. Literalization or prosification—taking the terms of a figure of speech at face value; restricting the sense of an expression more narrowly than is required by the context.

K.1 It is stated explicitly in the Torah and in the Prophets that God is not corporeal, as it is said, "For the Lord your God is God in the heaven above and on the earth below" (Josh. 2:11), and no body can be in two places (at once) (*Yesode Torah* 1.8).

> *Comment:* When Rahab exclaims that the fame of Israel's God and his invincibility have demoralized her townspeople and convinced them of his omnipotence, she does not enunciate a physical law, or intend it to be inferred. To be God above and below means to exercise dominion everywhere, and it is putting pressure on the language to draw the logical conclusion that Maimonides draws from Rahab's merism—a figure by which a whole is expressed through division into two, e.g., "young and old" = everyone; "heaven and earth" = everywhere.

K.2 Women and servants are exempt from the study of Torah, but a male minor's father is obligated to teach him Torah, as it is said,

"You shall teach them [God's commandments] to your sons to speak of them" (Deut. 11:19). A woman, however, is not obligated to teach her son, since only one who is obligated to study is obligated to teach (*Talmud Torah* 1.1).

Comment: The citation is from a general admonition to observe God's commandments and love him, addressed to the nation at large and bolstered by the promise of agricultural prosperity for obedience and the threat of famine and exile for disobedience. Teaching children the Torah is necessary, so that they may know their responsibility as members of the covenant people. In Deuteronomy 29:10 "little ones" (male and female) and women are included in the Israelite covenant partnership, and in 31:12 women and "little ones" are among those convoked in the septennial reenactment of the Sinaitic "day of assembly," in which God proclaimed the Decalogue, the basis of his covenant with Israel, in the hearing of the entire people. The purpose of the convocation is to make the adults "hear [the rehearsed Torah] . . . and learn to fear the Lord . . . and their sons [= children, equivalent to the preceding 'little ones'], who are ignorant, hear and learn to fear the Lord." In those rites, then, the obligation to hear the covenant stipulations (= the Torah) lies on all adults and all "little ones" regardless of sex. Hence, it is to be inferred that in our citation the obligation of teaching "sons" embraces daughters as well, and those addressed include all adults, women as well as men. Be it noted, too, that respecting the arch sin against the covenant—incitement to idolatry—women are explicitly named among those liable: "Should your . . . daughter or the wife of your bosom incite you" (Deut. 13:7), even though in the sequel only masculine forms are used. Now it is clear that women are liable only because they are supposed to know the covenant stipulation; but if they are not included among those who must be informed of these stipulations, they cannot be held responsible for violating them. There seems to be a certain tension between the halakhic exemption of women from learning the Torah and the general halakhic rule that "all negative commandments in the Torah obligate men and women equally" (*'Avodah Zarah* 12.3); but if women are exempt from learning, how are they to know these negative commandments that obligate them?

For Maimonides the obligation to learn is associated with liberty; servants and women are exempt because they are not sovereign over their time, and the study of Torah must be accorded set times (*Talmud Torah* 1.8). Since a married woman is subjugated to the needs of her husband and family, she is exempt from the duty to learn Torah; and since education of minors is preparation for adult responsibility, a minor female too is exempt from learning Torah. On the other hand, since adult males are obligated to study Torah at set times (a democratization of God's injunction to Joshua, "You shall study [or: recite] it day and night" (Josh. 1:8; see below, N), fathers are obligated to train their sons in the duty of fixed study of Torah.

The strict halakhic construction of "You shall teach them to your sons" (and not to your daughters) is thus the outcome of two factors: (1) the conception of Torah study as a routine, fixed in schedule and curriculum; and (2) a definite assignment of roles to adult males and females, whereby males retain some control over their time, while females are so much subject to the calls of familial responsibility and tasks as to lack any such control. Through the combination of these two factors, study of Torah in rabbinic Judaism is a "liberal art" (an art that requires some degree of liberty). This is not a biblical conception.

K.3 Some sins deserve punishment in this life, upon one's body or property or his minor children. For a person's minor children, whose minds have not yet been formed and who have not yet become liable to observe the commandments, are considered his possessions. Scripture says, "A man for his own sin shall be put to death" (Deut. 24:16) —the rule applies to grown men (*Teshuvah* 6:1).

Comment: The biblical injunction addresses a court, forbidding it to punish vicariously across generations: "Fathers shall not be put to death on account of sons, nor sons on account of fathers; a man [= each person] for his own offense shall be put to death." Both parts of the verse, the negative and the positive, deal with this single issue; the emphasis was justified in the light of ancient practice.[5]

Maimonides isolates the last clause and ascribes it to the working of divine punishment. That each person dies for his own sin is contradicted by infant mortality. A degree of rationalization is obtained by a literal construction of איש as "a (grown) man": only adults are judged as autonomous moral individuals.

This leaves open the status of the morally unformed person, the minor who does not yet have a full mental capacity and therefore cannot be responsible for what he does. Such a minor has not yet emerged into individuality, and is not to be regarded as an autonomous moral entity. His moral guardian is his parent, who is held answerable for his child's liabilities; the other side of the coin is the child's inclusion in the moral state of its parents: parents condemned by their conduct implicate their minor children in their punishment. By this conception Deuteronomy 24:16b, originally guarding minors from vengeance taken upon their parents (by an earthly agency), is understood as subjecting minors to the divine retribution dealt to their parents. Hermeneutics defeats the plain sense in the interest of theodicy.

L. Refinement—e.g., rationalization or spiritualization—of the primary sense.

L.1 Don't think that repentance applies only to sins in which there is some act, such as fornication, robbery, or theft. Just as one must repent of these, so must he examine his bad traits and repent of them—anger, hate, envy, competitiveness, mockery, pursuit of gain and glory, gourmandizing, and the like; of all such he must repent. Indeed, these offenses are worse than those in which there is some act, for when one becomes addicted to one of them he can forsake them only with difficulty. Hence Scripture says, "Let the wicked man forsake his way, and the base man his devisings" (Isa. 55:7; *Teshuvah* 7.3).

Comment: In biblical Hebrew a person's "way" refers to his actions; in Ezekiel 33:11 "the evil man's turning from his way" is spelled out in verses 14–15 to mean "doing what is just and right: returning [a poor borrower's] pledge, restoring what one has robbed [another of], following the statutes of life, and not acting crookedly." "Devisings" refers to planning specific actions, as the word implies. Maimonides carries the contrast between interiority and exteriority a step further by refining the concept of the former. The penitent must abandon not only his evil acts and his thoughts that led to them, but even those general character traits and tendencies that underlie the thought of evildoing.

L.2 Cognition of this matter (that the prime cause is God) is a positive commandment, as it is said, "I, the Lord, am your God" (Exod. 20:2). Whoever thinks that there is a god besides this One God transgresses a negative commandment, which is, "You shall have no other god beside me" (ibid., v. 3), and denies the basic principle on which everything depends (*Yesode Torah* 1.6).

Comment: The first two statements of the Decalogue, here cited, are related to each other as motive and command: "Since I, the Lord, am your God who has liberated you from the land of Egypt, from the house of bondage, you shall have no other god beside me." The divine claim on Israel for exclusive worship is historically grounded: The infinite benefaction that God has conferred upon Israel by liberating them created an infinite obligation on their part to be loyal servants to him alone.

To Maimonides recognition of God's existence is first of all an intellectual obligation, based on rational grounds (briefly outlined in the first five paragraphs of this chapter), independent of historical events. The first statement of the Decalogue, separated from the second already in Talmudic literature, and sundered from its continuation in which the Exodus is alluded to, is taken by Maimonides to imply a conclusion arrived at by reason; more, it includes a command to know this conclusion. "I, the Lord, am your God" means: you must acknowledge my being God (= the prime cause) as a postulate of reason. The next statement flows out of the first one as a logical conclusion: having recognized my Godhood as a postulate of reason you may not imagine the existence of an equal, a rival god (this is argued in detail in the following paragraphs).

The experiential motive in Scripture for Israel's obligation of exclusive acknowledgment of, and allegiance to, their God is transformed by Maimonides into an obligation to recognize the rational necessity of God's existence (as the prime cause of all that is), and a prohibition of conceiving the existence of another like him. The biblical expressions of the empirical ground of loyalty to God and the consequential ban of the worship of other gods are converted into positive and negative injunctions concerning intellection and ratiocination. The language of faith based on events is boldly transmuted into language of faith based on reason.

M. Metaphorization as a means of importing philosophical or spiritual meaning: Metaphors may serve theological, ethical, or pedagogical purposes.

M.1 Prophets cannot prophesy at will, except our master Moses: whenever he willed it, the holy spirit of prophecy rested upon him . . . as it is said, "Wait, that I may hear what the Lord commands concerning you" (Num. 9:8). God assured him of this, as it is said, "Go, say to them [the Israelites], 'Return to your tents,' but you stay here with me" (Deut. 5:27–28); from which you learn that other prophets return to their "tents," meaning their physical needs, when their prophecy is finished, just like other people, hence they do not withdraw from their wives. But our master Moses did not return to his former "tent," hence he withdrew permanently from his wife, and from the likes of her (*Yesode Torah* 7.6).

Comment: The ability of Moses to obtain divine responses (i.e., to prophesy) at will is shown by the passage in Numbers 9:8, in which he directs inquirers to stand by until he receives an oracle in reply to their inquiry. Maimonides says no more than what is implicit in the plain sense of Scripture.

Deuteronomy 5:27–28 is treated differently. According to its context the passage refers to God's acquiescence in the people's request, after the Sinai theophany, to be spared further exposure to the terrifying direct contact with him; they ask Moses to be their mediator in future communications with him. God concurs— the people are to return from their place of assembly at the foot of the mountain to their tents (away from the presence of God), while Moses remains at the mountain to receive further word on behalf of the people.

For Maimonides the surface meaning points to a deeper theological doctrine of the uniqueness of Moses' prophecy. Whereas other prophets had to make themselves ready spiritually to receive the holy spirit, and after prophesying they relapsed into mundane preoccupations, "the mind of Moses attached itself to the Rock Everlasting; the 'splendor' (Num. 27:20) never left him, the skin of his face radiated (Exod. 34:30–35), and he became as holy as the angels" (*Yesode Torah* 7.6, end). Such spiritual height required mental withdrawal from mundane affairs, particularly from the grossly corporeal and sensory ones. This is foreshadowed in Scripture's injunction that there must be a separation of the sexes three days prior to the Sinai theophany, thus readying the entire people for a prophetic experience (the mass receipt of direct revelation), Exodus 19:14–15. This serves as a basis for a "first storey" metaphorization of "return to your tents" in Deuteronomy 5:27: God allows the people after the theophany to resume normal (sexual) relations with their wives, while requiring Moses to continue his abstinence (verse 28, "but you stay here with Me")—so in midrashic literature; this is, in turn, the ground for Maimonides' "second storey" metaphor. For Maimonides "tents" = "wives" is itself metonymic for "physical needs," i.e., attention to corporeal and mundane affairs ("his wife and the likes of her"). Moses, in his view, never diverted his mind from godly thoughts after Sinai; he separated himself from his wife (the "first storey" metaphor, which Maimonides considers the plain historic sense of Scripture), and "stayed" forever "with" God—i.e., dedicated his mind to contemplating divine matters for the rest of his life.

This complex metaphorization illustrates the simultaneous levels of scriptural sense: the literal meaning of "return to your tents" is but a metaphor for "resume sexual relations with your wives." And this is a metonym for "relapse into attention to worldly matters," as is the wont of all prophets except Moses. The last sense is the timeless theological teaching of the passage, which yields itself only to a person capable of proper metaphorization.

M.2 One should regard himself always as on the verge of death— perhaps he may die within the hour and be permanently settled in his sins; he should therefore repent forthwith and not think, "When I get old I shall repent," lest he die before he grows old. That is what Solomon meant when he said, in his wisdom, "At all times let your clothes be white [clean], and let not the oil on your head be wanting" (Eccles. 9:8; *Teshuvah* 7.2).

Comment: The verse in Ecclesiastes is part of a passage (9:7–10) that urges the reader to enjoy the pleasures of this life, for the ability to do so is a manifest sign of divine approval; moreover, if one misses his pleasures, nothing after death can make up for them. This hedonistic advice, of a piece with Ecclesiastes' view of the vanity of existence, is converted by Maimonides into exalted ethical teaching by metaphorization: Laundered clothing and oiled head are metaphors for a person cleansed of sin by repentance. The sage urges one to hold himself "at all times" in a cleansed spiritual state, lest he be overtaken suddenly by death and thus lose forever the chance of expunging his sins.

M.3 A disciple who has not yet attained competence to render decisions but renders them nevertheless is foolish, wicked, and arrogant; of him it is said, "She has felled [*hippilah*] many [*rabbim*] corpses" (Prov. 7:26). Likewise a sage who has attained competence to render decisions but does not render them withholds Torah and puts stumbling blocks before the blind, and of him it is said, "and numerous [רבים] are all her slain" (ibid.) (*Talmud Torah* 5.4).

Comment: According to the context the verse sums up the menace of the "alien woman" who seduces innocent youths and sets them on the road to perdition. But the chapter opens with a contrast between Dame Wisdom (whom the young disciple is urged to embrace) and "the alien woman" (whom he must shun), a contrast that hints at the possible metaphorization of the latter, like that which occurs in Proverbs 9, where Dame Folly (vv. 13–18), opposed to Dame Wisdom (vv. 1–6), is described as a seductress of youth in terms recalling the "alien woman." This possibility is fully exploited by Maimonides: if Dame Wisdom is Torah personified, the "alien woman" is ignorance personified. Of her Proverbs 7:26a says that she has "aborted" (הפילה, "caused to fall," in the postbiblical Hebrew sense), i.e., brought forth before their time rabbis (a play on רבים) who are corpses. In other words, ignorance has produced abortions—unripe births—in the form of worthless teachers.

The second part of verse 26 describes metaphorically another ill effect of ignorance: עצומים evokes עצם "to shut (the eye)," and is understood as "blinded" or "shut off, withheld from light (= Torah)." The whole second clause will then mean blinded, or withheld from Torah, are all victims of ignorance. This is taken as the opposite of the preceding clause, in that it speaks not of the feckless teachers produced by ignorance but of an erring public that is left in the dark owing to the refusal of competent teachers to enlighten them.

By a metaphorization that has a foothold in the biblical text

Maimonides converts a worldly teaching into a precept of academic ethics.

N. Contemporization—adjustment to current circumstances of ideas and ordinances predicated on obsolete conditions, including democratic extension of precepts directed at the biblical elite.

N.1 One is obligated to be considerate of orphans and widows, because they are dejected and meek, even if they are wealthy. We must be considerate even of a king's widow and his orphans, as it is said, "Every widow and orphan you [plural] shall not afflict" (Exod. 22:21; De'ot 6.10).

Comment: The context enjoins the community to care for each and every widow and orphan, the plural subject and the two objects in the singular indicating collective responsibility for even a single case of violation. The continuation of the cited verse (21) reads: "Should you [plural] afflict him [singular, in effect "her or him"], for if he should cry for help to me, I shall surely heed his cry, my anger will be kindled, and I shall slay you [plural] by the sword, so that your [plural] wives shall become widows and your children orphans" (vv. 22–23). "Every" (*kol*) in verse 21 means "any, even one."

Maimonides takes "every" to mean "even a wealthy man's, even a king's"; in addition to obliterating the biblical point that punishment will be visited for even a single orphan's or widow's cry, Maimonides effaces the collective responsibility indicated by the biblical plural subject by his opening formulation "one [*'adam*] is obligated." This formulation in the singular converts a collective obligation into an individual one, and adjusts the biblical communal moral entity to the contemporary reality of a nation splintered and scattered over the earth. Maimonides has in fact reversed the biblical emphasis: The individual is under obligation to be considerate of every kind of orphan and widow.

N.2 It is a grave offense to despise the sages or hate them. Jerusalem was destroyed just because the people despised the disciples of the sages who were located there, as it is said, "They made light of the messengers of God, and despised his words and mocked at his prophets" (2 Chron. 36:16), that is, despised the teachers of his words (*Talmud Torah* 6.11).

Comment: The biblical citation is part of an indictment of Jerusalem, to the effect that its doom was sealed because its inhabitants refused to heed the warnings continuously given to them by generations of prophets sent by God to prod them into repentance. Maimonides contemporizes the lesson by equating the biblical messengers of God (= prophets) with the sages ("disciples of the wise") through his interpretation of "(despise) his words" as "(despise) the teachers of his words." Functionally the contemporary sages are equivalent to the biblical prophets and therefore may be understood as the referent of the biblical term; contemporization interprets the biblical text anachronistically as referring to present-day functionaries.

N.3 Every man in Israel is obligated to study Torah ... even if he is a beggar; even if he is saddled with wife and children, he is obligated to set aside times for study of Torah by day and by night, as it is said, "You must study it day and night" (Josh. 1:8) (*Talmud Torah* 1.8).

Comment: As the head of the polity of Israel, Joshua is commanded in the cited verse to study continuously ("day and night") —and observe—the Torah for as long as he lives. Maimonides democratizes the obligation, laying it on every adult Jewish male, as though the command to Joshua were grounded on his being an adult Jewish male (and needed special emphasis only because Joshua was a "king"; cf. Deuteronomy 17:19, where a similar obligation is laid on the king in order to keep him humble). Moreover, Maimonides derives a specification from the citation by taking a merism ("day and night" = continuously) literally: the study must be performed at set times by day and by night.

By democratizing the injunction to Joshua, Maimonides gives it a contemporary significance (and also sets a royal standard of study and observance for the rank and file of Jewish men).

These fifteen hermeneutical operations account for almost all of the meanings of Scripture found in *Sefer ha-maddaᶜ*. As a rule, the cited passage moves beyond its original sense in its new Maimonidean setting; only in a very few cases is the citation static, merely a scriptural flourish adorning Maimonides' statement, as in *Deᶜot* 1.1:

Then there is the avaricious person, who cannot be satisfied by any amount of money, in accord with the verse, "He who loves money will never be sated with money." (Eccles. 5.9)

Moreover, the vast majority of citations are interpreted in a transparent manner: The hermeneutic maneuver is self-explanatory and requires no special knowledge in order to follow it. Very seldom is the connection of the proof-text to the Maimonidean rule enigmatic. Here is an example:

Likewise, if one has made an idol with his own hands for others, even if for a Gentile, he is to be flogged, as it is said, "Molten gods you shall not make for yourselves" (Lev. 19:4; ᶜ*Avodah Zarah* 3.9).

A glance at the midrashic source of this ruling discloses the hermeneutic operation that yields a connection:

> From the verse "Molten gods you shall not make for yourselves" may I infer that if others make them for you it is allowed? No; the text reads "not for yourselves" (under any circumstances). If so, may I infer that if you make them for others it is permitted? No; the text reads "you shall not make not-for-yourselves" (i.e., you shall not make for others) (*Sifra Qedoshim*, end of sec. 1).

Maimonides refers to this last "piggyback" hermeneutical stage, which is extremely artificial, and unfathomable from his form of citation.

The relation of the original Scripture to the Scripture as presented in the *Sefer ha-madda*ᶜ illustrates Jonathan Z. Smith's insight:

> Where there is a canon (a closed list of authoritative texts), it is possible to predict the necessary occurrence of a hermeneute, of an interpreter whose task it is continually to extend the domain of the closed canon over everything that is known or everything that exists *without* altering the canon in the process.[6]

Let us spell this out by characterizing in general terms what our ideal reader (one who knew only the *Sefer ha-madda*ᶜ and the Bible) would have gathered from Maimonides' use of Scripture:

1. First, from the sheer abundance of citations, he would have gathered that rabbinic Judaism (a portion of which the *Sefer ha-madda*ᶜ epitomizes) is derived from—is indeed an elaborated expression of—the Bible. Both its theological and its legal precepts have their roots in Scripture, and this is what lends rabbinic Judaism its authority as an exposition of a divinely ordained canon. The frequency of citation and its distribution over several fields of religious life is an implicit retort to the Karaite accusation that rabbinic (Talmudic) Judaism is a human figment.[7]

2. However, the relation of Scripture to rabbinic Judaism is by no means static; to be sure, there are cases in which the citation retains its contextual sense when it is used by Maimonides to support a rabbinic precept, but far more often the citation has a fresh aspect in its Maimonidean setting. The primary sense of Scripture is extended by logical moves (e.g., generalization, specification) or it is left behind more radically as the citation is abstracted from its setting in Scripture and its semantic cargo released from the bounds of its original context. Underlying this dynamic interpretation is the view of the scriptural text as perfectly supercharged with meaning. The primary contextual

sense is not an exhaustive discharge of the text's meaning; the text continues to yield meanings when abstracted, fragmented, combined innovatively, all in accord with varying circumstances in, and purposes for, which it is addressed.

3. Unlike Maimonides, the ideal reader cannot be aware of the various ideological settings from which interpretations have been culled; to name the chief ones:

(a) the Talmudic-midrashic value world;

(b) philosophical and theological speculation;

(c) ascetic trends.[8]

This variety represents in fact a layering of Jewish thought, whereby the biblical basis was successively overlaid with more or less systematically developed ideational and value structures, each claiming biblical derivation. To the reader of Maimonides, historical perspective is denied by the harmonious amalgam of these layers—a triumph of consolidation unmatched before or after. The cosmos of Talmudic Judaism as presented by Maimonides is both uniquely organized and uniquely enriched by subsequent developments. As such, it is, for the reader of its time, contemporary and not obsolete, abreast of the best thought of the age. And since, as aforesaid, the Maimonidean presentation insisted on the biblical origin of contemporary Judaism, the effect is to portray the Bible as an enduringly adequate guide and inspiration for living through all time. Or, better said, the Bible is an adequate and enduring guide when interpreted by the rabbinic sage who knows how to evoke its multifaceted meanings.

A question may well arise in the mind of our ideal reader as he contemplates the great freedom of interpretation exhibited by Maimonides: Is there any control over that freedom? Are there limits to the liberty exercised by the exponents of rabbinic Judaism in their scriptural exegesis? To that question he will find no explicit answer in the *Code.* Nor will he be helped if he goes behind the *Code* to its Talmudic-midrashic-rabbinic sources. To be sure, lists of hermeneutical rules appear in that literature, but it is abundantly clear from the practice of the Talmudic-midrashic sages that in the vast majority of their interpretations of Scripture they were neither guided nor constrained by rules. It would therefore seem that the only bounds to hermeneutic liberty were considerations of harmony with the existing norms and value-complexes[9]—the conception of harmony, including strictures upon those norms and values. One of the most powerful impressions made by the *Code* on the reader is that of the harmony and coherence of the Judaism it portrays. To that impression the constant citation of the Bible contributes no little part.

The attempt to trace all wisdom to the Bible is not an attempt on our part to draw out what is objectively in it; it is an attempt on our part to unify our knowledge by reference to a single source of authority—and there are good philosophical and psychological reasons why we should attempt to do so.[10]

It is unlikely that our ideal reader could have taken so detached a view of the hermeneutic enterprise that we have described, but he surely would have endorsed this perceptive justification of it.

NOTES

1. *Sefer ha-maddaʿ* is cited according to the edition of Simon Rawidowicz (Jerusalem, 1974)—essentially the same as the standard editions. Translations of Maimonides and of the Bible are mine. The Talmudic-midrashic sources of Maimonides are conveniently available in Saul Lieberman, ed., *Sefer Hamada*, annotations of sources, notes and elucidations [by] Jacob Cohen (Jerusalem, 1964).

Sefer ha-maddaʿ comprises five treatises (*hilkhot*, "laws") concerning: 1. *Yesode Torah*, "Foundations of Torah (= religion)," mostly theology and the doctrine of prophecy; 2. *Deʿot*, "Ethical Characteristics"; 3. *Talmud Torah*, "Study of Torah"; 4. *ʿAvodah Zarah (we-ḥuqqot ha-goyyim)*, "Idolatry (and the Customs of the Gentiles)"; 5. *Teshuvah*, "Repentance."

The concept of citation prevailing in this essay accords with the careful definition of Stefan Morawski: "Quotation is the literal reproduction of a verbal text ... wherein what is reproduced forms an integral part of some work and can easily be detached from the new whole in which it is incorporated. ... The crucial features of the quotation are its literalness and its discreteness. ... To the former is related the question of accuracy or fidelity, the latter is responsible for its appearance in inverted commas. Thus the quotation is a semantic portion designed to perform a certain function in a new and extraneous semantic structure of a higher order ... through it one can examine the relationship between the original to which it properly belongs and the work which has borrowed it" ("The Basic Functions of Quotation," in A. J. Greimas et al., eds., *Signs. Language. Culture* (The Hague, 1970), 690–705; cited passage on p. 691).

The most common quotation marker in *Sefer ha-maddaʿ* is a phrase with the verb "said" (*ʾamar*)–most frequently, "(as) it is said (שנאמר)." Other phrases are "as David said (in Psalms)," or "that is (the meaning of) what Solomon said in his wisdom (in Eccles.)." In series the much less used Aramaic form "and it is written" (וכתיב) may appear. I have not included rhetorical allusions to Scripture, but have included a few references to stories significantly interpreted (e.g., E.2 below).

2. A few observations on Maimonides' use of Scripture are found in Isadore Twersky's grand *Introduction to the Code of Maimonides* (New Haven, 1980), 57, 145–50. A systematic attempt to describe Maimonides' own Bible exegesis, particularly its philosophic-rationalistic and philologically grounded character, is Wilhelm Bacher's *Die Bibelexegese Maimuni's* (Budapest, 1896). Bacher was not interested in the vast body of Talmudic-midrashic interpretation that Maimonides incorporated into his *Code*. The fundamental analysis of that mode of interpretation remains Isaac Heinemann's *The Methods of the Aggadah* [Hebrew] (Jerusalem, 1949).

Jacob I. Dienstag published a wide-ranging bibliography on "Biblical Exegesis of Maimonides in Jewish Scholarship," in G. Appel, ed., *Samuel K. Mirsky Memorial Volume* (Jerusalem: Sura Institute for Research and New York: Yeshiva University, 1970), 151–90. As far as I can see, none of the items registered there aim at classifying the quotations in Maimonides by the type of hermeneutical operation exhibited in their use.

3. See the illuminating article by Galit Hazan-Rokem, "The Biblical Verse as Prov-

erb and as Quotation," *Jerusalem Studies in Hebrew Literature* [Hebrew], 1 (1981): 155–66.

4. James L. Kugel has described well the rabbinic "forgetting" of parallelism in favor of distinction between parallel clauses in *The Idea of Biblical Poetry* (New Haven, 1981), 96–109.

5. See my discussion in Menahem Haran, ed., *Yehezkel Kaufmann Jubilee Volume* (Jerusalem, 1960), 20–7.

6. Jonathan Z. Smith, *Imagining Religion* (Chicago, 1982), p. 48.

7. See Twersky (note 2, above), 45, 145.

8. Twersky, ibid., 459–65.

9. The constituent of coherence in rabbinic thought; see Max Kadushin, *The Rabbinic Mind*, 2nd ed. (New York, 1965), especially 14–35.

10. Bernard Jackson, "Legalism," JJS 30 (1979):1–22; citation from 13f.

Bibliography of the Writings of Moshe Greenberg

1950
1. "A New Approach to the History of the Israelite Priesthood." JAOS 70: 41–47.

1951
2. "The Bible and Mythological Polytheism" by Yehezkel Kaufmann. Translated from the Hebrew by Moshe Greenberg. JBL 70: 179–197.
3. "Hebrew s*egullā*: Akkadian *sikiltu.* JAOS 71: 172–174.

1953
4. "Biblical Criticism and Judaism." *Commentary* 15: 298–304.

1955
5. *The Hab/piru.* New Haven: American Oriental Society.
6. Review of *Ancient Israel* by Harry M. Orlinsky. *The Reconstructionist* 21/13: 24–27.
7. Review of *The Jewish Commentary for Bible Readers, Book of Kings* by Leo L. Honor. *The Reconstructionist* 21/11: 30-32.
8. ‏"לחקר בעית החׄברו (חׄפרו)." תרביץ כד[תשט"ו]: 379–369‎.

1956
9. "Hebrew 'Alive' at the U. of P." *Women's League Outlook* 26/4: 6, 26.
10. "The Stabilization of the Text of the Hebrew Bible: Reviewed in the Light of the Biblical Materials from the Judean Desert." JAOS 76: 157–167. See no. 114.
11. Review of ‏קדמוניות ארצנו‎: *The Antiquities of Israel* by M. Avi-yonah and S. Yeivin. JBL 75: 257–258.
12. Review of *The Bible: A Modern Jewish Approach* by Bernard J. Bamberger. *Judaism* 5/1: 86–87.

1957
13. "Ezekiel 17 and the Policy of Psammetichus II." JBL 76: 304–309.
14. "The Hebrew Oath Particle *ḥay/ḥe.*" JBL 76: 34–39.

15. Review of *Israel and Revelation* by Eric Voegelin. *American Political Science Review* 51: 1101–1103.

1958

16. "On Ezekiel's Dumbness." JBL 77: 101–105.

1959

17. "The Biblical Conception of Asylum." JBL 78: 125–132. (See no. 136.)
18. "On Teaching the Bible in Religious Schools." *Jewish Education* 29/3: 45–53. (See nos. 60, 166.)
19. Review of *Rivers in the Desert: A History of the Negev* by Nelson Glueck. *The JWB Circle—In Jewish Bookland,* May 1959, 1, 7.

1960

20. *The Religion of Israel: From its Beginnings to the Babylonian Exile* by Yehezkel Kaufmann. Translated and abridged by Moshe Greenberg. Chicago: University of Chicago Press. (See nos. 72, 104, 193.)
21. "Some Postulates of Biblical Criminal Law." In *Yehezkel Kaufmann Jubilee Volume,* ed. Menahem Haran, 5–28. Jerusalem: Magnes Press. (See nos. 77, 99, 139, 169, 207.)
22. "The Teaching of the Bible." *Proceedings [of the] Seventh Annual Pedagogic Conference,* 1–9. Cleveland: Institute of Jewish Studies, Cleveland Bureau of Jewish Education.
23. "נסה in Exodus 20:20 and the Purpose of the Sinaitic Theophany." JBL 79: 273–276.
24. Review of הלשון והרקע הלשוני של מגילת ישעיהו השלמה ממגילות ים המלח: *The Language and Linguistic Background of the Isaiah Scroll* by Eduard Yechezkel Kutscher. JBL 79: 278–280.

1961

25. *Introduction to Hebrew.* Revised edition. Philadelphia: Department of Oriental Studies, University of Pennsylvania. (See no. 57.)

1962

26. "Another Look at Rachel's Theft of the Teraphim." JBL 81: 239–248.
27–40. Articles in *The Interpreter's Dictionary of the Bible,* ed. Keith Crim. Nashville: Abingdon Press. 27. "Avenger of Blood" (1: 321); 28. "Banishment" (1: 346); 29. "Bloodguilt" (1:449–450); 30. "Bribery" (1:465); 31. "City of Refuge" (1:638–639); 32. "Confiscation" (1:669); 33. "Crimes and Punishments" (1:733–744); 34. "Drunkenness" (1:872); 35. "Hanging" (2:522); 36. "Prison" (3:891–892); 37. "Scourging" (4:245–246); 38. "Stocks" (4:443); 39. "Stoning" (4:447); 40. "Witness" (4:864).
41. Review of בימי בית ראשון: מלכויות ישראל ויהודה: *The Kingdoms of Israel and Judah,* ed. A. Malamat. JBL 81: 299–300.

1963

42. "The Bible: A New Translation." *Hadassah Magazine* 43/6: 6, 21.
43. "The New Torah Translation." *Judaism* 12: 226–237.
44. "Reflections on a New Jewish Problem." *Jewish Exponent,* September 13.
45–48. "Text and Tradition I–IV". *Jewish Exponent,* February 1, 8, 15, 22 [four articles illustrating the Jewish Publication Society's *The Torah: The Five Books of Moses*].
49. "Yehezkel Kaufmann: In Memoriam." *Jewish Exponent,* November 8.
50. Review of *The Torah: The Five Books of Moses. Philadelphia Inquirer,* January 27.

51.   "לדמותו של שמואל ליב בלאנק המורה." שבילי החינוך 23/2 [תשכ"ג]: 74–73.

1964
52.   "Jewish Tradition vs. Prejudice." *Hadassah Magazine* 46/2: 6, 30.
53.   "Kaufmann on the Bible: An Appreciation." *Judaism* 13/1: 77–89.
54.   "Stocktaking 5725." *Jewish Exponent*, September 11.
55.   Review of *The Hebrew Scriptures: An Introduction to Their Literature and Religious Ideas* by Samuel Sandmel. JQR 54: 258–265.
56.   "יחזקאל כ' והגלות הרוחנית." בתוך: ע"ז לדוד, 442–433. ירושלים: קרית ספר [תשכ"ד].

1965
57.   *Introduction to Hebrew.* Englewood, NJ: Prentice Hall [revised edition of no. 25].
58.   "Anthropopathism in Ezekiel." In *Perspectives in Jewish Learning*, ed. Monford Harris, 1–10. Chicago: College of Jewish Studies.
59.   "The Impact of the New Translation." *The JPS Bookmark* 11/4: 4–6.
60.   "On Teaching the Bible in Religious Schools." In *Modern Jewish Educational Thought*, ed. David Weinstein and Michael Yizhar, 79–88. Chicago: College of Jewish Studies. (See nos. 18, 166.)
61.   "Response to Roland de Vaux's 'Method in the Study of Early Hebrew History.'" In *The Bible in Modern Scholarship*, ed. J. Philip Hyatt, 37–43. Nashville: Abingdon Press.
62.   "The Unbroken Chain." *Jewish Exponent*, February 5.

1967
63.   "The Biblical Grounding of Human Value." In *The Samuel Friedland Lectures, 1960–1966*, 39–52. New York: The Jewish Theological Seminary of America. (See nos. 73, 112, 166.)
64.   "Liberation and Spoliation—A Passover Message." *Jewish Exponent*, April 12.
65.   "The Thematic Unity of Exodus iii–xi." *Papers [of the] Fourth World Congress of Jewish Studies*, I, 151–155. Jerusalem: World Union of Jewish Studies.
66.   "ח'ברו (ח'פרו)—עברים." בתוך: ההיסטוריה של עם ישראל, כרך שני: האבות והשופטים, ערך בנימין מזר, 102–95. תל–אביב: החברה להוצאת ההיסטוריה של עם ישראל והוצאת מסדה, תשכ"ז. ראה מס' 74.

1968
67.   "Idealism and Practicality in Numbers 35:4–5 and Ezekiel 48." JAOS 88 [E. A. Speiser volume]: 59–66.
68.   "In Memory of E. A. Speiser." JAOS 88 [E. A. Speiser volume]: 1–2.

1969
69.   *Understanding Exodus: Part I.* New York: Behrman House.
70.   "על משמעות סיפור גן עדן ב'בראשית'." שדמות לג: 11–10 [תשכ"ט] ראה מס' 166.
71.   "תפקידה של התורה בחיי ישראל." בתוך: פרקי בית המדרש, 13–7. ירושלים: בית המדרש למורים העברי הממלכתי על שם דוד ילין [תשכ"ט]. ראה מס' 166.
72.   *Connaître La Bible* by Yehezkel Kaufmann. Paris: Presses Universitaires de France [unacknowledged French shortened translation of no. 20].
73.   "El Fundamento Biblico del Valor Humano." *Libro Anual* [Lima, Peru] 4: 160–170 [Spanish translation of no. 63].
74.   "Ḥab/piru and Hebrews." In *The World History of the Jewish People Vol.*

II: Patriarchs, ed. B. Mazar, 188–295. Tel Aviv: Massada Press. (See no. 66.)

75. "Prolegomenon." In *Pseudo-Ezekiel and the Original Prophecy*, by Charles Cutler Torrey and Critical Articles by Shalom Spiegel and Charles Cutler Torrey, xi–xxxv. New York: Ktav.

76. "Rabbinic Reflections on Defying Illegal Orders: Amasa, Abner, and Joab." *Judaism* 19/1: 30–37. (See nos. 143, 166.)

77. "Some Postulates of Biblical Criminal Law." In *The Jewish Expression*, ed. J. Goldin, 18–37. New York: Bantam Books. (See no. 21.)

78. Review of *Ezekiel's Prophecy on Tyre (Ez. 26, 1–28, 19): A New Approach* by H.J. Van Dijk. JAOS 90: 536–540.

1971

79–94. Articles in the *Encyclopaedia Judaica*, eds. Cecil Roth and Geoffrey Wigoder. Jerusalem: Encyclopaedia Judaica. 79. "Decalogue" (5: 1435–1446); 80. "Exodus, Book of" (6:1050–1067); 81. "Ezekiel" (6:1078–1095); 82. "Herem" (8:345–350); 83. "Labor" (10: 1320–1321); 84."Sabbatical Year and Jubilee" (14:577–578); 85. "Levitical Cities" (11:136–138); 86. "Ginsberg, Harold Louis" (7:580); 87. "Speiser, Ephraim Avigdor" (15:258–259); 88. "Moses" (12:371, 378–388); 89. "Oath" (12:1295–1298); 90. "Plagues of Egypt" (13:604–613); 91. "Resurrection" (14:96–98); 92. "Sabbath" (14:557–562); 93. "Semites" (14:1148–1149); 94. "Urim and Thummim" (16:8–9).

95. "Mankind, Israel and the Nations in the Hebraic Heritage." *In No Man is Alien*, ed. J. Robert Nelson, 15–40. Leiden: Brill. (See no. 166.)

96. "The Redaction of the Plague Narrative in Exodus." In *Near Eastern Studies in Honor of William Foxwell Albright*, ed. Hans Goedicke, 243–252. Baltimore: Johns Hopkins Press. (See no. 106.)

97. "Tribute (to W. F. Albright)." *Newsletter of the American Schools of Oriental Research* 6: [4–6].

98. Review of *A Rigid Scrutiny: Critical Essays on the Old Testament* by Ivan Engnell. *Judaism* 20: 248–249.

99. הנחות היסוד של החוק הפלילי המקראי: תורגם מאנגלית וללא כל שינוי מתוך ספר היובל לי. קויפמן, ירושלים תשכ"א. פנימי, לתלמידי החוג למקרא. ירושלים: האוניברסיטה העברית, הפקולטה למדעי הרוח—החוג למקרא [תשל"א]. [ללא עריכת המחבר] ראה מס' 169 ,21.

100. "חורבן וגאולה." שדמות מ"א, אביב תשל"א: 108–104. ראה 166.

101–102. ערכים בתוך: אנציקלופדיה מקראית, כרך ו, ערכו ב. מזר ואחרים. ירושלים: מוסד ביאליק [תשל"ב]. 101. "עברי, עברים" (51–48).

102. "ערי מקלט" (388–384).

103. "פרשת השבת בירמיהו." בתוך: עיונים בספר ירמיהו: ערך ב"צ לוריא, חלק ב, 37–27. [ירושלים]: החברה לחקר המקרא בישראל.

1972

104. *The Religion of Israel: From Its Beginnings to the Babylonian Exile*, by Yehezkel Kaufmann. Translated and abridged by Moshe Greenberg. New York: Schocken Books. [Paperback edition of no. 20].

105. Review of *Ancient Israel's Criminal Law: A New Approach to the Decalogue* by Anthony Philips. JBL 91: 535-538.

106. "אמנות הסיפור והעריכה בפרשת המכות (שמות ז-יא)." בתוך: המקרא ותולדות ישראל: מחקרים לזכרו של יעקב ליור, 75–.65 תל-אביב: אוניברסיטת תל-אביב, [תשל"ב]. ראה מס' 96.

107. ‏"המובאות בספר יחזקאל כרקע לנבואות." בית מקרא ג (נ), 273–278‏
‏[תשל"ב].‏

108. ‏"לשאלת היקפן ומידת גיבושן של התורה ומצוותיה." פתחים 20, ניסן‏
‏תשל"ב: 27–23. ראה מס' 166.‏

1973

109. "Prophecy in Hebrew Scripture." *Dictionary of the History of Ideas*, ed.
Philip P. Wiener, III: 657–664. New York: Charles Scribner's Sons.

110. Review of *Studies in the Bible and Ancient Orient, Vol. I: Biblical and
Canaanite Literatures* by U. Cassuto. *Ariel* 32: 205–207.

111. ‏"הרהורים על תפקידי המורה למקרא והכשרתו." בתוך: הגות במקרא‏
‏לזכר ישי רון, 128–119. תל-אביב: עם עובד והחברה לחקר המקרא‏
‏בישראל [תשל"ד]. ראה מס' 166.‏

112. ‏"ערך האדם במקרא." שדמות נ: 170–164 [עיבוד עברי של מס' 63].‏
‏ראה מס' 166.‏

1974

113. "Biblical Judaism (20th–4th centuries B.C.E.)." *EncBrit: Macropaedia*.
15th ed. Chicago: Encyclopaedia Britannica. 10: 303–310.

114. "The Stabilization of the Text of the Hebrew Bible: Reviewed in the
Light of the Biblical Materials from the Judean Desert." In *The Canon
and Masorah of the Hebrew Bible*, ed. Sid Z. Leiman, 298–326. New
York: Ktav. (See no. 10.)

115. ‏"מתוד מכתב פרופ' מ. גרינברג לבנו בצבא 26 בנובמבר 1973."‏
‏מידעון: עלון לתלמידי בתי-הספר העל-יסודיים 3: 15–12.‏
‏[ירושלים: משרד החינוך והתרבות, תשל"ד] ראה מס' 166.‏

116. ‏בקורת על: הנסיון, מאת יעקב ליכט. פתחים 27, טבת תשל"ב: 42–41.‏

1975

117. "Hope and Death." *Ariel* 39:21–39. (See no. 166.)

118. ‏"המקרא ובן דורנו: הוראת המקרא באוניברסיטה—למי ולמה." שדמות‏
‏נו: 18–11 [תשל"ה]. ראה מס' 166.‏

1976

119. "On Sharing the Scriptures." In *Magnalia Dei: The Mighty Acts of God*,
ed. F. M. Cross et al., 455–463. Garden City, N.Y.: Doubleday.

120. "On the Refinement of the Conception of Prayer in Hebrew Scriptures." *A[ssociation for] J[ewish] S[tudies] review* 1: 57–92. (See no.
122.)

121. ‏"הזיקה בין העם והארץ על פי המקרא." הציונות: סמינריון לקציני‏
‏אוגדת סיני, 19–11.‏

122. ‏"על עידון מושג התפילה במקרא." אשל באר שבע א: 33–9 [תשל"ו].‏
‏ראה מס' 120, 166.‏

123. ‏ראיון עם פרופ' משה גרינברג [על ביקורת המקרא והאמונה]. קשת‏
‏בענן 33 [תשל"ו]. ראה מס' 166.‏

1977

124. "Moses' Intercessory Prayer." *Tantur Yearbook* 1977–78: 21–36.

125. "*NHŠTK* (Ezek. 16:36): Another Hebrew Cognate of Akkadian *naḫāšu*.
In *Ancient Near Eastern Studies in Memory of J. J. Finkelstein*, ed. Maria
de Jong Ellis, 85–86. Hamden, Conn.: Archon Books.

126. "Two New Hunting Terms in Psalm 140:12." *Hebrew Annual Review*
1:149–153.

127. ‏"גישה להוראת המקרא בבית-הספר." פתחים 40: אלול תשל"ז: 22–18.‏
‏ראה מס' 166.‏

128. ‏"חקר המקרא והמציאות הישראלית—[חלק] א." הארץ 23.9.77.‏
‏[חלק] ב, 30.9.77. [קיצור של מס' 135] ראה מס' 166.‏

1978

129. "Rabbinic Reflections on Defying Illegal Orders: Amasa, Abner, and Joab." In *Contemporary Jewish Ethics*, ed. Menachem Marc Kellner, 211–220. New York: Sanhedrin Press. (See no. 76.)

130. "The Use of the Ancient Versions for Interpreting the Hebrew Text." *Congress Volume: Goettingen 1977.* Supplements to Vetus Testamentum 29: 131–148.

131. ‏"מזמור קמ." ארץ-ישראל: מחקרים בידיעת הארץ ועתיקותיה 14 [ספר‏
‏גינזברג]: 99–88 [תשל"ח].‏

132. ‏"על זהות, תבונה ודת." תכנים יהודיים בחינוך בישראל: הרצאות‏
‏ביום עיון לזכר סגן ישי רון ז"ל, 30–15. ירושלים: משרד החינוך‏
‏והתרבות [תשל"ח. ראה מם', 168, 166, 142.‏

133. ‏"תשובה לאזרח שחשש ל'חילול קדש' מהדפסת פסוקי מקרא בחוברת עבודה‏
‏לתלמיד." הלכה למעשה בתכנון לימודים 2: 147–145. ראה מס' 166.‏

1979

134. "Religion: Stability and Ferment." In *The World History of the Jewish People Vol. 5: The Age of the Monarchies: Culture and Society,* ed. A. Malamat, 79–123. Jerusalem: Massada Press. (See no. 148.)

135. ‏"חקר המקרא והמציאות הארצישראלית." בתוך: המקרא ואנחנו, ערך‏
‏אוריאל סימון, 85–70. תל-אביב: דביר [תשל"ט]. ראה מס' 166, 128.‏

136. "The Biblical Conception of Asylum." In *Jewish Law and Decision-making: A Study through Time*, by Aaron M. Schreiber, 140–143. Philadelphia: Temple University Press [abridged version of no. 17].

137. "Some Postulates of Biblical Criminal Law." In *Jewish Law and Decision-making: A Study through Time*, by Aaron M. Schreiber, 143–150. Philadelphia: Temple University Press [abridged version of no. 21].

138. "The Meaning and Location of the 'Lookout' Passage in Ezek. 3:16–21." *Proceedings of the American Academy for Jewish Research* 46–47 [Jubilee volume]: English section, 265–280.

1980

139. "Reflections on Job's Theology." In ספר איוב *The Book of Job: A New Translation According to the Traditonal Hebrew Text, With Introductions by Moshe Greenberg, Jonas C. Greenfield, and Nahum Sarna*, xvii–xxiii. Philadelphia: The Jewish Publication Society of America. (See nos. 145, 166.)

140. "The Vision of Jerusalem in Ezekiel 8–11: A Holistic Interpretation." In *The Divine Helmsman: Studies in God's Control of Human Events Presented to Lou H. Silberman,* eds. James L. Crenshaw and Samuel Sandmel, 143–164. New York: Ktav.

141. ‏"'אתם קרויים אדם . . .'." שדמות ע"ו אלול, תש"ם: 76–67. ראה מס'‏
‏166.‏

142. ‏"על זהות, תבונה ודת." פתחים 50–49, אדר תש"ם: 35–29. [קוצר‏
‏ממס' 132].‏

143. ‏"עמשא, אבנר ויואב: על הסירוב לפקודות בלתי-חוקיות במשנת חז"ל."‏
‏שדמות ע"ד, אדר תש"ם: 87–80. ראה מס' 166, 76.‏

1981

144. Review of *Ezekiel 1: A Commentary on the Book of the Prophet Ezekiel, Chapters 1–24* by Walther Zimmerli. *Association for Jewish Studies Newsletter* 28: 22–24.

145. ‏"הרהורים על התיאולוגיה של איוב." פתחים 56–55, אלול תשמ"א:‏
‏57–52 [נוסח מתוקן של מאמר באותו שם שהופיע בשיבושים‏
‏ב-פתחים 54–53, אדר תשמ"א; עיבוד עברי של מס' 138]. ראה מס'‏
‏166.‏

146. ‏"ואתה הסבת את לבם אחרנית." בתוך: מחקרים באגדה, תרגומים‏
‏ותפילות ישראל לזכר יוסף היינימן, ערכו עזרא פליישר ויעקב‏
‏פטוחובסקי, נב-סו. ירושלים: מאגנס והיברו יוניון קולג' פרס.‏

147. ‏"המשמעות האמיתית של המקרא." שדמות ע"ט, תמוז תשמ"א: 91–88.‏
‏ראה מס' 166.‏

1982

148. ‏"האמונה הישראלית בתקופת המלוכה: יציבות ותסיסה.". בתוך:‏
‏ההיסטוריה של עם ישראל: ימי המלוכה—תרבות וחברה, ערך אברהם‏
‏מלמט, 89–60. [תל-אביב]: עם עובד [תשמ"ב]. ראה מס' 134.‏

149. ‏"החג במקרא וזמן מקורש." *Proceedings of the 1981 Convention of the Rabbinical Assembly* 43: ד–א ראה מס' 166.‏

150–152. ‏ערכים בתוך: אנציקלופדיה מקראית, כרך ח, ערכו ב. מזר‏
‏ואחרים. ירושלים: מוסד ביאליק. [תשמ"ב] 150. "שמות, ס' (ואלה)‏
‏שמות" (112–97); 151. מתוך "תנ"ך, פרשנות": "הגדרת הנושא‏
‏והיקף הערך" (642–641); פרשנות חז"ל (647–642); "הפרשנות‏
‏בתרגומים הארמיים" (649–647) "פרשני צרפת" (703–689) [ראה מס'‏
‏156]; 152. "תפלה" (921–896).‏

153. ‏"תבניתה של תפילת הבקשה במקרא." ארץ ישראל: מחקרים בידיעת הארץ‏
‏ועתיקותיה 16 [ספר אורלינסקי]: 55–47. [תשמ"ב]‏

1983

154. *Biblical Prose Prayer.* Berkeley and Los Angeles: University of California Press.

155. *Ezekiel 1–20.* The Anchor Bible. Garden City, N.Y.: Doubleday.

156. ‏פרשנות המקרא היהודית: פרקי מבוא, ערך משה גרינברג. ירושלים:‏
‏מוסד ביאליק. מתוכו חיבר "מבוא" (2–1); "פרשנות חז"ל" (9–3);‏
‏"הפרשנות בתרגומים הארמיים" (13–11); "פרשני צרפת" (85–68);‏
‏"סוף דבר" (138–137). ראה מס' 151.‏

157. "Can Modern Critical Bible Scholarship Have a Jewish Character?" *Immanuel* 15: 7–12. (See no. 163.)

158. "Ezekiel 17: A Holistic Interpretation." JAOS 103 [S.N. Kramer Volume]: 149–154. (See no. 170.)

159. "Ezekiel's Vision: Literary and Iconographic Aspects." In *History, Historiography and Interpretation: Studies in Biblical and Cuneiform Literatures*, eds. H. Tadmor and M. Weinfeld, 159–168. Jerusalem: Magnes Press.

160. "*MSRT HBRYT*, 'The Obligation of the Covenant,' in Ezekiel 20:37." In *The Word of the Lord Shall Go Forth* [D.N. Freedman volume], eds. C.L. Meyers and M. O'Connor, 37–46. Winona Lake, Ind.: Eisenbrauns.

161. "Nebuchadnezzar at the Parting of the Ways." In *Ah, Assyria...: Studies in Assyrian History and Ancient Near Eastern Historiography presented to Hayim Tadmor*, eds. M. Cogan and I. Ephᶜal. Scripta Hierosolymitana 33: 267–271. Jerusalem: Magnes Press.

162. Review of *Ezechiel* by Bernhard Lang. JAOS 103: 472–473.

163. "הייתכן מדע מקרא ביקורתי בעל אופי יהודי?" בתוך: דברי הקונגרס
העולמי השמיני למדעי היהדות: ישיבות מרכזיות, מקרא ולשון
עברית, 98–95. ראה מס' 157.

164. "היחס בין פירוש רש"י לפירוש רשב"ם לתורה." בתוך: ספר יצחק
אריה זליגמן, ערכו א. רופא וי. זקוביץ, 567–559. ירושלים: אלחנן
רובינשטיין.

165. "מקומו ההיסטורי של יחזקאל בקהילת גולי בבל." בתוך: ההיסטוריה
של עם ישראל: שיבת ציון—ימי שלטון פרס, ערך חיים תדמור, 141–147.
ירושלים ותל-אביב: עם עובד.

1984

166. על המקרא ועל היהדות: קובץ כתבים, ערך אברהם שפירא. תל-אביב: עם
עובד [תשמ"ו]. מכיל: הדפסה חוזרת של מס' 111 ,108 ,100 ,71 ,70,
143 ,141 ,135 ,132 ,127 ,123 ,122 ,121 ,118 ,115 ,112
149 ,147 ,145; עיבוד עברי של מס' 117 ,95 ,18.

167. "The Design and Themes of Ezekiel's Program of Restoration." *Interpretation* 38: 181–208.

168. "על זהות, תבונה ודת." In *ללמד וללמד: Studies in Jewish Education and Judaica in Honor of Louis Newman*, eds. Alexander M. Shapiro and Burton I. Cohen, 183–192. New York: Ktav [abridgment of no. 132].

169. "הנחות יסוד של החוק הפלילי במקרא." בתוך: תורה נדרשת מאת משה
גרינברג, יוחנן מופס וגרשון דוד כהן. ערך א. שפירא. תל-אביב: עם
עובד [תשמ"ד]. [נוסח מתוקן של 99].

170. "יחזקאל י"ז—אינטרפרטציה הוליסטית." מחקרי ירושלים בספרות
עברית ד: 17–7. ראה מס' 158.

171. "עצמאות וטפילות תרבותית." ידיעות אחרונות 2 אוקטובר. ראה מס'
177.

1985

172. הסגולה והכוח. [תל-אביב]: הקיבוץ המאוחד/ ספרית פועלים [תשמ"ו].
מכיל גירסה עברית של מס' 201 ,185.

173. Review of *Les écoles et la formation de la Bible dans l'ancien Israël* by André Lemaire. IEJ 35: 208–209.

174. "מסורת עשרת הדיברות בראי הביקורת." בתוך: עשרת הדברות בראי
הדורות, ערך בן-ציון סגל, 94–65. ירושלים: מאגנס [תשמ"יו]. ראה
מס' 195.

175. "מפתח לחלק הראשון (ל"ב נתיבות התרגום') של ספר 'אוהב גר'
לשד"ל." שנתון למקרא ולחקר המזרח הקדום ט: 94–83.

176. מקרא לישראל: פירוש מדעי למקרא [פרוספקט עם דוגמת פירוש
ל-יחזקאל לז, א-יד]. תל-אביב: עם עובד.

177. "עצמאות וטפילות תרבותית או: הרהורים על אשרולולוגיה כמותרות."
ידיעון האיגוד העולמי למדעי היהדות 24: 8–5. [תשמ"ה] ראה מס'
171.

1986

178. "More Reflections on Biblical Criminal Law." In *Studies in Bible*, ed. Sara Japhet. Scripta Hierosolymitana 31:1–17. Jerusalem: Magnes Press.

179. "What Are Valid Criteria for Determining Inauthentic Matter in Ezekiel?" In *Ezekiel and His Book*, ed. J. Lust. Bibliotheca Ephemeridum Theologicarum Lovaniensium 74: 123–135. Leuven: University Press.

180. "חכמי ישראל וחכמה חיצונית." בתוך מחקרים במדעי היהדות, ערך
משה בר-אשר, 126–117. ירושלים: [תשמ"ו].

181. צרכי מדינת ישראל במחקר בסיסי: דין וחשבון של הוועדה להערכת
המחקר הבסיסי במקרא [ערך משה גרינברג]. ירושלים: האקדמיה
הלאומית הישראלית למדעים [תשמ"ז].

1987

182. "Exegesis." In *Contemporary Jewish Religious Thought*, eds. A.A. Cohen
and P. Mendes-Flohr, 211–218. New York: Charles Scribner's Sons.

183. "Ezekiel." *The Encyclopaedia of Religion*, ed. Mircea Eliade, 5: 239–
242. New York: Macmillan.

184. "Ezekiel 16: A Panorama of Passions." In *Love and Death in the Ancient
Near East: Essays in Honor of Marvin H. Pope*, eds. John H. Marks and
Robert M. Good, 143–150. Guilford, Conn.: Four Quarters Publishing
Co.

185. "Der Gebrauch der Bibel im heutigen Israel." In *Mitte der Schrift?: Ein
jued.-christl. Gespräch*, eds. Martin Klopfenstein et al., 343–353. Bern:
Lang. (See no. 172.)

186. "Job." In *The Literary Guide to the Bible*, eds. Robert Alter and Frank
Kermode, 283–304. Cambridge, Mass.: Harvard University Press.

187. Review of *Biblical Interpretation in Ancient Israel* by Michael Fishbane.
Numen 34/1: 128–130.

188. Review of *Critique Textuelle de L'Ancien Testament* by Dominique
Barthélemy. JQR 78: 137–140.

189. Review of *The Pennsylvania Tradition of Semitics: A Century of Near
Eastern and Biblical Studies at the University of Pennsylvania* by Cyrus
H. Gordon. JQR 77: 226–227.

1988

190. Review of *Le Livre de Jérémie* by P.-M. Bogaert, ed. JQR 79: 71–72.

191. Review of *Understanding Scripture: Exploration of Jewish and Christian
Traditions of Interpretation*, eds. Clemens Thoma and Michael
Wyschogrod. *Numen* 35/1: 154–156.

192. "מוסר יהודי במבחן השעה." עת לעשות 1 תשמ"ט: 17–11.

1989

193. Yehezkel Kaufmann, A *Religião de Israel*. São Paulo: Brasil: Perspectiva:
Editora da Universidade de São Paulo: Associação Universitária de
Cultura Judaica [Portuguese translation of no. 20].

194. "Bible Interpretation as Exhibited in the First Book of Maimonides'
Code." *The Judeo-Christian Tradition and the U. S. Constitution*: Proceedings of a Conference at The Annenberg Research Institute, November 16–17. A Jewish Quarterly Review Supplement: 29–56.

195. "Jewish Conceptions of the Human Factor in Biblical Prophecy." In *Justice and the Holy: Essays in Honor of Walter Harrelson*, eds. D.A. Knight
and P.J. Paris, 145–162. Atlanta: Scholars Press.

196. "Theological Reflections—Land, People and the State." In *People, Land
and State of Israel: Jewish and Christian Perspectives* = *Immanuel* 22/23:
25–34.

197. "השפעת המודרניות על הבנת העבר: מזווית ראייתו של מקרא." בתוך:
טורא: אסופת מאמרי הגות ומחקר במחשבת ישראל מוגשת לפרופ' שלמה
(סיימון) גרינברג בשנות גבורותיו, ערך מאיר אייליי, 19–13.
[חיפה] המרכז ללימודי יהדות באורנים והקיבוץ המאוחד.

198. "תפילה למען המדינה." ידיעון התנועה המסורתית בישראל, אביב
[תשמ"ט]ראה מס' 200.

199. תפילה למען המדינה." שיח מישרים: כתב עת על חיי שעה וחיי עולם
לישראל 17: 11 [תשמ"ט]. ראה ממ' 199.

1990

200. "The Decalogue Tradition Critically Examined." In *The Ten Command-ments in History and Tradition,* ed. Gershon Levi, 83–119. Jerusalem: Magnes Press. (See no. 174.)

201. "Biblical Attitudes toward Power: Ideal and Reality in Law and Proph-ets" and "Reply to the Comments of John Welch." In *Religion and Law: Biblical-Judaic and Islamic Perspectives,* eds. Edwin B. Firmage et al., 101–112; 120–125. Winona Lake: Eisenbrauns. (See no. 172.)

202. "On Teaching the Bible." In *Studies in Jewish Education, vol. 5,* eds. H. Deitcher and A.J. Tannenbaum, 27–34. Jerusalem: Magnes Press.

203. "The Task of Masorti Judaism." In *Deepening the Commitment: Zionism and the Conservative Movement,* eds. J.S. Ruskay and D. Szonyi, 137–145. New York: Jewish Theological Seminary of America.

204. "Three Conceptions of the Torah in Hebrew Scriptures." In *Die Hebräische Bibel und ihre zweifache Nachgeschichte: Festschrift für Rolf Rendtorff zum 65. Geburtstag,* eds. Erhard Blum et al., 365–378. Neukirchen: Neukirchener Verlag.

205. "To Whom and For What Should a Bible Commentator Be Responsi-ble?" *Proceedings of the Tenth World Congress of Jewish Studies: Divi-sion A: The Bible and its World:* 29–38.

206. "שרה קמין ז"ל". מדעי היהדות 114-115 :30.

1991

207. "Some Postulates of Biblical Criminal Law." In *Essential Papers on Israel and the Ancient Near East,* ed. Frederick E. Greenspahn, 333–352. New York: New York University Press. See no. 21.

208. Review of *Thinking Biblical Law,* ed. Dale Patrick. JAOS 111: 819–820.

209. "יחזקאל קויפמן—רשמים אישיים." איגרת האקדמיה הלאומית הישראלית
למדעים 9, שבט תשנ"א: [4-6]. ראה מס' 211.

210. "ערך החיים במקרא." בתוך: החיים: מהות וערך, ערכה לאה מזור,
141-108. ירושלים: מאגנס [תשנ"א].

211. "רשמים אישיים על יחזקאל קויפמן." מדעי היהדות 31 תשנ"א: 85-81.
ראה מס' 209.

212. "איוב היה או לא היה: סוגיה בפרשנות ימי הביניים." בתוך:
Sha'arei Talmon: Studies in the Bible, Qumran, and the Ancient Near East Presented to Shemaryahu Talmon, eds. Michael Fishbane and Emanuel Tov, 3°–11°. Winona Lake: Eisenbrauns.

Index